Lloyd's Maritime and Commercial Law Quarterly Index 1974–1990

Lloyd's

Maritime and Commercial Law Quarterly Index 1974 – 1990

LLP

LONDON NEW YORK HAMBURG HONG KONG

LLOYD'S OF LONDON PRESS LTD

1991

Lloyd's of London Press Ltd.
One Singer Street,
London EC2A 4LQ
Great Britain

USA AND CANADA
Lloyd's of London Press Inc.
Suite 308, 611 Broadway
New York, NY 10012 USA

GERMANY
Lloyd's of London Press GmbH
59 Ehrenbergstrasse
2000 Hamburg 50
Germany

SOUTH EAST ASIA
Lloyd's of London Press (Far East) Ltd.
Room 1101, Hollywood Centre
Hollywood Road
Hong Kong

ISBN 1–85044–335–1

Typeset in Linotron 202 Times by
Promenade Graphics Ltd., Cheltenham, Glos.
Printed in Great Britain by
Bookcraft (Bath) Ltd.
Midsomer Norton, Avon

Introduction

In 1986 we published a consolidated contents and index covering the years 1974–1985—the first twelve years of the *Quarterly's* life. This Index also marked the availability, for the first time, of a complete set of bound annual volumes 1974–1985, which now extends to 1990.

As the Index 1974–1985 was so much appreciated by the *Quarterly's* subscribers and librarians and researchers, it was decided to publish in this volume a consolidated contents and index 1974–1990 with the addition of tables of cases and legislation covering the period 1986–1990.

This book, therefore, consists of four parts: a contents list covering Part 1, 1974, to Part 4, 1990 and divided into Articles, Case and Comment, Other Features, Book Reviews and Book Notices. Using to the full electronic methods of storing and sorting information, we are able to include as parts 2 and 3 tables of cases and legislation covering the period 1986–1990. Finally, the fourth part is a consolidated index 1974–1990, with the year of publication preceding the page number in each index entry. Every article, case and comment and book review published from 1974–1990 has been indexed, and it is hoped that this will again form a key to the mine of maritime and commercial law contained in the *Quarterly*.

We hope that this volume will prove to be as useful as its predecessor and that we shall be publishing its successor in five years' time.

January, 1991 THE PUBLISHERS

Contents

Contents 1974–1990 1

Table of Cases 1986–1990 35

Table of Legislation 1986–1990 115

Index 1974–1990 141

Contents 1974–1990

ARTICLES

Some considerations of *The Johanna Oldendorff* and *The Loucas N* cases *Donald Davies* [1974] 1
The practice of scuttling *Donald R. O'May* [1974] 6
Hi-jacking in road transport law *G. W. Quick Smith* [1974] 11
Speed and consumption warranties *Cedric Barclay* [1974] 13
In perspective—ICC Rules for a combined transport document *N. R. McGilchrist* [1974] 25
Text of ICC Uniform Rules for a combined transport document [1974] 29
Receiver/contractor relationships *Michael Tugendhat* [1974] 39
Tanker voyage charterparties—need for modernisation *F. M. Ventris* [1974] 44
Time charter—doctrine of overlap-underlap in US courts *John P. Besman* [1974] 49
References to charterparties in bills of lading *Dr. S. Mankabady* [1974] 53
Second International Congress of Maritime Arbitrators [1974] 61
Who is to pay for the stevedore's negligence? *L. J. Kovats* [1974] 121
Interpretation of the Hague Rules *Dr. S. Mankabady* [1974] 125
Recommendations relating to the revision of the Hague Rules [1974] 134
An examination of Lloyd's Standard Form of Salvage Agreement *J. G. R. Griggs* [1974] 138
Lloyd's Standard Form of Salvage Agreement [1974] 145
Revision of the York-Antwerp Rules [1974] 151
The York-Antwerp Rules 1974 [1974] 153
The new York-Antwerp Rules examined *N. G. Hudson* [1974] 162
The concept of safe ports *John M. Reynolds* [1974] 179
The new Hague Rules *N. R. McGilchrist* [1974] 255
The Consumer Credit Act 1974 *Professor R. M. Goode* [1974] 264
International and national organisations concerned with shipping *Dr. S. Mankabady* [1974] 274
When payment is made *F. R. Ryder* [1974] 286
Copyright *Brian W. Haines* [1974] 289
Bank manuals and instructions to staff—some legal aspects *Dr. W. S. Weerasooria* [1974] 295
The Centrocon arbitration clause strikes again *N. G. Hudson* [1974] 301
Accommodations of the law of international trade *Dr. Stojan Cigoj* [1974] 309
The EEC and insurance *Dr. S. Mankabady* [1975] 1
The practical effects of *The Esso Malaysia* *Simon Gault* [1975] 5
Maritime pollution: Canada's approach *P. D. Lowry* [1975] 10
Judgments in foreign currencies *D. H. Hene* [1975] 19
The freight forwarder: his status from a comparative viewpoint *Professor D. J. Hill* [1975] 27
Arrest of ships *William Goffey* [1975] 34

New problems of financing oil shipments *F. M. Ventris* [1975] 38
Manifest disregard of law *Jack Berg* [1975] 129
The contractual relationship between shipper, forwarder and carrier by road *Professor D. J. Hill* [1975] 137
Dock work *J. Gifford Gordon* [1975] 142
"Time lost in waiting for berth to count as . . . laytime" *Attilio M. Costabel* [1975] 150
Collision cases 1974 *S. T. Harley* [1975] 156
The lawyer and the computer *G. E. Stephens* [1975] 166
Marine insurance law in South Africa *Senator B. R. Bamford* [1975] 171
Banks in Socialist Eastern Europe *L. J. Kovats* [1975] 173
Limitation of liability—at sea and in the air *Neil R. McGilchrist* [1975] 256
International sale of goods *Basil Eckersley* [1975] 265
Blow-out in the North Sea *Gunnar Brask* [1975] 271
Liability for contamination of mixed and refined cargoes shipped in distribution tankers *Allen Cameron* [1975] 281
Technical aspects of unseaworthiness *Cedric Barclay* [1975] 288
Legal relations of stevedores in comparative law *Dr. Stojan Cigoj* [1975] 296
Combined transport to Europe *Dr. D. J. Hill* [1975] 303
Report on the third session of the UN Conference on the Law of the Sea *Michael Lake* [1975] 383
Legal problems arising from the transport of liquefied natural gas [1975] 387
Ground for refusal to contribute in general average *Leslie J. Buglass* [1975] 390
Disclosure requirements imposed on arbitrators in maritime arbitrations under United States law *John P. Meade* [1975] 399
Charterparty disputes—withdrawals, repudiation, frustration *Cedric Barclay* [1975] 412
Note on the activities of the European Communities *Michael Lake* [1975] 418
CMR—an outline and its history *A. E. Donald* [1975] 420
International carriage of passengers and their luggage by rail and road *R. W. Hodgin* [1976] 1
Documentary Credits—the International Chamber of Commerce Code of Practice *B. S. Wheble* [1976] 8
Rules for Documentary Credits [1976] 15
Ship's delivery orders *Nigel Teare* [1976] 29
Products liability afloat *Alfred J. Kuffler* [1976] 33
Greek shipping case law *Gr. J. Timagenis* [1976] 46
Medical malpractice *L. J. Gusmano* [1976] 50
Rights and duties of insurance brokers *Senator B. R. Bamford* [1976] 59
Forwarding and sub-contracting complications *Dr. D. J. Hill* [1976] 63
General average adjustment and arbitration in the People's Republic of China *N. G. Hudson* [1976] 135
The Peking Adjustment Rules [1976] 141
The International Chamber of Commerce Uniform Rules for a Combined Transport Document *B. S. Wheble* [1976] 145
Uniform Rules for a Combined Transport Document [1976] 148
Combined transport to and from the United States *Gerald H. Ullman* [1976] 157
Maritime arbitration awards in New York involving shipowner withdrawals from charter upon late payment *Stephen J. Murray* [1976] 164
The insurance of household goods shipments *Andrew E. Rossmere* [1976] 173
War risks *Donald R. O'May* [1976] 180
Four new Protocols to the Warsaw Convention *Neil R. McGilchrist* [1976] 186
Simplification of documentation and document replacement *Kurt Gronfors* [1976] 250

Power of English arbitrators to make awards in foreign currencies *A London arbitrator* [1976] 255
Damages assessable against marine insurers for wrongful failure to pay property losses *Hervey C. Allen* [1976] 258
Time not of the essence in nominating arbitrator *R. G. Ashworth* [1976] 266
Obtaining security in aid of arbitration *Nicholas J. Healy, Jnr.* [1976] 267
Per package limitation—a diverging approach in Canadian courts *David F. McEwen* [1976] 269
Commercial arbitration in commodity trades *J. C. S. Mackie* [1976] 278
The common law liability of a public carrier by sea *D. Barry Kirkham* [1976] 282
Some rules of practice procedure and methods of appeal in arbitrations under Scots law *Ian G. Inglis* [1976] 289
The Austrian General Freight Forwarding Conditions and the Austrian Freight Forwarding Insurance Scheme *Dr. Gerhard Blasche* [1976] 374
Third International Congress of Maritime Arbitrators [1976] 377
"No fault" in America *Professor Derrick Owles* [1976] 396
The antitrust exemption in the US Shipping Act—should it be eliminated or modified? *John P. Meade* [1976] 401
Jurisdiction over claims for damage done by any ship *Dr. Malcolm Clarke* [1976] 412
General average—defences and "due diligence" disputes *N. Geoffrey Hudson* [1976] 416
Table of comparative maritime arbitration procedures *Michael Marks Cohen* [1976] 422
The Water Pollution Control Act—United States response to water pollution by ships *Alfred J. Kuffler* [1977] 1
Tug and tow—limitation of liability—the flotilla issue *L.J. Kovats* [1977] 19
Stare decisis et non quieta movere *Manfred W. Arnold* [1977] 24
CMR—Continental case law: loss by theft from a comparative viewpoint *Maitre R. Wijffels* [1977] 30
A method of drafting a "Code of Transport" *Professor H. Schadee* [1977] 37
The division of liability as between ship and cargo *Anthony Diamond, Q.C.* [1977] 39
Legal aspects of safety of offshore installations *Professor F. J. J. Cadwallader* [1977] 53
Aspects of industrial property rights in the European Economic Community *Brian W. Haines* [1977] 64
Convention on Limitation of Liability for Maritime Claims 1976 [1977] 73
Commercial and maritime law in Israel *P. G. Naschitz* [1977] 84
Some legal aspects of directors' liability insurance in the United States *Professor Derrick Owles* [1977] 163
Salvorial negligence and its consequences *D. R. Thomas* [1977] 167
Again, when payment is made *F. R. Ryder* [1977] 174
The Collision Regulations 1972 *S. T. Harley* [1977] 178
Modern factoring of debts—its framework of law *F. R. Salinger* [1977] 184
From radical revolution to questionable reformation *Professor G. Righetti* [1977] 192
New Maritime code of the German Democratic Republic *Dr. Dolly Richter-Hannes and Dr. Ralf Richter* [1977] 197
Exchange contracts and the international sale of goods *James P. Corbett* [1977] 310
Arbitration in Piraeus—a growing trend *Gr. J. Timagenis* [1977] 319
Crossing leading to collision at sea *Dr. Samir Mankabady* [1977] 330
The application of the International Convention on Civil Liability for Oil Pollution Damage to the *Urquiola* case *Ignacio Arroyo* [1977] 337
Impracticability of performance—is it grounds for breach? *Manfred W. Arnold* [1977] 346
Products liability in Australia *John Goldring* [1977] 351

Foreign currency claims and the English courts *Stuart L. Isaacs* [1977] 356
It isn't Hell: it's Purgatory—a trial lawyer's view of product liability in America *Forest L. Tozer* [1977] 488
Seaworthiness in time charters *Dr. Malcolm Clarke* [1977] 493
Like fleas to a dog *Professor Derrick Owles* [1977] 498
New forms for general average security *N. G. Hudson* [1977] 501
The Hague-Visby Rules now operative in United Kingdom [1977] 512
Double insurance and contribution *R. W. Hodgin* [1977] 515
Identity of the carrier—the Hague Rules, Visby Rules, UNCITRAL *William Tetley, Q.C.* [1977] 519
Quot homines tot sententiae *F. M. Ventris* [1977] 533
Rights and liabilities of underwriters on payment of a Constructive Total Loss *N. Geoffrey Hudson* [1978] 1
An iniquity unmatched by any requirement of society *Professor Derrick Owles* [1978] 9
CMI Conference—Rio de Janeiro 1977. Report of proceedings [1978] 14
Gold franc—replacement of unit of account *Miss L. Bristow* [1978] 31
Insurance intermediaries—recent and projected developments—Insurance Brokers (Registration) Act 1977 *Derek Morgan* [1978] 39
Damages under CMR: the decision of the House of Lords *A. C. Hardingham* [1978] 51
Transference of risk under comparative and internationally unified law *Dr. Stojan Cigoj* [1978] 56
The Unfair Contract Terms Act 1977 *F. M. B. Reynolds* [1978] 201
The Unfair Contract Terms Act 1977 [1978] 211
The Hague-Visby Rules *Anthony Diamond, Q.C.* [1978] 225
Need for reform of arbitration procedures—a High Court comment [1978] 267
Maritime liens: an American view *Richard E. Burke* [1978] 269
Lloyd's Standard Form of Salvage Agreement: a descriptive and analytical scrutiny *D. Rhidian Thomas* [1978] 276
Intertanktime *Hans Peter Michelet* [1978] 287
The businessman, the law and the EEC *F. R. Ryder* [1978] 291
The Pearson Report [1978] 399
Claims for short delivery of bulk oil cargoes: some recent trends *J. Weale* [1978] 405
The watchdog has no right, without the knowledge of his master, to take a sop from a possible wolf *Professor Derrick Owles* [1978] 422
Consortium and related operations in the United Kingdom *Dr. F. Wooldridge* [1978] 427
The Hamburg Rules [1978] 439
Some NYPE time charter problems *Michael Mabbs* [1978] 456
US letters rogatory and the English courts *Stuart Isaacs* [1978] 464
Fundamental breach of charterparty *Dr. Malcolm Clarke* [1978] 472
Legal problems associated with shipbuilding contracts *Dr. Samir Mankabady* [1978] 477
New York charter arbitrations and pre-hearing discovery: a concept whose time has come *Alfred J. Kuffler* [1978] 557
The integration of the CMR Rules in Swedish domestic road transportation regulations *Goran Petersson and Johan Wetter* [1978] 567
The future of Tovalop *A. F. Bessemer Clark* [1978] 572
Current consumer protection legislation in Finland *Leif Sevon* [1978] 592
The duties, obligations and liabilities of the ship's agent to his principal *Dr. Johannes Trappe* [1978] 595
Insurance companies freedom of establishment within the EEC—implementation in Italy *Attilio Costabel* [1978] 606
The Hamburg Rules: a commentary *William Tetley, Q.C.* [1979] 1

The 1976 Limitation Convention and oil pollution damage *Professor Erling Selvig* [1979] 21
General conditions for the transport of goods within the Netherlands *E. C. G. Klinkhamer* [1979] 26
Reforming the banking laws—Stage One *D. M. Morgan* [1979] 30
Tort liability of the shipowner or operator for physical injuries to persons in the sea *Dr. Branimir Luksic* [1979] 44
Resolution of collision claims in China *Patrick Griggs* [1979] 138
Manifest disregard of the law *R. Glenn Bauer* [1979] 142
Towage conditions and fundamental breach *Jonathan S. Lux* [1979] 148
The sister ship action *in rem* *D. Rhidian Thomas* [1979] 158
The special drawing right in liability conventions: an acceptable solution? *Dr. Aleksander Tobolewski* [1979] 169
A fundamental principle of insurance law *Charles Lewis* [1979] 275
The new German law on standard contract terms *Wolfgang Freiherr von Marschall* [1979] 278
Foreign exchange losses—the passing of risk? *Alex Maitland Hudson* [1979] 288
Some legal aspects of the *Amoco Cadiz* incident *Bernard A. Dubais* [1979] 292
Waybills and short form documents: a lawyer's view *Richard Williams* [1979] 297
The UNCTAD report on an international legal base for marine insurance contracts, as related to hull claims *Kenneth Goodacre* [1979] 315
Gold values in carriage of goods Conventions—an up-to-date review *Attilio M. Costabel* [1979] 326
The Himalaya Clause *D. G. Powles* [1979] 331
The Collision Regulations in question *Dr. J. F. Kemp* [1979] 347
A new competition—rivals for centres of arbitration *The Lord Hacking* [1979] 435
Some topical considerations in the event of a casualty to an oil tanker *Dr. D. W. Abecassis* [1979] 449
Sovereign immunity and the common law *Charles Lewis* [1979] 460
Piracy: the current crime *Alan D. Wiener* [1979] 469
Foreign currency judgments *D. G. Powles* [1979] 485
The State Immunity Act *Charles Lewis* [1980] 1
Problems in defining insurance contracts *R. W. Hodgin* [1980] 14
Charterer's authority to sign bills of lading under standard time charter terms *Russell W. Pritchett* [1980] 21
The Fourth Council Directive on Accounts *Dr. Frank Wooldridge* [1980] 27
The *Mareva* injunction—recent developments *Frank Meisel* [1980] 38
Limits of liability in the present economic situation *Dr. Aleksander Tobolewski* [1980] 47
The Protection of Trading Interests Bill *Professor Derrick Owles* [1980] 55
International agreements and the EEC: the practical implications of a constitutional conflict *Keith H. Hendry* [1980] 117
Policy disputes in America: damages against insurers *Jonathan Barrett* [1980] 131
Anti-trust implications of liner conferences: alternatives to the regulation of liner trades with emphasis on the European approach *Anne C. B. McIntosh* [1980] 139
The Hague-Visby Rules, forum, arbitration and choice of law clauses *Professor D. C. Jackson* [1980] 159
Salvage, General Average and the insurance of average disbursements *N. Geoffrey Hudson* [1980] 168
Alongside vessels or lighters reachable on her arrival *F. M. Ventris* [1980] 174
Losses in translation—some problems with foreign exchange: Part 1—Accounting *Derrick Owles* [1980] 179
Cargo recovery actions in the United States *J. Edwin Carey* [1980] 184
The role of Lloyd's Open Form *A. F. Bessemer Clark* [1980] 297

Lloyd's Standard Form of Salvage Agreement [1980] 304
Reservation of title by the unpaid seller *Charles Lewis* [1980] 309
Another Companies Act in the series *Derrick Owles* [1980] 315
Arrest of vessels in Japan *Tameyuki Hosoi* [1980] 322
The Demise clause in American courts *Russell W. Pritchett* [1980] 387
A fundamental breach of duty *F. D. Rose* [1980] 396
Maritime securities and the conflict of laws—some problems *A. M. Tettenborn* [1980] 404
Some problems with foreign exchange: Part 2—Taxation *Derrick Owles* [1980] 411
Recent developments in money transfer methods *Anu Arora* [1980] 416
The formation and repudiation of contracts by international telex *Charles Lewis* [1980] 433
The *Mareva* injunction—attachment *in personam* (Part 1) *F. D. Rose* [1981] 1
International commercial arbitration agreements and the enforcement of foreign arbitral awards *D. Rhidian Thomas* [1981] 17
The effect of bankruptcy upon mortgages of future property *Paul Matthews* [1981] 40
Future developments in money transfer *Anu Arora* [1981] 56
Prize competitions—the lottery of legality *R. M. Merkin* [1981] 66
The Anglo-American scene *R. D. Margo* [1981] 83
The *Mareva* injunction—attachment *in personam* (Part 2) *F. D. Rose* [1981] 177
An appraisal of the Arbitration Act 1979 *D. Rhidian Thomas* [1981] 199
In consideration of building ships *Dr. Malcolm Clarke* [1981] 234
British flag—a privilege or an encumbrance—or just an anachronism? *Philip P. Jones* [1981] 241
The EEC Convention on the law applicable to contractual obligations *Ross Williams* [1981] 250
The legal position of banks in Performance Bond cases *Anu Arora* [1981] 264
The wealth-time continuum revisited: set-off in marine collision claims *J. A. Knott* [1981] 269
The unpaid seller's reservation of title under the *Romalpa* clause is not effective in America *Professor D. E. Murray* [1981] 278
Insurance law reform *R. W. Hodgin* [1981] 284
Special charges on cargo. Part 1: The obligations of ship and cargo owners *N. Geoffrey Hudson* [1981] 315
Making the polluter pay for oil pollution damage to the environment: a note on *The Zoe Colocotroni* case *Professor E. D. Brown* [1981] 323
Foreign maritime liens in English courts—principle and policy *Professor David Jackson* [1981] 335
Passing off and unfair competition *Charles Lewis* [1981] 341
Insurance law and the Law Commission *R. M. Merkin* [1981] 347
Arrest of vessels in Japan *Tameyuki Hosoi and Yutaka Tsurusaki* [1981] 359
Extraterritorial jurisdiction of US antitrust laws: the new approach *Dr. M. Sornarajah* [1981] 365
Special charges on cargo. Part 2: Remedies, defences and insurers' liabilities *N. Geoffrey Hudson* [1981] 471
The bill of lading in the oil tanker trade *F. M. Ventris* [1981] 479
Group life assurance in Canada *R. M. Merkin* [1981] 485
Maritime law judgments in Canada reported in 1980 *Professor William Tetley, Q.C.* [1981] 489
Criminal liabilities of ships' masters *Silas W. Taylor* [1981] 499
The time-charterer, the one-ship company and the sister-ship action *in rem* *A. M. Tettenborn* [1981] 507
What has become of the US Fire Statute? *R. Glenn Bauer* [1982] 1

Some Admiralty law issues in Canadian offshore oil and gas development *W. Wylie Spicer* [1982] 5
Deductions from freight and hire under English law *F. D. Rose* [1982] 33
Debenture holders and judgment creditors—problems of priority *Diane M. Hare and David Milman* [1982] 57
US taxation and the Economic Tax Recovery Act of 1981 *Derrick Owles* [1982] 81
Development of common and civil law—the contrasts *Professor J. A. Jolowicz* [1982] 87
The case of the Cuban sugar *Charles Lewis* [1982] 96
The Gulf States and the control of marine pollution—regional arrangements and national legislation *Dr. S. H. Amin* [1982] 104
Restructuring the control of price indications *D. W. Oughton* [1982] 117
Nigeria's exclusive economic zone *Dr. B. Obinna Okere* [1982] 124
Risk sharing in LNG shipping—some aspects of the relationships between owners and charterers of LNG ships and third parties *D. W. Abecassis* [1982] 138
Construction problems at Lloyd's *Charles Christian* [1982] 152
American Express will not do, I am afraid *S. F. Heather* [1982] 157
From bailment to bailment *F. D. Rose* [1982] 200
Gaps in the action *in rem* *S. J. Hazelwood* [1982] 210
The port agent—his rights, liabilities and problems *Albert Morris* [1982] 218
Admiralty jurisdiction—The Supreme Court Act 1981 *Professor D. C. Jackson* [1982] 236
New Israeli Insurance Contract Law—1981 *P. G. Naschitz* [1982] 249
State taxes and business in the United States *Dr. Derrick Owles* [1982] 253
Arresting the misconception *Susan K. Robinson* [1982] 261
The Insurance Ombudsman Bureau: first annual report *R. M. Merkin* [1982] 266
Leave to appeal under the Arbitration Act 1979 *Charles Lewis* [1982] 271
"Barratry"—the scuttler's easy route to the "golden prize" *Steven J. Hazelwood* [1982] 383
The sleeping and the dead *P. B. Matthews* [1982] 401
Law of commercial contracts in Iran *Dr. S. H. Amin* [1982] 416
Gaps in the action *in rem*—plugged? *Steven J. Hazelwood* [1982] 422
Too remote *Dr. Johannes Trappe* [1982] 427
Maritime liens in Polish law in the context of the law of the European Socialist States *Professor Wojciech Adamczak* [1982] 433
Non-apparent damage to goods in transit *Dr. Malcolm Clarke* [1982] 533
Canadian maritime law judgments in 1981 *Professor William Tetley, Q.C.* [1982] 542
Continuing problems after the supposed demise of *Ryan* indemnity in US Admiralty law *Hon. D. A. Bagwell* [1982] 556
Contract damages for exchange losses—a New Zealand development *C. E. F. Rickett* [1982] 566
The theory of changed circumstances in international trade *Dr. S. H. Amin* [1982] 577
Arrest of ships owned by charterers *S. J. Tabbush* [1982] 585
Hongkong Fir revisited: the House of Lords and certainty in contracts *George Applebey and Frank Meisel* [1982] 592
Laws controlling mercury pollution: issues and implications for the United Kingdom *Dr. L. D. Guruswamy* [1982] 611
New Lines for Conference Lines *F. D. Rose* [1982] 636
American business and income tax *Derrick Owles* [1982] 650
The recognition and enforcement in England of foreign personal and proprietary judgments *P. A. Stone* [1983] 1
Definition and classification of maritime fraud *Peter Kapoor* [1983] 29
IMO and liability for oil pollution from ships: a retrospective *Dr. David Abecassis* [1983] 45

Crimes committed on board foreign ships on the high seas and the jurisdiction of the English courts *J. Kodwo Bentil* [1983] 60
Legal systems in the Gulf States *Dr. S. H. Amin* [1983] 71
The sea law changeth *S. T. Harley* [1983] 86
The US tax collector and the foreigner *Derrick Owles* [1983] 93
Releasing ships from arrest *P. B. Matthews* [1983] 99
The implied warranty of seaworthiness in time policies: the American view *Russell W. Pritchett* [1983] 195
Negligence in the commercial sphere *I. J. Dawson* [1983] 209
Registration defences and the Restrictive Trade Practices Act: three recent cases *R. M. Merkin* [1983] 224
The practice of maritime arbitrations in London: recent developments in the law *David A. McIntosh* [1983] 235
Iran-US claims settlement *Dr. S. H. Amin* [1983] 248
The foreshadowed global legal regime of deep seabed exploration and mining *J. Kodwo Bentil* [1983] 260
The peril of "pirates"—all "at sea" *S. J. Hazelwood* [1983] 283
When arbitration proceedings become stale *Charles Lewis* [1983] 289
Receiver's liability for negligence *Anu Arora* [1983] 294
Contracts of hire and the Supply of Goods and Services Act 1982 *Professor N. E. Palmer* [1983] 377
Petroleum shortage disputes: the difference between the legal and arbitration approach *James M. Textor* [1983] 392
Performance Bonds: use and usefulness *Karen Williams* [1983] 423
Fundamental changes in Italian arbitration law *Attilio M. Costabel* [1983] 440
Quis custodes custodiet *F. M. Ventris* [1983] 442
Law of personal injuries in the Middle East *Dr. S. H. Amin* [1983] 446
Anatomy of an arrest in Panama *Juan Francisco Pardini* [1983] 456
Environmental Law: EEC legislation controlling dangerous substances: legal odyssey or uncharted voyage of discovery? *Dr. L. D. Guruswamy* [1983] 464
Negligence and exclusion clauses again *Professor N. E. Palmer* [1983] 557
Insurance law: recent causes *Dr. M. A. Clarke* [1983] 576
The future of deviation in the law of the carriage of goods *C. P. Mills* [1983] 587
"Errors of navigation" in NYPE form: reflections on *The Emmanuel C* *Peter S. K. Koh* [1983] 597
Canadian maritime law judgments in 1982 *Professor William Tetley, Q.C.* [1983] 603
The master's negligence and charterers' warranty of safe port/berth *Lewis Herman and Steven E. Goldman* [1983] 615
Is there a right to wreck? *K. S. Goddard* [1983] 625
Equipment leasing: a decade of growth *I. R. Davies* [1983] 631
Contracts for the supply of services under the 1982 Act *J. R. Murdoch* [1983] 652
Communications of acceptance *E. J. Jacobs* [1983] 663
Fisheries in the Gulf *Dr. S. H. Amin* [1983] 671
Expenses in *custodia legis*, court costs and attorney's fees *Professor William Tetley, Q.C.* [1984] 1
Ship routeing schemes and the criminal liability of the master *C. J. Warbrick* [1984] 23
CMR: putting practice into theory *David Glass* [1984] 30
Reservation of title clauses: a legal quagmire? *Iwan Davies* [1984] 49
The dilemma of an issuing bank: to accept or reject documents tendered under a letter of credit *Dr. Anu Arora* [1984] 81
Arrest of ships in Greece *Gr. J. Timagenis* [1984] 90
The disclosure of criminal information to insurers *Philip H. Clarke* [1984] 100
Should accidents between pleasure craft fall within US admiralty jurisdiction—an analysis of *Foremost Insurance Co.* v. *Richardson* *Joan Taranto Sargent* [1984] 112

Mental distress damages in contract—a decade of change *A. S. Burrows* [1984] 119
Sea links—Maritime lawyers and the market-place *The Hon. Michael Summerskill* [1984] 205
Oil pollution of the sea and the Swedish *Tsesis* decision *Hugo Tiberg* [1984] 218
The staying of actions on the ground of *forum non conveniens* in England today *Adrian Briggs* [1984] 227
Charter-parties fixed "subject to details" *S. N. Ball* [1984] 250
Salvage agreements: the master's authority *K. S. Goddard* [1984] 255
Conflict between the fishing and sand and gravel industries in Scottish coastal waters: the role of law *A. D. M. Forte* [1984] 263
Service of documents in shipping cases under Greek law *Gr. J. Timagenis* [1984] 275
Romalpa clauses: further developments *J. R. Davies* [1984] 280
Protecting against maritime liens for supplies and services on chartered ships calling at US ports *John P. Love and John D. Kimball* [1984] 290
Commercial contracts and the Commercial Court *The Rt. Hon. Sir Robert Goff* [1984] 382
Salvage: Present and future *Geoffrey Brice, Q.C.* [1984] 394
Protection & Indemnity Clubs *T. G. Coghlin* [1984] 403
Changes in South African admiralty jurisdiction *Alan Rycroft* [1984] 417
Developments in maritime law in Hong Kong in 1983 *C. S. C. Quennell* [1984] 434
The proper law of a marine insurance policy *P. A. Stone* [1984] 438
The criminal liability of ships' masters: Provisions and changes *Silas W. Taylor* [1984] 446
The "Liggett" defence: a banker's last resort *E. P. Ellinger and C. Y. Lee* [1984] 459
Contracts with consignees and indorsees *P. N. Todd* [1984] 476
Admissibility and enforcement of foreign court decisions and arbitration awards in Greece *Gr. J. Timagenis* [1984] 488
Rights of rejection under c.i.f. sales *G. H. Treitel, Q.C.* [1984] 565
The Uniform Customs—their nature and the 1983 Revision *E. P. Ellinger* [1984] 578
United States admiralty and shipping law—recent developments *Nicholas J. Healy* [1984] 607
Consequential damages and the duty to mitigate in New York maritime arbitrations *L. C. Bulow* [1984] 622
The Polish insurance system—a comparative review *Wojciech Marek* [1984] 643
Freezing a joint bank account *Paul Matthews* [1984] 651
"Non-maritime" demurrage claims *F. M. Ventris* [1984] 657
The Data Protection Act 1984 *R. C. Austin* [1984] 663
General average, salvage and the contract of affreightment *John Crump* [1985] 19
Salvage and enhanced awards *Geoffrey Brice, Q.C.* [1985] 33
The New Zealand contract statutes *Francis Dawson* [1985] 42
Attachment, the *Mareva* injunction and *saisie conservatoire* *Professor William Tetley, Q.C.* [1985] 58
Economic loss in the maritime context *N. J. J. Gaskell* [1985] 81
Liability and compensation for pollution damage caused by ships revisited—report on an important international conference *A. H. E. Popp* [1985] 118
Performance bonds: are bankers free from the underlying contract? *Graham A. Penn* [1985] 132
The new Marine Policy and Institute Clauses *Donald R. O'May* [1985] 191
Insurance law downpour in Australia *A. T. Scotford* [1985] 201
Singapore—some recent developments in maritime and Admiralty law *G. P. Selvam* [1985] 209
Combating international commercial crime—a Commonwealth perspective *Barry A. K. Rider* [1985] 217
Charter-party fixtures "subject details"—further reflections *Charles Debattista* [1985] 241

Time charterer's third party liability in Japan *Tameyuki Hosoi* [1985] 254
The Admiralty Court of Sri Lanka sets aside its own order made *per incuriam* *V. Ratnasabapathy* [1985] 260
Decision-making in maritime law *The Rt. Hon. Sir Michael Mustill* [1985] 314
Canadian Admiralty decisions 1983–84 *Professor William Tetley, Q.C.* [1985] 326
Oilvoy demurrage clauses—what is a storm? *James M. Textor* [1985] 343
Forum non conveniens—an update *Adrian Briggs* [1985] 360
Shipowners' liens—preservation after release of goods *A. M. Tettenborn* [1985] 376
New definition of pollution damage *Professor Z. Brodecki* [1985] 382
Arrest of vessels in the States of the Arab Gulf Co-operation Council *Richard Price and Andreas Haberbeck* [1985] 392
Transnational fraud *The Hon. Tan Boon Tiek* [1985] 418
US maritime liens and the new arrest and attachment rules *David R. Owen* [1985] 424
Materiality in insurance contracts *Henry Brooke, Q.C.* [1985] 437
The regulation of wet marine and aviation insurance in the United States *Brooks White* [1985] 453
The implementation of the Admiralty Jurisdiction Regulation Act in South Africa *Hilton Staniland* [1985] 462
Warehouseman not entitled to benefit from Warsaw Convention limitation in Israel *P. G. Naschitz* [1985] 479
Unfair contract terms: evaluating an EEC perspective *A. D. M. Forte* [1985] 482
Time limitation in the English conflict of laws *P. A. Stone* [1985] 497
The law of marine insurance—has it a future? *Anthony Diamond, Q.C.* [1986] 25
New York arbitration as seen by a Londoner *H. C. Wodehouse* [1986] 43
A New Yorker looks at London maritime arbitration *Michael Marks Cohen* [1986] 57
Insurance coverage disputes in the United States: a period of uncertainty for the insurer *Arthur J. Liederman* [1986] 79
The significance of tort in claims in respect of carriage by sea *F. M. B. Reynolds* [1986] 97
The politically unsafe port *C. G. C. H. Baker and Paul David* [1986] 112
The new Canadian personal property security legislation *Jacob S. Ziegel* [1986] 160
The giro system and electronic transfers of funds *E. P. Ellinger* [1986] 178
The vindication of commercial security over commodities: equitable pledges and conversion *N. E. Palmer* [1986] 218
Arbitration: the basis and validity of a restricted reasons agreement *D. Rhidian Thomas* [1986] 235
Insurance under Saudi Arabian law *Andreas Haberbeck* [1986] 246
Laytime problems and comparison of law *Dr. Johannes Trappe* [1986] 251
Bills of lading and third parties *Professor G. H. Treitel, Q.C.* [1986] 294
The Lloyd's Open Form and contractual remedies *N. J. J. Gaskell* [1986] 306
United States admiralty and shipping law—recent developments *Nicholas J. Healy and Jerome Scowcroft* [1986] 350
Recent developments in maritime law in Hong Kong *C. S. C. Quennell* [1986] 382
Commodity futures contracts and the Gaming Act *Dr. David A. Chaikin and Brendan J. Moher* [1986] 390
The new Institute Cargo Clauses *Anthony George* [1986] 438
The bill of lading as a receipt—missing oil in unknown quantities *Charles Debattista* [1986] 468
The making of the marine insurance contract: a comparison of English and U.S. law *David G. Condon* [1986] 484
The validity of "floating" choice of law and jurisdiction clauses *Adrian Briggs* [1986] 508

The crystallization of floating charges, subordination agreements and priority conflicts *Loo Choon Chiaw* [1986] 519
Problems with and solutions for New York maritime arbitration *Robert M. Jarvis* [1986] 535
Marine insurance law: can the lawyers be trusted? *Donald R. O'May* [1987] 29
Uncollected goods: the penalties of delay *Professor N. E. Palmer* [1987] 43
Canadian maritime law decisions 1985–86 *Professor William Tetley, Q.C.* [1987] 82
The United Nations Convention on Conditions for Registration of Ships *S. G. Sturmey* [1987] 97
Products liability in US maritime law *Thomas M. DiBiagio* [1987] 118
Out-turn clauses in c.i.f. contracts in the oil trade *James J. Lightburn and Gawie M. Nienaber* [1987] 177
Disqualifying company directors *Brenda M. Hannigan* [1987] 188
Illegal insurance *Dr. Malcolm Clarke* [1987] 201
The transport of goods in refrigerated containers: an Australian perspective *R. C. Springall* [1987] 216
The Third Parties (Rights against Insurers) Act 1930 in a modern context *Keith Michel* [1987] 228
Maritime claims: the European Judgments Convention *Geoffrey Brice, Q.C.* [1987] 281
The new Carriage of Goods by Sea Act in South Africa *Hilton Staniland* [1987] 305
Proposed reforms of admiralty jurisdiction in Australia *B. J. Davenport, Q.C.* [1987] 317
The New Zealand Contractual Mistakes Act: a lesson in legislation *Andrew Beck* [1987] 325
The lack of uniformity and the very unfortunate state of maritime law in Canada, the United States, the United Kingdom and France *Professor William Tetley, Q.C.* [1987] 340
The USSR maritime arbitration commission (Part 1) *W. A. Timmermans* [1987] 350
Restitutionary damages for breach of contract *Peter Birks* [1987] 421
The insurance of average disbursements *N. Geoffrey Hudson* [1987] 443
The USSR maritime arbitration commission (Part 2) *W. A. Timmermans* [1987] 468
Liability under United States law for spills of oil or chemicals from vessels *David Ashley Bagwell* [1987] 496
Floating choice of law clauses *Andrew Beck* [1987] 523
The safe port/berth obligation and employment and indemnity clauses *Charles G. C. H. Baker* [1988] 43
Section 459 of the Companies Act 1985—a code of conduct for the quasi-partnership? *Brenda Hannigan* [1988] 60
Canadian maritime law decisions 1986–87 *Professor William Tetley, Q.C.* [1988] 82
Lis alibi pendens and *forum non conveniens* in collision actions after the Civil Jurisdiction and Judgments Act 1982 *Elizabeth Blackburn* [1988] 91
Lien holders and mortgagees: who should prevail? *Professor Francesco Berlingieri* [1988] 157
Interest on maximum sums *Dr. F. A. Mann and J. Kurth* [1988] 177
EEC competition rules and maritime transport *Dr. Dieter Rabe and Dr. Michael Schütte* [1988] 182
Maritime consumers?—the Consumer Protection Act and shipping law *A. M. Tettenborn* [1988] 211
Liability for injuries sustained by passengers in the event of hijacking of aircraft and other violations of aviation security *Henrik Gam* [1988] 217
United States federal income tax consequences to foreign corporations engaged in international shipping *Donna Marie Zerbo* [1988] 235
Fault and marine losses *Sir Michael John Mustill* [1988] 310
Understanding banking law *Ross Cranston* [1988] 360
Civil jurisdiction and judgments—recent decisions of the European Court *P. A. Stone* [1988] 383

Damages for breach of a c.i.f. contract *Professor G. H. Treitel* [1988] 457
Sub-bailment on terms *Professor N. E. Palmer* [1988] 466
CHAPS transfer of funds *Professor Benjamin Geva* [1988] 477
Liability for labelling of goods and instructions for use *Ian Brown* [1988] 502
The shipowners' right to a limitation of liability adrift on a sea of tort changes *Judge Lynn N. Hughes* [1988] 517
The bill of lading: do we really need it? *Sir Anthony Lloyd* [1989] 47
Dr. Lushington's contribution to the law of maritime salvage(1833–67) *Professor S. M. Waddams* [1989] 59
The higher altitudes of contract law *J. W. Carter* [1989] 81
Canadian maritime law decisions: 1987–88 *Professor William Tetley, Q.C.* [1989] 89
Transport deregulation in the Canadian maritime industry *Peter G. Cathcart, Q.C.* [1989] 104
Bills of lading and implied contracts *G. H. Treitel* [1989] 162
The Halcyon Isle revisited: a South African perspective *Hilton Staniland* [1989] 174
The juridical nature of a lien on sub-freights *Fidelis Oditah* [1989] 191
Reservation of title—the controversy continues *Gerard McCormack* [1989] 198
Wider still and wider: the bounds of Australian exorbitant jurisdiction *Adrian Briggs* [1989] 216
Misdirected funds: restitution from the recipient *Peter Birks* [1989] 296
"Dangerous" cargoes: the responsibilities and liabilities of the various parties *Lucienne Carasso Bulow* [1989] 342
Banks and extra-territorial orders *E. P. Ellinger* [1989] 363
Acting in the course of a business *Robert A. Pearce* [1989] 371
Sales from bulk *A. H. Hudson* [1989] 420
Mistaken settlements of disputable claims *N. H. Andrews* [1989] 431
Who has got his cross liabilities crossed? *Nicolas Wilmot* [1989] 450
Examination of judgment debtors as to their assets abroad: courts' powers and jurisdiction *Peter Kaye* [1989] 465
The Chinese Foreign Economic Contract Law of 19 October 1987 *Xu Guojian and Adam Samuel* [1989] 476
Third party rights against insurers *Keith Michel and Simon Congdon* [1989] 495
Administrative caution *John de Lacy* [1989] 506
The new Salvage Convention: green seas and grey areas *Geoffrey Brice, Q.C.* [1990] 32
The time of payment in paper-based and electronic funds transfer systems *Johanna Vroegop* [1990] 64
Worldwide *Mareva* injunctions: the position of international banks *Ali Malek and Caroline Lewis* [1990] 88
Canadian maritime law decisions 1988–1989 *Professor William Tetley, Q.C.* [1990] 99
The off-hire clause in the New York Produce Exchange time charterparty *Martin Davies* [1990] 107
Maritime arbitration in the People's Republic of China *Clement Shum* [1990] 114
EEC insurance market and 1992: significance of fiscal and tariff issues *Marc Dassesse* [1990] 176
The formation of international contracts *Adrian Briggs* [1990] 192
Wrongful trading *Fidelis Oditah* [1990] 205
Performance guarantees *Martin Coleman* [1990] 223
The legal implications of cheque truncation *Johanna Vroegop* [1990] 244
True and fair revisited *Hugh Evans* [1990] 255
Seller cure in the sale of goods *Rex J. Ahdar* [1990] 364
Recent developments in laytime cases *Johannes Trappe* [1990] 383
The courts and the Companies Acts: the judicial contribution to company law *David Milman* [1990] 401

Contributory negligence: a viable defence for auditors? *P. S. Marshall and A. J. Beltrami* [1990] 416
Services rendered under ineffective contracts *J. W. Carter* [1990] 495
Registration of company charges: the new law *G. McCormack* [1990] 520
The role of correspondent banks in direct funds transfers *Johnanna Vroegop* [1990] 547

CASE AND COMMENT

Anticipatory breach of condition (*The Afovos*) [1984] 189
Rejection of documents (*Gill & Duffus S.A.* v. *Berger & Co. Inc.*) [1984] 191
Incorporation of charter-party terms (*The Varenna*) [1984] 194
Baltime Clause 13 (*The TFL Prosperity*) [1984] 196
Deductions from freight for the carriage of goods by road (*R. H. & D. International Ltd.* v. *I. A. S. Animal Air Services Ltd.*) [1984] 199
Transhipment and the Hague-Visby Rules (*Mayhew Foods Ltd.* v. *Overseas Containers Ltd.*) [1984] 202
Limitation of shipowner's liability (*The Marion*) [1984] 363
Late payment of debt (*La Pintada*) [1984] 365
"Illegal" insurance (*Bedford Insurance Co.* v. *I. R. B.; B. A. Stewart* v. *Oriental Fire & Marine Insurance Co.*) [1984] 368
Arrest and arbitration (*The Andria; The Tuyuti*) [1984] 370
Admiralty jurisdiction: Tort claims (*The Antonis P. Lemos*) [1984] 374
Assumpsit duties (*The Zephyr*) [1984] 376
Limitation on relief for affirmed contracts (*The Alaskan Trader* (*No. 2*)) [1984] 378
Foreign tonnage limitation not a ground for refusing stay of action (*The Benarty*) [1984] 545
Arbitration appeals and charter-party construction (*The Antaios*) [1984] 547
Norwegian Saleform guarantee and indemnity clause (*The Barenbels*) [1984] 553
Contracts for the supply of services in Australia [1984] 557
The Macmillan doctrine reviewed in Hong Kong (*Tai Hing Cotton Mill Ltd.* v. *Liu Chong Hing Bank Ltd.*) [1984] 559
Restraining foreign proceedings (*British Airways Board* v. *Laker Airways Ltd.*) [1984] 563
Actions in tort for damaged cargo (*The Aliakmon*) [1985] 1
Variation and affirmation in insurance contracts (*Hadenfayre* v. *British Insurance Society Ltd.*) [1985] 3
A new approach for service of a writ out of the jurisdiction (*Cordoba Shipping Co.* v. *National State Bank* (*The Albaforth*)) [1985] 6
Sampling bunkers in oil tankers (*The Othoni; The Erikoussa*) [1985] 10
Insurance: accidental injury (*National & General Insurance Co. Ltd.* v. *Chick*) [1985] 12
"Romalpa" clauses (*Clough Mill Ltd.* v. *Martin*) [1985] 15
Arrest of ships (*Gatoil International Inc.* v. *Arkwright–Boston Manufacturers Mutual Insurance Co.*; *The Antonis P. Lemos*) [1985] 173
Jurisdiction clauses in bills of lading and the European Judgments Convention (*The Tilly Russ*) [1985] 177
Bank accounts, restitution and theft (*Attorney-General's Reference* (*No. 1 of 1983*)) [1985] 180
Arrest after judgment (*The Daien Maru No. 18*) [1985] 186
Proper law of a *Brandt* v. *Liverpool* contract (*The Elli* 2) [1985] 188
Stale arbitrations (*The Leonidas D*) [1985] 293
Norwegian Saleform (*The Barenbels*) [1985] 306
Substitution of ships' names on writ (*The Kusu Island*) [1985] 309
Economic loss in collision cases (*Candlewood Navigation Corporation Ltd.* v. *Mitsui O. S. K. Lines Ltd.* (*The Mineral Transporter*)) [1985] 407

Fixed charge over book debts (*Re Keenan Bros.*) [1985] 409
Effect of quotation of freight rate (*Aotearoa International Ltd.* v. *Scancarriers A/S*) [1985] 412
Assumpsit duties (*The Zephyr*) [1985] 414
Marine insurance—Wilful misconduct of the assured (*Wood* v. *Associated National Insurance Co. Ltd.* (*The Isothel*)) [1985] 415
Lien on sub-freights registrable as a charge (*In re Welsh Irish Ferries Ltd.* (*The Ugland Trailer*)) [1986] 1
Ownership of bulk cargoes (*The Gosforth*) [1986] 4
Return to the *Macmillan* doctrine (*Tai Hing Cotton Mill Ltd.* v. *Liu Chong Hing Bank Ltd.*) [1986] 8
Admiralty jurisdiction over agency contracts (*Peralta Shipping Corp.* v. *Smith & Johnson Corp.*) [1986] 12
Salvage of ancient treasure ships (*Subaqueous Exploration & Archaeology Ltd., and Atlantic Ship Historical Society Inc.* v. *The Unidentified, Wrecked and Abandoned Vessel, etc, et al.*) [1986] 16
The application of foreign overall limitation statutes (*The M/V Swibon*) [1986] 22
Interest on debts paid late (*Edmunds* v. *Lloyd's Italico & l'Ancora Cia. di Assicurazione & Riassicurazione S.p.A.*) [1986] 139
The end of Section 27? (*Kenya Railways* v. *Antares Co. Pte. Ltd.* (*The Antares*)) [1986] 142
Reinsurance—Follow settlements and claims co-operation clauses (*Insurance Co. of Africa* v. *SCOR* (*UK*) *Reinsurance Co. Ltd.*) [1986] 145
Insurance covenants in leases and the insurance provisions in charterparties (*Mark Rowlands Ltd.* v. *Berni Inns Ltd. and others*) [1986] 149
Enhancement of salvage awards (*Westar Marine Services* v. *Heerema Marine Contractors S. A.*) [1986] 152
The parol evidence rule (*Law Commission Report No. 154*) [1986] 157
Maritime liens [1986] 159
Non-maritime admiralty claims (*The Goring*) [1986] 276
Arrest of associated ship not retrospective in operation (*Euromarine International of Mauren* v. *The Ship Berg and others*) [1986] 279
Developments in Australia [1986] 283
Table tennis for marine lawyers [1986] 286
Warehouseman and the Warsaw Convention—another point of view [1986] 292
The relevance of "formal investigation" findings to civil liability proceedings (*The European Gateway*) [1986] 417
Effect of incorporation of UCP and question of leave to defend action to enforce documentary credit (*Forestal Mimosa Ltd.* v. *Oriental Credit Ltd.*; *Esal* (*Commodities*) *Ltd.* v. *Oriental Credit Ltd.*) [1986] 420
Lien on sub-freights need not be perfected under U.S. Uniform Commercial code (*In re Pacific Caribbean Shipping* (*USA*) *Inc.* (*The Alicia*)) [1986] 424
P. & I. liability for compulsory wreck removal (*East Coast Tender Services Inc.* v. *Robert T. Winzinger Inc.*) [1986] 427
Imported goods and negligence by customs officials: the laibility of the Crown (*Zien* v. *The Queen*) [1986] 430
Greek NAT tax illegal in Sri Lanka [1986] 434
Customary reduction of COGSA liability (*Sun Oil Co.* v. *Carlisle*) [1986] 436
Forum non conveniens—the last word? (*Spiliada Maritime Corporation* v. *Cansulex Ltd.*) [1987] 1
Insurer's liability extended (*Banque Keyser Ullman S.A.* v. *Skandia* (*U.K.*) *Insurance Ltd* [1987] 5

Contributory negligence in contract—again (*Forsikringsaktieselskapet Vesta* v. *Butcher*)	[1987] 10
Air and maritime transport and the EEC competition rules (*Ministère Publique* v. *Asjes, Nouvelles Frontières et al.*)	[1987] 14
Maritime terrorism and the law	[1987] 18
The insurance of pleasure craft and the doctrine of proximate cause (*J. J. Lloyd Instruments Ltd.* v. *Northern Star Insurance Co. Ltd.* (*The Miss Jay Jay*))	[1987] 22
Law determining ownership of shipwreck in the US (*Klein* v. *Unidentified Wrecked and Abandoned Vessel*)	[1987] 24
Publication of arbitration awards	[1987] 139
Damages on recission for breach of contract (*Lombard North Central plc* v. *Butterworth*)	[1987] 143
Extension of time, deck stowage and the time bar (*Kenya Railways* v. *Antares Pte. Ltd.* (The Antares))	[1987] 146
Fixed and floating charges (*Re Brightlife Ltd.*)	[1987] 147
In defense of *The Halcyon Isle*	[1987] 152
Silence may not be golden (*Excomm Ltd.* v. *Guan Guan Shipping* (*Pte.*) *Ltd.* (*The Golden Bear*))	[1987] 155
General average—the future of non-separation agreements (*Ellerman Lines Ltd.* v. *Gibbs, Nathaniel* (*Canada*) *Ltd. et al.*)	[1987] 160
Exclusion and limitation clauses (*Darlington Futures Ltd.* v. *Delco Australia Pty. Ltd.*)	[1987] 165
Sri Lanka Admiralty Rules upheld (*The Ayesha*)	[1987] 169
Costs and Lloyd's Form Salvage arbitrations (*The Ios I*)	[1987] 172
Order 29—Interim payment: having your cake and eating it? (*Shearson Lehman Brothers Inc.* v. *J. H. Rayner* (*Mincing Lane*) *Ltd.*)	[1987] 173
EEC bank secrecy provisions (*Hillegom Municipality* v. *Hillenius*)	[1987] 251
More points on the *Brandt* v. *Liverpool* contract (*The Aramis*)	[1987] 255
Third party rights on insurance contracts (*Trident General Insurance Co. Ltd.* v. *McNiece Bros. Pty. Ltd.*)	[1987] 258
The demise clause and the Hague Rules (*Kaleej International Pty. Ltd.* v. *Gulf Shipping Lines Ltd.*; *Carling O'Keefe Breweries of Canada Ltd.* v. *C. N. Marine Inc.* (*The Newfoundland Coast*))	[1987] 259
Salvage in non-tidal waters (*The Goring*)	[1987] 262
Abandonment of arbitration by silence or inactivity (*Food Corporation of India* v. *Antclizo Shipping Corporation* (*The Antclizo*))	[1987] 263
Wreck or wreccum maris? (*The Lusitania*)	[1987] 267
The application of the Hague Rules in post-revolutionary Iran	[1987] 273
Oil pollution (*The Patmos*)	[1987] 275
Lex mercatoria (*Deutsche Schachtbau- und Tiefbohrgessellschaft mbH* v. *The R'as Al Khaimah National Oil Co.*)	[1987] 277
Restraint of foreign proceedings (*SNIAS* v. *Lee*)	[1987] 391
The meaning of merchantable quality in sales of goods: quality or fitness for purpose? (*M/S Aswan Engineering Establishment Co.* v. *Lupdine Ltd.* *Rogers* v. *Parish* (*Scarborough*) *Ltd.* Law Commissions Report No. 160	[1987] 400
Direct recovery from P. & I. Associations (*The Fanti and The Padre Island*)	[1987] 406
Orders under charterparties (*The Kanchenjunga; The Epaphus*)	[1987] 408
Notice of Unreadiness (*Aktion Maritime Corporation of Liberia* v. *S. Kasmas & Bros. Ltd.* (*The Aktion*))	[1987] 410
Damages and the late payer (*The Lips*)	[1987] 414
Freezing foreign bank accounts (*Libyan Arab Foreign Bank* v. *Bankers Trust Co.*)	[1988] 1
Reinsurance, brokers and the conflict of laws (*Forsikringsaktieselskapet Vesta* v. *Butcher*)	[1988] 5

Torts in violation of international law (*Amerada Hess Shipping Corp.* v. *Argentine Republic* (*The Hercules*)) [1988] 10
Arbitration: hazards of invoking Indian law (*Oil & Natural Gas Commission* v. *Western Company of North America*) [1988] 12
Towage or salvage? (*The Manchester*) [1988] 16
Extent of auditors' liability (*Alexander* v. *Cambridge Credit Corp. Ltd.*) [1988] 19
Anticipating confusion (*Sanko Steamship Co. Ltd.* v. *Eacom Timber Sales Ltd.* (*The Sanko Iris and Sanko Venus*)) [1988] 21
International arbitration (*Naviera Amazonica Peruana S. A.* v. *Compania Internacional de Seguros del Peru*) [1988] 23
The insurer's duties of good faith and disclosure (*The Good Luck*) [1988] 27
Chipping away at *C. T. I.* v. *Oceanus* (*Barclay Holdings* (*Australia*) *Pty. Ltd.* v. *British National Ins. Co. Ltd.*) [1988] 30
Quasi-bailment (*Metaalhandel J. A. Magnus B. V.* v. *Ardfields Transport Ltd.*; *Transcontainer Express Ltd.* v. *Custodian Security Ltd.*) [1988] 34
Liability for defective ship (*Coltman* v. *Bibby Tankers Ltd.* (*The Derbyshire*)) [1988] 123
Illegality of contract, insurance of goods (*Euro-Diam Ltd.* v. *Bathurst*) [1988] 124
Personal restitution in equity (*Islamic Republic of Iran Shipping Lines* v. *Denby* [1988] 128
European Community instruments on air transport [1988] 135
Wrongful dishonour of cheques: general or special damages (*Rae* v. *Yorkshire Bank plc*) [1988] 138
Registration of retention of title clauses under s.395 of the Companies Act 1985 (*E. Pfeiffer Weinkellerei-Weineinkauf G.m.b.H. & Co.* v. *Arbuthnot Factors Ltd.*) [1988] 140
Liens on sub-freights and priorities (*The Attika Hope: The Annangel Glory*) [1988] 148
Carriage by air in the US Court of Appeals (*Re Korean Air Lines Disaster of September 1, 1983*) [1988] 150
The Italian Constitutional Court and the limits on the liability of the carrier of goods by sea [1988] 273
Measuring damages for breach of a chattel lease: the Supreme court of Canada liberalizes the rules (*Langille* v. *Keneric Tractor Sales Ltd.*) [1988] 276
Mortgagee's interest insurance (*The Alexion Hope*) [1988] 282
The demise clause (*The Jalamohan*) [1988] 285
Admixture of goods in English law (*Indian Oil Corp. Ltd.* v. *Greenstone Shipping S. A.* (*Panama*)) [1988] 286
A very comfortable comfort letter (*Kleinwort Benson Ltd.* v. *Malaysia Mining Corp. Bhd.*) [1988] 290
The red hand rule (*Interfoto Picture Library Ltd.* v. *Stiletto Visual Programmes Ltd.*) [1988] 294
Nemo dat and the Factors Act (*National Employers' Mutual Gen. Ins. Assn. Ltd.* v. *Jones*) [1988] 297
Mistake in contract (*Associated Japanese Bank* (*International*) *Ltd.* v. *Credit du Nord S. A.*) [1988] 300
Abandonment of arbitration by silence or inactivity (*The Antclizo; The Multitank Holsatia*) [1988] 302
The dog that slept [1988] 307
Containers supplied to a ship for her operation? (*The River Rima*) [1988] 423
Garnishment of English debt: foreign complications (*Deutsche Schachtbau* v. *S. I. T. Co.*) [1988] 429
Advice and consent (*Bank of Baroda* v. *Shah; Midland Bank* v. *Perry*) [1988] 436
Charterparties sub details (*The Junior K*) [1988] 439
Bank's duties to principal debtor and guarantor (*Barclays Bank Plc* v. *Quincecare Ltd.*) [1988] 441

Our law or theirs? (*Holmes* v. *Bangladesh Biman Corp.*; *McElderry* v. *Cathay Pacific Airways*) [1988] 445
Non-tidal salvage (*The Goring*) [1988] 449
Avoidance of policy or repudiation of claim? (*Gordon* v. *A. A. Mutual Ins. Assn. Ltd.*) [1988] 452
LOF salvage arbitrations: publication of awards, and appeals [1988] 454
P pays X for the physical damage due to D's negligence (*The Esso Bernicia*) [1989] 1
Self-induced frustration and *force majeure* clauses (*The Dan King*) [1989] 3
Guarantees undertaken without the request of the debtor (*The Zuhal K and Selin*) [1989] 7
In defence of *The Ioannis Daskalelis* [1989] 11
Recent amendments to the US Wreck Removal Act [1989] 15
Winding up a foreign company (*International Westminster Bank Plc* v. *Okeanos Maritime Corp.*) [1989] 20
Supply of goods and charge cards (*Re Charge Card Services Ltd.*) [1989] 22
Proof of scuttling (*The Captain Panagos D. P.*) [1989] 25
Liability for pilot's negligence under Belgian law [1989] 27
Apportionment of loss: collisions and contributions (*Fitzgerald* v. *Lane*) [1989] 30
Japanese agent's liability for delivery without presentation of bill of lading (*Daiwa Bank* v. *Mankai Shipping and Fast Marine* (*The Taichun*)) [1989] 35
Title to sue in the Warsaw Convention system: opening the gate wide? (*Gatewhite Ltd.* v. *Iberia Lineas Aereas de Espana Sociedad*) [1989] 37
Implied terms in the banker and customer relationship (*The Maira* (*No. 3*)) [1989] 40
The Merchant Shipping Act 1988 [1989] 133
Privity of contract in Australia: the beginning of the end? (*Trident General Insurance Co. Ltd.* v. *McNiece Bros. Pty. Ltd.*) [1989] 139
Forward trading in Brent crude (*The Aragon*) [1989] 143
Articles 22 and 25 of the Warsaw Convention—an Australian contribution (*S. S. Pharmaceutical Co. Ltd.* v. *Qantas Airways Ltd.*) [1989] 145
The gratuitous agent's liability (*Chaudhry* v. *Prabhakar*) [1989] 148
Notice of readiness—the persistence of uncertainty (*The Aktion*) [1989] 152
The unauthorized publication of arbitration awards [1989] 158
The duty of disclosure (*La Banque Financière* v. *Westgate* (*The Good Luck*)) [1989] 251
An inconsistency of approach? (*The Kyzikos*) [1989] 263
Carriage by air outside the international Conventions (*Holmes* v. *Bangladesh Biman corp.*) [1989] 267
Economic duress: clarity or confusion? (*Atlas Express Ltd. v. Kafco* (*Importers and Distributors*) *Ltd.* (*The Alev*)) [1989] 270
Hague Rules in Australia (*P. S. Chellaram & Co. Ltd.* v. *China Ocean Shipping Co.*) [1989] 277
"Small comfort" letters (*Kleinwort Benson Ltd.* v. *Malaysia Mining Corp. Bhd.*) [1989] 281
Reinsurance (*Forsikringsaktieselskapet Vesta* v. *Butcher*) [1989] 285
Earned freight: how sacrosanct? (*The Dominique*) [1989] 289
Multi-party insurances and the conflict of laws (*The Irish Rowan*) [1989] 389
Misdelivery and time bars (*The Captain Gregos*) [1989] 394
Rejection of goods, restitution for services and incontrovertible benefit (*The Manila*) [1989] 397
Sea waybills and the Carriage of Goods by Sea Act 1971 (*The European Enterprise*) [1989] 403

The use of reasonable endeavours to save a vessel from sinking (*The Talisman*) [1989] 408
Oppression and preferred shares—a heady Canadian brew (*Palmer* v. *Carling O'Keefe Breweries of Canada Ltd.*) [1989] 411
Orders under charterparties (*The Kanchenjunga*) [1989] 415
The Salvage Convention 1989—who pays? [1989] 416
Forward trading in Brent crude (*The Aragon*) [1989] 418
Passing of property under c.i.f. contracts and the Bills of Lading Act 1855 (*The Delfini*) [1990] 1
Duties of confidence and loyalty (*International Corona Services* v. *Lac Minerals*) [1990] 4
Security arrests in South Africa (*The Dimitris*) [1990] 9
Oil pollution: "ships" and "liability" (*The Stolt Avance*) [1990] 14
Penalties and the financial contract (*Esanda Finance Corp.* v. *Plessnig*) [1990] 16
The Companies Act 1989 [1990] 28
The construction of *force majeure* clauses and self-induced frustration (*The Super Servant Two*) [1990] 153
Penalties and forfeiture: contractual remedies specified by the parties (*Jobson* v. *Johnson*) [1990] 158
Offences on board ships: jurisdiction (*R.* v. *Cumberworth*) [1990] 162
Contract to carry passenger by sea (*The Mikhail Lermontov*) [1990] 164
Amendment of writ *in rem* (*The Kusu Island*) [1990] 169
Not such a common adventure (*The Alppi* v. *The Bjorn Eskil*) [1990] 173
The saga of the International Tin Council [1990] 305
Misdelivery and time bars (*The Captain Gregos*) [1990] 314
Interlocutory orders for inspection of property (*The Mare del Nord*) [1990] 319
Liability after discharge (*The Bunga Teratai*) [1990] 323
Lis Alibi Pendens: Staying or discontinuing English proceedings (*Australian Commercial* v. *ANZ Bank*; *Attorney-General* v. *Arthur Anderson*) [1990] 326
Restitution without counter-restitution (*Guinness Plc* v. *Saunders*) [1990] 330
A guarantee signed by mistake (*Lloyds Bank Plc* v. *Waterhouse*) [1990] 338
The travails of duress (*Crescendo Management* v. *Westpac Banking*; *Williams* v. *Roffey Bros.*; *The Evia Luck* (*No. 2*)) [1990] 342
The enactment of the 1989 Salvage Convention in English law: policy issues [1990] 352
The notions of waiver (*The Kanchenjunga*) [1990] 453
Description, reliance and the sale of goods (*Harlingdon and Leinster Enterprises Ltd.* v. *Christopher Hull Fine Art Ltd.*) [1990] 455
The remedies for abuse of confidential information (*Lac Minerals Ltd.* v. *International Corona Services Ltd.*; *Aquaculture Corp.* v. *N. Z. Mussel Co. Ltd.*) [1990] 460
F.o.b. contracts: substitution of vessels (*Cargill U.K. Ltd.* v. *Continental U.K. Ltd.*) [1990] 465
Set-off and counterclaim—the necessary connection (*Dole Dried Fruit and Nut Co.* v. *Trustin Kerwood Ltd.*) [1990] 471
Auditor's duties: a narrow approach (*Caparo Industries Plc.* v. *Dickman*) [1990] 477
Determining the indeterminate class (*The Morning Watch*) [1990] 481
The banker's right to compound interest (*The Maira* (*No. 3*)) [1990] 488
Foreign maritime liens not to be recognized in South Africa (*The Andrico Unity*) [1990] 491
The demise clause again (*Carling O'Keefe Breweries of Canada Ltd.* v. *C. N. Marine Inc.* (*The Newfoundland Coast*)) [1990] 493

OTHER FEATURES

International Case Notes [1974] 67
International Legislation [1974] 107
International Convention (For the Reciprocal Recognition and Enforcement of Judgments in Civil and Commercial Matters) [1974] 109
Legal Notes [1974] 118
International Case Notes [1974] 184
International Legislation [1974] 221
International Convention (For the Prevention of Pollution from Ships 1973) [1974] 232
Legal Notes [1974] 247
International Case Notes [1974] 316
International Legislation [1974] 357
Legal Notes [1974] 363
International Case Notes [1975] 45
International Legislation [1975] 101
International Convention on the Limitation Period in the International Sale of Goods [1975] 105
Legal Notes [1975] 117
International Case Notes [1975] 176
International Legislation [1975] 237
Legal Notes [1975] 243
International Case Notes [1975] 310
International Legislation [1975] 361
Legal Notes [1975] 367
International Case Notes [1975] 430
International Legislation [1975] 475
Legal Notes [1975] 484
International Case Notes [1976] 66
International Legislation [1976] 116
Legal Notes [1976] 120
International Case Notes [1976] 192
International Legislation [1976] 228
Legal, Maritime and Commercial Notes [1976] 230
International Case Notes [1976] 299
International Legislation [1976] 342
Legal, Maritime and Commercial Notes [1976] 346
International Case Notes [1976] 430
International Legislation [1976] 481
Legal, Maritime and Commercial Notes [1976] 486
Combined Transport: Freight liner conditions *Dr. D. J. Hill* [1977] 88
International Case Notes [1977] 94
International Legislation [1977] 130
Legal, Maritime and Commercial Notes [1977] 132
Carriage by Air: Air Traffic Control—the operator's liability *Neil R. McGilchrist* [1977] 204
Combined Transport: The interpretation of CMR in the English courts *Dr. D. J. Hill* [1977] 212
International Case Notes [1977] 218
International Legislation [1977] 262
Legal, Maritime and Commercial Notes [1977] 265
Carriage by Air: Special contracts and the Malta Agreement *Neil R. McGilchrist* [1977] 366
When does loss mean damage? *Neil R. McGilchrist* [1977] 370

Combined Transport: Warehousing and the sub-contractor *Dr. D. J. Hill* [1977] 373
International Case Notes [1977] 378
International Legislation [1977] 417
Legal, Maritime and Commercial Notes [1977] 419
Carriage by Air: Wilful misconduct and the Warsaw Convention *Neil R. McGilchrist* [1977] 539
Combined Transport: International carriage of perishable goods and ATP *Dr. D. J. Hill* [1977] 546
International Case Notes [1977] 552
International Legislation [1977] 603
Legal, Maritime and Commercial Notes [1977] 606
Carriage by Air: Legislative history as an aid to interpretation *Neil R. McGilchrist* [1978] 68
Combined Transport: The carriage of dangerous goods by land *Dr. D. J. Hill* [1978] 74
Recent Legislation: Torts (Interference with Goods) Act 1977 *R. W. Hodgin* [1978] 80
International Case Notes [1978] 83
International Legislation [1978] 133
Legal, Maritime and Commercial Notes [1978] 134
Carriage by Air: Aerial hi-jacking *Neil R. McGilchrist* [1978] 298
Centre View: Local authorities and offshore petroleum development *John Gibson* [1978] 305
Of soya beans, circles and strings *David Powles* [1978] 306
International Case Notes [1978] 308
International Legislation [1978] 365
Legal, Maritime and Commercial Notes [1978] 367
Recent Legislation: Benelux law on commercial agents now incorporated in Dutch Commercial Code *W. L. J. Calkoen* [1978] 395
Recent Publications [1978] 398
Carriage by Air: Claims against the product supplier *Neil R. McGilchrist* [1978] 487
Centre Comment: The delimitation of sea fisheries districts *John Gibson* [1978] 495
Damages—how remote can you get? *John Gibson* [1978] 497
Combined transport: Actions against successive carriers under CMR *A. C. Hardingham* [1978] 499
International Case Notes [1978] 506
International Legislation [1978] 555
Carriage by Air: Obtaining jurisdiction in the United States *Neil R. McGilchrist* [1978] 609
Centre Comment: On the Kingdom of the Shore *John Gibson* [1978] 616
The broker's duty of care *David Glass* [1978] 619
Recent Legislation: Insurance and the EEC *R. W. Hodgin* [1978] 621
International Case Notes [1978] 636
United Kingdom Legislation [1978] 693
Legal, Maritime and Commercial Notes [1978] 695
Carriage by Air: Punitive damages in aviation litigation *Neil R. McGilchrist* [1979] 48
Recent Legislation: State Immunity Act 1978 *R. W. Hodgin* [1979] 55
International Case Notes [1979] 62
International Legislation [1979] 113
Legal, Maritime and Commercial Notes [1979] 119
Recent Publications [1979] 137

OTHER FEATURES

Carriage by Air: Is Warsaw Convention liability contractual in nature? *Neil R. McGilchrist* [1979] 181

Centre Comment: Oil pollution: a circular argument *John Gibson* [1979] 186

The sub-contractor's lien *David Glass* [1979] 189

Combined Transport: The delay provisions of CMR *A.C. Hardingham* [1979] 193

International Case Notes [1979] 202

United Kingdom Legislation [1979] 257

Legal, Maritime and Commercial Notes [1979] 259

Carriage by Air: *The People ex rel. Air France* v. *Louis J. Giliberto* *Neil R. McGilchrist* [1979] 351

Airline passenger tickets and the duty to give notice *Neil R. McGilchrist* [1979] 353

Centre Comment: Compulsory pilotage: a jurisdictional collision *John Gibson* [1979] 356

Combined Transport: Aspects of the limitation of actions under CMR *A. C. Hardingham* [1979] 362

International Case Notes [1979] 380

International Legislation [1979] 412

Legal, Maritime and Commercial Notes [1979] 416

Carriage by Air: The airport operator's liability for bird-strikes *Neil R. McGilchrist* [1979] 494

Centre Comment: Oil pollution and the common law *John Gibson* [1979] 498

Combined Transport: The time bar regulations in the CMR Convention *Johan Wetter* [1979] 504

International Case Notes [1979] 517

International Legislation [1979] 570

Legal, Maritime and Commercial Notes [1979] 575

Carriage by Air: Aviation litigation in the United States—the pendulum swings? *Neil R. McGilchrist* [1980] 59

Centre Comment: The extra-legal extent of the territorial lore *John Gibson* [1980] 67

International Case Notes [1980] 76

Carriage by Air: Liability insurance claims in general aviation *Neil R. McGilchrist* [1980] 196

Centre Comment: Marine conservation and the right of navigation *John Gibson* [1980] 203

International Case Notes [1980] 215

International Legislation [1980] 295

Carriage by Air: The airline as plaintiff—recent developments in the United States *Neil R. McGilchrist* [1980] 328

Aviation insurance—a recent decision *R. D. Margo* [1980] 335

Centre Comment: Local sea fisheries: the legislative net *John Gibson* [1980] 340

International Case Notes [1980] 347

International Legislation [1980] 383

Carriage by Air: *Forum non conveniens*—the continuing debate *Neil R. McGilchrist* [1980] 439

International Case Notes [1980] 454

Carriage by Air: Denial of boarding to airline passengers *N. R. McGilchrist* [1981] 93

An air disaster and associated problems *R. Binney* [1981] 101

International Case Notes [1981] 115

International Legislation [1981] 175

Carriage by Air: Delivery of a passenger ticket *N. R. McGilchrist* [1981] 296

Centre Comment: The appointment of Customs ports *John Gibson* [1981] 303
Combined Transport: CMR: Safeguarding the parties' interests *A. C. Hardingham* [1981] 306
Carriage by Air: Delivery of a passenger ticket (reprise); BAA v. BAB. A licence upon terms—the requirement of reasonableness *Neil R. McGilchrist* [1981] 378
Centre Comment: CMR and hired trailers—a tilt too far? *David Glass* [1981] 384
Commercial arbitration: The injunctive jurisdiction of the Commercial Court with regard to consensual commercial arbitrations *D. Rhidian Thomas* [1981] 389
International Case Notes [1981] 397
Carriage by Air: Denial of boarding—a perspective from the Philippines *Neil R. McGilchrist* [1981] 518
Australian aviation policy rewritten to avoid effects of *Maclean* v. *Maclean* *Tony Pyne* [1981] 525
Commercial arbitration: Power of court to extend time for commencing arbitration proceedings *D. Rhidian Thomas* [1981] 529
International Case Notes [1981] 550
Carriage by Air: What is a Poincaré gold franc worth? *N. R. McGilchrist* [1982] 164
Centre Comment: CMR: Case update *David Glass* [1982] 173
Commercial arbitration: Removal of arbitrators by the court *D. R. Thomas* [1982] 186
Commercial Notes [1982] 198
Carriage by Air: The gold franc in the United States—after *Franklin Mint* *N. R. McGilchrist* [1982] 281
Commercial arbitration: Costs, discretion and issues of technical misconduct *D. Rhidian Thomas* [1982] 288
Commercial Notes [1982] 302
International Case Notes [1982] 308
Carriage by Air: Notices in the passenger ticket *N. R. McGilchrist* [1982] 444
Recovery under the Warsaw Convention for loss of valuable air cargo *Stanley H. Solomon and Steven E. Goldman* [1982] 453
Commercial arbitration: Security for costs in arbitration *D. Rhidian Thomas* [1982] 463
Commercial Notes [1982] 481
International Case Notes [1982] 484
Carriage by Air: When may domestic carriage be characterised as international? *Neil R. McGilchrist* [1982] 660
Commercial arbitration: The vexed issue of interest awards *D. Rhidian Thomas* [1982] 667
Commercial Notes [1982] 684
International Case Notes [1982] 687
Carriage by Air: Can the US courts denounce the Warsaw Convention? *N. R. McGilchrist* [1983] 111
Commercial arbitration: Judge—Arbitrators *D. Rhidian Thomas* [1983] 120
Commercial Notes [1983] 130
International Case Notes [1983] 132
Carriage by Air: Limitation of liability under the Warsaw Convention—further developments in the US *N. R. McGilchrist* [1983] 308
Commercial arbitration: The legal remedies for dilatoriness in the pre-hearing arbitral procedure *D. Rhidian Thomas* [1983] 315

Commercial Notes [1983] 335
International Case Notes [1983] 338
Carriage by Air: Article 25: an English approach to recklessness *Neil R. McGilchrist* [1983] 488
Commercial arbitration: Admiralty security and the arbitral process *D. R. Thomas* [1983] 495
Commercial Notes [1983] 513
International Case Notes [1983] 519
Carriage by Air: Does the Warsaw Convention govern non-contractual liability *N. R. McGilchrist* [1983] 685
Commercial arbitration: Restraining concurrent foreign legal proceedings *D. R. Thomas* [1983] 692
Commercial Notes [1983] 702
Environmental Law: Environmental protection and the United Nations Convention on the Law of the Sea *Dr. L. D. Guruswamy* [1983] 705
International Case Notes [1983] 718
Commercial Arbitration: Arbitration agreements as a signpost of the proper law *D. R. Thomas* [1984] 141
International Case Notes [1984] 150
International Case-Note: Maritime wrongful death—*Bodden* v. *American Offshore Inc.* [1984] 295
Commercial Arbitration: Proper law of arbitration agreements [1984] 304
Civil Aviation: Mental anguish—before and after the crash [1984] 311
Information [1984] 331
Briefs from *Lloyd's Law Reports* [1984] 333
Commercial Arbitration: The curial law of arbitration proceedings *D. Rhidian Thomas* [1984] 491
Aviation Law: *Franklin Mint Corpn.* v. *Trans World Airlines Inc.*—The opinion of the Supreme Court *N. R. McGilchrist* [1984] 499
Information [1984] 518
Briefs from *Lloyd's Law Reports* [1984] 521
International Case-note: Canadian marine insurance law (*The Bamcell II*) *D. F. and J. M. McEwan* [1984] 671
Information [1984] 690
Briefs from *Lloyd's Law Reports* [1984] 692
Commercial Arbitration: New South Wales Commercial Arbitration Bill 1984 *A. T. Scotford* [1985] 136
Information [1985] 149
Briefs from *Lloyd's Law Reports* [1985] 151
Commercial Arbitration: The power of arbitrators to cure accidental errors *D. Rhidian Thomas* [1985] 263
Information [1985] 281
Briefs from *Lloyd's Law Reports* [1985] 284
Information [1985] 405
Information [1985] 517
Information [1986] 556
Information [1987] 136
Information [1987] 559
Information [1989] 132

BOOK REVIEWS

Bamford: The Law of Shipping and Carriage in South Africa [1974] 314
Goodacre: Marine Insurance Claims [1975] 308

Office of Facilitation, Department of Transportation, Washington: Cargo Liability Study—Final Report [1976] 191
Security Gazette Ltd. (Publishers): Court, the Journal of Legal Practice in Magistrates' Courts [1976] 298
Reynolds and Davenport (Eds.): Bowstead on Agency [1977] 202
Inland Waterways Association: Report on Continental Waterways [1977] 203
Cremades: Panoramica Espanola del Arbitraje Comercial Internacional [1977] 538
Hadden: Company Law and Capitalism [1978] 65
Raistrick and Rees: Lawyers' Law Books; a Practical Index to Legal Literature [1978] 66
Riley: Consequential Loss and Insurance Claims [1978] 67
Cain, Marshall and Brindley: Charlesworth and Cain Company Law [1978] 296
Lawson: Exclusion Clauses after the Unfair Contract Terms Act [1978] 297
Everton: Trade Winds—an Introduction to the UK's Law of Competition [1978] 505
Tetley: Marine Cargo Claims [1978] 627
Mankabady: Collision at Sea—a Guide to the Legal Consequences [1978] 630
Rodière: Droit des Transports [1978] 632
Reynolds and Davenport: Bowstead on Agency [1978] 633
Stockholm Chamber of Commerce (Publishers): Arbitration in Sweden [1978] 634
Singh: Maritime Flag and International Law [1979] 58
UK Mutual Steam Ship Assurance Association (Bermuda) Ltd., and UK Freight Demurrage and Defence Association Ltd.: Legal Decisions and Developments [1979] 60
David & Charles (Publishers): Falconer's Marine Dictionary [1979] 61
Hansell: Elements of Insurance [1979] 199
Whiting: International Trade and Payments [1979] 201
International Chamber of Commerce (Publishers): Guide to Documentary Operations [1979] 371
Butler: Northeast Arctic Passage [1979] 372
Leifer: Malacca, Singapore and Indonesia [1979] 372
Mangone (Ed.): International Straits of the World (Vols. I and II) [1979] 372
McWhinney: The World Court and the Contemporary International Law-making Process [1979] 376
Grime: Shipping Law [1979] 378
Smith: Essential Business Law—Law and the Legal System [1979] 510
Birds: Essential Business Law—Insurance [1979] 512
Ramazani: The Persian Gulf and the Strait of Hormuz [1979] 513
Sweeney (Ed.): International Regulations of Maritime Transportation. Annual Proceedings of the Fordham Corporate Law Institute [1979] 514
Duckworth: Kitchin's Road Transport Law [1979] 515
Elias: New Horizons in International Law [1980] 71
Rosenne (Ed.): Documents on the International Court of Justice [1980] 72
Ivamy: Payne & Ivamy's Carriage of Goods by Sea [1980] 73
Rodière: Droit Maritime Precis [1980] 208
Yates: Essential Business Law—Leases of Business Premises [1980] 210
Morse: Essential Business Law Series—Company Finance, Takeovers and Mergers [1980] 212
Farrar: Essential Business Law Series—Company Insolvency [1980] 212
Sorkin: How to Recover for Loss or Damage to Goods in Transit—1977 Supplement and Revision [1980] 344
Ivamy: Marine Insurance [1980] 447
Kitchen: The Employment of Merchant Seamen [1980] 448
Margo: Aviation Insurance [1980] 451
Cusine and Grant (Eds.): The Impact of Marine Pollution [1980] 451

Speiser: Lawsuit	[1981] 110
Ivamy: Personal Accident, Life and Other Insurances	[1981] 111
Voskvil and Wade (Eds.): The Hague-Zagreb Essays 3	[1981] 112
Lasok (Ed.): Fundamental Duties	[1981] 294
Lambeth (Ed.): Templeman on Marine Insurance	[1981] 373
Lord Denning: The Family Story	[1981] 374
Guest (Gen. Ed.): Benjamin's Sale of Goods	[1981] 510
Neale and Goyder: The Antitrust Laws of the USA	[1981] 512
Thomas: Maritime Liens	[1981] 514
Buglass: Marine Insurance and General Average in the US. An Average Adjuster's Viewpoint	[1981] 516
Hoyle (Ed.): Cases and Materials on the Law of International Trade	[1982] 160
Hoyle: The Law of International Trade	[1982] 160
Simmonds (Gen. Ed.): Commercial Business and Trade Laws (United Kingdom)	[1982] 162
Newman and Wypyski (Eds.): United States International Trade Reports	[1982] 162
Ivamy: Dictionary of Insurance Law	[1982] 277
Mark: Chalmers' Sale of Goods	[1982] 278
Schmitthoff: Commercial Law in a Changing Economic Climate	[1982] 279
Lord Denning: What next in the Law?	[1982] 438
Amin: International and Legal Problems of the Gulf	[1982] 441
Ellen and Campbell: International Maritime Fraud	[1982] 442
Watson: Finance of International Trade	[1982] 655
Honnold: Uniform Law for International Sales	[1982] 657
Hollingshead and Harris (Eds.): 1982 International Handbook and Legal Guide for the Insurer and Reinsurer	[1982] 659
Goodacre: Marine Insurance Claims	[1983] 103
Fischer: A Collection of International Concessions and Related Instruments. Contemporary Series, Vol. 1	[1983] 105
Parks: The Law of Tug, Tow and Pilotage	[1983] 107
Harley: How to Secure a Maritime Lien	[1983] 109
Meinhardt and Davis: Company Law in Great Britain	[1983] 301
Gold: Maritime Transport	[1983] 304
Summerskill: Laytime	[1983] 306
Jess: A Guide to the Insurance of Professional Negligence Risks	[1983] 481
Bassett and Smith: Farwell's Rules of the Nautical Road	[1983] 484
Ivamy: A Casebook on Partnership	[1983] 486
Mustill and Gilman: Arnould's Law of Marine Insurance	[1983] 679
Clarke: International Carriage of Goods by Road: CMR	[1983] 681
Woodcock: Raising Finance: The Guardian Guide for the Small Business	[1983] 682
Clayton: Law for the Small Business: The Daily Telegraph Guide	[1983] 682
Waring: Charterparties, a Comparative Study of South African, English and American Law	[1984] 135
McLaren and Palmer: The Law and Practice of Commercial Arbitrations	[1984] 137
Brice: Maritime Law of Salvage	[1984] 139
Brocker: 1910 Salvage Convention and Lloyd's Open Form under Pressure	[1984] 139
Collins: The Civil Jurisdiction and Judgments Act 1982	[1984] 320
Colman: The Practice and Procedure of the Commercial Court	[1984] 322
Herman: Shipping Conferences	[1984] 325
Goode: Payment Obligations in Commercial and Financial Transactions	[1984] 327
Singh: International Maritime Law Conventions	[1984] 329
Lewis: Lord Atkin	[1984] 506
Lowe: Extraterritorial Jurisdiction	[1984] 507
Douglas: Harbour Law	[1984] 509
Hartley: Civil Jurisdiction and Judgments	[1984] 511

Simpson: Biographical Dictionary of the Common Law [1984] 512
Geen and Douglas: The Law of Pilotage [1984] 514
Rose: The Modern Law of Pilotage [1984] 514
Slabotzky: Grain Contracts and Arbitration [1984] 679
Megrah and Ryder: Byles on Bills of Exchange [1984] 682
O'Connell: The International Law of the Sea (Vol. II) [1984] 684
Hague Convention: Service of Process Abroad [1984] 685
Borrie: The Development of Consumer Law and Policy—Bold Spirits and Timorous Souls [1984] 685
Korah: Exclusive Dealing Agreements in the EEC [1984] 688
Holdert and Buzek: Collision Cases—Judgments and Diagrams [1985] 141
Sturt: The Collision Regulations [1985] 141
Acomb, Jr. (Ed.): Damages Recoverable in Maritime Matters [1985] 141
McDorman, Beauchamp and Johnston: Maritime Boundary Delimitation [1985] 144
Mankabady (Ed.): The International Maritime Organization [1985] 146
Ventris: Bankers' Documentary Credits [1985] 273
Merkin and Williams: Competition Law: Antitrust Policy in the UK and the EEC [1985] 276
Coulson: Commercial Law in the Gulf States: The Islamic Legal Tradition [1985] 279
Kay: Legal Aspects of Business in Saudi Arabia [1985] 279
Ziadeh: Property Law in the Arab World [1985] 279
Sassoon and Merren: C.I.F. and F.O.B. Contracts [1985] 398
Hodgson: The Profits of Crime and their Recovery [1985] 401
Williams and Hepple: Foundations of the Law of Tort [1985] 403
Mocatta, Mustill and Boyd: Scrutton on Charterparties [1985] 513
McConnell, Jr.: The US Shipping Act of 1984 [1985] 515
Arroyo (Ed.): Anuario de Derecho Maritimo (Vol. 1) [1985] 516
Patchett: Recognition of Commercial Judgments and Awards in the Commonwealth [1986] 129
Hill and Messent: CMR: Contracts for the International Carriage of Goods by Road [1986] 131
Grinnings: Arbitration: A Practical Guide [1986] 134
Ivamy: Payne & Ivamy's Carriage of Goods by Sea (12th edn.) [1986] 136
Colinvaux: Law of Insurance (The) (5th edn.) [1986] 260
Bennion: Statutory Interpretation [1986] 262
Stein: Legal Institutions—The Development of Dispute Settlement [1986] 265
Sanders (General Ed.): Yearbook, Commercial Arbitration (Vol. X, 1985) [1986] 267
Hoyle: Law of International Trade (The) (2nd edn.) [1986] 268
Rubin and Sugarman (Eds.): Law, Economy and Society, 1750–1914: Essays in the History of English Law [1986] 270
Brown: Sea-bed Energy and Mineral Resources and the law of the Sea. Vol. 1: The Areas within National Jurisdiction [1986] 272
Hill: Maritime Law (2nd edn.) [1986] 400
Geva: Financing Consumer Sales and Product Defences (In Canada and the United States) [1986] 401
Ivamy (Ed.): Encyclopedia of Shipping Law Sources (U.K.) [1986] 402
Lee: Encyclopedia of Arbitration Law [1986] 402
Lee: Encyclopedia of International Commercial Arbitration [1986] 402
Fawcett: Outer Space (New Challenges to Law and Policy) [1986] 404
Werner (Ed.): Journal of International Arbitration [1986] 405
Paulsson (Ed.): Arbitration International [1986] 405
Penn (Ed.): Journal of International Banking Law [1986] 405
Lerrick and Mian: Saudi Business and Labour Law (Its Interpretation and Application) [1986] 406
d'Alessio: Nazionalita Della Nave: Tra Codificazioné e Decodificazione [1986] 408

Baldwin: Regulating the Airlines (Administrative Justice and Agency Discretion)	[1986] 409
Hoyle: The *Mareva* Injunction and Related Orders	[1986] 410
Powles: The *Mareva* Injunction and Associated Orders	[1986] 410
Australian Government Publishing Service: Asian Pacific Regional Trade Law Seminar	[1986] 412
Tettenborn: An Introduction to the Law of Obligations	[1986] 413
Steel and Rose (Shaw, Consulting Ed.): Kennedy's Law of Salvage (5th Edn.)	[1986] 539
Birks: An Introduction to the Law of Restitution	[1986] 540
Ademuni-Odeke: Protectionism and the Future of International Shipping	[1986] 542
Prott and O'Keefe: Law and the Cultural Heritage (Vol. 1: Discovery and Excavation)	[1986] 546
Korah: Patent Licensing and EEC Competition Rules: Regulation 2349/84	[1986] 547
Whish: Competition Law	[1986] 548
Davies (Ed.): Financial Times Law Reports	[1986] 551
St. John Smart (Ed.): Law Reports of the Commonwealth 1985: Commercial Law Reports	[1986] 551
Reynolds: Bowstead on Agency (15th Edn.)	[1987] 125
Goode (Ed.): Electronic Banking: The Legal Implications	[1987] 126
Smith: Exclusive Economic Zone Claims	[1987] 128
Korah: An Introductory Guide to EEC competition Law and Practice (3rd Edn.)	[1987] 129
Gorton and Ihre: A Practical Guide to Contracts of Affreightment and Hybrid Contracts	[1987] 130
Walker: The Law of Contracts and Related Obligations in Scotland (2nd Edn.)	[1987] 131
Kiantou-Pampouki: Naftiko Dikeo (Maritime Law)	[1987] 132
Brennan: Provisional Damages: A Guide to the New Procedures	[1987] 133
Carmichael and Wolstenholme: Taxation of Lloyd's Underwriters (2nd Edn.)	[1987] 134
Woon: Commercial Law of Singapore	[1987] 134
Tan Lee Meng: The Law in Singapore on Carriage of Goods by Sea	[1987] 235
Furmston (Ed.): The Law of Tort	[1987] 236
Korah: R & D and the EEC Competition Rules Regulation 418/85	[1987] 238
Beale, Bishop and Furmston: Contract Cases and Materials	[1987] 239
Tillotson: Contract Law in Perspective (2nd Edn.)	[1987] 239
Collins: The Law of Contract	[1987] 242
Jess: The Insurance of Commercial Risks: Law and Practice	[1987] 244
Booth: Law, Force and Diplomacy at Sea	[1987] 245
Wallace: International Law	[1987] 247
Foskett: The Law and Practice of Compromise (2nd Edn.)	[1987] 248
Schwampe: Charterers' Liability Insurance	[1987] 373
Abecassis and Jarashow: Oil Pollution from Ships	[1987] 374
Soni: Control of Marine Pollution in International Law	[1987] 375
Smit and Pechota (Eds.): World Arbitration Reporter	[1987] 376
Green: Commercial Agreements and Competition Law	[1987] 378
Buchan: Mortgages of Ships: Marine Security in Canada	[1987] 379
Hedley: Bills of Exchange and Bankers' Documentary Credits	[1987] 380
Arroyo: Convenios Internacionales Maritimos	[1987] 381
Mann: Foreign Affairs in English Courts	[1987] 383
Hudson and Allen: The Institute Clauses Handbook	[1987] 385
Price and Whelan: The Maritime Laws of the Arabian Gulf Co-operation Council States	[1987] 386

Mankabady: The International Maritime Organisation (2nd Edn., Vol. 1) [1987] 387
Furmston: Cheshire, Fifoot & Furmston's Law of Contract (11th Edn.) [1987] 387
Schlechtriem: Uniform Sales Law [1987] 534
Sarcevic and Volken (Eds.): International Sale of Goods [1987] 534
Yates and Hawkins: Standard Business Contracts: Exclusions and Related Devices [1987] 535
Jackson: Enforcement of Maritime Claims [1987] 537
Read (Ed.): Law Reports of the Commonwealth: Commercial Law Reports 1986 [1987] 544
Parritt: Violence at Sea [1987] 546
Gabriel: Legal Aspects of Syndicated Loans [1987] 549
Jones and Goodhart: Specific Performance [1987] 551
Ventris: Tanker Voyage Charterparties [1987] 553
Townsend: The Financing of Countertrade [1987] 554
Koburger Jr.: Vessel Traffic Systems [1987] 556
Ivamy: Merchant Shipping (Liner Conferences) Act 1982 [1987] 557
Jacobs-Wustefeld: Law Dictionary (English-German) [1987] 558
Ramsay (Ed.): Debtors and Creditors (A Socio-Legal Perspective) [1988] 103
Cripps: The legal Implications of Disclosure in the Public Interest [1988] 105
Bernstein: Handbook of Arbitration Practice [1988] 107
Crawford: Crawford & Falconbridge: Banking and Bills of Exchange (8th Edn.) [1988] 108
Gold: Handbook on Marine Pollution [1988] 109
Arroyo (Gen. Ed.): Yearbook Maritime Law (Vol. 1: 1984) [1988] 110
Hendry and Wood: The Legal Status of Berlin [1988] 112
Lindgren, Carter and Harland: Contract Law in Australia [1988] 113
Golding (Ed. Louw): The Law and Practice of Reinsurance [1988] 116
Institute of Maritime Law: Limitation of Shipowners' Liability: The New Law [1988] 117
Griggs and Williams: Limitation of Liability for Maritime Claims [1988] 117
Dashwood, Hacon and White: A Guide to the Civil Jurisdiction and Judgments Convention [1988] 118
Gee and Andrews: *Mareva* Injunctions: Law and Practice [1988] 120
Ough: The *Mareva* Injunction and Anton Piller Order (Practice and Precedents) [1988] 120
Kapoor and Kerr: A Guide to Maritime Boundary Delimitation [1988] 121
Craig, Park and Paulsson: International Chamber of Commerce Arbitration [1988] 246
Saleh: Commercial Arbitration in the Arab Middle East [1988] 246
McGovern: International Trade Regulation (GATT, the United States and the European Community) (2nd Edn.) [1988] 248
Schofield: Laytime and Demurrage [1988] 249
Rose (Ed.): New Foundations for Insurance Law [1988] 251
University of East Asia (Ed.): Statutes and Regulations of the People's Republic of China [1988] 253
Butler and Merkin: Reinsurance Law [1988] 254
Schmitthoff: Schmitthoff's Export Trade (The Law and Practice of International Trade) (8th Edn.) [1988] 256
Walker: Export Practice and Documentation (3rd Edn.) [1988] 256
Koh Soon Kwang (Ed.): Carriage of Goods by Sea [1988] 258
Merkin: Richards Butler on Latent Damage [1988] 260
Shaw: International Law (2nd Edn.) [1988] 261
Geva (Ed.): Banking & Finance Law Review [1988] 262
Ivamy: Encyclopedia of Oil and Natural Gas Law [1988] 263
Christou: International Agency, Distribution and Licensing Agreements [1988] 264
Dugard: Recognition and the United Nations [1988] 265

Milnes Holden: The Law and Practice of Banking (Vol. 1 Banker and Customer (4th Edn.); Vol. 2 Securities for Bankers' Advances (7th Edn.))	[1988] 266
Schadee and Claringbould (Eds.): Transport: International Transport Treaties	[1988] 267
Ivamy (Ed.): Encyclopedia of Carriage Law Sources	[1988] 267
Albrecht and Heward (Eds.): Maritime Law Handbook	[1988] 267
Bos and Brownlie (Eds.): Liber Amicorum for Lord Wilberforce	[1988] 396
Redfern and Hunter: The Law and Practice of International Commercial Arbitration	[1988] 398
Cuyvers: The Strait of Dover	[1988] 400
Rozakis and Stagos: The Turkish Straits	[1988] 400
Goldrein and Wilkinson: Commercial Litigation: Pre-emptive Remedies	[1988] 403
Shashikumar: US Shipping Act of 1984: A Scrutiny of Controversial Proposals	[1988] 404
Markesinis: (A Comparative Introduction to) the German Law of Tort	[1988] 405
Butler (Ed.): The Law of the Sea and International Shipping (Anglo-Soviet Post-UNCLOS Perspectives)	[1988] 407
Downes: A Textbook on Contract	[1988] 408
Schiels: Tramp Ship Agency Practice	[1988] 410
Carbone (Ed.): La Giurisprudenzia Italiana in Tema di Trasporti	[1988] 411
Howarth: Freshwater Fishery Law	[1988] 412
Beseler and Williams: Anti-Dumping and Anti-Subsidy Law: The European Communities	[1988] 414
Schwebel: International Arbitration: Three Salient Problems	[1988] 416
Lawson: Sales Promotion Law	[1988] 417
Savage and Bradgate: Business Law	[1988] 418
Dassesse and Isaacs: EEC Banking Law	[1988] 420
Ryder: Legal Problems of International Banking	[1988] 421
Bourguignon: Sir William Scott, Lord Stowell	[1988] 528
Adams: Understanding Contract Law	[1988] 529
Tetley: Maritime Liens and Claims	[1988] 533
Lasok and Stone: Conflict of Laws in the European Community	[1988] 535
Kaye: Civil Jurisdiction and Enforcement of Foreign Judgments	[1988] 535
Todd: Modern Bills of Lading	[1988] 538
Sharpe and Spicer (Eds.): New Directions in Maritime Law	[1988] 538
Akehurst: A Modern Introduction to International Law (6th Edn.)	[1988] 540
Campbell (Ed.): Legal Aspects of Doing Business in Eastern Europe and the Soviet Union	[1988] 541
Gaskell, Debattista and Swatton: Chorley & Giles' Shipping Law	[1988] 543
Silvertown: The Law of Lien	[1988] 545
Lee: Commercial Disputes Settlement in China	[1988] 546
Meeson: The Practice and Procedure of the Admiralty Courts (Forms and Precedents)	[1988] 547
Goff and Jones: Law of Restitution (The) (3rd Edn.)	[1989] 115
Goode: Proprietary Rights and Insolvency in Sales Transactions	[1989] 116
Parris: Effective Retention of Title Clauses	[1989] 118
Dickson: Reservation of Title Clauses	[1989] 118
Burrows: Remedies for Torts and Breach of Contract	[1989] 121
Davies: Commencement of Laytime	[1989] 122
Horner: Parallel Imports	[1989] 123
Verwer: Liability for Damage to Luggage in International Air Transport	[1989] 124

Trebilcock: Common Law of Restraint of Trade (The): A Legal and Economic Analysis [1989] 126
Lambeth: Templeman on Marine Insurance: Its Principles and Practice (6th Edn.) [1989] 126
Merkin (Ed.): Encyclopedia of Competition Law [1989] 127
Goode (Ed.): Conflicts of Interest in the Changing Financial World [1989] 128
Moser (Ed.): Foreign Trade, Investment and the Law in the People's Republic of China [1989] 129
Wesley-Smith: An Introduction to the Hong Kong Legal System [1989] 130
Freedman: Product Liability Actions by Foreign Plaintiffs in the United States [1989] 131
McGuinness: The Law of Guarantee (A Treatise on Guarantee, Indemnity and the Standby Letter of Credit) [1989] 225
Newns and Parrington: Double Taxation Relief for Shipping [1989] 226
Carter (Ed.): Journal of Contract Law [1989] 228
Neale and Stephens: International Business and National Jurisdiction [1989] 229
Kemicha (Ed.): Euro–Arab Arbitration [1989] 231
Chatterjee (Ed.): Lloyd's Arbitration Reports [1989] 231
Zahn, Eberding and Ehrlich: Zahlung und Zahlungssicherung im Aussenhandel (6th Edn.) [1989] 234
Kelly and Ball: Insurance Legislation Manual [1989] 234
McNeil: Motor Carrier Cargo Claims [1989] 236
Theunis (Ed.): International Carriage of Goods by Roads (CMR) [1989] 236
Goyder: EEC Competition Law [1989] 237
de Lupis: The Law of War [1989] 238
Tyree: Australian Law of Cheques and Payment Orders [1989] 239
Penn, Shea and Arora: Banking Law. Vol. 1: The Law Relating to Domestic Banking. Vol. 2: The Law and Practice of International Banking [1989] 240
Mbanefo (Ed.): Nigerian Shipping Cases. Vol. 2: 1980–1986 [1989] 242
Chiaw (Ed.): Butterworths Banking and Financial Law Review 1987 [1989] 243
Merrills: International Dispute Settlement [1989] 246
Merkin and McGee: Insurance Contract Law [1989] 246
Parkington (Ed.): MacGillivray & Parkington on Insurance Law [1989] 246
Ivamy: Marine Insurance (4th Edn.) [1989] 246
Goodacre: Institute Time Clauses Hulls [1989] 246
Brown: Marine Insurance. Vol. 1: Principles and Basic Practice [1989] 246
Witherby & Co. Ltd.: Reference Book of Marine Insurance Clauses (58th Edn.) [1989] 246
Goodacre: Goodbye to the Memorandum [1989] 246
Shaw: Admiralty Jurisdiction and Practice in South Africa [1989] 382
Hetherington: Annotated Admiralty Legislation [1989] 382
North and Fawcett: Cheshire & North's Private International Law (11th Edn.) [1989] 385
Jacobs (Ed.): Yearbook of European Law 7: 1987 [1989] 387
van den Berg (Gen. Ed.): Yearbook on Commercial Arbitration [1989] 513
Hames and McBain: Aircraft Finance: Registration, Security and Enforcement [1989] 515
Nordquist (Ed.): United Nations Convention of the Law of the Sea 1982: A Commentary [1989] 517
Ivamy: General Principles of Insurance Law (5th Edn.) [1989] 520
Churchill: EEC Fisheries Law [1989] 521

Dahmani: The Fisheries Regime of the Exclusive Economic Zone	[1989] 521
Mendes (Ed.): Review of International Business Law	[1989] 524
Netherlands (The) Institute for the Law of the Sea (NILOS): International Organizations and the Law of the Sea (Vol. 2.1986)	[1989] 525
Reid: Shiphandling with Tugs	[1989] 525
Amin: Middle East Legal Systems; Commercial Law of Iran; Islamic Law in the Contemporary World	[1990] 119
Ballantyne: Commercial Law in the Arab Middle East: The Gulf States	[1990] 119
Tetley: Marine Cargo Claims (3rd Edn.)	[1990] 126
Finn (Ed.): Equity and Commercial Relationships	[1990] 128
Rose (Ed.): International Commercial and Maritime Arbitration	[1990] 130
Fleming: The American Tort Process	[1990] 132
Tarr (Gen. Ed.): Insurance Law Journal	[1990] 133
Margo: Aviation Insurance (2nd Edn.)	[1990] 135
McGregor: The Law of Damages (15th Edn.)	[1990] 137
McBryde: The Law of Contract in Scotland	[1990] 138
Woolman: An Introduction to the Scots Law of Contract	[1990] 138
Cusine and Forte: Scottish Cases and Materials in Commercial Law	[1990] 139
Hartley: The Foundations of European Community Law (2nd Edn.)	[1990] 141
Lew (Ed.): Contemporary Problems in International Arbitration	[1990] 142
Joyner and Chopra (Eds.): The Antarctic Legal Regime	[1990] 144
Anton: Civil Jurisdiction in Scotland	[1990] 146
Allen: Misrepresentation	[1990] 147
Dore: Arbitration and Conciliation under the UNCITRAL Rules: A Textual Analysis	[1990] 268
Goode: Consumer Credit Law	[1990] 269
Zweigert and Kotz: An Introduction of Comparative Law (2nd Edn.)	[1990] 271
Bridge: Sale of Goods	[1990] 272
Dickson, Rosenor and Storm (Eds.): Security on Moveable Property and Receivables in Europe	[1990] 273
Harris: Remedies in Contract and Tort	[1990] 275
Tilbury, Noone and Kercher: Remedies (Commentary and Materials)	[1990] 276
Jacob (Gen. Ed.): Private International Litigation	[1990] 277
Parks: Law and Practice of Marine Insurance and Average (The)	[1990] 278
Circus: Towards a General Duty to Trade Fairly?	[1990] 279
Collier: Conflict of Laws	[1990] 282
Jaffey: Introduction to the Conflict of Laws	[1990] 282
Kumar: Control of Exclusion Clauses in England and India	[1990] 284
Van Niekerk: Roman-Dutch Insurance Law	[1990] 285
Capper: Mareva Injunctions	[1990] 286
Gray: Futures and Options for Shipping	[1990] 287
Zachcial and Heidelhoff (Eds.): Shipping Statistics Yearbook 1988	[1990] 288
Kittichaisaree: Law of the Sea and Maritime Boundary Delimitation in South-East Asia (The)	[1990] 289
Elagab: Legality of Non-forcible Countermeasures in International Law (The)	[1990] 290
Booker: Containers: Conditions, Law and Practice of Carriage and Use	[1990] 291
Kingsley: Braekhus & Rein's Handbook on P. & I. Insurance (3rd Edn.)	[1990] 292
Usher: Legal Aspects of Argiculture in the European Community	[1990] 293
Butler: Soviet Law (2nd Edn.)	[1990] 294
Born and Westin: International Civil Litigation in United States Courts	[1990] 296
Strivens (Ed.): Merger Control in the EEC	[1990] 297
Fox, Jr.: International Commercial Agreements	[1990] 298

Pineus: Ship's Value (2nd Edn.) [1990] 299
Kaikobad: Shatt-al-Arab Boundary Question (The) [1990] 300
Lewison: Interpretation of Contracts (The) [1990] 428
Storme and Demeulenaere: International Commercial Arbitration in Belgium [1990] 429
Goode: Legal Problems of Credit and Security (2nd Ed.) [1990] 431
Cooke and Oughton: Common Law of Obligations (The) [1990] 432
Llewellyn: Regulation and Supervision of Financial Institutions (The) [1990] 434
Penn: Banking Supervision (Regulation of the UK Banking Sector under the Banking Act 1987) [1990] 434
Vincenzini: International Regulation of Salvage at Sea [1990] 436
Rose (Ed.): Blackstone's Statutes on Commercial Law [1990] 438
Pitt (Ed.): Butterworth's Commercial Law Handbook [1990] 438
Raybould: Comparative Law of Monopolies [1990] 439
Mangone: Marine Policy for America (2nd Edn.) [1990] 440
Bernaerts: Bernaerts' Guide to the United Nations Convention on the Law of the Sea [1990] 441
Tarr: Australian Insurance Law [1990] 443
Birds: Modern Insurance Law (2nd Edn.) [1990] 445
de Alba: Maritime Codes—1: Panama [1990] 446
de Alba: Ship Registries—1: Panama [1990] 448
Ademuni-Odeke: Shipping in International Trade Relations [1990] 448
Schreuer: State Immunity: Some Recent Developments [1990] 450
International Chamber of Commerce: Retention of Title—A Practical Guide to 19 National Legislations [1990] 451
Guest (Gen. Ed.): Chitty on Contracts (26th Edn.) [1990] 555
Harris and Tallon (Eds.): Contract Law Today (Anglo-French Comparisons) [1990] 556
Horn (Ed.): Law of International Trade Finance (The) (Studies in Transnational Economic Law, Vol. 6) [1990] 558
Jess: Insurance of Professional Negligence Risks (The): Law and Practice (2nd Edn.) [1990] 559
Churchill and Lowe: Law of the Sea (The) (2nd Edn.) [1990] 561
Howarth: Water Pollution Law [1990] 562
Howarth: Law of the National Rivers Authority (The) [1990] 562
United Nations Office for Ocean Affairs and the Law of the Sea (Ed.): Annual Review of Ocean Affairs: Law and Policy, Main Documents 1985–1987, Vols. I and II [1990] 563
Korea Maritime Institute: Changes in the World Shipping Environments and Counter-Strategies toward the Year 2000 [1990] 564
Williams and Bonnick: Commentaries on Tanker Voyage Charterparties [1990] 565
Campbell (Ed.): Legal Aspects of Business Transactions and Investment in the Far East [1990] 566
Gold: Exchange Rates in International Law and Organization [1990] 567
Sands (Ed.): Chernobyl: Law and Communication [1990] 568
McArdle (Ed.): International Ship Arrest [1990] 570

BOOK NOTICES

Commonwealth Lawyer's Association: The Commonwealth Lawyer [1984] 516
Bolton: Marine Transport: A Guide to Libraries and Sources of Information in Great Britain [1984] 516
Permanent Bureau of the Hague Conference (Ed.): The Hague Conference on Private International Law: Collection of Conventions (1951–1980) [1984] 516

Eales and de Vos: A Guide to Bankruptcy	[1984] 517
United Nations: The Law of the Sea (Official Text of the United Nations Convention on the Law of the Sea with Annexes and Index)	[1984] 689
Prentice: Butterworths Company Law Cases 1983	[1984] 689
Mbanefo: Nigerian Shipping Laws	[1985] 147
Martin (Ed.): A Concise Dictionary of Law	[1985] 147
Commonwealth Secretariat: 1983 Meeting of Commonwealth Law Ministers: Memoranda	[1985] 147
MacElrevey: Shiphandling for the Mariner	[1985] 148
Hooyer: Behaviour and Handling of Ships	[1985] 148
Ashworth (Ed.): Product Liability Casebook	[1985] 404
Hudson and Allen: Marine Claims Handbook (4th Edn.)	[1985] 404
Pineus: Time-Barred Actions	[1986] 274
Pineus & Röhreke: Limited Liability in Collision Cases	[1986] 274
Astle: Limitation of Liability	[1986] 274
Modern Liner Contracts	[1986] 414
McCune: The Asbatankvoy Charter	[1986] 414
A Guide to the Hague and Hague-Visby Rules	[1986] 414
Ivamy (Ed.): Dictionary of Shipping Law	[1986] 414
Ivamy (Ed.): Casebook on Carriage by Sea	[1986] 415
Hay (Ed.): Professional Liability Today	[1986] 415
Kapoor and Gray: Maritime Fraud: An Overview	[1986] 415
Kon: The Business Men's Guide to EEC Legal Developments	[1986] 415
Cranston: Consumers and the Law	[1986] 553
Calverley: Country Risk Analysis	[1986] 553
Hudson (Ed.): Butterworths Insurance Law Handbook (2nd. Ed.)	[1986] 553
Encyclopedia of Shipping Law Sources (U.K.) Service Issue No. 4	[1986] 554
Thomas R. Miller & Co.: Legal Decisions 1985	[1986] 554
Astle: Time Charter Withdrawals	[1986] 554
Colman: The Practice and Procedure of the Commercial Court (2nd Ed.)	[1986] 554
Brodie: Dictionary of Shipping Terms	[1986] 555
Maw and Williams (Eds.): What Law Now for the Seas?	[1987] 248
Cone: The Regulation of Foreign Lawyers (3rd Edn.)	[1987] 248
Williams (Ed.): Career Preparation and Opportunities in International Law	[1987] 248
Consumer Law Statutes (5th Edn.)	[1987] 248
Hamilton: All Jangle and Riot (A Barrister's History of the Bar)	[1987] 249
Rose: Civil Liability Statutes (Contract, Tort and Restriction)	[1987] 249
Vaughan: The Banking Act 1979	[1987] 249
Murphy, Rowley and Hunnings (Eds.): North American Commercial Law	[1988] 269
Jowell and McAuslan (Eds.): Lord Denning: The Judge and the Law	[1988] 269
Hudson (Ed.): Butterworths Insurance Law Handbook (2nd Edn.)	[1988] 270
Bates: UK Oil Pollution Legislation	[1988] 270
Ivamy: Merchant Shipping Act 1970	[1988] 270
Calwell: Sea Lawyer: A Guide for Yachtsmen (2nd Edn.)	[1988] 270
Amin: Law and Justice in Contemporary Yemen	[1988] 270
Mawer: Tales from a Palm Court	[1988] 270
Ivamy (Ed.): Casebook on Agency (3rd Edn.); Casebook on Shipping Law (4th Edn.); Casebook on Sale of Goods (5th Edn.)	[1988] 271
Jackson: Arrests, Liens and Mortgages: Modern Needs and Modern Developments	[1988] 548
Bates: UK Marine Pollution Law	[1988] 548
Schwampe: Charterers' Liability Insurance	[1988] 548
Thomas Miller & Co.: Legal Decisions 1987	[1988] 548
Degenhardt (Ed.): Maritime Affairs—A World Handbook	[1988] 548

Sullivan: The Marine Encyclopaedic Dictionary (2nd Edn.) [1988] 549
Brodie: Dictionary of Shipping Terms: Italian-English and English-Italian [1988] 549
Brodie: Dictionary of Shipping Terms: Spanish-English and English-Spanish [1988] 549
Ivamy: Merchant Shipping Act 1979 [1988] 549
Patterson (Ed.): The City Directory 1988 [1988] 549
Tetley: Maritime Liens and Claims [1989] 249
Ivamy (Ed.): Mozley & Whiteley's Law Dictionary (10th Edn.) [1989] 528
Healy and Sharpe: Cases and Materials on Admiralty (2nd Edn.) [1990] 151
Henry: The Carriage of Dangerous Goods by Sea [1990] 151
Douglas: The Pilotage Act 1987 [1990] 151
Ignarski (Ed.): The Underwiters' Bedside Book [1990] 151
Graham and Hughes: Containerisation in the Eighties [1990] 152
Hayuth: Intermodality: Concept and Practice [1990] 152
Campbell (Ed.): Legal Aspects of Doing Business in Africa [1990] 152
Swedish Transport Research Board: A Directory of 154 Periodicals Useful to Transport Researchers; Information Databases in the Field of Transportation [1990] 152
Schmitthoff and Goode (Eds.): International Carriage of Goods: Some Legal Problems and Possible Solutions [1990] 302
Hill: Maritime Law (3rd Edn.) [1990] 302
Guest (Gen. Ed.): Benjamin's Sale of Goods (3rd Edn.) [1990] 302
Hodgin: Insurance Intermediaries and the Law [1990] 302
Fernandes: Marine Insurance Law of Canada [1990] 303

Table of Cases 1986–1990

A. *v*. C. [1981] Q.B. 956 .... [1987] 251
A & D Properties Inc. *v*. M.V. *Volta River*, 1984 AMC 464 (E.D. Louisiana) .... [1989] 353
A.B. Marintrans *v*. Comet Shipping Co. Ltd. [1985] 1 W.L.R. 1270 .. [1987] 10; [1988] 8, 55; [1990] 418
A.B.D. (Metals & Waste) Ltd. *v*. Anglo Chemical & Ore Co. Ltd. [1955] 2 Lloyd's Rep. 456 .... [1990] 310, 311
AB Consolidated Ltd. *v*. Europe Strength Food Co. [1978] 2 N.Z.L.R. 515 .... [1990] 464
Abadesa, The [1967] P. 265 .... [1989] 32
Aberdeen Railway Co. *v*. Blaikie Brothers (1854) 1 Macq. 461 (H.L.) .... [1990] 331
Abeyesekere *v*. Jayatilaka (1931) 33 N.L.R. 291 .... [1987] 171
Abidin Daver, The [1984] A.C. 398 .... [1986] 441, 513; [1987] 3; [1988] 91, 391; [1990] 13
Abitibi-Price Sales Corp. *v*. The *Wilhelm Wesch* [1987] 2 F.C. 579 (F.C.) .... [1989] 90
Abu Dhabi Gas Liquefaction Co. *v*. Eastern Bechtel Corp. [1982] 2 Lloyd's Rep. 425 (C.A.) .[1986] 66
A Company No. 004475/82 (*Re*) [1983] 2 All E.R. 36, 44; [1983] Ch. 178 .... [1988] 61; [1990] 411
A Company No. 002612/84 (*Re*) [1985] B.C.L.C. 80 .... [1988] 72
A Company No. 005287/85 (*Re*) 1 W.L.R. 281 .... [1988] 77
A Company No. 008699/85 (*Re*) B.C.L.C. 382, at 387 .... [1988] 65, 78
A Company (*Re*) [1986] B.C.L.C. 391 .... [1988] 60
A Company (No. 00477 of 1986) [1986] P.C.C. 372 (*Re*) [1986] B.C.L.C. 376 .... [1988] 62; [1989] 508; [1990] 411
A Company No. 001761/86 [1987] B.C.L.C. 141, at 143 .... [1988] 64
A Company No. 004377/86 (*Re*) [1987] 1 W.L.R. 102 .... [1988] 62
A Company No. 005136/86 (*Re*) [1987] B.C.L.C. 82 .... [1988] 75
A Company No. 007623/86 (*Re*) [1986] B.C.L.C. 362 .... [1988] 62
A Company (No. 00359 of 1987) (*Re*) [1988] Ch. 210 .... [1989] 20 *et seq*., 393
A Company (No. 00370 of 1987) (*Re*) [1988] 1 W.L.R. 1068 .... [1990] 411
A Company (No. 00789 of 1987) (*Re*) (1989) 5 B.C.C. 792 .... [1990] 411
A Company (No. 823 of 1987) (*Re* Sam Weller & Sons Ltd.) (*Re*) [1989] 3 W.L.R. 923 .... [1990] 411
A Company (No. 005009 of 1987), *ex p*. Copp (*Re*) [1989] B.C.L.C. 13 .... [1990] 209, 213
A Company (No. 005685 of 1988) *ex p*. Schwartz (No. 2) (*Re*) [1989] B.C.L.C. 427 .... [1990] 411
A.C. & S. Inc. *v*. Aetna Casualty & Surety Co., Nos. 83–1927/28 (3 Cir. 17 June 1985) .... [1986] 91
Acland *v*. Lewis (1860) K. & G. 334 .... [1990] 402
Acmetrack Ltd. *v*. Bank Canadian National (1984) 12 D.L.R. (4th) 428 (Ont. C.A.) .... [1986] 174
Acrow Ltd. *v*. Rex Chainbelt Inc. [1971] 1 W.L.R. 1676 .... [1990] 88
Acrux, The [1965] P. 391 .... [1989] 179
Actis Co. Ltd. *v*. Sanko Steamship Co. Ltd. (*The Aquacharm*) [1982] 1 Lloyd's Rep. 7 .... [1990] 107, 110, 111
Adamastos Shipping Co. Ltd. *v*. Anglo-Saxon Petroleum Co. Ltd. [1959] A.C. 133, 170 .... [1986] 482
Addis *v*. Gramophone Ltd. [1909] A.C. 488, 495 .... [1988] 139
Addison *v*. Cox (1872) L.R. 8 Ch. 76 .... [1989] 197
Addystone Pipe and Steel (1889) 175 U.S. 211 .... [1986] 550
Adelaide Electric Supply Co. *v*. Prudential Assurance Co. [1934] A.C. 122 .... [1990] 407
Adler *v*. Dickson [1955] 1 Q.B. 158 .... [1986] 344
Admiral Oriental Lines *v*. U.S., 86 F. 2d 201 (2 Cir. 1936) .... [1986] 13
Adolf Warski, The [1976] 2 Lloyd's Rep. 241 .... [1987] 538
Adrabell Ltd., Airborne Accessories Ltd. *v*. Goodman (*Re*) [1984] 3 All E.R. 407 .... [1986] 168
A.E. & C.I. Ltd. *v*. King and Sons, 1979 (2) SA 36 (A) .... [1987] 315

Aetna Casualty & Surety Co. *v.* General Reinsurance Corp., Superior Ct., New Britain, Hartford, Conn. (reported in Mealey's Litigation Reports: "Insurance", 28 May 1985, at p. 590) .... [1986] 81
Aetna Financial Services Ltd. *v.* Feigelman (S.C.C., p. 276) .... [1987] 545
Afovos, The [1983] 1 W.L.R. 195 .... [1987] 145, 412; [1989] 87
Afovos Shipping Co. S.A. *v.* Pagnan [1983] 1 W.L.R. 195 .... [1987] 145, 212; [1989] 87
Africa, The (1854) 1 Sp. 299 .... [1989] 78
A.-G. *v.* Guardian Newspapers (No. 1) [1987] 1 W.L.R. 1248 .... [1987] 423; [1989] 159
A.-G. *v.* Guardian Newspapers Ltd. (No. 2) [1988] 3 W.L.R. 776; [1990] A.C. 109 .... [1990] 7, 462
AGIP (Africa) Ltd. *v.* Jackson, *The Times*, 5 June 1989 .... [1989] 296, 338, 339, 340
A-G of Canada *v.* Fishing Vessel Owners' Assoc. of B.C. [1985] 1 F.C. 791 .... [1987] 94
A.-G.'s Reference (No. 1 of 1983) [1985] Q.B. 182 .... [1985] 180; [1989] 305
A.-G.'s Reference (No. 1 of 1985) [1986] Q.B. 491 .... [1988] 130; [1990] 463
Agia Erini II, The (1974) S.M.A. No. 875 .... [1989] 355
Agrebele, The [1985] 2 Lloyd's Rep. 496 .... [1987] 158; [1988] 308
Agricultores Federados Argentinos *v.* Ampro S.A. [1965] 2 Lloyd's Rep. 157 .... [1990] 467
Agri-Trans Corp. *v.* Gladders Barge Line Inc., 721 F. 2d 1005, 1008–09 (5 Cir. 1983) .... [1986] 379
Agro Co. of Canada Ltd. *v.* The *Regal Scout* [1984] 2 F.C. 851 .... [1987] 87
Ailsa Craig Fishing Co. Ltd. *v.* Malvern Fishing Co. Ltd. [1983] 1 W.L.R. 964 (H.L.) .... [1987] 167; [1989] 396; [1990] 155
Ainsbury *v.* Millington [1987] 1 W.L.R. 379 .... [1988] 303
Air Ecosse Ltd. *v.* Civil Aviation Authority [1988] P.C.C. 252 .... [1990] 405
A.J. Bekhor & Co. Ltd. *v.* Bilton [1981] Q.B. 923 .... [1990] 323
A.K.A.S. Jamal *v.* Moola Dawood Sons & Co. [1916] A.C. 175 (P.C.) .... [1990] 310, 312
Akerblom *v.* Price (1881) 7 Q.B.D. 129, 132 .... [1988] 19
Aktieselskabet Olivebank *v.* Dansk Svovlslyre Fabrik [1919] 2 K.B. 162 .... [1987] 409
Aktieselskabet Reidar *v.* Arcos Ltd. [1927] 1 K.B. 352 .... [1987] 419
Akties Nord-Osterso Rederiet *v.* E.A. Casper Edgar & Co. Ltd. (1923) 28 Com. Cas. 222 .... [1989] 85
Aktion, The [1987] 1 Lloyd's Rep. 283 .... [1987] 410; [1989] 152 *et seq.*
Aktion Maritime Corp. of Liberia *v.* S. Kasmas & Bros. Ltd. (*The Aktion*) [1987] 1 Lloyd's Rep. 283 .... [1987] 410; [1989] 152 *et seq.*
Al Hofuf, The [1981] 1 Lloyd's Rep. 81 .... [1987] 62; [1989] 81
Al Saudi Banque *v.* Clarke Pixley [1990] 2 W.L.R. 344 .... [1990] 208
Al Wahab, The [1982] 1 W.L.R. 961; aff'd [1984] A.C. 50 .... [1990] 125, 194, 197
Alan (W.J.) & Co. Ltd. *v.* El Nasr Export & Import Co. [1972] 2 Q.B. 189 .... [1989] 23; [1990] 66
Alaska Trainship Corp. *v.* Pacific Pilotage Authority [1981] 1 S.C.R. 261; *confirming* [1980] 2 F.C. 54 and [1978] 1 F.C. 411 .... [1989] 98
Alaskan Trader, The [1983] 2 Lloyd's Rep. 647 .... [1986] 124
Albacora S.R.L. *v.* Westcott & Laurance Line [1966] 2 Lloyd's Rep. 53 .... [1990] 126
Albatross, The (1853) 1 Sp. 175n .... [1989] 69
Albazero, The [1977] A.C. 774 .... [1986] 100, 304; [1988] 38; [1989] 9; [1990] 319
Albeko Schuhmaschinen A.G. *v.* Kamborian Shoe Machine Co. Ltd. (1961) 111 L.J. 519 .... [1989] 220, 386; [1990] 192
Albert & Son *v.* Armstrong Rubber Co., 178 F. 2d (2 Cir. 1949) .... [1986] 336
Albion, The (1861) Lush. 282 .... [1989] 59, 71
Alchemist, The (1980) S.M.A. No. 1473 .... [1989] 350, 361
Aldora, The [1975] 1 Lloyd's Rep. 617 .... [1986] 316
Alec Lobb (Garages) Ltd. *v.* Total Oil (G.B.) Ltd. [1985] 1 W.L.R. 173 .... [1989] 272
Alenquer, The and The *Rene* [1955] 1 Lloyd's Rep. 101 .... [1990] 51
Alert, The (1893) 56 F. 721 .... [1990] 36
Aletheia, The (1864) 13 W. Rep. 279 .... [1989] 67
Alev, The [1989] 1 Lloyd's Rep. 138 .... [1989] 270 *et seq.*; [1990] 345, 346
Alexander *v.* Burchfield (1842) 7 Man. & G. 1061 .... [1990] 71
Alexander *v.* Nat'l Union, 1939 A.M.C. 923 (2 C.A.), 38 C.J. 1051 .... [1986] 498
Alexander *v.* Westeel-Rosco Ltd. (1978) 93 D.L.R. (3d) 116 (Ont. H.C.) .... [1989] 412
Alexion Hope, The [1988] 1 Lloyd's Rep. 311; [1987] 1 Lloyd's Rep. 60, 282; (1986) (Unrep.) .... [1987] 39; [1988] 325
Alfa Nord, The [1977] 2 Lloyd's Rep. 434 (C.A.) .... [1987] 83; [1989] 292
Alfen, The (1857) Swab. 189 .... [1989] 65
Algoma Central Rwy. *v.* The *Cielo Bianco* (1987) 73 N.R. 321 (Fed. C.A.) .... [1988] 86

Aliakmon, The [1985] Q.B. 350 (C.A.); [1986] 2 W.L.R. 902; [1986] A.C. 785 (H.L.) .... [1986] 6, 97, 294, 295, 296, 297, 298, 299, 300, 301, 302, 303, 304, 305, 405; [1987] 9, 54, 84, 238, 258; [1988] 40, 257, 259, 366, 469, 505; [1989] 5, 54, 55, 117, 167, 237, 422, 423; [1990] 317
Alicia, The (1986) 789 F. 2d 1406, 1986 A.M.C. 2308 (9 Cir. 1986) .... [1986] 424, 426; [1989] 192
Alland *v.* Consumers Credit Corp., 476 F. 2d 951, 956 (2 Cir. 1973) .... [1986] 49
Allanson *v.* Atkinson (1813) 1 M. & S. 583 .... [1989] 312
Allen *v.* Coltart (1883) 11 Q.B.D. 782 .... [1987] 256
Allen *v.* Gold Reefs of W. Africa Ltd. [1900] 1 Ch. 656 .... [1988] 75
Allen *v.* Gulf Oil Refinery Ltd. [1981] A.C. 1004 .... [1988] 419
Allen *v.* Royal Bank of Canada (1925) 95 L.J.P.C. 17 .... [1990] 66
Allen *v.* Sir Alfred McAlpine & Sons Ltd. [1968] 1 Q.B. 299 .... [1987] 155
Allen-Qualley Co. *v.* Shellmar Products Co. (1929) 36 F. 2d 623 (7th Cir.) .... [1990] 461
Allied Arab Bank Ltd. *v.* Hajjar [1988] Q.B. 787 .... [1989] 469
Allied Arab Bank Ltd. *v.* Hajjar (No. 2) [1988] 3 W.L.R. 33; [1988] 3 All E.R. 103 .... [1989] 330
Allied Marine Transport Ltd. *v.* Vale do Rio Doce Navegacao S.A. (*The Leonidas D*) [1985] 1 W.L.R. 925 .... [1986] 68, 105; [1988] 304, 307
Allied Towing Corp. (*In re*), 478 F. Supp. 398 (E.B. Va., 1979) .... [1987] 502
Allobrogia, The [1979] 1 Lloyd's Rep. 190 .... [1987] 232, 234, 407; [1989] 393, 499
Allseas Maritime S.A. *v.* M.V. *Mimosa* (1987) 812 F. 2d 243 (5th Cir.) .... [1988] 520
Allstate *v.* Klock Oil Co., 2426 N.Y.S. 2d 603 (1980) .... [1986] 93
Allstate Ins. Co. *v.* Pietrosh, 85 Nev. 310, 454 P. 2d 106, 110 (1969) .... [1986] 84
Alpha, The (1865) 13 W.R. 927 .... [1989] 61
Altus, The [1985] 1 Lloyd's Rep. 423, 430 .... [1986] 252
Aluminium Industrie Vaassen B.V. *v.* Romalpa Aluminium Ltd. [1976] 1 W.L.R. 676 .... [1986] 168; [1988] 141; [1989] 119, 198, 510, 511; [1990] 403
Alva S.S. Co. Ltd. *v.* City of New York (1980) 616 F. 2d 605 .... [1990] 53
Alyeska Pipelines Service Co. *v* Wilderness Society, 421 U.S. 240 (1975) .... [1986] 47
A.M. Satterthwaite & Co. Ltd. *v.* New Zealand Shipping Co. Ltd. (*The Eurymedon*) [1975] A.C. 154 .... [1990] 127, 319
Amalgamated Investments and Property Co. Ltd. *v.* Texas Commerce International Bank Ltd. [1982] Q.B. 84 .... [1990] 498
Amatex Corp., *In re*, Case No. 82–05220 (E.D. Pa., 9 November 1982) .... [1986] 80
Amerada Hess Corp. *v.* S.S. *Phillips Oklahoma* (1983) S.M.A. No. 1794 (S.D.N.Y.) .... [1989] 354
Amerada Hess Shipping Corp. *v.* Argentine Republic (*The Hercules*) 830 F. 2d 421 .... [1988] 10
American Accord, The [1983] 1 A.C. 168 .... [1989] 234; [1990] 234, 235, 552
American Airlines *v.* Hope [1973] 1 Lloyd's Rep. 233 (C.A.); [1974] 2 Lloyd's Rep. 301 (H.L.) .... [1990] 136
American Commercial Barge Line Co. *v.* Eagle Marine Indus. Inc., 1977 A.M.C. 475 (E.D. Mo. 1976) [1986] 379
American Cyanamid Co. *v.* Ethicon [1975] A.C. 396 .... [1988] 404
American Express Ltd. *v.* British Airways Board [1983] 1 W.L.R. 701 .... [1987] 73
American Home Products Corp. *v.* Liberty Mutual Ins. Co., 565 F. Supp. 1484 (S.D.N.Y 1983), aff'd 748 F. 2d 760 (2 Cir. 1984) .... [1986] 82, 88, 90
American Metal Co. *v.* M/V *Belleville*, 1970 AMC 633; 284 F. Supp. 1002 .... [1990] 35
American States Ins. Co. *v.* Maryland Cas. Co., 587 F. Supp. 1549 (E.D. Mich. 1984) .... [1986] 93
American Steel Barge Co. *v.* Chesapeake & O. Coal Agency Co. (1903) 115 F. 669 .... [1989] 192
American Tobacco Co. *v.* Goulandris (1960) 281 F. 2d 179 (2nd Cir.) .... [1989] 351
AMEV-UDC Finance Ltd. *v.* Austin (1986) 60 A.L.J.R. 741; (1986) 162 C.L.R. 170 .... [1987] 146; [1990] 23
Amin Rasheed Corp. *v.* Kuwait Insurance Co. (*The Al Wahab*) [1984] A.C. 50 (H.L.); [1982] 1 W.L.R. 961; [1983] 1 W.L.R. 228 (C.A.) .... [1986] 441, 511, 514, 516; [1987] 2, 523, 525, 526, 528, 529; [1989] 219; [1990] 125, 194, 197
Amo Containers Ltd. *v.* Drake Insurance Co. Ltd. (1985) 51 Nfld. & P.E.I.R. 55; 150 A.P.R. 55 .... [1987] 90
Amoco Cadiz, The (*In re*), 1984 A.M.C. 2123 (N.D. Ill., 1984) .... [1987] 520
Amoco Transport Co. *v.* S/S *Mason Lykes*, No. 83–2219 (5 Cir. 16 August 1985) .... [1986] 362
Ampthill Peerage Case, The [1977] A.C. 547 .... [1989] 000
Amstar Corp. *v.* SS *Alexandros T.*, 644 F. 2d 904 (4 Cir. 1981) .... [1986] 350
Amstar Corp. *v.* S/S *Juanita Halkias*, No. 83–3326 (E.D. Pa., 19 December 1983) .... [1986] 359
Anaconda, The *v.* American Sugar Co., 322 U.S. 42 (1944) .... [1986] 67
Anco Princess, The, 1978 A.M.C. 2471; [1978] 1 Lloyd's Rep. 293 (E.D.La., 1977) .... [1987] 344

Andalusia, The (1865) 12 L.T. 584 .... [1989] 65, 79
Anderson *v.* Earlanger [1980] C.L.Y. 133 .... [1987] 46, 57, 58
Anderson *v.* Schultz (1975) 62 D.L.R. (3d) 762 .... [1990] 505
Anderson Marine Enterprises Ltd. *v.* Ship *Mei Hai* 25 F.T.R. 74 (Can. F.C.) .... [1990] 100
Anderson's (Pacific) Trading Co. Pty. Ltd. *v.* Karlander New Guinea Line Ltd. [1980] 2 N.S.W.L.R. 870 .... [1987] 260; [1988] 285
Andrabell Ltd. (*Re*) [1984] 3 All E.R. 407 .... [1988] 147; [1989] 202, 203
Andreas Lemos, The [1983] Q.B. 647 .... [1990] 164
Andree, The (1939) 39 Ll.L.Rep. 213 .... [1987] 449
Andre et Cie *v.* Marine Transocean Ltd. (*The Splendid Sun*) [1981] Q.B. 694; [1981] 2 Lloyd's Rep. 29 (C.A.) .... [1986] 68; [1987] 156; [1988] 304, 308
Andrew Wilson, The (1863) Br. & Lush. 56 .... [1989] 68
Andrews *v.* Essex Mar. Ins. Co. (1882) 3 Mas. C.C. 6 .... [1988] 334
Andrews *v.* Hopkinson [1957] 1 Q.B 229 .... [1988] 502
Andria, The now renamed *Vasso* [1984] Q.B. 477 .... [1987] 540
Andrico Unity, The, 1987 (3) S.A. 794 (C) .... [1989] 175 *et seq.*
Andrico Unity, The, 1989 (4) S.A. 325(A) .... [1990] 491
Angbats AB Kalmarsund *v.* Pakistan Edible Oils Corp. (*The Corina*), S.M.A. No. 1567 (1981) .... [1986] 72
Angelakis (G. & N.) Shipping Co. S.A. *v.* Compagnie Nationale Algerienne de Navigation (*The Attika Hope*) [1988] 1 Lloyd's Rep. 439 .... [1988] 148; [1989] 191, 193
Angeliki, The [1973] 2 Lloyd's Rep. 226 .... [1986] 142, 285
Anglia Commercial Properties Ltd. *v.* North East Essex Building Co. Ltd. (1983) 266 E.G. 1096 .... [1987] 62
Anglia Television Ltd. *v.* Reed [1972] 1 Q.B. 60 .... [1986] 335; [1990] 148
Anglo-Austrian Printing & Publishing Co. (*Re*) [1895] 2 Ch. 891 .... [1990] 217
Anglo Auto Finance Co. Ltd. *v.* James [1963] 1 W.L.R. 1042, pet. diss. *ibid.*, 1049 .... [1990] 19
Anglo-Canadian Shipping Co. *v.* Pulp, Paper & Woodworkers, Local (1988) 27 B.C.L.R. (2d) 378 (B.C.C.A.) .... [1990] 102
Anglo Eastern Bulkships Ltd. *v.* Ameron Inc., 556 F. Supp. 1198 (S.D.N.Y. 1982) .... [1986] 361
Anglo-French Co-operative Society (*Re*) (1882) 21 Ch.D. 492 .... [1990] 222
Anglo-Iranian Oil Co. Ltd. *v.* Jaffrate (*The Rose Mary*) [1953] 1 W.L.R. 246 .... [1986] 435
Anita, The [1971] 1 Lloyd's Rep. 487, rvsg. [1970] 2 Lloyd's Rep. 365 .... [1988] 435
Ann Stathatos, The (1949) 83 Ll.L.Rep. 228 .... [1986] 125; [1988] 57
Anna M. Fahy, The, 153 F. 866 (2 Cir. 1907) .... [1986] 379
Annangel Glory C.N.S.A. *v.* M. Golodetz Ltd. (*The Annangel Glory*) [1988] 1 Lloyd's Rep. 45 .... [1988] 145, 150; [1989] 191, 192, 193, 194, 196, 197; [1990] 523
Annapolis, The (1861) Lush. 355 .... [1989] 77
Anne Quinn Corp. *v.* American Manufacturers Mutual Ins. Co., 1974 A.M.C. 655 (S.D.N.Y.) .... [1986] 500
Annefield, The [1971] P. 168 .... [1987] 87
Anns *v.* Merton London Borough Council [1978] A.C. 728 .... [1987] 9, 84; [1988] 366; [1989] 42; [1990] 479
Antaios Compania Naviera S.A. *v.* Salen Rederierna A.B. (*The Antaios*) [1985] A.C. 191 .... [1986] 143, 238, 242, 552; [1988] 396, 409; [1989] 122; [1990] 556
Antares, The (1985) LMLN 162; [1986] 2 Lloyd's Rep. 626, 633; [1987] 1 Lloyd's Rep. 424 .... [1986] 142; [1987] 146, 260; [1990] 315
Antares, The (No. 2) [1987] 1 Lloyd's Rep 424; [1986] 2 Lloyd's Rep. 626 .... [1987] 146; [1989] 396; [1990] 315
Antclizo, The [1987] 2 Lloyd's Rep. 130; [1988] 1 W.L.R. 603 .... [1987] 155, 263; [1988] 302, 303, 307, 308
Anterist *v.* Crédit Lyonnais [1987] 1 C.M.L.R. 333 .... [1988] 388
Anticosti Shipping Co. *v.* St. Amand [1959] S.C.R. 372 .... [1987] 82
Antilles Steamship Co. Ltd. *v.* Union Carbide Corp. (*The Alchemist*) (1980) S.M.A. No. 1473 .... [1989] 350
Antique Porcelain Ltd. *v.* Trust House Forte Ltd. 11 December 1977. (Unrep.) .... [1987] 80
Anton Piller K.G. *v.* Manufacturing Processes Ltd. [1976] Ch. 55 .... [1990] 321
Antonis P. Lemos, The [1985] A.C. 711 .... [1986] 97; [1987] 85
Aotearoa International Ltd. *v.* Scancarriers A/S (*The Barranduna and Tarago*) [1985] 2 Lloyd's Rep. 419 (P.C.) .... [1986] 105

Apex Oil Co. *v.* United States, 530 F. 2d 1291; 1976 A.M.C. 2119 (8th Cir., 1976), cert. denied 429 U.S. 827 (1976) .... [1987] 499
Apex Supply Co. Ltd. (*Re*) [1942] 1 Ch. 108 .... [1989] 509
Apiliotis, The [1985] 1 Lloyd's Rep. 255 .... [1988] 53
A.P.J. Priti, The [1987] 2 Lloyd's Rep. 37 (C.A.) .... [1988] 52
Apollo, The [1978] 1 Lloyd's Rep. 200 .... [1990] 108, 111
Apollon, The [1983] 1 Lloyd's Rep. 409 .... [1990] 387
Apollon, The [1985] 1 Lloyd's Rep. 597 .... [1986] 235, 237, 238
Applewood Lane West Ltd. *v.* Scott (1987) 35 D.L.R. (4th) 287 .... [1988] 396
Aquacharm, The [1982] 1 Lloyd's Rep. 7 .... [1986] 126; [1990] 107, 110, 111
Aquaculture Corp. *v.* N.Z. Mussel Co. Ltd., C.A., as yet unreported; judgment 11 June 1990; first instance (1986) 1 N.Z.I.P.R. 678 .... [1990] 464
Aquila, The (1798) 1 C.Rob. 37 .... [1987] 272
Arab Bank Ltd. *v.* Barclays Bank (D.C.O.) [1954] A.C. 495 .... [1989] 364; [1990] 71
Aragon, The, 15 April 1987 .... [1989] 143 *et seq.*, 418, 419
Aramis, The [1987] 2 Lloyd's Rep. 58; (1988) LMLN 238; [1989] 1 Lloyd's Rep. 213 .... [1987] 255; [1988] 38; [1989] 53, 162 *et seq.*, 423, 430; [1990] 319
Aratra Potato Co. Ltd. *v.* Egyptian Navigation Co. (*The El Amria*) [1981] 2 Lloyd's Rep. 119 .... [1986] 517; [1987] 396
Arawa,The [1977] 2 Lloyd's Rep. 416 .... [1987] 80
Arbutus Park Estates Ltd. *v.* Fuller (1977) 74 D.L.R. (3d) 257 .... [1987] 428
Arcado *v.* Haviland, Case 9/87, 8 March 1988 .... [1988] 384
Archbolds (Freightage) Ltd. *v.* S. Spanglett Ltd. [1961] 1 Q.B. 374 (C.A.) .... [1987] 202, 203, 204, 205, 206; [1988] 126; [1989] 521
Archital Luxfer Ltd. *v.* Henry Boot Construction Ltd. [1981] 1 Lloyd's Rep. 642 .... [1987] 173
Arcos Ltd. *v.* E.A. Ronaasen & Son [1933] A.C. 470 .... [1990] 457
Arctic Engineering Ltd. (*Re*) [1986] B.C.L.C. 253 .... [1987] 190
Arctic Explorer, The (1984) 590 F. Supp. 1346; 1984 A.M.C. 2413 (S.D. Tex.) .... [1989] 13
Arctic Offshore Marine Services Ltd. *v.* M.N.R. (1986) 4 F.T.R. 183 (F.C.) .... [1989] 102
Arcweld Constructions Pty. Ltd. *v.* Smith (1968) Unrep., Victoria Sup. Ct. .... [1988] 36
Ardennes (Cargo Owners) *v.* *Ardennes* (Owners) [1951] 1 K.B. 55 .... [1986] 316; [1988] 286
Arenson *v.* Casson, Beckman Rutley & Co. [1977] A.C. 405 .... [1989] 160
Argo, The (1856) Swab. 112 .... [1989] 61
Argonaut, The [1982] 2 Lloyd's Rep. 214 .... [1988] 307
Aries Tanker Corp. *v.* Total Transport Ltd. (*The Aries*) [1977] 1 W.L.R. 185 .... [1986] 387; [1989] 291, 292, 293, 294; [1990] 172, 474
Arietta Venizelos, The, 1973 A.M.C. 1012 .... [1986] 127
Armadora Occidental S.A. *v.* Horance Mann Insurance Co. [1977] 1 W.L.R. 1098 .... [1986] 508, 515, 516, 518; [1987] 528
Armagas Ltd. *v.* Mundogas S.A. (*The Ocean Frost*) [1985] 1 Lloyd's Rep. 1 .... [1986] 109
Armagh Shoes Ltd. (*Re*) [1982] N.I. 59; [1984] B.C.L.C. 405 .... [1989] 194; [1990] 209
Armar, The [1981] 1 W.L.R. 207 .... [1986] 508, 512, 513, 517; [1987] 523, 525, 526; [1990] 194
Armar Shipping Co. Ltd. *v.* Caisse Algériènne d'Assurance et de Reassurance (*The Armar*) [1981] 1 W.L.R. 207 .... [1986] 508, 512, 513, 517; [1987] 523, 525, 526; [1990] 194
Armonia, The (1853) 17 Jur. 354n .... [1989] 74
Armory *v.* Delamirie (1722) 1 Str. 505 .... [1988] 289
Armour & Co. *v.* Ft. Morgan S.S. Co., 270 U.S. 253 (1926) .... [1986] 12
Armour *v.* Thyssen Edelstahlwerke A.G., 1989 S.L.T. 182 .... [1990] 527
Armstrong *v.* Toler, 11 Wheat. 258 (S. Ct., U.S., 1826) .... [1987] 214
Arnold *v.* National Westminster Bank [1988] 3 W.L.R. 1229 .... [1989] 433, 434
Arris *v.* Stukely (1677) 2 Mod. 260 .... [1989] 297
Arrow Transfer Co. Ltd. *v.* Royal Bank of Canada (1972) 27 D.L.R. (3rd) 81 .... [1986] 8
Arta, The [1985] 1 Lloyd's Rep. 534 .... [1988] 50
Arthur, The (1862) 6 L.T. 556 .... [1989] 73, 76
Arthur Young & Co. *v.* W.A. Chip and Pulp Co. Pty. Ltd. [1988] 13 A.C.L.R. 283 .... [1990] 419, 421
AS-Autoteile *v.* Malhé, Case 220/84; [1986] 3 C.M.L.R. 321 .... [1989] 472
A/S Awilco of Oslo *v* Fulvia S.p.A. di Navigazione of Cagliari (*The Chikuma*) [1981] 1 W.L.R. 314 .... [1986] 214; [1989] 367
A/S Gunnstein & Co. K/S *v.* Jenson, Krebs & Nielsen (*The Alfa Nord*) [1977] 2 Lloyd's Rep 434 (C.A.) .... [1987] 83; [1989] 292
A/S Ivarans, 1982 A.M.C. 2493 (1 C.A.) .... [1986] 498

A/S Ornen *v*. The *Duteous* [1987] 1 F.C. 270 (F.C.) .... [1988] 86
A.S. James Pty. Ltd. *v*. C.B. Duncan [1970] V.R. 705 .... [1990] 419
Asfar v. Blundell [1896] 1 Q.B. 123 .... [1988] 257; [1990] 475
Ashbury Carriage Co. *v*. Riche (1875) L.R. 7 H.L. 653 .... [1990] 402
Ashington Piggeries Ltd. *v*. Christopher Hill Ltd. [1972] A.C. 441 .... [1988] 515; [1990] 457
Ashtiani *v*. Kashi [1987] Q.B. 888 (C.A.) .... [1989] 469; [1990] 89
Asiatic Electric Co. Pty. Ltd. (*Re*) (1970) 92 W.N. (N.S.W.) 361 .... [1990] 217
Askew *v*. American Waterways Operators, 411 U.S. 325, 1973 A.M.C. 811, 2493 (1973) .... [1986] 376, 377; [1987] 502
Aslan *v*. Murphy (Nos. 1 and 2) [1989] 3 All E.R. 130 .... [1990] 8
Aspen Trader, The [1981] 1 Lloyd's Rep. 273 .... [1986] 144
Associated Distributors *v*. Hall [1938] 2 K.B. 83 .... [1990] 471
Associated Japanese Bank (International) Ltd. *v*. Credit du Nord S.A. [1988] N.L.J.L.R. 109; [1989] 1 W.L.R. 255 .... [1988] 300; [1989] 432, 437, 442, 443; [1990] 456, 506
Associated Provincial Picture Houses *v*. Wednesbury Corporation [1948] 1 K.B. 223 .... [1987] 233
Associated Travel Ltd. (*In re*) [1978] 1 W.L.R. 547 .... [1986] 384
Astley *v*. Reynolds (1731) 2 Str. 915 .... [1990] 344
Astro Amo Compania Naviera S.A. *v*. Elf Union S.A. (*The Zographia M*) [1976] 2 Lloyd's Rep. 382 .... [1986] 214
Astrovlanis Compania Naviera S.A. *v*. Linard (*The Gold Sky*) [1972] 2 Lloyd's Rep. 187 .... [1987] 39; [1988] 355
Aswan (M/S) Engineering Establishment Co. *v*. Lupdine Ltd. [1987] 1 W.L.R. 1 .... [1987] 400, 402
Athanasia Comninos, The and the *Georges Chr Lemos* [1981] Com L.R. 132 .. [1988] 53, 58; [1989] 347
Athenic, The [1984] L.M.L.N. 134 .... [1986] 78
Athens Maritime Enterprises Corp. *v*. Hellenic Mutual War Risks Assn. (Bermuda) Ltd. (*The Andreas Lemos*) [1983] Q.B. 647 .... [1990] 164
Athos, The [1981] 2 Lloyd's Rep. 74 .... [1990] 453
Atkins International S.A. *v*. Islamic Republic of Iran Shipping Lines (*The A.P.J. Priti*) [1987] 2 Lloyd's Rep. 37 (C.A.) .... [1988] 52
Atlantic Baron, The [1979] Q.B. 705 .... [1986] 313; [1987] 426; [1989] 272; [1990] 344
Atlantic Emperor, The [1989] 1 Lloyd's Rep. 54 .... [1990] 132, 192
Atlantic Lines & Navigation Co. Inc. *v*. The *Didymi* [1988] 1 Lloyd's Rep. 97; [1985] 1 F.C. 240 (Fed. C.A.) .... [1987] 87; [1989] 98
Atlantic Song, The [1983] 2 Lloyd's Rep. 395 ....[1986] 261
Atlantic Star, The [1974] A.C. 436; [1972] 2 Lloyd's Rep. 446 ....[1987] 5, 315; [1989] 222, 223, 224
Atlas, The (1862) Lush. 518 .... [1989] 72, 74, 80
Atlas Express Ltd. *v*. Kafco (Importers and Distributors) Ltd. [1989] 1 All E.R. 641; [1989] Q.B. 833 ....[1989] 270 *et seq.*; [1990] 345
Attika Hope, The [1988] 1 Lloyd's Rep. 439 .... [1988] 148; [1989] 191, 193; [1990] 523
Attock Cement Co. Ltd. *v*. Romanian Bank for Foreign Trade, 21 December 1988, unreported (C.A.) .... [1989] 365
Attorney-General *v*. Arthur Anderson & Co., *The Times*, 13 October 1987; [1989] E.C.C. 224 (C.A.) .... [1990] 277, 327
Attorney-General *v*. Nissan [1970] A.C. 179 .... [1987] 384
Attorney-General *v*. Sun Hung Kai Bank Ltd. (Hong Kong C.A., p.677) .... [1987] 546
Attorney-General *v*. Technical Construction Co. Ltd. .... [1986] 552
Attorney-General for the Dominion of Canada *v*. Attorney-General for the Provinces of Ontario, Quebec and Nova Scotia [1898] A.C. 700 (P.C.) ....[1988] 90
Attorney General of Ceylon *v*. Scindia Steam Navigation Co. Ltd. [1962] A.C. 60 .... [1986] 388, 478
Attorney-General of Hong Kong *v*. Ng Yuen Shiu [1983] 2 A.C. 629 .... [1990] 435
Attorney-General's Reference (No. 1 of 1985) [1986] Q.B. 491 .... [1987] 435; [1989] 196
Attorney-General's Reference (No. 1 of 1988) [1989] A.C. 971 .... [1990] 413
Attwood *v*. Small (1836) 6 Cl. & Fin. 232 .... [1986] 318
Atwool *v*. Merryweather (1867) L.R. 5 Eq. 464 ....[1988] 77
Audi-NSU *v*. Adelin Petit (1979) Journal des Tribunaux 625 .... [1988] 385
August 8, The [1983] 2 A.C. 450 .... [1990] 171
Augustus Barnett & Son Ltd. (*Re*) [1986] B.C.L.C. 170 .... [1988] 294; [1990] 210
Aurora, The (1842) 1 W. Rob. 322 .... [1989] 61, 66
Austotel Pty. Ltd. *v*. Franklins Selfserve Pty. Ltd., 8 June 1989 (N.S.W.C.A.), unreported .. [1990] 502

Australia and New Zealand Banking Group Ltd. *v.* Westpac Banking Corp. (1988) 164 C.L.R. 662; (1988) 62 A.L.J.R. 292; (1988) 78 A.L.R. 157 ....[1989] 303, 304; [1990] 496, 518, 550
Australian Commercial Research and Development Ltd. *v.* ANZ McCaughan Merchant Bank Ltd. [1989] 3 All E.R. 65 .... [1990] 327
Australian National Airlines Commission *v.* Robinson [1977] V.R. 87 .... [1989] 85
Austrian Lloyd Steamship Co. *v.* Gresham Life Assurance Society Ltd. [1903] 1 K.B. 249 ... [1987] 311
AVX Ltd. *v.* EGM Solders Ltd. (1982) *The Times*, 7 July .... [1986] 232; [1987] 43, 48, 56
Avery *v.* Bowden (1855) 5 E. & B. 714 .... [1989] 84
Avon C.C. *v.* Howlett [1983] 1 W.L.R. 605 .... [1989] 438, 441; [1990] 147
Avon Finance Co. Ltd. *v.* Bridger [1985] 2 All E.R. 281 .... [1987] 125; [1988] 436; [1990] 338
Awad *v.* Pillai [1982] R.T.R. 266 (C.A.) .... [1986] 227; [1987] 44
Ayache *v.* Cie Air-France (1984) 38 R.F.D.A. 450 (T.G.I. Paris) .... [1988] 219
B. & G. Construction Co. *v.* Bank of Montreal [1954] 2 D.L.R. 753 .... [1986] 8
B. & S. Contracts of Design Ltd. *v.* Victor Green Publications Ltd. [1984] I.C.R. 419 [1989] 7, 273, 274
Babanaft International Co. S.A. *v.* Avant Petroleum Inc. (*The Oltenia*) [1982] 2 Lloyd's Rep. 99 (C.A.) .... [1986] 59
Babanaft International Co. S.A. *v.* Bassatne [1988] 2 F.T.L.R. 116; [1989] 2 W.L.R. 232 (C.A.) .... [1989] 465, 469, 470, 472, 474; [1990] 88, 89, 90, 91
Bache & Co. (London) Ltd. *v.* Banque Vernes et Commerciale de Paris S.A. [1973] 2 Lloyd's Rep. 437 .... [1990] 239, 241, 242
Bad Boy Appliances and Furniture Ltd. *v.* Toronto Dominion Bank (1972) 25 D.L.R. (3rd) 257 .... [1986] 8
Baden, Delvaux and Lecuit *v.* Société Générale pour Favoriser le Développement du Commerce et de l'Industrie en France S.A. [1983] B.C.L.C. 325 .... [1988] 364; [1989] 298 *et seq.*
Bahr *v.* Nicolay (No. 2) (1988) 62 A.L.J.R. 268 .... [1989] 85
Baker (G.L.) Ltd. *v.* Medway Building & Supplies Ltd. [1958] 1 W.L.R. 1216 (Ch. D.); [1958] 1 W.L.R. 1225 (C.A.) .... [1989] 314, 316, 331, 334
Balder Offshore Canada *v.* Federal Commerce and Nav. Ltd., 1986 A.M.C. 1279 (F.C.) ....[1988] 88
Balmoral Supermarket Ltd. *v.* Bank of New Zealand [1974] 2 N.Z.L.R. 155 .... [1989] 367; [1990] 65
Balodis *v.* The *Prince George* [1985] 1 F.C. 890 .... [1987] 90
Balsamo *v.* Medici and Morris [1984] 1 W.L.R. 951 .... [1986] 226; [1987] 44, 54; [1990] 550
Bamburi, The [1982] 1 Lloyd's Rep. 312 .... [1986] 119
Bamcell II, The [1983] S.C.R. 47; [1986] 2 Lloyd's Rep. 524 .... [1984] 671; [1988] 87; [1990] 106
Bamford *v.* Bamford [1970] Ch. 212 .... [1988] 72
Banco, The [1971] P. 137 .... [1988] 96
Banco do Brasil S.A. *v.* The *Alexandros G. Tsavliris*, 1987 A.M.C. 2452 (F.C.) .... [1989] 94
Banco Nacional de Cuba *v.* Sabbatino (1964) 376 U.S. 398 .... [1989] 230
Bankers Trust Co. *v.* Shapira [1980] 1 W.L.R. 1274 .... [1987] 251
Bankers Trust International Ltd. *v.* Todd Shipyards Corp. (*The Halcyon Isle*) [1981] A.C. 221; [1980] 2 Lloyd's Rep. 325; 1980 A.M.C. 1221 (P.C.) .... [1987] 153, 321; [1988] 82; [1989] 11 *et seq.*, 174 *et seq.*; [1990] 492
Bank Line Ltd. *v.* Arthur Capel & Co. [1919] A.C. 435 .... [1986] 346; [1990] 156
Bank Mellat *v.* Helliniki Techniki S.A. [1984] Q.B. 291 (C.A.) .... [1986] 63; [1988] 25; [1989] 473
Bank Negara Indonesia 1946 *v.* Lariza (Singapore) Pte. Ltd. [1988] A.C. 583 .... [1990] 559
Bank of Australasia *v.* Palmer [1897] A.C. 540, 545 .... [1986] 157
Bank of Baroda *v.* Shah [1988] N.L.J. L.R. 98 .... [1988] 436
Bank of Boston Connecticut *v.* European Grain & Shipping Ltd. (*The Dominique*) [1989] 2 W.L.R. 440 .... [1989] 289 *et seq.*
Bank of British North America *v.* Haslip (1914) 20 D.L.R. 922 .... [1990] 71, 74, 248
Bank of England *v.* Cutler [1908] 2 K.B. 208 .... [1989] 9
Bank of England *v.* Vagliano [1891] A.C. 107, 144 .... [1986] 27
Bank of Ireland *v.* Evans' Trustees (1855) 5 H.L.C. 389, 410–411 .... [1986] 9
Bank of New South Wales *v.* Milvain (1884) 10 V.L.R., L3 .... [1988] 139
Bank of Nova Scotia *v.* Angelica-Whitewear Ltd. [1987] 1 S.C.R. 591 .... [1989] 524
Bank of Nova Scotia *v.* Gaudreau (1984) 48 O.R. (2d) 478 .... [1986] 167
Bank of Nova Scotia *v.* Hellenic Mutual War Risks Association (Bermuda) Ltd. (*The Good Luck*) [1988] 1 Lloyd's Rep. 514; [1989] 2 Lloyd's Rep. 238; [1990] 2 W.L.R. 547 .... [1989] 251 *et seq.*; [1990] 318, 417, 419
Bank of St. Thomas *v.* British Brigantine *Julia Blake* (1882) 107 U.S. 418 .... [1987] 163
Bank of Tokyo *v.* Karoon [1986] 3 W.L.R. 414; [1987] A.C. 45n .... [1987] 5, 391
Bannerman *v.* White (1861) 10 C.B.N.S. 844 .... [1990] 456

Banque Belge pour l'Etranger *v*. Hambrouck [1921] 1 K.B. 321 .... [1987] 437; [1989] 118–119, 306, 310, 339
Banque Financière de la Cité S.A. *v*. Westgate Insurance Co. Ltd. [1989] 3 W.L.R. 25; [1990] 3 W.L.R. 364 (C.A.) .... [1990] 318, 445, 560
Banque Keyser Ullmann S.A. *v*. Skandia (U.K.) Ins. Co. Ltd. [1988] 1 F.T.L.R. 360; [1987] 2 W.L.R. 1300; [1989] 3 W.L.R. 25; [1990] Q.B. 665 .... [1987] 5, 245; [1988] 29, 252; [1989] 248, 251; [1990] 134, 418, 485
Barameda Enterprises Pty. Ltd. *v*. O'Connor (*The Tiruna and the Pelorus*) [1987] 2 Lloyd's Rep. 667 .... [1988] 178
Barber Lines A/S *v*. M/V *Donau Maru*, 764 F. 2d 50 (1 Cir. 1985) .... [1986] 362
Barboni *v*. Cie Air-France (1982) 36 RFDA 355 (T.G.I. Paris) .... [1988] 227
Barclay Holdings (Australia) Pty. Ltd. *v*. British National Insurance Co. Ltd., 3 April 1987 ...[1988] 31
Barclay-Johnson *v*. Yuill [1980] 1 W.L.R. 1259 .... [1988] 135
Barclays Bank Ltd. *v*. Customs and Excise [1963] 1 Lloyd's Rep. 81 .... [1989] 395; [1990] 316
Barclays Bank *v*. TOSG Trust Ltd. [1984] B.C.L.C. 1, r'vsd on other grounds [1984] A.C. 626 .... [1990] 412
Barclays Bank Ltd. *v*. W.J. Simms & Son [1980] Q.B. 677 .... [1989] 305, 307, 440; [1990] 334
Barclays Bank Plc *v*. Bank of England [1985] 1 All E.R. 385 .... [1988] 478; [1990] 71, 72, 73, 75, 76, 244, 245, 246, 247, 249
Barclays Bank Plc *v*. Quincecare Ltd. [1988] 1 F.T.L.R. 507 .... [1988] 441
Barclays Bank Plc *v*. Willowbrock International Ltd. [1987] 1 F.T.L.R. 386; [1986] B.C.L.C. 45 .... [1987] 150; [1989] 195
Barefoot, The (1850) 14 Jur. 841 .... [1989] 72
Barker *v*. Moore & McCormack Inc. (1930) 40 F. 2d 410 .... [1990] 107
Barley (Y.P.) Producers Ltd. *v*. E.C. Robertson Pty. Ltd. [1927] V.L.R. 194 .... [1989] 81
Barnes *v*. Addy (1874) L.R. 9 Ch. App. 244 .... [1988] 365; [1989] 245, 304, 323, 324, 337, 338
Barnett *v*. Sanker (1925) 41 T.L.R. 660 .... [1986] 395
Barnouw *v*. S.S. *Ozark*, 304 F. 2d 717, 1962 A.M.C. 1675 (5 Cir. 1962) .... [1986] 356
Barranduna, The [1985] 2 Lloyd's Rep. 419 (P.C.) .... [1986] 105
Barras *v*. Aberdeen Steam Trawling & Fishing Co. [1933] A.C. 402 .... [1987] 268
Barrett Bros. (Taxis) Ltd. *v*. Davies [1966] 1 W.L.R. 1334 .... [1987] 233; [1989] 498, 508
Barrow Borough Transport Ltd. (*Re*) [1989] 3 W.L.R. 858; (1989) 5 B.C.C. 646 .... [1990] 405
Barrow *v*. Isaacs [1891] 1 Q.B. 417 .... [1989] 442
Barry *v*. Croskey (1861) 2 J. & H. 1, 29 .... [1986] 393, 394
Bart *v*. British West Indian Airways Ltd. [1967] 1 Lloyd's Rep. 239 .... [1989] 38–39
Barth *v*. Atlantic Container Line, 597 F. Supp. 1254, 1985 A.M.C. 1196 (D. Md. 1984) . [1986] 367, 368
Bartley, The (1857) Swab. 198 .... [1989] 69, 78
Barton *v*. Armstrong [1976] A.C. 104 .... [1989] 272, 276; [1990] 342, 343
Bartus *v*. Riccardi (1967) 55 Misc. 2d 3; 284 N.Y.S. 2d 222 (Utica City Ct.) .... [1990] 370
Basildon District Council *v*. J.E. Lesser (Properties) Ltd. [1985] Q.B. 839 ....[1987] 10; [1988] 513; [1990] 418
Bass Anglers Sportsman Soc'y *v*. United States Steel Corp., 324 F. Supp. 412 (N.D., M.D., S.D. Ala.), aff'd *per curiam sub. nom.* Bass Anglers Sportsman Soc'y *v*. Koppers Co., 447 F. 2d 1304 (5th Cir., 1971) .... [1987] 517
BAT and R.J. Reynolds *v*. Commission ("Philip Morris/Rothmans"). Joined Cases 142 and 156/84, [1988] 4 C.M.L.R. 24 .... [1988] 187
Batavier, The (1853) 1 Sp. 169 ....[1989] 69
Batis, The [1990] 1 Lloyd's Rep. 345 .... [1990] 454
Batistoni *v*. Dance. *The Times*, 18 January 1908 ....[1987] 64
Baton Rouge Marine Contractors Inc. *v*. Rosa Roth, No. 83–7153 (S.D.N.Y. 22 March 1984) .... [1986] 355
Batut *v*. Hartley (1872) 26 L.T. 968 .... [1986] 226
Bayer A.G. *v*. Winter [1986] 1 W.L.R. 497 .... [1986] 412
Baylis *v*. Barnett, *The Times*, 28 December 1988 .... [1989] 260
Baylis *v*. Bishop of London [1913] 1 Ch. 127 .... [1989] 305
B. Elliott (Canada) Ltd. *v*. John T. Clark & Son (1982) 542 F. Supp. 1367 (U.S.D.C., My.), aff'd (1983) 704 F. 2d 1305 (4 Cir.) .... [1990] 315
Beale *v*. Taylor [1967] 1 W.L.R. 1193 .... [1988] 508
Bear, The tug, 1924 A.M.C. 620 (Wash. S. Ct.) .... [1986] 494, 500
Beattie (R.K.) Ltd. *v*. C.N. Marine Inc. (1986) 74 N.B.R. (2d) 221; (1987) 187 A.P.R. 221 (N.B.Q.B.) ....[1988] 84

Beauchamp *v.* Coastal Corp. (*The Wayward Princess*) [1984] 2 F.C. 511; [1986] 2 F.C. 298 (Fed. C.A.) .... [1987] 93; [1988] 90
Beauchamp *v.* Winn (1873) L.R. 6 H.L. 223 .... [1989] 442
Beaverford, The *v.* The *Kafiristan* [1983] A.C. 136 .... [1986] 308; [1990] 38
Bebr van Veelde Scheepvaartkantor B.V. *v.* Compania Naviera Sea Orient S.A. (*The Agrebele*) [1985] 2 Lloyd's Rep. 496 .... [1987] 158
Becker, Gray & Co. *v.* London Assurance Corp. [1918] A.C. 101 .... [1986] 119; [1988] 252
Beco Inc. *v.* Minnechaug Golf Course Inc. (1968) 256 A. 2d 522 .... [1990] 374
Bedford Insurance Co. Ltd. *v.* Instituto de Resseguros do Brasil [1985] Q.B. 966; [1984] 1 Lloyd's Rep. 210; .... [1987] 36, 201, 203, 206; [1988] 254; [1989] 494
Beesly *v.* Hallwood Estates Ltd. [1960] 1 W.L.R. 549; aff'd [1961] Ch. 105 .... [1989] 169
Bekhor (A.J.) & Co. Ltd. *v.* Bilton [1981] Q.B. 923 .... [1990] 323
Belcore Maritime Corp. *v.* F. Lli. Moretti Cereali S.p.A. (*The Mastro Giorgis*) [1983] 2 Lloyd's Rep. 66 .... [1990] 107, 108, 111, 112
Belgian State *v.* Fromageries Franco-Suisse Le Ski, Judgment 27 May 1971 (Belgium) .... [1989] 29
Bell *v.* Carstairs (1811) 14 East. 374 .... [1988] 333
Bell *v.* Gardiner (1842) 4 Man. & G. 11 .... [1989] 431, 442
Bell *v.* Hood, 71 F. Supp. 813 (S.D. Cal., 1947) .... [1987] 503
Bell *v.* Lever Bros. [1932] A.C. 161 .... [1986] 320, 324; [1988] 300, 530; [1989] 119, 432, 437, 438, 440, 443, 444, 447, 448; [1990] 456
Bell Production Engineers Ass'n *v.* Bell Helicopter Textron, 688 F. 2d 997, 999 (5 Cir. 1982) .. [1986] 72
Bella Steamship Co. *v.* Ins. Co. of North America, 1925 A.M.C. 751 .... [1986] 503
Bellador Silk Ltd. (*Re*) [1965] Ch. 667 .... [1990] 410
Belmont Finance Corp. Ltd. *v.* Williams Furniture Ltd. [1979] Ch. 250 .... [1990] 426
Belmont Finance Corp. Ltd. *v.* Williams Furniture Ltd. (No. 2) [1980] 1 All E.R. 393 .... [1988] 365; [1989] 325
Belvoir Finance Co. Ltd. *v.* Stapleton [1971] 1 Q.B. 201 .... [1988] 39
Belzetta Shipping Co. *v.* Dynamic Export Corp. (*The Leage*), S.M.A. No. 1320 (1979) .... [1986] 72
Benjamin Cope & Sons Ltd. (*Re*) [1914] 1 Ch. 800 .... [1986] 525, 532
Bennet *v.* Griffiths (1861) 3 E. & E. 119 .... [1990] 323
Bennett *v.* Bennett [1952] 1 All E.R. 413 .... [1987] 212
Benton *v.* Aetna Cas. & Surety, 50 Cal. Rptr. 824, 241 C.A. 2d 768 (1966) .... [1986] 501
Beresford *v.* Royal Insurance Co. Ltd. [1938] A.C. 586 .... [1987] 210, 212, 213; [1988] 125, 319
Berg, The, 1984(4) SA 647(N) .... [1986] 279
Berg (V.) & Son Ltd. *v.* Vanden Avenne-Izegem P.V.B.A. [1977] 1 Lloyd's Rep. 499 (C.A.) .... [1989] 399 *et seq.*
Berger and Light Diffusers Pty. Ltd. *v.* Pollock [1973] 2 Lloyd's Rep. 442, 463 .... [1986] 31; [1988] 33
Berger & Co. Inc. *v.* Gill & Duffus S.A. [1984] A.C. 382 .... [1989] 88
Berghoefer *v.* ASA, Case 221/84 [1986] 1 C.M.L.R. 13 .... [1988] 389
Berk (F.W.) *v.* Style [1956] 1 Q.B. 180 .... [1986] 444
Berkeley Applegate (Investment Consultants) Ltd. (*Re*) [1988] 3 All E.R. 71 .... [1990] 336
Berkeley Curtis Bay Co. (Matter of), 557 F. Supp. 335, 1984 A.M.C. 1126, 1934 (S.D.N.Y. 1983), aff'd on other grounds *sub nom.* B.C. Bay Co. *v.* American Dredging Co., 742 F. 2d 1431, opinion published at 1984 A.M.C. 1941 (2 Cir. 1983) .... [1986] 375; [1987] 503
Berkshire, The [1974] 1 Lloyd's Rep. 185 .... [1987] 260; [1988] 285
Bernstein *v.* Pamson Motors (Golders Green) Ltd. [1987] 2 All E.R. 220 .... [1987] 404; [1988] 506; [1990] 365
Berry and Stewart *v.* Tottenham Hotspur Football Co. Ltd. [1935] Ch. 718 .... [1988] 79
Beshada *v.* Johns-Manville Products Corp., 90 N.J. 191, 447 A. 2d 539 (1982) .... [1986] 80
Besseler Waechter Glover & Co. *v.* South Derwent Coal Co. [1938] 1 K.B. 408 .... [1990] 471
Bethlehem Steel Corp. *v.* Marriott Corp. (*The Steelton*) (1980) 631 F. 2d 441; 1980 A.M.C. 2122 (6th Cir.); *upholding* 1977 A.M.C. 2252; [1979] 1 Lloyd's Rep. 431 (N.D. Oh.) .... [1989] 13
Betsey, The (1843) 2 W. Rob. 167 .... [1989] 75
Beverley Acceptances Ltd. *v.* Oakley [1982] R.T.R. 417 (C.A.) .... [1986] 225
Bhoja Trader, The [1981] 2 Lloyd's Rep. 256 .... [1990] 241
BICC Plc *v.* Burndy Corp. [1985] Ch. 232 (C.A.) .... [1986] 149; [1990] 161
Biakh *v.* Hyundai [1988] 1 Lloyd's Rep. 187 .... [1989] 513
Bibby Bulk Carriers Ltd. *v.* Cansulex (*The Cambridgeshire*) (Unrep.) .... [1987] 3
Bier B.V. *v.* Mines de Potasse d'Alsace [1976] E.C.R. 1735 .... [1987] 286
Bigane Vessel Fueling Co. *v.* Bolton Steam Shipping Co., No. 79–2041 (N.D. Ill. 15 October 1981) .... [1986] 355

Biggerstaff *v*. Rowatt's Wharf Ltd. [1896] 2 Ch. 93, 101 .... [1986] 521
Binder *v*. Alachouzos [1972] 2 Q.B. 151 .... [1989] 436
Binladen BSB Landscaping *v*. M/V *Nedlloyd Rotterdam*, 759 F. 2d 1006, 1017 n. 12; [1985] A.M.C. 2113 .... [1986] 368; [1989] 280
Bird *v*. Appleton (1800) 8 T.R. 562 .... [1987] 215
Bird Precision Bellows Ltd. (*Re*) [1984] Ch. 419; [1986] Ch. 658 .... [1988] 62, 63
Bissell & Co. *v*. Fox Bros. & Co. (1885) 53 L.T. 193 .... [1990] 69
Bisso *v*. Inland Waterways Corp., 349 U.S. 85 (1955) .... [1986] 374
Bize *v*. Dickason (1786) 1 T.R. 285 .... [1989] 436
Black *v*. Freedman & Co. (1910) 12 C.L.R. 105 .... [1990] 332
Black Diamond Steamship Corp. *v*. Robert Stewart and Sons Ltd. (*The Norwalk Victory*), 336 U.S. 386; 1949 A.M.C. 393 (1949) .... [1986] 23
Black Sea, The (1855) Pritch. Dig. 337 .... [1989] 75
Blackburn Low *v*. Vigors (1886) 17 Q.B.D. 553; (1887) 12 App. Cas. 531 .... [1989] 256
Blain (*ex p., re* Sawers) (1879) 12 Ch. D. 522 .... [1989] 268
Blakemore *v*. Bellamy [1983] R.T.R. 303 (D.C.) .... [1989] 372
Blanckaert & Williams PVBA *v*. Trost, Case 139/80 [1981] E.C.R. 819; [1982] 2 C.M.L.R. 1 .... [1987] 287; [1988] 387
Bligh *v*. Brent (1837) 2 Y. & Co. Ex. 268 .... [1990] 402
Bliss *v*. South East Thames R.H.A. [1987] I.C.R. 700 (C.A.) .... [1990] 137
Blue Arrow Plc (*Re*) [1987] B.C.L.C. 585 .... [1989] 414
Blue Metal Industries *v*. Dilley [1970] A.C. 827 .... [1990] 405
Blue Wave, The [1981] 1 Lloyd's Rep. 151 .... [1987] 538
Blundell (*Re*) (1888) 40 Ch. D. 370 .... [1989] 333, 337
B.N.I.C. *v*. Clair (123/83) [1985] E.C.R. 392; [1985] 2 C.M.L.R. 430 .... [1987] 16
Board of Trade *v*. Christie Grain & Stock Co., 198 U.S. 236 (1905) .... [1986] 397
Boardman *v*. Phipps [1967] 2 A.C. 46 .... [1987] 429, 436; [1988] 129; [1989] 158, 159, 161, 203, 335; [1990] 130, 335, 336, 463
Boehringer-Mannheim Diagnostics Inc. *v*. Pan American World Airways Inc. (1984) 737 F. 2d (5th Cir.) .... [1988] 179
Bold Buccleugh, The (1851) 7 Moo. P.C. 267 .... [1987] 322, 543; [1988] 161; [1989] 187, 188
Bolivinter Oil S.A. *v*. Chase Manhattan Bank N.A. [1984] 1 Lloyd's Rep. 251 .... [1990] 223, 241
Bolt & Nut Co. (Tipton) Ltd. *v*. Rowlands, Nicholls & Co. [1964] 2 Q.B. 10 .... [1990] 66
Bolton *v*. Mahadeva [1972] 1 W.L.R. 1009 .... [1990] 512
Bolwell Fibreglass Pty. Ltd. *v*. Foley [1984] V.R. 97, 98–99, 117 .... [1986] 228; [1990] 514
Bonacina (*Re*) [1912] 2 Ch. 394 .... [1990] 203
Bond Worth Ltd. (*Re*) [1980] Ch. 228 .... [1989] 117, 119, 120, 200, 204, 209, 210
Bonner *v*. City of Pritchard, 661 F. 2d 1206 (11th Cir., 1981) .... [1987] 26
Bonython *v*. Commonwealth of Australia [1951] A.C. 201 .... [1987] 529
Booth Fisheries Canadian Co. Ltd. *v*. Banque Provinciale du Canada (1972) 7 N.B.R. (2d) 138 [1986] 8
Borax Co. (*Re*) [1901] 1 Ch. 326 .... [1986] 523
Borden (U.K.) Ltd. *v*. Scottish Timber Products Ltd. [1981] Ch. 25 .... [1988] 289; [1989] 119, 510
Boreas, The, 1988 A.M.C. 1000 (N.D. Cal.) .... [1989] 95
Bornier *v*. Cie Air-Inter (1983) 37 R.F.D.A. 49 (Cour de Cass.) .... [1988] 232
Borrowman, Phillips & Co. *v*. Free & Hollis (1878) 4 Q.B.D. 500 .... [1990] 365
Bosch *v*. Van Rijn (13/61) [1962] E.C.R. 45; [1962] C.M.L.R. 1 .... [1987] 16
Boss *v*. Hopkinson (1870) 18 W.R. 725 .... [1989] 197
Bottacchi, The (1985) 773 F. 2d 1528; 1986 A.M.C. 1 .... [1989] 12
Boudreau *v*. Registrar of Shipping [1984] 1 F.C. 990 .... [1987] 90
Boulton *v*. Jones (1857) 2 H. & N. 564; 27 L.J. Exch. 117 .... [1989] 332; [1990] 506
Bovey Hotel Ventures Ltd. (*Re*). Unrep., 13 January 1982 (Ch. D.); 10 June 1982 (C.A.) .... [1988] 66
Bovrill *v*. R.H.M. [1982] 1 W.L.R. 668 .... [1990] 322
Bowen *v*. Paramount Builders [1977] 1 N.Z.L.R. 394 .... [1986] 111
Bowes *v*. Chaleyer (1923) 32 C.L.R. 159 (H.C.A.) .... [1989] 84
Bowes *v*. Shand (1877) 2 App. Cas. 455 .... [1988] 457; [1990] 457
Bowlay Logging Ltd. *v*. Domtar Ltd. [1978] 4 W.W.R. 105 .... [1986] 336
Bowling *v*. Cox [1926] A.C. 751 (P.C., British Honduras) .... [1989] 315
Bowmakers Ltd. *v*. Barnet Instruments Ltd. [1945] K.B. 65 (C.A.) .... [1987] 213; [1988] 126
Boyd *v*. Emmerson (1834) 2 Ad. & E. 184 .... [1990] 69, 70
Boyd *v*. Moses (1869) 74 U.S. 316 .... [1989] 353

B.P. Exploration Co. (Libya) Ltd. *v.* Hunt (No. 2) [1979] 1 W.L.R. 783; aff'd [1981] 1 W.L.R. 232; aff'd [1983] 2 A.C. 352 .... [1989] 304, 399; [1990] 518
BP Kemi-DDSF [1979] O.J. No. L286/32 .... [1988] 189
Bracewell *v.* Appleby [1975] Ch. 408 .... [1987] 428
Bradburn *v.* G. W. Rly. (1874) L.R. 10 Ex. 1 .... [1986] 295
Bradbury Gretorex Co. (Colonial) Ltd. *v.* Standard Trading Co. (Pty.) Ltd., 1953 3 S.A. 529 (W) .... [1990] 12
Bradley *v.* Eagle Star Ins. Co. Ltd. [1989] 2 W.L.R. 568 .... [1989] 496, 504, 505
Brady *v.* Brady [1989] A.C. 755 .... [1990] 405
Brady *v.* S.S. *African Queen*, 179 F. Supp. 321 (E.D. Va., 1960) .... [1987] 24
Brady-Hamilton Stevedore Co. *v.* M.V. *Kalantiao*, 1987 (4) S.A. 250 (D), 263 .... [1989] 175–181, 188
Braemar Investments Ltd. (*Re*) [1989] Ch. 54 .... [1990] 533
Bragg *v.* Bragg [1925] P. 20 .... [1988] 395
Brainard *v.* Aetna Casualty & Surety Co., 187 N.Y.S. 2d 435, 437 (1959) .... [1986] 80
Braithwaite *v.* Foreign Hardwood Co. [1905] 2 K.B. 543 .... [1989] 81, 82, 83, 84, 85, 87, 88
Brandon *v.* Leckie (1972) 29 D.L.R. (3d) 633 (Alb. S.C.) .... [1988] 298
Brandt *v.* Liverpool, Brazil and River Plate Steam Navigation Co. Ltd. [1924] 1 K.B. 575 .... [1986] 101, 296, 298; [1987] 255; [1989] 52, 53, 164, 165, 166, 168, 169, 171, 172, 173, 422, 423, 429; [1990] 1
Brandt's Sons & Co. *v.* Dunlop Rubber Co. Ltd. [1905] A.C. 454, 462 .... [1986] 197
Branwhite *v.* Worcester Works Finance Ltd. [1969] 2 Ch. 67 .... [1990] 334
Bray *v.* Ford [1896] A.C. 44 .... [1987] 433
Brazlumber Ltd. *v.* S.P.S. Management, No. 83–9310 (S.D.N.Y. 17 September 1984) .... [1986] 359
Brede, The [1974] Q.B. 233 .... [1986] 387; [1990] 475
Breen *v.* Breen [1964] P. 144 .... [1989] 386
Bremen (M/S) and Unterweser Reederei *v.* Zapata Offshore Co., 1972 A.M.C. 1407 .... [1986] 486
Bremer Handelsgesellschaft m.b.H. *v.* C. Mackprang Jr. [1979] 1 Lloyd's Rep. 221 .... [1989] 6, 399
Bremer Handelsgesellschaft m.b.H. *v.* Continental Grain Co. [1983] 1 Lloyd's Rep. 269 .... [1989] 6, 7; [1990] 156
Bremer Vulkan Schiffbau und Maschinenfabrik *v.* South India Shipping Corp. Ltd. [1981] A.C. 909; [1981] 1 Lloyd's Rep. 253 .... [1986] 68; [1987] 156, 264; [1988] 306, 307; [1989] 170
Bridge *v.* Campbell Discount Co. Ltd. [1962] A.C. 600 .... [1990] 19
Brien *v.* Dwyer (1978) 141 C.L.R. 378; (1979) 22 A.L.R. 485 .... [1989] 87; [1990] 251
Brightlife Ltd. (*Re*) [1986] 3 All E.R. 673; [1987] Ch. 200 .... [1987] 147; [1989] 211, 244; [1990] 209, 275, 403, 404, 414, 528, 539, 540
Brikom Investments Ltd. *v.* Carr [1979] Q.B. 467 .... [1986] 472

Brimnes, The [1975] 1 Q.B. 929 .... [1986] 213; [1989] 367; [1990] 67, 68, 81, 82
Brinkibon Ltd. *v.* Stahag Stahl G.m.b.H. [1983] 2 A.C. 34 .... [1988] 396; [1990] 85
Brisbane *v.* Dacres (1813) 5 Taunt. 143, 160 .... [1987] 430; [1989] 436
Bristol Tramways &c. Carriage Co. Ltd. *v.* Fiat Motors Ltd. [1910] 2 K.B. 831 .... [1988] 509
Bristow *v.* Eastman (1794) 1 Peake 291 .... [1989] 306
Britain, The (1839) 1 W. Rob. 40 .... [1989] 76
Britannia Steamship Ins. Assn. Ltd. *v.* Ausonia Assicurazioni S.p.A. [1984] 2 Lloyd's Rep. 98 .... [1990] 192
British Airways Board *v.* Laker Airways Ltd. [1985] A.C. 58 .... [1987] 384, 393, 395
British and Beningtons Ltd. *v.* N.W. Cachar Tea Ltd. [1923] A.C. 48; *sub nom.* North Western Cachar Tea Co. Ltd. *v.* British & Benningtons Ltd. (1921) 10 Ll.L.Rep. 381 .... [1988] 22; [1989] 81, 82, 84, 85, 86
British Columbia *v.* Consolidated Churchill Copper Corp. Ltd. [1978] 5 W.W.R. 652 .... [1990] 540
British Eagle International Airlines Ltd. *v.* Campagnie Nationale Air France [1975] 1 W.L.R. 758 .... [1990] 75, 248, 275, 407
British Empire, The (1842) 6 Jur. 608 .... [1989] 74, 76
British Motor Trade Association *v.* Gilbert [1951] 2 All E.R. 641 .... [1987] 430
British Nylon Spinners Ltd. *v.* Imperial Chemical Industries Ltd. [1953] Ch. 19; [1955] Ch. 37 .... [1989] 230
British Oil and Cake Co. Ltd. *v.* J. Burstall & Co. (1923) 39 T.L.R. 406 .... [1988] 515
British & Overseas Trading (Bristles) Ltd. *v.* Brooks Wharf and Bull Wharf Ltd. [1967] 2 Lloyd's Rep. 51 .... [1986] 226; [1988] 469
British Road Services Ltd. *v.* Arthur V. Crutchley & Co. Ltd. [1968] 1 All E.R. 811, 820 .... [1988] 36
British Steel Corp. *v.* Cleveland Bridge and Engineering Co. Ltd. [1984] 1 All E.R. 504 .... [1990] 498

British Syphon Co. *v.* Homewood [1956] 1 W.L.R. 1190 .... [1990] 6, 462, 463
British Union and National Ins. Co. *v.* Rawson [1916] 2 Ch. 476 .... [1989] 497
Broere *v.* Two Thousand One Hundred Thirty-three Dollars, 72 F. Supp. 115, 1947 A.M.C. 1523 (1947) .... [1986] 17
Broken Hill Pty. Co. Ltd. *v.* Hapag-Lloyd Aktiengesellschaft [1980] 2 N.S.W.L.R. 572 .... [1986] 105; [1989] 281
Brook Bond Liebig (Spices) [1978] O.J. No. L 53/20 .... [1988] 189
Brooks Robinson Pty. *v.* Rothfield [1951] V.L.R. 405 .... [1990] 514
Broome *v.* Cassell & Co. [1972] A.C. 1072 .... [1987] 427
Broome *v.* Speak [1903] 1 Ch. 586, affmd. *sub nom.* Shepheard *v.* Broome [1904] A.C. 342 . [1988] 463
Brostrom *v.* Dreyfus (1932) 38 Com. Cas. 79 .... [1988] 48
Brown *v.* British Abrasive Wheel Co. [1919] 1 Ch. 280 .... [1988] 75
Brown *v.* Litton (1711) 1 P. Wms. 140 .... [1990] 335
Brown *v.* New Jersey Insurance Co., 14 P. 2d 272 (1932) .... [1987] 214
Brown & Root Inc. *v.* M/V *Peisander*, 648 F. 2d 415, 1982 A.M.C. 929 (5 Cir. 1981) .... [1986] 367
Brown (P.) Jun. & Co. *v.* Minas de Matahambre (*The Nordamerika*), 1931 A.M.C. 1637 .... [1989] 345
Brown Jenkinson & Co. Ltd. *v.* Percy Dalton (London) Ltd. [1957] 2 Q.B. 621 .... [1986] 269
Brown Shipley & Co. Ltd. *v.* Alicia Hosiery [1966] 1 Lloyd's Rep. 668 .... [1990] 478
Browner International Transport Ltd. *v.* Monarch S.S. Co. Ltd. (*The European Enterprise*) [1989] 2 Lloyd's Rep. 185 .... [1989] 404
Browning *v.* Morris (1778) 2 Cowp. 790 .... [1987] 207
B.R.T. *v.* SABAM (127/73) [1974] E.C.R. 51; [1974] 2 C.M.L.R. 238 .... [1987] 16
Brush Aggregates Ltd. (*Re*) [1983] B.C.L.C. 320 .... [1988] 144, 145
B.T.C. *v.* Gourley [1956] A.C. 185 .... [1990] 134
Btesh *v.* Royal Insurance Co. Ltd., 40 F. 2d 659 (S.D.N.Y., 1930); 1931 A.M.C. 1044 (2 C.A.) .... [1986] 498; [1987] 211
Buchanan (Peter) Ltd. and Macharg *v.* McVey [1954] I.R. 89, 107, [1955] A.C. 516n., 529 ... [1986] 435
Buchanan-Jardine *v.* Hamilink, 1983 S.L.T. 149 .... [1989] 374
Buckey Union Ins. Co. *v.* Liberty Solvents and Chemical Co. Inc., C.A. 11598, Ohio Ct. of Appeals, 11 July 1984 .... [1986] 92
Bucknell *v.* Bucknell [1969] 1 W.L.R. 1204 .... [1987] 251
Buenos Aires Maru, The [1986] 1 S.C.R. 752; 1986 A.M.C. 2580 .... [1987] 95, 343–344; [1988] 82; [1990] 102
Buffalo, The (1937) 58 Ll. L. Rep. 302 .... [1986] 153
Bulk Distribution Centers Inc. *v.* Monsanto Co., 589 F. Supp. 1437 (S.D. Fla., 1984) ... [1987] 505, 510
Bulk Transport Group Shipping Co. Ltd. *v.* Sea Crystal Shipping Ltd. (*The Kyzikos*) [1987] 1 Lloyd's Rep. 48; [1987] 1 W.L.R. 1565; [1988] 3 W.L.R. 858 ....[1989] 263 *et seq.*
Buller *v.* Plunkett (1860) 1 J. & H. 441 .... [1989] 197
Bulmer *v.* Norris (1860) 9 C.B.N.S. 19 .... [1990] 402
Bunga Teratai, The, 4 February 1987 Sup. Ct. N.S.W., unreported; (1988) 12 N.S.W.L.R. 730 (C.A.); (1989) 63 A.L.J.R. 468 .... [1990] 324, 325
Bunge Corp. *v.* Agri-Trans Corp. (1982) 542 F. Supp. 961; 1983 A.M.C. 1931 (N.D. Miss.); *modified on appeal sub nom.* Agri-Trans Corp. *v.* Gladders Barge Line Inc. (1983) 721 F. 2d 1005 (5th Cir.) .... [1989] 16
Bunge Corp. *v.* Tradax Export S.A. [1980] 1 Lloyd's Rep. 294; [1981] 1 W.L.R. 711 (H.L.) ....[1986] 128; [1987] 62, 145; [1988] 396; [1989] 143, 144
Buques Centroamericanos *v.* Akti Compania Naviera, 1976 A.M.C. 424 (S.D.N.Y) ....[1986] 59
Burden *v.* Burden (1813) 1 V. & B. 170 .... [1990] 331
Burdon *v.* Zeller's Ltd. (1981) 16 B.L.R. 59 (Ont. H.C.) .... [1989] 412
Burgess *v.* M/V *Tamano*, 564 F. 2d 964, 1977 A.M.C. 1892, reh'g denied, 1977 A.M.C. 1922 (1 Cir. 1977), cert. denied *sub nom.* M/V *Tamano v.* United States, 435 U.S. 941, 1978 A.M.C. 1895 (1978) .... [1986] 375; [1987] 503
Burnett *v.* Trans World Airlines Inc. (1973) 368 F. Supp. 1152 (New Mex. D.C.); 12 Avi. 18, 405 .... [1988] 228
Burns *v.* U.S., 200 F. 2d 106 (4th Cir., 1952) .... [1987] 211
Burrows *v.* Delta Transp. Co., 106 Mich. 582; 64 N.W. 501; 29 L.R.A. 468 (1895) .... [1987] 521
Burrows *v.* Rhodes [1899] 1 Q.B. 816 .... [1987] 208; [1988] 125
Burstall *v.* Grimsdale (1906) 11 Com. Cas. 280, 289 .... [1986] 303
Bushell *v.* Faith [1970] A.C. 1099 .... [1990] 409
Business Computers Ltd. *v.* Anglo African Leasing Ltd. [1977] 1 W.L.R. 578 .... [1990] 475
Busk *v.* Royal Exchange Assurance Co. (1818) 2 B. & Ald. 73 .... [1988] 330

Butler *v.* Banimar Shipping S.A., 1978 (4) S.A. 753 (SE) .... [1990] 12
Butler *v.* Broadhead [1975] Ch. 97 .... [1989] 315; [1990] 401
Butler Machine Tool Co. Ltd. *v.* Ex-Cell-O Corp. (England) Ltd. [1979] 1 W.L.R. 401 ...... [1987] 536; [1989] 394, 396; [1990] 498
Buttenlandsche Bankvereeniging *v.* Hildesheim (1903) 10 T.L.R. 641 (C.A.) .... [1986] 394
Buttes Gas & Oil Co. *v.* Hammer [1982] A.C. 888 .... [1987] 384
B.V. Bureau Wijsmuller *v.* U.S., 702 F. 2d 333 (2 Cir. 1983) .... [1986] 153, 347
C.A. Venezolana de Navegacion *v.* Bank Line Ltd. (*The Roachbank*) [1987] 2 Lloyd's Rep. 498; [1988] 2 Lloyd's Rep. 337 (C.A.) .... [1990] 107, 109
Cadogan Finance Ltd. *v.* Lavery and Fox (1982) 132 N.L.J. 1101 .... [1986] 225
Caernbahn, The [1914] P. 25 (C.A.) .... [1989] 33
Cairns, Noble & Co. Ltd. *v.* Ashwin & Co. (1920) 5 Ll.L.Rep. 120 .... [1990] 550, 551
Calico Printers Association *v.* Barclays Bank Ltd. (1931) 36 Com. Cas. 197; (1930) 36 Com. Cas. 71 .... [1986] 201; [1990] 549, 550, 551
California *v.* Sierra Club, 451 U.S. 287 (1981) .... [1987] 518
Calisher *v.* Forbes (1871) L.R. 7 Ch. App. 109 .... [1989] 197
Callaham *v.* Bank of Anderson (1904) 48 S.E. 293 .... [1988] 376
Calland *v.* Loyd (1840) 6 M. & W. 26 .... [1989] 317
Calliope, The [1970] P. 172 .... [1989] 30
Caltex Oil Pty. Ltd. *v.* The Dredge *Willemstad* (1976) 136 C.L.R. 529 .... [1986] 97
Calzaturificio Brennero *v.* Wendel [1984] E.C.R. 3971 .... [1989] 386
Camanche, The, 75 U.S. (8 Wall) 448 (1869) .... [1986] 307
Cambridgeshire, The (Unrep.) .... [1987] 3
Cameron *v.* H.M. Advocate, 1971 S.L.T. (Rep.) 333 .... [1990] 163
Camidge *v.* Allenby (1827) 6 B. & C. 373 .... [1990] 66
Campbell (R.M.) (Vehicle Sales) Pty. Ltd. *v.* Machnig, 22 May 1981, unrep., N.S.W.S.C. .... [1988] 40, 469
Camphor, The, S.M.A. No. 1549 (1980) .... [1986] 72
Canada Rice Mills *v.* Union Marine and General Insurance [1941] A.C. 55 .. [1986] 286; [1990] 127, 154
Canada Steamship Lines Ltd. *v.* The King [1952] A.C. 192 (P.C.) .... [1988] 82; [1990] 155
Canadian Acceptance Corp. Ltd. *v.* Regent Park Butcher Shop Ltd. (1939) 3 D.L.R. (3d) 304 .... [1988] 277
Canadian Aero Services Ltd. *v.* O'Malley (1973) 40 D.L.R. (3d) 371 .... [1987] 421, 436
Canadian Imperial Bank of Commerce *v.* Campbell (1984) 7 D.L.R. (4th) 252 .... [1987] 91
Canadian Imperial Bank of Commerce *v.* F.B.D.B. [1985] 3 W.W.R. 318 (Alberta Q.B. Ct.) [1989] 197
Canadian Saltfish Corp. *v.* Rasmusson [1986] 2 F.C. 500 (Fed. C.A.) .... [1988] 90
Candler *v.* Crane Christmas & Co. [1951] 2 K.B. 164 .... [1990] 420
Candlewood Navigation Corp. Ltd. *v.* Mitsui O.S.K. Lines Ltd. (*The Mineral Transporter*) [1986] A.C. 1; [1985] 3 W.L.R. 381 .... [1985] 407; [1986] 98, 151; [1987] 237; [1989] 1
Cane *v.* Jones [1980] 1 W.L.R. 1451 .... [1990] 403
Canficorp *v.* Cormorant Bulk Carriers 1985 A.M.C 1444 (Fed. C.A.) .... [1987] 83, 261
Canova, The (1866) L.R. 1 A. & E. 54 .... [1989] 75
Cantamar Holdings Ltd. *v.* Tru-View Aluminium Products (1979) 23 O.R. (2d) 572 .... [1986] 169
Cantiere Navale Triestina *v.* Handelsvertretung der Russische Soviet Republik Naphtha Export (1925) 21 Ll. L. Rep. 204 .... [1986] 252
Cantieri Navali Riuniti S.p.A. *v.* N.V. Omne Justitia (*The Stolt Marmaro*) [1985] 2 Lloyd's Rep. 428 .... [1986] 515, 516, 518; [1988] 6
Caparo Industries Plc *v.* Dickman [1990] 2 W.L.R. 358 (H.L.); [1989] Q.B. 653; [1989] 2 W.L.R. 316 .... [1990] 208, 263, 419, 478, 479, 485, 553
Cap Blanco, The [1913] P. 130 .... [1987] 311
Cap Bon-, The [1967] 1 Lloyd's Rep. 543 .... [1987] 540
Cap Palos, The [1921] P. 458 .... [1986] 318
Cape Packet, The (1848) 3 W. Rob. 122 .... [1989] 72
Cape Race, The (1927) 18 F. 2d 79 .... [1990] 53
Cape Town Municipality *v.* F. Robb and Co. Ltd., 1966 (4) SA 345 (C) .... [1986] 280
Capital Associates Ltd. *v.* Royal Bank of Canada (1970) 15 D.L.R. 3d 234 .... [1990] 70, 75, 244
Capital Finance Co. Ltd. *v.* Bray [1964] 1 W.L.R. 623 (C.A.) .... [1987] 76
Captain Gregos, The [1990] 1 Lloyd's Rep. 310; [1989] 2 All E.R. 54 .... [1989] 394, 396; [1990] 314
Captain Panagos D.P., The [1986] 2 Lloyd's Rep. 470; [1989] 1 Lloyd's Rep. 33 (C.A.) .... [1987] 40; [1988] 283; [1989] 25 *et seq.*
Cardiff Workmen's Cottage Co. Ltd. (*Re*) [1906] 2 Ch. 627 .... [1989] 211

Cardinal Shipping Corp. *v.* M/S *Seisho Maru*, 744 F. 2d 461 (5 Cir. 1984) .... [1986] 353, 355
Care Shipping Corp. *v.* Latin American Shipping Corp. (*The Cebu*) [1983] Q.B. 1005, [1983] 1 Lloyd's Rep. 320 .... [1986] 425; [1989] 193
Cargill U.K. Ltd. *v.* Continental U.K. Ltd. [1989] 1 Lloyd's Rep. 193; [1989] 2 Lloyd's Rep. 290 (C.A.) .... [1990] 466
Cargo ex *Capella* (1867) L.R. 1 A. & E. 356 .... [1989] 65
Cargo ex Schiller, The (1877) 2 P.D. 145 .... [1987] 270
Cargo Laden and Latterly Laden on Board the M.V. *Thalassini Avgi v.* M.V. *Dimitris* (*The Dimitris*), 1989 (3) S.A. 820(A) .... [1990] 9
Carlen *v.* Drury (1812) 1 Ves. & B. 154 .... [1988] 80
Carlill *v.* Carbolic Smoke Ball Co. Ltd. [1893] 1 Q.B. 256 .... [1986] 315; [1988] 114, 502
Carling O'Keefe Breweries of Canada Ltd. *v.* C.N. Marine Inc. (*The Newfoundland Coast*) 1987 AMC 954; (1989) 104 N.R. 166 .... [1987] 259, 260; [1988] 84, 285; [1990] 494
Carl Zeiss Stiftung *v.* Herbert Smith & Co. (No. 2) [1969] 2 Ch. 276 .... [1989] 324, 326, 327, 329, 332, 336
Carl Zeiss Stiftung *v.* Rayner & Keeler Ltd. [1967] 1 A.C. 853 .... [1987] 384
Carmania II, The [1963] 2 Lloyd's Rep. 152 .... [1988] 96
Carmarthen & Cardigan Ry. Co. *v.* Manchester & Wilford Ry. Co. (1873) L.R. 8 C.P. 685 .... [1990] 66, 68
Carney *v.* Herbert [1985] A.C. 301 .... [1988] 409
Caroline, The (1861) Lush. 334 .... [1990] 353
Carpenters' Co. *v.* British Mutual Banking Co. Ltd. [1938] 1 K.B. 511 .... [1990] 69
Carreras Rothmans Ltd. *v.* Freeman Mathews Treasure Ltd. [1985] Ch. 207 ...... [1986] 542; [1990] 129
Carriage Co-operative Supply Assn. (*Re*) (1884) 27 Ch.D. 322 .... [1990] 222
Carrier Dove, The (1863) 2 Moo. P.C. (N.S.) 243; Br. & Lush. 113 .... [1988] 450; [1989] 59
Carrington Slipways Pty. Ltd. *v.* Pacific Austral Pty. Ltd. (1989) (unreported, N.S.W. Sup. Ct.) .... [1989] 142
Carrington Viyella Plc (*Re*) (1983) 1 B.C.C. 98, 951 .... [1988] 63; [1990] 411
Carruthers *v.* Sydebotham (1815) 4. & S. 77 .... [1988] 332
Carse *v.* Coppen, 1951 S.C. 233 .... [1990] 402
Carter *v.* Boehm (1766) 3 Burr 1905; 97 E.R. 1162 .... [1986] 29; [1987] 7; [1988] 30; [1989] 255
Casati, Case 203/80, judgment of 11 November 1981; [1981] E.C.R. 2595 .... [1990] 177
Case Concerning Military and Paramilitary Activities In and Against Nicaragua [1986] I.C.J. Rep. 14 .... [1990] 561
Case of the S.S. *Lotus* (1927) P.C.I.J., Ser. A. No. 10 .... [1990] 89
Casey *v.* Highlands Ins. Co., 100 Idaho 505, 600 P. 2d 1387, 1391 (1979) .... [1986] 82
Cassaboglou *v.* Gibb (1883) 11 Q.B.D. 797 .... [1989] 117
Cassone, *In re*, 63 N.Y. 2d 756 (1984) .... [1986] 68
Castanho *v.* Brown & Root (U.K.) Ltd. [1981] A.C. 557 .... [1987] 3, 393; [1988] 391
Castle Insurance Co. Ltd. *et al. v.* Hong Kong Islands Shipping Co. Ltd. [1984] A.C. 226 .... [1987] 164
Cato, The (1866) 35 L.J. Adm. .... [1989] 75, 76
Catt *v.* Marac Australia Ltd. (1986) 9 N.S.W.L.R. 639 .... [1990] 464
Cattle *v.* Stockton Waterworks Co. (1875) L.R. 10 Q.B. 453 .... [1986] 299; [1989] 1
Caxton Publishing Co. Ltd. *v.* Sutherland Publishing Co. Ltd. [1939] A.C. 178; [1936] Ch. 323 .... [1990] 462
C.C.C. Films (London) Ltd. *v.* Impact Quadrant Films Ltd. [1985] Q.B. 16 .... [1986] 335, 336; [1990] 148
C.C.R. Fishing Ltd. *v.* Tomenson Inc. (1989) 55 D.L.R. (4d) 429 (B.C.C.A.) .... [1990] 106
C.C.R. Fishing Ltd. *v.* Tomenson Inc. (*The La Pointe*) [1986] 2 Lloyd's Rep. 513 (B.C.S.C.) .... [1988] 87
CDN Research *v.* Bank of Nova Scotia (1981) 32 O.R. (2d) 568 .... [1990] 235
Cebu, The [1983] Q.B. 1005, [1983] 1 Lloyd's Rep. 320 .... [1986] 425; [1989] 193
Cedric, The [1920] P. 193 .... [1989] 32
Cehave N.V. *v.* Bremer Handelsgesellschaft m.b.H. (*The Hansa Nord*) [1976] Q.B. 44 .... [1986] 158; [1987] 400; [1988] 506; [1990] 457
Celthene Pty. Ltd. *v.* W.J.K. Hauliers Ltd. [1981] 1 N.S.W.L.R. 606 .... [1986] 105
Cenco Inc. *v.* Seidman & Seidman (1982) 686 F. 2d 449 .... [1990] 426
Central London Property Trust Ltd. *v.* High Trees House Ltd. [1947] K.B. 130 .. [1986] 472; [1987] 388
Central R.R. Co. of New Jersey (*In re*), 469 F. 2d 857, 1983 A.M.C. 222 (3 Cir. 1972), cert. denied, 411 U.S. 938 (1973) .... [1986] 354
Centrovincial Estates Plc *v.* Merchant Investors Insurance Co. Ltd. (1983) C.L.R. 158 .... [1986] 323

Century Ins. Co. of Canada *v.* Case Existological Laboratories Ltd. (*The Bamcell II*) [1983] S.C.R. 47; [1986] 2 Lloyd's Rep. 524 .... [1984] 671; [1988] 87
Century Ins. Co. of Canada *v.* N.V. Bocimar S.A. [1987] 1 S.C.R. (Can. S.C.) .... [1989] 89, 93
Cephalonian Shipping Co. (*In re*), 1979 A.M.C. 1451 n. 1 (S.D.N.Y. 1979) .... [1986] 358
Chamberland *v.* Fleming (1985) 12 D.L.R. (4th) 688 .... [1987] 85
Chambers *v.* Miller (1862) 13 C.B. (N.S.) 125 .... [1989] 367; [1990] 65
Champion, The (1863) Br. & Lush. 690 .... [1989] 78
Champion International Corp. *v.* Continental Casualty Corp., 546 F. 2d 502 (2 Cir. 1976) .... [1986] 95
Champlain Ship Supply Ltd. *v.* The *Felicia V* [1984] 1 F.C. 476 .... [1987] 91
Chanda, The [1985] 1 Lloyd's Rep. 563 .... [1989] 498
Chandris *v.* Argo Insurance Co. Ltd. [1963] 2 Lloyd's Rep. 65 .... [1986] 140
Chandris *v.* Isbrandstsen-Moller Co. [1951] 1 K.B. 240 .... [1988] 55
Channel Island Ferries Ltd. *v.* Sealink U.K. Ltd. [1988] 1 Lloyd's Rep. 323 .... [1989] 7
Channon *v.* English Scottish & Australian Bank (1918) 18 S.R. (N.S.W.) 30 .... [1988] 371
Chanter *v.* Hopkins (1838) 4 M. & W. 399 .... [1990] 456
Chan *v.* Zacharia (1984) 154 C.L.R. 178 .... [1988] 365
Chaplin & Co. *v.* Brammall [1908] 1 K.B. 233 .... [1987] 126
Chapman *v.* Chapman [1954] A.C. 429 .... [1989] 435
Chapman *v.* G.W. Ry. Co. (1880) 5 Q.B.D. 278 .... [1987] 45, 66
Chapronière *v.* Mason (1905) 21 T.L.R. 633 .... [1988] 508
Charge Card Services (*Re*) [1986] 3 W.L.R. 697 .... [1987] 152
Charge Card Services Ltd. (*Re*) [1988] 3 W.L.R. 764; [1987] Ch. 150; [1989] Ch. 497 .... [1989] 22 *et seq.*, 244; [1990] 275, 528
Charles Adolphe, The (1856) Swab. 153 .... [1989] 61, 63, 66
Charles *v.* Blackwell (1877) 2 C.P.D. 151 .... [1990] 66, 251
Charles (L.H.) & Co. Ltd. (*Re*) [1935] W.N. 15 .... [1990] 533
Charles Rickards Ltd. *v.* Oppenhaim [1950] 1 K.B. 616 .... [1987] 65
Charlotte, The (1848) 3 W. Rob. 68 .... [1989] 65
Charnock *v.* Liverpool Corp. [1968] 1 W.L.R. 1498 .... [1989] 171
Charter *v.* Sullivan [1957] 2 Q.B. 117 .... [1990] 310
Charterhouse Credit Ltd. *v.* Tolley [1963] 2 Q.B. 683 .... [1990] 284
Chas. Davis *v.* Gilyott & Scott [1975] 2 Lloyd's Rep. 422 .... [1990] 292
Chase Manhattan Bank N.A. *v.* Israel-British Bank (London) Ltd. [1981] Ch. 105 .... [1987] 437; [1988] 362; [1989] 120–121, 438; [1990] 332, 550
Chateauqay Ore & Iron Co. *v.* Eastern Transportation Co., 1935 A.M.C. 1320 (E.D.N.Y.) .... [1986] 495
Chaudhry *v.* Prabhakhar [1989] 1 W.L.R. 29 .... 148 *et seq.*
Chauffeurs Teamsters & Helpers *v.* Stroehmann Bros., 625 F. 2d 1092, 1094 (3 Cir. 1980) .... [1986] 72
Cheall *v.* APEX [1983] 2 A.C. 180 .... [1989] 4; [1990] 157
Cheetham & Co. Ltd. *v.* Thornham Shipping Co. Ltd. [1964] 2 LLoyd's Rep. 17 .... [1990] 2
Chellaram & Sons (London) Ltd. *v.* Butlers Warehousing and Distribution Ltd. [1978] 2 Lloyd's Rep. 412 .... [1988] 469
Chellaram (P.S.) & Co. Ltd. *v.* China Ocean Shipping Co. [1989] 1 Lloyd's Rep. 413 (N.S.W. Sup. Ct.) .... [1989] 277 *et seq.*, 396; [1990] 315
Chellentis *v.* Luckenbach S.S. Co. (1917) 247 U.S. 372 .... [1990] 34
Chemco Leasing S.p.A. *v.* Rediffusion plc, *The Times*, 19 December 1986 .... [1987] 157; [1988] 291
Chernoff *v.* Chilcott and Kinakin (1988) 27 B.C.L.R. (2d) 283 (B.C.C.A.) .... [1990] 100
Cherry *v.* Allied Insurance Brokers [1978] 1 Lloyd's Rep. 274 .... [1987] 208
Chesneau *v.* Interhome, *The Times*, 9 June 1983 .... [1986] 319
Chess (Oscar) Ltd. *v.* Williams [1957] 1 W.L.R. 370 .... [1990] 148
Chester *v.* Maritima del Litoral S.A., 586 F. Supp. 192 (E.D. Wis. 1983) .... [1986] 367
Chevron U.S.A. Inc. *v.* Hammond, 726 F. 2d 483, 1984 A.M.C. 1027, 1985 A.M.C. 2395 (9 Cir. 1984), cert. denied, 105 S. Ct. 2 (1985) 86 L. Ed2d 703 (1985) .... [1986] 376; [1987] 502
Chicago, Milwaukee, St. Paul & Pacific RR Co. *v.* United States, 575 F. 2d 839 (Ct. Cl. 1978) .... [1987] 500
Chieftain, The (1846) 2 W. Rob. 450 .... [1989] 77
Chikuma, The [1981] 1 W.L.R. 314 .... [1986] 214; [1989] 367; [1990] 85, 86
China, The (1869) 74 U.S. (7 Wall.) 53 .... [1988] 161
China Mutual Trading Co. Ltd. *v.* Banque Belge pour l'Etranger (Extreme Orient) S.A. (1954) 39 H.K.L.R. 144 .... [1989] 369

China Pacific S.A. *v.* Food Corporation of India (*The Winson*) [1982] A.C. 939 .... [1986] 308, 326, 340, 345, 349; [1988] 37, 546; [1990] 34
Choko Star, The [1990] 1 Lloyd's Rep. 516 (C.A.); reversing [1989] 2 Lloyd's Rep. 42 ....[1990] 35, 353, 359
Chotin Transportation Inc. *v.* United States (1987) 819 F. 2d 1342; 1988 A.M.C. 2375 (6th Cir.) (16 judges *en banc*, seven dissenting) ....[1989] 18
Chow Yoong Hong *v.* Choong Fah Rubber Manufactury [1962] A.C. 209 .... [1989] 208
Christensen *v.* Hindustan Steel Ltd. [1971] 1 Lloyd's Rep. 395; [1971] 1 W.L.R. 1369 .... [1987] 411; [1990] 396
Christie *v.* Secretan (1799) 8 T.R. 192 .... [1988] 343
Christine Isle, The, 1974 A.M.C. 331 (Bermuda) .... [1987] 153, 380; [1989] 179
Christopher *v.* Police. 22 April 1974 (Wellington M 36/74) ....[1987] 55
Cia. Mar. San Basilio S.A. *v.* Oceanus Mutual Indemnity Assn. (*The Eurysthenes*) [1977] Q.B. 49 .... [1988] 353
Cia Naviera Maropan S.A. *v.* Bowaters Lloyd Pulp and Paper Mills (*The Stork*) [1955] 2 Q.B. 68 ....[1987] 408; [1988] 43
Cia. Naviera Sea Orient S.A. *v.* Gebr. Van Weelde Scheepvartkantoor N.V., 21 May 1987 (C.A.) .... [1987] 263
Cia. Portorafti Commerciale S.A. *v.* Ultramar Panama Inc. (*The Captain Gregos*) [1989] 2 All E.R. 54; [1990] 1 Lloyd's Rep. 310 .... [1989] 394; [1990] 314
Cie Air-France *v.* Consorts Teichner (1985) 39 R.F.D.A. 232 (Israel S.C.) .... [1988] 224
Cie Air-Inter *v.* Bornier (1983) 37 RFDA 47 (Cour de Cass.); *cf.* (1979) 33 R.F.D.A. 340 .... [1988] 219
Cie Francaise d'Importation et de Distribution S.A. *v.* Deutsche Continental Handelsgesellschaft [1985] 2 Lloyd's Rep. 592 .... [1987] 158
Cie. Tunisienne *v.* Cie. d'Armement [1971] A.C. 572 .... [1986] 261
Cielo Bianco, The [1987] F.C. 592 ....[1989] 94
Cielo Rosso, The, 1980 A.M.C. 2088, S.M.A. No. 1498 (1980) ....[1986] 73
Cincinnati Milacron Ltd. *v.* M/V *American Legend*, 1985 A.M.C. 1065 (D. Md. 1984) .. [1986] 367, 368
Cinnaminson Township Board of Educ. *v.* U.S. Gypsum Co., 552 F. Supp. 855 (D.C.N.J., 1982) .... [1987] 124
Citadel Insurance Co. *v.* Atlantic Union Insurance Co. S.A. [1982] 2 Lloyd's Rep. 543 .... [1988] 6
Citibank N.A. *v.* Hobbs Savill & Co. Ltd. (*The Panglobal Friendship*) [1978] 1 Lloyd's Rep. 368 .... [1989] 192
Citicorp Australia Ltd. *v.* Hendry (1985) 4 N.S.W.L.R. 1 ....[1990] 23
City and Westminster Properties *v.* Mudd [1959] Ch. 129 .... [1986] 316
City Equitable Fire Insurance Co. Ltd. (*Re*) [1925] Ch. 407 .... [1987] 200
City of Chicago *v.* Dunham Towing & Wrecking Co., 161 Ill. App. 307 (1st Dist., 1911), 175 Ill. App. 549 (1st Dist., 1912) .... [1987] 521
City of Milwaukee *v.* Illinois, 451 U.S. 304 (1981) .... [1987] 504
City of New Orleans *v.* Firemen's Charitable Associaton, 9 So. 486 (1891) .... [1987] 427
City of Norwich, The, 118 U.S. 468 (1886) .... [1986] 380; [1987] 345; [1988] 518
Civica Investments Ltd. (*Re*) [1983] B.C.L.C. 456 .... [1987] 190
C.L. Nye Ltd. (*Re*) [1971] 1 Ch. 442 ....[1990] 534, 535
Clandeboye, The, 70 F.631 (4 Cir. 1895) .... [1986] 322
Clare & Co. *v.* Dresdner Bank [1915] 2 K.B. 576 ....[1990] 71
Clarets Ltd. (*Re*), unreported, 22 November 1978 .... [1990] 531
Clarisse, The (1856) 12 Moo. P.C. 340 ....[1989] 59
Clark, *et al v.* Manufacturer's Ins. Co., 49 U.S. 235 .... [1986] 500
Clark (John T.) & Sons *v.* The S.S. *Al Kulsum*, 1974 A.M.C. 1489 (S.D.N.Y 1974) .... [1986] 355
Clarke *v.* Bruce Lance & Co. [1988] 1 W.L.R. 881 .... [1988] 439
Clarke *v.* Dickson (1858) E.B. & E. 148 .... [1986] 318
Clarke *v.* Shee and Johnson (1774) 1 Cowp. 197 ....[1989] 301, 316, 339
Clattenburg *v.* Canada (1986) 2 F.T.R. 116 (F.C.) .... [1989] 102
Claude Neon Lights (Vic.) Ltd. *v.* Gorham [1962] V.R. 493 (Vic. Full Ct.) ....[1990] 22
Claydon *v.* Bradley [1987] 1 All E.R. 522 .... [1990] 231
Cleadon Trust Ltd. (*Re*) [1939] Ch. 286 ....[1989] 10
Cleaver *v.* Mutual Reserve Fund Life Assn. [1892] 1 Q.B. 147 .... [1987] 210; [1988] 125
Clemens *v.* Clemens Bros. Ltd. [1976] 2 All E.R. 268 ....[1988] 71
Clemens (E.) Horst Co. *v.* Biddell Bros. [1911] 1 K.B. 934, 957; [1912] A.C. 18 .... [1986] 299
Cleobulos Shipping Co. Ltd. *v.* Intertanker Ltd. (*The Cleon*) [1983] 1 Lloyd's Rep. 586 .... [1989] 292
Cleon, The [1983] 1 Lloyd's Rep. 586 .... [1989] 292

Cleveland Museum of Art *v.* Capricorn International S.A. (1989) 5 B.C.C. 860; 17 October 1989 .... [1990] 542
Clifford Maersk, The [1982] 1 W.L.R. 1292 .... [1988] 83
Clipper Ship Supply Inc. *v.* Sematour Shipping (1988) 19 F.T.R. 15 (Can. F.C.) .... [1990] 105
Clotilde, The, F. Cas. 2903 (D. Me. 1872) .... [1986] 324
Clough Mill Ltd. *v.* Martin [1984] 1 W.L.R. 1067; [1985] 1 W.L.R. 111 .... [1985] 15; [1987] 75; [1988] 146, 257; [1989] 119, 194, 201, 212, 509; [1990] 129, 527, 529
Cluden, The 1982 A.M.C. 2321 .... [1988] 440
Clydebank Engineering & Shipbuilding Co. Ltd. *v.* Don Jose Ramos Yzquierdo y Castaneda [1905] A.C. 6 .... [1990] 18
Coal Exporter Corp. *v.* Notias (1962) E.A. 220 (East African C.A. in Aden) .... [1989] 179
Coast Lines Ltd. *v.* Hudig & Veder Chartering N.V. [1972] 2 Q.B. 34 .... [1986] 512
Cobb Coin Company Inc. *v.* The Unidentified, Wrecked and Abandoned Sailing Vessel, etc., 549 F. Supp. 540, 550–551, 1983 A.M.C. 1018, 1029 (1982) .... [1986] 18
Cochran *v.* McDonald (1945) 161 P. 2d 305 (Wash, S.C.) .... [1988] 510
Coco *v.* A.N. Clark (Engineers) Ltd. [1969] R.P.C. 41 .... [1989] 159
Codex Corp. *v.* Racal-Milgo [1984] F.S.R. 87 .... [1990] 462
Codrington *v.* Codrington (1875) L.R. 7 H.L. 854 .... [1988] 474
Cognet-Centre Leclerc, Case 355/85, judgment of 23 October 1986; [1986] E.C.R. 3231 .... [1990] 187
Coggs *v.* Bernard (1703) Ld. Raym. 909 .... [1989] 149
Colchester Estates (Cardiff) *v.* Carlton Industries plc [1986] 1 Ch. 80 .... [1987] 12
Coldunell Ltd. *v.* Gallon [1986] Q.B. 1184, pet. diss. [1986] 1 W.L.R. 994 .... [1987] 125; [1988] 436; [1990] 158, 338
Coleman *v.* Bucks and Oxon Union Bank [1897] 2 Ch. 243 .... [1989] 304
Coleman *v.* Myers [1977] 2 N.Z.L.R. 225 .... [1990] 464
Colin *v.* Holden (unreported, Victoria Sup. Ct., July 1988) .... [1989] 279
Collins *v.* Atlantic Pilotage Authority (1985) 149 A.P.R. 323 .... [1987] 93
Collins *v.* Blantern (1767) 2 Wils. K.B. 341 .... [1988] 125
Collister *v.* Nationwide Life Ins. Co., 475 Pa. 579, 388 A. 2d 1346, 1353 (1978), cert. denied, 439 U.S. 1089 (1979) .... [1986] 86
Colombine, The (1843) 2 W. Rob. 186 .... [1989] 76
Colonial Bank *v.* European Grain & Shipping Ltd. (*The Dominique*) [1987] 1 Lloyd's Rep. 239; [1988] 3 W.L.R. 60 .... [1989] 195, 289 *et seq.*
Colonial Bank of Australasia *v.* Marshall [1906] A.C. 559 (P.C. affg. (1904) 1 C.L.R. 632 .... [1986] 10
Colonial Trusts Corp. (*Re*) *ex parte* Bradshaw (1879) 15 Ch. D. 465, 472–73 .... [1986] 524
Colorado, The [1923] P. 102 .... [1989] 13, 174, 179, 180, 181, 190
Coltman *v.* Bibby Tankers Ltd. (*The Derbyshire*) [1986] 1 W.L.R. 751; [1987] I.C.R. 619; [1987] 2 W.L.R. 1098 (C.A.); [1987] 3 W.L.R. 1181 (H.L.) .... [1988] 123, 211
Columbia Picture Industries Inc. *v.* Robinson [1987] Ch. 38 .... [1988] 120
Comex Houlder Diving Ltd. *v.* Colne Fishing Co. Ltd. 1987 S.L.T. 443 (H.L.) .... [1989] 3
Commercial Banking Co. of Sydney Ltd. *v.* Mann [1961] A.C. 1 .... [1988] 474
Commercial Standard Ins. Co. *v.* General Trucking Co., 423 So. 2d 168 (Ala. 1982) .... [1986] 82
Commission *v.* Belgium, Case 155/82, judgment of 2 March 1983; [1983] E.C.R. 531 .... [1990] 183
Commission *v.* France (167/73) [1974] E.C.R. 359; [1974] 2 C.M.L.R. 216 .... [1987] 16
Commission *v.* France, Case 270/83, judgment of 28 January 1986; [1986] E.C.R. 273 .... [1990] 181
Commission *v.* Germany, Case 205/84, judgment of 4 December 1986; [1986] E.C.R. 3755 .... [1990] 177
Commissioner of Income Tax *v.* Vazir Sultan & Sons, A.I.R. 1959 S.C. 814, 821 .... [1988] 15
Commissioners of Taxation *v.* English, Scottish and Australian Bank Ltd. [1920] A.C. 683 (P.C.) .... [1989] 41
Committee for Justice and Liberty *v.* National Energy Board [1978] 1 S.C.R. 369 .... [1989] 92
Commodore, The (1853) 1 Sp. 175n .... [1989] 69
Commonwealth Coatings Corp. *v.* Continental Cas. Co., 393 U.S. 145 (1969) .... [1986] 62
Commonwealth Insurance *v.* Groupe Sprinks [1983] 1 Lloyd's Rep. 67, 78 .... [1986] 31
Commonwealth Oil Refining Co. (*In re*), 805 F. 2d 1175 (5th Cir., 1986) .... [1987] 507
Commonwealth Oil Refining Co. (Matter of), 734 F. 2d 1079 (5 Cir. 1984) .... [1986] 371
Commonwealth of Puerto Rico *v.* S.S. *Zoe Colocotroni*, 456 F. Supp. 1327; 1979 A.M.C. 12 (D.P.R., 1978), aff'd in part, vacated in part 628 F. 2d 652; 1981 A.M.C. 2099 (1st Cir., 1980), cert. denied 450 U.S. 912 (1981) .... [1987] 500, 502, 504, 507
Commonwealth Trading Bank of Australia *v.* Sydney Wide Stores Pty. Ltd. (1981) 35 A.L.R. 513 .... [1986] 10

Comoco Marine Serv. *v.* M.V. *El Centro Americano*, 1984 A.M.C. 2592 (D. Ore.) .... [1987] 153
Compagnie d'Armement Maritime S.A. *v.* Compagnie Tunisienne de Navigation S.A. [1971] A.C. 572 .... [1986] 513; [1987] 529, 531, 532; [1989] 218
Compania de Navegación y Financiera Bosnia *v.* National Unity Marine Salvage Corp., 457 F. Supp. 1013 (S.D.N.Y. 1978) .... [1986] 67
Compania Española de Petroleos S.A. *v.* Nereus Shipping S.A., 527 F. 2d 966 (2 Cir. 1975), cert. denied, 426 U.S. 936 (1976) .... [1986] 66, 536
Compania Maritima San Basilio S.A. *v.* Oceanus Mutual Underwriting Association (*The Eurysthenes*) [1977] 1 Q.B. 49 .... [1986] 41
Compania Merabello San Nicolas S.A. (*Re*) [1973] 1 Ch. 75 .... [1986] 384; [1987] 231; [1989] 393
Compania Naviera Martiartu *v.* Royal Exchange Assurance Corporation [1923] 1 K.B. 650, 657; (1924) 19 Ll.L.Rep. 95 .... [1986] 287; [1987] 41
Compania Portorafti Commerciale *v.* Kaiser Int'l Corp., 616 F. Supp. 236 (S.D.N.Y 1985) .... [1986] 59
Competitive Insurance *v.* Davies Investments [1975] 1 W.L.R. 1240 .... [1989] 325
Complaint of American Export Lines Inc., 620 F. Supp. 490 (S.D.N.Y., 1986) .... [1987] 118
Complaint of Caribbean Sea Transport Ltd., 748 F. 2d 622 (11th Cir., 1984) .... [1987] 345
Comptoir d'Achat et de Vente du Boerenbond Belge S.A. *v.* Luis de Ridder Limitada (*The Julia*) [1949] A.C. 293 .... [1987] 183
Comunale *v.* Traders and General Ins. Co., 50 Cal. 2d 654, 328 P. 2d 198, 201–202 (1958) ..... [1986] 81
Concordia Fjord, The [1984] 1 Lloyd's Rep. 385 .... [1986] 121, 149, 150; [1988] 46
Cone (Frederick H.) & Co. *v.* *The Tai Shan*, 218 F. 2d 822, 1955 A.M.C. 420 (2 Cir. 1955) .. [1986] 369
Connor *v.* Aerovox Inc., 730 F. 2d 835 (1st Cir., 1984) .... [1987] 503
Connors Marine *v.* British & Foreign, 1938 A.M.C. 645 (N.Y.A.D.) .... [1986] 498
Constable's Case (1601) 5 Co. Rep. 106a .... [1987] 269
Con-stan Industries of Australia Pty. Ltd. *v.* Norwich Winterthur Insurance (Australia) Ltd. (Aust. High Ct.) Judgment 11 April 1986 .... [1986] 284
Constantine (Joseph) S.S. Ltd. *v.* Imperial Smelting Corp. Ltd. [1942] A.C. 154 .... [1989] 5
Constitution Insurance *v.* Kosmopoulos (1987) 34 D.L.R. (4d) 208 .... [1990] 135
Consumer and Industrial Press Ltd. (*Re*) [1988] B.C.L.C. 177 .... [1989] 507; [1990] 414
Consumers Glass *v.* Farrell Lines 1986 A.M.C. 443 .... [1987] 84
Container Transport International Inc. *v.* Oceanus Mutual Underwriting Association (Bermuda) Ltd. [1982] 2 Lloyd's Rep. 178; rev'd. [1984] 1 Lloyd's Rep. 476 .... [1986] 29; [1987] 8; [1988] 30; [1989] 48
Conti Shipping *v.* Bomar Resources Inc. (*The Continental Trader*) (1986) S.M.A. No. 2211 .... [1989] 354, 358, 361
Continental Bank of Canada *v.* Reidel International (1988) 49 D.L.R. (4th) 737 (Can. F.C.) .. [1990] 99
Continental C. & G. Rubber Co. Pty. Ltd. (*Re*) (1919) 27 C.L.R. 294 .... [1990] 502
Continental Caoutchouc & Gutta Percha Co. *v.* Kleinwort, Sons & Co. (1904) 90 L.T. 474 .... [1989] 303, 313
Continental Contractors Ltd. *v.* Medway Oil & Storage Co. Ltd. (1925) 23 Ll. L. Rep. 125 .... [1989] 81
Continental Grain Export Corp. *v.* S.T.M. Grain Ltd. [1979] 2 Lloyd's Rep. 460 .... [1989] 7
Continental Illinois National Bank & Trust Co. of Chicago *v.* Alliance Ins. Co. Ltd. (*The Captain Panagos D.P.*) [1986] 2 Lloyd's Rep. 470; [1989] 1 Lloyd's Rep. 33 (C.A.) .... [1987] 40; [1989] 25 *et seq.*
Continental Oil Co. *v.* Bonanza Corp., 706 F. 2d 1365 (5 Cir. 1983) .... [1986] 428, 429
Continental Sea Foods *v.* N.H. Fire Ins. Co., 1964 A.M.C. 196 (S.D.N.Y.) .... [1986] 489
Continental Trader, The (1986) S.M.A. No. 2211 .... [1989] 354, 358, 361
Contractors (I.E.) Ltd. *v.* Lloyds Bank Plc [1989] 2 Lloyd's Rep. 205 .... [1990] 223, 243
Cooden Engineering Co. Ltd. *v.* Stanford [1953] 1 Q.B. 86 .... [1990] 19, 22
Cook *v.* Deeks [1916] 1 A.C. 554 .... [1988] 77, 134
Cooke (Sidney) Ltd. *v.* Hapag-Lloyd [1980] 2 N.S.W.L.R. 587 .... [1989] 281
Coomber *v.* Coomber [1911] 1 Ch. 723 .... [1987] 436
Coombes *v.* Hayward [1913] 1 K.B. 150 .... [1990] 321
Cooper *v.* Australian Electric Co. (1922) 25 W.A.L.R. 66 .... [1990] 518
Cooper *v.* General Dynamics, 533 F. 2d 163 (5th Cir., 1976) .... [1987] 505
Cooper *v.* Phibbs (1867) L.R. 2 H.L. 149 .... [1989] 119; [1990] 335
Cooper *v.* Stubbs [1925] 2 K.B. 753 (C.A.) .... [1986] 394
Cooper (*ex p.*) (1875) L.R. 10 Ch.App. 510 .... [1990] 219
Cooper Ewing & Co. Ltd. *v.* Hamel Horley Ltd. (1922) 13 Ll. L. Rep. 590 .... [1989] 81
Cope *v.* Rowlands (1836) 2 M. & W. 149 .... [1987] 202

Cordial Manufacturing Co. Ltd. *v.* Hong Kong/America Air Transport Ltd. [1976] H.K.L.R. 555 .... [1989] 39
Corfield *v.* Sevenways Garage Ltd. [1985] R.T.R. 109 (D.C.) .... [1989] 372
Corina, The, S.M.A. No. 1567 (1981) .... [1986] 72
Cornelius *v.* Phillips [1918] A.C. 199 .... [1987] 202, 203
Coromandel, The (1857) Swab. 205 .... [1989] 78
Corse *v.* The Queen (1892) 3 Ex. C.R. 13 .... [1986] 432
Cory Bros. & Co. Ltd. *v.* U.S., 57 F. 2d 1010 (1931) .... [1986] 14
Cosh *v.* Larsen [1971] 1 Lloyd's Rep. 557 .... [1990] 15
Costa *v.* ENEL, Case 6/64, judgment of 15 July 1964; [1964] E.C.R. 585 .... [1990] 181
Couchman *v.* Hill [1947] K.B. 554 .... [1988] 504
Coulon *v.* Ozolins [1984] 1 N.Z.L.R. 489 .... [1987] 327, 329
Coupland *v.* Arabian Gulf Oil Co. [1983] 1 W.L.R. 1136 .... [1986] 99; [1988] 364
Court Line Ltd. *v.* Dant & Russell Inc. (1939) 64 Ll.L.Rep. 212 .... [1990] 107, 110, 111
Couturier *v.* Hastie (1856) 5 H.L.C. 673 .... [1986] 317
Cowie *v.* Barber (1814) 4 Camp. 100 .... [1987] 212
Coxwold, The [1942] A.C. 691 .... [1986] 28; [1987] 30
Crabb *v.* Arun District Council [1976] Ch. 179 .... [1986] 472
Crabtree-Vickers Pty. Ltd. *v.* Australian Direct Mail Advertising & Addressing Co. Pty. Ltd. (1975) 133 C.L.R. 72 .... [1988] 396
Craig *v.* Anyon (1925) 212 App. Div. 55; 208 N.Y.S. 259 .... [1990] 423
Craven-Ellis *v.* Canons Ltd. [1936] 2 K.B. 403 .... [1987] 433; [1990] 334, 337, 507
Craythorne *v.* Swinburne (1807) 14 Ves. 160 .... [1989] 9
Cremer *v.* General Carriers S.A. (*The Dona Mari*) [1974] 1 W.L.R. 341 .... [1986] 226; [1988] 469; [1989] 165, 172, 422
Crescendo Management Pty. Ltd. *v.* Westpac Banking Corp., C.A. 492 of 1986; judgment 23 December 1988 .... [1990] 343
Crippen (*Re*) [1911] P. 108 .... [1988] 125, 318
Cristina, The [1938] A.C. 485 .... [1990] 171
Crooks *v.* Allen (1879) 5 Q.B.D. 38 .... [1988] 295
Crooks & Co. *v.* Agricultural Co-operative Union Ltd., 1922 AD 423 .... [1989] 176
Cross *v.* S.S. *Kaimana*, 401 F. 2d 182 (9 Cir. 1968), cert. denied, 393 U.S. 1095 (1969) .... [1986] 356
Crown Central Petroleum Corp. *v.* Ibrahim, 27 April 1988 (unreported) .... [1990] 91
Crown Forest Industries *v.* Valley Towing (1988) 19 F.T.R. 48 (Can. F.C.) .... [1990] 99
Crown Zellerbach Corp. *v.* Ingram Industries, 745 F. 2d 995, 1985 A.M.C. 305 (5 Cir. 1984) (*per curiam*), reh'g *en banc* granted, 745 F. 2d 1005 (5 Cir. 1985) .... [1986] 381
Crus V, The (1862) Lush. 583 .... [1986] 314; [1989] 76
Crystal, The [1894] A.C. 508 .... [1990] 358
C.T.I. *v.* Oceanus [1984] 1 Lloyd's Rep. 476 (C.A.) .... [1986] 31, 498, 499; [1987] 245; [1988] 116; [1990] 134, 444, 556, 560
C.U.M. *v.* Eastern Canada Shipping (1972) Inc. 1985 C.A. 106 .... [1987] 95
Cuba, The (1860) Lush 14 .... [1989] 68
Cudgen Rutile (No. 2) Pty. Ltd. *v.* Chalk [1975] A.C. 520 .... [1990] 497
Cumana Ltd. (*Re*) [1986] B.C.L.C. 430 (C.A.) .... [1988] 66
Cumberland, The (1845) 9 Jur. 191 .... [1989] 66, 73
Cundy *v.* Lindsay (1878) 3 App. Cas. 459 .... [1986] 323
Cunningham *v.* Woodchester Investments Ltd. (1984) unreported, 16 November (H.C.) .... [1989] 373
Cunningham (J. & J.) *v.* Robert A. Munro (1922) 28 Com. Cas. 42 .... [1990] 466
Curacao Trading Co. *v.* Federal Ins. Co., 1942 A.M.C. 1079 (S.D.N.Y.) .... [1986] 490, 492
Currie (M.R.) & Co. *v.* Bombay Native Ins. Co. (1869) L.R. 3 P.C. 72 .... [1988] 355
Curtis *v.* Chemical Cleaning and Dyeing Co. [1951] 1 K.B. 805 .... [1986] 316
Curtis *v.* Johannesburg Municipality, 1906 TS 308 .... [1986] 280
Customs Brokers (R. & B.) Co. Ltd. *v.* United Dominions Trust Ltd. [1988] 1 W.L.R. 321 .... [1989] 371, 375, 377, 380, 381
Cutter *v.* Powell (1797) 6 T.R. 320; 101 E.R. 573 .... [1988] 409
C.V.G. Siderurgicia del Orinoco S.A. *v.* London Steamship Owners Mutual Insurance Association Ltd. (*The Vainqueur Jose*) [1979] 1 Lloyd's Rep. 557 .... [1987] 232
Cyona Distributors Ltd. (*Re*) [1967] Ch. 889 .... [1990] 221
Czarnikow *v.* Roth, Schmidt & Co. [1922] 2 K.B. 478, 488 .... [1986] 58, 239
D'Amico Societa di Navigazione *v.* World Wide Transp. (*The Cielo Rosso*), 1980 A.M.C. 2088, S.M.A. No. 1498 (1980) .... [1986] 73

Dadon *v.* Air France, Civil Appeal 20/83, 38(3) P.D. (1984) 785 .... [1986] 292
Dafen Tinplate Co. Ltd. *v.* Llanelly Steel Co. (1907) Ltd. [1920] 2 Ch. 124 ....[1988] 75
Daff *v.* Midland Colliery Owners' Mutual Indemnity Co. Ltd. (1913) 109 L.T. 418 .... [1989] 503
Dagenham (Thames) Dock Co. (*Re*) (1873) L.R. 8 Ch. App. 1022 .... [1990] 160, 161
Dagmar, The [1968] 2 Lloyd's Rep. 563 ....[1988] 48
Daiwa Bank *v.* Mankai Shipping and Fast Marine (*The Taichun*), 20 July 1987, Kobe Dist. Ct., Japan .... [1989] 35 *et seq.*
Dakin *v.* Oxley (1864) 15 C.B. (N.S.) 646 .... [1990] 475
Dallal *v.* Bank Mellat [1986] Q.B. 441 .... [1987] 525
Dallas (*Re*) [1904] 2 Ch. 385 .... [1989] 197
Dalmas *v.* Stathatos (*The Maria Stathatos*), 84 F. Supp. 828 (S.D.N.Y. 1949) .... [1986] 344
Daly *v.* General Steam Navigation Co. Ltd. (*The Dragon*) [1979] 1 Lloyd's Rep. 257 .... [1990] 165
Damisetal, Cases 16–20/79, judgment of 6 November 1979; [1979] E.C.R. 3327 .... [1990] 182
Dammers & Vanderheide & Scheepvaart Maats Christina B.V. *v.* Corona (1988) 836 F. 2d 750 (2d Cir.) .... [1988] 519
Dan King, The (1988) L.M.L.N. 225 ....[1989] 3 *et seq.*
Daniels *v.* Daniels [1978] Ch. 406 ....[1988] 77
Daniels *v.* R. White & Sons Ltd. [1938] 4 All E.R. 258 .... [1988] 576
Darby *v.* Newton (1816) 6 Taunt. 544 .... [1987] 202
Darlington Futures Ltd. *v.* Delco Australia Pty. Ltd., 10 May 1985 (Unrep.); 28 February 1986 (Unrep.); (1986) 161 C.L.R. 500; (1987) 61 A.L.J.R. 76 ....[1987] 165, 166, 167; [1990] 155, 325
Darrah, The [1976] 1 Lloyd's Rep. 285; [1976] 2 Lloyd's Rep. 359; [1977] A.C. 157 .... [1986] 255; [1989] 401; [1990] 391
David *v.* Frowd (1833) 1 My. & K. 200 ....[1989] 313, 314, 329
Davie *v.* New Merton Board Mills Ltd. [1959] A.C. 604 .... [1988] 123
Davies *v.* Parry, 29 March 1988, unrep. .... [1988] 471
Davies *v.* Summer [1984] 1 W.L.R. 1301 .... [1989] 374, 376, 378, 380, 381
Davies *v.* Swan Motor Co. (Swansea) Ltd. [1949] 2 K.B. 291; [1949] 1 All E.R. 620 ....[1989] 35
Davis (Chas.) *v.* Gilyott & Scott [1975] 2 Lloyd's Rep. 422 .... [1990] 292
Davis Contractors Ltd. *v.* Fareham U.D.C. [1956] A.C. 696 .... [1986] 345; [1988] 301, 530; [1990] 156, 346, 347
Davis *v.* Colonial Mobile Homes [1975] 28 N.C.App. 13; 220 S.E. 2d 802 .... [1990] 376
Davis *v.* Henry Birks & Sons Ltd. [1981] 5 W.W.R. 559; (1983) 142 D.L.R. (3d) 356 .. [1987] 44, 60, 66
Day *v.* Mead [1987] 2 N.Z.L.R. 443 .... [1990] 464
Day *v.* Trans World Airlines Inc. (1975) 528 F. 2d 31 (2nd Cir.); 13 Avi. 18, 144, cert. denied (1976) 429 U.S. 890; *cf.* (1975) 13 Avi. 17, 647 .... [1988] 222
Dearle *v.* Hall (1828) 3 Russ. 1 .... [1988] 142, 149; [1989] 195, 197, 212, 213, 214, 215
De Beers Consolidated Mines Ltd. *v.* Howe [1906] A.C. 455 .... [1989] 386
De Bloos *v.* Bouyer, Case 14/76 [1976] E.C.R. 1497; [1977] 1 C.M.L.R. 60 .... [1987] 285, 287; [1988] 385; [1989] 472
De Bussche *v.* Alt (1878) 8 Ch.D. 286 .... [1990] 550, 551
De Hahn *v.* Hartley (1786) 1 T.R. 343; 99 E.R. 1130 ....[1986] 37
De Lovio *v.* Boit, C.C. Mass., 7 Fed. Cas. 418 No. 3, 776 (1815) ....[1986] 14, 488
De Meza and Stuart *v.* Apple, Van Straten, Shena and Stone [1974] 1 Lloyd's Rep. 508; aff'd [1975] 1 Lloyd's Rep. 498 ....[1987] 10; [1988] 8, 55; [1990] 420, 422, 425, 427
De Nicols *v.* Curlier [1900] A.C. 21 .... [1989] 386
Decro-Wall S.A. *v.* Practitioners in Marketing Ltd. [1971] 1 W.L.R. 361 .... [1990] 474
Deglman *v.* Guaranty Trust Co. of Canada [1954] 3 D.L.R. 785 .... [1990] 511
Degrace *v.* Central Garage Sales & Service Ltd. (1979) 24 N.B.R. (2d) 557 (New Brunswick Sup. Ct., App. Div.) .... [1987] 66, 68, 71
Deichland, The [1989] 3 W.L.R. 478 .... [1990] 171, 278
Delano *v.* Equitable Trust (1920) 181 N.Y. Supp. 852 .... [1988] 376
Delbrueck & Co. *v.* Manufacturers Hanover Trust Co., 609 F. 2d 1047 (1979) (U.S. Ct. of App., 2 Cir.), affirming 464 F. Supp. 989 (1979) (U.S. Dist. Ct., S.D.N.Y., 2 Cir.) .... [1986] 198, 209; [1989] 368; [1990] 79
Delfini, The [1988] 2 Lloyd's Rep. 599; [1990] 1 Lloyd's Rep. 252 (C.A.) .....[1989] 51, 57, 395; [1990] 1
Delian Spirit, The [1972] 1 Q.B. 103; [1971] 1 Lloyd's Rep. 506 (C.A.) .... [1986] 258; [1990] 390
Demosthenes, The (No. 1) [1982] 1 Lloyd's Rep. 275 .... [1987] 411
Denbigh, Cowan & Co. *v.* Atcherley (1921) 90 L.J.K.B. 836 .... [1987] 183
Denilauler *v.* S.n.c. Couchet Frères [1980] E.C.R. 1553 (Case No. 125/79) ....[1990] 90
Denmark Productions *v.* Boscobel Productions [1969] 1 Q.B. 699 .... [1989] 5

Denny Mott & Dickson Ltd. *v*. James B. Fraser & Co. Ltd. [1944] A.C. 265 .... [1990] 156
Department of the Environment *v*. Thomas Bates & Son Ltd. [1990] 3 W.L.R. 457 .... [1990] 482
Deposit & Investment Co. Ltd. *v*. Kaye (1962) 63 S.R. (N.S.W.) 453 .... [1990] 512
Dept. of Trade *v*. St. Christopher's Motorists Assn. Ltd. [1974] 1 Lloyd's Rep. 7 .... [1987] 214
Derby & Co. Ltd. *v*. Weldon (No. 1) [1989] 2 W.L.R. 276 (C.A.) .... [1989] 465; [1990] 89, 91
Derby & Co. Ltd. *v*. Weldon (Nos. 3 and 4) [1989] 2 W.L.R. 412 (C.A.) .. [1989] 465, 475; [1990] 92, 94
Derbyshire, The [1986] 1 W.L.R. 751; [1987] I.C.R. 619, [1987] 2 W.L.R. 1098 (C.A.); [1987] 3 W.L.R. 1181 (H.L.) .... [1988] 123, 211
Derry *v*. Peek (1889) 14 App. Cas. 337 .... [1986] 314; [1989] 441; [1990] 410
Deterding *v*. United States, 109 Ct. Cl. 851; 69 F. Supp. 214 (Ct. Cl. 1947) .... [1987] 436
Deutsche Bank *v*. Banque des Marchands de Moscou (1931) 4 L.D.A.B. 293 .... [1989] 44; [1990] 490
Deutsche Schachtbau- und Tiefbohr-Gesellschaft m.b.H. *v*. Shell International Petroleum Co. Ltd. (trading as Shell International Trading Co.) [1988] 3 W.L.R. 230; also reported sub nom. Deutsche Schachtbau- und Tiefbohrgesellschaft m.b.H. *v*. Ras al-Khaimah National Oil Co. (D.S.T. *v*. Rakoil) [1988] 2 All E.R. 833 (*q.v.*) .... [1988] 429
Deutsche Schachtbau- und Tiefbohrgesellschaft m.b.H. *v*. Ras al-Khaimah National Oil Co. (No. 2) (D.S.T. v. Rakoil (No. 2)) [1988] 1 Lloyd's Rep. 164; [1987] 3 W.L.R. 1023; [1988] 3 W.L.R. 230 (H.L.) .... [1987] 279; [1988] 429; [1989] 467
Deveron, The (1841) 1 W. Rob. 180 .... [1989] 67
DFDS *v*. U.S.A., 1988 A.M.C. 1530 (S. Dist., Fla.) .... [1990] 53
Diana Prosperity, The [1976] 1 W.L.R. 989 .... [1988] 462, 506; [1990] 457
Dias, The [1978] 1 Lloyd's Rep. 325; [1978] 1 W.L.R. 261 (H.L.) .... [1986] 253; [1987] 419; [1988] 251; [1990] 393, 394
Dias Compania Naviera *v*. Louis Dreyfus Corporation (*The Dias*) [1978] 1 Lloyd's Rep. 325; [1978] 1 W.L.R. 261 (H.L.) .... [1986] 253; [1987] 419; [1988] 251
Dick Bentley Productions Ltd. *v*. Harold Smith (Motors) Ltd. [1965] 1 W.L.R. 623 .... [1990] 148
Dickow *v*. Cincinnati, 23 Ohio N.P.N.S. 1; 31 Ohio Dec. 266 (Hamilton Comm. Pl. 1920) ... [1987] 521
Dickson *v*. Devitt (1916) 21 Com. Cas. 291, 294 .... [1988] 8
Dictator, The [1892] P. 304 .... [1987] 322, 543; [1990] 171
Dien Danielsen, The, 1982 (3) SA 534 (N); 1983 (4) SA 275 (N) .... [1987] 309, 311
Diligenti *v*. RWMD Operations Kelowna Ltd. [1976] 1 BCLR 36 (B.C.S.C.) .... [1988] 70
Dillon *v*. Charter Travel Co. Ltd. (*The Mikhail Lermontov*), N.S.W.S.C., 20 November 1989 .... [1990] 164
Dimbleby & Sons Ltd. *v*. N.U.J. [1984] 1 W.L.R. 427 .... [1990] 406
Dimitris, The, 1989 (3) S.A. 820 (A) .... [1990] 9
Dimond (H.H.) (Rotorua 1966) Ltd. *v*. Australia and New Zealand Banking Group Ltd. [1979] 2 N.Z.L.R. 739 .... [1990] 72, 73, 75, 76, 244, 245, 247
Dimskal Shipping Co. S.A. *v*. International Transport Workers Federation (*The Evia Luck (No. 2)*) [1990] 1 Lloyd's Rep. 319 (C.A.); [1989] 1 Lloyd's Rep. 166 ...... [1990] 347, 348, 349, 350, 351
Diplock (*Re*) [1948] Ch. 465 (C.A.), aff'd as Ministry of Health *v*. Simpson [1951] A.C. 251 .... [1987] 437; [1989] 313, 314, 316, 317, 328, 331, 334
Director, Office of Workers' Compensation Programs *v*. Perini North River Associates, 459 U.S. 297, 1983 A.M.C. 609 (1983) .... [1986] 372
Discounter Catalogue Showrooms Ltd. (*Re*) (1987) unreported .... [1989] 508
Dixon *v*. Monkland Canal Co. (1831) 5 W. & S. 445 .... [1989] 320
Doak *v*. Weekes and another (*The Marandoo*) [1986] 4 A.N.Z. Insurance Cases 60–697 ...... [1986] 287
Dole Dried Fruit and Nut Co. *v*. Trustin Kerwood Ltd. (1990) L.M.L.N. 276 .... [1990] 472
Domangue *v*. Eastern Air Lines Inc. (1984) 772 F. 2d 256 (5th Cir.) .... [1988] 179
Domar Ocean Transp. Ltd. *v*. M/V *Andrew Martin*, No. 83–3348 (5 Cir. 8 March 1985) ...... [1986] 362
Dome Petroleum Ltd. *v*. Burrard Yarrows Corp. [1984] 48 B.C.L.R. 370 .... [1987] 87
Domestic Converters *v*. Arctic Steamship Line [1984] 1 F.C. 211 .... [1987] 94
Domingo de Larrinaga, The, 1928 A.M.C. 64 .... [1987] 163
Dominique, The [1987] 1 Lloyd's Rep. 239; [1988] 3 W.L.R. 60; [1989] A.C. 1056; [1989] 2 W.L.R. 440 .... [1989] 195, 289 *et seq.*; [1990] 472
Dona Mari, The [1974] 1 W.L.R. 341 .... [1988] 469; [1989] 165, 172, 422
Donoghue *v*. Stevenson [1932] A.C. 562 .... [1988] 214, 366, 406; [1989] 150
Doorman *v*. Jenkins (1834) 2 Ad. & El. 256 .... [1989] 149
Dora, The, 7 September 1976 (Unrep.) .... [1987] 90
Dorset C.C. *v*. Southern Felt Roofing Co. Ltd., *Financial Times*, 24 November 1989 .... [1990] 155
Dorset Yacht Co. Ltd. *v*. Home Office [1970] A.C. 1004 .... [1987] 9; [1988] 406
Dorval *v*. Bouvier [1968] S.C.R. 288 .... [1989] 89

Dosseitei, The (1846) 10 Jur. 865 ....[1989] 72
Doto, The, 1985 AMC 1152 (S.D. Alabama) ....[1989] 353, 354
Double-M Constr. Corp. *v*. Central School District No. 1, 61 A.D. 2d 981, 402 N.Y.S. 2d 442 (N.Y. App. Div. 1978) ....[1986] 64
Dougherty (P.) Co. *v*. U.S.A. (*The Mohawk*), 1953 A.M.C. 1541 (U.S.C.A., 3rd Cir.) ....[1990] 52
Doust & Co. *v*. The *Nyon III* (1986) 3 F.T.R. 192 (F.C.) ....[1989] 91
Dow Chemical Co. *v*. Barge *U.M.-23B*, 1970 A.M.C. 1622 ....[1990] 52
Dow Chemical Pacific Ltd. *v*. Rascator Maritime S.A., 594 F. Supp. 1490 (S.D.N.Y. 1984) ....[1986] 47
Dowson and Mason Ltd. *v*. Potter [1986] 1 W.L.R. 1419 ....[1990] 464
Doyle *v*. Olby (Ironmongers) Ltd. [1969] 2 Q.B. 158 ....[1990] 148
D.P.C. Estates Pty. Ltd. *v*. Consul Developments Pty. Ltd. [1974] 1 N.S.W.L.R. 443 .... [1988] 129; [1989] 327, 336
D.P.P. *v*. Schildkamp [1971] A.C. 1 ....[1990] 405
Dragon, The [1979] 1 Lloyd's Rep. 257 ....[1990] 165
Drew *v*. Nunn (1879) 4 Q.B.D. 661, 665–6 ....[1986] 206
Drilling (706) Co. Ltd. *v*. Pierson (1984) 7 D.L.R. (4th) 374 ....[1987] 88
Driver *v*. Broad [1893] 1 Q.B. 744, 748–49 ....[1986] 522
Drummond Coal Co. *v*. Interocean Shipping Co. (*The Doto*), 1985 A.M.C. 1152 (S.D. Alabama) ....[1989] 353, 354
D/S A/S Idaho *v*. Colossus Maritime S.A. (*The Concordia Fjord*) [1984] 1 Lloyd's Rep. 385 ....[1986] 121; [1988] 46
DSV Silo-und Verwaltungsgesellschaft mbH *v*. Owners of the *Sennar* and 13 other ships [1985] 1 W.L.R. 490 ....[1987] 392, 396
D.T.R. Nominees Pty. Ltd. *v*. Mona Homes Pty. Ltd. (1978) 138 C.L.R. 423 ....[1989] 86
Dubai Electricity Co. *v*. Islamic Republic of Iran (*The Iran Vojdan*) [1984] 2 Lloyd's Rep. 380 ....[1986] 508, 509, 510, 511, 513, 515, 516, 517, 518; [1990] 196
Dudgeon *v*. Pembroke (1874) L.R. 9 Q.B. 581; (1877) 2 App. Cas. 284 ....[1986] 39; [1988] 350
Dudley, 1928 A.M.C. 1806 ....[1986] 492
Duijnstee *v*. Goderbauer, Case 288/82 [1983] E.C.R. 3663 ....[1989] 472
Duke *v*. Jackson, 1921 S.C. 362 ....[1988] 508
Duke of Beaufort *v*. Neeld (1845) 12 Cl. & F. 248 ....[1989] 442
Duke of Norfolk's Settlement Trusts (*Re*) [1982] Ch. 61 ....[1990] 336
Dunbar *v*. A. & B. Painters Ltd. [1985] 2 Lloyd's Rep. 616; [1986] 2 Lloyd's Rep. 38 (C.A.) ....[1987] 208; [1990] 560
Duncan Stevenson Macmillan *v*. Knott Becker Scott Ltd. [1990] 1 Lloyd's Rep. 98 ....[1990] 318
Dundee, The (1827) 2 Hagg. 137 ....[1988] 179
Dunelmia, The [1970] 1 Q.B. 289 ....[1986] 99
Dunkirk Colliery Co. *v*. Lever (1878) 9 Ch.D. 20 ....[1990] 310, 312
Dunlop Pneumatic Tyre Co. Ltd. *v*. New Garage and Motor Co. Ltd. [1915] A.C. 79 .... [1989] 437, 503, 504; [1990] 19
Duomatic Ltd. (*Re*) [1969] 2 Ch. 365 ....[1990] 403
Dupleix, The [1911] P. 8 ....[1990] 171
Durham Bros. *v*. Robertson [1898] 1 Q.B. 765 ....[1986] 198
Dutch *v*. Warren (1720) 1 Strange 406 ....[1987] 430
Dyestuffs [1972] E.C.R. 619 ....[1986] 549
Eads *v*. H.D. Bacon (1853) Fed. Cas. 224 ....[1990] 36
Eagle, The [1977] 2 Lloyd's Rep. 70 ....[1990] 164
Eagle Ins. Corp. *v*. Hartford Fire Ins. Co., 540 F. 2d 1257 (5 Cir. 1976) ....[1986] 84
Eagle Leasing Corp. *v*. Hartford Fire Ins. Co., 540 F. 2d 1257, 1261 4 (8 Cir. 1976) ....[1986] 84
Eagle-Picher Ind. Inc. *v*. Liberty Mut. Ins., 682 F. 2d 12, 17 (1 Cir. 1982), cert. denied, 460 U.S. 1028 (1983) ....[1986] 83, 88
Eagle Star & British Dominions *v*. Tadlock, 22 F. Supp. 545 (S.D. Cal., 1938) ....[1986] 502
Eagle Term, The *v*. Ins. Co. of U.S.S.R., 1981 A.M.C. 137 (2nd Cir.) ....[1988] 89
Eagle Terminal Tankers Inc., As Owner of the *Eagle Courier* *v*. Insurance Company of U.S.S.R. (Ingosstrakh) Ltd., 1981 A.M.C. 137 ....[1987] 163
Earhart *v*. William Low Co. (1979) 600 P. 2d 1344 ....[1990] 504
Earl Grey, The (1853) 1 Sp. 180 ....[1989] 69
Earl of Eglinton, The (1855) Swab. 7 ....[1989] 79
Earle & Stoddart *v*. Ellerman's Wilson Line, 287 U.S. 420 (1932) ....[1986] 369
Earle (G. & T.) Ltd. *v*. Hemsworth R.D.C. (1928) 140 L.T. 69 ....[1990] 545

East Coast Tender Services Inc. *v.* Robert T. Winzinger Inc., 759 F. 2d 280 (3 Cir. 1985) .... [1986] 427, 428, 429
East River S.S. Corp. *v.* Delaval Turbine Inc., 752 F. 2d 903, 1985 A.M.C. 913 (3rd Cir., 1985) (*en banc*), aff'd. on other grounds *sub nom.* East River Steamship Corp. *v.* Transamerica Delaval Inc., 106 S. Ct. 2295 (1986) .... [1986] 361; [1987] 118, 119
Eastern Assoc. Coal *v.* Aetna Casualty & Surety Co., 632 F. 2d 1068 (3 Cir. 1980), cert. denied, 451 U.S. 786 (1981) .... [1986] 84
Eastern City, The [1958] 2 Lloyd's Rep. 127, 131 .... [1986] 112; [1988] 45
Eastern Construction Co. Ltd. *v.* National Trust Co. Ltd. [1914] A.C. 197 (P.C.) .... [1987] 72
Eastern Prince—U.S.S. *Roustabout*, 1944 A.M.C. 727 (W.D. Wash) .... [1986] 484
Eastern Saga, The [1984] 2 Lloyd's Rep. 373 .... [1986] 66
Eastman Chemical International A.G. *v.* N.M.T. Trading Ltd. [1972] 2 Lloyd's Rep. 25 .... [1988] 35
Ebrahimi *v.* Westbourne Galleries Ltd. [1973] A.C. 360 .... [1988] 62
E. Clemens Horst Co. *v.* Biddell Bros. [1911] 1 K.B. 934, 957; [1912] A.C. 18 .... [1986] 299
ECS/AKZO [1985] O.J. No. L 374/1 .... [1988] 193
Eckman *v.* Midland Bank Ltd. [1973] Q.B. 519 .... [1987] 251
E.D. & F. Man Ltd. *v.* Nigerian Sweets & Confectionery Co. Ltd. [1977] 2 Lloyd's Rep. 50 ... [1990] 66
Eddis *v.* Chichester Constable [1969] 1 W.L.R. 385 .... [1989] 315
Edgington *v.* Fitzmaurice (1885) 29 Ch. D. 459 .... [1986] 315; [1988] 464
Edinburgh Assurance Co. *v.* R.L. Burns, 1980 A.M.C. 1261 (C.D. Cal.) .... [1986] 486, 496
Edmunds *v.* Lloyd's Italico & l'Ancora Cia. di Assicurazione & Riassicurazione S.p.A. [1986] 1 W.L.R. 492 .... [1986] 139
Edward Hawkins, The (1861) 31 L.J. Adm. 46; affmd. (1862) 15 Moo. P.C. 486 .... [1989] 77
Edward Owen Engineering Ltd. *v.* Barclays Bank International Ltd. [1978] Q.B. 159 .... [1990] 223, 224, 229, 231, 233, 236
Edwards *v.* Newlands & Co. [1950] 2 K.B. 534 .... [1988] 34
Edwards *v.* Skyways Ltd. [1964] 1 W.L.R. 349 .... [1988] 291; [1989] 283
E.E. & Brian Smith (1928) Ltd. *v.* Wheatsheaf Mills Ltd. [1939] 2 K.B. 302 .... [1990] 365
Effy, The [1972] 1 Lloyd's Rep. 18 .... [1990] 82, 83
Egerton *v.* Brownlow (1853) 4 H.L.C. 1 .... [1987] 211; [1989] 59
Egremont Castle, The, 1934 A.M.C. 1317 .... [1986] 501
Egyptian International Foreign Trade Co. *v.* Soplex Wholesale Supplies Ltd. [1985] 2 Lloyd's Rep. 36 .... [1990] 223, 232
Ehrmann Bros. Ltd. (*Re*) [1906] 2 Ch. 697 .... [1990] 530, 531
E.I. Du Pont de Nemours & Co. *v.* I.C. Agnew, *Financial Times*, 24 July 1987 (Judgment 21 July 1987) [1987] 398
E.L. Oldendorff & Co. G.m.b.H. *v.* Tradax Export S.A. (*The Johanna Oldendorff*) [1974] A.C. 479 .... [1989] 122, 264
El Al *v.* Na'amat Israel Airlines, Civil Appeal 192/83, 38(4) P.D. (1984) 57 .... [1986] 292
El Amria, The [1981] 2 Lloyd's Rep. 119 (C.A.) .... [1986] 261, 517; [1987] 396; [1989] 218; [1990] 13
Elafi, The [1981] 2 Lloyd's Rep. 679; [1982] 1 All E.R. 208; [1981] 2 Lloyd's Rep. 679 .... [1986] 6, 297, 299; [1987] 54, 257; [1989] 167, 422; [1990] 3
Elbe Maru, The [1978] 1 Lloyd's Rep. 206 .... [1986] 105, 344; [1987] 80; [1990] 292
Elder *v.* Elder & Watson Ltd. 1952 S.C. 49 .... [1988] 61
Elder Dempster & Co. Ltd. *v.* Paterson Zochonis & Co. Ltd. [1924] A.C. 522 ... [1986] 107; [1988] 472
Elefanten Schuts *v.* Jacqmain [1981] E.C.R. 1671 .... [1988] 119
Eleftheria, The [1969] 2 All E.R. 641 .... [1987] 310
Elena Shipping Ltd. *v.* Aidenfield Ltd. (*The Elena*) [1986] 1 Lloyd's Rep. 425 .... [1989] 292
Eleni 2, The [1985] 1 Lloyd's Rep. 107 .... [1986] 102
Eleonore, The (1863) 9 L.T. 397 .... [1989] 73
Eley *v.* Positive Life Assurance (1876) 1 Ex. D. 88 .... [1990] 409, 410
Elfie A. Issaias *v.* Marine Insurance Co. Ltd. (*The Elias Issaias*) (1923) 15 Ll. L. Rep. 186 .... [1987] 39; [1989] 26
Elfrida, The, 172 U.S. 186, 19 S. Ct. 146 (1898) .... [1986] 17, 312
Eli Lilly *v.* Home Insurance Co., C.A. No. 82–0669 (D.D.C. 12 April 1984) .... [1986] 90
Eli Lilly & Co. *v.* Home Ins. Co., No. 84–5404, 54–5, 5406, 5407 (2 Cir. 18 June 1985) .... [1986] 84
Eli Lilly Argentina S.A. *v.* Aerolineas Argentinas (1986) 508 N.Y.S. 2d 865 (N.Y. City Civ. Ct.) .... [1988] 180
Elian & Rabbath *v.* Matsas & Matsas [1966] 2 Lloyd's Rep. 495 .... [1990] 223, 230, 240
Elias Issaias, The (1923) 15 Ll. L. Rep. 186 .... [1987] 39; [1989] 26
Elise, The (1859) Swab. 436 .... [1989] 61

Eliza, The (1862) Lush. 536 .... [1989] 67
Elizabeth, The (1844) 8 Jur. 365 .... [1989] 73
Ellerman Lines Ltd. *v.* Gibbs Ltd. (1984) 4 D.L.R. (4th) 645; [1984] 1 F.C. 411; 1984 A.M.C. 2579 .... [1987] 87, 161
Ellerman Lines Ltd. *v.* Gibbs, Nathaniel (Canada) Ltd. [1986] 2 F.C. 463; 26 D.L.R. (4th) 161 (Fed. C.A.) .... [1987] 160; [1988] 89
Ellerman Lines Ltd. *v.* Lancaster Maritime Co. Ltd. (*The Lancaster*) [1980] 1 Lloyd's Rep. 497 .... [1988] 150
Elli 2, The [1985] 1 Lloyd's Rep. 107 .... [1986] 102; [1989] 52, 165, 172
Elliott (B.) (Canada) Ltd. *v.* John T. Clark & Son (1982) 542 F. Supp. 1367 (My. D.C.); aff'd (1983) 704 F. 2d 1305 (U.S. C.A., 4th Cir.) .... [1989] 395; [1990] 315
Eloc Electro-Optieck and Communicatie B.V. (*Re*) [1982] Ch. 43 .... [1989] 21, 393
Elsey *v.* Hyde, 1926 (unreported) .... [1990] 19
Elvin Powell & Co. Ltd. *v.* Plummer Roddis Ltd. (1933) 50 T.L.R. 158 .... [1986] 231; [1987] 64
Elwin *v.* O'Regan [1971] N.Z.L.R. 1124 (N.Z.S.C.) .... [1988] 298
Ema *v.* Compagnie Generale Transatlantique, 353 F. Supp. 1286 (D.P.R. 1972) .... [1986] 380
Embiricos *v.* Sydney Reid & Co. [1914] 3 K.B. 45, at 54 .... [1988] 22
Emeh *v.* Kensington & Chelsea & Westminster Area Health Authority [1985] Q.B. 1012 .... [1988] 50
Emerson G.M. Diesel Inc. *v.* Alaskan Enterprise, 732 F. 2d 1468, 1985 A.M.C. 2069, 2074 (9 Cir. 1984) .... [1986] 360; [1987] 119
E.M.I. (New Zealand) Pty. Ltd. *v.* William Holyman & Sons Pty. Ltd. [1976] 2 N.Z.L.R. 567 . [1988] 34
E.M.I. Ltd. *v.* Pandit [1975] 1 W.L.R. 302 .... [1990] 320
Emma, The (1844) 2 W. Rob. 315 .... [1989] 62
Emons Industries Inc. *v.* Liberty Mutual Ins. Co., 567 F. Supp. 335 (S.D.N.Y. 1983) .... [1986] 83
Employers' Liability Assn. Corp. Ltd. *v.* Sedgwick Collins & Co. Ltd. [1927] A.C. 95 .... [1988] 429
Empresa Cubana de Fletes *v.* Lagonisi Shipping Co. Ltd. (*The Georgios C*) [1971] 1 Q.B. 488 .... [1986] 214
E.M.S. Industrie S.A. *v.* Polski Towarzystwo Okretowe, No. 83–4279 (E.D.N.Y. 9 May 1985) .... [1986] 368
Emu, The (1838) 1 W. Rob. 15 .... [1989] 60, 69
Emulous, The (1832) 1 Sumn. 207; 8 Fed. Cas. 704, 708 (Case 4480) (Mass. Cir. Ct.) .... [1986] 153
Enchantress, The (1860) Lush. 93 .... [1989] 76
Endeavour, The (1847) 6 N.o.C. 56; aff'd. (1848) 6 Moo. P.C. 334 .... [1989] 69
Engineering Plastics Ltd. *v.* J. Mercer & Sons Ltd. [1985] 2 N.Z.L.R. 72 .... [1987] 332
Enpatria-San Juan, The, 1929 A.M.C. 540 (9 C.A.) .... [1986] 494
Ensley City, The, 1947 AMC 568; 71 F. Supp. 444 (D. Md.), aff'd 1948 A.M.C. 1589; 170 F. 2d 25 (4th Cir.) .... [1989] 353
Ente Nazionale per l'Energia Elettrica *v.* Baliwag Navigation Inc. (*The Kuniang*), 1986 A.M.C. 1184, reversing 774 F. 2d 648 (4th Cir.) .... [1989] 359
Envtl Defense Fund Inc. *v.* Gorsuch, 17 Env't Rep. Cas. (BNA) 1099 (D.D.C., 1982) .... [1987] 511
E. Pfeiffer Weinkellerei-Weineinkauf G.m.b.H. & Co. *v.* Arbuthnot Factors Ltd. [1988] 1 W.L.R. 150 .... [1989] 198 *et seq.*; [1990] 530
E.P. Finance Co. Ltd. *v.* Dooley [1963] 1 W.L.R. 1313 .... [1990] 19
Epaphus, The [1986] 2 Lloyd's Rep. 387; [1987] 2 Lloyd's Rep. 215 (C.A.) ....[1987] 408, 409; [1988] 51
Epar, The [1985] 2 M.L.J. 3 .... [1987] 235
Equipements de Ferme Lambo Inc. *v.* C.P. Steamships Ltd. (1987) 8 F.T.R. 75 (F.C.) .... [1989] 94
Equitable Trust Co. of New York *v.* Dawson Partners Ltd. (1927) 27 Ll. L. Rep. 49 .... [1986] 200; [1990] 232, 550, 551
Equiticorp Int. Plc (*Re*) (1989) 5 B.C.C. 599 .... [1989] 507
Erb *v.* German-American Insurance Co. of New York, 67 N.W. 583 (1896) .... [1987] 214
Erechthion, The [1987] 2 Lloyd's Rep. 180 .... [1988] 58
Eric Holmes Ltd. (*Re*) [1965] 1 Ch. 1052 .... [1990] 534
Erich Schroeder, The [1974] 1 Lloyd's Rep. 192 .... [1987] 172
Erie RR Co. *v.* Tompkins, 304 U.S. 64 (1938) .... [1987] 502
Erlanger *v.* New Sombrero Phosphate Co. (1878) 3 App. Cas. 1218 .... [1986] 318
Ernest *v.* Nicholls (1857) 6 H.L.C. 401 .... [1990] 30
Esal (Commodities) Ltd. *v.* Oriental Credit Ltd. [1985] 2 Lloyd's Rep. 546 .... [1986] 420, 422; [1990] 223, 228
Esanda Finance Corp. Ltd. *v.* Plessnig (1989) 63 A.L.J.R. 238; (1989) A.S.C. 55–533; 55–595 .... [1990] 17
Escambia Trading Co. *v.* Aetna Casualty & Surety, 1977 A.M.C. 1285 (N.D. Fla.) .... [1986] 499, 501

Eschersheim, The [1976] 1 W.L.R. 430 (H.L.) .... [1986] 333; [1988] 86
Esmail *v*. J. Rosenthal & Sons Ltd. [1964] 2 Lloyd's Rep. 447 .... [1989] 81, 82
Esperanza, The, 1939 A.M.C. 293 (2 C.A.) .... [1986] 494
Esso *v*. Southport Corp. [1956] A.C. 218 .... [1990] 41
Esso Malaysia, The [1975] Q.B. 198 .... [1988] 215
Esso Petroleum Co. Ltd. *v*. Customs and Excise Commissioners [1976] 1 W.L.R. 1 .... [1988] 502
Esso Petroleum Co. Ltd. *v*. Hall, Russell & Co. Ltd. (*The Esso Bernicia*) [1988] 3 W.L.R. 730 ...[1989] 1 *et seq*., 45
Esso Petroleum Co. Ltd. *v*. Harper's Garage (Stourport) Ltd. [1968] A.C. 269 .... [1989] 126
Esso Petroleum Co. Ltd. *v*. Mardon [1976] 1 Q.B. 801 .... [1990] 149
Estasis Salotti *v*. RUWA, Case 24/76 [1976] E.C.R. 1831; [1977] 1 C.M.L.R. 345 .... [1988] 389
Estmanco (Kilner House) Ltd. *v*. Greater London Council [1982] 1 W.L.R. 2 .... [1988] 77
Etablissement Esefka International Anstalt *v*. Central Bank of Nigeria [1979] 1 Lloyd's Rep. 445 .... [1990] 234
Ethyl Corp. *v*. United Steelworkers, 768 F. 2d 180, 184 (7 Cir. 1985) .... [1986] 75
Etic Ltd. (*Re*) [1928] Ch. 861 .... [1990] 218
E.U., The (1853) 1 Sp. 63 .... [1989] 70, 71, 77
Eugene F. Morgan, The, 212 U.S. 466 (1909) .... [1986] 18
Eugenia, The [1963] 2 Lloyd's Rep. 381 .... [1986] 127
Eureka Ins. Co. *v*. Robinson, 56 P.A. 256, 6 P.F. Smith 256 (1857) .... [1986] 489
Eurico S.p.A. *v*. Philipp Bros. (*The Epaphus*) [1986] 2 Lloyd's Rep. 387; [1987] 2 Lloyd's Rep. 215 (C.A.) .... [1987] 408, 409; [1988] 51
Euroclean Canada Inc. *v*. Forest Glade Investments Ltd. (1985) 16 D.L.R. (4th) 289 (Ont. C.A.) .... [1986] 174
Euro-Diam Ltd. *v*. Bathurst [1987] 1 Lloyd's Rep. 178; [1987] 2 W.L.R. 1368; [1988] 2 W.L.R. 517 .... [1987] 211, 212, 213; [1988] 125; [1989] 366; [1990] 134, 426
Eurolines Shipping Co. S.A. *v*. Metal Transport Corp., 491 F. Supp. 590, 1980 A.M.C. 2442 (S.D.N.Y. 1980) .... [1986] 358, 536
Euromarine International of Mauren *v*. The Ship *Berg* and others, 1984(4) SA 647(N) .... [1986] 279
European Asian Bank A.G. *v*. Punjab and Sind Bank (No. 2) [1983] 1 W.L.R. 642, 656 .... [1986] 199
European Bank, Agra Bank's Claim (*Re*) (1872) L.R. 8 Ch. App. 41 .... [1989] 365
European Enterprise, The [1989] 2 Lloyd's Rep. 185 .... [1989] 404
European Gateway, The, *The Times*, 27 May 1986 .... [1986] 417
Eurostem Maritime Ltd. (*Re*) [1987] P.C.C. 190 .... [1990] 404
Eurymedon, The [1975] A.C. 154 .... [1986] 97; [1987] 536; [1988] 396, 505; [1989] 23, 142, 164, 170, 171, 172, 423; [1990] 127, 319
Eurysthenes, The [1977] 1 Q.B. 49 .... [1986] 41; [1988] 353
Evaggelos Th, The [1971] 2 Lloyd's Rep. 200, 206 .... [1986] 119, 126; [1988] 52
Evangelinos *v*. Trans World Airlines Inc. (1977) 550 F. 2d 152 (3rd Cir.); 14 Avi. 17, 612; *cf.* (1976) 14 Avi. 17, 101 and 13 Avi. 18, 051 .... [1988] 222
Evangelismos, The (1858) Swab. 378 .... [1987] 323
Evans *v*. Rival Granite Quarries Ltd. [1910] 2 K.B. 979, 999 .... [1986] 521, 524, 529, 530
Evans *v*. Triplex Safety Glass Co. Ltd. [1936] 1 All E.R. 283 .... [1988] 516
Evans (J.) & Son (Portsmouth) Ltd. *v*. Andrea Merzario Ltd. [1976] 1 W.L.R. 1078 .... [1986] 316
Evendon *v*. Guildford City Association Football Club Ltd. [1975] Q.B. 917 .... [1986] 472
Everet *v*. Williams (1725), noted in (1893) 9 L.Q.R. 197 .... [1988] 125
Evia, The (No. 2) [1981] 2 Lloyd's Rep. 613,620; [1982] 1 Lloyd's Rep. 334, 338 (C.A.); [1983] 1 A.C. 736 .... [1986] 112, 114, 115, 116, 122, 124, 149; [1987] 408; [1988] 45, 48; [1990] 453
Evia Luck, The (No. 2) [1990] 1 Lloyd's Rep. 319 (C.A.); [1989] 1 Lloyd's Rep. 166 .... [1989] 273; [1990] 347, 348, 349, 350, 351
Evpo Agnic, The [1988] 1 W.L.R. 1090 .... [1989] 383, 384
Evra Corp. *v*. Swiss Bank Corp., 522 F. Supp. 820 (1981); revsd. on another ground, 673 F. 2d 951 (1982) .... [1986] 202; [1990] 549, 552
Excel Metal Fab Ltd. *v*. The *Ogopogo I* (1987) 11 F.T.R. 202 (F.C.) .... [1989] 102
Exchange Banking Co. (*Re*) (1882) 21 Ch.D. 519 .... [1990] 222
Excomm Ltd. *v*. Guan Guan Shipping (Pte.) Ltd. (*The Golden Bear*) [1987] 1 Lloyd's Rep. 330 .... [1987] 155, 263; [1988] 307, 308
Executive Jet Aviation Inc. *v*. City of Cleveland, 409 U.S. 249 (1972) .... [1987] 118
Exim Industries Inc. *v*. Pan American World Airways Inc. (1985) 754 F. 2d 106 (2nd Cir.) ... [1988] 180
Ex p. Cooper (1875) L.R. 10 Ch. App. 510 .... [1990] 219

Ex p. Gardom (1808) 15 Ves. 286 .... [1990] 224
Export Credits Guarantee Department *v.* Universal Oil Products Co. [1983] 1 W.L.R. 399 (H.L.) .... [1987] 81; [1990] 159
Eyles *v.* Ellis (1827) 4 Bing. 112 .... [1990] 81, 82
Eyre *v.* Measday [1986] 1 All E.R. 488 (C.A.) .... [1987] 80
Fablo Pty. Ltd. *v.* Bloore [1983] 1 Qd. R. 107 .... [1990] 512
Faccenda Chicken Ltd. *v.* Fowler [1987] Ch. 117 .... [1988] 107
Facey *v.* Rawthorne (1925) 35 C.L.R. 566 .... [1989] 86
Fagertind, The, Hamburg Award 8.6.1977 .... [1990] 390
Fairline Shipping Corp. *v.* Adamson [1975] Q.B. 180 .... [1987] 80
Falcke *v.* Scottish Imperial Insurance Co. (1886) 34 Ch.D. 234 .... [1990] 356
Falconbridge Nickel Mines Ltd. *v.* Chimo Shipping Ltd. [1974] S.C.R. 933; [1973] 2 Lloyd's Rep. 469 .... [1990] 315
Falstria, The [1988] 1 Lloyd's Rep. 495 .... [1990] 278
Fanetti *v.* Hellenic Lines, 678 F. 2d 424, 1982 A.M.C. 1521 (2 Cir. 1982), cert. denied *sub nom.* Hellenic Lines Ltd. *v.* Fanetti, 463 U.S. 1206 (1983) .... [1986] 373
Fanti, The [1987] 2 Lloyd's Rep. 299 .... [1987] 406; [1989] 495 *et seq.*, 500, 505
Fanti, The and the *Padre Island* [1989] 1 Lloyd's Rep. 239 .... [1989] 495 *et seq.*, 501
Farm Bureau Mut. Ins. Co. *v.* Horinck, 23 Kan. 175, 660 P. 2d 1374 (1983) .... [1986] 83
Farm Bureau Mut. Ins. Co. *v.* Waugh, 159 Md. 115, 188 A.2d 889 (1963) .... [1986] 82
Farrell *v.* Federated Employers Mutual Insurance Association [1970] 1 Lloyd's Rep. 170; [1970] 1 W.L.R. 1400 .... [1987] 233; [1989] 498, 503
Farrow's Bank Ltd. (*Re*) [1923] 1 Ch. 41 .... [1990] 72, 75, 76, 247
Favorite, The (1844) 2 W. Rob. 255 .... [1989] 70
Favorite, The (1882) 12 F. 213 (N.D. Ill.) .... [1988] 179
Fawcus *v.* Sarsfield (1856) 5 El. & Bl. 192; 119 E.R. 836 .... [1986] 38
FDC Co. *v.* Chase Manhattan Bank, 17 October 1984, unreported .... [1989] 369
Featherstonehaugh *v.* Turner (1858) 25 Beav. 382 .... [1990] 335
Federal Business Development Bank *v.* The *Winder 4135* (1985) 11 D.L.R. (4th) .... [1987] 91
Federal Commerce and Navigation Co. Ltd. *v.* Eisenerz [1974] S.C.R. 1225 .... [1987] 83
Federal Commerce and Navigation Co. Ltd. *v.* M/V *Marathonian*, 528 F. 2d 907 (2nd Cir., 1975), cert. denied 425 U.S. 975 (1976) .... [1987] 512
Federal Commerce & Navigation Co. Ltd. *v.* Molena Alpha Inc. (*The Nanfri*) [1978] Q.B. 927; [1979] A.C. 757; [1979] 1 Lloyd's Rep. 201 (H.L.) .... [1986] 426; [1988] 149; [1989] 191, 193, 292
Federal Commerce & Navigation Co. Ltd. *v.* Tradax Export S.A. (*The Maratha Envoy*) [1975] 1 W.L.R. 1372 .... [1986] 51
Federal Sugar Refining Co. *v.* United States Sugar Equalization Board Inc., 268 F. 575 (1920) .... [1987] 428
Fehmarn, The [1958] 1 W.L.R. 159 (C.A.) .... [1988] 88
Felix, The (1853) 1 Sp. 175n .... [1989] 69
Felix Hadley & Co. *v.* Hadley [1898] 2 Ch. 680 .... [1990] 66, 68
Felthouse *v.* Bindley (1862) 11 C.B. (N.S.) 869 .... [1987] 155
Fender *v.* St. John-Mildmay [1938] A.C. 1 .... [1987] 212
Fercometal S.A.R.L. *v.* Mediterranean Shipping Co. S.A. (*The Simona*) [1988] 3 W.L.R. 200; [1986] 1 Lloyd's Rep. 171; [1987] 2 Lloyd's Rep. 236 .... [1989] 82
Fergusson *v.* Fyffe (1841) 8 Cl. and Finn. 121 .... [1989] 44; [1990] 490
Ferrier *v.* Bottomer (1972) 126 C.L.R. 597 .... [1990] 220
Ferryboat Orange, The, 1972 A.M.C. 627 .... [1986] 499
Fertilizer (C. & J.) *v.* Allied Mutual Ins. Co., 227 N. W. 2d 169, 176–177 (Iowa 1975) .... [1986] 86
Fibrosa Spolka Akcyjna *v.* Fairbairn Lawson Combe Barbour Ltd. [1943] A.C. 32 .... [1990] 505
FIDC *v.* European American Bank and Trust Co. (1983) 576 F. Supp. 950 .... [1986] 199; [1989] 368
Fidias, The, 1986 (1) S.A. 714 (D) .... [1989] 174, 177, 178, 179, 185
Fielden, The (1862) 11 W.R. 156 .... [1989] 61
Fielding & Platt Ltd. *v.* Najjar [1969] 1 W.L.R. 357 (C.A.) .... [1988] 125
Figueiredo (L.) Navegacas S.A. *v.* Reederei Richard Schroeder K.G. (*The Erich Schroeder*) [1974] 1 Lloyd's Rep. 192 .... [1987] 172
Filartiga *v.* Pena-Irala, 630 F. 2d 876 .... [1988] 10
Films Rover International Ltd. *v.* Cannon Film Sales Ltd. [1988] 2 F.T.L.R. 536 (C.A.) .... [1989] 302
Fils et Cables d'Acier de Lens *v.* Midland Metals Corp., 584 F. Supp. 240 (S.D.N.Y. 1984) .... [1986] 75
Finance (E.P.) Co. Ltd. *v.* Dooley [1963] 1 W.L.R. 1313 .... [1990] 19
Financings Ltd. *v.* Baldock [1963] 2 Q.B. 104 .... [1987] 143; [1988] 277; [1990] 20, 470

Financings Ltd. *v*. Stimson [1962] 1 W.L.R. 1184 .... [1986] 402
Finix, The [1975] 2 Lloyd's Rep. 415; [1978] 1 Lloyd's Rep. 16 .... [1990] 388
Finlay *v*. Metro Toyota Ltd. (1978) 82 D.L.R. (3d) 440 .... [1990] 377, 379
Finning Ltd. *v*. Federal Business Development Bank (1989) 34 B.C.L.R. (2d) 237 (B.C.S.C.) .... [1990] 105
Fire & All Risks Insurance Co. *v*. Powell [1966] V.R. 513 (S. Ct., Victoria) .... [1987] 211
Firefly, The (1857) Swab. 240 .... [1989] 76
Fireman's Fund *v*. Wilburn Boat, 1962 A.M.C. 1593 (5 C.A.) .... [1986] 498
Firestone Tire & Rubber Co. *v*. Almacenes Miramar Inc. (1978) 452 F. Supp. 670 (U.S.D.C., Puerto Rico); 1980 A.M.C. 1590 .... [1989] 395; [1990] 316
Fisher *v*. Harrods Ltd. [1966] 1 Lloyd's Rep. 500 .... [1988] 512
Fitzgerald *v*. Lane [1988] 3 W.L.R. 356 (H.L.); [1987] Q.B. 781 (C.A.) .... [1989] 30 *et seq.*
Fjordaas, The [1988] 1 Lloyd's Rep. 336 .... [1989] 266
Fleece, The (1850) 3 W. Rob. 278 .... [1989] 72
Fletcher *v*. Sledmore [1973] R.T.R. 371 .... [1989] 380
Flintoft *v*. Royal Bank of Canada [1964] S.C.R. 631 .... [1986] 168
Flippo *v*. Mode O'Day Frock Shops of Hollywood (1970) 449 S.W. 2d 692 .... [1988] 508
Florence, The (1852) 16 Jur. 572 .... [1989] 77
Florence Land and Public Works (*Re*) (1878) 10 Ch. D. 530 .... [1986] 529
Florida Department of State *v*. Treasure Salvors Inc., et al, 458 U.S. 670, 102 S. Ct. 3304, 1983 A.M.C. 144 (1982) .... [1986] 17, 18
Foley *v*. Hill (1848) 2 H.L. Cas. 28 .... [1988] 139, 375; [1989] 202
Follett *v*. Hoppe (1847) 5 C.B. 226 .... [1989] 312
Fomento (Sterling Area) Ltd. *v*. Selsdon Fountain Pen Co. [1958] 1 W.L.R. 45 .... [1990] 421
Fontevivo, The [1975] 1 Lloyd's Rep. 339 .... [1988] 49
Food Corp. of India *v*. Antclizo Shipping Corp. (*The Antclizo*) [1987] 2 Lloyd's Rep. 130; [1988] 1 W.L.R. 603 .... [1987] 155, 263; [1988] 302, 303, 307, 308
Food Corp. of India *v*. Marastro Cia. Naviera S.A. (*The Trade Fortitude*) [1986] 2 Lloyd's Rep. 209 .... [1987] 417
Forbes *v*. Aberdeen Motors Ltd. 1965 S.C. 193 .... [1987] 52, 66
Foreman & Ellams *v*. Federal Steam Navigation Co. (1928) 30 Ll.L.Rep. 52 .... [1987] 223
Foremost Ins. Co. *v*. Richardson, 457 U.S. 668 (1982) .... [1987] 118
Forestal Mimosa Ltd. *v*. Oriental Credit Ltd. [1986] 1 W.L.R. 631 .... [1986] 420
Forget *v*. Ostigny [1895] A.C. 318 (P.C.) .... [1986] 395
Forman *v*. Bank of England (1902) 18 T.L.R. 339 .... [1990] 71
Forman & Co. Pty. Ltd. *v*. The Ship *Liddesdale* [1900] A.C. 190 .... [1990] 517
Forsikringsaktieselskapet Vesta *v*. Butcher [1986] 2 All E.R. 488; [1986] 2 Lloyd's Rep. 179; [1988] 1 Lloyd's Rep. 19; [1988] 3 W.L.R. 565; aff'd on other grounds [1989] 2 W.L.R. 290 .... [1987] 7, 10, 528; [1988] 5, 28, 56, 513; [1989] 285 *et seq.*, 358; [1990] 52, 417, 418, 420, 425
Forster *v*. Silvermere Golf and Equestrian Centre (1980) N.L.J. 549 .... [1988] 135
Forsythe Int'l *v*. *Ruth Venture* (1985) 633 F. Supp. 74; 1986 A.M.C. 621 (D. Ore.) .... [1989] 12
Foss *v*. Harbottle (1843) 2 Hare 461 .... [1988] 61; [1990] 402
Foster *v*. Driscoll [1929] 1 K.B. 470 (C.A.) .... [1987] 215; [1988] 127
Foster *v*. Stewart (1814) 3 M. & S. 191 .... [1987] 433
Fothergill *v*. Monarch Airlines [1981] A.C. 251, 290, 293 .... [1986] 292; [1990] 355
Foulder *v*. Canadian Pacific [1968] 2 Lloyd's Rep. 366 .... [1986] 401
Four Point Garage Ltd. *v*. Carter [1985] 3 All E.R. 12 .... [1989] 511
Foxton *v*. Manchester and Liverpool District Banking Co. (1881) 44 L.T. 406 .... [1989] 304
Franco-Canadian Fisheries Arbitration of 1986 (1986) 90 R.G.D.I.P. 713 .... [1990] 561
Frangos *v*. Sun Insurance Office (1934) 49 Ll. L. Rep. 354, 358–359 .... [1986] 40
Frank B. Hall Inc. *v*. Jefferson Insurance Co. *et al*, 279 Fed. 892 (S.D.N.Y. 1921) .... [1986] 490, 492
Frank Pais, The [1986] 1 Lloyd's Rep. 529 .... [1986] 508, 516, 517, 518
Franklin Ins. Co. *v*. Humphrey, 65 Ind. 549, 43 Am. Jur. 2, p. 739 (1879) .... [1986] 489
Franklin Mint Corp. *v*. Trans World Airlines (1982) 640 F. 2d 303; rev'd (1984) 466 U.S. 243 [1989] 146
Frankston Hastings Corp. *v*. Cohen [1960] 102 C.L.R. 607 (H.C.A.) .... [1990] 419
Fraser *v*. Furman [1967] 1 W.L.R. 898 .... [1989] 521
Fraser *v*. Whalley (1894) 2 Hem. & M. 10 .... [1988] 72
Freccia del Nord, The [1989] 1 Lloyd's Rep. 388 .... [1990] 278
Frederick E. Bouchard Inc. *v*. United States, 583 F. Supp. 477; 1985 A.M.C. 668 (D. Mass., 1984) .... [1987] 501

Freeman & Lockyer *v.* Buckhurst Park Properties (Mangal) Ltd. [1964] 2 Q.B. 480 .... [1988] 396; [1990] 403
Freighters (Steamship Agents) Co. *v.* M/V *Jalavihar*, 1982 A.M.C. 2182 (E.D. La. 1981) .... [1986] 355
Freightmarine Shipping Ltd. *v.* S. Wainstein & Co. (Pty.) Ltd. and Others, 1984 (2) SA 425 (D) .... [1987] 315
Friend *v.* Burgh (1679) Cas *temp.* Finch 437 .... [1990] 18
Frost *v.* Aylesbury Dairy Co. Ltd. [1905] 1 K.B. 608 .... [1988] 508, 515; [1989] 259
Fuentes *v.* Shevin, 407 U.S. 67 (1972) .... [1986] 350
Furbank *v.* Anderson (1966) 57 W.W.R. 647 (B.C. Co. Ct.) .... [1987] 52, 66
Fusilier, The (1865) Br. & Lush. 341 .... [1989] 59, 77, 78, 79
G. & N. Angelakis Shipping Co. S.A. *v.* Compagnie Nationale Algerienne de Navigation (*The Attika Hope*) [1988] 1 Lloyd's Rep. 439 .... [1989] 191, 193
G. & T. Earle Ltd. *v.* Hemsworth R.D.C. (1928) 140 L.T. 69 .... [1990] 545
Gabbiano, The [1940] P. 166 .... [1987] 183; [1990] 2
Galatea, The (1858) Swab. 349 .... [1989] 75
Galatia, The [1979] 2 Lloyd's Rep. 450, 457, aff'd [1980] 1 Lloyd's Rep. 453, [1980] 1 W.L.R. 495, 509, 517 .... [1986] 422, 479
Gale *v.* Denman [1930] 1 K.B. 588 .... [1990] 322
Gallie *v.* Lee [1971] A.C. 1004 .... [1989] 442
Galway Bay, The [1985] 3 A.N.Z. Insurance Cases 60–610 .... [1986] 289
Gansfjord, The (1928) 25 F. 2d 736; 1928 AMC 1283 (E.D. La.) .... [1989] 19
Gapp *v.* Bond (1887) 19 Q.B.D. 200 .... [1990] 275
Gardner *v.* Moore [1984] A.C. 548; [1984] 2 Lloyd's Rep. 135 .... [1987] 210, 211, 212; [1988] 126
Gardom (*ex p.*) (1808) 15 Ves. 286 .... [1990] 224
Garlick *v.* W.H. Rycroft & Co. [1982] C.A.T. 277; (1984) 134 N.L.J. 607 .... [1987] 52, 56, 63, 64
Garnac Grain Co. Inc. *v.* H.M.F. Faure & Fairclough Ltd. [1968] A.C. 130 (H.L.) .... [1990] 310, 312
Garnett *v.* M'Kewan (1872) L.R. 8 Ex. 10 .... [1989] 365
Gary, The *v.* *Sherman*, The, F. Cas. 5229 (C.S.C., 1869) .... [1986] 330
Gas Float Whitton No. 2, The [1895] P. 301, aff'd. [1897] A.C. 337 .... [1987] 270; [1990] 352
Gassner *v.* Locket, 101 So. 2d 33 (Fla., 1958) .... [1987] 436
Gatewhite Ltd. *v.* Iberia Lineas Aereas de Espana Sociedad (1988) LMLN 230 .... [1989] 37 *et seq.*
Gatoil International Inc. *v.* Arkwright-Boston Manufacturers Mutual Ins. Co. (*The Sandrina*) [1985] A.C. 255 .... [1988] 425
Gaunt *v.* British and Foreign Marine Insurance Co. [1921] 2 A.C. 41 .... [1986] 442
GB-Inno *v.* ATAB, Case 13/77, judgment of 16 November 1977; [1977] E.C.R. 2115 .... [1990] 182
Gebr. Bellmer KG. *v.* Terminal Servs. Houston Inc., 711 F. 2d 622 (5 Cir. 1983) .... [1986] 367, 368
Gebr. Broere B.V. *v.* Saras Chimica S.p.A. [1982] 2 Lloyd's Rep. 436, 438 .. [1986] 252, 257; [1990] 390
Geddling *v.* Marsh [1920] 1 K.B. 668 .... [1988] 508
Gedeh, The, S.M.A. No. 1534 (1981) .... [1986] 72
Geestland, The [1980] 1 Lloyd's Rep. 628 .... [1986] 342
Geismar *v.* Sun Alliance & London Insurance Co. Ltd. [1978] Q.B. 383 .... [1987] 212, 213, 215; [1988] 125
Gem Shipping Co. of Monrovia *v.* Babanaft (Lebanon) S.A.R.L. (*The Fontevivo*) [1975] 1 Lloyd's Rep. 339 .... [1988] 49
Gemma, The [1899] P. 285 .... [1990] 171
General Capinpin, The [1989] 1 Lloyd's Rep. 232 .... [1990] 398, 399, 400
General Elec. Co. *v.* S.S. *Nancy Lykes*, 706 F. 2d 80, 1983 A.M.C. 1947 (2 Cir.), cert. denied, 104 S. Ct. 157 (1983) .... [1986] 369
General National Maritime Transport Co. *v.* Gotaverken Arendal A.B. (1980) Rev. Arb. 524 (Cour d'appel de Paris) .... [1989] 231
General Palmer, The (1844) 5 N.o.C. 159n .... [1989] 65, 79
General Reinsurance Corp. *v.* Aetna Casualty & Surety Co., Sup. Ct. New York (reported in Mealey's Litigation Reports: "Insurance", March 1985, at p. 329) .... [1986] 81
General Reinsurance Corp. *v.* Forsakringsaktiebolaget Fennia Patria [1983] Q.B. 856 .. [1988] 116, 371
General S.A., General Trade Enterprises & Agencies *v.* P. Consorcio Pesquero del Peru S.A. (*The Stylianos Restis*), 66 Civ. 3394; 1974 AMC 2343 (S.D.N.Y) .... [1989] 350, 361
General Trading Co. Ltd. and Van Stolk's Commissiehandel (*Re*) (1911) 16 Com. Cas. 95 ... [1988] 457
General Valdes, The [1981] 1 Lloyd's Rep. 170; [1982] 1 Lloyd's Rep. 17 (C.A.) .... [1986] 236
Generous, The (1868) L.R. 2 A. & E. 57 .... [1986] 314
Gennessee, The (1848) 12 Jur. 401 .... [1989] 66, 71
Gentiruco A.G. *v.* Firestone S.A. (Pty.) Ltd., 1972 (1) S.A. 589 (A) .... [1989] 178

George, The (1866) Pritch. Dig. 381a .... [1989] 78
George *v*. Roach (1942) 67 C.L.R. 253 .... [1990] 518
George Inglefield Ltd. (*Re*) [1933] Ch. 1 .... [1989] 194, 204
George Mitchell (Chesterhall) Ltd. *v*. Finney Lock Seeds Ltd. [1983] 2 A.C. 803; [1983] Q.B. 284 .... [1987] 167; [1988] 297; [1990] 155, 284
Georges Chr. Lemos, The (1979) unreported. .... [1988] 58
Georgios C, The [1971] 1 Q.B. 488 .... [1986] 214
Get Out! Inc. *v*. Exxon Corp., 586 F. 2d 726 (9th Cir., 1978) .... [1987] 518
Getty Refining and Marketing Co. *v*. M.T. *Fadi B*, 766 F. 2d 829 (3 Cir. 1985) .... [1986] 362
Gewa Chartering BV *v*. Remco Shipping Lines Ltd. (*The Remco*) [1984] 2 Lloyd's Rep. 205 [1987] 261
G.H. Renton *v*. Palmyra Trading Corp. of Panama [1957] A.C. 149 .... [1990] 316
Gian Singh & Co. Ltd. *v*. Banque de l'Indochine [1974] 1 W.L.R. 1234 .... [1990] 235
Giannis Xilas, The [1982] 2 Lloyd's Rep. 511 .... [1990] 399
Gibbons *v*. Trapp Motors Ltd. (1970) 9 D.L.R. (3d) 742 .... [1990] 377
Gibbons *v*. Westminster Bank Ltd. [1939] 2 K.B. 882 .... [1988] 139
Gibbs Nathaniel (Canada) Ltd. *v*. The Vessel *City of Colombo*, T–1896–76 (Unrep.) .... [1987] 161
Gibson *v*. Manchester City Council [1979] 1 W.L.R. 294 .... [1987] 536; [1989] 170
Gibson *v*. Small (1853) 4 H.L.C. 353; 10 E.R. 499 .... [1986] 38; [1988] 347
Gilbert-Ash (Northern) Ltd. *v*. Modern Engineering (Bristol) Ltd. [1974] A.C. 689 .... [1989] 501; [1990] 50
Gilia, The (1975) S.M.A. No. 931 .... [1989] 351
Gill & Duffus *v*. Berger [1984] A.C. 382 .... [1990] 273
Gillespie *v*. Alexander (1827) 3 Russ. 130 .... [1989] 313
Gillespie Bros. & Co. Ltd. *v*. Roy Bowles Transport Ltd. [1973] Q.B. 400 .... [1986] 158; [1988] 469; [1990] 292
Gilpatrick *v*. Hartford (1923) 98 Conn. 471 .... [1989] 304
Gino d'Alessandro Constructions Pty. Ltd. *v*. Powis [1987] 2 Qd. R. 40 .... [1990] 511
Girgis *v*. Flaherty [1984] 1 N.S.W.L.R. 56; [1985] 4 N.S.W.L.R. 248; [1987] 162 C.L.R. 574 .... [1989] 217, 222
GKN Contractors Ltd. *v*. Lloyds Bank Plc (1985) 30 B.L.R. 48 .... [1990] 223, 224, 233, 236, 237
G.L. Baker Ltd. *v*. Medway Building & Supplies Ltd. [1958] 1 W.L.R. 1216 (Ch. D.); [1958] 1 W.L.R. 1225 (C.A.) .... [1989] 314, 316, 331, 334
Glafki Shipping Co. S.A. *v*. Pinios Shipping Co. No. 1 (*The Maira*) [1982] 1 Lloyd's Rep. 257 .... [1989] 40
Glafki Shipping Co. S.A. *v*. Pinios Shipping Co. No. 1 (*The Maira*) (No. 2) [1986] 2 Lloyd's Rep. 12 .... [1989] 40
Glaholm *v*. Hays (1841) 2 M. & G. 257 .... [1987] 145
Glasgow Assurance Corp. Ltd. *v*. William Symondson & Co. (1911) 16 Com. Cas. 109 .... [1987] 8; [1989] 256
Glasgow Packet, The (1844) 2 W. Rob. 306 .... [1989] 78
Glendarroch, The [1894] P. 226 .... [1990] 154
Globe Nova, The, S.M.A. No. 1733 (1982) .... [1986] 73
Globe Transp. & Trading Co. *v*. Egyptian Co. (*The Globe Nova*), S.M.A. No. 1733 (1982) ... [1986] 73
Gloria de Maria, The (1856) Swab. 106 .... [1989] 69
Glory, The (1850) 14 Jur. 676 .... [1989] 68, 72
Gluckstein *v*. Barnes [1990] A.C. 240 .... [1990] 331
Godina *v*. Patrick Operations Pty. Ltd., C.A. N.S.W., 7 February 1983 .... [1986] 105
Gokal Chand Jagan-Nath *v*. Nand Ram Das-Atma Ram [1939] A.C. 106 .... [1987] 58
Gold Sky, The [1972] 2 Lloyd's Rep. 187 .... [1987] 39; [1988] 355
Golden Acres Ltd. *v*. Queensland Estates Pty. Ltd. [1969] Qd. L.R. 378 .... [1986] 510
Golden Bear, The [1987] 1 Lloyd's Rep. 330 .... [1987] 155, 263; [1988] 307, 308
Golden Lake, The [1982] 2 Lloyd's Rep. 632 .... [1986] 107
Golden Panagia SS. *v*. Flota Mercante Grancolombiana (*The Golden Panagia*), S.M.A. No. 1866 (1983) .... [1986] 73
Golden Trader, The [1975] Q.B. 348 .... [1987] 540
Goldman *v*. Thai Airways International Ltd. [1983] 1 W.L.R. 1186 .... [1989] 146
Goldstein *v*. Jefferson Title & Trust Co. (1928) 95 Pa. Superior Ct. 167 .... [1988] 376
Goldsworthy *v*. Brickell [1987] Ch. 378 .... [1988] 368
Golodetz (M.) & Co. Ltd. *v*. Czarnikow-Rionda Inc. (*The Galatia*) [1980] 1 W.L.R. 495, 509, 517 .... [1986] 422
Golodetz (M.) Export Corp. *v*. S.S. *Lake Anja*, 1985 A.M.C. 891 (2nd Cir.) .... [1989] 359

Gomer *v.* Pitt & Scott (1922) 12 Ll. L. Rep. 115 .... [1989] 149
Good Helmsman, The [1981] 1 Lloyd's Rep. 377 .... [1990] 107, 111
Good Luck, The [1988] 1 Lloyd's Rep. 514 .... [1988] 27; [1989] 251 *et seq.*
Good Luck, The [1989] 2 Lloyd's Rep. 238; [1990] 2 W.L.R. 547; [1990] Q.B. 818 .... [1990] 318, 417, 419, 556
Goodclaims (Pty.) Ltd. *v.* Globus-Reederei GmbH and Others, 1981 (3) SA 485 (D) .... [1987] 315
Goodwin *v.* Robarts (1875) L.R. 10 Exch. 337; (1876) 1 App. Cas. 476 .... [1988] 362
Goodwin Squires Securities Ltd. (*In re*), *The Times*, 22 March 1983 .... [1988] 369
Gordon *v.* A.A. Mutual Ins. Assn. Ltd. 1988 (1) S.A. 398 .... [1988] 452
Gordon *v.* London City & Midland Bank Ltd. [1902] 1 K.B. 242 .... [1990] 69
Goring, The [1986] 2 W.L.R. 219; [1987] 2 W.L.R. 1151; [1987] Q.B. 687; [1988] 2 W.L.R. 460; [1988] A.C. 831 .... [1986] 152, 170; [1987] 55, 262; [1988] 449; [1989] 80, 137; [1990] 33, 355, 356
Gorwyn Holdings Ltd. (*Re*). Unrep., 4 June 1985 (C.A.) .... [1988] 66
Gosforth, The (Rotterdam Comm. Ct., 20 February 1985, unreported) .... [1986] 4; [1989] 56, 58, 421, 425, 427, 430
Goulandris Brothers Ltd. *v.* B. Goldman & Sons Ltd. [1958] 1 Q.B. 74 .... [1987] 83
Gould *v.* Cornhill Insurance Co. Ltd. (1983) 43 Nfld. & P.E.I.R. 355; 127 A.P.R. 355 .... [1987] 90
Government of India *v.* Taylor [1955] A.C. 491, 514 .... [1986] 435
Government of Newfoundland *v.* Newfoundland Ry. Co. (1888) 13 App. Cas. 199 (P.C.) .... [1989] 293, 294; [1990] 475
Government of the Republic of Spain *v.* North of England S.S. Co. (1938) 61 Ll. L. Rep. 44 [1986] 128
Government of U.S.A. *v.* Ship *Valiant Enterprise* (1961) 63 N.L.R. 337 .... [1987] 170
Government Stock and Other Securities Investment Co. *v.* Manila Ry. Co. [1897] A.C. 81, 86 .... [1986] 521, 529
Governor, The, 1923 A.M.C. 741 .... [1986] 490
Governors of the Peabody Donation Fund *v.* Sir Lindsay Parkinson & Co. Ltd. [1985] A.C. 210 .... [1987] 9; [1990] 486
Gowers *v.* Lloyds and National Provincial Foreign Bank Ltd. [1938] 1 All E.R. 766 .... [1989] 303
Grace (G.W.) & Co. *v.* General S.N. Co. [1950] 2 K.B. 383 .... [1988] 43
Graces, The (1844) 2 W. Rob. 294 .... [1989] 63, 74
Grainger & Son *v.* Gough [1896] A.C. 325 .... [1989] 374
Grand Champion Tankers Ltd. *v.* Norpipe A/S (*The Marion*) [1984] A.C. 563 .... [1988] 523
Grant *v.* Australian Knitting Mills Ltd. [1936] A.C. 85 .... [1988] 515; [1990] 456
Grant *v.* John Grant & Sons Ltd. (1950) 82 C.L.R. 1 .... [1990] 409
Grant *v.* Norway (1851) 10 C.B. 665, (1851) 20 L.J.C.P. 93 .... [1986] 109, 401, 469, 470, 472, 473, 474, 475, 481, 482, 483
Grant *v.* Southwestern and County Properties Ltd. [1975] Ch. 185 .... [1990] 322
Grant, Smith & Co. *v.* Seattle Construction & Dry Dock Co. [1920] A.C. 162 .... [1986] 40; [1988] 350
Gray *v.* Barr [1971] 2 Q.B. 554; [1971] 2 Lloyd's Rep. 1 .... [1986] 261; [1987] 209, 211, 212; [1988] 320
Gray *v.* Johnston (1868) L.R. 3 H.L. 1 .... [1989] 304
Gray *v.* Zurich Ins. Co., 65 Cal. 2d 263, 419 P. 2d 168, 54 Cal. Rptr. 104 (1966) .... [1986] 87
Great American Ins. Co. *v.* Weyl (1938) 94 F. 2d 31 (3rd Cir.) .... [1989] 435
Great Lakes Container Corp. *v.* National Union Fire Ins. Co., 727 F. 2d 30 (1 Cir. 1984) .... [1986] 93
Great Lakes Pilotage Authority Ltd. *v.* Misener Shipping Ltd. [1987] 2 F.C. 431 (F.C.) .... [1989] 98
Great Outdoors Co. Ltd. (The) (*Re*) (N.Z. H.C., p. 549) .... [1987] 545
Great Pacific, The (1869) L.R. 2 P.C. 516 .... [1988] 158
Greater Nottingham Co-operative Soc. Ltd. *v.* Cementation Piling & Foundations Ltd. [1988] 3 W.L.R. 396; [1989] Q.B. 71 (C.A.) .... [1988] 470, 505; [1990] 318
Greathouse (J. P.) Steel Erectors Inc. *v.* Blount Brothers Construction Co., 374 F. 2d 324, 325 (D.C. Cir. 1967) .... [1986] 49
Green *v.* Cafarella (1934) (unreported) .... [1990] 21
Green *v.* Portsmouth Stadium [1953] 2 Q.B. 190; [1953] 1 W.L.R. 487 .... [1989] 436
Green Star Shipping Co. Ltd. *v.* London Assurance (*The Andree*) (1939) 39 Ll.L.Rep. 213 .. [1987] 449
Greenbrae, 1935 A.M.C. 221 .... [1986] 492
Greenhalgh *v.* Arderne Cinemas Ltd. [1946] 1 All E.R. 512; [1950] 2 All E.R. 1120 .... [1988] 71, 75
Greenhalgh *v.* Mallard [1947] 2 All E.R. 255 .... [1989] 442
Greenman *v.* Yuba Power Products Inc., 59 Cal. 2d 57, 27 Cal. Rptr. 697, 377 P. 2d 897 (1963) .... [1986] 80
Greenstone Shipping Co. *v.* Transworld Oil Ltd., 588 F. Supp. 574 (D. Del. 1984) .... [1986] 359
Greenwood *v.* Francis [1899] 1 Q.B. 312 .... [1990] 225
Greenwood *v.* Martins Bank Ltd. [1933] A.C. 51 .... [1986] 8, 9; [1988] 363

Greenwood *v.* United States, 350 U.S. 366 (1956) .... [1987] 512
Gregerso, The [1973] Q.B. 274 .... [1986] 153; [1990] 353, 362
Grierson Oldham and Adams Ltd. (*Re*) [1968] Ch. 17 .... [1990] 260
Grieve (*Re*) [1899] 1 Q.B. 794 .... [1986] 394
Griffin *v.* Weatherby (1868) L.R. 3 Q.B. 753 .... [1990] 246, 249
Grigorios, The [1924] A.C. 431 .... [1986] 27; [1987] 32; [1988] 324
Grist *v.* Bailey [1967] Ch. 532 .... [1987] 243; [1988] 301; [1989] 442
Grizewood *v.* Blane (1851) 11 C.B. 526 .... [1986] 393, 394
Groves *v.* John Wunder Co., 286 N.W. 23 (1939) .... [1987] 432
Groves-Raffin Construction Ltd. *v.* Bank of Nova Scotia [1976] 1 Lloyd's Rep. 373 .... [1988] 443
Guadano *v.* Hamburg Chicago [1973] F.C. 726 .... [1989] 94
Guaranty Trust Co. of New York *v.* Lyon, 124 N.Y.S. 2d 680 (1953) .... [1986] 208; [1990] 84
Gubisch Maschinenfabrik A.G. *v.* Palumbo, Case 144/86, 8 December 1987 .... [1988] 392
Guerin *v.* The Queen (1984) 13 D.L.R. (4th) 321 .... [1987] 436
Guertin *v.* Royal Bank of Canada (1983) 1 D.L.R. (4th) 68 .... [1987] 421
Guinness Plc *v.* Saunders [1990] 2 W.L.R. 324 (H.L.), affirming [1988] 1 W.L.R. 863 (C.A.) and [1988] B.C.L.C. 43 (Ch.D.) .... [1989] 303; [1990] 222, 330, 407, 465
Gulf *v.* Tug *Mary Mackin* (1983) 52 N.R. 282 .... [1987] 93
Gulf and Fraser *v.* Almas & Almas (1984) 55 B.C.L.R. 301 .... [1987] 91
Gulf Trading & Transp. Co. *v.* M.V. *Hoegh Shield*, 658 F. 2d 363, 1982 A.M.C. 1138 (5 Cir. 1981), reh'g and reh'g *en banc* denied, 670 F. 2d 182 (5 Cir.), cert. denied, 457 U.S. 1119, 1982 A.M.C. 2108 (1982) .... [1986] 353; [1987] 153
Gulf Trading & Transp. Co. *v.* M.V. *Tento*, 694 F. 2d 1191 (9th Cir., 1982), cert. denied, 461 U.S. 929 (1983) .... [1987] 153
Gulf Trollers Association *v.* Canada (1987) 72 N.R. 31 (Fed. C.A.) .... [1989] 89
Gulf Trollers Association *v.* Minister of Fisheries and Oceans [1984] 2 F.C. 398 .... [1987] 94
Gulf Venture, The [1985] 1 Lloyd's Rep. 131 .... [1989] 94
Gulfcoast Transit Co. *v.* The *Anco Princess*, 1978 A.M.C. 2471; [1978] 1 Lloyd's Rep. 293 (E.D. La. 1977) .... [1987] 344
Gulfstream Cargo Ltd. *v.* Reliance Ins. Co. (1969) 409 F. 2d 974 .... [1988] 347
Gulliver *v.* Unifund Assurance Co. (1985) 53 Nfld. & P.E.I.R. 242 .... [1987] 66
Guy *v.* Churchill (1889) 40 Ch.D. 481 .... [1990] 219
G.W. Jones, The (1982) 48 F. 925 .... [1990] 35
Gyda, The, 1970 A.M.C. 84; 304 F. Supp. 1204; 1971 A.M.C. 2041; 304 F. Supp. 1204 (D.C. Michigan); 1971 A.M.C. 2032; 438 F. 2d 803 (6th Cir.), aff'd 1971 A.M.C. 2070; 406 F. 2d 1039 (6th Cir.); 723 F. 2d 994 (1st Cir.) *cert.* denied 1972 A.M.C. 597 .... [1989] 352, 357
Gyler *v.* Mission Ins. Co., 10 Cal. 3d 216, 514 P. 2d 1219, 110 Cal. Rptr. 139 (1973) .... [1986] 88
H. & E. van der Sterren *v.* Cibernetics (Holdings) Pty. Ltd. (1970) 44 A.L.J.R. 157 .... [1987] 168
Haddad *v.* Cie Air-France (1982) 36 RFDA 342 (Cour de Cass.); *cf.* (1979) 33 RFDA 327, 329 .... [1988] 219
Hadjepateras *v.* Pacifica S.A., 1961 A.M.C. 1417, 290 F. 2d 697 (5 Cir. 1961) .... [1986] 13
Hadley *v.* Baxendale (1854) 9 Ex. 341; 156 E.R. 145 .... [1987] 122, 415; [1988] 277
Haeuber *v.* Can-do, 666 F. 2d 275 (1984) .... [1986] 496
Hafton Properties Ltd. *v.* McHugh [1987] S.T.C. 16 .... [1988] 369
Hagan *v.* Scottish Ins. Co., 186 U.S. 423 (U.S.S. Ct., 1902) .... [1986] 492
Haidee, The (1842) 1 N.o.C. 594 .... [1989] 61
Hain S.S. Co. *v.* Minister of Food [1949] 1 K.B. 492 .... [1986] 255
Hain S.S. Co. *v.* Tate & Lyle Ltd. (1936) 41 Com. Cas. 350 .... [1987] 147
Halcyon Isle, The [1981] A.C. 221; [1980] 2 Lloyd's Rep. 325; 1980 A.M.C. 1221 (P.C. (Singapore)) .... [1986] 352; [1987] 153, 321, 380; [1988] 82, 534; [1989] 11 *et seq.*, 174 *et seq.*; [1990] 101, 492
Halifax Longshoremen's Assn. *v.* Maritime Employers Assn. (1988) 200 A.P.R. 405 (N.S.S.C.) .... [1989] 99
Hall *v.* Hvide Hull No. 3, 746 F. 2d 294, 1985 A.M.C. 1408 (5 Cir. 1984) .... [1986] 372
Hall *v.* Wickins Motors (Gloucester) Ltd. [1972] 1 W.L.R. 1418 .... [1989] 380
Hallett's Estate (*Re*) (1880) 13 Ch. D. 696 .... [1989] 203
Halley, The (1868) 2 L.R. 2 P.C. 193 .... [1990] 201
Halls *v.* David [1989] 1 W.L.R. 745 .... [1990] 214, 220
Halt Garage (1964) Ltd. (*Re*) [1982] 3 All E.R. 1016 .... [1988] 77
Halterm Ltd. *v.* National Harbours Board (1985) 55 N.R. 118 .... [1987] 95
Hambly *v.* Trott (1776) 1 Cowp. 371 .... [1987] 433

Hamilton Fraser *v*. Pandorf (*The Inchrhona*) (1887) 12 App. Cas. 518 .... [1986] 39
Hamilton's Windsor Ironworks (*Re*) *ex parte* Pitman and Edwards (1879) 12 Ch. D. 707, 710 [1986] 524
Hamlet *v*. Richardson (1833) 9 Bing. 644 .... [1989] 436
Hamlyn & Co. *v*. Talisker Distillery [1894] A.C. 202 .... [1987] 528
Hamlyn *v*. Tallisker Distillery [1984] A.C. 202 .... [1986] 509, 510; [1989] 219, 365
Hammer & Sohne *v*. H.W.T. Realisations Ltd., 1985 S.L.T. (Sh. Ct.) 21 .... [1986] 552
Hamzeh Malas & Sons *v*. British Imex Industries Ltd. [1958] 2 Q.B. 127 .... [1990] 552
Hanak *v*. Green [1958] 2 Q.B. 9 .... [1990] 50, 475
Haniotis *v*. Dimitriou [1983] V.R. 498 .... [1987] 55
Hannah Blumenthal, The [1983] 1 A.C. 854; [1983] 1 Lloyd's Rep. 103 .... [1986] 68; [1987] 156, 264; [1988] 304, 307; [1989] 5, 170, 442; [1990] 156, 157, 555
Hansa Nord, The [1976] Q.B. 44 .... [1987] 400; [1988] 506; [1990] 457
Hansen *v*. The *Ocean Victoria* [1975] 1 F.C. 451 .... [1987] 92
Happy Pioneer, The [1983] H.K.L.R. 43 .... [1986] 97
Har Rai (The Ship) *v*. Marlex Petroleum Inc. [1987] 1 S.C.R. 57 (Can. S.C.); upholding Fed. C.A. [1984] 2 F.C. 345; (1984) 4 D.L.R. (4th) 739; 1984 A.M.C. 1649 .... [1987] 154; [1988] 82; [1989] 12, 14
Harbottle (R.D.) (Mercantile) Ltd. *v*. National Westminster Bank Ltd. [1978] Q.B. 146 .... [1990] 223, 236, 239
Harbutts Plasticine *v*. Wayne Tank & Pump Co. [1970] 1 Q.B. 477 .... [1990] 284
Hardie *v*. Hanson (1960) 105 C.L.R. 451 .... [1990] 221
Hardy *v*. MIB [1964] 2 Q.B. 745; [1964] 1 Lloyd's Rep. 397 .... [1987] 209, 210, 211; [1988] 323
Hare *v*. Henty (1861) 10 C.B.N.S. 65 .... [1990] 71, 72, 247
Harisiades *v*. Shaughnessy, 342 U.S. 580, 594 (1952) .... [1986] 377
Harland & Wolff *v*. Burns & Laird Lines (1931) 40 Ll.L.Rep. 286 .... [1990] 127
Harlem, The, 1931 A.M.C. 995 (2 C.A.) .... [1986] 492
Harlingdon and Leinster Enterprises Ltd. *v*. Christopher Hull Fine Art Ltd. [1990] 3 W.L.R. 13 .... [1990] 456
Harlowe's Nominees Pty. Co. Ltd. *v*. Woodside (Lake Entrance) Oil Co. Ltd. (1968) 121 C.L.R. 483 .... [1988] 72
Harmon *v*. Chicago, 110 Ill. 400; 51 Am. Rep. 698 (1884) .... [1987] 521
Harmony Shipping Co. S.A. *v*. Saudi-Europe Line Ltd. (*The Good Helmsman*) [1981] 1 Lloyd's Rep. 377 .... [1990] 107, 111
Harold Meyers Travel Serv. *v*. Magid, 16 O.R. (2d) 1; 77 D.L.R. (3d) 32 (C.A.) .... [1987] 154
Harriett, The (1857) Swab. 218 .... [1989] 61, 68, 71, 78
Harrington Motor Co. Ltd. (*In re*) *ex parte* Chaplin [1928] Ch. 105 .... [1987] 229
Harriot, The (1842) 1 W. Rob. 439 .... [1989] 61, 62, 78
Harris *v*. Empress Motors [1984] 1 W.L.R. 212 (C.A.) .... [1990] 138
Harris *v*. Watson (1791) Peake N.P. 72 .... [1990] 345
Harris *v*. Wyre Forest D.C. [1988] 1 All E.R. 691; [1988] 2 W.L.R. 1173; [1989] 2 W.L.R. 790 .... [1988] 367, 471; [1990] 486
Harris & Sheldon Group Ltd. (*Re*) [1971] 1 W.L.R. 899 .... [1990] 407
Harris Simons Construction Ltd. (*Re*) [1989] 1 W.L.R. 368; [1989] B.C.L.C. 202 .... [1989] 507;
Harrison (T. & J.) *v*. Knowles & Foster [1927] 2 K.B. 606; aff'd on other grounds [1928] 1 K.B. 608 .... [1990] 456
Harrison *v*. Knowles & Foster [1918] 1 K.B. 608 .... [1986] 401 [1990] 405, 413
Harrowing *v*. Katz (1894) 10 T.L.R. 115, 400, (1895) 12 T.L.R. 66 (H.L.) .... [1986] 473, 474
Harry Escombe, The, 1920 A.D. 187, 199 .... [1988] 16
Hartford Fire Ins. Co. *v*. Martin, 1965 A.M.C. 874 .... [1986] 504
Harvela Investments Ltd. *v*. Royal Trust Co. of Canada (C.I.) Ltd. [1986] A.C. 207 .... [1987] 553; [1989] 169
Hassel, The [1959] 2 Lloyd's Rep. 82 .... [1986] 331
Hatcher *v*. White (1953) 53 S.R. (N.S.W.) 285 .... [1987] 208
Hauser *v*. American Central Ins. Co., 1964 A.M.C. 526 .... [1986] 503
Havering L.B.C. *v*. Stevenson [1970] 1 W.L.R. 1375 .... [1989] 374
Haverkate *v*. Toronto Harbour Commissioners (1986) 30 D.L.R. (4th) 125 (Ont. H.Ct.) .... [1988] 84
Haverkate *v*. Toronto Harbour Commissioners (1988) 62 O.R. 447 (Ont. C.A.) .... [1990] 103
Hayes-Leger Associates Inc. *v*. M.V. *Oriental Knight* [1986] AMC 1724 .... [1989] 280
Hayn *v*. Culliford (1879) 4 C.P.D. 182, 185 .... [1986] 105
Hayward *v*. Bank of Nova Scotia (1985) 19 D.L.R. (4th) 758 .... [1988] 379

H.E. Kane Agencies Ltd. *v.* Coopers & Lybrand (1983) 22 N.B.R. (2d) 374; 23 C.C.L.T. 233; 116 A.P.R. 374 (Q.B.) .... [1990] 425
Hebe, The (1844) 2 W. Rob. 246 .... [1989] 71, 75
Hedley Byrne & Co. Ltd. *v.* Heller & Partners Ltd. [1964] A.C. 465 .... [1986] 202, 310, 314, 317, 423; [1988] 361, 365, 406, 462; [1989] 150, 151; [1990] 149, 485, 553
Hedwig, The (1853) 1 Sp. 19 .... [1989] 61, 69
Heil *v.* Hedges [1951] 1 T.L.R. 512 .... [1988] 512
Heilbut, Symons & Co. *v.* Buckleton [1913] A.C. 30 .... [1988] 505
Heindl-Evans *v.* Reliance Ins., 1980 A.M.C. 2823 .... [1986] 495
Heinrich Hanno & Co. B.V. *v.* Fairlight Shipping Co. Ltd. (*The Kostas K*) [1985] 1 Lloyd's Rep. 231 .... [1986] 66
Helbert Wagg & Co. Ltd. (*Re*) [1956] Ch. 323 .... [1987] 528
Helby *v.* Matthews [1895] A.C. 471 .... [1986] 173
Helen & George, The (1858) Swab. 368 .... [1989] 76
Helen L, The, 1937 A.M.C. 1170 (Wash. S. Ct.) .... [1986] 486
Helen Miller, The [1980] 2 Lloyd's Rep. 95 .... [1986] 118
Hellenic Shipping & Industries Co. Ltd. *v.* American Maritime Navigation Co. (*The Mesologi*) (1971) S.M.A. No. 642 .... [1989] 355
Helle Skou, The [1976] 2 Lloyd's Rep. 205 .... [1990] 396
Helson *v.* McKenzies (Cuba St.) Ltd. [1950] N.Z.L.R. 878 .... [1987] 51
Hely-Hutchinson *v.* Brayhead Ltd. [1968] 1 Q.B. 549 .... [1990] 331
Henderson *v.* Henderson (1843) 3 Hare 100, 115 .... [1989] 442
Hendy Lennox (Industrial Engines) Ltd. *v.* Grahame Puttick Ltd. [1984] 1 W.L.R. 485 .... [1987] 75; [1989] 202, 203
Hener *v.* United States, 525 F. Supp. 350, 355 (S.D.N.Y 1981) .... [1986] 17
Henjes *v.* Aetna Ins. Co. (1943) 132 F. 2d 715 .... [1988] 347
Hennessey v. Craigmyle & Co. Ltd. [1986] I.C.R. 461 .... [1989] 276
Hennessey *v.* Rohmann Osbourne (1877) 36 L.T. 51 .... [1990] 321
Henrik Sif, The [1982] 1 Lloyd's Rep. 456 .... [1986] 472; [1987] 260; [1988] 441
Henriksens Rederi A/S *v.* T.H.Z. Rolimpex (*The Brede*) [1973] 1 Q.B 233 .... [1986] 387
Henry, The (1851) 15 Jur. 183 .... [1989] 74, 75, 76, 79
Henry *v.* Hammond [1913] 2 K.B. 515 .... [1989] 202
Henry Smith & Co. *v.* The Bedouin Steam Navigation Co. Ltd. [1986] A.C. 70, 77, 80 .... [1986] 471, 473, 474
Henry Steers Jr., The (1901) 110 F. 578 .... [1990] 53
Hercules, The, 830 F. 2d 321 .... [1988] 10
Hercules Carriers Inc. *v.* State of Florida, 720 F. 2d 1201, 1984 A.M.C. 2962 (11 Cir. 1983), aff'd 728 F. 2d 1359 (11 Cir.) (*en banc*), cert. denied, 105 S. Ct. 128 (1984) .... [1986] 361; [1987] 512
Heriteau *v.* W.D. Morris Realty Ltd. [1944] 1 D.L.R. 28 .... [1987] 45
Her Majesty's A-G. *v.* Wellington Newspapers [1988] 1 N.Z.L.R. 129 .... [1990] 464
Herman *v.* Trans World Airlines Inc. (1972) 337 N.Y.S. 2d 827; 12 Avi. 17, 634; (1972) 12 Avi. 17, 304 .... [1988] 221
Herman *v.* Trans World Airlines Inc. (1974) 34 N.Y. 2d 385; 13 Avi. 17, 231 .... [1988] 228
Hermine, The [1979] 1 Lloyd's Rep. 212 (C.A.), rvrsg. [1978] 2 Lloyd's Rep. 37 .... [1986] 113; [1988] 49, 53, 54
Hernandez *v.* Air France (1976) 545 F. 2d 279 (1st Cir.); 14 Avi. 17, 421, cert. denied (1977) 97 S. Ct. 1592; *cf. In re* Tel Aviv (1975) 13 Avi. 18, 166 .... [1988] 222
Herne Bay Steamboat Co. *v.* Hutton [1903] 2 K.B. 683 .... [1988] 115
Heron II, The [1969] 1 A.C. 350 .... [1986] 338; [1990] 433
Herrington *v.* British Railways Board [1972] A.C. 877 (H.L.) .... [1987] 56, 64
Hertha Engeline Fritzen, The, Gdynia Award 13.2.1967 .... [1990] 391
Heskell *v.* Continental Express Ltd. [1950] 1 All E.R. 1033 .... [1986] 109, 269, 471, 472, 473
Hewett *v.* Court (1983) 46 A.L.R. 87 (H.C.A.) .... [1986] 552
Heydon's Case (1584) 3 Co. Rep. 7a .... [1990] 410
H.H. Dimond (Rotorua 1966) Ltd. *v.* Australia and New Zealand Banking Group Ltd. [1979] 2 N.Z.L.R. 739 .... [1990] 72, 73, 75, 76, 244, 245, 247
Hickman *v.* Berens [1895] 2 Ch. 638 .... [1989] 443
Highlands Insurance Co. *v.* Continental Insurance Co. [1987] 1 Lloyd's Rep. 109 .... [1987] 8, 245
Highway Properties Ltd. *v.* Kelly, Douglas & Co. Ltd. [1971] S.C.R. 562; 17 D.L.R. (3d) 710 .... [1988] 279
Hill *v.* James Crowe (Cases) Ltd. [1977] 2 Lloyd's Rep. 450 .... [1988] 516

Hill *v.* William Hill (Park Lane) Ltd. [1949] A.C. 530 .... [1989] 436
Hillegom Municipality *v.* Hillenius [1986] 3 C.M.L.R. 422 .... [1987] 251, 252
Hinderlider *v.* La Plata & Cherry Creek Ditch Co., 304 U.S. 92 (1938) .... [1987] 503
Hines Inc. *v.* U.S. (1977) 551 F. 2d 717; 1977 A.M.C. 380 (6th Cir.) .... [1989] 17, 18
Hinkins Steamship Agency *v.* Freighters Inc., 1973 A.M.C. 348, 351 F. Supp. 373 (N.D. Cal. 1972); aff'd 1974 A.M.C. 1397, 498 F. 2d 411 (9 Cir. 1974) .... [1986] 13
Hirji Mulji *v.* Cheong Yue Steamship Co. Ltd. [1926] A.C. 497 .... [1990] 156
Hobbs *v.* Marlowe [1978] A.C. 16 .... [1989] 9, 10
Hobbs *v.* Petersham Transport Co. Pty. Ltd. (1971) 45 A.L.J.R. 356; (1971) 124 C.L.R. 220, ... [1987] 63; [1988] 36
Hochster *v.* De La Tour (1853) 2 El. & Bl. 678; 118 E.R. 922 .... [1988] 531
Hockley *v.* Goldstein (1922) 90 L.J.K.B. 111 .... [1986] 197
Hodgson *v.* Malcolm (1806) 2 Bos. & Pul. (N.R.) 336 .... [1988] 331
Hodgson *v.* Shaw (1834) 3 My. & K. 183 .... [1989] 9
Hoenig *v.* Isaacs [1952] 2 All E.R. 176 .... [1990] 512
Hoffmann *v.* Kreig, Case 145/86, 4 February 1988 .... [1988] 393
Hoffman-La Roche *v.* Commission [1979] E.C.R. 461 .... [1988] 189
Hofing GMC Truck Inc. *v.* Kay Wheel Sales Co., 543 F. Supp. 414 (E.D. Pa. 1982) .... [1986] 83
Hogg *v.* Cramphorn Ltd. [1967] Ch. 254 .... [1988] 72
Hokkaido Fisheries Co. Ltd. (*In re*), 506 F. Supp. 631; 1981 A.M.C. 1468 (D. Alas., 1981) .. [1987] 504
Holden *v.* Chief Constable of Lancashire [1987] Q.B. 380 .... [1990] 138
Holiday *v.* Sigil (1826) 2 Car. & P. 177 .... [1989] 306, 315
Holland *v.* Arthur Andersen & Co. (1984) 469 N.E. 2d 419 (Ill. App. 1 Dist.) .... [1990] 426, 427
Hollandia, The [1982] 1 Q.B. 872; [1983] A.C. 565; *sub nom.* The *Morviken* [1983] 1 Lloyd's Rep. 1, 5 .... [1986] 143, 511; [1987] 146, 235, 528; [1989] 405
Holles (Lady) *v.* Wyse (1693) 2 Vern. 289 .... [1990] 18
Hollingworth *v.* Southern Ferries Ltd. (*The Eagle*) [1977] 2 Lloyd's Rep. 70 .... [1990] 164
Hollins *v.* Fowler (1875) L.R. 7 H.L. 757, 766–767 .... [1986] 220
Hollister *v.* Luke Construction Co., 517 F. 2d 920 (5 Cir. 1975) .... [1986] 373
Holman *v.* Johnson (1775) 1 Cowp. 341, 343 .... [1986] 435
Holmes *v.* Ashford [1950] 2 All E.R. 76 .... [1988] 512
Holmes *v.* Bangladesh Biman Corp. [1987] 2 Lloyd's Rep. 192 (C.A.); [1988] 2 Lloyd's Rep. 120; [1989] 2 W.L.R. 481 .... [1988] 445; [1989] 267 *et seq.*
Holroyd *v.* Marshall (1862) 10 H.L. Cas. 191 .... [1986] 520
Holsworthy U.D.C. *v.* Holsworthy R.D.C. [1907] 2 Ch. 62 .... [1989] 433
Holt *v.* Jesse (1876) 3 Ch. D. 177 .... [1989] 444
Holwell Securities Ltd. *v.* Hughes [1974] 1 W.L.R. 155 .... [1988] 257
Holzer Watch Co. Inc. *v.* Seaboard and Western Airlines Inc. (1957) 5 Avi. Cas. 17854 (N.Y. Cty. Ct.) .... [1989] 38
Home Insurance Co. *v.* Administratia Asigurarilor de Stat [1983] 2 Lloyd's Rep. 674 .... [1988] 116
Home Insurance Co. *v.* Aetna Cas. & Surety Co., 1975 Fire and Cas. Cases. 793 (S.D.N.Y. 74 Civ. 4164, 24 April 1975) .... [1986] 96
Home Insurance Co. *v.* Ipec Holdings Ltd. (1983) (unreported, N.S.W. Sup. Ct.) .... [1989] 139, 142
Home Insurance Co. *v.* Merchant's Transportation Co., 1927 A.M.C. 57 (9 C.A.) .... [1986] 496
Home Insurance Co. *v.* Victoria-Montreal Fire Ins. Co. [1907] A.C. 59 .... [1988] 9; [1989] 287
Hone (*Re*) [1951] 1 Ch. 85 .... [1990] 67, 68
Hong Kong and Shanghai Banking Corp. *v.* Kloeckner & Co. A.G. [1989] 2 Lloyd's Rep. 323 .... [1990] 223, 242
Hong Kong Fir Shipping Co. Ltd. *v.* Kawasaki Kisen Kaisha Ltd. [1962] 2 Q.B. 26 .... [1988] 396; [1990] 149, 457
Hong Kong Producer, The [1969] 2 Lloyd's Rep. 536 .... [1990] 292
Hood *v.* Anchor Line (Henderson Bros.) Ltd. [1918] A.C. 837 .... [1988] 295; [1990] 164
Hood's Trustees *v.* Southern Union General Insurance Co. of Australasia Ltd. [1928] Ch. 793 .... [1987] 229
Hopewell, The (1855) 2 Sp. 249 .... [1989] 61, 69
Horcal Ltd. *v.* Gatland [1984] B.C.L.C. 43 .... [1989] 448
Horton *v.* Jones (1934) 34 S.R. (N.S.W.) 359, aff'd on other grounds (1935) 53 C.L.R. 475 .. [1990] 511
Horton *v.* Jones (No. 2) (1939) 39 S.R. (N.S.W.) 305 .... [1990] 506
Hospital Products Ltd. *v.* U.S. Surgical Corp. (1984) 156 C.L.R. 41; 58 A.L.J.R. 587; 55 A.L.R. 417 .... [1986] 552; [1987] 125, 423, 434, 438, 439; [1990] 6, 130
Hotson *v.* East Berkshire Area Health Authority [1987] A.C. 750 .... [1990] 138

Houghland *v.* R.R. Low (Luxury Coaches) Ltd. [1962] 1 Q.B. 694 .... [1987] 56; [1989] 150
Houldsworth *v.* City of Glasgow Bank (1880) 5 App. Cas. 317 .... [1990] 410
House of Fraser *v.* AGCE Investments Ltd. [1987] Ch. 387 .... [1990] 401, 404
Household Products Co. Ltd. (*Re*) (1981) 124 D.L.R. (3d) 325 .... [1986] 525
Houston City, The [1956] A.C. 266; (1954) 91 C.L.R. 233; [1954] 2 Lloyd's Rep. 148 .... [1986] 116; [1987] 409; [1988] 43
Houthandel, The (1853) 1 Sp. 25 .... [1989] 64, 71
Howard *v.* Pickford Tool Co. Ltd. [1951] 1 K.B. 417 .... [1989] 84
Howard *v.* Wood (1679) 2 Show. K.B. 21 .... [1989] 297
Howard Marine and Dredging Co. Ltd. *v.* A. Ogden and Sons (Excavations) Ltd. [1978] Q.B. 574 .... [1986] 314
Howard Smith Ltd. *v.* Ampol Petroleum Ltd. [1974] A.C. 821 .... [1988] 72
Howe Richardson Scale Co. Ltd. *v.* Polymex-Cekop [1978] 1 Lloyd's Rep. 161 .... [1990] 223, 224, 229, 240
Hubbock *v.* Helms (1887) 56 L.J. Ch. 536, 537–38 .... [1986] 523, 524, 530
Huddersfield Banking Co. Ltd. *v.* Lister [1895] 2 Ch. 273 .... [1989] 431, 445
Huddleston *v.* Central Risks Information Services Ltd. [1987] 1 W.L.R. 701 .... [1990] 322
Hughes *v.* Metropolitan Railway (1877) 2 App. Cas. 439 .... [1990] 471
Hugney *v.* Consolidation Coal Co., 345 F. Supp. 1079 (W.D. Pa., 1971) .... [1987] 345
Huilerie l'Abeille *v.* Société des Huileries du Niger (*The Kastellon*) [1978] 2 Lloyd's Rep. 203 [1988] 458
Humarock, The (1916) 234 F. 716 .... [1990] 36
Humble Oil & Refining Co. *v.* Tug *Crochet* (1970) 422 F. 2d 602; 1972 AMC 1843 (5th Cir.) ... [1989] 18
Humphrey (H.M.F.) Ltd. *v.* Baxter, Hoare & Co. Ltd. (1933) 149 L.T. 603 .... [1986] 226; [1988] 469
Hunt *v.* Silk (1804) 5 East 449; 102 E.R. 1142 .... [1988] 530
Hunter *v.* Handley, 1955 S.C. 200 (Ct. of Sess.) .... [1990] 259
Hunter *v.* Shell Oil Co. (1952) 198 F. 2d 485 (5th Cir.) .... [1990] 461
Hunter Engineering Co. *v.* Syncrude Canada Ltd. (1989) 57 D.L.R. (4th) 321 .... [1990] 461
Huron Portland Cement Co. *v.* City of Detroit, 362 U.S. 440 (1960), noted in 59 Mich. L. Rev. 964 (1961); 1960 U. Ill. L.F. 450 (1960) .... [1987] 522
Hurona, The, 1929 A.M.C. 258 (N.Y.A.D.) .... [1986] 494
Husserl *v.* Swiss Air Transport Co. Ltd. (1972) 351 F. Supp. 702 (SDNY); 12 Avi. 17, 637 ... [1988] 220
Husserl *v.* Swiss Air Transport Co. Ltd. (1975) 388 F. Supp. 1238 (SDNY); 13 Avi. 17, 603 .. [1988] 224
Hyde *v.* Tameside A.H.A. [1981] C.L.Y. 1854 (C.A.) .... [1990] 137
Hyosung (America) Inc. *v.* Japan Air Lines Co. Ltd. and Flying Tigers (1985) 19 Aviation Cases (CCH) 18, 034 (U.S.D.C., SDNY) .... [1988] 153
Hyundai *v.* Pournaras [1978] 2 Lloyd's Rep. 502 .... [1986] 400
Hyundai Heavy Industries Co. Ltd. *v.* Papadopoulos [1980] 1 W.L.R. 1129 .... [1986] 400; [1990] 502
I.A.C. (Leasing) Ltd. *v.* Humphrey (1972) 126 C.L.R. 131 (H.C.A.) .... [1987] 146; [1990] 22
I.D.C. Ltd. *v.* Cooley [1972] 1 W.L.R. 443 .... [1987] 429
I.E. Contractors Ltd. *v.* Lloyds Bank Plc [1989] 2 Lloyd's Rep. 205 .... [1990] 223, 243
Illingworth *v.* Houldsworth [1904] A.C. 355 .... [1986] 522, 529; [1989] 210
Illinois *v.* City of Milwaukee, 731 F. 2d 403 (7th Cir., 1984); 406 U.S. 91 (1972); 451 U.S. 304 [1987] 503
Illyria Cia. Naviera S.A. *v.* Bamaodah (*The Elli 2, Toulla and Eleni 2*) [1985] 1 Lloyd's Rep. 107 .... [1986] 102
Ilse, The, Hamburg Award 18.9.1974, unreported .... [1990] 392
Imperial Bank of Canada *v.* Bank of Hamilton [1903] A.C. 49 .... [1990] 250
Imperial Mercantile Credit Association *v.* Coleman (1873) L.R. 6 H.L. 189 .... [1990] 331
Imperial Motors Ltd. (*Re*) (1989) 5 B.C.C. 214 .... [1989] 507
Imperial Oil Ltd. *v.* The *Expo Spirit* (1987) 80 N.R. 259 (Fed. C.A.) .... [1989] 91
In the matter of a Company (No. 00477 of 1986) [1986] P.C.C. 372 .... [1989] 508
INA Corporation *v.* The Government of the Islamic Republic of Iran, Mealey's Litigation Reports: Iranian Claims, August 1985, 2084 .... [1987] 139
Inca, The (1858) Swab. 371; 12 Moo. P.C. 189 .... [1989] 68, 73, 78
Incas and Monterey Printing and Packaging Ltd. *v.* M/V *Sang Jin*, 747 F. 2d 958, 1985 A.M.C. 968, reh'g *en banc* denied, 751 F. 2d 1258 (5 Cir. 1985) .... [1986] 352
Inchmaree, The (1887) 12 App. Cas. 484 .... [1986] 39; [1987] 30
Inchmaree, The [1899] P. 111 .... [1986] 327
Inchrhona, The (1887) 12 App. Cas. 518 .... [1986] 39
Ind, Coope & Co. Ltd. (*Re*) [1911] 2 Ch. 223 .... [1989] 197
Independent Automatic Sales Ltd. *v.* Knowles & Foster [1962] 1 W.L.R. 974 .... [1988] 143, 144; [1989] 207, 208, 209; [1990] 524, 529

India, The (1842) 1 W. Rob. 406 .... [1989] 77
Indian Oil Corp. Ltd. *v.* Greenstone Shipping S.A. (Panama) [1988] 1 Q.B. 345 .... [1988] 287
Industrial Development Consultants Ltd. *v.* Cooley [1972] 1 W.L.R. 443 .... [1988] 133
Industrie Chimiche Italia Centrale and Cerealfin S.A. *v.* Alexander Tsavliris & Sons Maritime Co. (*The Choko Star*) [1990] 1 Lloyd's Rep. 516 (C.A.); reversing [1989] 2 Lloyd's Rep. 42 .... [1990] 35, 353, 359
Ingham *v.* Agnew (1812) 15 East 517 .... [1987] 202
Inglis *v.* Stock (1885) 10 App. Cas. 263 .... [1989] 423
Ingram *v.* Little [1961] 1 Q.B. 31 .... [1986] 323
Ingram River Equipment Inc. *v.* Pott Industries Inc., 756 F. 2d 649, 1985 A.M.C. 2062 (8 Cir. 1985) .... [1986] 361
Initial Services Ltd. *v.* Putterill [1968] 1 Q.B. 396 .... [1986] 237
Insurance Company of Africa *v.* Scor (U.K.) Reinsurance Co. Ltd. [1985] 1 Lloyd's Rep. 312 .... [1986] 145; [1988] 7
Insurance Co. of North America *v.* Electronics Purification Co., 63 Cal. Rptr. 382, 390 (1967) . [1986] 80
Insurance Co. of North America *v.* Forty Eight Insulations Inc., 633 F. 2d 1212 (6 Cir. 1980), cert. denied, 454 U.S. 1109 (1981) .... [1986] 88
Insurance Co. of North America *v.* John J. Bordlee Contractors, 543 F. Supp. 597 (E.D. La. 1982) .... [1986] 84
Insurance Co. of North America *v.* S/S *American Argosy*, 732 F. 2d 299, 1984 A.M.C. 1547 (2 Cir. 1984) .... [1986] 370
Integrated Container Services Inc. *v.* B.T.I. [1984] 1Lloyd's Rep. 154 (C.A.) .... [1986] 487
Inter-Americas Oil Co. *v.* Cosmopolitan Tankers, S.M.A. No. 1574 (1981) .... [1986] 72
Interbulk Ltd. *v.* Aiden Shipping Co. Ltd. (*The Vimeira*) [1984] 2 Lloyd's Rep. 66 (C.A.) [1986] 66, 72
Interfoto Picture Library Ltd. *v.* Stiletto Visual Programmes Ltd. [1988] 2 W.L.R. 615; [1989] Q.B. 433 .... [1988] 286, 295; [1990] 149
International Ass'n of H.F.I. & A. Workers *v.* General Pipe Covering, 613 F. Supp. 858, 860 (D. Minn. 1985) .... [1986]68
International Corona Services *v.* Lac Minerals (1986)25 D.L.R. (4th) 504; (1988) 44 D.L.R. (4th) 529; (1989) 61 D.L.R. (4th) 14; 11 August 1989 (Can. S.C.) .... [1987] 436; [1990] 4, 8
International Factors Ltd. *v.* Rodriguez [1979] 1 Q.B.1; [1979] 1 Q.B. 351 (C.A.) .... [1986] 228; [1987] 149; [1988] 41; [1989] 195
International Hotels Corp. *v.* Golden, 15 N.Y. 2d 9; 202 N.E. 2d 568; 254 N.Y.S. 2d 527 (1964) .... [1987] 154
International Leasing Corp. (Vic.) Ltd. *v.* Aiken (1967) 85 W.M. (Part 1) (N.S.W.) 766 (N.S.W. C.A.) .... [1990] 22
International Marine Development Corp. *v.* Lakes Shipping and Trading Corp. (*The Gilia*) (1975) S.M.A. No.931 .... [1989] 351
International Mercantile Marine Co. *v.* Fels (1909) 170 F. 275 (2nd Cir.) .... [1989] 342
International (R.H. & D.) Ltd. *v.* I.A.S. Animal Air Services Ltd. [1984] 1 W.L.R. 573 .... [1987] 83
International Sales and Agencies Ltd. *v.* Marcus [1982] 3 All E.R. 551 .... [1989] 303, 325; [1990] 332, 412
International Terminal Operators *v.* Miida Electronics(*The Buenos Aires Maru*) [1986] 1 S.C.R. 752; 1986 A.M.C. 2580 .... [1987] 343–344
International Westminster Bank Plc *v.* Okeanos Maritime Corp. [1987] B.C.L.C. 450 .. [1989] 20 *et seq.*
Internav Ltd. *v.* Scanbulk Ltd. (*The Wismar*) (1980) S.M.A. No. 1454 .... [1989] 343
Interoffice Telephones Ltd. *v.* Robert Freeman Co. Ltd. [1958] 1 Q.B. 190 .... [1988] 279
Interpool Ltd. *v.* Galani [1988] Q.B. 738 .... [1989] 466, 469, 470, 473, 474
Interstate Lighterage & Transportation Co. *v.* Newton Creek Towing Co. (1920) 267 F. 989 ... [1990] 53
Intertradex S.A. *v.* Lesieur Tourteaux S.A.R.L. [1978] 2 Lloyd's Rep. 509 .... [1989] 6, 7; [1990] 156
Interview Ltd. (*Re*) [1975] I.R. 382 .... [1989] 205
Investigator, The (1880) 6 Q.B.D. 51 .... [1987] 30
Investment Co. Institute *v.* Camp (1971) 401 U.S. 617 .... [1988] 381
Ioannis Daskalelis, The [1974] S.C.R. 1248; [1974] 1 Lloyd's Rep. 174; 1973 A.M.C. 176; (1973) 32 D.L.R. (3d) 572 ....[1986] 401; [1987] 154, 380; [1988] 82; [1989] 11 *et seq.*; [1990] 101
Iodine, The (1844) 3 N.o.C. 140 .... [1989] 68, 71
Ionmar Cia. Naviera S.A. *v.* Central of Georgia Railroad Co. (The M.V. *Nicolaos D.L.*), 1979 A.M.C. 1747; 471 F. Supp. 942 (S.D. Ga.), vacated 1982 A.M.C. 1489; 666 F. 2d 897 (5th Cir.) .... [1989] 343, 349, 358
Ios I, The [1987] 1 Lloyd's Rep. 321 .... [1987] 172

Iran Vojdan, The [1984] 2 Lloyd's Rep. 380 ....[1986] 508, 509, 510, 511, 513, 515, 516, 517, 518; [1987] 523, 524, 528, 531; [1990] 196
Irani *v.* Southampton and South-West Hampshire Health Authority [1985] I.C.R. 590 .... [1987] 552
I.R.C. *v.* Collco Dealings Ltd. [1962] A.C. 1 .... [1987] 384
Irene's Success, The [1982] Q.B. 481; [1981] 2 Lloyd's Rep. 635 .... [1986] 6, 97, 299; [1987] 54, 84; [1988] 257, 259; [1989] 47, 54
Irish National Ins. Co. and Sedgwick *v.* Oman Ins. Co. [1983] 2 Lloyd's Rep. 453 .... [1986] 261
Irish Rowan, The [1989] 2 Lloyd's Rep. 144 ....[1989] 389 *et seq.*
Irish Shipping Ltd. *v.* Commercial Union Assurance Co. Plc (*The Irish Rowan*) [1989] 2 Lloyd's Rep. 144 ....[1989] 389 *et seq.*
Irish Shipping Ltd. *v.* The Queen, 1984 2 F.C. 777; (1984) 52 N.R. 25, (aff'g. 1977 1 F.C. 485 .[1987] 94
Ironmonger & Co. *v.* Dyne (1926) 44 T.L.R. 497 .... [1986] 394
Irving A. Burton Ltd. *v.* Canadian Imperial Bank of Commerce (1982) 134 D.L.R. (3d) 369 (Ont. C.A.) .... [1986] 168
Irwin *v.* Eagle Star Ins., 1973 A.M.C. 1184 (5 C.A.) .... [1986] 485
Isabelle, The [1984] 1 Lloyd's Rep. 366 .... [1990] 388
Isbrandsten (H. & J.) Ltd. *v.* Executive International Movers, 1986 A.M.C. 2977 (F.C.) .... [1987] 88; [1988] 88
Ishizaki Kisen Co. Ltd. *v.* U.S.A. (1975) 510 F. 2d 875; 1975 A.M.C. 287 (9th Cir.) ....[1989] 13
Islamic Republic of Iran Shipping Lines *v.* Denby [1987] 1 Lloyd's Rep. 367 .... [1988] 128, 129, 131, 133; [1990] 463
Island Creek Coal Sales Co. *v.* City of Gainesville,729 F. 2d 1046 (6 Cir. 1984) .... [1986] 359
Islander Shipping Enterprises S.A. *v.* Empresa Maritima del Estado S.A. (*The Khian Sea*) [1979] 1 Lloyd's Rep. 545(C.A.) ....[1988] 47
Ismail *v.* Polish Ocean Lines [1976] Q.B. 908 (C.A.) .... [1986] 237
Italmare S.p.A. *v.* Stellar Chartering & Brokerage Inc. (*The Marina di Cassano*) [1984] 2 Lloyd's Rep. 577 ....[1986] 72
ITO *v.* Miida Electronics Inc. (*The Buenos Aires Maru*) [1986] 1 S.C.R. 752 .... [1987] 95; [1988] 82
Itobar Pty. Ltd. *v.* Mackinnon and another (*The Galway Bay*) [1985] 3 A.N.Z Insurance Cases 60–610 .... [1986] 289
Iveco Fiat *v.* Van Hool, Case 313/85 [1988] 1 C.M.L.R. 57 .... [1988] 388
Ivenel *v.* Schwab, Case 133/81 [1982] E.C.R. 1891; [1983] 1 C.M.L.R. 538 .... [1987] 285; [1988] 385; [1989] 472
J'Aire Corp. *v.* Gregory, 598 P. 2d 60 (Cal., 1979) .... [1987] 237
J. & J. Cunningham *v.* Robert A. Munro (1922) 28 Com.Cas. 42 .... [1990] 466
Jackson *v.* Horizon Holidays Ltd. [1975] 1 W.L.R. 1468 .... [1990] 169
Jackson *v.* Renownden [1965] V.R. 315 .... [1990] 419
Jackson *v.* Watson & Sons [1909] 2 K.B. 193 .... [1988] 515
Jackson Township Municipal Utilities Authority *v.* Hartford Accident & Indemnity Co., 451 A. 2d 990 (N.J. 1982) ....[1986] 93
Jaensch *v.* Coffey (1984) 58 A.L.J.R. 426 .... [1986] 111
Jag Shakti, The [1986] A.C. 337 (P.C.) ....[1988] 38
Jalamohan, The [1988] 1 Lloyd's Rep. 393, 443 .... [1988] 285; [1990] 494
James *v.* Bradley [1980] W.A.R. 11 ....[1987] 76, 77
James *v.* Thomas H. Kent & Co. Ltd. [1950] 2 All E.R.1099; [1951] 1 K.B. 551 .... [1990] 506, 510
James (A.S.) Pty. Ltd. *v.* C.B. Duncan [1970] V.R.705 .... [1990] 419
James Dixon, The (1860) 2 L.T. 696 ....[1989] 64
James Finlay & Co. Ltd. *v.* N.V. Kwik Hoo Tong Handel Maatschappij [1928] 2 K.B. 604; [1929] 1 K.B. 400 .... [1988] 458
Jamieson's Tow & Salvage Ltd. *v.* Murray [1984] 2 N.Z.L.R. 144 ....[1987] 55, 126
Jan Hendrik, The (1853) 1 Sp. 181 ....[1989] 79
Jan Herman, The [1966] 1 Lloyd's Rep. 402 .... [1989] 123
Jarvis (*Re*) [1958] 1 W.L.R. 815 .... [1990] 335
Jarvis *v.* Swan Tours Ltd. [1973] 1 Q.B. 233 .... [1990] 169
J.E. Construction *v.* General Motors [1985] C.A. 275 ....[1987] 85
JEB Fasteners *v.* Marks, Bloom & Co. [1981] 3 All E.R. 289 .... [1990] 481
Jebsen *v.* Cargo of Hemp, 228 F. 143 (D. Mass. 1915) .... [1986] 425
Jefferson Ltd. *v.* Burton Group Ltd. 13 April 1984. (Unrep.) .... [1987] 55, 58, 63
Jefferson *v.* Paskell [1916] 1 K.B. 57 ....[1989] 85
Jenki, The, Hamburg Award 8.6.1977 .... [1990] 390
Jenkins *v.* Heycock (1853) 8 Moo. P.C. 351 .... [1988] 347

Jennings *v*. Wolfe [1950] 3 D.L.R. .... [1986] 442
Jernigan *v*. Allstate Insurance Co., 272 F. 2d 857 (5th Cir., 1959) .... [1987] 212
J.H. Rayner (Mincing Lane) Ltd. *v*. Dept. of Trade and Industry [1989] 3 W.L.R. 969; [1989] 3 All E.R. 523 (H.L.), affirming [1989] Ch. 72; [1988] 3 All E.R. 272 (C.A.) .... [1990] 305
J.H. Rayner (Mincing Lane) Ltd. *v*. Dept. of Trade and Industry [1989] 3 W.L.R. 969; [1989] 3 All E.R. 523 (H.L.), affirming [1989] Ch. 253; [1988] 3 All E.R. 364 (C.A.), affirming [1988] Ch. 1; [1987] 3 All E.R. 787 .... [1990] 306
Jirna Ltd. *v*. Mister Do-Nut of Canada, 1973 40 D.L.R. (3d) 303 .... [1987] 434
J.J. Lloyd Instruments Ltd. *v*. Northern Star Insurance Co. Ltd. (*The Miss Jay Jay*) (1986) L.M.L.N. 182 (15 October 1986) (C.A.); [1985] 1 Lloyd's Rep. 264; [1987] 1 Lloyd's Rep. 32 .... [1987] 22; [1988] 348
J. Lauritzen A.S. *v*. Wijsmuller B.V. (*The Super Servant Two*) [1989] 1 Lloyd's Rep. 148; [1990] 1 Lloyd's Rep. 1 .... [1989] 3; [1990] 153
J. Lauritzen A.S. *v*. Wijsmuller B.V. (*The Dan King*) (1988) L.M.L.N. 225 .... [1989] 3 *et seq.*
Joachimson *v*. Swiss Bank Corp. [1921] 3 K.B. 110 .... [1989] 364; [1990] 71
Jobson *v*. Johnson [1989] 1 All E.R. 621; [1989] 1 W.L.R. 1026 (C.A.) .... [1990] 158 *et seq.*
Jogia (*Re*) [1988] 1 W.L.R. 484 .... [1990] 350
Johanna Oldendorff, The [1973] 2 Lloyd's Rep. 285; [1974] A.C. 479 .... [1986] 51, 258; [1989] 122, 264; [1990] 390
Johannes, The (1860) Lush. 182 .... [1989] 77, 78
Johannes Christoph, The (1854) 2 Sp. 93 .... [1989] 61, 70
Johannsen *v*. Minnesota Valley Ford Tractor Co. (1981) 304 N.W. 2d 654 (Minn.) .... [1990] 374
Johansen *v*. Cal. State Auto Ass'n. Inter-Ins. Bureau, 15 Cal. 3d 9, 20, 538 P. 2d 744, 747, 123 Cal. Rptr. 288, 295 (1975) .... [1986] 81
John, The (1860) Lush. 11 .... [1989] 70
John *v*. Dodwell & Co. Ltd. [1918] A.C. 563 .... [1989] 321, 322
John *v*. Rees [1970] 1 Ch. 345 .... [1989] 392
John G. Stevens, The (1898) 170 U.S. 113 .... [1988] 160
John Martin of London Ltd. *v*. Russell [1960] 1 Lloyd's Rep. 554 .... [1986] 445
John Michalos, The [1987] 2 Lloyd's Rep. 188 .... [1990] 394
John Snow & Co. Ltd. *v*. D.B.G. Woodcroft & Co. Ltd. [1985] B.C.L.C. 54 .... [1988] 148
John Whitbread *v*. Walley (1988) 45 D.L.R. (4th) 729; 1988 A.M.C. 902 (B.C.S.C.); *rev'd*. 13 May 1988, unrep. (B.C.S.C.) .... [1989] 95
Johns-Manville Corporation, *In re*, Case No. 82–B–11656 (S.D.N.Y. 26 August 1982) .... [1986] 80
Johnson *v*. Agnew [1980] A.C. 367 .... [1987] 144; [1989] 86, 302
Johnson County, Tenn. *v*. U.S. Gypsum Co., 580 F. Supp. 284 (E.D. Tenn., 1984) .... [1987] 124
Johnson Matthey & Co. Ltd. *v*. Constantine Terminals Ltd. [1976] 2 Lloyd's Rep. 215, 222 .... [1986] 106, 226, 231; [1987] 56, 68; [1988] 39, 467
Johnson's Tyne Foundry Pty. Ltd. *v*. Maffra Corp.(1948) 77 C.L.R. 544 .... [1990] 508
Johnstone *v*. Cox (1880) 16 Ch. D. 571; aff'd (1881) 19 Ch. D. 17 (C.A.) .... [1989] 197
Johnstone & Wilmot Pty. Ltd. *v*. Kaine (1928) 23 Tas.L.R. 43 .... [1987] 70, 72
Jones *v*. Barkley (1781) 1 Doug. 272 .... [1989] 84
Jones *v*. Bender Welding & Machine Works Inc., 581 F. 2d 1313 (9 Cir. 1978) .... [1986] 361
Jones *v*. Just (1868) L.R. 3 Q.B. 197 .... [1987] 400
Jones *v*. Livox Quarries Ltd. [1952] 2 Q.B. 608 .... [1990] 421
Jones *v*. *The Flying Clipper*, 116 F. Supp. 386, 1954 A.M.C. 259 (S.D.N.Y. 1953) .... [1986] 369
Jones & Laughlin Steel Corp. *v*. Pfeiffer, 462 U.S. 523, 1983 A.M.C. 1881 (1983) .... [1986] 373
Jones (R.E.) *v*. Waring & Gillow Ltd. [1926] A.C. 670 .... [1989] 305, 306, 439
Jonge Andries, The (1857) Swab. 226 .... [1989] 75
Joseph Constantine Steamship Ltd. *v*. Imperial Smelting Corp. Ltd. [1942] A.C. 154 .... [1989] 5, 442; [1990] 156, 157
Joseph Thorley Ltd. *v*. Orchis S.S. Co. [1907] 1 K.B. 660 .... [1987] 147
Joseph Travers & Sons Ltd. *v*. Longel Ltd. (1948) 44 T.L.R. 150 .... [1990] 458
Jourdain *v*. Miller and Nova Corp. [1988] E.T.L. 460 (Can. F.C.) .... [1990] 101
Jowitt & Sons *v*. Union Cold Storage Co. [1913] 3 K.B. 1 .... [1988] 469
J.P. Donaldson, The (1897) 167 U.S. 599 .... [1990] 173
Julia, The (1861) Lust. 224 .... [1989] 59
Julia, The [1949] A.C. 293 .... [1987] 183; [1989] 422
Julianae Shipping Corp. *v*. Amalgamet Inc., *re* M.V. *Kapetan Antonis* (1988) S.M.A. No. 2516 .... [1989] 356
Julius Young Manufacturing Co. *v*. Delta Airlines, 414 N.Y.S. 2d 528 (1979) .... [1986] 292

Junior K, The (1988) 25 February, unrep. .... [1988] 439
Junior Books Ltd. *v.* Veitchi Co. Ltd. [1983] 1 A.C. 520 .... [1986] 97, 232, 302, 303; [1987] 236; [1988] 252, 260, 406, 470, 505; [1989] 1, 55; [1990] 318, 485
Just *v.* Chambers, 312 U.S. 383, 388; 61 S. Ct. 687, 691; 1941 A.M.C. 430, 433 (1941) .... [1986] 19
Kabelmetal (*Re*) [1975] 2 C.M.L.R. D40 .... [1988] 265
Kacianoff *v.* China Traders Ins. Co. [1914] 3 K.B. 1121 .... [1986] 119
Kafiristan, The [1938] A.C. 136 .... [1986] 313, 327, 344
Kahler *v.* Midland Bank [1950] A.C. 24 .... [1989] 365; [1990] 550
Kalantiao, The, 1987 (4) S.A. 250 (D), 263 .... [1989] 175–181, 188
Kaleej International Pty. Ltd. *v.* Gulf Shipping Lines Ltd. (1986) 6 N.S.W.L.R. 569 .... [1987] 260; [1988] 285
Kalemian *v.* Liberty Mutual Fire Ins. Co., 1963 A.M.C. 1730 .... [1986] 492
Kalfelis *v.* Schröder, Münchmeyer, Hengst & Co., Case No. 189/87, 27 September 1988; *The Times*, 5 October 1988 .... [1989] 132; [1990] 193
Kalliopi A, The [1988] 2 Lloyd's Rep. 101 (C.A.); [1987] 2 Lloyd's Rep. 263 .... [1990] 394
Kanchenjunga, The [1987] 2 Lloyd's Rep. 509; [1989] 1 Lloyd's Rep. 354; [1990] 1 Lloyd's Rep. 391 .... [1987] 408; [1988] 46; [1989] 415; [1990] 453
Kane (H.E.) Agencies Ltd. *v.* Coopers & Lybrand (1983) 22 N.B.R. (2d); 23 C.C.L.T. 233; 116 A.P.R. 374 (Q.B.) .... [1990] 425
Kapetan Antonis, The (*Re*) (1988) S.M.A. No. 2516 .... [1989] 356
Kapetan Markos N.L., The (No. 2) [1987] 2 Lloyd's Rep. 321 .... [1988] 468; [1989] 171
Karak Rubber Co. Ltd. *v.* Burden (No. 2) [1972] 1 W.L.R. 602 .... [1988] 443; [1989] 43, 336
Karfunkel *v.* Cie Nationale Air France (1977) 427 F. Supp. 971 (SDNY); 14 Avi. 17, 674 [1988] 218, 229
Karin Vatis, The [1988] 2 Lloyd's Rep. 330 .... [1989] 290
Karinjee Jivanjee & Co. *v.* William F. Malcolm & Co. (1926) 25 Ll.L.Rep. 28 .... [1987] 184
Karl Snider Trucking Ltd. *v.* P.G. du Quebec [1986] R.J.Q. 363 .... [1987] 84
Kartini, The (1984) S.M.A. No. 1958 .... [1989] 347, 348, 353, 355, 360
Kastellon, The [1978] 2 Lloyd's Rep. 203 .... [1988] 458
Katagum Wholesale Commodities Co. Ltd. *v.* The M.V. *Paz*, 1984 (3) S.A. 261(N) .... [1990] 9
Kate, The (1864) Br. & Lush. 218 .... [1989] 69
Kathmer Investment Ltd. *v.* Woolworths (Pty.) Ltd., 1970 (2) SA 498 (A) at 504 H .... [1987] 314
KDS Construction Services Pty. Ltd. (*Re*) [1986] 4 A.C.L.C. 250 .... [1990] 67, 68
Keech *v.* Sandford (1726) Sel.Cas.t.King (Macnaghten) 61 .... [1988] 134; [1989] 335
Keenan Bros. Ltd. (*Re*) [1985] I.R. 401; [1985] I.L.R.M. 254, 641 (S.C.); [1986] B.C.L.C. 242 .... [1987] 150; [1989] 194, 211
Keene Corp. *v.* Ins. Co. of North America, 597 F. Supp. 946, 953 (D.D.C. 1985) .... [1986] 83
Keene Corp. *v.* Ins. Co. of North America, 667 F. 2d 1034 (D.C. Cir. 1981), cert. denied 455 U.S. 1007 (1982) .... [1986] 88, 89
Kelly *v.* Solari (1841) 9 M. & W. 54 .... [1989] 305, 319, 320, 431, 439 *et seq.*
Kelo, The [1985] 2 Lloyd's Rep. 85 .... [1986] 304; [1987] 255; [1989] 163, 172
Kemp *v.* R. [1988] Q.B. 645 .... [1990] 413
Kendall (Henry) & Sons *v.* William Lillico & Sons Ltd. [1969] 2 A.C. 31 .... [1987] 400, 403
Kenerick Tractor Sales Ltd. *v.* Langille (1987) 43 D.L.R. (4th) 171 .... [1990] 17
Kennedy *v.* Panama, New Zealand and Australian Royal Mail Co. Ltd. (1867) L.R. 2 Q.B. 580 .... [1988] 300, 530; [1989] 432; [1990] 339
Kenney *v.* Ship *Cape York* (1989) 25 F.T.R. 139 (Can. F.C.) .... [1990] 100
Kenya Railways *v.* Antares Co. Pte. Ltd. (*The Antares*) [1986] 2 Lloyd's Rep. 626, 633; [1987] 1 Lloyd's Rep. 424; (1985) L.M.L.N. 162 .... [1986] 142; [1987] 146, 260
Kenyon Swansea Ltd. (*Re*) [1987] B.C.L.C. 514 .... [1988] 64
Kepitigalla Rubber Estates Ltd. *v.* National Bank of India [1909] 2 K.B. 1010, 1025–1026 .... [1986] 9
Kerasan, The, 1927 A.M.C. 577 (N.Y.A.D.) .... [1986] 485, 500
Ketteman *v.* Hensel Properties Ltd. [1987] A.C. 189 .... [1990] 172
Keyes *v.* Royal Bank of Canada [1947] S.C.R. 377 .... [1990] 251
Khalij Sky, The, 1986 (1) S.A. 485 (C) .... [1989] 12, 174, 175, 181, 187
Khedive, The (1882) 7 App. Cas. 795 .... [1990] 50
Khian Captain (No. 2), The, [1986] 1 Lloyd's Rep. 429 .... [1989] 293
Khian Sea, The [1979] 1 Lloyd's Rep. 545 (C.A.) .... [1986] 115; [1988] 47
Kievet *v.* Loyal Protective Life Ins. Co., 34 N.J. 475, 170 A 2d 22 (1961) .... [1986] 87
Kievet *v.* Loyal Protective Life Ins. Co., 65 Cal. 2d 263, 419 P. 2d 168, 54 Cal. Rptr. 104 (1966) .... [1986] 79
Kilsby *v.* Williams (1822) 5 B. & Ald. 815 .... [1990] 69

Kinahan's Trusts (*Re*) [1907] Ir. R. 321 .... [1989] 197
King, The *v*. Forty Nine Casks of Brandy (1836) 3 Hagg. 257 .... [1987] 269
King, The *v*. Two Casks of Tallow (1837) 3 Hagg. 294 .... [1987] 269
King *v*. Aetna Ins. Co., 1931 A.M.C. 1940 (2 C.A.) .... [1986] 499
King *v*. Greig [1931] V.L.R. 413 .... [1990] 272
King *v*. Victoria Ins. Co. Ltd. [1896] A.C. 250 (P.C.) .... [1989] 9
Kingalock, The (1854) 1 Spinks E. & A. 263 .... [1986] 312, 317, 321; [1989] 67, 74
Kings North Trust Ltd. *v*. Bell [1986] 1 W.L.R. 119 .... [1987] 125; [1988] 436; [1990] 338
Kingston *v*. Preston (1773) 2 Doug. 689; 99 E.R. 437 .... [1988] 409
Kingston Cotton Mill Co. (No. 2) (*Re*) [1986] 2 Ch. 279 .... [1990] 423
Kinlan *v*. Ulster Bank Ltd. [1928] I.R. 171 .... [1988] 139
Kirchner & Co. *v*. Gruban [1909] 1 Ch. 413 .... [1987] 311
Kiriri Cotton Co. Ltd. *v*. Dewani [1960] A.C. 192 (P.C.) .... [1987] 207; [1989] 441
Kitchen *v*. RAFA [1958] 1 W.L.R. 563 (C.A.) .... [1990] 138
Klein *v*. Unidentified Wrecked and Abandoned Sailing Vessel, 758 F. 2d 1511 (11th Cir., 1985); 568 F. Supp. 1562, 1655 (S.D. Fla., 1983) .... [1987] 24
Kleinjan & Holst N.V. Rotterdam *v*. Bremer Handelsgesellschaft m.b.H. Hamburg [1972] 2 Lloyd's Rep. 11 .... [1988] 458
Kleinwort, Sons & Co. *v*. Dunlop Rubber Co. (1907) 94 L.T. 263 .... [1989] 303, 313
Kleinwort Benson Ltd. *v*. Malaysia Mining Corp. Bhd. [1988] 1 W.L.R. 799; [1989] 1 W.L.R. 379 (C.A.) .... [1988] 290; [1989] 281 *et seq*.; [1990] 210
Kleinwort Benson Ltd. *v*. Sherkate Sahami Sakht (*The Myrto*) (No. 2) [1984] 2 Lloyd's Rep. 341 .... [1989] 8
Klos *v*. Mobil Oil Co., 55 N.J. 1171, 259 A. 2d 889 (1969) .... [1986] 87
Knauer *v*. Callens [1978] II Pas. Belge 871 .... [1988] 385
Knickerbocker Ice Co. *v*. Stewart, 253 U.S. 149 (1920) .... [1987] 118
Knight *v*. U.S. Fire Ins., Docket No. 83 Civ. 5102 (10 February 1986, S.D.N.Y.) .... [1986] 505
Knight of St. Michael, The [1898] 8 Asp. M.L.C. P. 30; 360; 3 Com. Cas. 62 .... [1987] 458
Kodros Shipping Corp. *v*. Empresa Cubana de Fletes (*The Evia (No. 2)*) [1981] 2 Lloyd's Rep. 613, 620, [1982] 1 Lloyd's Rep. 334, 338 (C.A.); [1983] 1 A.C. 736 .... [1986] 112, 114, 115, 116, 122, 124, 149; [1988] 45
Kolfor Plant Hire Ltd. *v*. Tilbury Plant Hire Ltd. *The Times*, 17 May 1977; discussed in (1978) 128 N.L.J. 763 .... [1987] 53, 62, 78
Komatsu Ltd. *v*. States Steamship Co., 674 F. 2d 806, 1982 A.M.C. 2152 (9 Cir. 1982) .... [1986] 367
Koragang Cement Pty. Ltd. *v*. Australian Shipping Commission (Unrep., judgment 10 February 1986) .... [1986] 285
Korchenski (S.R.), Deputy Marshal *v*. *The Galaxias*, 1989 A.M.C. 348; [1989] 1 F.C. 375 (Can. F.C.) .... [1990] 101
Korean Airlines Disaster of September 1, 1983 (*Re*) (*sub nom*. Chan *et al*. *v*. Korean Air Lines Ltd. (No. 87–1055, U.S. Sup. Ct.)); (1987) 829 F. 2d 1171; (1985) 664 F. Supp. 1463 .... [1988] 151; [1989] 269
Kosak *v*. United States, 465 U.S. 848 (1984) .... [1987] 512
Koskas *v*. Standard Marine Insurance Co. Ltd. (1927) 27 Ll.L.Rep. 59 .... [1987] 536
Kossick *v*. United Fruit Co., 365 U.S. 731, 1961 A.M.C. 833 (U.S.S. Ct.) ... [1986] 488, 505; [1987] 123
Kostas K, The [1985] 1 Lloyd's Rep. 231 .... [1986] 66
Koufos *v*. C. Czarnikow Ltd. (*The Heron II*) [1969] 1 A.C. 350 .... [1986] 338
Kovacs *v*. Cooper, 336 U.S. 77, 96 (1949) .... [1986] 76
Kratzmann (N.A.) Pty. Ltd. *v*. Tucker (1968) 123 C.L.R. 295 .... [1990] 220
Krell *v*. Henry [1903] 2 K.B. 740 .... [1988] 115
Kristiansands Tankrederi A/S *v*. Standard Tankers (Bahamas) Ltd. (*The Polyglory*) [1977] 2 Lloyd's Rep. 353 .... [1988] 50
Krohn & Co. *v*. Mitsui & Co. [1978] 2 Lloyd's Rep. 419 .... [1987] 184
Kruger & Co. *v*. Moel Tryvan S.S. Co. [1907] A.C. 272 .... [1986] 121
Kruger Inc. *v*. Baltic Shipping Co. [1988] 1 F.C. 262 (F.C.) .... [1989] 93
Kruger Inc. *v*. Naviera Lavinel C.A. and the M.V. *Maria Elena* (1988) 15 F.T.R. 123; 1988 AMC 554; 1988 E.T.L. 57 (F.C.) .... [1989] 93
Kruppstahl A.G. *v*. Quitmann Products Ltd. [1982] I.L.R.M. 551 .... [1988] 147
Krystal *v*. British Overseas Airways Corporation (1975) 403 F. Supp. 1322 (Cal. D.C.); 14 Avi. 17, 128 .... [1988] 229
K/S Arnt J. Moreland *v*. Kuwait Petroleum Corp. (*The Fjordaas*) [1988] 1 Lloyd's Rep. 336 . [1989] 266
Kum *v*. Wah Tat Bank Ltd. [1971] 1 Lloyd's Rep. 439 .... [1989] 167

Kuniang, The, 1986 AMC 1184, reversing 774 F. 2d 648 (4th Cir.) .... [1989] 359
Kusu Island, The [1985] 1 M.L.J. 342; 14 September 1989 (Sing. C.A.) .... [1985] 309; [1990] 169, 170
Kwei Tek Chao *v*. British Traders & Shippers Ltd. [1954] 2 Q.B. 459 .... [1988] 458; [1990] 273
Kyoju Maru, The, 1984 (4) SA 210(D) .... [1986] 279
Kyzikos, The [1987] 1 Lloyd's Rep. 48; [1987] 1 W.L.R. 1565; [1988] 3 W.L.R. 858 (H.L.) ....[1989] 263 *et seq*.; [1990] 384, 388, 393
La Banque Financière de la Cité S.A. *v*. Westgate Ins. Co. Ltd. (formerly named Hodge General & Mercantile Ins. Co. Ltd.) [1988] 2 Lloyd's Rep. 513 .... [1989] 247, 251 *et seq*.
La Compania Martiartu *v*. Royal Exchange Ass. Corp. [1923] 1 K.B. 650 ....[1989] 26
La Pintada, The [1985] A.C. 104; [1984] 2 Lloyd's Rep. 9 (H.L.) ....[1986] 73, 76, 140; [1987] 415; [1988] 177
La Pointe, The [1986] 2 Lloyd's Rep. 513 (B.C.S.C.) ....[1988] 87
Lacey (William) (Hounslow) Ltd. *v*. Davis [1957] 1 W.L.R. 932 .... [1990] 503
Lacks *v*. Fidelity & Casualty Co., 306 N.Y. 357, 118 N.D. 2d 555 (1954) ....[1986] 87
Lac Minerals Ltd. *v*. International Corona Services Ltd. (1989) 61 D.L.R. (4th) 14 .... [1990] 4, 460
Laconia, The [1977] 1 Lloyd's Rep. 315; [1977] A.C. 850 ....[1986] 123, 149, 214, 405; [1988] 373, 481; [1989] 367; [1990] 83
Ladbroke & Co. *v*. Todd (1914) 30 T.L.R. 433 ....[1989] 41
Lady Katherine Barham, The (1861) 5 L.T. 693 ....[1989] 73
Lady Worsley, The (1855) 2 Sp. 253 ....[1989] 72
Lagunas Nitrate Co. *v*. Lagunas Syndicate [1899] 2 Ch. 392 .... [1986] 318
Lake *v*. Bayliss [1974] 1 W.L.R. 1073 .... [1987] 436
Laker Airways Ltd. *v*. Department of Trade [1977] Q.B. 643 .... [1986] 409
Lambert *v*. Lewis [1982] A.C. 225 .... [1988] 502
Lamdon Trust *v*. Hurrell [1955] 1 W.L.R. 391 ....[1990] 19
Lamine *v*. Dorrell (1701) 2 Ld. Ray. 1216 .... [1987] 430
Lamson Store Service Co. Ltd. *v*. Russell Wilkins & Sons Ltd. (1906) 4 (1) C.L.R. 672 (H.C.A.) ....[1990] 22
Lamson Store Service Co. Ltd. *v*. Weidenback & Co. Trustees (1904) 7 W.A.L.R. 166 (W.A. Full Ct.) ....[1990] 22
Lancaster, The [1980] 2 Lloyd's Rep. 497, 500 .... [1986] 150; [1988] 150
Landall Holdings Ltd. *v*. Caratti [1970] 3 W.A.R. 97, 108 .... [1986] 522
Lane County Escrow Service Inc. *v*. Smith, 560 P. 2d 608 (Ore.) .... [1990] 332
Langille *v*. Keneric Tractor Sales Ltd. [1987] 2 S.C.R. 440; *sub nom*. Keneric Tractor Sales Ltd. *v*. Langille (1987) 43 D.L.R. (4th) 171; (1985) 67 N.S.R. (2d) 404, 406–408 .... [1988] 277
Lansco Inc. *v*. Dept. of Environment Protection, 350 A. 2d 520 (N.J. Ch. 1975), aff'd 363 A. 2d 363 N.J. App. Div., cert. denied 372 A. 2d 322 (N.J. 1977) ....[1986] 92
Lariza (Singapore) Pte. Ltd. *v*. Bank Negara Indonesia (Singap. C.A., p. 70) .... [1987] 545
Larner *v*. L.C.C. [1949] 2 K.B. 683 .... [1989] 304
Laura Prima, The [1982] 1 Lloyd's Rep. 1 (H.L.) .... [1986] 55, 253; [1989] 263, 265
Laurelgates Ltd. *v*. Lombard North Central Ltd. (1983) 33 N.L.J. 720 .... [1990] 366
Lauritzen *v*. Larsen, 345 U.S. 571; 1953 A.M.C. 1210 ....[1986] 23
Lauritzen (J.) A.S. *v*. Wijsmuller B.V. (*The Super Servant Two*) [1989] 1 Lloyd's Rep. 148; [1990] 1 Lloyd's Rep. 1 .... [1989] 3; [1990] 153
Lauritzen (J.) A.S. *v*. Wijsmuller B.V. (*The Dan King*) (1988) L.M.L.N. 225 ....[1989] 3 *et seq*.
Law *v*. Garret (1878) 8 Ch. D. 26 .... [1987] 311
Law *v*. Hollingsworth (1797) 7 T.R. 160 .... [1988] 331
Lawyers Title and Guarantee Co. (*Re*) (1945) 58 N.Y.S. 2d 857 .... [1989] 317
L'Estrange *v*. F. Graucob Ltd. [1934] 2 K.B. 394 .... [1986] 315; [1990] 284, 341
Le Cheminant *v*. Pearson (1812) 4 Taunt. 367 .... [1986] 438
Leaf *v*. International Galleries [1950] 2 K.B. 86 .... [1986] 318; [1990] 459
Leage, The, S.M.A. No. 1320 (1979) ....[1986] 72
Leakey *v*. National Trust [1980] Q.B. 485 (C.A.) .... [1987] 56, 64, 78
Learoyd Bros. & Co. *v*. Pope & Sons (Dock Carriers) Ltd. [1966] 2 Lloyd's Rep. 142 .... [1988] 467
Leda, The (1856) Swab. 40 ....[1989] 70
Leduc *v*. Ward (1888) 20 Q.B.D. 475 .... [1988] 286
Lee *v*. York Coach and Marine [1977] R.T.R. 35 .... [1990] 366
Lee Cooper Ltd. *v*. C.H. Jeakins & Sons Ltd. [1967] 2 Q.B. 1 .... [1988] 467
Leeds Shipping Co. *v*. Francaise Bunge (*The Eastern City*) [1958] 2 Lloyd's Rep. 127, 131 ...... [1988] 45
Legatus, The (1856) Swab. 168 ....[1989] 68

Legione *v*. Hateley (1983) 152 C.L.R. 406 .... [1989] 87
Leigh and Sillivan Ltd. *v*. Aliakmon Shipping Co. Ltd. (*The Aliakmon*) [1985] Q.B. 350 (C.A.); [1986] 2 W.L.R. 902; [1986] A.C. 785 (H.L.) .... [1986] 97, 232; [1987] 9, 54, 84, 238, 255; [1988] 257, 259, 366, 505; [1989] 5, 54, 55, 117, 167, 237; [1990] 317
Leise Maersk, The [1958] 2 Lloyd's Rep. 341 .... [1986] 144
Lem *v*. Barotto Sports Ltd. (1977) 69 D.L.R. (3) 276 (Alb. S.C.) .... [1988] 510
Lenfest *v*. Coldwell, 1975 A.M.C. 2489 (2 C.A.) .... [1986] 485, 490
Leni, The, Hamburg Award 8.6.1977 .... [1990] 390
Lensen S.S. Co. *v*. Anglo-Soviet S.S. Co. (1935) 40 Com. Cas. 320, 329 .... [1988] 58
Leon Blum, The [1915] P. 90 .... [1986] 344
Leon *v*. Casey [1932] 2 K.B. 576 .... [1986] 284
Leonidas D, The [1985] 1 W.L.R. 925; [1985] 2 Lloyd's Rep. 18 (C.A.) .... [1986] 68, 105; [1987] 67, 155, 264; [1988] 304, 307
Leppo *v*. Trans World Airlines Inc. (1977) 392 N.Y.S. 2d 660; *cf*. 1976 U.S. Aviation Reports 23 ... 222
Leslie (R.) Ltd. *v*. Sheill [1914] 3 K.B. 607 .... [1990] 336
Les Produits Alimentaires Grandma *v*. Zim Israel Nav., 1987 A.M.C. 1474 (F.C.) .... [1988] 85
Lessors (Aust.) Pty. Ltd. *v*. Westley [1965] N.S.W.R. 2091 .... [1990] 20
Letnik *v*. Toronto (Municipality of) [1988] 2 F.C. 399 (Fed. C.A.) .... [1990] 99
Lever Bros. Ltd. *v*. Bell [1931] 1 K.B. 557 .... [1989] 446
Levison *v*. Patent Steam Carpet Cleaning Co. Ltd. [1978] Q.B. 69 (C.A.) .... [1986] 158; [1987] 49
Levy Bros. Co. Ltd. *v*. The Queen [1959] 20 D.L.R. (2d) 459, 26 D.L.R. (2d) 760 .... [1986] 432
Lewes Sanitary Steam Laundry Co. Ltd. *v*. Barclay & Co. Ltd. (1906) 95 L.T. 444 .... [1986] 9
Lewis *v*. Averay [1972] 1 Q.B. 198 .... [1986] 323; [1989] 437, 442
Leyland Shipping Co. Ltd. *v*. Norwich Union Fire Insurance Society Ltd. [1918] A.C. 350 .... [1986] 40; [1988] 338
L.H. Charles & Co. Ltd. (*Re*) [1935] W.N. 15 .... [1990] 533
Liberian Insurance Agency *v*. Mosse [1977] 2 Lloyd's Rep. 560 .... [1986] 449
Liberian Shipping Corp. "Pegasus" *v*. A. King & Sons Ltd. (*The Pegasus*) [1967] 2 Q.B. 86 . [1986] 144
Liberian Vertex Transports Inc. *v*. Associated Bulk Carriers Ltd., 738 F. 2d 85, 86–87, 1984 A.M.C. 2841, 2843–45 (2 Cir. 1984) .... [1986] 358, 536
Libyan Arab Foreign Bank *v*. Bankers Trust Co. [1988] 1 Lloyd's Rep. 259; [1987] 2 F.T.L.R. 509 .... [1988] 1, 362, 371, 375; [1989] 242, 363 *et seq*.; [1990] 93
Libyan Arab Foreign Bank *v*. Manufacturers Hanover Trust Co. (No. 2) [1989] 1 Lloyd's Rep. 608 .... [1990] 81
Lickbarrow *v*. Mason (1784) 5 T.R. 683 .... [1989] 162
Lietz *v*. The Queen [1985] 1 F.C. 845 .... [1987] 92
Life Savers (Australasia) Pty. Ltd. *v*. Frigmobile Pty. Ltd. [1983] 1 N.S.W.L.R. 431 .... [1986] 105; [1987] 166
Lightburn *v*. Belmont Sales Ltd. (1969) 6 D.L.R. (3d) 692 .... [1990] 377, 379
Lightly *v*. Clouston (1808) 1 Taunt. 112 .... [1987] 433
Lilley *v*. Doubleday (1881) 7 Q.B.D. 510 .... [1988] 34
Lilly *v*. Stevenson (1895) 22 Rett. 278 .... [1988] 250
Limako B.V. *v*. Hentz & Co. Inc. [1978] 2 Lloyd's Rep. 400 .... [1986] 391
Lincoln Grain Inc. *v*. Coopers & Lybrand (1984) 216 Neb. 433; 345 N.W. 2d 300 .... [1990] 422, 426
Lincoln Pulpwood Co. Ltd. (The) *v*. M/V *Rio Casma* [1935] Ex. C.R. 123 .... [1988] 86
Lind (Peter) & Co. Ltd. *v*. Mersey Docks and Harbour Board [1972] 2 Lloyd's Rep. 234 ..... [1990] 503
Linda, The [1988] 1 Lloyd's Rep. 175 .... [1990] 278
Linda, The (1987) L.M.L.N. 210 (21 November 1987) .... [1988] 96
Lin Securities Pte. Ltd. (*Re*) (1988) 2 M.L.J. 137 .... [1989] 244
Lion Laboratories Ltd. *v*. Evans [1985] Q.B. 526 .... [1989] 159
Lipkin Gorman *v*. Cass (1985) *The Times*, 29 May .... [1986] 412
Lipkin Gorman *v*. Karpnale Ltd. and Lloyds Bank Plc (1986) 136 N.L.J. 659; [1987] 1 W.L.R. 987 ..[1987] 14; [1988] 56, 365, 443; [1989] 297, 301, 303, 309, 310, 316, 321, 329, 330, 331, 335, 339
Lipkin Gorman *v*. Karpnale Ltd. [1989] 1 W.L.R. 1340 .... [1990] 417
Lips, The, [1987] 3 W.L.R. 572; [1987] 2 W.L.R. 906 .... [1987] 414, 415; [1988] 177
Lisboa, The [1980] 2 Lloyd's Rep. 546 .... [1987] 396, 540
Lista, The (1946) 79 Ll. L. Rep. 401 .... [1986] 347
Lister *v*. Forth Dry Dock and Engineering Co. Ltd. [1989] I.C.R. 341 .... [1990] 412
Lister *v*. Romford Ice and Cold Storage Co. Ltd. [1957] A.C. 555 .... [1988] 407; [1989] 43, 236; [1990] 445

Lister *v.* Stubbs (1890) 45 Ch. D. 1 .... [1987] 436, 440; [1988] 128, 131; [1989] 196; [1990] 286, 463
Litsion Pride, The [1985] 1 Lloyd's Rep. 437 .... [1987] 8; [1989] 257; [1990] 560
Litt *v.* Martindale (1856) 18 C.B. 314 .... [1989] 318
Little Joe, The (1860) Lush. 88 .... [1989] 67, 69
Lively, The (1848) 3 W. Rob. 64 .... [1989] 67
Liverpool and London War Risks Assoication Ltd. *v.* Ocean Steamship Co. Ltd. (*The Priam*) [1948] A.C. 243 .... [1987] 31
Liverpool City Council *v.* Irwin [1977] A.C. 239 .... [1988] 127, 506; [1989] 42, 171, 259
Lloyd *v.* Grace, Smith & Co. [1912] A.C. 716 .... [1986] 109
Lloyd Cheyham *v.* Littlejohn [1987] B.C.L.C. 303 .... [1990] 256, 259, 260
Lloyds and Scottish Finance Ltd. *v.* Cyril Lord Ltd. (1979) 129 N.L.J. 366 .... [1989] 208, 211
Lloyds Bank Ltd. *v.* Bundy [1975] 1 Q.B. 326 .... [1986] 313; [1988] 367, 419
Lloyd's Bank Plc *v.* Waterhouse, *The Independent*, 27 February 1990 .... [1990] 338
Loblaw Inc. *v.* Employers Liability Assurance Corp., 85 A.D. 2d 880, 446 N.Y.S. 2d 743 (4th Dept. 1981) .... [1986] 84
Local 149, Boot & Shoe Workers Union *v.* Faith Shoe Co., 201 F. Supp. 234 (M.D. Pa. 1962) [1986] 68
Loch Tulla, The (1950) 84 Ll. L. Rep. 62, 69 .... [1986] 330, 334, 340
Lock *v.* Portsmouth Co. (1905) 141 Fed. Rep. 182 .... [1988] 52
Lockwoods, The (1845) 9 Jur. 1017 .... [1989] 64, 77
Logan *v.* Bank of Scotland (No. 2) [1906] 1 K.B. 141 .... [1987] 311
Logicrose Ltd. *v.* Southend Football Club [1988] 1 W.L.R. 1256 .... [1989] 303, 336
Lombank Ltd. *v.* Cook [1962] 1 W.L.R. 1133 .... [1990] 21
Lombank Ltd. *v.* Excell [1964] 1 Q.B. 415 .... [1990] 19
Lombard North Central Plc *v.* Butterworth [1987] 2 W.L.R. 7; [1987] Q.B. 527 (C.A.) ...... [1987] 143; [1988] 279; [1989] 502; [1990] 470
London, Chatham and Dover Railway Co. *v.* South Eastern Railway Co. [1893] A.C. 429 .... [1987] 416; [1988] 177
London & Cheshire Insurance Co. Ltd. *v.* Laplagrene Property Co. Ltd. [1971] Ch. 499 ...... [1990] 525
London and Counties Securities (in liquidation) *v.* Caplan, 26 May 1978 (unreported) .... [1990] 94, 95, 96
London and General Bank (No. 2) (*Re*) [1895] 2 Ch. 673 .... [1990] 264, 421
London Borough of Bromley *v.* Ellis [1971] 1 Lloyd's Rep. 97 .... [1986] 202
London Borough of Southwark *v.* Charlesworth (1983) 147 J.P. (Rep.) 470 .... [1989] 373
London Joint Stock Bank Ltd. *v.* Macmillan [1918] A.C. 777 .... [1986] 8; [1988] 363
London School of Electronics Ltd. (*Re*) [1986] Ch. 211 .... [1988] 66, 68; [1990] 411
London Wine Company (Shippers) Ltd. (*Re*) (1975), unreported .... [1989] 116
London Wine Co. (*Re*) [1986] P.C.C. 121 .... [1989] 421, 429
Long Island Tankers Corp. *v.* S.S. *Kaimana*, 265 F. Supp. 723, 1967 A.M.C. 2467, 2470–71 (N.D. Cal. 1967), aff'd *per curiam* on opinion below *sub nom.* Cross *v.* S.S. *Kaimana*, 401 F. 2d 182 (9 Cir. 1968), cert. denied, 393 U.S. 1095 (1969) .... [1986] 356
Lonrho *v.* Bond (No. 2) (1989) 5 B.C.C. 776 .... [1990] 407, 414
Lorac Transport Ltd. *v.* The *Atra* [1985] 1 F.C. 459; [1987] 1 F.C. 108 (Fed. C.A.) . [1987] 96; [1988] 87
Lord Chesham (*Re*) (1886) 31 Ch. D. 466 474
Lotus, The (Case of) (1927) P.C.I.J., Ser. A, No. 10 .... [1990] 89
Louisa, The (1842) 7 Jur. 182 .... [1989] 71
Louisa, The (1843) 2 W. Rob. 22 .... [1989] 76
Louisa, The (1848) 3 W. Rob. 99 .... [1989] 74
Louisa, The (1863) Br. & Lush. 59 .... [1989] 70
Louisiana Ship Management Inc. (*In re*), Civ. No. 85–2321, 14 May 1985 .... [1986] 354
Louisville and Nashville Rd. Co. *v.* M/V *Bayou Lacombe*, 597 F. 2d 469 (5th Cir., 1979) ..... [1987] 511
Loveland (S.C.) Co. *v.* U.S.A., 1963 A.M.C. 260 .... [1990] 173
Lowe *v.* Ingalls Shipbuilding, 723 F. 2d 1173 (5 Cir. 1984) .... [1986] 373
Lowery *v.* Tug *Ellen S. Bouchard*, 128 F. Supp. 16, 1955 A.M.C. 572 (N.D.N.Y. 1955) .... [1986] 379
Lowry (F.A.) *v.* Conn Fire Ins. Co., 1934 A.M.C. 581 (2 C.A.) .... [1986] 495
Lubbock *v.* Potts (1806) 7 East 449 .... [1987] 214
Lucena *v.* Craufurd (1806) 2 Bos. & P.N.R. 269 .... [1990] 560
Lucille, The [1984] 1 Lloyd's Rep. 244 (C.A.); [1983] 1 Lloyd's Rep. 387 .... [1986] 121, 126, 149; [1988] 46
Luis de Ridder Ltda. S.A.C. *v.* Nivose Societa di Navigazione (1935) 53 Ll. L. Rep. 21 .... [1986] 144
Luisi and Carbone, Joined Cases 286/82 and 26/83, judgment of 31 January 1984; [1984] E.C.R. 377 .... [1990] 177

Luisi and Carbone *v.* Ministero del Tesoro [1985] 3 C.M.L.R. 52 .... [1988] 420
Luna, The (1919) 1 Ll. L. Rep. 475 .... [1986] 316
Lundie Bros. Ltd. (*Re*) [1965] 1 W.L.R. 1051 .... [1988] 61; [1990] 410
Lundquist Rederierna A/B *v.* Great Northern Paper Co. [1983] 1 F.C. 350 (Fed. C.A. 1982) [1988] 111
Lundy *v.* Litton Systems Inc., 624 F. 2d 590 (5 Cir.), reh'g denied, 629 F.2d 1349 (5 Cir. 1980), cert. denied, 450 U.S. 913 (1981) .... [1986] 373
Lusitania, The [1986] Q.B. 384 .... [1987] 267
Luxor (Eastbourne) Ltd. *v.* Cooper [1941] A.C. 108 .... [1989] 171
Lykes Brothers S.S. Co. *v.* Tug *Bayou La Fourche* 1974 A.M.C. 1783 (S.D. Tex.) .... [1988] 518
Lyus *v.* Prowsa Developments Ltd. [1982] 1 W.L.R. 1044 .... [1990] 530
Maasdam, The (1893) 7 Asp. M.L.C. 400 .... [1986] 329, 334
Macaura *v.* Northern Assurance Co. Ltd. [1925] A.C. 619 .... [1989] 236; [1990] 135, 443
MacDonald *v.* Air Canada (1971) 439 F. 2d 1402 (1st Cir.); 11 Avi. 18, 029 .... [1988] 223
MacDonald *v.* Prudential Assurance Co. Ltd. (1972) 24 D.L.R. (3d) 185 (S. Ct., New Brunswick) .... [1987] 212
Maché *v.* Cie Air France (1966) 20 R.F.D.A. 228 (Cour de Cass.) .... [1988] 223
Mackay *v.* Dick (1881) 6 App. Cas. 251 .... [1986] 332; [1988] 409
Mackender *v.* Feldia A.G. [1967] 2 Q.B. 590 .... [1986] 260–261, 319; [1987] 211; [1990] 192
Mackeney *v.* Ramsays, Bonars & Co. (1843) 9 C. & F. 818 .... [1990] 550, 551
Mackenzie *v.* Imperial Bank [1938] 2 D.L.R. 764 .... [1986] 8
Mackersy *v.* Ramsays, Bonar & Co. (1843) 9 Cl. & F. 846, 851 .... [1986] 200
MacKinnon *v.* Canada (Fisheries and Oceans) [1987] 1 F.C. 490 (F.C.) .... [1988] 89
Mackinnon *v.* Donaldson, Lufkin & Jenrette Securities Corp. [1986] Ch. 482 .... [1988] 362; [1989] 364, 369, 469; [1990] 93, 95
Maclaine Watson & Co. Ltd. *v.* Dept. of Trade and Industry [1988] 3 W.L.R. 1169; [1988] 3 All E.R. 359 (C.A.); affirming *sub nom. Re* International Tin Council [1987] 1 All E.R. 890 .... [1990] 306
Maclaine Watson & Co. Ltd. *v.* International Tin Council (No. 2) [1989] Ch. 286; [1987] 1 W.L.R. 1711; [1988] 3 All E.R. 376 (C.A.) ....[1989] 467, 470, 475; [1990] 306, 323
Macrae (P. & J.) Ltd. (*In re*) [1961] 1 W.L.R. 229 .... [1986] 385
MacRobertson Miller Airline Services *v.* Commissioner of State Taxation (WA) (1975) 133 C.L.R. 125 .... [1989] 220; [1990] 165
MacShannon *v.* Rockware Glass Ltd. [1978] A.C. 795 ....[1986] 513; [1987] 2, 393; [1988] 91
Macy & Co., *In re*, 39 N.Y. 2d 268, 271 (1976) .... [1986] 68
Magdalen, The (1861) 31 L.J. Adm. 22 .... [1989] 71, 72
Magee *v.* Pennine Insurance Co. Ltd. [1969] 2 Q.B. 507 .... [1988] 301; [1989] 431, 437 *et seq.*, 445
Maggie Hammond, The, 76 U.S. (9 Wall.) 435 (1869) .... [1987] 152
Magnolia, The Steamboat, 53 U.S. (12 How.) 466 (1851) .... [1987] 497
Magnus *v.* Buttermer (1852) 11 C.B. 876; 138 E.R. 720 .... [1986] 39
Mahesan *v.* Malaysia Housing Society [1979] A.C. 374 .... [1987] 429
Mahfoud *v.* Eastern Air Lines Inc. (1984) 729 F. 2d 777 (5th Cir.) .... [1988] 179
Mahmoud and Ispahani (*In re*) [1921] 2 K.B. 716 (C.A.) ....[1987] 202, 203, 204, 205
Mahoney *v.* Lindsay (1980) 55 A.L.J.R. 118 .... [1989] 84
Maira, The [1982] 1 Lloyd's Rep. 257 .... [1989] 40
Maira, The [1989] 3 W.L.R. 185 .... [1990] 318
Maira, The (No. 2) [1986] 2 Lloyd's Rep. 12 .... [1989] 40
Maira, The (No. 3) [1988] 2 Lloyd's Rep. 126; [1990] A.C. 637 .... [1989] 40 *et seq.*, 171; [1990] 489
Makefjell, The [1976] 1 Lloyd's Rep. 29 .... [1986] 97
Malente, The, Award 19 November 1982, unreported .... [1990] 385, 390
Malilang *v.* M.V. Houda Pearl 1986 (3) S.A. 960 (A) .... [1990] 493
Man (E.D. & F.) Ltd. *v.* Nigerian Sweets & Confectionery Co. Ltd. [1977] 2 Lloyd's Rep. 50 . [1990] 66
Manchester, The, 1981 (2) S.A. 798 (C.) .... [1988] 16
Manchester Trust *v.* Furness [1895] 2 Q.B. 539 .... [1989] 165
Manhattan Novelty Corp. *v.* Seaboard and Western Airlines Inc. (1958) 5 Avi. Cas. 17229 (N.Y.S.C.) .... [1989] 38
Manhattan Prince, The [1985] 1 Lloyd's Rep. 140 .... [1990] 108
Manila, The [1988] 3 All E.R. 843 .... [1989] 397 *et seq.*, 402
Manion *v.* Pan American World Airways Inc. (1980) 15 Avi. 18, 337 (N.Y.S.C.), on appeal (1981) 16 Avi. 17, 473 .... [1988] 221
Manlon Trading Ltd. (*Re*) (1988) 4 B.C.C. 455 .... [1990] 414
Mann, Macneal & Steeves Ltd. *v.* Capital & Counties Ins. Co. Ltd. [1921] 2 K.B. 300 .... [1988] 257

Mantovani *v.* Carapelli [1980] 1 Lloyd's Rep. 375 .... [1987] 397
Manurewa Transport Ltd. (*Re*) [1971] N.Z.L.R. 909 .... [1990] 540
Manus Asia Co. Inc. *v.* Standard Chartered Bank, 22 September 1988, unreported .... [1989] 369
Maralinga Pty. Ltd. *v.* Major Enterprises Pty. Ltd. [1973] 128 C.L.R. 336 .... [1986] 316
Marandoo, The [1986] 4 A.N.Z. Insurance Cases 60–697 .... [1986] 287
Maratha Envoy, The [1977] 2 Lloyd's Rep. 301; [1975] 1 W.L.R. 1372 .... [1986] 51, 258, 259
Marbrook Freight Ltd. *v.* K.M.I. (London) Ltd. [1979] 2 Lloyd's Rep. 341 .... [1989] 39
Marc Rich & Co. A.G. *v.* Societa Italiana Impianti P.A. (*The Atlantic Emperor*) [1989] 1 Lloyd's Rep. 54 .... [1990] 132
March Cabaret Club & Casino Ltd. *v.* London Assurance [1975] 1 Lloyd's Rep. 169 .[1987] 8; [1989] 257
Marchessini (P.D.) & Co. *v.* Oceanic Operations Corp., 1964 A.M.C. 1538, 227 F. Supp. 17 (S.D.N.Y. 1964) .... [1986] 13
Marcial Ucin S.A. *v.* S.S. *Galicia* (1983) 723 F. 2d 994 (1st Cir.) .... [1989] 352
Marcy Lee Mfg. Co. *v.* Cortley Fabrics Co., 354 F. 2d 42 (2 Cir. 1965) .... [1986] 72
Mardorf Peach & Co. Ltd. *v.* Attica Sea Carriers Corp. of Liberia (*The Laconia*) [1977] A.C. 850 .... [1986] 214; [1988] 373, 481; [1989] 367; [1990] 83
Mare del Nord, The [1990] 1 Lloyd's Rep. 40 .... [1990] 320
Marene Knitting Mills Pty. Ltd. *v.* Greater Pacific General Insurance Ltd. (1976) 11 A.L.R. 166, 172; [1976] 2 Lloyd's Rep. 631, 642 .... [1988] 30
Mareva, The [1975] 2 Lloyd's Rep. 509 .... [1986] 410; [1987] 320; [1990] 241, 286
Mareva Compania Naviera S.A. *v.* International Bulk Carriers S.A. (*The Mareva*) [1975] 2 Lloyd's Rep. 509 .... [1986] 410; [1987] 320; [1990] 241, 286
Mareva Navigation Co. Ltd. *v.* Canaria Armadora S.A. (*The Mareva A.S.*) [1977] 1 Lloyd's Rep. 368 .... [1989] 98; [1990] 107, 110
Margarine Union G.m.b.H. *v.* Cambay Prince S.S. Co. Ltd. (*The Wear Breeze*) [1969] 1 Q.B. 219 .... [1986] 97; [1987] 84; [1988] 40; [1989] 54
Maria das Dores, The (1863) Br. & Lush. 27 .... [1989] 66
Maria Stathatos, The, 84 F. Supp. 828 (S.D.N.Y. 1949) .... [1986] 344
Mariannina, The [1983] 1 Lloyd's Rep. 12 (C.A.) .... [1987] 530
Marilyn O, The (*Re*) (1987) S.M.A. No. 2402 .... [1989] 348
Marina di Cassano, The [1984] 2 Lloyd's Rep. 577 .... [1986] 72
Marine Leasing Servs. Inc. (*In re*), 328 F. Supp. 589, 598, 1971 A.M.C. 1329, 1344 (E.D. La. 1971), aff'd *per curiam*, 471 F. 2d 255, 1974 A.M.C. 534 (5 Cir. 1973) .... [1986] 379
Marine Midland Grace Trust Co. *v.* Banco del Pais S.A., 261 F. Supp. 884 (1966) .... [1986] 422
Marine Transit Corp. *v.* Dreyfus, 284 U.S. 263 (1932) .... [1986] 67
Marine Voyager, The *v.* O'Connell Construction (1988) 19 F.T.R. 233 (Can. F.C.) .... [1990] 103
Marintrans (A.B.) *v.* Comet Shipping Co. Ltd. (*The Shinjitsu Maru No. 5*) [1985] 1 W.L.R. 1270 .... [1990] 418
Mariola Marine Corp. *v.* Lloyd's Register of Shipping (*The Morning Watch*) [1990] 1 Lloyd's Rep. 547 .... [1990] 482
Marion, The [1984] A.C. 563 .... [1988] 523
Maritime Bulk Carriers *v.* Garnac Grain Co. (*The Polyfreedom*), 1975 A.M.C. 1826, S.M.A. No. 926 (1975) .... [1986] 57
Maritime Coastal Containers *v.* Shelburne Marine (1982) 52 N.S.R. (2d) 51 .... [1986] 230; [1987] 46, 57, 65, 66, 67, 68
Maritime National Fish Ltd. *v.* Ocean Trawlers Ltd. [1935] A.C. 524; [1934] 1 D.L.R. 621; [1934] 4 D.L.R. 288 .... [1989] 5; [1990] 156
Maritime Trader, The [1981] 2 Lloyd's Rep. 153 .... [1987] 540
Maritime Underwater Surveys Inc. *v.* Unidentified Wrecked and Abandoned Sailing Vessel, 717 F. 2d 6 (1st Cir., 1983) .... [1986] 19; [1987] 26
Mark Rowlands Ltd. *v.* Berni Inns Ltd. and others [1985] 2 Lloyd's Rep. 437; [1986] Q.B. 211 (C.A.) .... [1986] 123, 149; [1988] 57; [1990] 135, 560
Markappa Inc. *v.* N.W. Spratt & Son Ltd. (*The Arta*) [1985] 1 Lloyd's Rep. 534 .... [1988] 50
Markt & Co. Ltd. *v.* Knight Steamship Co. [1910] 2 K.B. 1021 .... [1989] 390
Marlex Petroleum Inc. *v.* The Ship *Har Rai*, 1984 A.M.C. 1649 (Can. Fed. Ct. App., Ottawa, 1984) .... [1986] 353
Marquardt *v.* French, 53 Fed. 603 (S.D.N.Y. 1893) .... [1986] 12
Marreco *v.* Richardson [1908] 2 K.B. 584 .... [1990] 66, 68
Marriott *v.* Hampton (1797) 7 T.R. 269; 2 Esp. 546; 2 Sm. L.C. 386 .... [1987] 430; [1989] 436
Marsh *v.* Keating (1834) 1 Bing. (N.C.) 198 .... [1989] 307, 319, 320
Marston *v.* American Employers Ins. Co., 439 F. 2d 1035, 1038 (1 Cir. 1971) .... [1986] 83

Marston Construction Co. Ltd. *v*. Kigass Ltd. [1989] *Construction Industry Law Letter* 476 .. [1989] 402
Martha, The (1859) Swab. 489 .... [1989] 62, 65, 72
Martin Luther, The (1857) Swab. 287 .... [1989] 65
Maru Shipping Co. *v*. Burmeister & Wain American Corp., 528 F. Supp. 210, 1982 A.M.C. 1320 (S.D.N.Y. 1981) .... [1986] 361
Marubeni Corp. *v*. Gearbulk Ltd. (1986) 4 F.T.R. 265 (F.C.) .... [1989] 97
Mary, The (1842) 1 W. Rob. 448 .... [1989] 77
Mary Lou, The [1981] 2 Lloyd's Rep. 272 .... [1986] 114; [1988] 47
Mary Pleasants, The (1857) Swab. 224 .... [1989] 61, 78
Mary T. Tracy, The (1920) 298 F. 528, 530 (S.D.N.Y.) .... [1988] 51
Maryland Casualty Co. *v*. Cushing, 347 U.S. 409, 1954 A.M.C. 837 (1954) .... [1986] 380
Marzetti *v*. Williams (1830) 1 B. & Ad. 415 .... [1988] 139
Mash & Murrell *v*. Joseph I. Emmanuel Ltd. [1962] 1 W.L.R. 16 .... [1986] 269
Maskell *v*. Horner [1915] 3 K.B. 106 .... [1990] 344
Massalia, The (No. 2) [1962] 2 Q.B. 416 .... [1990] 393, 395, 396
Massein *v*. The King [1935] 1 D.L.R. 701 .... [1986] 432
Mastro Giorgis, The [1983] 2 Lloyd's Rep. 66 .... [1990] 107, 108, 111, 112
Matter of Berkeley Curtis Bay Co., 557 F. Supp. 335, 1984 A.M.C. 1934 (S.D.N.Y. 1983), aff'd on other grounds *sub nom*. B.C. Bay Co. *v*. American Dredging Co., 742 F. 2d 1431, opinion published at 1984 A.M.C. 1941 (2 Cir. 1983) .... [1986] 375
Matter of Commonwealth Oil Refining Co., 734 F. 2d 1079 (5 Cir. 1984) .... [1986] 371
Matthes *v*. Carter (1955) 55 S.R. (N.S.W.) 357 .... [1990] 511
Matthew Ship Chartering Ltd. *v*. Industria Azucarera Nacional S.A., *re* M.V. *Marilyn O* (1987) S.M.A. No. 2402 .... [1989] 348
Matthews *v*. Williams, Brown & Co. (1894) 10 T.L.R. 386 .... [1989] 41
Maude, The (1876) 3 Asp. M.L.C. 338 .... [1986] 330, 331
Maugnie *v*. Cie Nationale Air France (1977) 549 F. 2d 1256 (9th Cir.); 14 Avi. 17, 534, cert. denied (1977) 431 U.S. 974 .... [1988] 222
Maurice Pincoffs Co. *v*. St. Paul Fire & Marine Ins. Co., 447 F. 2d 204 (5 Cir. 1971) .... [1986] 95
Mavor *v*. Pyne (1825) 3 Bing. 285 .... [1990] 514
Mayhew Foods Ltd. *v*. Overseas Containers Ltd. [1984] 1 Lloyd's Rep. 317 .... [1987] 219, 306
Mayne Nickless *v*. Pegler [1974] 1 N.S.W.L.R. 228, 239 .... [1988] 30; [1989] 236; [1990] 444
Maynegrain Pty. Ltd. *v*. Compafina Bank [1984] 1 N.S.W.L.R. 258 (P.C.); (1984) 58 A.L.J.R. 389 .... [1986] 218, 220; [1987] 44, 56, 126; [1988] 37
McAllister Lighterage Line *v*. I.N.A. & Scott Paper, 1957 A.M.C. 1774 (2 C.A.) .... [1986] 501
McCann *v*. Richmond Lodge Motors and Allied Irish Finance Co. (N.I.) Ltd. 1984 N.I.L.R. Bulletin of Judgments, No. 16, p. 11 (N.I. High Ct.) .... [1987] 76
McCarthy *v*. The Bark *Peking*, 716 F. 2d 130, 1984 A.M.C. 1 (2 Cir. 1983), cert. denied *sub nom*. South Street Seaport Museum *v*. McCarthy, 104 S. Ct. 1439 (1984) .... [1986] 372
McCullough *v*. McGrath's Stock & Poultry Ltd. [1981] 2 N.Z.L.R. 428 .... [1987] 326
McCutcheon *v*. MacBrayne [1964] 1 W.L.R. 125 .... [1990] 284
McDonald *v*. Dennys Lascelles Ltd. (1933) 48 C.L.R. 457 .... [1989] 291; [1990] 519
McDougall *v*. Aeromarine of Emsworth Ltd. [1958] 1 W.L.R. 1126 .... [1990] 377
McElderry *v*. Cathay Pacific Airways (1988) 21 Avi. 17, 159 .... [1988] 447
McEntire *v*. Crossley Bros. Ltd. [1895] A.C. 457 .... [1988] 148
McGuinness *v*. Bremner Plc [1988] B.C.L.C. 673 .... [1990] 415
McKenzie *v*. Bank of Montreal (1976) 70 D.L.R. (3d) 113 (Ontario C.A.) .... [1988] 367
McKinnon *v*. Acadian Lines Ltd. (1978) 81 D.L.R. (3d) 480 (N.S. Sup. Ct.), noted (1979) 57 Can. Bar Rev. 117 .... [1987] 45; [1988] 469
McRae *v*. Commonwealth Disposals Commission (1951) 84 C.L.R. 377 .... [1986] 316, 335, 336; [1988] 301; [1989] 442, 443; [1990] 456, 506
Mead *v*. Lord Orrery (1745) 3 Atk. 235 .... [1989] 321
Mears *v*. London & South West Railway Co. (1862) 11 C.B.N.S. 850 .... [1988] 39
Mears *v*. Western Canada Pulp & Paper Co. [1905] 2 Ch. 353 .... [1990] 67
Mechanisations Eaglescliffe Ltd. (*Re*) [1966] 1 Ch. 20 .... [1990] 534
Medora, The (1847) 5 N.o.C. 156 .... [1989] 59
Medora, The (1853) 1 Sp. 17 .... [1989] 61, 63
Meehan *v*. Jones (1982) 149 C.L.R. 571 .... [1990] 497
Meeth *v*. Glacetal [1978] E.C.R. 2133; [1979] 1 C.M.L.R. 520 .... [1988] 388
Mengel's W.T. (*Re*) [1962] Ch. 791 .... [1988] 474
Menier *v*. Hooper's Telegraph Works (1874) 9 Ch. App. 350 .... [1988] 77

Mente & Co. *v.* Isthmian S.S. Co. (*The Quarrington Court*), 36 F. Supp. 278, 1940 A.M.C. 1546 (S.D.N.Y. 1940), aff'd, 122 F. 2d 266, 1941 A.M.C. 1234 (2 Cir. 1941) .... [1986] 365
Mercantile Bank of India Ltd. *v.* Chartered Bank of India, Australia and China [1937] 1 All E.R. 231 .... [1990] 524, 531, 532
Mercantile Investment and General Trust Co. *v.* International Co. of Mexico [1893] 1 Ch. 484 .... [1989] 437
Mercedes Benz Aust. Pty. Ltd. *v.* Scan Carriers S.A., 25 November 1987, unreported .... [1989] 281
Merchants and Manufacturers Ins. Co. Ltd. *v.* Hunt & Thorne [1941] 1 K.B. 295 .... [1989] 257, 258
Merchants Fire Assurance Corp. *v.* Lattimore, 263 F. 2d 232 (9 C.A. 1959) .... [1986] 502
Merchants' Mutual Auto Insurance Co. *v.* Smart, 267 U.S. 126 (1925) .... [1987] 212
Merchants Nat'l Bank of Mobile *v.* The Dredge *General G.L. Gillespie*, 663 F. 2d 1338, 1982 A.M.C. 1 (5 Cir. 1981), cert. dismissed, 456 U.S. 966 (1982) .... [1986] 350
Merchants' Trading Co. *v.* Universal Marine Insurance Co. (1870) 2 Asp. M.C. (2nd) 431, n.(a) .... [1986] 39
Mercury Bell, The *v.* Amosin [1986] 3 F.C. 454; (1986) 27 D.L.R. (4th) 641 (Fed. C.A.) .... [1988] 88
Merrimac, The, 242 F. 572, 574 (S.D. Fla. 1917) .... [1986] 20
Merry *v.* Green (1841) 7 M. & W. 623 .... [1989] 315
Mesologi, The (1971) S.M.A. No. 642 .... [1989] 355
Messenger, The (1857) Swab. 191 .... [1989] 68
Metaalhandel J.A. Magnus B.V. *v.* Ardfields Transport Ltd. [1987] 2 F.T.L.R. 319 .... [1988] 35
Metallgesellschaft A.G. *v.* M/V *Captain Constante*, No. 85–7443, Slip Opinion (2 Cir. 19 May 1986) .... [1986] 536
Metallurgical & Commercial *v.* Metal Sales Co. Ltd., 1977 (2) SA 388 (W) at 391 E-H .... [1987] 314
Metaxas *v.* Ship *The Galaxias* [1989] 1 F.C. 386 (Can. F.C.) .... [1990] 101
Metcalfe *v.* The Britannia Ironworks Co. (1877) 2 Q.B.D. 423 .... [1990] 518
Metropolitan Bank *v.* Heiron (1880) L.R. 5 Ex. D. 319 .... [1988] 131
Mexico I, The [1990] 1 Lloyd's Rep. 507; [1988] 2 Lloyd's Rep. 149 .... [1990] 394, 395, 396, 397, 398
Meyer *v.* Scottish Wholesale Co-operative Society, 1954 S.C. 381, affmd. *sub nom.* Scottish Wholesale Co-operative Society *v.* Meyer [1959] A.C. 324 .... [1988] 66
M. Golodetz Export Corp. *v.* S.S. *Lake Anja*, 1985 A.M.C. 891 (2nd Cir.) .... [1989] 359
Michael, The [1979] 1 Lloyd's Rep. 55; [1979] 2 Lloyd's Rep. 1 (C.A.) .... [1987] 39; [1989] 26
Michaels *v.* Mariforum Shipping S.A., 624 F. 2d 411, 1980 A.M.C. 1901 (2 Cir. 1980) .... [1986] 358
Michalos (N.) and Sons Maritime S.A. *v.* Prudential Assurance Co. Ltd. (*The Zinovia*) [1984] 2 Lloyd's Rep. 264 .... [1987] 40
Michelin *v.* Commission [1983] E.C.R. 3461 .... [1988] 188
Michigan Chemical Corp. *v.* Amer. Home Assur. Co., 728 F. 2d 374, 378 (6 Cir. 1984) .... [1986] 83
Micosta S.A. *v.* Shetland Islands Council (*The Mihalis*) [1984] 2 Lloyd's Rep. 525 .... [1988] 263
Midland Bank Ltd. *v.* Seymour [1955] 2 Lloyd's Rep. 147, 168 .... [1986] 199
Midland Bank Plc *v.* Laker Airways Ltd. [1986] Q.B. 689 .... [1987] 394, 395
Midland Bank Plc *v.* Perry [1988] 1 Fam. L.R. 161 .... [1988] 436
Midland Bank Trust Co. Ltd. *v.* Hett, Stubbs & Kemp [1979] Ch. 384 .... [1988] 443; [1990] 553
Midland Bank Trust Co. Ltd. *v.* Green [1981] A.C. 513 .... [1990] 530
Midland Silicones Ltd. *v.* Scruttons Ltd. [1962] A.C. 446 (H.L.) .... [1986] 105; [1990] 103
Midwest Shipping Co. *v.* Henry [1971] 1 Lloyd's Rep. 375 .... [1988] 46
Mihalis, The [1984] 2 Lloyd's Rep. 525 .... [1988] 263
Mike Trading & Transport Ltd. *v.* Pagnan & Fratelli (*The Lisboa*) [1980] 2 Lloyd's Rep. 546 [1987] 396
Mikhail Lermontov, The, N.S.W.S.C., 20 November 1989 .... [1990] 164
Miles *v.* New Zealand Alford Estate (1886) 32 Ch. D. 266, 285 .... [1989] 436
Miles *v.* Wakefield Metropolitan District Council [1987] A.C. 539 .... [1990] 515
Miliangos *v.* George Frank (Textiles) Ltd. [1976] A.C. 443 .... [1988] 396
Millars' Karri and Jarrah Co. (1902) *v.* Weddel Turner & Co. (1908) 14 Com. Cas. 25, at 29, 31 .... [1988] 23
Millars of Falkirk Ltd. *v.* Turpie, 1976 S.L.T. (Notes) 66 .... [1987] 403; [1988] 506
Miller *v.* Continental Insurance Co., 389 N.Y.S. 2d 565 (1976) .... [1987] 209, 212
Miller *v.* Race (1758) 1 Burr. 452 .... [1989] 301
Miller Indus. Inc. *v.* Caterpillar Tractor Co., 473 F. Supp. 1147 (S.D. Ala. 1979), vacated on other grounds, 516 F. Supp. 84 (S.D. Ala. 1980) .... [1986] 361
Miller Industries *v.* Caterpillar Tractor Co., 733 F. 2d 813, 1984 A.M.C. 2559 (11 Cir. 1984) [1986] 361
Minasian *v.* Aetna Life Insurance Co., 3 N.E. 2d 17 (S. Ct., Mass., 1939) .... [1987] 209, 211
Mineral Transporter, The [1985] 3 W.L.R. 381; [1986] A.C. 1 .... [1985] 407; [1986] 98, 151, 299, 552; [1987] 237; [1989] 1

Minerva, The (1854) 1 Sp. 271 .... [1989] 63, 66
Minister for Environmental Planning *v.* San Sebastian Pty. Ltd. [1983] 2 N.S.W.L.R. 268 .... [1986] 111
Ministère Publique *v.* Asjes, Nouvelles Frontières et al (209–213/84) [1986] 3 C.M.L.R. 173 .... [1987] 14; [1988] 135
Ministry of Housing and Local Government *v.* Sharp [1970] 2 Q.B. 223 .... [1988] 439; [1990] 553
Minnehaha, The (1861) Lush. 335 .... [1989] 59, 72
Minturn *v.* Maynard, 58 U.S. 477 (1854) .... [1986] 13
Miraflores, The and the *Abadesa* [1967] 1 A.C. 826 .... [1989] 31, 32, 35
Miramar Maritime Corp. *v.* Holborn Oil Trading Ltd. [1984] 3 W.L.R. 1, 4 .... [1986] 242
Miss Jay Jay, The (1986) L.M.L.N. 182 (15 October 1986) (C.A.); [1985] 1 Lloyd's Rep. 264; [1987] 1 Lloyd's Rep. 32 .... [1986] 40; [1987] 22; [1988] 348
Mitchell *v.* Davis (1920) 27 T.L.R. 68 .... [1987] 45, 46, 48
Mitchell *v.* Ealing L.B.C. [1979] Q.B. 1, noted (1980) 54 A.L.J. 30 .... [1987] 46, 48, 50, 71, 78
Mitchell *v.* W.T. Grant Co., 416 U.S. 600 (1974) .... [1986] 350
Mitsubishi Corp. *v.* Aristidis I. Alafouzos [1988] 1 Lloyd's Rep. 191 .... [1990] 242
Mobil Sales & Supply Corp. *v.* *SS Pacific Bear*, 1980 A.M.C. 1409 (N.D. Cal., 1979) .... [1987] 153
Mobile Sales & Supply Corp. *v.* M/V *Banglar Kakoli*, No. 81–7704 (S.D.N.Y., 13 June 1984) .... [1986] 369
Modern Engineering (Bristol) Ltd. *v.* Gilbert-Ash (Northern) Ltd. [1974] A.C. 689 .... [1990] 475
Moens *v.* Heyworth (1842) 10 M. & W. 147 .... [1989] 256
Moffatt *v.* Kazana [1969] 2 Q.B. 152 .... [1989] 315
Mogul S.S. Co. *v.* McGregor, Gow & Co. (1889) 23 Q.B.D. 598, affmd. 1892 A.C. 25 .... [1988] 182
Mohawk, The, 1953 A.M.C. 1541 (U.S.C.A, 3rd Cir.) .... [1990] 52
Molkerei-Zentrale, Case 28/67, judgment of 3 April 1968; [1968] E.C.R. 143 .... [1990] 181
Molthes Rederi Aktieselskabet *v.* Ellerman's Wilson Line Ltd. [1927] 1 K.B. 710 .... [1986] 2; [1987] 541; [1989] 191, 192, 193, 195
Momm *v.* Barclays Bank International Ltd. [1977] 1 Q.B. 790; *sub nom.* Delbrueck *v.* Barclays Bank International Ltd. [1976] 2 Lloyd's Rep. 341 .... [1986] 208; [1989] 367; [1990] 81, 82
Mondel *v.* Steel (1841) 8 M. & W. 858 .... [1990] 515
Monica S, The [1968] P. 741 .... [1987] 322, 380
Monk Corp. *v.* Island Fertilizers Ltd. (1988) 19 F.T.R. 220 (Can. F.C.) .... [1990] 102
Monks *v.* Poynice Pty. Ltd. (1987) 8 N.S.W.L.R. 662 .... [1990] 507
Monkwearmouth, The (1845) 9 Jur. 72 .... [1989] 65
Monolithic Building Co. (*In re*) [1915] 1 Ch. 643 .... [1986] 177; [1990] 530
Montagu's Settlement Trusts (*Re*) [1987] Ch. 264 .... [1988] 365; [1989] 299, 300, 301, 304, 311, 312, 328, 329, 330, 331, 332, 334, 335, 339
Montan, The [1984] 1 Lloyd's Rep. 389; [1985] 1 Lloyd's Rep. 189 (C.A.) .... [1986] 235, 236, 238, 239, 240, 241, 242, 243, 244
Moore *v.* Fulham Vestry [1895] 1 Q.B. 399 .... [1989] 436
Moore *v.* Mourgue (1776) 2 Cowp. 479 .... [1989] 149
Moore *v.* Woolsey (1854) 4 El. & Bl. 243 .... [1987] 212
Moore & Co. and Landauer & Co. (*Re*) [1921] 2 K.B. 519 .... [1990] 457
Moorcock, The (1889) 14 P.D. 64 .... [1987] 554; [1988] 506
Moorgate Mercantile Co. Ltd. *v.* Finch [1962] 1 Q.B. 701 .... [1986] 226
Moorgate Mercantile Co. Ltd. *v.* Twitchings [1977] A.C. 890 .... [1986] 225
Moorhouse *v.* Angus & Robertson (No. 1) Pty. Ltd. [1981] 1 N.S.W.L.R. 700 .... [1987] 48, 68, 70, 73, 75
Moralice (London) Ltd. *v.* E.D. & F. Man [1954] 2 Lloyd's Rep. 526 .... [1989] 144
Morania Barge No. 140 Inc. *v.* M. and J. Tracy Inc. (1962) 312 F. 2d 78; 1963 A.M.C. 678 (2d Cir.) .... [1989] 18
Morelli *v.* Fitch & Gibbons [1928] 2 K.B. 636 .... [1988] 508
Morgan Crucible Co. *v.* Hill Samuel Bank Ltd., *The Financial Times*, 27 July 1990 .... [1990] 481
Morgan Guaranty Trust Co. of New York *v.* Hellenic Lines, 593 F. Supp. 1004, 1985 A.M.C. 800 (S.D.N.Y. 1984) .... [1986] 356
Morgan Guaranty Trust Co. of New York *v.* Hellenic Lines, 1984 A.M.C. 1074, 38 B.R. 987 (S.D.N.Y. 1984), modified by 585 F. Supp. 1227, A.M.C. 2409 (S.D.N.Y. 1984) .... [1986] 353
Morison *v.* Thompson (1874) L.R. 9 Q.B. 480 .... [1987] 435
Morning Star, The [1987] 1 Lloyd's Rep. 401 .... [1989] 383
Morning Watch, The [1990] 1 Lloyd's Rep. 547 .... [1990] 482
Morrell *v.* Wootten (1852) 16 Beav. 197, 204 .... [1986] 198
Morris *v.* C.W. Martin & Sons Ltd. [1966] 1 Q.B. 716 (C.A.) .... [1986] 105, 226, 303, 431; [1987] 68, 77; [1988] 36, 466

Morris *v.* Howell (1888) 22 L.R. Ir. 77 .... [1990] 321
Morris *v.* Kanssen [1946] A.C. 459 .... [1990] 405, 408, 409
Morris *v.* Martin & Sons Ltd. [1966] 1 Q.B. 716 .... [1990] 319
Morrison-Knudsen Construction Co. *v.* Director, Office of Workers' Compensation Programs, 461 U.S. 624 (1983) .... [1986] 356
Morrison Steamship Co. Ltd. *v.* *Greystoke Castle* (Cargo Owners) [1947] A.C. 265 .... [1986] 342
Morse Dry Dock & Repair Co. *v.* Northern Star, 1926 A.M.C. 977 .... [1988] 173
Moschi *v.* Lep Air Services Ltd. [1973] A.C. 331 .... [1990] 224
Moses H. Cone Memorial Hosp. *v.* Mercury Const. Corp., 460 U.S. 1 (1983) .... [1986] 359
Moses *v.* MacFerlan (1760) 2 Burr. 1005; 1 W. Bl. 219; 97 E.R. 676 .. [1987] 429; [1989] 436; [1990] 496
Moss *v.* Elphick [1910] 1 K.B. 846 .... [1990] 407
Mostyn, The [1928] A.C. 57 .... [1986] 401
Motor Mart Ltd. *v.* Webb [1958] N.Z.L.R. 773 .... [1989] 201
Motor Oil Hellas (Corinth) Refineries S.A. *v.* Shipping Corp. of India (*The Kanchenjunga*) [1987] 2 Lloyd's Rep. 509 .... [1987] 408; [1988] 46
Mount *v.* Jay & Jay [1960] 1 Q.B. 159 .... [1990] 273
Mount Royal/Walsh In. *v.* *The Jensen Star*, 1988 A.M.C. 1590 (Can. F.C.); 23 May 1989 (No. A–621–88, T–1654–84) (unreported) (Can. Fed. C.A.) .... [1990] 104
Mozart, The [1985] 1 Lloyd's Rep. 239 .... [1989] 498
M/S Aswan Engineering Est. Co. v. Lupdine Ltd. [1987] 1 W.L.R. 1 .... [1988] 505, 514
Muduroglu *v.* T.C. Ziraat Bankasi [1986] 3 W.L.R. 606 .... [1987] 2
Muirhead *v.* Industrial Tank Specialities Ltd. [1985] 3 W.L.R. 993; [1985] 3 All E.R. 705; [1986] Q.B. 507, pet. diss. [1986] 1 W.L.R. 1380 .... [1986] 98, 302; [1987] 236; [1988] 260, 471, 505; [1989] 1
Mullings *v.* Trinder (1870) L.R. 10 Eq. 449 .... [1989] 64
Multi Guarantee Co. Ltd. (*Re*) [1986] 2 F.T.L.R. 301 .... [1988] 255
Multiservice Book Binding Ltd. *v.* Marden [1979] Ch. 84 .... [1989] 272
Multitank Holsatia, The [1988] 2 Lloyd's Rep. 486; (1988) L.M.L.N. 222 .... [1988] 303, 308; [1989] 171
Muncaster Castle, The [1961] A.C. 807 .... [1987] 554
Municipal Committee, Amritsar *v.* Hazara Singh, A.I.R. 1975 S.C. 1087, 1088–89 .... [1988] 15
Munroe *v.* Minister of Fisheries and Oceans (1987) 6 F.T.R. 149 (F.C.) .... [1989] 101
Munt *v.* Stokes (1892) 4 T.R. 561 .... [1989] 436
Murphy *v.* Brentwood D.C. [1990] 2 W.L.R. 944 .... [1990] 482
Murray *v.* Legal & General Insurance Society Ltd. [1970] 2 Q.B. 495 .... [1987] 234
Murray *v.* Shuter [1976] Q.B. 972 .... [1990] 138
Muschinski *v.* Dodds (1985) 160 C.L.R. 583 .... [1990] 496
Musyka *v.* Charpat Transportation Inc. and the *Tusker* (1986) 3 F.T.R. 237 (F.C.) .... [1989] 102
Mutual & Federal Ins. Co. Ltd. *v.* Oudtshoorn Municipality 1985 (1) S.A. 419 .... [1988] 453
Mutual Life Insurance Co. of New York *v.* Armstrong, 117 U.S. 591 (1886) .... [1987] 210
Mutual (Q'ld) Knitting Mills Pty. Ltd. (*Re* [1959] Q.L.R. 357 (Q'ld S.C.) .... [1990] 22
My Kinda Town *v.* Soll [1983] R.P.C. 407 (C.A.) .... [1987] 428; [1990] 462
Mycenae, The, Hamburg Award 15.12.1976, Vers R 1978, 1040 .... [1990] 390, 391
Myrto, The [1977] 2 Lloyd's Rep. 243; [1978] 1 Lloyd's Rep. 11 (C.A.) .... [1989] 94
Myrto, The (No. 2) [1984] 2 Lloyd's Rep. 341 .... [1989] 8
Nacap Ltd. *v.* Moffat Plant Ltd. [1987] S.L.T. 221 .... [1988] 40
Nacirema Operating Co. *v.* The S.S. *Al Kulsum*, 407 F. Supp. 1222, 1224–26, 1976 A.M.C. 609, 611–14 (S.D.N.Y. 1975) .... [1986] 355
Naidoo *v.* Marine & Trade Ins. Co. Ltd., 1978 (3) S.A. 666 (A) .... [1989] 178
Nance *v.* British Columbia Electric Ry. [1951] A.C. 601 .... [1990] 422, 424
Nanfri, The [1978] Q.B. 927; [1979] A.C. 757; [1979] 1 Lloyd's Rep. 201 (H.L.) .... [1986] 386, 426; [1988] 149; [1989] 191, 193, 292; [1990] 476, 524
Natalie, The, 1959 A.M.C. 2359 .... [1986] 41
Nat. Life Ins. Co. *v.* Minch (1873) 53 N.Y. 144 .... [1989] 435
National Bank of Greece S.A. *v.* Pinios Shipping Co. (*The Maira*) [1989] 3 W.L.R. 185 ...... [1990] 318
National Bank of Greece S.A. *v.* Pinios Shipping Co. No. 1 (*The Maira*) (No. 3) [1990] A.C. 637; [1988] 2 Lloyd's Rep. 126 .... [1989] 40 *et seq.*; [1990] 489
National Bank of New Zealand Ltd. *v.* Walpole and Patterson Ltd. [1975] 2 N.Z.L.R. 7 .... [1986] 9
National Carriers Ltd. *v.* Panalpina (Northern) Ltd. [1981] A.C. 675 .... [1990] 156
National Employer's Mutual Gen. Ins. Assn. Ltd. *v.* Jones [1988] 2 W.L.R. 952; [1987] 3 W.L.R. 901 .... [1988] 297
National Mercantile Bank Ltd. *v.* Rymill (1881) 44 L.T. 767 .... [1986] 220

National Motor Mail-coach Co. Ltd. (*Re*) [1908] 2 Ch. 228 .... [1990] 67
National Mutual Life Assn. of Australasia Ltd. *v*. Walsh [1987] 8 N.S.W.L.R. 585 .... [1990] 334
National Provincial and Union Bank of England *v*. Charnley [1924] 1 K.B. 431 .... [1990] 534
National Slag *v*. Canadian Imperial Bank of Commerce (1982) 140 D.L.R. 3d 473 .... [1990] 73, 76
National Surety Corp. *v*. Lybrand (1939) 256 App. Div. 226; 9 N.Y.S. 2d 554 .... [1990] 423
National Trailer Convoy (Can.) Ltd. *v*. Bank of Montreal (1980) 10 B.L.R. 196 (Ont.) .... [1986] 167
National Trust Co. Ltd. *v*. Wong Aviation Ltd. (1969) 3 D.L.R. (3d) 55 (S.C.C.) .... [1987] 49
National Westminster Bank Ltd. *v*. Barclays Bank International Ltd. [1975] Q.B. 654 .... [1989] 304
National Westminster Bank Ltd. *v*. Halesowen Presswork and Assemblies Ltd. [1972] A.C. 785 .... [1989] 365
National Westminster Bank Plc *v*. Morgan [1983] 3 All E.R. 85; reversed [1985] A.C. 686 .... [1986] 313; [1987] 399; [1988] 361, 367; [1989] 272; [1990] 158, 340
Nationwide Mutual Insurance Co. *v*. Roberts, 134 S.E. 2d 654 (S. Ct., N. Carolina, 1964) ... [1987] 212
Nautilus, The (1856) Swab. 105 .... [1989] 69
Navegación Goya S.A. *v*. Mutual B &M Ins. Co., 1972 A.M.C. 650 (S.D..N.Y.), 1977 A.M.C. 175 .... [1986] 485, 486, 503
Naviera Amazonica Peruana S.A. *v*. Compania Internacional de Seguros del Peru [1988] 1 Lloyd's Rep. 116; 1 F.T.L.R. 100 .... [1988] 23; [1989] 514
Navigation Sonamar Inc. *v*. Algoma Steamships Ltd. [1987] R.J.Q. 1346 (Queb. Super. Ct.) .. [1989] 92
Navigest Inc. *v*. Laurentian Pilotage Authority (1987) 11 F.T.R. 183 (F.C.) .... [1989] 91
Naylor *v*. Preston A.H.A. [1987] 1 W.L.R. 958 .... [1989] 434
Naylor (Isaac) & Sons Ltd. *v*. New Zealand Cooperative Wool Marketing Association Ltd. [1981] 1 N.Z.L.R. 361 .... [1987] 419
Nea Agrex S.A. *v*. Baltic Shipping Co. Ltd. [1976] 1 Q.B. 933 .... [1986] 142, 285
Nea Karteria Maritime Co. Ltd. *v*. Atlantic & Great Lakes S.S. Corp. (No. 1) (*The Athanasia Comninos and the Georges Chr Lemos*) [1981] Com. L.R. 132 .... [1988] 53; [1989] 347
Nea Tyhi, The [1982] 1 Lloyd's Rep. 606 .... [1986] 107, 299; [1987] 54, 84; [1988] 257, 259
Neate *v*. Harding (1851) 6 Exch. 349 .... [1989] 306
Nelson *v*. Dahl (1879) 12 Ch. D. 568 .... [1988] 370
Nelson *v*. Larholt [1948] 1 K.B. 339 .... [1989] 309, 312, 314, 318, 319, 327, 334
Nelson Guarantee Corp. Ltd. *v*. Hodgson [1958] N.Z.L.R. 609 .... [1990] 419, 423
Nelson H. Leo *v*. I.N.A., 1960 A.M.C. 832 .... [1986] 504, 506
Nema, The [1982] A.C. 724 .... [1986] 46, 75, 238, 345, 346, 552; [1988] 396; [1989] 122; [1990] 556
Nemeth *v*. General Steamship Corp., 694 F. 2d 609, 1983 A.M.C. 855 (9 Cir. 1982) .... [1986] 367
Neptune, The (1841) 1 W. Rob. 297 .... [1989] 61, 63
Neptune, The (1858) 12 Moo. P.C. 346 .... [1989] 59, 68, 71
Neptune Maritime Co. *v*. Koninklijke Bunge B.V. (*The Argonaut*) [1982] 2 Lloyd's Rep. 214 [1988] 307
Nereide S.p.A. di Navigazione *v*. Bulk Oil International Ltd. (*The Laura Prima*) [1982] 1 Lloyd's Rep. 1 .... [1986] 55; [1989] 263, 265
Neste Oy *v*. Lloyds Bank Plc [1983] 2 Lloyd's Rep. 63 .... [1989] 318
Netty, The [1981] 2 Lloyd's Rep. 57 .... [1988] 93
Neubros Corp. *v*. Northwestern Nat'l Ins., 1972 A.M.C. 2443 (E.D.N.Y.) .... [1986] 499
Nevill (*Re*), ex p. White (1871) 6 Ch. 397 .... [1989] 202
New Amsterdam Casualty Co. *v*. Jones, 135 F. 2d 191 (6th Cir., 1943) .... [1987] 209, 212
New Chinese Antimony Co. Ltd. *v*. Ocean S.S. Co. Ltd. [1917] 2 K.B. 664 .... [1986] 475, 478
New England Marine Ins. Co. *v*. Dunham, 78 U.S. 1 (1871) .... [1986] 488
New Jersey *v*. Ruckelshaus, Civil Action No. 84–1668 (JWB) (D.C.N.J. 1984) .... [1987] 511
New Orleans, The [1904] 1 K.B. 943 .... [1990] 323
New York Life Insurance Co. *v*. National Bank Trust Co. (1975) 528 F. 2d 802 (4th Cir.) .... [1990] 230
New York, New Haven and Harfford Railroad Co. *v*. Nothnagle, 1953 A.M.C. 1228 .... [1988] 274
New York Dock Co. *v*. Steamship *Poznan*, 274 U.S. 117, 122, 1927 A.M.C. 723, 726–27 (1927) .... [1986] 356
New York Star, The (1980) 144 C.L.R. 300; [1981] 1 W.L.R. 138 (P.C.) ...... [1987] 223; [1989] 280, 396
New Zealand Netherlands Society *v*. Kuys [1973] 1 W.L.R. 1126 .... [1987] 433, 436
New Zealand Shipping Co. Ltd. *v*. A.M. Satterthwaite & Co. Ltd. (*The Eurymedon*) [1975] A.C. 154 .... [1988] 362, 396; [1989] 23, 142, 164, 170, 171, 172
New Zealand Shipping Co. *v*. Société des Ateliers de France [1919] A.C. 1 .... [1989] 4
Newbros *v*. Northwestern Insurance, 359 F. Supp. 310 (1972) .... [1986] 41
Newfoundland Coast, The, 1987 A.M.C. 954 (Can. F.C.) (1989) 104 N.R. 166 .... [1987] 259, 260; [1988] 285; [1990] 494
Newfoundland Processing Ltd. *v*. Ship *South Angela* (No. 1) [1989] 1 F.C. 259 (Can. F.C.) .. [1990] 104

Newmarch *v.* Newmarch [1978] Fam. 79 .... [1988] 395
Ngo Chew Hong Edible Oil Pte. Ltd. *v.* Scindia S.N. Co. Ltd. (*The Jalamohan*) [1988] 1 Lloyd's Rep. 443 .... [1988] 285
Ngurli Ltd. *v.* McCann (1953) 90 C.L.R. 425 .... [1988] 72
Niagara County *v.* Utica Mutual Ins. Co., 439 N.Y.S. 2d 538 (1981) .... [1986] 92
Niblett Ltd. *v.* Confectioners' Materials Co. Ltd. [1921] 3 K.B. 387 .... [1988] 509
Nicaragua *v.* U.S.A. [1984] I.C.J. Rep. 392 .... [1988] 541
Nichimen Corp. *v.* Gearbulk Ltd. 1986 A.M.C. 593 .... [1987] 88
Nichols *v.* Jessup. Unrep. C.A., 26 September 1986 .... [1987] 329
Nicolai Heinrich, The (1853) 17 Jur. 329 .... [1989] 60, 61, 67
Nicolaos D.L., The, 1979 A.M.C. 1747; 471 F. Supp. 942 (S.D. Ga.), vacated 1982 A.M.C. 1489; 666 F. 2d 897 (5th Cir.) .... [1989] 343, 349, 358
Nicolina, The (1843) 2 W. Rob. 175 .... [1989] 61
Niel Maersk, The (1936) 18 F. Supp. 824; (1937) 91 F. 2d 932 (2nd Cir.), *cert.* denied (1937) 302 U.S. 753; 58 S. Ct. 281; 82 L. Ed. .... [1989] 351
Nightingale *v.* Tildsley [1980] C.L.Y. 134 .... [1988] 546
Nimrod, The (1850) 7 N.o.C. 570 .... [1989] 64, 73
Nina's Bar Bistro Pty. Ltd. *v.* MBE Corporation (Sydney) Pty. Ltd. [1984] 3 N.S.W.L.R. 613 [1989] 84
Nippon Seiko K.K. *v.* Council. Case 258/84, judgment 7 May 1987, unrep. .... [1988] 187
Nippon Shosen Kaisha K.K. *v.* United States, 238 F. Supp. 55 (N.D. Cal., 1964) .... [1987] 26
Nippon Yusen Kaisha *v.* Acme Shipping Corp. [1972] 1 W.L.R. 74 .... [1988] 46
Nippon Yusen Kaisha *v.* Karageorgis [1975] 1 W.L.R. 1093 .... [1986] 410
Nissho Iwai Australia Ltd. *v.* Malaysian International Shipping Corp. Bhd. (*The Bunga Teratai*), 4 February 1987 Sup. Ct. N.S.W., unreported; (1988) 12 N.S.W.L.R. 730 (C.A.); (1989) 63 A.L.J.R. 468 .... [1990] 324, 325
Nissos Samos, The [1985] 1 Lloyd's Rep. 378 .... [1988] 440
Nixon *v.* Furphy (1925) 25 S.R. (N.S.W.) 151 .... [1987] 426; [1990] 344
No, The (1853) 1 Sp. 184 .... [1989] 62
Noah's Ark, The (1961) 292 F. 437; (1963) 322 F. 2d 3 .... [1990] 51
Noble (R.A.) & Sons (Clothing) Ltd. (*Re*) [1983] B.C.L.C. 273 .... [1988] 67
Nogar Marin, The [1988] 1 Lloyd's Rep. 412 .... [1990] 455
Nora, The, 181 Fed. 845 (S.D. Fla 1910) .... [1986] 20
Nordamerika, The, 1931 A.M.C. 1637 .... [1989] 345
Nordglimt, The [1987] 2 Lloyd's Rep. 470; [1988] Q.B. 183 .... [1988] 94; [1990] 171, 278
Norma, The (1860) Lush. 124 .... [1989] 68
Norman, The [1960] 1 Lloyd's Rep. 1 .... [1988] 523
Norse River, The, Hamburg Award 1.3.1976 .... [1990] 391
Norse Viking, The, S.M.A. No. 1665 (1982) .... [1986] 72
North Atlantic and Gulf Steamship Co. Inc. (*In re*), 204 F. Supp. 899, 1963 A.M.C. 871 (S.D.N.Y. 1962), aff'd 320 F. 2d 628 (2 Cir. 1963) .... [1986] 424
North Georgia Finishing Inc. *v.* Di-Chem Inc., 419 U.S. 601 (1975) .... [1986] 350
North Ocean Shipping Co. *v.* Hyundai Construction Co. Ltd. (*The Altantic Baron*) [1979] Q.B. 705 .... [1986] 313; [1987] 426; [1989] 272; [1990] 344
North Pacific S.S. Co. *v.* Hall Brothers Marine Ry. & S. Co., 249 U.S. 119 (1918) .... [1986] 14
North Princess, The, 1960 A.M.C. 1897 .... [1986] 257
North Scottish Helicopters Ltd. *v.* United Technologies Corp. Inc. Unrep., [1988] S.L.T. 77 (Ct. of Sess., Outer House) .... [1988] 40
Northern Fishing Co. (Hull) Ltd. *v.* Eddom (*The Norman*) [1960] 1 Lloyd's Rep. 1 .... [1988] 523
Northern Native Fishing Corp. *v.* Canada (1988) 13 F.T.R. 153 (F.C.) .... [1989] 97
Northern Shipping Co. *v.* S/S *Glory*, 1983 A.M.C. 1499 (E.D. La. 1982) .... [1986] 355
Northumbria, The (1869) L.R. 3 A. & E. 6 .... [1988] 178
Northwest Amusement Co. Inc. *v.* Aetna Casualty & Surety Co., 107 P. 2d 110 (1940) .... [1987] 212
Northwestern Autoservices Ltd. (*Re*) [1980] 2 N.Z.L.R. 302 .... [1990] 409
Northwestern Mutual L.I. *v.* Lenard, 1974 A.M.C. 877 (2 C.A.) .... [1986] 484
Northwestern Mutual Life Insurance Co. *v.* Johnson (1920) 254 U.S. 96 .... [1988] 320
Northwestern Mutual Life Insurance Co. *v.* Linard (1974) 498 F. 2d 556 .... [1988] 319
Norwalk Victory, The, 336 U.S. 386; 1949 A.M.C. 393 (1949) .... [1986] 23
Norway's (A State) Application (No. 2) (*Re*) [1988] 3 W.L.R. 603; [1989] 2 W.L.R. 458 (H.L.) .... [1989] 433
Norwich & New York Transportation Co. *v.* Wright (1871) 80 U.S. 104 .... [1988] 518

Norwich City Council *v.* Harvey, 2 November 1987, unrep.; [1989] 1 W.L.R. 828 (C.A.) .... [1988] 468; [1990] 318
Norwich Co. *v.* Wright, 80 U.S. 104 (1871) .... [1987] 345
Norwich Union Fire Ins. Society *v.* William H. Price Ltd. [1934] A.C. 455 .... [1989] 431, 439, 445
Nova (Jersey) Knit *v.* Kammgarn Spinnerei G.m.b.H. [1977] 1 W.L.R. 463; [1977] 1 Lloyd's Rep. 463 (H.L.) .... [1986] 59
Nova Mink Ltd. *v.* Trans-Canada Airlines (1951) 2 D.L.R. 241 .... [1990] 486
N.S. Tractors *v.* Tarros Gage, 1986 A.M.C. 2050 (F.C.) .... [1988] 83
Nugent *v.* Gifford (1738) 1 Atk. 463 .... [1989] 321
Nunley *v.* M/V *Dauntless Colocotronis*, 513 F. Supp. 720, 1981 A.M.C. 1915 (E.D. La. 1981), vacated and remanded, 696 F. 2d 1141 (5 Cir. 1983), rev'd and remanded, 727 F. 2d 455, 1984 A.M.C. 2920 (5 Cir. 1984) (*en banc*) .... [1986] 379; [1989] 16
Nuschlag, The *v.* Atlantic Mutual, 1942 A.M.C. 391 (2 C.A.) .... [1986] 494
N.V. Bocimar S.A. *v.* Century Ins. Co. of Canada (1984) 53 N.R. 383 .... [1987] 86; [1989] 93
N.V. Slavenburg's Bank *v.* Intercontinental Natural Resources Ltd. [1980] 1 W.L.R. 1076 .... [1986] 2; [1990] 537, 541
Nye Ltd. (C.L.) (*Re*) [1971] 1 Ch. 442 .... [1990] 534, 535
O'Callaghan *v.* Hamilton Leasing [1984] I.L.R.M. 146 .... [1989] 373
O'Connell *v.* Jackson [1972] 1 Q.B. 270 .... [1990] 422
O'Connor *v.* Kirby [1971] 1 Lloyd's Rep. 454 .... [1990] 560
O'Dea *v.* Allstates Leasing System (W.A.) Pty. Ltd. (1983) 152 C.L.R. 359 .... [1990] 23
O'Donnell T & T Co. *v.* Marine Transit Co., 1932 A.M.C. 1520 (N.Y.A.D.) .... [1986] 492
O'Farrell *v.* Manpower Services Commission, EAT 754/84, 2 September 1985 .... [1989] 273
O'Rourke *v.* Eastern Air Lines Inc. (1984) 730 F. 2d 842 (2nd Cir.) .... [1988] 180
O'Sullivan *v.* Management & Music Ltd. [1985] Q.B. 428 .... [1989] 272; [1990] 130, 331, 335, 465
Obestain Inc. *v.* National Mineral Development Corp. Ltd. (*The Sanix Ace*) [1987] 1 Lloyd's Rep. 465 .... [1988] 38
Ocean, The (1842) 1 W. Rob. 334; (1843) 2 W. Rob. 91 .... [1989] 60, 71
Ocean Frost, The [1985] 1 Lloyd's Rep. 1; [1985] 3 All E.R. 795 (C.A.) .... [1986] 109, 224
Ocean Prince (*In re* Tug), 584 F. 2d 1151; 1979 A.M.C. 2018 (2nd Cir., 1978) .... [1987] 504
Ocean Ship Supply Ltd. *v.* The M/V *Leah* (1984) 729 F. 2d 971; 1984 A.M.C. 2089 (4th Cir.) .... [1986] 353; [1987] 152; [1989] 12
Ocean Transport Line Inc. *v.* American Philippine Fiber Industries Inc., 743 F.2d 85, 1985 A.M.C. 741 (2 Cir. 1984) .... [1986] 371
Oceanic Steam Navigation Co. *v.* Mellor (*The Titanic*), 233 U.S. 718 (1913) .... [1986] 23
Oceanic Sun Line Special Shipping Co. Inc. *v.* Fay (1988) 165 C.L.R. 197; 79 A.L.R. 10; 62 A.L.J.R. 389 .... [1989] 217, 220, 221, 222, 223, 224; [1990] 165, 195
Odeon Associated Theatres Ltd. *v.* Jones [1971] 1 W.L.R. 442 .... [1990] 258
Office of Supply *v.* New York Navigation Co., 469 F. 2d 377 (2 Cir. 1972) .... [1986] 59
Official Custodian for Charities *v.* Parway Estates Ltd. [1985] Ch. 151 .... [1990] 412
Ogden *v.* Graham (1861) 1 B. & S. 773 .... [1986] 116
Ohio Oil Co. *v.* Sharp (1943) 135 F. 2d 303 (10th Cir.) .... [1990] 461
Oil & Natural Gas Commission *v.* Western Company of North America, A.I.R. 1987 S.C. 674 [1988] 13
Oil Spill by the *Amoco Cadiz* off the Coast of France (*Re*), 659 F. 2d 789 (7 Cir. 1981) .... [1986] 319
Old Bushmills Distillery Co. (*Re*) [1897] 1 I.R. 488, 507 .... [1986] 522
Old Colony Trust *v.* Wood (1947) 74 N.E. 2d 144 .... [1989] 304
Oldendorff (E.L.) & Co. G.m.b.H. *v.* Tradax Export S.A. (*The Johanna Oldendorff*) [1974] A.C. 479 .... [1986] 51; [1989] 122, 264
Olds Discount Co. Ltd. *v.* Cohen [1938] 3 All E.R. 281n. .... [1989] 194
Olds Discount Co. Ltd *v.* John Playfair Ltd. [1938] 3 All E.R. 275 .... [1989] 194, 208
Oliver B. Cannon & Son, Fidelity & Cas. Co., 519 F. Supp. 668 (D. Del. 1981) .... [1986] 84
Oliver J. Olson & Co. *v.* American Steamship *Marine Leopard*, 356 F. 2d 728 (9th Cir., 1966) .... [1987] 345
Olivier *v.* Ashman [1962] 2 Q.B. 210 .... [1990] 138
Oltenia, The [1982] 2 Lloyd's Rep. 99 (C.A.) .... [1986] 59
Olympic, The [1913] P. 92 .... [1987] 268
Olympic Airways *v.* Kalimi, Civil Appeal 74/81, 37(1) P.D. (1983) 1 .... [1986] 292
Olympic Brilliance, The [1981] 2 Lloyd's Rep. 176, [1982] 2 Lloyd's Rep. 205 .... [1986] 468
Olympic Towing Corp. *v.* Nebel Towing Co., 419 F. 2d 230, 1969 A.M.C. 1571 (5 Cir. 1969), cert. denied, 397 U.S. 989, 1981 A.M.C. 815 (1970) .... [1986] 380
Oman *v.* Johns-Manville Corp., 764 F. 2d 224 (4th Cir., 1985) (*en banc*) .... [1987] 118

Onisilos, The [1971] 2 Lloyd's Rep. 29; [1971] 2 Q.B. 500 (C.A.), pet. all. [1971] 2 W.L.R. 1402 (H.L.) .... [1986] 254; [1990] 395
Ooregum Gold Mining Co. of India *v.* Roper [1892] A.C. 125 .... [1990] 401, 402
Opera Photographic Ltd. (*Re*) [1989] 1 W.L.R. 634 .... [1990] 406
Oppenheim & Co. *v.* Mahomed Haneef, 49 I.A. 174; A.I.R. 1922 P.C. 120 (P.C.) .... [1988] 13
Orakpo *v.* Manson Investments Ltd. [1978] A.C. 95 .... [1989] 9, 10, 192
Orbona, The (1853) 1 Sp. 161 .... [1989] 63
Ore & Chem. Corp. *v.* Stinnes Interoil, 606 F. Supp. 1510, supplemented, 611 F. Supp. 237 (S.D.N.Y. 1985) .... [1986] 66, 536
Ore Prince, The, Judgment 15 December 1983 (Belgium) .... [1989] 28
Oregon *v.* Tug *Go-Getter* (1972) 468 F. 2d 1270; 1973 A.M.C. 243 (9th Cir.) .... [1989] 96
Oriel Ltd. (*Re*) [1986] 1 W.L.R. 180 .... [1990] 542
Oriental Commercial Shipping Co. Ltd. *v.* M.V. *Fidias*, 1986 (1) S.A. 714 (D) .... [1989] 174, 177, 178, 179, 185
Oriental Credit Ltd. (*Re*) [1988] Ch. 204 .... [1990] 323
Oriental Envoy, The [1982] 2 Lloyd's Rep. 266; [1988] 2 Lloyd's Rep. 149 .... [1990] 395
Oriental Hero-Castor, 1976 A.M.C. 1306 (S.D.N.Y. 1976) .... [1987] 344
Oscar Chess Ltd. *v.* Williams [1957] 370 .... [1990] 148
Oswego Barge Corp. (*In re*), 439 F. Supp. 312; 1978 A.M.C. 392 (N.D.N.Y, 1977) .... [1987] 502
Oswego Bargo Corp. (*In re*), 664, F. 2d 327; 1982 A.M.C. 769 (2nd Cir., 1981) .... [1987] 501, 502
OTM Ltd. *v.* Hydranautics [1981] 2 Lloyd's Rep. 211 .... [1990] 503
Otto Herman, The (1864) 33 L.J. Adm. 189 .... [1989] 65, 68, 78, 79
Oughtred *v.* I.R.C. [1960] A.C. 206 .... [1988] 132
Ovens (*Re*) (1979) 103 D.L.R. (3d) 353 (Ont. C.A.) .... [1986] 176
Overstone Ltd. *v.* Shipway [1962] 1 W.L.R. 117 .... [1990] 21
Owen *v.* Tate [1976] Q.B. 402 .... [1989] 7, 8, 9, 10
Owen (*Re*) [1949] 1 All E.R. 901 .... [1990] 67
Owen & Co. *v.* Cronk [1895] 1 Q.B. 265 .... [1989] 303
Owners of Cargo lately laden on board the Ship *Aramis v.* Aramis Maritime Corp. (*The Aramis*) [1987] 2 Lloyd's Rep. 58; (1988) LMLN 238; [1989] 1 Lloyd's Rep. 213 .... [1989] 53, 162 *et seq.*
Owners of the Motor Vessel *Tojo Maru v.* N.V. Bureau Wijsmuller (*The Tojo Maru*) [1972] A.C. 242, 292H .... [1986] 308, 344
Oxford Peerage Case (1625) W. Jones 96 .... [1989] 49
Oxford Shipping Co. *v.* Nippon Yusen Kaisha (*The Eastern Saga*) [1984] 2 Lloyd's Rep. 373 .... [1986] 66
Paal Wilson & Co. A/S *v.* Partenreederei Hannah Blumenthal (*The Hannah Blumenthal*) [1983] 1 A.C. 854; [1983] 1 Lloyd's Rep. 103 .... [1986] 68; [1988] 304, 307; [1989] 5, 170, 442
Pacific Acceptance Corp. *v.* Forsythe (1970) 92 W.N. (N.S.W.) 29 .... [1990] 420, 425
Pacific Associates Inc. *v.* Baxter [1989] 3 W.L.R. 1150 (C.A.) .... [1990] 318
Pacific Caribbean Shipping (USA) Inc. (*Re*) (*The Alicia*) (1986) 789 F. 2d 1406, 1986 A.M.C. 2308 (9 Cir. 1986) .... [1986] 424, 426; [1989] 192
Pacific Inland Navig. Co. (*In re*), 263 F. Supp. 915 (D. Hawaii 1967) .... [1986] 381
Pacific Molasses Co. *v.* Entre Rios Cia. Naviera S.A. (*The San Nicholas*) [1976] 1 Lloyd's Rep. 8 .... [1986] 101
Pacific Resources *v.* Oswego Sh., 1984 A.M.C. 1276 (S.D.N.Y.) .... [1986] 488
Pacol Ltd. *v.* Trade Lines Ltd. (*The Henrik Sif*) [1982] 1 Lloyd's Rep. 456 .... [1987] 260; [1988] 441
Padre Island, The [1984] 2 Lloyd's Rep. 408; [1987] 2 Lloyd's Rep. 529 .... [1987] 233, 406; [1989] 495 *et seq.*, 499, 500, 502, 505, 521
Pagnan S.p.A. *v.* Tradax Ocean Transportation S.A. [1987] 2 Lloyd's Rep. 342 .... [1989] 228
Palagonia *v.* Trans World Airlines Inc. (1978) 110 Misc. 2d 478 (N.Y.S.C.); 16 Avi. 18, 152 . [1988] 229
Palamisto General Enterprises S.A. *v.* Ocean Marine Insurance Co. Ltd. [1972] 2 Q.B. 625, 647 .... [1986] 289
Palm Shipping Inc. *v.* Kuwait Petroleum Corp. (*The Sea Queen*) [1988] 1 Lloyd's Rep. 500 .. [1989] 266
Palmer *v.* Bugler (1988) *The Independent*, 10 November (D.C.) .... [1989] 372
Palmer *v.* Carling O'Keefe Breweries of Canada Ltd. (1989) 67 O.R. 161 .... [1989] 411 *et seq.*
Palmer *v.* Rouse (1858) 3 H. & N. 504 .... [1987] 270
Pan American World Airways Inc. *v.* California Stevedore & Ballast Co., 559 F. 2d 1173, 1978 A.M.C. 1834 (9 Cir. 1977) (*per curiam*) .... [1986] 367
Pan American World Airways Inc. *v.* S.A. Fire & Accident Ins. Co. Ltd. (1965) (3) S.A.L.R. 150 .... [1989] 38
Pan Atlantic Ins. Co. Ltd. *v.* Pine Top Ins. Co. Ltd. [1989] 1 Lloyd's Rep. 568 .... [1989] 390

Panama, New Zealand and Australian Royal Mail Co. (*Re*) (1870) 5 Ch. App. 318 .... [1986] 521; [1990] 402
Panama Centroamericana de Navigación *v.* Sierra Leone (*The Norse Viking*), S.M.A. No. 1665 (1982) .... [1986] 72
Panamanian Oriental S.S. Corp. *v.* Wright (*The Anita*) [1971] 1 Lloyd's Rep. 487, rvsg. [1970] 2 Lloyd's Rep. 365; [1971] 1 W.L.R. 882 .... [1986] 446; [1988] 435
Panchaud Freres S.A. *v.* Etablissements General Grain Co. [1970] 1 Lloyd's Rep. 53 .... [1989] 87, 397 *et seq.*
Panda O.H.G. *v.* Circle Products Ltd. [1970] 1 Lloyd's Rep. 499 (C.A.) .... [1987] 179
Panglobal Friendship, The [1978] 1 Lloyd's Rep. 368 .... [1989] 192
Panorama Developments *v.* Fidelis Furnishings [1971] 2 Q.B. 711 .... [1990] 403
Pao On *v.* Lau Yiu Long [1980] A.C. 614 .... [1987] 426; [1989] 275; [1990] 342, 343
Papadimitriou *v.* Henderson (1939) 64 Ll.L.Rep. 345 .... [1988] 342
Papoose, The, 1969 A.M.C. 781 (5 Cir.) .... [1986] 41, 500
Paradine *v.* Jane (1647) Aleyn 26 .... [1989] 6
Paradise Holdings Inc. (*In re*) (1986) 795 F. 2d 757 (9th Cir.) .... [1988] 519
Parekh *v.* Shah Jehan Cinemas (Pty.) Ltd. and Others, 1980 (1) SA 301 (D) .... [1987] 310
Paris, The (1854) 1 Sp. 289 .... [1989] 63, 69
Park Gate Waggon Works Co. (*Re*) (1881) 17 Ch. D. 234 .... [1990] 217
Parke *v.* Daily News Ltd. [1962] Ch. 927 .... [1990] 410
Parke Davis & Co. *v.* B.O.A.C. (1958) (N.Y. Cty. Ct.) .... [1989] 38
Parker *v.* Hoefer, 2 N.Y. 2d 612; 142 N.E. 2d 194; 162 N.Y.S. 2d 13, cert. denied, 355 U.S. 833 (1957) .... [1987] 154
Parker *v.* South Eastern Ry. Co. (1877) 2 C.P.D. 416 .... [1987] 65, 80; [1988] 294; [1990] 284
Parkin *v.* Dick (1809) 11 East 502 .... [1987] 212
Parklines S.A. *v.* *Mercandian Senator*, No. 84–3793 (D.N.J. 7 November 1984) .... [1986] 356
Parkside Leasing Ltd. *v.* Smith [1985] 1 W.L.R. 310 .... [1990] 67, 68
Parlement Belge, The (1880) 5 P.D. 197 .... [1990] 171
Parott *v.* Wells Fargo & Co. (1872) 82 U.S. 524 .... [1989] 353
Parouth, The [1982] 2 Lloyd's Rep. 351 .... [1989] 220; [1990] 192
Parr's Bank Ltd. *v.* Thomas Ashby & Co. (1898) 14 T.L.R. 563 .... [1990] 72, 73, 76, 247
Parr's Banking Co. Ltd. *v.* Yates [1898] 2 Q.B. 460 .... [1990] 491
Parry *v.* Cleaver [1970] A.C. 1 .... [1986] 150
Partabmull Rameshwar *v.* K.C. Sethia (1944) Ltd. [1951] 2 Lloyd's Rep. 89 (H.L.) .... [1987] 207
Partenreederei M.S. Tilly Russ *v.* Haven & Vervoebedrijf Nova N.V., Case 71/83 [1985] Q.B. 931; [1984] E.C.R. 2417; [1984] 3 C.M.L.R. 499 .... [1988] 389
Patapsco Ins. Co. *v.* Coulter (1830) 3 Pet. S.C.R. 222 .... [1988] 334
Paterson Zochonis & Co. Ltd. *v.* Merfarken Packaging Ltd. [1986] 3 All E.R. 522 .... [1987] 9
Patmos, The, 1st Civil Div., Messina, 7 July 1986 .... [1987] 275
Paton *v.* Inland Revenue Commissioners [1938] A.C. 341 .... [1990] 491
Patrick & Lyon Ltd. (*Re*) [1933] Ch. 786 .... [1990] 206
Patterson *v.* Harris (1861) 1 B. & S. 336; 121 E.R. 740 .... [1986] 39
Patton-Tully Transportation Co. (*In re*) (1986) 797 F. 2d 206 (5th Cir.) .... [1988] 519
Paul *v.* National Steamship Co. Ltd. (1937) 43 Com. Cas. 68 .... [1987] 257
Paul *v.* Pavey & Matthews Pty. Ltd. [1985] 3 N.S.W.L.R. 114 .... [1990] 509
Paul and Frank Ltd. *v.* Discount Bank (Overseas) Ltd. [1967] Ch. 348 .... [1988] 144; [1989] 207, 209; [1990] 527
Pavey & Matthews Pty. Ltd. *v.* Paul (1987) 162 C.L.R. 221 .... [1989] 141; [1990] 337, 496
Pavlides *v.* Jensen [1956] Ch. 565 .... [1988] 66
Paz, The, 1984 (3) S.A. 261 (N) .... [1990] 9
P. Dougherty Co. *v.* U.S.A. (*The Mohawk*) 1953 A.M.C. 1541 (U.S.C.A., 3rd Cir.) .... [1990] 52
Peabody Donation Fund *v.* Sir Lindsay Parkinson Ltd. [1985] A.C. 210, 240 .... [1986] 97
Peace, The (1856) Swab. 115 .... [1989] 61
Peachdart Ltd (*Re*) [1984] Ch. 131 .... [1986] 168; [1988] 147; [1989] 119, 120
Pearce *v.* Brooks (1866) L.R. 1 Ex. 213 .... [1988] 127
Pedrick *v.* Morning Star Motors Ltd. 14 February 1979 (Unrep.) .... [1987] 43
Peffer *v.* Rigg [1977] 1 W.L.R. 285 .... [1990] 530
Pegasus, The [1967] 2 Q.B. 86 .... [1986] 144
Peggy Doreen, The [1970] 2 Lloyd's Rep. 347 .... [1989] 94
Pelorus, The [1987] 2 Lloyd's Rep. 667 .... [1988] 178
Penarth Dock Engineering *v.* Pounds [1963] 1 Lloyd's Rep. 359 .... [1987] 428

Pendrecht, The [1980] 2 Lloyd's Rep. 56 .... [1986] 115
Penfolds Wines Pty. Ltd. *v.* Elliott (1946) 74 C.L.R. 204, 217–218 .... [1986] 232
Pennell *v.* Venida Investments Ltd. Unrep., 25 July 1974 .... [1988] 71
Pennsylvania Glass Sand *v.* Caterpillar Tractor Co., 652 F. 2d 1165 (3rd Cir., 1981) .... [1987] 119
Pennsylvania Mftrs. Ins. Co. *v.* Aetna Casualty & Surety Ins. Co., 426 Pa. 453, 457, 233 A.2d 548, 551 (1967) .... [1986] 82
Pensacola, The (1864) Br. & Lush. 306 .... [1989] 73, 76
People *v.* Cunard White Star Ltd., 280 N.Y. 413; 21 N.E. 2d 489 (1939) .... [1987] 521
People *v.* Detroit, B.I. & W. Ferry Co., 187 Mich. 177; 153 N.W. 799 (1915) .... [1987] 521
People *v.* United National Life Insurance Co., 427 P. 2d 199 (S.C. Cal., 1967) .... [1987] 208
People of the State of Illinois *v.* Giliberto (1978) 383 N.E. 2d 977 (IU.); 15 Avi. 17, 429, cert. denied (1979) 99 S. Ct. 2052 .... [1988] 224
People's Ferry Co. *v.* Beers, 20 How. 673 (U.S. 1857) .... [1986] 12
Peralta *v.* Smith & Johnson, 739 F. 2d 798 (1984); cert. denied 105 S. Ct. 1405 .... [1986] 12
Peralta (*Re*) and the Queen (1985) 16 D.L.R. (4th) 259; 49 O.R. (2d) 705 .... [1987] 89
Percival *v.* Wright [1902] 2 Ch. 421 .... [1988] 80
Perdana Properties Bhd. *v.* United Orient Leasing Co. Sdn. Bhd. [1981] 1 W.L.R. 1496 (P.C.) .... [1987] 63
Perez & Co. *v.* *Mexico I* (1987) 826 F. 2d 1449; 1988 A.M.C. 1930 (5th Cir.) .... [1989] 12
Pericles, The (1863) Br. & Lush. 80 .... [1989] 75
Perla, The (1857) Swab. 230 .... [1989] 66, 72
Permanent Houses (Holdings) Ltd. (*Re*) [1988] B.C.L.C. 563 .... [1990] 209, 403, 528
Persia, The (1842) 1 W. Rob. 327 .... [1989] 69
Persia, The (1853) 1 Sp. 166 .... [1989] 73
Peter Cassidy Seed Co. Ltd. *v.* Osuustukkukauppa [1957] 1 W.L.R. 273 .... [1987] 207
Peter Lind & Co. Ltd. *v.* Mersey Docks and Harbour Board [1972] 2 Lloyd's Rep. 234 .... [1990] 503
Peter Pan Manufacturing Corp. *v.* Corsets Silhouette [1964] 1 W.L.R. 96 .... [1987] 428; [1990] 462
Peter Symmons & Co. *v.* Cook (1981) 131 N.L.J. 758 .... [1989] 374, 375, 378, 381
Peter Turnbull & Co. Pty. Ltd. *v.* Mundus Trading Co. (Australasia) Pty. Ltd. (1954) 90 C.L.R. 235 .... [1989] 84
Peters *v.* South Netherlands Contractors' Association, Case 34/82 [1983] E.C.R. 987; [1984] 2 C.M.L.R. 605 .... [1988] 384
Peters *v.* ZNAV, Case 34/82 [1983] E.C.R. 987 .... [1990] 193
Petrofina *v.* Magnaload [1984] Q.B. 127 .... [1990] 135
Petroleum Helicopters Inc. *v.* Boeing-Vertol Co., 478 F. Supp. 84 (E.D. La.), aff'd *per curiam* on basis of opinion below, 606 F. 2d 114 (5 Cir. 1979) .... [1986] 359
Petros Hadjikyriakos, The [1988] 2 Lloyd's Rep. 56 .... [1990] 387
Pettus *v.* Jones & Laughlin Steel Corp., 322 F. Supp. 1078, 1972 A.M.C. 170 (W.D. Pa. 1971) .... [1986] 381
Peveril Gold Mines Ltd. (*Re*) [1898] 1 Ch. 122 .... [1990] 407
Peyman *v.* Lanjani [1985] 2 W.L.R. 154 .... [1986] 318
Pfeiffer (E.) Weinkellerei-Weineinkauf G.m.b.H. & Co. *v.* Arbuthnot Factors Ltd. [1988] 1 W.L.R. 150 .... [1988] 141; [1989] 198 *et seq.*; [1990] 530
P.G. du Quebec *v.* Vincent [1984] C.S. 1037 .... [1987] 96
Phantom, The (1866) L.R. 1 A. & E. 58 .... [1989] 76
Phibro Energy Inc. *v.* Coastal (Bermuda) Ltd. (*The Aragon*) 15 April 1987 .... [1989] 143 *et seq.*
Philip Morris (Aust.) Pty. Ltd. *v.* Transport Commission [1975] Tas. S.R. 128 .... [1988] 467
Phillips *v.* Brooks Ltd. [1919] 2 K.B. 243 .... [1986] 323
Phillips *v.* Ellinson Bros. Pty. Ltd. (1941) 65 C.L.R. 221 .... [1990] 511, 515
Phillips *v.* Eyre (1870) L.R. 6 Q.B. 1 (Ex. Ch. 1870) .... [1986] 99; [1987] 154
Phillips *v.* Homfray (1883) 24 Ch. D. 439 .... [1987] 433
Phillips *v.* Hunter (1795) 2 H. Bl. 414 .... [1987] 430
Phillips Products Ltd. *v.* Hyland [1987] 1 W.L.R. 659 .... [1988] 475
Philp *v.* Bennet & Co. (1901) 18 T.L.R. 128 .... [1986] 395
Phipps *v.* Boardman [1964] 1 W.L.R. 993 .... [1988] 133
Phoenix General Insurance Co. of Greece S.A. *v.* A.D.A.S. [1988] Q.B. 216 .... [1988] 126, 254
Phoenix General Insurance Co. of Greece S.A. *v.* Halvanon Insurance Co. Ltd. [1985] 2 Lloyd's Rep. 599; [1986] 2 Lloyd's Rep. 552 (C.A.); [1987] 2 W.L.R. 512; [1988] Q.B. 216 .... [1987] 37, 202, 203, 204, 205, 206, 207, 208, 210, 244; [1989] 248, 494; [1990] 134
Phoenix Indemnity *v.* Steiden Stores Inc. (1954) 267 S.W. 2d 733, 735 (Kentucky C.A.) [1989] 434, 439
Phoenix Ins. Co. *v.* Erie W. Transp. Co., 117 U.S. 312 (U.S.S. Ct., 1886) .... [1986] 495

Phonogram Ltd. *v.* Lane [1982] Q.B. 938 ... [1990] 411
Phonographic Equipment (1958) Ltd. *v.* Muslu [1961] 1 W.L.R. 1379 ... [1990] 19
Photo Production Ltd. *v.* Securicor Transport Ltd. [1980] A.C. 367; [1980] A.C. 827 (H.L.) ... [1986] 341; [1987] 63, 126, 144, 147, 166, 236; [1988] 115, 297, 474, 512; [1989] 396; [1990] 155, 498, 555
Pickett *v.* British Rail Engineering [1980] A.C. 136 ... [1990] 138
Pickstone *v.* Freemans Plc [1989] A.C. 66 ... [1990] 412
Pickup *v.* Thames & Mersey Marine Insurance Co. Ltd. (1878) 3 Q.B.D. 594 ... [1988] 345
Pickwick, The (1852) 16 Jur. 669 ... [1989] 71
Pierce *v.* Bemis (*The Lusitania*) [1986] Q.B. 384 ... [1987] 267
Piercy *v.* Mills & Co. Ltd. [1902] 1 Ch. 77 ... [1988] 72
Piermay Shipping Co. S.A. and Brandt's Ltd. *v.* Chester (*The Michael*) [1979] 1 Lloyd's Rep. 55; [1979] 2 Lloyd's Rep. 1 (C.A.) ... [1987] 39; [1989] 26
Piggly Wiggly Operators' Warehouse Inc. *v.* Piggly Wiggly Operators' Warehouse Independent Truck Drivers Union, Local No. 1, 611 F. 2d 580, 583 (5 Cir. 1980) ... [1986] 49
Piggott *v.* Anglo-American Telegraph Co. (1868) 19 L.T. 46 ... [1990] 323
Pilgrim Apparel Inc. *v.* National Union Fire Ins. Co. (1958) 6 Avi. Cas. 17733 (N.Y. Cty. Ct.) [1989] 38
Pine Top Insurance Co. Ltd. *v.* Unione Italiana Anglo Saxon Reinsurance Co. [1987] 1 Lloyd's Rep. 476 ... [1988] 9
Pink *v.* Fleming (1890) 25 Q.B.D. 396; 6 Asp. M.L.C. 554 ... [1987] 458
Pioneer Concrete (U.K.) Ltd. *v.* National Employers Mutual General Insurance Association Ltd. [1985] 1 Lloyd's Rep. 274 ... [1987] 233
Pioneer Shipping Ltd. *v.* B.T.P. Tioxide Ltd. (*The Nema*) [1982] A.C. 724 ... [1986] 46, 75, 345, 346; [1988] 396
Piper Aircraft Co. *v.* Reyno, 454 U.S. 235 (1981) (U.S. Sup. Ct.) ... [1987] 5
Pipon *v.* Cope (1808) 1 Camp. 434 ... [1988] 338
Pirelli General Cable Works Ltd. *v.* Oscar Faber & Partners [1983] 2 A.C. 1 ... [1988] 260
Pitria Star, The, 1986 A.M.C. 2966 (U.S.D.C., E.D. Louisiana) ... [1989] 357
Pitria Star Navigation Co. *v.* Monsanto Co. (*The Pitria Star*), 1986 A.M.C. 2966 (U.S.D.C., E.D. Louisiana) ... [1989] 357
Pitsa T, The [1987] 2 Lloyd's Rep. 404 ... [1990] 97
Pitts (*Re*) [1931] 1 Ch. 546 ... [1987] 210
Place *v.* Norwich & New York Transportation Co. (*The City of Norwich*) (1886) 118 U.S. 468 ... [1986] 380; [1987] 345; [1988] 518
Planché *v.* Colburn (1831) 8 Bing. 14 ... [1990] 502
Planche *v.* Fletcher (1779) 1 Doug. 251 ... [1987] 211
Planet Shipping Co. *v.* S.A. Marocaine de l'Industrie de Raffinage (*The Athenic*) [1984] L.M.L.N. 134 ... [1986] 78
Plata American Trading *v.* Lancashire, 1958 A.M.C. 2329 (N.Y.A.D.) ... [1986] 492
Platoro Limited Inc. *v.* The Unidentified Remains of a Vessel, etc., et al., 614 F. 2d 1051, 1055; 1981 A.M.C. 1097, 1102–1103 (5 Cir. 1980) ... [1986] 20
Pleschell *v.* Allnutt (1813) 4 Taunt. 792 ... [1987] 212
Plymouth, The, 3 Wall. 20 (1866) ... [1987] 118
PMPA Insurance Co. Ltd. *v.* New Ireland Assurance Co., *Irish Times*, 23 October 1975 (Irish H.C.) ... [1986] 64
Polar Shipping Ltd. *v.* Oriental Shipping Corp., 680 F. 2d 627, 1982 A.M.C. 2330 (9 Cir. 1982) ... [1986] 350
Polhill *v.* Walter (1832) 2 B. & Ad. 114 ... [1988] 464
Polish Steamship Co. *v.* Atlantic Maritime Co. [1985] 1 Q.B. 41 ... [1990] 310
Poliskie Line Oceanicze *v.* Hooker Chemical Corp., 1980 A.M.C. 1748; 499 F. Supp. 94 (S.D.N.Y.) ... [1989] 355, 360
Pollock *v.* Bank of New Zealand (1901) 20 N.Z.L.R. 174 ... [1990] 251
Polyfreedom, The, 1975 A.M.C. 1826, S.M.A. No. 926 (1975) ... [1986] 57; [1990] 390
Polyglory, The [1977] 2 Lloyd's Rep. 353 ... [1988] 50
Polypropylene [1986] O.J. No. L 230/1 ... [1988] 193
Pool *v.* Pool (1889) 58 L.J.P. 67 ... [1986] 206
Popi M, The [1985] 1 W.L.R. 948 ... [1986] 40, 286; [1987] 40; [1988] 350
Port Colborne Warehousing *v.* Board of Steamship Inspection (1987) 73 N.R. 126 (Fed. C.A.) ... [1989] 92

Port Jackson Stevedoring Pty. Ltd. *v.* Salmond & Spraggon (Australia) Pty. Ltd. (*The New York Star*) (1978) 139 C.L.R. 231; (1980) 144 C.L.R. 300; [1981] 1 W.L.R. 138 (P.C.) .... [1986] 344; [1987] 166, 223; [1989] 280, 395; [1990] 326
Port Line Ltd. *v.* Ben Line Steamers Ltd. [1958] 2 Q.B. 146 .... [1986] 149
Port Swettenham Authority *v.* T.W. Wu & Co. (M) Sdn. Bhd. [1979] A.C. 580 (P.C.) [1987] 45, 49, 126
Porta-Leasing *v.* Prestige, Case 784/79 [1980] E.C.R. 1517; [1981] 1 C.M.L.R. 135 .... [1988] 389
Porter *v.* American Optical Corp., 641 F. 2d 1128 (5 Cir.), cert. denied 455 U.S. 1109 (1981) . [1986] 88
Porter *v.* General Guarantee Corp. [1982] R.T.R. 384 .... [1987] 126; [1990] 366
Porteus *v.* Watney (1878) 2 Q.B.D. 534 .... [1990] 394
Posgate & Denby (Agencies) Ltd. (*Re*) [1987] B.C.L.C. 8 .... [1988] 62
Posner *v.* Scott-Lewis [1987] Ch. 25 .... [1987] 552
Post Chaser, The [1982] 1 All E.R. 19 .... [1990] 454
Post Office *v.* Norwich Union Fire Insurance Society Ltd. [1967] 2 Q.B. 363 .... [1987] 230, 406; [1989] 504, 505
Potton Homes Ltd. *v.* Coleman Contractors Ltd. (1984) 28 B.L.R. 19 .... [1990] 223, 233, 236, 240, 242
Powell and Thomas *v.* Evan Jones & Co. [1905] 1 K.B. 11 .... [1988] 128; [1990] 550, 551
Power Curber International Ltd. *v.* National Bank of Kuwait S.A.K. [1981] 1 W.L.R. 1233 .... [1990] 90, 93, 240
Powstaniec Wielkopolski, The [1988] 3 W.L.R. 723; (1988) 228 L.M.L.N. (12 July) .... [1988] 452; [1989] 137
Practice Direction (Arbitration Award: Appeal) [1985] 1 W.L.R. 959 .... [1986] 72
Practice Note (C.A.: Skeleton Arguments) [1983] 1 W.L.R. 1055 .... [1986] 72
Pre-Cam Exploration and Development Ltd. *v.* McTavish (1966) 57 D.L.R. (2nd) 557 .... [1990] 462
President Brand, The [1967] 2 Lloyd's Rep. 338 .... [1990] 393
President of India *v.* La Pintada Compania Navigación S.A. (*The La Pintada*) [1985] A.C. 104; [1984] 2 Lloyd's Rep. 9 (H.L.) .... [1986] 73, 76, 140; [1987] 415; [1988] 177
President of India v. Lips Maritime Corp. (*The Lips*) [1987] 3 W.L.R. 572; [1987] 2 W.L.R. 906 .... [1987] 414, 415; [1988] 177
President of India *v.* Metcalfe Shipping Co. Ltd. (*The Dunelmia*) [1970] 1 Q.B. 289 .... [1986] 99, 481
Press Caps Ltd. (*Re*) [1949] Ch. 434 .... [1990] 260, 264
Preveze, The [1971] 1 Lloyd's Rep. 202 .... [1990] 172
Priam, The [1948] A.C. 243 .... [1987] 31
Pride of Canada, The (1863) Br. & Lush. 208 .... [1989] 76
Prideaux *v.* Criddle (1869) L.R. 4 Q.B. 455 .... [1990] 71
Primlaks Ltd. (*Re*) (1989) 5 B.C.C. 710 .... [1989] 507; [1990] 413
Prince *v.* Oriental Bank Corp. (1878) 3 App. Cas. 325 .... [1990] 71
Prince of Wales, The (1848) 6 N.o.C. 39 .... [1989] 61
Princess Alice, The (1848) 3 W. Rob. 138 .... [1988] 16; [1989] 64, 69
Princess Cruises Corp. *v.* Bayly, Martin & Fay Inc., 1974 A.M.C. 433 (N.D. Cal.) .... [1986] 496
Princess Helena, The (1861) Lush. 190 .... [1989] 65
Prins Frederik, The (1820) 2 Dods. 451 .... [1988] 11
Procter & Gamble Philippine Manufacturing Corp. *v.* Kurt A. Becher [1988] 2 Lloyd's Rep. 21 (affmg. [1988] 1 Lloyd's Rep. 88) .... [1988] 457
Procter & Gamble Philippine Manufacturing Corp. *v.* Peter Cremer G.m.b.H. & Co. (*The Manila*) [1988] 3 All E.R. 843 .... [1989] 397
Produce Brokers New Company (1924) Ltd. *v.* Wray, Sanderson & Co. Ltd. (1931) 39 Ll.L.Rep. 257 .... [1987] 185
Produce Marketing Consortium Ltd. (*Re*) [1989] 1 W.L.R. 745; (1989) 5 B.C.C. 569 .... [1990] 207, 212, 214, 215, 216
Produits Alimentaires Gradma Ltee *v.* Zim Israel Navigation Co. (1988) 86 N.R. 39 (Fed. C.A.) .... [1990] 103
Progressive Mailing House Pty. Ltd. *v.* Tabili Pty. Ltd. (1985) 157 C.L.R. 17 .... [1987] 146
Progress Marine Inc. *v.* Foremost Ins. Co., 642 F. 2d 816 (5 Cir. 1981) .... [1986] 427, 428, 429
Project Development Co. Ltd. S.A. *v.* KMK Securities Ltd. [1982] 1 W.L.R. 1470 .... [1990] 97
Prometheus, The [1974] 1 Lloyd's Rep. 350 .... [1986] 258, 259
Proodos Marine Carriers Co. *v.* Overseas Shipping and Logistics, 578 F. Supp. 207, 1984 A.M.C. 2392 (S.D.N.Y. 1984) .... [1986] 357
Propeller Genesee Chief, The (1851) 53 U.S. 443 .... [1989] 15
Property Life Ltd. *v.* Edgar. 15 March 1980 (N.Z. Sup. Ct.) (Unrep.) .... [1986] 231; [1987] 64
Prosperity Ltd. *v.* Lloyds Bank Ltd. (1923) 39 T.L.R. 372 .... [1989] 41

Proudfoot *v.* Montefiore (1867) L.R. 2 Q.B. 511 .... [1986] 320
Prudential Assurance *v.* Newman Industries Ltd. (No. 2) [1982] Ch. 204 .... [1990] 402
Prudential Insurance Co. of America *v.* Goldstein, 43 F. Supp. 765 (E.D.N.Y., 1942) .... [1987] 212
Prudential Lines *v.* Exxon, 704 F. 2d 59, 67 (2 Cir. 1983) .... [1986] 58
P.S. Chellaram & Co. Ltd. *v.* China Ocean Shipping Co. [1989] 1 Lloyd's Rep. 413 (N.S.W. Sup. Ct.) .... [1989] 277 *et seq.*; [1990] 315
Pt. Karana Line *v.* Eddie Steamship Co. Ltd. (*The Kartini*) (1984) S.M.A No. 1958 .... [1989] 347, 348, 353, 355
Public Utilities Commission of City of Waterloo *v.* Burroughs Business Machines (1975) 52 D.L.R. (3d) 481 .... [1990] 379
Public Works Commissioner *v.* Hills [1906] A.C. 368 (P.C.) .... [1990] 158
Puerto Buitrago, The [1976] 1 Lloyd's Rep. 250 .... [1986] 124
Puerto Rico Maritime Shipping Auth. *v.* Star Lines Ltd., 454 F. Supp. 368 (S.D.N.Y. 1978) . [1986] 358
Pugh *v.* Pugh [1951] P. 482 .... [1989] 386
Pukallus *v.* Cameron (1982) 56 A.L.J.R. 907 .... [1986] 316
Punch *v.* Savoy's Jewellers Ltd. (1986) 26 D.L.R. (4th) 546 .... [1987] 49; [1988] 469
Punt *v.* Symons & Co. Ltd. [1903] 2 Ch. 506 .... [1988] 72
Purden's Curator Bonis *v.* Boyd, 1963 S.L.T. 157 (H.L.) .... [1989] 2
Purissima Concepcion, The (1849) 3 W. Rob. 181; (1850) 7 N.o.C. 503 .... [1989] 60, 67
Puritan Ins. *v.* Eagle S.S. Co., Docket No. 85–7320 (Slip Opinion, 18 December 1985) .... [1986] 506
Pye Ltd. *v.* B.G. Transport Service Ltd. [1966] 2 Lloyd's Rep. 300 .... [1987] 213; [1988] 125
Pyrene Co. Ltd. *v.* Scindia Navigation Co. Ltd. [1954] 2 Q.B. 402 .... [1986] 269; [1988] 84; [1989] 171, 395; [1990] 316
Pythia, The [1979] Q.B. 645 .... [1990] 287, 320
Q.N.S. Paper Co. *v.* Chartwell Shipping Ltd. [1985] C.A. 413 (Quebec C.A.) .... [1987] 82
Quebec Marine Insurance Co. *v.* Commercial Bank of Canada (1870) L.R. 3 P.C. 234, 244 .... [1986] 37
Queen, The (1853) 1 Sp. 175n .... [1989] 69
Queen, The *v.* The *Sun Diamond* [1984] 1 F.C. 3 .... [1987] 95
Queen Ins. Co. of America *v.* Globe & Rutgers Fire Ins. Co., 263 U.S. 487 (S. Ct., 1923) .... [1986] 484
Queensland Electricity Generating Board *v.* New Hope Collieries Pty. Ltd. [1986] 2 B.C.L. 86 .... [1989] 232
Quinn *v.* Burch Bros. (Builders) Ltd. [1966] 2 Q.B. 370 .... [1990] 417
Quistclose Investments Ltd. *v.* Rolls Razor Ltd. [1970] A.C. 567 .... [1988] 362; [1989] 120, 258
Qureshi *v.* Qureshi [1972] Fam. 173 .... [1988] 395
R. *v.* Austen (1985) 82 L.S. Gaz. 2499 .... [1987] 189
R. *v.* Belliveau (1987) 200 A.P.R. 382 (N.S. Co. Ct.) .... [1989] 101
R. *v.* Bradley [1961] 1 W.L.R. 398 .... [1987] 198
R. *v.* Campbell [1984] B.C.L.C. 83; (1984) 78 Cr. App. R. 95 .... [1987] 197
R. *v.* Campbell (1987) 62 Nfld. & P.E.I.R. 176; 190 A.P.R. 176 (P.E.I. C.A.) .... [1988] 89
R. *v.* Corbin (1984) 6 Cr. App. R. (S.) 17 .... [1987] 189
R. *v.* Crown Zellerbach Canada Ltd. [1988] 1 S.C.R. 401 (Can. S.C.) .... [1990] 101
R. *v.* Cuthbertson [1981] A.C. 470 .... [1987] 214
R. *v.* Empire Sandy Inc. (1988) 24 O.A.C. 219 (Ont. C.A.) .... [1989] 92
R. *v.* Frei (1988) 216 A.P.R. 368 (N.S. C.A.) .... [1990] 105
R. *v.* Gallant (1987) 62 Nfld. & P.E.I.R. 62; 190 A.P.R. 62 (Nfld. S.C.) .... [1988] 89
R. *v.* Gray [1900] 2 Q.B. 36 .... [1990] 88
R. *v.* Green & Green [1981] 3 Cr. App. R. (S.) 22 .... [1987] 191
R. *v.* Grossman (1981) 73 Cr. App. R. 302 .... [1988] 362; [1989] 365; [1990] 93
R. *v.* Guignard (1987) 201 A.P.R. 389 (N.B.Q.B.) .... [1989] 100
R. *v.* Hopkins (1988) 206 A.P.R. 203 (Nfld. C.A.) .... [1989] 102
R. *v.* Howson (1966) 55 D.L.R. (2d) 582 .... [1987] 55
R. *v.* Johnson and Wilson (1987) 198 A.P.R. 411 (N.B. Prov. Ct.) .... [1989] 101
R. *v.* Kelly [1982] A.C. 665 .... [1990] 163
R. *v.* Kelsey (1985) 162 A.P.R. 154; 55 Nfld. & P.E.I.R. 154 (Nfld. D.C.) .... [1987] 86
R. *v.* Kelton and Cumberworth, *sub nom.* R. *v.* Cumberworth, *The Times*, 8 May 1989 .... [1990] 162
R. *v.* Kemp [1988] Q.B. 645 (pet. diss. [1988] 1 W.L.R. 846 (H.L.)) .... [1990] 206
R. *v.* Lefevre (1987) 191 A.P.R. 85 (N.S.S.C. in Appeal) .... [1989] 99
R. *v.* Lesley (1860) Bell 226 .... [1990] 163
R. *v.* Liverpool JJ., *ex p.* Molyneux [1972] 2 Q.B. 384 .... [1990] 163, 164
R. *v.* Lovitt [1912] A.C. 212 .... [1990] 71
R. *v.* Otero (1988) 209 A.P.R. 115 (Nfld. S.C.) .... [1989] 101

R. *v*. Panel on Take-overs and Mergers, *ex p*. Datafin Plc [1987] Q.B. 815 .... [1990] 403, 410, 436
R. *v*. Panel on Take-overs and Mergers, *ex p*. Guinness Plc [1989] 2 W.L.R. 863 .... [1990] 403
R. *v*. Paul (1987) 194 A.P.R. 268 (Nfld. S.C.) .... [1989] 101
R. *v*. Registrar of Companies, *ex p*. Central Bank of India [1986] Q.B. 1114 .... [1990] 401, 534
R. *v*. Robertson (1984) 43 C.R. (3d) 39 .... [1989] 101
R. *v*. Roman and Alonso (1987) 204 A.P.R. 319 (Nfld. C.A.); (1989) 92 N.R. 322 (Can. S.C.) .... [1989] 100; [1990] 105
R. *v*. Secretary of State for the Home Dept., *ex p*. Khan [1984] 1 W.L.R. 1337 .... [1990] 435
R. *v*. Secretary of State for the Home Office, *ex p*. Ruddock [1987] 1 W.L.R. 1482 .... [1990] 435
R. *v*. Secretary of State for Trade and Industry, *ex p*. R. [1989] 1 W.L.R. 372 .... [1990] 406
R. *v*. Shadrokh-Cigari [1988] Crim.L.R. 465 .... [1989] 305
R. *v*. Skinner (1985) 147 A.P.R. 313; 65 N.S.R. (2d) 313 .... [1987] 90
R. *v*. Skinner (1987) 200 A.P.R. 115 (N.S. Co. Ct.) .... [1989] 100
R. *v*. Squires (1987) 62 Nfld. & P.E.I.R. 48; 190 A.P.R. 48 (Nfld. Prov. Ct.) .... [1988] 89
R. *v*. Starvish (1987) 196 A.P.R. 136 (N.S.S.C. App. Div.) .... [1989] 99
R. *v*. Sussex Justices [1924] 1 K.B. 256 .... [1989] 92
R. & B. Customs Brokers Co. Ltd. *v*. United Dominions Trust Ltd. [1988] 1 W.L.R. 321 .... [1989] 371, 375, 377, 380, 381
Rabin *v*. Gerson Berger Association Ltd. [1986] 1 All E.R. 374 .... [1986] 157
Radford *v*. De Froberville [1977] 1 W.L.R. 1262 .... [1987] 432
Radnor, The [1956] 1 Q.B. 333 .... [1990] 388
Rae *v*. Yorkshire Bank plc [1988] F.L.R. 1 .... [1988] 138
Raffles *v*. Wichelhaus (1864) 2 H. & C. 906; 159 E.R. 375 .... [1987] 337
Rafuse Motors *v*. Mardo Construction Ltd. (1964) 41 D.L.R. (2d) 340 .... [1990] 379
Rajasthan, The (1856) Swab. 171 .... [1989] 78
Ralli Bros. *v*. Compania Naviera Sota y Aznar [1920] 1 K.B. 614; [1920] 2 K.B. 287 .... [1987] 211, 384; [1989] 386
Ram Narain *v*. Radha Kishen Moti Lal Chamaria Firm (1929) L.R. 57 Ind. App. 76 .... [1990] 530
Rama Corp. Ltd. *v*. Proved Tin Investments [1952] 2 Q.B. 147 .... [1990] 405
Ramsay *v*. Hartley [1977] 1 W.L.R. 686 .... [1990] 219
Ramsay Scarlett *v*. M.V. *Koh Eun*, 462 F. Supp. 277; 1979 A.M.C. 970 (E.D. Va., 1978) .... [1987] 153
Ramsay Scarlett & Co. *v*. S.S. *Koh Eun*, 462 F. Supp. 1286, 1978 A.M.C. 1477 (E.D. Va. 1978) .... [1986] 355
Ranger, The (1845) 3 N.o.C. 589 .... [1989] 64, 69
Raphael, The [1982] 2 Lloyd's Rep. 42 .... [1990] 155
Rasbora Ltd. *v*. J.C.L. Marine Ltd. [1977] 1 Lloyd's Rep. 645 .... [1989] 373
Rasmussen and S/LF Bordoyarvik *v*. Canadian Saltfish Corp. (1986) 68 N.R. 379 .... [1989] 90
Rasnoimport (V/O) *v*. Guthrie & Co. Ltd. [1966] 1 Lloyd's Rep. 1 .... [1986] 269; [1989] 173
Raven, The [1980] 2 Lloyd's Rep. 132 .... [1990] 475
Rawson *v*. Samuel (1839) 1 Cr. & Ph. 161 .... [1989] 293, 294; [1990] 474
Ray *v*. Atlantic Richfield Co., 435 U.S. 151, 1978 A.M.C. 527 (1978) .... [1986] 377
Rayner (J. H.) (Mincing Lane) Ltd. *v*. Bank fur Gemeinwirtschaft A.G. [1983] 1 Lloyd's Rep. 462 (C.A.) .... [1986] 399
Rayner (J.H.) (Mincing Lane) Ltd. *v*. Dept. of Trade and Industry [1989] 3 W.L.R. 969; [1989] 3 All E.R. 523 (H.L.), affirming [1989] Ch. 72; [1988] 3 All E.R. 272 (C.A.) .... [1990] 305
Rayner (J.H.) (Mincing Lane) Ltd. *v*. Dept. of Trade and Industry [1989] 3 W.L.R. 969; [1989] 3 All E.R. 523 (H.L.), affirming [1989] Ch. 253; [1988] 3 All E.R. 364 (C.A.), affirming [1988] Ch. 1; [1987] 3 All E.R. 787 .... [1990] 306
R.D. Harbottle (Mercantile) Ltd. *v*. National Westminster Bank Ltd. [1978] Q.B. 146 .... [1990] 223, 236, 239
R.E. Jones Ltd. *v*. Waring & Gillow Ltd. [1926] A.C. 670 .... [1989] 305, 306
Reading *v*. Attorney-General [1951] A.C. 507; [1948] 2 K.B. 268; [1949] 2 K.B. 232 ..... [1987] 434, 435
Reardon Smith Line Ltd. *v*. Australian Wheat Board (*The Houston City*) [1956] A.C. 266; (1954) 91 C.L.R. 233; [1954] 2 Lloyd's Rep. 148 .... [1986] 116; [1987] 409; [1988] 43
Reardon Smith Line Ltd. *v*. Ministry of Agriculture [1962] 1 Q.B. 42; aff'd. in part on other grounds [1963] A.C. 691 .... [1987] 409; [1988] 51, 54
Reardon Smith Line Ltd. *v*. Yngvar Hansen-Tangen and Sanko Steamship Co. (*The Diana Prosperity*) [1976] 1 W.L.R. 989 .... [1986] 242; [1987] 35; [1988] 462, 506; [1990] 457
Reckitt *v*. Barnett, Pembroke and Slater Ltd. [1929] A.C. 176 .... [1989] 321
Red Rover, The (1850) 3 W. Rob. 150 .... [1989] 69, 78
Red Star Towing & Transp. Co. *v*. Woodburn, 18 F. 2d 77, 1927 A.M.C. 597 (2 Cir. 1927) .. [1986] 379

Reddie *v.* Williamson (1863) 1 Macph. 228 (Ct. of Sess.) .... [1990] 491
Redler Grain Silos Ltd. *v.* BICC Ltd. [1982] 1 Lloyd's Rep. 435 .... [1986] 223
Reece *v.* Yeager Ford Sales Inc. (1971) 155 W. Va. 453; 184 S.E. 2d 722 .... [1990] 374
Reed *v.* Wiser, 14 Avi 17, 481 (1977) 17, 848 .... [1986] 292
Reference re Industrial Relations and Disputes Investigation Act [1955] S.C.R. 529 ....[1987] 89
Regal (Hastings) Ltd. *v.* Gulliver [1967] 2 A.C. 134n.; [1942] 1 All E.R. 378 .... [1987] 429
Regal Sword, The, 1983 A.M.C. 2240 (S.D.N.Y. 1983) .... [1986] 425, 426
Regazzoni *v.* K.C. Sethia (1944) Ltd. [1958] A.C. 301 .... [1987] 384; [1989] 366
Regent, The, 1945 A.M.C. 25 (E.D.N.Y.) .... [1986] 494
Regent OHG Aisenstadt und Barig *v.* Francesco of Jermyn Street Ltd. [1981] 3 All E.R. 327 . [1989] 83
Regina *v.* General Motors of Canada Ltd. (1985) 48 O.R. (2d) 204 ....[1987] 96
Regina *v.* Martin; Regina *v.* MacIntyre (1985) 154 A.P.R. 52; 59 N.B.R. (2d) 52; (N.B.Q.B. Trial Div.) ....[1987] 86
Regina *v.* Rocher (1985) 14 D.L.R. (4th) 210 ....[1987] 89
Regina *v.* Saul (1984) 10 D.L.R. (4th) 736 ....[1987] 89
Regina *v.* Tower Hamlets L.B.C., ex p. Chetnik Developments Ltd. [1988] A.C. 858 .... [1989] 304
Reibor International Ltd. *v.* Cargo Carriers (KACZ–Co.) Ltd., 759 F. 2d 262, 1985 A.M.C. 885 (2 Cir. 1985), aff'g 1984 A.M.C. 885 (S.D.N.Y. 1984) .... [1986] 352
Reid *v.* Rigby & Co. [1894] 2 Q.B. 40 ....[1989] 307, 320
Reid *v.* Rush & Tompkins Group [1990] 1 W.L.R. 212 .... [1990] 485
Reid Newfoundland Co. *v.* Anglo-American Telegraph Co. Ltd. [1912] A.C. 555; [1910] A.C. 560; (1910) 9 Nfld. L.R. 307 .... [1987] 433
Reinante Transoceanic Navegacion S.A. *v.* President of India (*The Apiliotis*) [1985] 1 Lloyd's Rep. 255 ....[1988] 53
Reischer *v.* Borwick [1894] 2 Q.B. 548 ....[1986] 40
Rejfek *v.* McElroy (1965) 112 C.L.R. 517 .... [1986] 288
Rekstin *v.* Severo Sibirsko Gosudarstvennoe Akcionernoe Obschestvo Komseverputj and Bank for Russian Trade [1933] 1 K.B. 47 ....[1986] 207; [1988] 372; [1990] 81
Remco, The [1984] 2 Lloyd's Rep. 205 .... [1987] 261
Remia *v.* Commission [1985] E.C.R. 2566 .... [1988] 187
Rena K, The [1979] Q.B. 377 .... [1987] 87, 300, 540
Renssalaer, 1925 A.M.C. 1116 (N.Y.A.D.) .... [1986] 486
Renton (G.H.) & Co. *v.* Palmyra Trading Corp. of Panama [1957] A.C. 149 ...... [1989] 395; [1990] 316
Republic of China *v.* Nat. Union F.I. Co., 1958 A.M.C. 1529 (D. Md.) .... [1986] 489
Republic of Haiti *v.* Duvalier [1989] 2 W.L.R. 261 (C.A.) ....[1989] 465, 475; [1990] 91
Republic Insurance Co. *v.* Gatoil International Inc., 5 July 1985 (unreported) ....[1990] 97
Repulse, The (1845) 2 W. Rob. 396 ....[1989] 76
Resultatet, The (1853) 17 Jur. 353 ....[1989] 61, 62, 74, 76
Revelstoke Credit Union *v.* Miller (1984) 28 C.C.L.T. 17 .... [1990] 422, 424
Rex *v.* International Trustee for the Protection of Bondholders Aktiengesellschaft [1937] A.C. 500 .... [1987] 529
Reyners, Case 2/74, judgment of 21 June 1974; [1974] E.C.R. 631 .... [1990] 176
Rhadamanthe, The (1813) 1 Dods. 201 .... [1988] 158
Rhesa Shipping Co. S.A. *v.* Edmunds (*The Popi M*) [1985] 1 W.L.R. 948 ....[1986] 40, 286; [1987] 40; [1988] 350
Rhodesian Railways Ltd. *v.* Mackintosh, 1932 AD 359 .... [1987] 310
Rhodian River, The [1984] 1 Lloyd's Rep. 373 .... [1986] 225
Rhone, The *v.* The *Peter A.B. Widener* (1988) 18 F.T.R. 81 (F.C.) ....[1989] 97
Richard *v.* Pringle, 293 F. Supp. 981 (E.D.N.Y., 1968) ....[1987] 26
Richards *v.* James (1848) 2 Exch. 71 .... [1986] 141
Richardson *v.* Richardson (National Bank of India Ltd. garnishees) [1927] P. 228 .... [1989] 467; [1990] 71
Riches *v.* Westminster Bank Ltd. [1947] A.C. 390 .... [1988] 177
Richmond Gate Ltd. (*Re*) [1965] 1 W.L.R. 335 .... [1990] 334
Richmond Shipping Ltd. *v.* D/S & A/S Vestland (*The Vestland*) [1980] 2 Lloyd's Rep. 171 ... [1989] 192
Rickford *v.* Ridge (1810) 2 Camp. 537 ....[1990] 71
Rickless *v.* United Artists Corp. [1985] 12 F.S.R. 502; [1987] 2 W.L.R. 945 (C.A.); [1988] Q.B. 40 .... [1987] 428; [1990] 462
Rideau St. Lawrence Cruise Ships *v.* Canada (1988) 19 F.T.R. 1 (Can. F.C.) .... [1990] 100
Ridyard *v.* Roberts. 16 May 1980. (Unrep.) .... [1987] 47, 57, 67
Riedell *v.* Commercial Bank of Australia [1931] V.L.R. 382 ....[1990] 73, 76, 245, 247

Rightside Properties Ltd. *v.* Gray [1975] Ch. 72 .... [1989] 83
Rio Sun (No. 2), The [1982] 1 W.L.R. 158 .... [1989] 498
Rio Tinto Zinc Corp. *v.* Westinghouse Electric Corp. [1978] A.C. 547 .... [1988] 4
Ripon City, The [1897] P. 226 .... [1989] 193
Rivard *v.* The Queen [1979] 2 F.C. 345 .... [1987] 94
River Jimini, The (1984) 127 *Schip en Schade* 335 .... [1988] 424
River Rima, The [1987] 2 Lloyd's Rep. 106; [1988] 1 W.L.R. 758 .... [1988] 423
R.J.Moran, The, 299 F. 500 (2 Cir. 1924) .... [1986] 379
R. Leslie Ltd. *v.* Sheill [1914] 3 K.B. 607 .... [1990] 336
Roachbank, The [1987] 2 Lloyd's Rep. 498; [1988] 2 Lloyd's Rep. 337 (C.A.) .... [1990] 107, 109
Roadway Express Inc. *v.* Piper, 447 U.S. 752 (1980) .... [1986] 49
Roanoake, The (1892) 50 F. 574 .... [1990] 36
Robbie (N.W.) & Co. Ltd. *v.* Witney Warehouse Co. Ltd. [1963] 1 W.L.R. 1324 .... [1990] 220
Robert Simpson Co. Ltd. *v.* Shadlock (1981) 119 D.L.R. (3d) 417 (Ont.) .... [1986] 167
Robert Sist Development Corp. Ltd. (*Re*) (1977) 17 O.R. (2d) 305 .... [1986] 176
Robins Dry Dock & Repair Co. *v.* Flint, 275 U.S. 303, 1928 A.M.C. 61 (1927) ... [1986] 361; [1987] 511
Robinson, McLaren *v.* Public Trustee (*Re*) [1911] 1 Ch. 502 .... [1989] 310, 312, 334
Rodocanachi *v.* Milburn Bros. (1887) 18 Q.B.D. 67 .... [1986] 469, 476
Rodrigues *v.* Campbell Indus. 87 Cal. App. 3d 494, 151 Cal. Rptr. 90, 92 (1978) .... [1986] 361
Rogers *v.* Parish (Scarborough) Ltd. [1987] 1 Q.B. 933; [1987] 2 W.L.R. 353 .... [1987] 400, 402; [1990] 380
Rolimpex (Ch. E.) Ltd. *v.* Avra Shipping Co. Ltd. (*The Angeliki*) [1973] 2 Lloyd's Rep. 226 [1986] 285
Rolin *v.* Steward (1854) 23 L.J.C.P. 148 .... [1988] 139
Rolled Steel Products (Holdings) Ltd. *v.* BSC [1986] Ch. 246 .... [1987] 203
Rolls Razor Ltd. *v.* Cox [1967] 1 Q.B. 552 .... [1990] 473
Romalpa Case, The [1976] 1 W.L.R. 676 .... [1989] 119, 198, 510, 511
Roman Ceramics Corp. *v.* People International Bank (1983) 714 F. 2d 1207 (3rd Cir.) .... [1990] 241
Romero *v.* International Terminal Operating Co., 358 U.S. 354 (1959) .... [1987] 118
Ronning *v.* Société Navale Chargeurs Delmas Vieljeux (Kenya C.A.) .... [1986] 552
Rookes *v.* Barnard [1964] A.C. 1129 .... [1987] 427
Ropner Shipping Co. Ltd. *v.* Cleeves Western Valleys Anthracite Collieries Ltd. (1927) 27 Ll. L. Rep. 317, 319 .... [1986] 252
Rosalie, The (1853) 1 Sp. 188 .... [1989] 70, 71
Rose, The (1986) 100 L.Q.R. 185 .... [1987] 55
Rose & Lucy *v.* Resolute Ins. Co. and Lloyd's Underwriters and/or Institute of London Companies, 1965 A.M.C. 1953 .... [1986] 504
Rose Mary, The [1953] 1 W.L.R. 246 .... [1986] 435
Rosehaugh, The (1854) 1 Sp. 267 .... [1989] 61
Roseline, The, 1985 A.M.C. 551 .... [1986] 102
Roseline, The, 1985 A.M.C. 1474; [1987] 1 Lloyd's Rep. 18 (F.C.) .... [1988] 84
Rosen (P.) & Co. Ltd. *v.* Dowley and Selby [1943] 2 All E.R. 172 .... [1987] 172
Rösler *v.* Rottwinkel, Case 241/83 [1985] ECR 99 .... [1989] 472
Rosman *v.* Trans World Airlines Inc. (1974) 34 N.Y. 2d 385; 13 Avi. 17, 231 .... [1988] 228
Ross *v.* Caunters [1980] Ch. 297 .... [1988] 439; [1990] 553
Ross *v.* Edwards & Co. (1895) 73 L.T. 100 (H.L.) .... [1987] 72
Ross Isle and Ariel, The [1982] 2 Lloyd's Rep. 589, 593 .... [1986] 236, 237, 241, 242
Ross T. Smyth & Co. Ltd. *v.* T. D. Bailey, Son & Co. [1940] 3 All E.R. 60, 66 .... [1986] 300
Rossano *v.* Manufacturers' Life Insurance Co. [1963] 2 Q.B. 352 .... [1987] 211
Rotea *v.* Izuel (1939) 95 P. 2d 927 .... [1990] 504
Roundwood Colliery Co. (*In re*) [1897] 1 Ch. 373 .... [1986] 524
Roux *v.* Salvador (1836) 3 Bing. N.C. 266 .... [1988] 257
Rover International Ltd. *v.* Cannon Film Sales Ltd. [1989] 1 W.L.R. 912 .... [1990] 334, 518
Rover International Ltd. *v.* Cannon Film Sales Ltd. [1988] 2 F.T.L.R. 536 (C.A.). Beatson (1989) 105 L.Q.R. 179 .... [1989] 302
Rowe *v.* Hopkins & Partners [1980] 2 N.Z.L.R. 550 .... [1990] 419
Rowland *v.* Divall [1923] 2 K.B. 500 .... [1989] 303; [1990] 518
Rowlands (Mark) *v.* Berni Inns [1986] Q.B. 211 .... [1990] 135, 560
Rowlandson *v.* National Westminster Bank Ltd. [1978] 1 W.L.R. 798 .... [1989] 44, 336
Rowling *v.* Takaro Properties Ltd. [1988] A.C. 473 .... [1990] 484
Royal Bank *v.* G. M. Homes Inc. (1984) 26 Bus. L. Rep. 297, 306; 4 P.P.S.A.C. 116, 124 .... [1986] 175

Royal Bank of Canada *v.* L.V.G. Auctions Ltd. (1983) 43 O.R. (2d) 582 (Ont. H.C.), (1984) 47 O.R. (2d) 800 (Out C.A.) .... [1986] 552, 553
Royal Bank of Ireland *v.* O'Rourke [1962] I.R. 159 .... [1990] 74, 75, 76, 244, 248
Royal British Bank *v.* Turquand (1856) 6 E. & B. 327 .... [1990] 402
Royal Exchange Assurance *v.* Compania Naviera Santi S.A. (*The Tropaioforos* (No. 2)) [1962] 1 Lloyd's Rep. 410 .... [1987] 396
Royal Greek Government *v.* Minister of Transport (*The Ann Stathatos*) (1949) 83 Ll.L.Rep. 228 .... [1986] 125; [1988] 57
Royal Mail Steam Co. Ltd. *v.* English Bank of Rio de Janeiro Ltd. (1887) 19 Q.B.D. 362 .... [1987] 163
Royal Products Ltd. *v.* Midland Bank Ltd. [1981] 2 Lloyd's Rep. 194 .... [1986] 199; [1989] 368; [1990] 84, 550, 551, 552
Royal Trust Bank *v.* Buchler [1989] B.C.L.C. 130 .... [1989] 507
Royal Typewriter Co., Division Litton Business Systems Inc. *v.* M.V. *Kulmerland* and Hamburg-Amerika Linie [1973] 2 Lloyd's Rep. 428 .... [1989] 280
Royle *v.* Trafford Borough Council [1984] I.R.L.R. 184 .... [1990] 515
Ruapehu, The (1925) 21 Ll. L. Rep. 310, 315 .... [1987] 49
Rumbelows Ltd. *v.* A.M.K. (1980) 19 Build. L.R. 25 .... [1988] 470
Runnymede Iron and Steel Ltd. *v.* Rossen Engineering Co. [1962] S.C.R. 26 .... [1990] 456
Rural Municipality of Storthoaks *v.* Mobil Oil of Canada Ltd. (1975) 55 D.L.R. (3d) 1 .... [1989] 304
Ruskin *v.* Canada All-News Radio Ltd. (1979) 7 B.L.R. 142 (Ont. H.C.) .... [1989] 412
Rustenburg Platinum Mines *v.* South African Airways [1979] 1 Lloyd's Rep. 19 .... [1987] 126
Ruth, The, 1923 A.M.C. 357 .... [1986] 495
Ryan-Walsh Stevedoring Co. *v.* M/V *Khalij Star*, 507 F. Supp. 36, 1981 A.M.C. 1478 (W.D. Wa. 1980) .... [1986] 355
Sabemo Pty. Ltd. *v.* North Sydney Municipal Council [1977] 2 N.S.W.L.R. 880 .... [1990] 502
Sabine Towing & Transp. Co. Inc. *v.* United States, 666 F. 2d 561 (Ct. Cl., 1981) .... [1987] 503
Sachs *v.* Miklos [1948] 2 K.B. 23 .... [1987] 46, 58, 80
Saco-Lowell Shops *v.* Reynolds (1944) 141 F. 2d 587 (4th Cir.) .... [1990] 461
Saif Ali *v.* Mitchell & Co. Ltd. [1980] A.C. 198 .... [1990] 553
Sailing-Ship *Garston* Co. *v.* Hickie & Co. (1885) 15 Q.B.D. 580 .... [1986] 52
Salem, The [1982] 1 Q.B. 946 (C.A.), aff'd [1983] 2 A.C. 375 .... [1986] 439; [1987] 32; [1989] 57
Salerno *v.* American League of Professional Baseball Clubs, 429 F. 2d 1003 (2nd Cir., 1970) [1987] 512
Salerno *v.* Pan American World Airways Inc. (1985) 19 Avi. 17, 705 (SDNY) .... [1988] 220
Salford Corp. *v.* Lever [1891] 1 Q.B. 168 .... [1988] 289
Salmon *v.* Pan American World Airways Inc. Index No. 096917, Sup. Ct. N.Y. County, 16 March 1971 .... [1988] 221
Salmond & Spraggon (Australia) Pty. Ltd. *v.* Port Jackson Stevedoring Pty, Ltd. (*The New York Star*) [1981] 1 W.L.R. 138 .... [1986] 97
Salomon *v.* Salomon & Co. Ltd. [1897] A.C. 22 .... [1986] 520; [1990] 205, 402, 407
Salt *v.* Chamberlain (Inspector of Taxes) [1979] S.T.C. 750, 53 T.C. 143 .... [1986] 394
Salton *v.* New Beeston Cycle Co. [1900] 1 Ch. 43 .... [1986] 206
Sammi Line Co. Ltd. *v.* Altamar Navegación S.A., 605 F. Supp. 72 (S.D.N.Y. 1985) .....[1986] 72, 536
Samos Shipping Enterprises Ltd. *v.* Eckhardt & Co. K.G. (*The Nissos Samos*) [1985] 1 Lloyd's Rep. 378 .... [1988] 440
Samson & Samson Ltd. *v.* Proctor [1975] 1 N.Z.L.R. 655 .... [1987] 432
Samuel, The (1851) 15 Jur. 407 .... [1989] 68, 72
Samuel (No. 2) (*Re*) [1945] Ch. 408 .... [1986] 220
Samuel (P.) & Co. Ltd. *v.* Dumas (*The Grigorios*) [1924] A.C. 431 ...... [1986] 27; [1987] 32; [1988] 324
Samuel Sanday & Co. *v.* British & Foreign M.I. Co. [1916] 1 A.C. 650 .... [1988] 252
San Nicholas, The [1976] 1 Lloyd's Rep. 8 .... [1986] 101, 297; [1989] 167, 422; [1990] 3
San Sebastian Pty. Ltd. *v.* Minister Administering Environmental Planning and Assessment Act 1979 (1986) 68 A.L.R. 161; 162 C.L.R. 340 .... [1988] 366; [1989] 140
Sanday *v.* Strath S.S. Co. Ltd. (1920) 26 Com. Cas. 163, 167 .... [1986] 475
Sandeman & Sons *v.* Tyzack and Branfoot S.S. Co. Ltd. [1913] A.C. 680 .... [1988] 288
Sanders *v.* Van der Putte, Case 73/77 [1977] ECR 2383 .... [1989] 472
Sanders Bros. *v.* Maclean & Co. (1883) 11 Q.B.D. 327 .... [1986] 299; [1988] 443
Sandgate, The (1929) 35 Ll.L.Rep. 9 .... [1990] 399
Sandrina, The [1985] A.C. 255; [1985] 1 Lloyd's Rep. 181 .... [1986] 382; [1988] 425; [1989] 384
Sanicentral *v.* Collin [1979] E.C.R. 3423; [1980] 2 C.M.L.R. 164 .... [1988] 388
Sanix Ace, The [1987] 1 Lloyd's Rep. 465 .... [1987] 257; [1988] 38
Sanko Iris, The [1987] 1 Lloyd's Rep. 487 (B.C.S.C.); (1987) 8 B.C.L.R. (2d) 69 .... [1988] 21, 85

Sanko Steamship Co. Ltd. *v.* Eacom Timber Sales Ltd. (*The Sanko Iris and Sanko Venus*) [1987] 1 Lloyd's Rep. 487; (1987) 8 B.C.L.R. (2d) 69 (B.C.S.C.) .... [1988] 21, 85
Sanko Steamship Co. Ltd. *v.* Fearnley and Egar A/S (*The Manhattan Prince*) [1985] 1 Lloyd's Rep. 140 .... [1990] 108
Sanko Venus, The [1987] 1 Lloyd's Rep. 487 .... [1988] 21, 85
Sankyo KKK *v.* Opia (Unrep.) .... [1987] 175
Santa Christina, The, 1928 A.M.C. 1074 (2 C.A.) .... [1986] 492
Santa Marina Shipping *v.* Madeg Holdings (1987) 6 F.T.R. 269 (F.C.) .... [1989] 98
Santipore, The (1854) 1 Sp. 231 .... [1989] 65, 71
Santor *v.* A and M Karagheusian Inc., 207 A. 2d 305 (1965) .... [1987] 118
Sarah, The (1849) 6 N.o.C. 677 .... [1989] 69
Saratoga, The (1861) Lush. 318 .... [1989] 75
Sargent (J.) (Garages) Ltd. *v.* Motor Auctions (West Bromwich) Ltd. [1977] R.T.R. 121 (C.A.) .... [1986] 225
Saskatchewan Govt. Insurance *v.* Spot Pack Inc. (1957) 242 F. 2d 385; 1957 A.M.C. 6455 (5 Cir.) .... [1986] 41; [1988] 347
Sassoon *v.* Western Assurance Co. [1912] A.C. 561 .... [1986] 40
Satanita, The [1895] P. 248; *aff's sub nom.* Clarke *v.* Dunraven [1897] A.C. 59 .... [1989] 170
Satterthwaite (A.M.) & Co. Ltd. *v.* New Zealand Shipping Co. Ltd. (*The Eurymedon*) [1975] A.C. 154 .... [1986] 97; [1988] 505; [1990] 127, 319
Saturnia, The [1984] 2 Lloyd's Rep. 366, aff'd [1987] 2 Lloyd's Rep. 43 .... [1986] 254; [1990] 395
Saturnus, The (1918) 250 F. 407 (2nd Cir.) .... [1988] 160
Saudi Crown, The [1986] 1 Lloyd's Rep. 261; (1986) L.M.L.N. 163 .... [1986] 109, 305; [1988] 462
Saunders *v.* Anglia Building Society [1971] A.C. 1004 .... [1990] 339, 340
Saunders *v.* Edwards [1987] 1 W.L.R. 1116 (C.A.) .... [1988] 126; [1990] 426
Savvas, The [1982] 1 Lloyd's Rep. 22 (C.A.) .... [1986] 256; [1990] 387
Sawers (*Re*), ex p. Blain (1879) 12 Ch. D. 522 .... [1989] 268
Sawyer & Vincent *v.* Window Brace Ltd. [1943] 1 K.B. 32 .... [1989] 433, 436
Saxton (*Re*) [1962] 1 W.L.R. 859 .... [1990] 322
Sayers *v.* Harlow U.D.C. [1958] 1 W.L.R. 623 .... [1987] 10; [1990] 418, 420
Sayers *v.* International Drilling Co. N.V. [1971] 1 W.L.R. 1176 .... [1986] 99
S.C.F. Finance Co. Ltd. *v.* Masri [1985] 1 W.L.R. 876 .... [1986] 412
S.C.F Finance Ltd. *v.* Masri (No. 2) [1986] 1 Lloyd's Rep. 293; [1986] 1 All E.R. 40; [1987] 1 All E.R. 175; [1986] 2 Lloyd's Rep. 366; [1987] Q.B. 1002 (C.A.) ...... [1987] 201, 209; [1988] 126, 368
S.C.F Finance Co. Ltd. *v.* Masri (No. 3) [1987] Q.B. 1028 .... [1989] 467
Scandinavian Bank Plc (*Re*) [1988] Ch. 87 .... [1990] 407, 408, 412
Scandinavian Trading Co. A/B *v.* Zodiac Petroleum S.A. (*The Al Hofuf*) [1981] 1 Lloyd's Rep. 81 .... [1989] 81
Scandinavia Trading Tanker Co. A.B. *v.* Flota Petrolera Ecuatoriana (*The Scaptrade*) [1983] 2 A.C. 694, 703–704; [1983] 2 Lloyd's Rep. 253, 258–259, affirming [1983] Q.B. 529, 540–541; [1983] 1 Lloyd's Rep. 146, 153 .... [1986] 75, 123, 149; [1990] 161
Scaptrade, The [1983] 2 A.C. 694; [1983] 2 Lloyd's Rep. 253, 258–259, affirming [1983] Q.B. 529, 540–541; [1983] 1 Lloyd's Rep. 146, 153 .... [1986] 75, 123, 149; [1989] 501, 502; [1990] 161
Schacht *v.* Brown (1983) 711 F. 2d 1343 (7th Cir.) .... [1990] 426, 427
Schering Chemicals Ltd. *v.* Falkman Ltd. [1982] Q.B. 1 .... [1989] 158
Schering Corp. *v.* Home Ins. Co., 712 F. 2d 4, 9 (2 Cir. 1983) .... [1986] 84
Scherrens *v.* Maenhout, Case No. 158/87, 6 July 1988; *The Times*, 5 September 1988 .... [1989] 132
Schiffahrt & Kohlen G.m.b.H. *v.* Chelsea Maritime Ltd. (*The Irene's Success*) [1982] 1 Q.B. 481 .... [1986] 6, 97, 299; [1987] 54, 84; [1988] 257, 259; [1989] 47, 54
Schiffahrtsgesellschaft Leonhardt & Co. *v.* A. Bottachi S.A. de Navegación, 732 F. 2d 1543, 1984 A.M.C. 2113, reh'g *en banc* granted, 743 F. 2d 763 (11 Cir. 1984) .... [1986] 350
Schiffahrtsgesellschaft Leonhardt & Co. *v.* A. Bottacchi S.A. de Navegación, 773 F. 2d 1528, 1986 A.M.C. 1 (11 Cir. 1985) (*en banc*) .... [1986] 425; [1989] 12
Schiffshypothekenbank Zu Luebeck A.G. *v.* Compton (*The Alexion Hope*) [1988] 1 Lloyd's Rep. 311; [1987] 1 Lloyd's Rep. 60 .... [1987] 39; [1988] 282, 325
S.C. Loveland Co. *v.* U.S.A., 1963 A.M.C. 260 .... [1990] 173
Schnell *v.* The *Vallescura*, 293 U.S. 296; 1934 A.M.C. 1573 .... [1989] 359, 360
Schroeder (A.) Music Publishing Co. Ltd. *v.* Macaulay [1974] 1 W.L.R. 1308 .... [1987] 243; [1988] 409; [1989] 126
Schuler (L.) A.G. *v.* Wickman Machine Tool Sales Ltd. [1974] A.C. 235 .... [1988] 531
Schwarstein *v.* Watson [1985] 3 N.S.W.L.R. 134 .... [1990] 509

Schweizerische *v.* Atlantic Container Line Ltd. (1985) 63 N.R. 104 (Fed. C.A.) .... [1988] 83
Scindia, The (1866) L.R. 1 P.C. 241 .... [1989] 59
SCL Building Services Ltd. (*Re*) (1989) 5 B.C.C. 746 .... [1990] 413
Scotia, The, 35 Fed. 907 (S.D.N.Y., 1888) .... [1987] 153
Scotson *v.* Pegg (1861) 7 H. & N. 295 .... [1989] 164
Scott Group *v.* Macfarlane [1978] 1 N.Z.L.R. 553 .... [1986] 111
Scott *v.* Pattison [1923] 2 K.B. 723 .... [1990] 512
Scottish Special Housing Association *v.* Wimpey Construction U.K. Ltd. [1986] 2 All E.R. 957 .... [1990] 155
Scow No. 9, The (1907) 152 F. 548 (D. Mass.) .... [1989] 19
Scruttons Ltd. *v.* Midland Silicones Ltd. [1962] A.C. 446 .... [1988] 466; [1990] 318
S.C. Schenk, The (1907) 158 F. 54 .... [1990] 53
SCWS *v.* Meyer [1959] A.C. 324 .... [1990] 410
Sea Crystal Shipping *v.* Bulk Transport Group Shipping Co. Ltd. (*The Kyzikos*) [1987] 1 Lloyd's Rep. 48; [1987] 1 W.L.R. 1565 (C.A.); [1988] 3 W.L.R. 858 (H.L.) .... [1989] 263; [1990] 384, 388, 393
Sea Dragon Inc. *v.* Gebr. van Weelde Scheepvaartkantoor B.V., 574 F. Supp. 367, 1984 A.M.C. 699 (S.D.N.Y. 1983) .... [1986] 357
Sea Fever v. Hartford Fire Ins. Co., 1983 A.M.C. 1276 (D. Mass.) .... [1986] 496
Sea Pioneer, The [1982] 1 Lloyd's Rep. 13, 16 (C.A.) .... [1986] 253; [1990] 393, 395
Sea Queen, The [1988] 1 Lloyd's Rep. 500 .... [1989] 266
Seaboard Shipping Corp. *v.* Jocharanne Tugboat Corp., 461 F. 2d 500 (2d Cir. 1972) .... [1986] 428, 429
Seager *v.* Copydex [1967] 1 W.L.R. 293 .... [1986] 542; [1987] 429
Seager *v.* Copydex Ltd. (No. 2) [1969] 1 W.L.R. 809 .... [1989] 159; [1990] 464
Seale *v.* Perry (1982) V.L.R. 193 .... [1989] 139
Sears *v.* Ceres Stevedoring Ltd. (1988) 88 N.R. 296 (Fed. C.A.) .... [1990] 103
Seas Shipping Co. *v.* Sieracki, 328 U.S. 85 (1946) .... [1987] 120
Sebel Products Ltd. *v.* Commissioners for Customs and Excise [1949] Ch. 409 .... [1989] 435
Secretary of State for Trade and Industry *v.* Hart [1982] 1 W.L.R. 481 .... [1990] 406
Securities Fund Services Inc. *v.* American National Bank and Trust Co., 542 F. Supp. 323 (1982) .... [1986] 202; [1990] 550, 552
Security America Corp. *v.* Schacht, No. 82–C–2132 (N.D. Ill., filed 31 January 1983) .... [1990] 426
Sedco *v.* Petroleos Mexicanos, 767 F. 2d 1140 (5 Cir. 1985) .... [1986] 58
Sedco Inc. *v.* S.S. *Strathewe*, 1986 A.M.C. 2801 .... [1987] 147
Seear *v.* Lawson (1880) 15 Ch.D. 426 .... [1990] 219
Seely *v.* White Motor Co., 63 Cal. 2d 9, 403 P.2d 145, 45 Rptr. 17 (1965) .... [1986] 360; [1987] 118
Segoura *v.* Bonakdarian, Case 25/76 [1976] E.C.R. 1851; [1977] 1 C.M.L.R. 361 .... [1988] 388
Segur *v.* Franklin (1934) 34 S.R. (N.S.W.) 67 .... [1990] 517
Seguros Banvenez S.A. *v.* S/S *Oliver Drescher*, 587 F. Supp. 172, 1984 A.M.C. 427 (S.D.N.Y. 1984), aff'd in pertinent part, 761 F. 2d 855, 861 (2 Cir. 1985) .... [1986] 370
Selangor United Rubber Estates *v.* Cradock (No. 3) [1968] 1 W.L.R. 1555 .... [1988] 361, 364, 443; [1989] 43, 44, 245, 322, 323, 336
Sellasia, The [1926] C.P.D. 437, 444 .... [1988] 16, 19
Sennar, The (No. 2) [1985] 1 W.L.R. 490 .... [1986] 97, 319, 417; [1987] 392, 396
Serrano *v.* U.S. Lines Co., 1965 A.M.C. 1038; 238 F. Supp. 383 (S.D.N.Y.) .... [1989] 355
Serviss *v.* Ferguson (1897) 84 F. 202 .... [1990] 53
Severna Shipping Panama S.A. *v.* Canada and St. Lawrence Seaway Authority (1987) 6 F.T.R. 87 (F.C.) .... [1989] 90
Sevonia Team, The [1983] 2 Lloyd's Rep. 640 .... [1989] 163, 422
Sewell *v.* Burdick (1884) 10 App. Cas. 74 .... [1986] 102, 298; [1989] 163, 164, 166, 167, 422, 428, 429; [1990] 4
Shaddock (L.) & Associates Pty. Ltd. *v.* Paramatta City Council (1981) 150 C.L.R. 225 ...... [1986] 111
Shaffer *v.* Heitner, 433 U.S. 186 (1977) .... [1986] 350
Shamia *v.* Joory [1958] 1 Q.B. 448 .... [1989] 297
Shamrock (The Barge), 335 F. Supp. 1150, 1972 A.M.C. 597 (D. Md. 1971) .... [1986] 381
Shanklin Pier Ltd. *v.* Detel Products Ltd. [1951] 2 K.B. 854 .... [1988] 502
Shannon, The (1847) 11 Jur. 1045 .... [1989] 69
Shapiro *v.* Glekel (1974) 380 F. Supp. 1053 .... [1990] 423
Sharneyford Supplies Ltd. *v.* Edge [1985] 3 W.L.R. 1 .... [1986] 319
Sharp *v.* Batt (1930) 25 Tas. L.R. 33 .... [1987] 54
Shaw (*Re*) (1977) 31 F.L.R. 118 .... [1990] 68, 69, 76

Shearer *v.* Bercain Ltd. [1980] 3 All E.R. 295 .... [1990] 410
Shearson Lehman Bros. Inc. *v.* Maclaine Watson & Co. Ltd. [1987] 1 W.L.R. 480; [1987] 2 All E.R. 181 (C.A.) .... [1987] 174, 175; [1990] 307
Shearson Lehman Bros. Inc. *v.* Maclaine Watson & Co. Ltd. (No. 2) [1988] 1 W.L.R. 16, 946; [1988] 1 All E.R. 116 (H.L.); [1989] 1 All E.R. 1056 .... [1990] 307
Shearson Lehman Hutton Inc. *v.* Maclaine Watson & Co. Inc. [1989] 2 Lloyd's Rep. 570; [1990] 1 Lloyd's Rep. 441 .... [1990] 308, 309
Sheffield and South Yorks Building Society (*Re*) (1889) 22 Q.B.D. 470 .... [1990] 402
Shell Canada Ltd. *v.* St. Lawrence Seaway Authority (1987) 36 D.L.R. (4th) 304 (Ont. C.A.) [1989] 90
Shell International Petroleum Co. Ltd. *v.* Gibbs (*The Salem*) [1983] 2 A.C. 375 .... [1987] 32
Shenavai *v.* Kreischer, Case 266/85 [1987] 3 C.M.L.R. 782 .... [1988] 386; [1989] 472
Shepherd (F.C) & Co. Ltd. *v.* Jerrom [1987] 1 Q.B. 301 .... [1989] 442
Shevill *v.* Builders Licensing Board (1982) 149 CL.R. 620 .... [1987] 146; [1990] 25
Shiells *v.* Blackburne (1789) 1 Hy. Bl. 158 .... [1989] 149
Shiloh Spinners Ltd. *v.* Harding [1973] A.C. 691 .... [1988] 126; [1990] 159, 162
Shine *v.* General Guarantee Corp. Ltd. [1988] 1 All E.R. 911 .... [1990] 381
Shinjitsu Maru No. 5, The [1985] 1 W.L.R. 1270 .... [1990] 418
Ship *Antonis P. Lemos v.* Samick Lines Co. (1985) 61 N.R. 288, *sub nom.* Samick Lines Co. Ltd. *v.* Owners of the Antonis P. Lemos (*The Antonis P. Lemos*) [1985] A.C. 711 .... [1987] 85
Ship *Lady Marquis* (*Re*) (1985) 73 N.S.R. (2) 38; 176 A.P.R. 38 (N.S.S.C.) .... [1988] 86
Shipley *v.* Marshall (1863) 14 C.B.N.S. 566 .... [1989] 207; [1990] 524
Shirlaw *v.* Southern Foundries (1926) Ltd. [1939] 2 K.B. 206; aff'd [1940] A.C. 701 .... [1988] 300; [1989] 171, 260
Shotter *v.* Westpac Banking Corp., Unrep., High Ct., Auckland, 12 February 1987 .... [1987] 335
Shuttleworth *v.* Cox Bros. & Co. (Maidenhead) Ltd. [1927] 2 K.B. 9, at 18 .... [1988] 75
Siboen, The and the *Sibotre* [1976] 1 Lloyd's Rep. 293 .... [1987] 422, 426; [1990] 344
Sibtree *v.* Tripp (1846) 15 M. & W. 23 .... [1990] 66
Sidaway *v.* Governors of the Bethlem Royal Hospital [1985] A.C. 871 .... [1990] 258, 259
Siddell *v.* Vickers (1892) 9 R.P.C. 152 .... [1987] 428; [1990] 462
Sidebottom *v.* Kershaw, Leese & Co. Ltd. [1920] 1 Ch. 154 .... [1988] 75
Sidermar S.p.A. *v.* Apollo Corp. (*The Apollo*) [1978] 1 Lloyd's Rep. 200 .... [1990] 108, 111
Sidney Cooke Ltd. *v.* Hapag-Lloyd Aktiengesellschaft [1980] 2 N.S.W.L.R. 587 .... [1986] 105; [1989] 281
Siebe Gorman & Co. Ltd. *v.* Barclays Bank Ltd. [1979] 2 Lloyd's Rep. 142 .... [1987] 149; [1989] 194, 210, 211, 244
Silver *v.* Ocean SS. Co. Ltd. [1930] 1 K.B. 416 .... [1986] 296
Silver Bullion, The (1854) 2 Sp. 70 .... [1989] 61, 74, 76, 78
Silverstein *v.* Chartered Bank, 392 N.Y.S. 2d 296 (1977) .... [1986] 202; [1990] 552
Simaan General Contracting Co. *v.* Pilkington Glass Ltd. (No. 2) [1988] 2 W.L.R. 761 .... [1988] 471
Simona, The [1988] 3 W.L.R. 200; [1986] 1 Lloyd's Rep. 171; [1987] 2 Lloyd's Rep. 236 .... [1989] 82
Simonius Vischer & Co. *v.* Holt & Thompson [1979] 2 N.S.W.L.R. 322 .... [1990] 419, 421, 422, 425
Simpson *v.* Thomson (1877) 3 App. 279 .... [1989] 54
Sinason-Teicher Inter-American Grain Corp. *v.* Oilcakes and Oilseeds Trading Co. Ltd. [1954] 1 W.L.R. 935 .... [1989] 84
Sinclair *v.* Brougham [1914] A.C. 398 .... [1987] 437; [1990] 65, 336, 337
Sindell *v.* Abbott Laboratories, 26 Cal. 3d 588, 163 Cal. Rptr. 132, 607 P.2d 924 (1980) .... [1986] 80
Singbeil *v.* Hansen (1985) 19 D.L.R. (4th) 48; 63 B.C.L.R. 332 .... [1987] 89
Singer Co. (U.K.) Ltd. *v.* Tees & Hartlepool Port Authority [1988] 2 Lloyd's Rep. 164; [1988] 1 F.T.L.R. 442 .... [1988] 466; [1990] 319
Singer *v.* Yokohama Specie Bank, 47 N.Y.S.2d 881 (1944); affd. 48 N.Y.S.2d 799 (1944) but rev'sd. 58 N.E.2d 726 (1946); 85 N.E.2d 894 (1949) .... [1986] 207; [1990] 84
Singh *v.* Thaper, *The Times*, 7 August 1987 .... [1988] 545
Sinoe, The [1971] 1 Lloyd's Rep. 514; [1972] 1 Lloyd's Rep. 201 (C.A.) .... [1986] 252; [1990] 117
Sio Export Trading Co. *v.* The *Dart Europe* [1984] 1 F.C. 256 (Fed. C.C.) .... [1987] 88
Siporex Trade S.A. *v.* Banque Indosuez [1986] 2 Lloyd's Rep. 146 .... [1990] 223, 232, 234
Sir Ralph Abercrombie, The (1867) L.R. 1 P.C. 454 .... [1989] 67
Skagway Terminal Co. *v.* The *Daphne* (1988) 15 F.T.R. 63 (F.C.) .... [1989] 96
Skandia Insurance Co. Ltd. *v.* Skoljarev (1979) 142 C.L.R. 375 .... [1986] 40, 287, 290
Skarp, The [1935] P. 134 .... [1986] 109
Skeate *v.* Beale (1841) 11 Ad. & E. 983 .... [1990] 344

Skibs A/S Gylfe *v.* Hyman-Michaels Co. (*The Gyda*), 1971 A.M.C. 2041; 304 F. Supp. 1204 (D.C. Michigan); 1971 A.M.C. 2032; 438 F. 2d 803 (6th Cir.), *cert.* denied 1972 A.M.C. 597 .... [1989] 352, 357
S.L. Sethia Liners Ltd. *v.* State Trading Corp. of India Ltd. [1985] 1 W.L.R. 1398, 1401 ...... [1986] 421
Slade's Case (1602) 4 Co. Rep. 91a; 92b .... [1990] 18, 496
Slattery *v.* Mance [1962] 1 Lloyd's Rep. 60; [1962] 1 Q.B. 676 .... [1987] 39; [1988] 283, 325
Slavenburg's Bank (N.V.) *v.* Intercontinental Natural Resources Ltd. [1980] 1 W.L.R. 1076 .... [1986] 2; [1990] 401, 537, 541
Slazenger & Sons *v.* Spalding & Bros. [1910] Ch. 257 .... [1990] 462
Smerchanski *v.* Minister of National Revenue [1979] 1 F.C. 801 .... [1987] 93
Smith *v.* Chadwick (1884) 9 App. Cas. 187 .... [1986] 317
Smith *v.* Croft [1987] 1 W.L.R. 580 .... [1988] 77
Smith *v.* Eric S. Bush [1990] A.C. 831 .... [1990] 480, 485, 487, 553
Smith *v.* Eric S. Bush [1987] 3 W.L.R. 889 .... [1988] 367
Smith *v.* Hughes (1871) L.R. 6 Q.B. 597 .... [1987] 266, 327; [1988] 114; [1989] 438; [1990] 340
Smith *v.* Littlewoods Organisation Plc [1987] A.C. 241 .... [1989] 336
Smith *v.* Rubel (1932) 13 P. 2d 1078 .... [1989] 304
Smith *v.* Smith (1975) 5 Fam. Law 125 .... [1989] 437, 444
Smith *v.* Union Bank of London (1875) 1 Q.B.D. 31 .... [1988] 371
Smith and Baldwin *v.* Barclays Bank Ltd. (1944) 5 L.D.A.B. 370 .... [1988] 371, 372
Smith and Fawcett Ltd. (*Re*) [1942] Ch. 304 .... [1988] 79
Smith (E.E. & Brian) (1928) Ltd. *v.* Wheatsheaf Mills Ltd. [1939] 2 K.B. 302 .... [1990] 365
Smith (Henry) & Co. *v.* Bedouin Steam Navigation Co. Ltd. [1896] A.C. 70 .... [1986] 388
Smith Kline and French Laboratories Ltd. *v.* Bloch [1983] 1 W.L.R. 730 .... [1988] 99
SNIAS *v.* Lee (See Société Nationale Industrielle Aerospatiale *v.* Lee Kui Jak)
SNW Commodities *v.* Falik [1984] 2 Lloyd's Rep. 224, 228 .... [1986] 391
Sneath *v.* Valley Gold Ltd. [1893] 1 Ch. 477 .... [1989] 437
Snepp *v.* United States, 100 S. Ct. 763 (1980), reversing in part United States *v.* Snepp, 595 F. 2d 926 (1979) and reinstating the judgment of the Dist. Ct., 456 F. Supp. 176 (1978); 100 S. Ct. 763 .... [1987] 423, 424, 425
Sniadach *v.* Family Finance Corp., 395 U.S. 337 (1969) .... [1986] 350
Soames *v.* British Empire Shipping Co. (1860) 8 H.L.C. 338 .... [1988] 546
Soc. SAR Schotte GmbH *v.* Soc. Parfums Rothschild S.a.r.l., Case 218/86, 9 December 1987 [1988] 387
Socanav Inc. and Enercham Shipmanagement Inc. *v.* Greater Sarnia Investment Corp. (1989) 21 F.T.R. 162 (Can. F.C.) .... [1990] 102
Sociedad Anonima de Navegación Petrolera *v.* Cia de Petroleos de Chile S.A., No. 85 Civ. 7776 (S.D.N.Y. 7 May 1986) .... [1986] 536
Société Canadienne des Métaux Reynolds Ltée *v.* Francoeur (1984) 9 D.L.R. (4th) 364 .... [1987] 89
Société de Traction *v.* Kamani Engineering Co., A.I.R. 1964 S.C. 558 .... [1988] 15
Société Nationale Industrielle Aerospatiale (SNIAS) *v.* Lee Kui Jak [1987] 3 W.L.R. 59 ..... [1987] 391
Socony Mobil Oil Co. Inc. *v.* West of England Shipowners Mutual Insurance Association (London) Ltd. (*The Padre Island*) [1984] 2 Lloyd's Rep. 408 .... [1987] 233
Solholt, The [1981] 2 Lloyd's Rep. 574 (affd. [1983] 1 Lloyd's Rep. 605) .... [1987] 146; [1988] 440; [1990] 455
Solle *v.* Butcher [1950] 1 K.B. 671 .... [1986] 324, 325; [1988] 301; [1989] 437
Somafer S.A. *v.* Saar-Ferngas A.G., Case 33/78 [1978] E.C.R. 2183; [1979] 1 C.M.L.R. 490 .... [1987] 287; [1988] 387
Somerset *v.* Cox (1865) 33 Beav. 634 .... [1989] 197
Sonia S, The [1983] 2 Lloyd's Rep. 63 .... [1988] 424
Sophie, The, 1926 A.M.C. 447 (2 C.A.) .... [1986] 490, 494
Sorrell *v.* Paget [1950] 1 K.B. 252 .... [1990] 356
Sotiros Shipping Inc. *v.* Sameiet Solholt (*The Solholt*) [1981] 2 Lloyd's Rep. 574 (affmd. [1983] 1 Lloyd's Rep. 605) .... [1988] 440
Sottomayor *v.* De Barros (No. 2) (1879) 5 P.D. 94 .... [1989] 386
Souch *v.* Strawbridge (1846) 2 C.B. 808 .... [1990] 510, 511
South African Railways and Harbours *v.* Johnson Navigation Co. S.A. (*The Manchester*) 1981 (2) S.A. 798 (C.) .... [1988] 16
South Australian Insurance Co. Ltd. *v.* Randell (1869) L.R. 3 P.C. 101 .... [1989] 202
South Carolina Insurance Co. *v.* Assurantie Maatschappij "de Zeven Provincien" N.V. [1987] A.C. 24 .... [1987] 391, 392
South Staffs. Waterworks Case [1978] 1 W.L.R. 1387 .... [1990] 557

Southard & Co. (*In re*) [1979] 1 W.L.R. 1198 .... [1986] 385
Southern Seas Navigation *v.* Petroleos Mexicanos, 606 F. Supp. 692 (S.D.N.Y. 1985) .... [1986] 67
Southern S.S. Agency Inc. *v.* *Khalij Sky*, 1986 1 S.A.L.R. 485; 1985 A.M.C. 2794 (S. Africa) .... [1987] 153; [1989] 12, 174, 175, 181, 187
Southern Water Authority *v.* Carey [1985] 2 All E.R. 1077 .... [1986] 232, 302; [1988] 468
Southern Water Authority *v.* Lewis & Duvivier (1984) 27 Build. L.R. 111 .... [1986] 106
Soya GmbH *v.* White [1983] 1 Lloyd's Rep. 122 .... [1986] 262
Spalding & Bros. *v.* A.W. Gamage Ltd. (1915) 84 L.J.Ch. 449 .... [1990] 462
Spalmatori, The [1964] A.C. 868 .... [1988] 251; [1990] 394
Spanish Prospecting Co. Ltd. (*Re*) [1911] 1 Ch. 92 .... [1990] 260
Span Terza, The [1982] 1 Lloyd's Rep. 225; 7 [1984] 1 W.L.R. 27 (H.L.) .... [1986] 401; [1987] 63
Sparling *v.* Javelin International Ltd. [1986] R.J.Q. 1073 (Que. S.C.) .... [1989] 413
Spartan Steel & Alloys Ltd. *v.* Martin & Co. (Contractors) Ltd. [1973] Q.B. 27 .... [1987] 236; [1988] 406; [1989] 1
Spedding *v.* Spedding (1913) 3 W.N. (N.S.W.) 81 .... [1990] 332
Speed, The (1844) 2 W. Rob. 225 .... [1989] 63
Spence *v.* Crawford [1939] 3 All E.R. 271 .... [1986] 318
Sperry Int'l Trade *v.* Israel, 689 F.2d 301 (2 Cir. 1982) .... [1986] 67
Spiers *v.* Halliday [1984] C.L.Y. 1040 .... [1990] 137
Spiliada, The [1985] 2 Lloyd's Rep. 116; [1986] 3 All E.R. 843, reversing [1985] 2 Lloyd's Rep. 116; [1987] A.C. 460 .... [1986] 516; [1987] 1, 391, 393, 538; [1988] 84, 91, 252, 547; [1989] 216, 218, 221, 223, 224, 392; [1990] 13, 277, 327
Spiliada Maritime Corp. *v.* Cansulex Ltd. (*The Spiliada*) [1985] 2 Lloyd's Rep. 116; [1986] 3 All E.R. 843, reversing [1985] 2 Lloyd's Rep. 116; [1987] A.C. 460 .... [1986] 516; [1987] 1, 391, 393, 538; [1988] 84, 91, 252, 547; [1989] 216, 218, 221, 223, 224; [1990] 13, 277, 327
Spirit of the Age, The (1857) Swab. 209 .... [1989] 61, 65, 69
Spiro *v.* Lintern [1973] 1 W.L.R. 1002 .... [1988] 441
Splendid Sun, The [1981] Q.B. 694; [1981] 2 Lloyd's Rep. 29 (C.A.) .... [1986] 68; [1987] 156; [1988] 304, 308
Sport International Bussum BV *v.* Inter-Footwear Ltd. [1984] 1 W.L.R. 776 .... [1986] 149; [1990] 158, 161
Spurling (J.) Ltd. *v.* Bradshaw [1956] 1 W.L.R. 461 .... [1988] 295
Spurrier *v.* La Cloche [1902] A.C. 441 .... [1986] 509
S.R. Korchenski, Deputy Marshal *v.* *The Galaxias*, 1989 A.M.C. 348; [1989] 1 F.C. 375 (Can. F.C.) .... [1990] 101
S.S. *Ardennes* (Cargo Owners) *v.* S.S. *Ardennes* (Owners) [1951] 1 K.B. 55 .... [1987] 261
S.S. Pharmaceutical Co. Ltd. *v.* Qantas Airways Ltd., 22 September 1988 (N.S.W. Sup. Ct.) .... [1989] 145 *et seq.*
S/S Steamship Co. Ltd. *v.* Eastern Caribbean Container Line [1985] 2 F.C. 284 (Fed. C.C.); [1986] 2 F.C. 27; (1986) 26 D.L.R. (4th) 472 (Fed. C.A.) .... [1987] 84; [1988] 85
S/S Steamship Co. Ltd. *v.* The *Alchatby* (1986) 5 F.T.R. 253 (F.C.) .... [1989] 103
St. Anna, The [1983] 1 W.L.R. 895 .... [1989] 383
St. John Shipping Corp. *v.* Joseph Rank Ltd. [1957] 1 Q.B. 267 .... [1987] 204; [1988] 126
St Joseph, The [1933] P. 119 .... [1986] 102
St. Lawrence Construction Ltd. *v.* Federal Commerce and Navigation [1985] 1 F.C. 767 (summary); (1985) 56 N.R. 174 (complete text) (Fed. C.A.) .... [1987] 82, 85
St. Nicholas, The (1860) Lush. 29 .... [1989] 71
St. Paul Fire & M.I. Co. *v.* Morice (1906) 11 Com. Cas. 153 .... [1989] 287
St. Paul Fire & M.I. Co. *v.* Vest Transportation Co. Inc. (1980) 500 F. Supp. 1365; 1982 A.M.C. 450 (N.D. Miss.); *aff'd per curiam* (1982) 666 F. 2d 932 (5th Cir.) .... [1989] 19
St. Pierre *v.* South American Stores (Gath & Chaves) Ltd. [1936] 1 K.B. 382 .... [1989] 221, 222, 385
Standard Investments Ltd. *v.* Canadian Imperial Bank of Commerce (1985) 22 D.L.R. (4th) 410 .... [1987] 436, 546; [1988] 379
Standard Rotary Machine Co. (*Re*) (1906) 95 L.T. 829 .... [1990] 545
Star S.S. Soc. *v.* Beogradska Plovidba (*The Junior K*) (1988) 25 February, unrep. .... [1988] 439
State *v.* Leary, 46 R.I. 197; 125 A. 353 (1924) .... [1987] 521
State of Idaho *v.* Bunker Hill Co., 635 F. Supp. 665 (D. Idaho, 1986) .... [1987] 509

State of Louisiana *ex rel.* Guste *v.* M/V *Testbank*, 524 F. Supp. 1170, 1982 A.M.C. 2246, 2250–51 (E.D. La. 1981), aff'd on other grounds, 728 F. 2d 748, 1984 A.M.C. 2951 (1984), aff'd after rehearing *en banc*, 752 F. 2d 1019, 1985 A.M.C. 1521 (5 Cir. 1985), cert. denied, 90 L. Ed. 2d 872 (1986) .... [1986] 361; [1987] 512
State of New York *v.* Shore Realty Corp., 759 F. 2d 1032 (2nd Cir., 1985) .... [1987] 505, 508
State Trading Corp. of India *v.* Golodetz [1989] 2 Lloyd's Rep. 277 .... [1990] 559
States Steamship Co. *v.* Aetna Ins. Co., 1985 A.M.C. 2749 .... [1986] 487
Steedman *v.* Drinkle [1916] 1 A.C. 275 .... [1990] 161
Steel, Young & Co. *v.* Grand Canary Coaling Co. (1902) 7 Com. Cas. 213 .... [1988] 250
Steele *v.* Tardiani (1946) 72 C.L.R. 386 .... [1990] 512, 515
Steelmet *v.* Caribe Towing, 1985 A.M.C. (11 C.A.) .... [1986] 495, 501
Steelton, The (1980) 631 P. 2d 441; 1980 A.M.C. 2122 (6th Cir); *upholding* 1977 A.M.C. 2252; [1979] 1 Lloyd's Rep. 431 (N.D. Ohio) .... [1989] 13
Stein *v.* Saywell (1969) 121 C.L.R. 529 .... [1986] 530
Stein *v.* The *Kathy K* [1967] 2 S.C.R. 802 .... [1989] 89
Steljes *v.* Ingram (1903) 19 T.L.R. 534 .... [1987] 63
Stellar Chartering & Brokerage *v.* Claybridge Shipping (*The Gedeh*), S.M.A. No. 1534 (1981) .... [1986] 72
Stena Nautica, The (No. 2) [1982] 2 Lloyd's Rep. 336 .... [1986] 149
Stephen *v.* Scottish Boatowners Mutual Ins. Assn. (*The Talisman*) [1989] 1 Lloyd's Rep. 535 (H.L.) .... [1989] 408, 410
Stephens *v.* Elwall (1815) 4 M. & S. 259 .... [1986] 220
Stephens Travel Service International Pty. Ltd. *v.* Qantas Airways Ltd. (1988) 13 N.S.W.L.R. 331 .... [1989] 304, 330
Sterling Bank of Canada *v.* Laughlin (1912) 1 D.L.R. 383 .... [1990] 74, 248
Sterling Navigation Co. Ltd. (*In re*) (*The Regal Sword*), 1983 A.M.C. 2240 (S.D.N.Y. 1983) .... [1986] 425, 426
Steuart Transportation Co. *v.* Allied Towing Corp., 596 F. 2d 609, 1097 A.M.C. 1187 (4 Cir. 1979) .... [1986] 375; [1987] 500, 502
Steuart Transp. Co. (*In re*), 435 F. Supp. 798; 1978 A.M.C. 1906 (E.D. Va., 1977), aff'd 596 F. 2d 609; 1979 A.M.C. 1187 (4th Cir., 1978) .... [1987] 504
Stevenson *v.* Beverley Bentinck Ltd. [1976] 1 W.L.R. 483 .... [1989] 373
Stewart *v.* Bohnert's Estate, 101 Cal. App.3d 978, 162 Cal. Rptr. 126, 131–32 (1980) .... [1986] 86
Stewart *v.* Oriental Fire & Marine Insurance Co. Ltd. [1985] Q.B. 988; [1984] 2 Lloyd's Rep. 109 .... [1987] 37, 201, 203, 204, 207, 208; [1988] 254; [1989] 494
Stewart *v.* Reavell's Garage [1952] 2 Q.B. 545 .... [1990] 550, 551
Stilk *v.* Myrick (1809) 2 Camp. 317; 6 Esp. 129 .... [1990] 344
Stinchcombe *v.* Thomas [1957] V.R. 509 .... [1990] 508
Stockloser *v.* Johnson [1954] 1 Q.B. 476 .... [1989] 443, 501; [1990] 158, 162
Stoddard *v.* Union Trust Ltd. [1912] 1 K.B. 181 .... [1989] 213
Stolt Avance, The, 24 May 1989 (Sing. H.C.) .... [1990] 15
Stolt Marmaro, The [1985] 2 Lloyd's Rep. 428 .... [1986] 515, 516, 518
Stork, The [1955] 2 Q.B. 68 .... [1987] 408; [1988] 43; [1990] 453
Strand Electric & Engineering Co. Ltd. *v.* Brisford Entertainments Ltd. [1952] 2 Q.B. 246 .. [1987] 428
Strandhill, The [1926] S.C.R. (Can.) 680; 1927 A.M.C. 244 .... [1987] 154
Strandhill, The *v.* Walter W. Hodder Co. Inc. [1926] 4 D.L.R. 801 .... [1989] 182, 183
Strathlorne S.S. Co. *v.* Andrew Weir & Co. (1934) 40 Com. Cas. 168; 50 Ll.L.Rep. 185 .... [1986] 125; [1988] 57
Strongman (1945) Ltd. *v.* Sincock [1955] 2 Q.B. 525 (C.A.) .... [1987] 207; [1989] 171
Stylianos Restis, The, 66 Civ. 3394; 1974 AMC 2343 (S.D.N.Y.) .... [1989] 350, 361
Subaqueous Exploration & Archaeology Ltd., and Atlantic Ship Historical Society Inc. *v.* The Unidentified, Wrecked and Abandoned Vessel, etc., et al, 577 F. Supp. 597, 1984 A.M.C. 913 (1983) .... [1986] 16
Sucrest Corp. *v.* M.V. *Jennifer*, 1978 AMC 2520; 455 F. Supp. 371 (Maine N.D.) .... [1989] 343, 345, 349, 361
Suiker Unie *v.* Commission [1975] E.C.R. 1663 .... [1988] 189
Suisse Atlantique Société d'Armement Maritime S.A. *v.* N.V. Rotterdamsche Kolen Centrale [1967] 1 A.C. 361 .... [1988] 532
Sumpter *v.* Hedges [1898] 1 Q.B. 673 .... [1990] 513
Sun Life Assurance Co. of Canada *v.* Jervis [1944] A.C. 111 .... [1988] 303
Sun Mutual Ins. Co. *v.* Ocean Ins. Co., 107 U.S. 485 (1882) .... [1986] 498

Sun Oil Co. *v.* Carlisle 1986 A.M.C. 305 .... [1986] 436
Sunbird Plaza Pty. Ltd. *v.* Maloney (1988) 62 A.L.J.R. 195 .... [1989] 85
Sundell *v.* Yannoulatos (1956) 56 S.R. (N.S.W.) 323 .... [1987] 426; [1990] 344
Sunkist Growers Inc. *v.* Adelaide Shipping Lines Ltd., 603 F. 2d 1327, 1979 A.M.C. 2787 (9 Cir. 1979), cert. denied, 444 U.S. 1012, 1980 A.M.C. 2102 (1980) .... [1986] 368
Sunrise Co. Ltd. *v.* The *Lake Winnipeg* (1987) 12 F.T.R. 57 (F.C.) .... [1989] 97
Super Servant Two, The [1989] 1 Lloyd's Rep. 148; [1990] 1 Lloyd's Rep. 1 .... [1989] 3; [1990] 153
Supreme Commandery of the Knights of the Golden Rule *v.* Ainsworth (1882) 71 Ala. 436 .. [1988] 319
Sutherland Shire Council *v.* Heyman (1985) 59 A.L.J.R. 564; (1985) 60 A.L.R. 1 . [1986] 98; [1990] 486
Swan, The (1839) 1 W. Rob. 68 .... [1989] 71
Swedish Central Rail Co. Ltd. *v.* Thompson [1924] 2 K.B. 255 .... [1989] 386
Swibon, The, 1985 A.M.C. 722 .... [1986] 22
Swift Indus. *v.* Botany Indus., 466 F. 2d 1125, 1136 (3 Cir. 1972) .... [1986] 72
Swiss Bank Corp. *v.* Boemische Industrial Bank [1923] 1 K.B. 673 .... [1988] 429
Swiss Bank Corp. *v.* Brinks M.A.T. Ltd. [1986] 2 Lloyd's Rep. 79; [1986] Q.B. 853 .... [1988] 180, 473; [1989] 147
Switzerland Gen. Ins. *v.* Logistec Navigation (1987) 7 F.T.R. 196 (F.C.) .... [1989] 96
Sybron Corp. *v.* Rochem [1984] Ch. 112 .... [1989] 438, 448, 449
Sydney Corporation *v.* West (1965) 114 C.L.R. 481 .... [1987] 168
Sylvania Technical Systems Inc. *v.* The Government of the Islamic Republic of Iran, separate opinion of H.M. Holtzmann, Iranian Assets Litigation Reporter, p. 10, 860 at 10, 863 .. [1987] 139
Symmons (Peter) & Co. *v.* Cook (1981) 131 N.L.J. 758 .... [1989] 374, 375, 378, 381
Syrian, The (1866) 14 L.T. 833 .... [1989] 78, 79
Sze Hai Tong Bank Ltd. *v.* Rambler Cycle Co. Ltd. [1959] A.C. 576 (P.C.) .... [1986] 389; [1989] 396; [1990] 315
Sztejn *v.* Henry Schroder Banking Corp. (1941) 31 N.Y.S. 2d 631 .... [1990] 234
Ta Chi Navigation (Panama) Corp. (*In re*), 677 F. 2d 225, 1982 A.M.C. 1710 (2 Cir. 1982) ... [1986] 369
Tagart, Beaton & Co. *v.* James Fisher & Sons [1903] 1 K.B. 391 .... [1987] 541; [1989] 191, 193, 195; [1990] 524
Tage Berglund *v.* Montoro Shipping Corp. (*The Dagmar*) [1968] 2 Lloyd's Rep. 563 .... [1988] 48
Tagus, The [1903] P. 44 .... [1986] 401
Tai Hing Cotton Mill Ltd. *v.* Liu Chong Hing Bank Ltd. [1984] 1 Lloyd's Rep. 555; [1985] 3 W.L.R. 317; [1986] A.C. 80; (P.C.) .... [1986] 8, 98; [1987] 9, 545;
Tai Ping Ins. Co. *v.* M/V *Warschau*, 731 F. 2d 1141 (5 Cir. 1984) .... [1986] 359
Taichun, The, 20 July 1987, Kobe Dist. Ct., Japan .... [1989] 35 *et seq.*
[1988] 363, 443; [1989] 41, 43, 45, 244, 259; [1990] 318
Tailby *v.* Official Receiver (1888) 13 App. Cas. 523 .... [1986] 300; [1988] 144; [1990] 272
Tailby *v.* Official Receiver [1931] 2 Ch. 255 .... [1989] 208
Takamine, The [1980] 2 Lloyd's Rep. 204 .... [1987] 172
Talisman, The [1989] 1 Lloyd's Rep. 535 (H.L) .... [1989] 408, 410
Tamvaco *v.* Simpson (1865) 19 C.B.N.S. 453 .... [1990] 344
Tanker Hygrade No. 18 Inc. *v.* United States, 526 F. 2d 805 (Ct. Cl. 1975) .... [1987] 500
Tankexpress A/S *v.* Compagnie Financiere Belge de Petroles S.A. [1949] A.C. 76 .... [1986] 214; [1990] 65
Tankrederei Ahrenkiel G.m.b.H. *v.* Frahuil S.A. (*The Multitank Holsatia*) (1988) L.M.L.N. 222 .... [1988] 303, 308
Tappenden *v.* Artus [1964] 2 Q.B. 185 .... [1988] 545
Tarago, The [1985] 2 Lloyd's Rep. 419 (P.C.) .... [1986] 105
Tarjan Construction Co. Pty. Ltd. (*Re*) 1964 N.S.W.R. 1054 .... [1986] 532
Tasmania, The (1890) 15 App. Cas. 223, 225 .... [1988] 39
Tasman Pulp and Paper Co. Ltd. *v.* Brambles J.B. O'Loghlen Ltd. [1981] 2 N.Z.L.R. 255 ..... [1989] 39
Tassos N, The [1983] 1 Lloyd's Rep. 648, 651 .... [1986] 252; [1990] 390
Tate & Lyle Industries Ltd. *v.* Greater London Council [1983] 2 A.C. 509, 530–531 .... [1986] 97
Tatung (U.K.) Ltd. *v.* Galex Telesure Ltd. (1989) 5 B.C.C. 325 .... [1989] 198, 206, 510, 511
Taupo Machinery Services (1977) Ltd. *v.* Field Equipment Ltd. Unrep., High Ct., Rotorua, 30 June 1986 .... [1987] 333
Taylor *v.* Bank of Athens (1922) 27 Com. Cas. 142 .... [1988] 457
Taylor *v.* Blakelock (1886) 32 Ch. D. 560 .... [1989] 195
Taylor *v.* Caldwell (1863) 3 B. & S. 826; 122 E.R. 309 .... [1988] 530
Taylor *v.* Chester (1869) L.R. 4 Q.B. 309 .... [1988] 125

Taylor *v.* Combined Buyers Ltd. [1924] N.Z.L.R. 627 .... [1990] 456
Taylor *v.* Johnson (1983) 151 C.L.R. 422 .... [1990] 506
Taylor *v.* Johnson (1983) 57 A.L.J.R. 197 .... [1986] 323
Taylor *v.* McGirr [1986] Crim.L.Rev. 544 .... [1990] 406
Taylor *v.* Oakes Roncoroni & Co. (1922) 27 Com. Cas. 261 .... [1989] 82
Taylor *v.* Plumer (1815) 3 M. & S. 562 .... [1989] 118
T.D.K. Tape Distributor (U.K.) Ltd. *v.* Videochoice Ltd. [1986] 1 W.L.R. 141 .... [1986] 412
Teacher *v.* Calder (1899) 1 F. 39; [1899] A.C. 451 (H.L. (Sc.)) .... [1987] 422
Techalloy Co. Inc. *v.* Reliance Ins. Co., 487 A.2d 820 (Pa. Superior Ct. 1984) .... [1986] 93
Teck Corporation Ltd. *v.* Millar (1972) 33 D.L.R. (3d) 288 .... [1988] 72
Tees, The and the *Pentucket* (1862) Lush. 505 .... [1988] 450
Teh Hu, The [1970] P. 106 .... [1990] 437
Tehno-Impex *v.* Gebr. van Weelde Scheepvaartkantoor B.V. [1981] 1 Q.B. 648 .... [1987] 416
Tel Aviv (*In re*) (1975) 13 Avi. 18, 166 .... [1988] 222
Tel-Oren *v.* Libyan Arab Republic, 517 F. Supp. 542; 726 F. 2d .... [1988] 10
Tenax Steamship Co. Ltd. *v.* *Brimnes* (owners of) (*The Brimnes*) [1975] Q.B. 929 .... [1986] 213; [1989] 367
Tennant Radiant Heat Ltd. *v.* Warrington Development Corp. [1988] 11 E.G. 71 .. [1990] 417, 418, 419
Tennants (Lancashire) Ltd. *v.* C.S. Wilson & Co. Ltd. [1917] A.C. 495 .... [1989] 7
Tennessee Valley Authority *v.* Hall, 437 U.S. 153 (1978) .... [1987] 498
Tennessee Valley Sand & Gravel Co. *v.* M/V *Delta*, 598 F. 2d 930, 934 (5 Cir. 1979) .... [1986] 379
Tervaete, The [1922] P. 259 .... [1989] 187
Tesaba, The [1982] 1 Lloyd's Rep. 397 .... [1986] 333; [1990] 359, 361
Tessili *v.* Dunlop, Case 12/76 [1976] E.C.R. 1473; [1977] 1 C.M.L.R. 26 .... [1987] 286; [1988] 385
Tessler Bros. (B.C.) Ltd. *v.* Italpacific Line, 494 F. 2d 438, 1974 A.M.C. 937 (9 Cir. 1974) .... [1986] 367; [1988] 274
T.H. Knitwear Ltd. (*Re*) [1988] Ch. 275 .... [1989] 9
Thacker *v.* Hardy (1878) 4 Q.B.D. 685, 695 .... [1986] 392
Thackwell *v.* Barclays Bank Plc [1986] 1 All E.R. 676 .... [1987] 213; [1988] 126; [1990] 426, 427
Thake *v.* Maurice [1986] Q.B. 644 (C.A.) .... [1987] 80; [1989] 438
Thames, The, 10 Fed. 848 (S.D.N.Y. 1881) .... [1986] 12
Thames and Mersey Marine Insurance Co. *v.* Hamilton, Fraser & Co. (*The Inchmaree*) (1887) 12 App. Cas. 484 .... [1986] 39; [1987] 30
Thames Towboat Co. *v.* The Schooner *Francis McDonald*, 254 U.S. 242 (1920) .... [1987] 123
Theems, The [1938] P. 197 .... [1988] 178
Theodore, The (1858) Swab. 351 .... [1989] 76
Theraios, The [1971] 1 Lloyd's Rep. 209 (C.A.) .... [1990] 399
Thetis, HMS (1835) 3 Hagg. 228 .... [1987] 269
Third Chandris Shipping Corp. *v.* Unimarine S.A. (*The Pythia*) [1979] Q.B. 645 .... [1990] 287, 320
Thomas *v.* Houston Corbett & Co. [1969] N.Z.L.R. 151 .... [1989] 304
Thomas *v.* H.W. Thomas Ltd. [1984] 1 N.Z.L.R. 686 .... [1988] 63
Thomas National Transport (Melbourne) Pty. Ltd. *v.* May & Baker (Australia) Pty. Ltd. (1966) 115 C.L.R. 353 .... [1987] 166
Thomas Wilson Sons & Co. *v.* The owners of the cargo per the *Xantho* (*The Xantho*) (1887) 12 App. Cas. 503 .... [1986] 39
Thompson *v.* Dominy (1845) 14 M. & W. 403 .... [1986] 100
Thompson *v.* Hopper (1856) 5 El. & Bl. 171; 119 E.R. 828; (1858) El. B. & El. 1038; 120 E.R. 796 .... [1986] 38; [1988] 334
Thompson *v.* L.M. & S. Ry. Co. [1930] 1 K.B. 41 .... [1988] 295
Thompson (W.L.) Ltd. *v.* Robinson (Gunmakers) Ltd. [1955] Ch. 177 .... [1990] 310, 311
Thomson *v.* Clydesdale Bank Ltd. [1893] A.C. 282 (H.L. (Sc.)) .... [1989] 320, 321
Thornton *v.* Shoe Lane Parking Ltd. [1971] 2 Q.B. 163 .... [1986] 313; [1988] 295
Thyssen Inc. *v.* S/S *Fortune Star*, 596 F. Supp. 865 (S.D.N.Y. 1984) .... [1986] 370
Tidewater Terminals Inc. *v.* General Metals Export Corp., No. 81–6761 (S.D.N.Y. 1982) ... [1986] 358
Tiger Motor Co. *v.* McMurtry (1969) 284 Ala. 283; 224 So. 2d 638 .... [1990] 377
Tilden Rent-a-Car *v.* Glendenning (1978) 83 D.L.R. (3d) 400 .... [1987] 536; [1990] 341
Tillmans & Co. *v.* S.S. Knutsford Ltd. [1908] 1 K.B. 185, affmd. [1908] 2 K.B. 385, affmd. *sub nom.* S.S. Knutsford Ltd. *v.* Tillmans & Co. [1908] A.C. 406 .... [1988] 54
Timko *v.* Useful Homes Corp., 114 N.J. Eq. 433; 168 A. 824 (1933) .... [1987] 436
Tinline *v.* White Cross Insurance Assn. [1921] 3 K.B. 327 .... [1987] 210
Tippens *v.* Metropolitan Life Insurance Co., 99 F. 2d 671 (5th Cir., 1938) .... [1987] 211

Tiruna, The [1987] 2 Lloyd's Rep. 667 .... [1988] 178
Titanic, The, 233 U.S. 718 (1913) .... [1986] 23
Tito *v*. Waddell (No. 2) [1977] Ch. 106 .... [1987] 422, 431, 437
Tobago, The (1804) 5 C. Rob. 218 .... [1988] 158
Todd Shipyards Corp. *v*. Altema Cia. Maritima S.A. (*The Ioannis Daskalelis*) [1974] S.C.R. 1248; [1974] 1 Lloyd's Rep. 174; 1973 A.M.C. 176; (1973) 32 D.L.R. (3d) 572 .... [1988] 82; [1989] 11 *et seq*.
Todd Shipyards Corp. *v*. Auto Transp., 763 F. 2d 745 (5 Cir. 1985) .... [1986] 73
Tojo Maru, The [1972] A.C. 242, 268, 292H .... [1986] 277, 308, 332, 337, 344, 540; [1990] 46
Tokyo Shipping Co. *v*. Scrap Disposal (*The Camphor*), S.M.A. No. 1549 (1980) .... [1986] 72
Tolten, The [1946] P. 135 .... [1989] 188, 193
Tomlinson (Hauliers) Ltd. *v*. Hepburn [1966] A.C. 451 .... [1990] 319
Toprak Mahsulleri Ofisi *v*. Finagrain Compagnie Commerciale Agricole et Financiere S.A. [1979] 2 Lloyd's Rep. 98 .... [1989] 366
Torenia, The [1983] 2 Lloyd's Rep. 210 .... [1987] 49
Torres *v*. Interstate Fire and Casualty Co., 275 F. Supp. 784, 1968 A.M.C. 367 (D.P.R. 1967) .... [1986] 380
Torrington Co. *v*. Metal Products Workers Union, Local 1645, 362 F. 2d 677, 680–81 & n.6 (2 Cir. 1966) .... [1986] 49
Toulla, The [1985] 1 Lloyd's Rep. 107 .... [1986] 102
Tournier *v*. National Provincial Bank [1924] 1 K.B. 461 .... [1987] 251
Towan, The (1844) 2 W. Rob. 259 .... [1989] 63
Tower Bridge, The [1936] P. 30 .... [1986] 346
Towne *v*. Eisner, 245 U.S. 418 (1917) .... [1986] 79
Tractech Inc. *v*. Costa Line, No. 83–5942 (S.D.N.Y., 10 October 1984) .... [1986] 367, 368
Trade Fortitude, The, 1974 A.M.C. 2198 .... [1986] 127
Trade Fortitude, The [1986] 2 Lloyd's Rep. 209 .... [1987] 417
Trade Indemnity Co. *v*. Workington Harbour Board [1937] A.C.1 .... [1986] 261
Tramountana Armadora S.A. *v*. Atlantic Shipping Co. S.A. [1978] 1 Lloyd's Rep. 391 .... [1986] 73; [1987] 172
Tramp Oil and Marine Ltd. *v*. M/V *Mermaid I*, 743 F. 2d 48, 1985 A.M.C. 459 (1 Cir. 1984) . [1986] 353
Tramp Shipping Co. Inc. *v*. Sanko Steamship Co. Ltd. (*The Agia Erini II*) (1974) S.M.A. No. 875 .... [1989] 355
Trans-Asiatic Oil Ltd. *v*. Apex Oil Co., 743 F. 2d 956, 1985 A.M.C. 1 (1 Cir. 1984) .... [1986] 350, 351
Trans Trust SPRL *v*. Danubian Trading Co. [1952] 2 Q.B. 297 .... [1987] 416
Transatlantic Schiffahrtskontor GmbH *v*. Vincor Shipping Co. Ltd. (December 1985, not yet reported) .... [1986] 385
Transcontainer Express Ltd. *v*. Custodian Security Ltd., 6 April 1986, unrep.; [1988] 1 Lloyd's Rep. 128; [1988] 1 F.T.L.R. 54 .... [1988] 38, 473
Transcontinental Insurance Co. of New York *v*. Minning, 135 F. 2d 479 (6th Cir., 1943) .... [1987] 214
Transmarine Seaways Corp. *v*. Marc Rich & Co., 1979 A.M.C. 1496 (S.D.N.Y. 1979) .... [1986] 73
Transmotors Ltd. *v*. Robertson, Buckley & Co. Ltd. [1970] 1 Lloyd's Rep. 224 .... [1987] 49
Transoceanic Petroleum Carriers *v*. Cook Industries Inc. (*The Mary Lou*) [1981] 2 Lloyd's Rep. 272 .... [1986] 114; [1988] 47
Transol Bunker B.V. *v*. M.V. *Andrico Unity*, 1987 (3) S.A. 794 (C) .... [1989] 175; [1990] 13, 491
Transvaal and Delagoa Bay Investment Co. *v*. Atkinson [1944] 1 All E.R. 579 .... [1989] 303, 307, 313, 338, 339
Transvaal Land Co. *v*. New Belgium (Transvaal) Land & Development Co. [1914] 2 Ch. 488 (C.A.) .... [1990] 331
Transvenezuelan Shipping Co. S.A. *v*. Czarnikow-Rionda Co. Inc., S.D.N.Y. 81 4987 Civ. (RCC), S.M.A. No. 1572B, 1982 A.M.C. 1458 (S.D.N.Y. 1981) .... [1986] 48, 70, 72, 536
Transworld Oil Ltd. *v*. Assurance Groupe de Paris, 17th Chamber of the Tribunal de Commerce de Paris, 20 February 1985 .... [1987] 185
Trask *v*. Maddox (*The Carrier Dove*) (1863) 2 Moo. P.C. (N.S.) 243 .... [1988] 450
Travers (Joseph) & Sons Ltd. *v*. Longel Ltd. (1948) 44 T.L.R. 150 .... [1990] 458
Trawnik *v*. Lennox [1985] 1 W.L.R. 532 .... [1988] 113
Trax Cargo Inc. *v*. C.P. Ambassador [1986] 3 F.C. 377 (Fed. C.A.) .... [1988] 83
Treasure Salvors Inc. *v*. Unidentified Wrecked and Abandoned Sailing Vessel, 569 F. 2d 330 (5th Cir., 1978) .... [1987] 25
Tremaine *v*. Phoenix Assurance Co., 1935 A.M.C. 753 .... [1986] 500
Trendtex Trading Corp. *v*. Credit Suisse [1982] A.C. 679 .... [1987] 3; [1989] 2; [1990] 220

Trengrouse & Co. *v.* Official Assignee of Steeds (1896) 14 N.Z.L.R. 636 .... [1990] 550, 551
Trent Rubber Services *v.* Polarctic (1987) 12 F.T.R. 140 (F.C.) ....[1989] 94
Tres Flores, The [1972] 2 Lloyd's Rep. 384, 391; [1973] 2 Lloyd's Rep. 247; [1974] Q.B. 264 ....[1986] 235, 258; [1987] 411; [1990] 387, 389, 390, 396
Trevor *v.* Whitworth (1887) 12 App. Cas. 409 ....[1990] 402, 403, 406, 407
Triangle Steel & Supply Co. *v.* Korean United Lines Inc. (1985) 63 B.C.L.R. 66 (B.C. S.C.) .. [1987] 83
Tribels, The [1985] 1 Lloyd's Rep. 129 .... [1986] 349
Trident General Insurance Co. Ltd. *v.* McNiece Bros. Pty. Ltd. (1987) 8 N.S.W.L.R. 270; (1988) 80 A.L.R. 574 ....[1987] 258; [1989] 139 *et seq.*
Trident General Ins. Co. Ltd. *v.* McNiece Bros. Pty. Ltd. (1988) 165 C.L.R. 107; noted (1989) 105 L.Q.R. 1 ....[1989] 139; [1990] 319, 505, 551
Trinder, Anderson & Co. *v.* Thames & Mersey Marine Insurance Co. [1898] 2 Q.B. 114 ..... [1988] 337
Trinidad, The, 10 F. 2d 849 (D.Ore., 1925) .... [1986] 322
Trinidad Corp. *v.* Sea Hire Serv. S.A., 1984 A.M.C. 2371 (E.D.N.Y.), aff'd 742 F. 2d 1441, 1984 A.M.C. 2374 (2 Cir. 1983), cert. denied, 104 S. Ct. 3514 (1984) .... [1986] 355
Tritonia, The (1847) 2 W. Rob. 522 ....[1989] 60
Troilus (Cargo owners) *v.* *Glenogle* (Owners, Master and Crew) [1951] A.C. 820 .... [1986] 329, 333
Tropaioforos, The (No. 2) [1962] 1 Lloyd's Rep. 410 .... [1987] 396
Tropical Marine Products Inc. *v.* Birmingham Fire Ins. Co. of Pennsylvania (1957) 247 F. 2d 116 .... [1988] 347
Tropwave, The [1981] 2 Lloyd's Rep. 159 .... [1990] 399
True Blue, The (1843) 2 W. Rob. 176 .... [1989] 75, 76
True Blue, The (1866) L.R. 1 P.C. 250 ....[1989] 59
Trussel *v.* Litton Systems, 753 F. 2d 366 (5 Cir. 1984) .... [1986] 372
Trustee of Rousou *v.* Rousou [1955] 1 W.L.R. 545 .... [1989] 315
TTT Stevedores of Texas Inc. *v.* Jagat Vijeta, 696 F. 2d 1135, 1983 (5 Cir. 1983) .... [1986] 355
Tubantia, The [1924] P. 78 .... [1987] 269
Tug Huntington Lim. Procs., 683 F. 2d 42; 1982 A.M.C. 2588 (2nd Cir., 1982), modifying 1980 A.M.C. 213 .... [1987] 345
Tukan Timber Ltd. *v.* Barclays Bank Plc [1987] 1 Lloyd's Rep. 171 .... [1990] 229, 236
Turnbull & Co. *v.* Duval [1902] A.C. 429 .... [1987] 126
Turnbull (Peter) & Co. Pty. Ltd. *v.* Mundus Trading Co. (Australasia) Pty. Ltd. (1954) 90 C.L.R. 235 ....[1989] 84
Turner *v.* Bladin (1951) 82 C.L.R. 463 .... [1990] 510
Turner *v.* Merrylees (1892) 8 T.L.R. 695 .... [1989] 149
Turner & Goudy *v.* McConnell [1985] 1 W.L.R. 898 (C.A.) ....[1986] 58
Turriff Construction Ltd. *v.* Regalia Knitting Mills Ltd. [1972] E.G.D. 257 .... [1990] 497
Tuyuti, The [1984] Q.B. 838 .... [1987] 540
Tweddle *v.* Atkinson (1861) 1 B. & S. 393 .... [1989] 139
Twin Disc Inc. *v.* Big Bud Tractor, 772 F. 2d 1329 (7th Cir., 1985) .... [1987] 122
Twins Transport Ltd. *v.* Patrick & Brocklehurst (1983) 25 Build L.R. 70 .... [1986] 232; [1988] 470
Two Hundred and Two Tons of Coal, The (1874) 24 Fed. Cas. 451 ....[1990] 36
UBAF Ltd. *v.* European American Banking Corp. [1984] Q.B. 713 .... [1989] 241
U.D.T. *v.* Western [1976] Q.B. 513 .... [1989] 442
Ugland Trailer, The [1985] 2 Lloyd's Rep. 372, [1986] Ch. 471 ....[1986] 1, 424, 426; [1988] 150, 545; [1989] 191, 193, 194, 195, 196; [1990] 410, 523
Ulrich Ammann Building Equipment Ltd. *v.* M/V *Monsun*, No. 83–2752 (S.D.N.Y., 21 March 1985) .... [1986] 368
UNR Industries *v.* Continental Insurance Co., *et al.* No. 83 A2523 (U.S.D.C., N.D. Ill. Decision 9 April 1985) ....[1986] 82
Unarco Industries Inc., *In re*, Case No. 82–B–00984 (N.D. Ill., 29 July 1982) ....[1986] 80
Undaunted, The (1860) Lush. 90 .... [1986] 308; [1989] 70, 77, 78
Unicorn Shipping Ltd. *v.* Demet Navy Shipping Co. Ltd. (*The Pitsa T*) [1987] 2 Lloyd's Rep. 404 ....[1990] 97
Unimarine S.A. *v.* Interessentslskapet Wind Endeavor, 1984 A.M.C. 405 (S.D.N.Y. 1981) . [1986] 358
Uni-Ocean Lines Pte. Ltd. *v.* C-Trade S.A. (*The Lucille*) [1984] 1 Lloyd's Rep. 244 (C.A.); [1983] 1 Lloyd's Rep. 387 ....[1986] 121, 126; [1988] 46
Union Amsterdam, The [1982] 2 Lloyd's Rep. 432 .... [1986] 252
Union Bank of Australia Ltd. *v.* McClintock [1922] 1 A.C. 240 .... [1988] 474
Union Carbide Corp. *v.* Travelers Indemnity Co., 399 F.Supp. 12 (W.D. pa. 1975) ....[1986] 96

Union Industrielle et Maritime *v*. Petrosul International Ltd. (*The Roseline*) 1985 A.M.C. 551, 1474; [1987] 1 Lloyd's Rep. 18 (F.C.) .... [1986] 102; [1988] 84
Union Insurance Co. *v*. Smith (1888) 124 U.S. 405 .... [1988] 347
Union Oil Co. *v*. Oppen, 501 F. 2d 558, 1975 A.M.C. 416 (9 Cir. 1974) .... [1986] 361
Union of India *v*. Compania Naviera Aeolus S.A. (*The Spalmatori*) [1964] A.C. 868 .... [1988] 251
Union Trust Co. *v*. Gilpin (1925) 84 A. 448 .... [1989] 304
Unique Mariner, The (No. 1) [1978] 1 Lloyd's Rep. 438 .... [1986] 309, 310, 313, 319, 321, 322, 323, 324, 325, 342, 349; [1990] 35, 353
Unique Mariner, The (No. 2) [1979] 1 Lloyd's Rep. 37, 50–51 .... [1986] 308, 309, 310, 318, 328, 331, 332, 333, 334, 335, 336, 337, 338, 341, 343, 344, 345, 348, 349; [1990] 353
United Australia Ltd. *v*. Barclays Bank Ltd. [1941] A.C. 1 .... [1987] 427; [1989] 258
United Brands *v*. Commission [1978] E.C.R. 207 .... [1988] 187
United City Merchants (Investments) Ltd. *v*. Royal Bank of Canada (*The American Accord*) [1983] A.C. 168 .... [1990] 234, 235, 552
United Dominions Corp. Ltd. *v*. Brian Pty. Ltd. (1985) 157 C.L.R. 1 .... [1990] 7
United Dominions Trust Ltd. *v*. Kirkwood [1966] 2 Q.B. 431 .... [1988] 362; [1990] 319
United Railways of the Havana and Regla Warehouse Ltd. (*Re*) [1960] Ch. 52 .... [1989] 365
United Scientific Holdings Ltd. *v*. Burnley B.C. [1978] A.C. 904 .... [1987] 421
United States. *See also* U.S.
United States *v*. Abbott, 89 F. 2d 166, 1957 A.M.C. 533 (2 Cir. 1957) .... [1986] 362
United States *v*. Barge *Shamrock*, 635 F. 2d 1108 (4th Cir., 1980) (not decided) .... [1987] 504
United States *v*. Bass, 404 U.S. 336 (1971) .... [1987] 512
United States *v*. Baycon Industries, 744 F. 2d 1505 (11 Cir. 1984) .... [1986] 379
United States *v*. Bear Marine Services, 696 F. 2d 1117; 1983 A.M.C. 2407 (5th Cir., 1983) .... [1986] 374; [1987] 501
United States *v*. Bear Marine Servs., 509 F.Supp. 710, 718–19 (E.D. La. 1980) .... [1986] 375
United States *v*. Beatty Inc., 401 F. Supp. 1040 (W.D. Ky., 1975) .... [1987] 498
United States *v*. Boyd, 491 F. 2d 1163 (9th Cir., 1973) .... [1987] 498
United States *v*. Boyd, 520 F. 2d 642 (6th Cir., 1975) .... [1987] 504
United States *v*. Burns, 512 F. Supp. 916 (W.D. Pa., 1981) .... [1987] 501
United States *v*. California, 332 U.S. 19 (1947) .... [1987] 27
United States *v*. Chevron Oil Co., 583 F. 2d 1357; 1979 A.M.C. 602 (5th Cir., 1978) .... [1987] 498, 499
United States *v*. Chotin Transp. Inc., 649 F. Supp. 356 (S.D. Ohio, 1986) .... [1987] 500
United States *v*. *City of Redwood City*, 640 F. 2d 963 (9th Cir., 1981) .... [1987] 501
United States *v*. Conservation Chemical Co., 619 F. Supp. 162 (W.D. Mo., 1985) .... [1987] 508
United States *v*. C & R Trucking Co., 537 F.Supp. 1080 (N.D.W. Va. 1982) .... [1986] 376
United States *v*. Dae Rim Fishery Co., No. 84–108 (D.Ala. 8 November 1984) .... [1986] 376
United States *v*. Dae Rim Fishery Co. Ltd., 794 F. 2d 1392 (9th Cir., 1986) .... [1987] 504
United States *v*. Dixie Carriers Inc., 627 F. 2d 736 (5th Cir., 1980) .... [1987] 501
United States *v*. Dixie Carriers Inc., 736 F. 2d 180; 1985 A.M.C. 815 (5th Cir., 1984) .... [1986] 375; [1987] 500
United States *v*. Ebinger (1967) 386 F. 2d 557 (2d Cir.) .... [1989] 96
United States *v*. Embassy Restaurant Inc., 359 U.S. 29 (1959), 720 F. 2d at 1099–101, 1984 A.M.C. at 322–324 .... [1986] 356
United States *v*. Gen'l American Trnsp. Corp., 367 F. Supp. 1284 (D.N.J., 1973) .... [1987] 499
United States *v*. Healy Tibbits Constr. Co., 607 F. 2d 540 (N.D. Cal. 1985) .... [1986] 376
United States *v*. Healy Tibbits Constr. Co., 713 F. 2d 1469 (9 Cir. 1984) .... [1986] 377
United States *v*. Hollywood Marine Inc., 519 F. Supp. 688; 1982 A.M.C. 1936 (S.D. Tex., 1981) .... [1987] 503, 504
United States *v*. Hougland Barge Line Inc., 387 F. Supp. 1110 (W.D. Pa. 1974) .... [1987] 499
United States *v*. Independent Bulk Transport Inc., 480 F. Supp. 474; 1979 A.M.C. 2846 (S.D.N.Y., 1979) .... [1987] 500
United States *v*. Ira S. Bushey & Sons Inc., 363 F. Supp. 110; 1973 A.M.C. 2639 (D. Vt.), aff'd without reported opinion, 487 F. 2d 1393 (1st Cir., 1973), cert. denied 417 U.S. 976 (1974) .... [1987] 501
United States *v*. Kennecott Copper Corp., 523 F. 2d 821; 1976 A.M.C. 208 (9th Cir., 1975) .... [1987] 499
United States *v*. Le Beouf Bros. Towing Co., 621 F. 2d 787, 1981 A.M.C. 1947, reh'g denied, 629 F. 2d 1350 (5 Cir. 1980), cert. denied, 452 U.S. 906, 1981 A.M.C. 2104 (1981) .... [1986] 375; [1987] 503
United States *v*. Louisiana, 394 U.S. 11 (1969) .... [1987] 518

United States *v.* Maine, 420 U.S. 515 (1975) .... [1987] 27
United States *v.* Malitovsky Cooperage Co., 472 F. Supp. 454 (E.D. Pa., 1979) .... [1987] 504
United States *v.* Messer Oil Co., 391 F. Supp. 577 (W.D. Pa., 1975) .... [1987] 499
United States *v.* Mobil Oil Corp., 464 F. 2d 1124; 1973 A.M.C. 427 (5th Cir., 1972) .... [1987] 499
United States *v.* Morania Barge 200 Inc., 1983 A.M.C. 2761 (E.D.N.C., 1982) .... [1987] 504
United States *v.* Mottolo, No. 83–547 (D.N.H., 15 March 1985) .... [1986] 376
United States *v.* M/V *Big Sam*, 681 F. 2d 432, 1983 A.M.C. 2730, reh'g denied, 693 F. 2d 451, 1983 A.M.C. 2749 (5 Cir. 1982), cert. denied, 103 S. Ct. 3112, 1983 A.M.C. 2111 (1983) .... [1986] 374; [1987] 501
United States *v.* Northeastern Pharm. & Chem. Co., 579 F. Supp. 823 (W.D. Mo., 1984) .... [1987] 508, 509, 510
United States *v.* P/B STCO 213, 756, F. 2d 364; 1985 A.M.C. 2763 (5th Cir., 1985) .... [1986] 375; [1987] 504
United States *v.* Poughkeepsie Housing Auth., No. 80–1998 (S.D.N.Y., 16 October 1981) .. [1986] 376
United States *v.* Price, 577 F. Supp. 1103 (D.N.J., 1983) .... [1987] 509
United States *v.* Reliable Transfer Co. Inc., 1975 A.M.C. 541; 421 U.S. 397, reversing 1974 A.M.C. 756; 497 F. 2d 1036 (2nd Cir.) .... [1986] 379; [1989] 358, 359; [1987] 118, 344; [1990] 52
United States *v.* Republic Marine Inc. (1987) 829 F. 2d 1399; 1988 A.M.C. 2507 (7th Cir.) .... [1989] 18
United States *v.* Republic Steel Corp., 362 U.S. 482 (1959) .... [1987] 517
United States *v.* Shell Oil Co., 605 F. Supp. 1064 (D. Colo., 1985) .... [1987] 510
United States *v.* Slade Inc., 447 F. Supp. 638; 1978 A.M.C. 1938 (E.D. Tex., 1978) .... [1987] 500, 504
United States *v.* S.S. *Lucy Schulte*, 343 F. 2d 897, 1965 A.M.C. 1516 (2 Cir. 1965) .... [1986] 355
United States *v.* Standard Oil Co. 384 U.S. 224 (1966) .... [1987] 517
United States *v.* T/B *Arcadian 95*, 714 F. 2d 470; 1984 A.M.C. 2659 (5th Cir., 1983) .... [1986] 374; [1987] 501
United States *v.* Texas Pipe Line Co., 611 F. 2d 345 (10th Cir., 1979) .... [1987] 500
United States *v.* Tex-Tow Inc., 589 F. 2d 1310 (7th Cir., 1978) .... [1987] 500
United States *v.* The Barge *Shamrock*, 1980 A.M.C. 1921 (D. Md. 1979), rev'd on other grounds, 635 F. 2d 1108, 1981 A.M.C. 1021 (4 Cir. 1980), cert. denied *sub nom.* Shell Oil Co. *v.* United States, 454 U.S. 803, 1982 A.M.C. 2111 (1981) .... [1986] 376
United States *v.* Ward, 448 U.S. 242 (1980) .... [1986] 377; [1987] 498, 499
United States *v.* Water Quality Ins. Syndicate, No. 84–7737 (S.D.N.Y., 11 July 1985) .... [1986] 376
United States *v.* W.B. Enterprises Inc., 378 F. Supp. 420; 1974 A.M.C. 1285 (S.D.N.Y., 1974) .... [1987] 498
United Steel Workers *v.* American Mfg. Co., 363 U.S. 564 (1960) .... [1986] 59
United Trading Corp. S.A. *v.* Allied Arab Bank Ltd. [1985] 2 Lloyd's Rep. 554 .... [1990] 223, 235, 236, 238, 242
Unitramp *v.* Garnac Grain Co. Inc. (*The Hermine*) [1979] 1 Lloyd's Rep. 212 (C.A.), rvrsg. [1978] 2 Lloyd's Rep. 37 .... [1988] 49, 54
Universal Cargo Carriers Corp. *v.* Citati [1957] 2 Q.B. 401, affmd. [1957] 1 W.L.R. 979 .... [1987] 412; [1988] 21, 54; [1989] 86
Universal Cargo Carriers Corp. *v.* Citati (No. 2) [1958] 2 Q.B. 254 .... [1988] 22
Universal Guarantee *v.* Jarvis (1937) (unreported) .... [1990] 19
Universal Guarantee Pty. Ltd. *v.* Carlile [1957] V.R. 68 .... [1990] 22
Universal Stock Exchange Ltd. *v.* David Strachan [1896] A.C. 166 .... [1986] 393
Universal Stock Exchange Ltd. *v.* Stevens (1892) 66 L.T. 612 .... [1986] 395
Universe Sentinel, The [1983] A.C. 366 .... [1989] 272; [1990] 347, 348
Universe Tankships Inc. of Monrovia *v.* I.T.W.F. (*The Universe Sentinel*) [1983] A.C. 366 .... [1987] 426; [1989] 272; [1990] 347, 348
University of Texas *v.* U.S., 535 F. 2d 438 (5 Cir. 1977) .... [1986] 429
University of Texas Medical Branch at Galveston *v.* U.S. (1977) 557 F. 2d 438; 1977 A.M.C. 2607 (5th Cir.) .... [1989] 18
Unwin *v.* Hanson [1891] 2 Q.B. 115 .... [1990] 257
Upper Lakes Shipping Ltd. *v.* Saint John Shipbuilding & Dry Dock Co. (1988) 86 N.R. 40 (Fed. C.A.) .... [1990] 106
Urman (*In re*) (1984) 44 O.R. (2d) 248 (C.A.) .... [1986] 168
U.S. *v.* Flood, 247 F. 2d 209 .... [1987] 91
U.S. *v.* Bethlehem Steel Corp. (1963) 319 F. 2d 512; 1963 A.M.C. 1673 (9th Cir.) .... [1989] 16
U.S. *v.* Cornell Steamboat Co., 202 U.S. 184 (1906) .... [1986] 152
U.S. *v.* Moran Towing and Transportation Co. (1967) 374 F. 2d 656; 1967 A.M.C. 1733 (4th Cir.) .... [1989] 16

U.S. *v.* Nassau Marine Corp. (1985) 577 F. Supp. 1475; 1985 A.M.C. 474 (E.D. La.); aff'd (1985) 778 F. 2d 1111 (5th Cir.) .... [1989] 17, 18
U.S. *v.* Ohio Barge Lines Inc. (1979) 607 F. 2d 624; 1980 A.M.C. 2199 (3d Cir.) ... [1986] 429; [1989] 16
U.S. *v.* S/S *Helena*, 295 F. Supp. 610 (E.D.La., 1969) .... [1987] 345
U.S. Shipping Board *v.* Bunge y Born (1925) 42 T.L.R. 174 .... [1987] 147
Vacwell Engineering Co. Ltd. *v.* B.D.H. Chemicals Ltd. [1971] 1 Q.B. 88 .... [1988] 509
Vagres Compania Maritima S.A. *v.* Nissho-Iwai American Corp. (*The Karin Vatis*) [1988] 2 Lloyd's Rep. 330 .... [1989] 290
Vainqueur, The [1974] 2 Lloyd's Rep. 398 .... [1986] 289
Vainqueur Jose, The [1979] 1 Lloyd's Rep. 557 .... [1987] 232; [1989] 498
Vale Chemical Co. *v.* Hartford Accident & Indemnity, *et al.*, Nos. 169, 170, Pa. Sup. Ct. (Philadelphia) 22 March 1985 .... [1986] 91
Vallescura, The, 293 U.S. 296; 1934 A.M.C. 1573 .... [1989] 359, 360
Valletort Sanitary Steam Laundry Co. Ltd. (*Re*) [1903] 2 Ch. 654 .... [1990] 545
Valley Auto Wrecking & Demolition Ltd. *v.* Colonial Motors Ltd. [1977] 1 W.W.R. 759 .... [1987] 66
Valley Towing Service *v.* S.S. *American Wheat*, 1981 A.M.C. 445 (E.D.La., 1975) .... [1987] 503
Valsesia, The [1927] P. 115 .... [1986] 311, 343, 344
Van Binsbergen, Case 37/74, judgment of 3 December 1974; [1974] E.C.R. 1299 .... [1990] 177
Van Camp Chocolates Ltd. *v.* Aulsebrooks Ltd. [1984] 1 N.Z.L.R. 354 .... [1990] 464
Van der Linde *v.* Calitz, 1967 (1) S.A. 239 (A) .... [1989] 177, 178
Van Eycke *v.* ASPA, Case 267/86, judgment of 21 September 1988 (unreported) .... [1990] 182
Van Oppen *v.* Clerk to the Bedford Charity Trustees [1990] 1 W.L.R. 235 .... [1990] 486
Van Wyck Assoc. *v.* St. Paul Fire & Marine Ins. Co., 115 Misc. 2d 447, 454 N.Y.S. 2d 266 (1982) .... [1986] 82
Van Wyk *v.* Rondalia 1967 (1) SA 373 (T) .... [1986] 280
Vana Trading Co. Inc. *v.* S.S. *Mette Skou*, 1977 A.M.C. 702; 556 F. 2d 100 (2nd Cir.) .... [1989] 359
Vantage Navigation Corp. *v.* Suhail & Saud Bahwan Building Materials LLC (*The Alev*) [1989] 1 Lloyd's Rep. 138 .... [1989] 270 *et seq.*
Vardinoyannis *v.* Egyptian General Petroleum Corp. (*The Evaggelos Th*) [1971] 2 Lloyd's Rep. 200 .... [1986] 119, 126; [1988] 52
Vargas Pena Apezteguia y Cia SAIC *v.* Peter Cremer G.m.b.H. [1987] 1 Lloyd's Rep. 394 .. [1988] 461
Varker *v.* Commercial Banking Co. of Sydney Ltd. [1972] 2 N.S.W.R. 967 .... [1986] 10
Varley *v.* Whipp [1900] 1 Q.B. 513 .... [1990] 456
Vastric, The [1966] 2 Lloyd's Rep. 219 .... [1990] 393, 396
Vatican Shrimp Co. Inc. *v.* Gabriel Solis (1987) 820 F. 2d 674; 1987 A.M.C. 2426 (5th Cir.) . [1988] 519
Vechscroon, The [1982] 1 Lloyd's Rep. 301 .... [1989] 405 *et seq.*
Velox, The [1906] P. 263 .... [1986] 347; [1990] 436
Venezolana (C.A.) de Navegacion *v.* Bank Line Ltd. (*The Roachbank*) [1987] 2 Lloyd's Rep. 498; [1988] 2 Lloyd's Rep. 337 (C.A.) .... [1990] 107, 109
Ventura Navigation Inc. *v.* Port of Singapore Authority (*The Stolt Avance*), 24 May 1989 (Sing. H.C.) .... [1990] 15
Verwayen *v.* The Commonwealth of Australia, Australian Torts Rep. 80–222 .... [1989] 279
Vest Transp. Co. Inc. (*In re*), 434 F. Supp. 748; 1977 A.M.C. 788 (N.D. Miss., 1977) .... [1987] 500
Vesta *v.* Butcher [1986] 2 All E.R. 488 .... [1988] 255
Vestland, The [1980] 2 Lloyd's Rep. 171 .... [1989] 192
Via Assur. I.A.R.D. Nord *v.* Alimenta, 1985 A.M.C. 667 (N.D. Ga.) .... [1986] 487
Victoria Fur Traders Ltd. *v.* Roadline (U.K.) Ltd. [1981] 1 Lloyd's Rep. 570 .... [1988] 476
Videan *v.* British Transport Commission [1963] 2 Q.B. 650 .... [1990] 485
Viger *v.* Commercial Ins. Co. 707 F. 2d 769 (3 Cir. 1983) .... [1986] 83
Vigers *v.* Pike (1842) 8 Cl. & Fin. 562 .... [1986] 318
Vigo S.S. Corp. *v.* Marship Corp., 26 N.Y. 2d 157, cert. denied, 400 U.S. 819 (1970) .... [1986] 66
Vimeira, The [1984] 2 Lloyd's Rep. 66 (C.A.) .... [1986] 66, 72
Violet *v.* Piccillo, 648 F. Supp. 1283 (D.R.I., 1986) .... [1987] 508, 509
Vita Food Products Inc. *v.* Unus Shipping Co. Ltd. [1939] A.C. 277 .... [1986] 510; [1987] 203, 209, 524; [1988] 126; [1989] 386, 393; [1990] 194
Vladimir Ilich, The [1975] 1 Lloyd's Rep. 322 .... [1987] 413
V/O Rasnoimport *v.* Guthrie & Co. Ltd. [1966] 1 Lloyd's Rep. 1 ... [1986] 110, 469, 472, 473; [1989] 173
Voest Alpine Intertrading G.m.b.H. *v.* Chevron International Oil Co. Ltd. [1987] 2 Lloyd's Rep. 547 .... [1989] 143
Voisin *v.* ODECO Drilling Co., 557 F. Supp. 715 (E.D. Tex. 1982), rev'd on other grounds, 744 F. 2d 1174, 1985 A.M.C. 635 (5 Cir. 1984) .... [1986] 373

Volta River, The, 1984 A.M.C. 464 (E.D. Louisiana) .... [1989] 353
Volvox Hollandia, The [1987] 2 Lloyd's Rep. 520 .... [1987] 281; [1988] 101
Vorras, The [1983] 1 Lloyd's Rep. 579 .... [1986] 257
Vrac Mar Inc. *v*. Karamanlis [1972] F.C. 430 .... [1987] 90
Vrede, The (1861) Lush. 322 .... [1989] 65
Vynior's Case (1609) 8 Co. Rep. 81b .... [1989] 160
Wabasso Ltd. *v*. National Drying Machinery Co. [1981] 1 S.C.R. 578 .... [1987] 83
Waddle *v*. Wallsend Shipping Co. Ltd. [1952] 2 Lloyd's Rep. 105 .... [1986] 418
Wadsworth *v*. Lydall [1981] 1 W.L.R. 598 .... [1987] 416
Wadsworth Lighterage & Coaling Co. *v*. Sea Ins. Co. (1929) 34 Ll.L.Rep. 98 .... [1988] 350
Wait *v*. Baker (1842) 2 Exch. 1,8 .... [1986] 300
Wait (*Re*) [1927] 1 Ch. 606, 635–636, 686 ....[1986] 6, 300; [1989] 116, 118, 119, 163; [1990] 272
Walker *v*. Boyle [1982] 1 W.L.R. 495 .... [1986] 319
Walker *v*. Bradford Old Bank Ltd. (1884) 12 Q.B.D. 511 .... [1986] 198
Walker *v*. Hungerfords (1987) 44 S.A.S.R. 532 .... [1990] 424
Walker *v*. Maitland (1821) 5 B. & Ald. 171 .... [1988] 333
Wallersteiner *v*. Moir (No. 2) [1975] Q.B. 373 .... [1990] 407
Wallis *v*. Smith (1882) 21 Ch.D. 243 .... [1990] 17
Wallis, Son & Wells *v*. Pratt & Haynes [1910] 2 K.B. 1003 .... [1990] 456
Walter and Sullivan Ltd. *v*. Murphy & Sons Ltd. [1955] 2 Q.B. 584 .... [1986] 198
Walters *v*. Morgan (1861) 3 De. G. F. & J. 718 .... [1986] 320
Walton (Grain and Shipping) Ltd. *v*. British Italian Shipping Co. [1959] 1 Lloyd's Rep. 223 .... [1987] 207; [1989] 171
Waltons Stores (Interstate) Ltd. *v*. Maher (1988) 164 C.L.R. 387; (1988) 62 A.L.J.R. 110 .... [1989] 140, 279; [1990] 498
Wanata, The (1873) 95 U.S. 461 .... [1988] 179
Wanganui Motors (1963) Ltd. *v*. Broadlands Finance Ltd., and Inwood (1988) 2 N.Z.B.L.C. 103; (1987) 1 N.Z.B.L.C. 102 .... [1990] 366
Ward *v*. Aeyre (1615) 2 Bulst. 323, 324 .... [1988] 288
Ward *v*. Byham [1956] 1 W.L.R. 496 (C.A.) .... [1990] 345
Ward *v*. Fielden [1985] C.L.Y. 2000 .... [1988] 545
Ward *v*. Griffiths Bros. Ltd. (1928) 28 S.R. (N.S.W.) 425 .... [1990] 519
Ward *v*. Royal Exchange Shipping Co. (1888) 58 L.T. 174 .... [1989] 197
Warde *v*. Feedex International Inc. [1984] 1 Lloyd's Rep. 310 .... [1986] 245
Ware *v*. Johnson [1984] 2 N.Z.L.R. 518 .... [1987] 327
Waren *v*. Internationale Graanhandel [1975] 1 Lloyd's Rep. 146 .... [1989] 422
Warwick Shipping Ltd. *v*. The Queen [1984] 1 F.C. 998 .... [1987] 93
Wash Gray, The, 277 U.S. 66 (U.S.S. Ct.), 1928 A.M.C. 923 .... [1986] 499
Washington Metropolitan Area Transit Authority *v*. Johnson, 104 S. Ct. 2827 (1984) .... [1986] 372
Waste Management of Carolina Inc. *v*. Peerless Ins. Co., 323 S.E. 2d 726 (N. Carolina Ct. App. 1984) .... [1986] 94
Watermark Ass'n Inc. *v*. Celotex Corp., 784 F. 2d 1183 (4th Cir., 1986) .... [1987] 118
Waterside Ocean Navigation Co. *v*. International Navigation Ltd., 737 F. 2d 150 (2 Cir. 1984) .... [1986] 359
Watson *v*. Duff Morgan and Vermont (Holdings) Ltd. [1974] 1 W.L.R. 450 .... [1990] 530
Watson *v*. Holliday (1882) 20 Ch. D. 780 .... [1987] 421, 428
Watt, The (1843) 2 W. Rob. 70 .... [1989] 66, 70
Watt & Scott Inc. *v*. Chantry Shipping S.A. [1988] 1 F.C. 537; (1987) 11 F.T.R. 242 (F.C.) ....[1989] 90
Watteau *v*. Fenwick [1893] 1 Q.B. 346 .... [1986] 225
Watts *v*. Public Trustee (1980) W.A.R. 97 .... [1989] 139
Waugh *v*. Morris (1873) L.R. 8 Q.B. 202 .... [1987] 203
Wauton *v*. Coppard [1899] 1 Ch. 92 .... [1986] 314
Way *v*. Latilla [1937] 3 All E.R. 759 .... [1990] 506
Wayne Tank & Pump Co. Ltd. *v*. Employers' Liability Assurance Corp. Ltd. [1974] Q.B. 57 ..[1987] 23
Wayward Princess, The [1986] 2 F.C. 298 (Fed. C.A.) .... [1988] 90
Wear Breeze, The [1969] 1 Q.B. 219 .... [1986] 6, 97, 299; [1987] 84; [1988] 40; [1989] 54
Wear Packet, The (1855) 2 Sp. 256 .... [1989] 72
Webb *v*. Griffin (1872) L.R. 5 H.L. 711 .... [1990] 221
Webb *v*. Ireland. 29 July 1986 (Sup. Ct., Ireland) (Unrep.) .... [1987] 72
Webster *v*. Bosanquet [1912] A.C. 394 .... [1990] 19
Webster *v*. Webster (1862) 31 Beav. 393 .... [1989] 197

Weddell *v.* Pearce & Major [1988] Ch. 26 .... [1990] 219
Weddle, Beck & Co. *v.* Hackett [1929] 1 K.B. 321, 330 .... [1986] 394
Wehner *v.* Dene S.S. Co. [1905] 2 K.B. 92 .... [1987] 541; [1989] 191, 195
Weinhouse *v.* Cowie (1811) 4 Taunt. 178 .... [1987] 202
Welch *v.* Bank of England [1955] Ch. 508 .... [1986] 9
Welch *v.* Bowmaker (Ireland) Ltd. [1980] I.R. 251 .... [1990] 545
Welded Tube *v.* Hartford Fire Ins., 1973 A.M.C. 555 (E.D. Pa.) .... [1986] 493, 498
Wellington Ins. Co. Ltd. *v.* Armac Diving Service Ltd. (1987) 38 D.L.R. 462 (B.C.C.A.) ......[1989] 96
Wellington Woollen Manufacturing Co. Ltd. *v.* Patrick [1935] N.Z.L.R. 23 .... [1990] 220
Wells *v.* Gas Float Whitton No. 2 (Owners) (*The Gas Float Whitton No. 2*) [1895] P. 301, aff'd. [1897] A.C. 337 .... [1987] 270
Wells (Merstham) Ltd. *v.* Buckland Sand & Silica Co. Ltd. [1965] 2 Q.B. 170 .... [1988] 502
Welsh Irish Ferries Ltd. (*In re*) (*The Ugland Trailer*) [1985] 2 Lloyd's Rep. 372, [1986] Ch. 471 ....[1986] 1, 424, 426; [1988] 150, 545; [1989] 191, 193, 194, 195, 196; [1990] 410, 523
Welsh *v.* Marentette (1985) 21 D.L.R. (4th) 276 ....[1987] 92
Werra, The (1887) 12 P.D. 52 .... [1986] 330
West *v.* National Motor and Accident Ins. Union Ltd. [1954] 2 Lloyd's Rep. 461 .... [1989] 261
West India and Panama Telegraph Co. Ltd. *v.* Home and Colonial Marine Insurance Co. Ltd. (*The Investigator*) (1880) 6 Q.B.D. 51 ....[1987] 30
West Side Bank *v.* Marine National Exchange Bank (1968) 155 N.W. 2d 587 . [1990] 74, 75, 76, 244, 248
West Winds Inc. *v.* The *Resolute*, 720 F. 2d 1097, 1984 A.M.C. 319 (9 Cir. 1983) .... [1986] 356
Westar Marine Services *v.* Heerema Marine Contractors S.A. Unreported (18 November 1985) USDC, N. Dist. of California .... [1986] 152
Westbourne Galleries Ltd. (*Re*) [1970] 1 W.L.R. 1378 ....[1988] 61
Westchester Fire Ins. Co. *v.* Buffalo Housewrecking & Salvage Co., 1941 A.M.C. 1601; 40 F. Supp. 378 (W.D.N.Y.), aff'd 1942 AMC 1052; 129 F. 2d 319 (2nd Cir.) .... [1989] 344–345, 355
Western Australian Insurance Co. Ltd. *v.* Dayton (1924) 35 C.L.R. 355 ....[1988] 32
Western Electric Co. (Australia) Ltd. *v.* Ward (1933) 51 W.N. (N.S.W.) 19 (N.S.W. Full Ct.) ....[1990] 22
Western Sahara case [1975] I.C.J. Rep. 3 .... [1988] 398
Western Stevedoring *v.* Ship *Anadolu Guney* (1988) 18 F.T.R. 9; 1989 E.T.L. 62 (Can. F.C.) .... [1990] 104
Western Stevedoring Co. *v.* Ship *Anadolu Guney* (cargo) (1989) 23 F.T.R. 117 (Can. F.C.) .... [1990] 104
Westerton (*Re*) [1919] 3 Ch. 104 .... [1989] 213
Westinghouse Electric Corp. *v.* M/V *Leslie Lykes*, 734 F. 2d 199, 207, 1985 A.M.C. 247, 257 (5 Cir. 1984) .... [1986] 369
Westinghouse Uranium Contract (*Re*) [1978] A.C. 547 .... [1989] 369
Westminster Bank Ltd. Hilton (1926) 43 T.L.R. 124 .... [1988] 443
Westpac Banking *v.* Savin [1985] 2 N.Z.L.R. 41 ....[1989] 321, 326, 327, 336
Westshore Terminals Ltd. *v.* The Ship *Genkui Maru* (T. 2894–72, 2 June 1976, unrep.) ....[1989] 96
Westview Sable Fish Co. *v.* The Ship *Neekis* (1986) 31 D.L.R. (4th) 709 (F.C.) ....[1988] 86
Westwake Price & Co. *v.* Ching [1957] 1 W.L.R. 45 .... [1987] 231, 245
Weyerhaeuser *v.* *Atropos Island* (1985) 777 F. 2d 1344; 1986 A.M.C. 1016 (9th Cir.) ....[1989] 96
Weyerhauser Co. *v.* Western Seas Shipping Co., 568 F. Supp. 1220, 1984 A.M.C. 765 (N.D. Cal. 1983), aff'd 743 F. 2d 635, 1985 A.M.C. 30 (9 Cir.), cert. denied, 105 S. Ct. 544 (1984) .... [1986] 66, 360, 536
Weyerhouse Co. *v.* Anglo Canadian Shipping Co. [1985] E.T.L. 309 (Fed. C.C.) ....[1987] 83
Whincup *v.* Hughes (1871) L.R. 6 C.P. 78 .... [1988] 530; [1990] 518
Whippingham, The (1934) 48 Ll. L. Rep. 49 .... [1986] 153
White *v.* Elmdene Estates Ltd. [1960] 1 Q.B. 1 ....[1990] 84
White *v.* Metropolitan Police Commission [1982] C.L.Y. 898 .... [1990] 138
White and Carter (Councils) Ltd. *v.* McGregor [1962] A.C. 413 .... [1986] 124; [1988] 531
White Star, The (1866) L.R. 1 A. & E. 68 ....[1989] 75
Whitecross Wire Co. *v.* Savill (1882) 8 Q.B.D. 653 .... [1986] 347
Whiteman *v.* Sadler [1910] A.C. 514 .... [1987] 203
Whitwham *v.* Westminster Brymbo Coal & Coke Co. [1896] 2 Ch. 538 .... [1987] 428
Whitworth Street Estates Ltd. *v.* James Miller and Partners Ltd. [1970] A.C. 583 .... [1987] 528, 529
Whyte (*Re*), 1984 S.L.T. 330; (1983) 1 B.C.C. 99.044 ....[1988] 64
Wichita Eagle & Beacon Publishing Co. Inc. *v.* Pacific National Bank (1971) 343 F. Supp. 332; reversed (1974) 493 F. 2d 1285 .... [1990] 226, 227

Wickman Machine Tools Ltd. *v*. Schuler A.G. [1974] A.C. 235 .... [1988] 265
Wiggins *v*. 1100 Tons, More or Less, of Italian Marble, 186 F. Supp. 452 (E.D. Va., 1960) ..... [1987] 26
Wight *v*. Foran (1987) 11 N.S.W.L.R. 470 .... [1989] 85
Wigsell *v*. School for the Indigent Blind (1882) 8 Q.B.D. 357 .... [1987] 432
Wilburn Boat *v*. Fireman's Fund, 348 U.S. 310, 1955 A.M.C. 467 .... [1986] 485, 487, 488, 497, 505, 506, 507
Wilh. Wilhelmsen *v*. Canadian Transport Co. (*The Takamine*) [1980] 2 Lloyd's Rep. 204 ..... [1987] 172
Wilhelmine, The (1842) 1 W. Rob. 335; (1843) 2 N.o.C. 213 .... [1989] 60, 61, 64, 69
Wilkinson *v*. Coverdale (1793) 1 Esp. 74 .... [1989] 149
William, The (1847) 2 W. Rob. 521 .... [1989] 68, 69
William A. Frame *v*. Canada (1987) 9 F.T.R. 161 .... [1989] 92
William Andrews (In the matter of), 266 F. Supp. 162, 165 (D. Fla 1967) .... [1986] 16
William Brandt Junior, The (1842) 2 N.o.C. Supp. lxvii .... [1989] 75
William C. Leitch Bros. Ltd. (No. 2) (*Re*) [1933] Ch. 261 .... [1990] 221
William Hannington, The (1845) 9 Jur. 631 .... [1989] 71
William & John, The (1863) Br. & Lush. 49 .... [1989] 70
William Lacey (Hounslow) Ltd. *v*. Davis [1957] 1 W.L.R. 932 .... [1990] 503
William Lushington, The (1850) 7 N.o.C. 361 .... [1989] 74
Williams *v*. Atlantic Assurance Co. Ltd. [1933] 1 K.B. 81, 100 .... [1986] 198
Williams *v*. Everett (1811) 14 East. 582 .... [1986] 198
Williams *v*. Roffey Bros. & Nicholls (Contractors) Ltd. [1990] 2 W.L.R. 1153 (C.A.) .... [1990] 344
Williams *v*. Williams (1881) 17 Ch. D. 437 .... [1989] 304, 332, 337
Williamson *v*. Cia Anonima Venezolana de Navegacion, 1971 A.M.C. 2083; 446 F. 2d 1339 (2nd Cir.) .... [1989] 355
Williamson *v*. Diab [1988] 1 Qd. R. 210 .... [1990] 512
Williamson *v*. Williamson (1869) L.R. 7 Eq. 542 .... [1989] 41
Willis *v*. FMC Machinery & Chemicals Ltd. (1976) 68 D.L.R. (3d) 127 (P.E.I. S.C.) .... [1988] 509
Willis (R.H.) & Sons *v*. British Car Auctions Ltd. [1978] 1 W.L.R. 438 .... [1986] 220
Willmott *v*. Barber (1880) 15 Ch.D. 96 .... [1989] 280
Willmott *v*. London Celluloid Co. (1884) 34 Ch.D. 147 .... [1990] 219
Wills *v*. Wood, *The Times*, 24 March 1984 .... [1987] 126
Willson *v*. Love [1896] 1 Q.B. 626 .... [1990] 19
Wilson *v*. Darling Island Stevedoring and Lighterage Co. Ltd. (1955) 95 C.L.R. 43 .... [1988] 472
Wilson *v*. Kelland [1910] 2 Ch. 306 .... [1990] 545
Wilson *v*. Moore (1834) 1 My. & K. 337 .... [1989] 321
Wilson *v*. Rickett Cockerell & Co. Ltd. [1954] 1 Q.B. 598 .... [1988] 508
Wilson *v*. Scampoli (1967) 228 A. 2d 848 (D.C. Ct. App.) .... [1990] 371
Wilson and M'Lellan *v*. Sinclair (1830) 4 W. & S. 398 .... [1989] 320
Wimble Sons & Co. Ltd. *v*. Rosenberg & Sons [1913] 3 K.B. 743 .... [1986] 269
Wimpey Construction (U.K.) Ltd. *v*. Martin Black & Co. (Wire Ropes) Ltd., 1982 S.L.T. 239 (O.H.) .... [1987] 238
Winbourne *v*. Eastern Air Lines Inc. (1984) 758 F. 2d 1016 (5th Cir.) .... [1988] 179
Windsor *v*. Chalcraft [1939] 1 K.B. 279 .... [1987] 230
Winkenson Impex Co. Ltd. *v*. Haverton Shipping Ltd. [1985] H.K.L.R. 141 .... [1986] 387
Winkfield, The [1902] P. 42 .... [1986] 432; [1988] 38
Winson, The [1982] A.C. 939 (H.L.) .... [1986] 308, 326, 340, 345, 349; [1987] 45, 55, 59, 60, 63, 78, 79; [1988] 37, 546; [1990] 34
Wishing Star Fishing Co. Ltd. *v*. B.C. Baron (1988) 81 N.R. 309; 1988 AMC 1657 (Fed. C.A.) [1989] 95
Wismar, The (1980) S.M.A. No. 1454 .... [1989] 343, 354
W.J. Alan & Co. Ltd. *v*. El Nasr Export & Import Co. [1972] 2 Q.B. 189 .... [1989] 23; [1990] 66
W.L. Thompson Ltd. *v*. Robinson (Gunmakers) Ltd. [1955] Ch. 177 .... [1990] 310, 311
Wondoflex Textiles Ltd. (*Re*) [1951] V.L.R. 458, at 467 .... [1988] 65
Wood *v*. Associated National Insurance Co. Ltd. [1985] 1 Qd. R. 297 .... [1986] 290
Wood *v*. Wood [1957] P. 254 .... [1988] 395
Wood *v*. Woodhouse & Rawson United [1896] W.N. 4 .... [1990] 217
Woodar Investment Development Ltd. *v*. Wimpey Construction U.K. Ltd. [1980] 1 W.L.R. 277 .... [1986] 106, 319; [1987] 53; [1990] 551
Woodhouse A.C. Israel Cocoa Ltd. S.A. *v*. Nigerian Produce Marketing Co. Ltd. [1972] A.C. 741 .... [1987] 265
Woodland *v*. Fear (1857) 7 El. & Bl. 519 .... [1990] 71
Woodroffes (Musical Instruments) Ltd. (*Re*) [1986] Ch. 366 .... [1986] 519, 524, 525, 530; [1990] 540

Woods *v.* Martins Bank Ltd. [1959] 1 Q.B. 55 .... [1988] 379
Woodworth *v.* Conroy [1976] Q.B. 884 .... [1988] 545
Woolcott *v.* Excess Insurance [1979] 1 Lloyd's Rep. 231 .... [1986] 260
Woolwich Equitable Building Society *v.* Inland Revenue Commissioners [1989] 1 W.L.R. 137 .... [1989] 403, 435
Wormell *v.* R.H.M. Agriculture (East) Ltd. [1987] 1 W.L.R. 1091, rvsng. [1986] 1 W.L.R. 336 .... [1987] 536; [1988] 511
Woudrichem, The, 278 Fed. 568 (E.D.N.Y. 1921) .... [1987] 152
Wren *v.* Holt [1903] 1 K.B. 610 .... [1988] 515
Wright *v.* Maman Cargo Terminals Ltd., Civil Action 288/81, Dist. Ct. cases (1984) Vol. 3, 341 .... [1986] 292
Wright *v.* U.S.A., 1989 A.M.C. 1338 .... [1990] 53
Wrotham Park Estate Co. Ltd. *v.* Parkside Homes Ltd. [1974] 1 W.L.R. 798 .... [1987] 428
Wuerttembergische *v.* M/V *Stuttgart Express*, 711 F. 2d 621, 1984 A.M.C. 2738 (5 Cir. 1983) .... [1986] 367, 368
Wyandotte Transportation Co. *v.* U.S. (1967) 389 U.S. 191; 1967 A.M.C. 2553 .... [1989] 16
Wycombe Marsh Garages Ltd. *v.* Fowler [1972] 1 W.L.R. 1156 .... [1989] 372
X, Y & Z *v.* B [1983] 2 Lloyd's Rep. 535; [1983] 2 All E.R. 464 .... [1989] 364, 369; [1990] 93
Xantho, The (1887) 12 App. Cas. 503 .... [1986] 39; [1990] 154
Yagerphone Ltd. (*Re*) [1935] Ch. 392 .... [1990] 220
Yango Pastoral Co. Pty. Ltd. *v.* First National Chicago Australia Ltd. (1978) 139 C.L.R. 410 .... [1987] 201, 203
Yasin, The [1979] 2 Lloyd's Rep. 45 .... [1986] 118, 150, 295
Yates *v.* Finn (1880) 13 Ch.D. 839 .... [1990] 335
Yellowtail, The, 1939 A.M.C. 1278 .... [1986] 495
Yeoman Credit Co. *v.* Waragowski [1961] 1 W.L.R. 1124 .... [1988] 279
Yeoman Credit Ltd. *v.* Apps [1962] 2 Q.B. 508 .... [1990] 284
Yeoman Credit Ltd. *v.* McLean [1962] 1 W.L.R. 131 .... [1990] 21
Yeramex Int'l *v.* S.S. *Tendo*, S.S. *Lindo*, 595 F. 2d 943, 1979 A.M.C. 1282 (4 Cir. 1979) .... [1986] 365
Yessenin-Volpin *v.* Novosti Press Agency (1978) 443 F. Supp. 849 .... [1988] 397
Yew Bon Tew *v.* Kenderaan Bas Maru [1982] 3 All E.R. 833 .... [1986] 280
Y.J.D. Restaurant Supply Co. *v.* Dib, 413 N.Y.S. 2d 835 (1979) .... [1987] 440
Yolland, Husson and Birkett Ltd. (*Re*) [1908] 1 Ch. 152 .... [1990] 520
Yone Suzuki *v.* Central Argentine R.R., 27 F. 2d 795, 804 (2 Cir. 1928), cert. denied, 278 U.S. 652 (1929) .... [1986] 371
Yorigami Maritime Construction Co. Ltd. *v.* Nissho-Iwai Co. Ltd., 1977 (4) SA 682 (C) .... [1987] 310
York-Shipley *v.* Atlantic Mutual, 1973 A.M.C. 584 .... [1986] 492
Yorkshire Dale S.S. Co. *v.* Minister of War Transport (*The Coxwold*) [1942] A.C. 691 .... [1986] 28; [1987] 30
Yorkshire Insurance Co. Ltd. *v.* Nisbet Shipping Co. Ltd. [1962] 2 Q.B. 330 .... [1989] 10, 236; [1990] 445
Yorkshire Woolcombers Association Ltd. (*Re*) [1903] 2 Ch. 284 .... [1989] 210
Young *v.* Grote (1827) 4 Bing. 233 .... [1986] 8
Young (Arthur) & Co. *v.* W.A. Chip and Pulp Co. Pty. Ltd. [1988] 13 A.C.L.R. 283 .... [1990] 419, 421
Younge *v.* Reynell (1852) 9 Hare 809 .... [1989] 9
Yourell *v.* Hibernian Bank Ltd. [1918] A.C. 372 .... [1990] 491
Y.P. Barley Producers Ltd. *v.* E.C. Robertson Pty. Ltd. [1927] V.L.R. 194 .... [1989] 81
Ypatianna, The [1988] Q.B. 345 .... [1989] 421
Yuen Kun Yeu *v.* Attorney-General of Hong Kong [1988] 1 A.C. 175 (P.C.) .... [1987] 545; [1988] 366; [1989] 42; [1990] 486
Z Ltd. *v.* A-Z and AA-LL [1982] Q.B. 558 .... [1990] 88, 89, 97
Zabriskie Chevrolet Inc. *v.* Smith (1968) 240 A. 2d 195 .... [1990] 375
Zelger *v.* Salinitri [1980] E.C.R. 89; [1984] E.C.R. 2397 .... [1987] 286, 292
Zelger *v.* Salinitri (No. 2), Case 129/83 [1984] E.C.R. 2397; [1985] 3 C.M.L.R. 366 .... [1988] 96, 392
Zelo, The (1924) 19 Ll.L.Rep. 41 .... [1990] 50
Zephyr, The [1984] 1 Lloyd's Rep. 58, revsd. on appeal [1985] 2 Lloyd's Rep. 529 .... [1986] 202; [1987] 208
Zephyrus, The (1842) 1 W. Rob. 329 .... [1989] 77
Zien *v.* The Queen [1984] 15 D.L.R. (4th) 283 (Fed. Ct., Trial Div.) .... [1986] 430
Zigurds, The [1923] P. 113 .... [1989] 179
Zinovia, The [1984] 2 Lloyd's Rep. 264 .... [1986] 339, 342; [1987] 40

Zographia M, The [1976] 2 Lloyd's Rep. 382 .... [1986] 214; [1990] 83
Zuchner *v.* Bayerische Vereinsbank [1981] E.C.R. 2021 .... [1988] 420
Zuhal K, The and the Selin [1987] 1 Lloyd's Rep. 151 .... [1989] 7 *et seq.*
Zygos Corp. *v.* Salen Rederiena A.B., 1985 (2) S.A. 486 (C); 1984 (444)(C) .... [1990] 14

Table of Legislation 1986–1990

Accession Convention 1978 (Convention on Accession of Denmark, Ireland, and United Kingdom to the EEC Convention on Jurisdiction and the Enforcement of Judgments in Civil and Commercial Matters 1968) .... [1988] 93, 119
art. 25(2) .... [1987] 293
34 .... [1989] 473
(1) .... [1987] 295
(3) .... [1987] 281, 295
36 .... [1987] 301
37, paras. 2, 41 .... [1987] 282
Act of Spanish and Portuguese Accession to the Communities, art. 3(2) .... [1988] 383
Act to prevent Pollution from Ships 1980 (33 U.S.C., s. 1901 *et seq*) .... [1987] 521
Acts Interpretation Act 1901 (Cth), s. 15AB .... [1989] 235
Administration of Justice Act 1956—
s. 1 .... [1988] 450
(1)(*h*) .... [1987] 417; [1988] 425
(*j*) .... [1988] 450
(4) .... [1988] 450
ss. 25, 26 .... [1987] 541
Administration of Justice Act 1969, s. 12 .... [1987] 418
Administration of Justice Act 1982—
Part III .... [1986] 139; [1987] 417
s. 15 .... [1987] 417
Administration of Justice Law, No. 44 of 1973 (Sri Lanka)—
Chap. 1 (repealed) .... [1987] 171
s. 3(2) .... [1987] 171
Administrative Procedure Act (U.S.) .... [1987] 515
Admiralty Act 1988 (Australia)—
s. 4(3)(*s*) .... [1989] 384
(*u*) .... [1989] 385
ss. 6, 19 .... [1989] 384
s. 29 .... [1989] 385
34 .... [1989] 384, 385
Admiralty Court Act 1840 .... [1987] 318
s. 6 .... [1988] 450
Admiralty Court Act 1861 .... [1987] 318
Admiralty Jurisdiction Act No. 40 of 1983 (Sri Lanka)—
s. 2(1) .... [1987] 169, 170, 171
Admiralty Jurisdiction Act No. 40 of 1983 (Sri Lanka)—*cont.*
s. 12 .... [1987] 170
Admiralty Jurisdiction (Hong Kong) Order in Council 1962 .... [1988] 259
Admiralty Jurisdiction Regulation Act No. 105 of 1983 (South Africa)—
s. 1(1)(ii)(*x*) .... [1987] 313
5(2)(*e*) .... [1987] 314
(3)(*a*)(ii) .... [1987] 314
(*c*) .... [1987] 314
7(1)(*a*) .... [1987] 311, 313
(*b*) .... [987] 312, 313
(2)(*a*) .... [1987] 313
Admiralty Jurisdiction Regulation Act No. 105 of 1983 of (South Africa) .... [1989] 382
s. 1(1)(ii)(*h*)(*r*) .... [1989] 383
(*j*) .... [1988] 16
(*x*) .... [1987] 313; [1989] 383
3(4), (5) .... [1990] 11
(4)(*a*) .... [1989] 183
(5) .... [1988] 16
(6), (7) .... [1990] 10, 11
(6) .... [1986] 279, 280, 281, 282
(7) .... [1986] 279, 280, 281, 282; [1989] 383; [1990] 14
(*b*)(ii) .... [1986] 282
(9) .... [1986] 282; [1989] 383
5(1) .... [1989] 383
(2)(*e*) .... [1987] 314; [1989] 383
(3) .... [1986] 280, 281, 282; [1989] 383; [1990] 9, 11, 14
(*a*)(ii) .... [1987] 314
(*c*) .... [1987] 314
(4) .... [1989] 385
ss. 6(1), 11 .... [1990] 493
s. 6(1) .... [1989] 177, 382
(*a*) .... [1986] 282; [1988] 16; [1989] 177, 178, 184
(2) .... [1989] 184
(3) .... [1986] 282
(3), (4) .... [1990] 13
7(1)(*a*) .... [1987] 311, 313
(*b*) .... [1987] 312, 313
(2)(*a*) .... [1987] 313; [1988] 16; [1989] 176
11 .... [1986] 282; [1989] 183, 184, 185, 187, 189
12 .... [1989] 178

Admiralty Jurisdiction Regulation Act No. 105 of 1983 (South Africa)—*cont.*
s. 16(2) .... [1989] 176
Antarctic Treaty 1959—
art. IV .... [1990] 144, 145
arts. VI, IX .... [1990] 145
art. VIII(1) .... [1990] 146
Arbitration Act 1950—
s. 1 .... [1987] 267; [1989] 160
4 .... [1986] 58
9 .... [1986] 62
10(1)(*a*) .... [1988] 24
12(1)(4) .... [1989] 159
(6) .... [1988] 303
(*a*) .... [1986] 63
(*b*)-(*d*)(*g*) .... [1989] 159
19(A)(i) .... [1987] 417
25(2)(*b*) .... [1987] 267
27 .... [1986] 58, 142, 143, 144; [1987] 146
Arbitration Act 1975 .... [1988] 430
Arbitration Act 1979 .... [1987] 280; [1989] 58; [1990] 384
s. 1(1) .... [1986] 235, 236
(5) ....[1986] 236, 243, 244, 245
(6) ....[1986] 236, 243, 244, 245
(7) .... [1990] 109
4 .... [1986] 74
5 .... [1986] 68; [1990] 556
6(2) .... [1986] 62
8(2) .... [1986] 235
Arbitration Act 1979 (Commencement) Order 1979 (S.I. 1979 No. 750) ... [1986] 235
Arbitration Act 1985 (Belgium) .... [1990] 429
Arbitration Act 1986 (Netherlands) ... [1989] 513
Arbitration Act (Act X of 1940) (India)—
ss. 2(*c*), 14, 17 .... [1988] 14
s. 47 .... [1988] 15
Arbitration Act No. 42 of 1965 (South Africa) .... [1987] 312
s. 6(1) .... [1987] 314
Arbitration (Protocol and Convention) Act (Act VI of 1937) (India) .... [1988] 13
Arctic Waters Pollution Prevention Act (Canada) .... [1989] 106
Arctic Waters Pollution Prevention Act, R.S.C. 1985, c. A–12 (amended by S.C. 1987, c. 7) (Canada) .... [1987] 348
Arrest Convention 1952 .... [1990] 354
Assignment of Book Debts Act, R.S.O. 1970, c. 33 .... [1986] 161
Athens Convention Relating to the Carriage of Passengers and their Luggage by Sea 1974 ...... [1988] 268; [1990] 354, 363
arts. 7, 8, 10(2) .... [1988] 178
Atlantic Fishery Regulations, C.R.C. 1978, c. 807 (Canada)—
s. 57(2), para. 1; Sched. XIV, para. 1 .... [1989] 100
Item 3, Sched. VIII, s. 41, 1985 P.C. 1985–3662, pursuant to the Fisheries Act .... [1989] 101
Atlantic Fishing Registration and Licensing Regulations, C.R.C. 1978, c. 808 (Canada), ss. 2, para. 5; 9(1)(*c*), paras. 1, 5, 9 .... [1989] 101
Australian Insurance (Agents and Brokers) Act 1985 .... [1987] 125
Australian Insurance Contracts Act 1984, s. 21 .... [1988] 30
Australian Sea Carriage of Goods Act 1924, s. 9(2) .... [1987] 312
Avtallsvillkorslagen (Sweden), art. 36 .... [1989] 493
Baghdad Treaty and River Frontier Protocol 1975 .... [1990] 300
Bangladesh Carriage by Air Act 1934 . [1988] 445
Bank Holding Company Act 1956— (U.S.) .... [1988] 381
Banking Act 1979 ..... [1987] 137, 249; [1988] 368
Banking Act 1987 .... [1987] 249; [1988] 368, 549; [1990] 434 *et seq.*
Bankruptcy Act 1914, s. 31 .... [1987] 151; [1988] 255
Bankruptcy Act (Rev. Stat. Can. 1970), c.B-3 as am. .... [1986] 176
Bankruptcy Code—
Chap. 7(11 U.S.C., ss. 701–766 (1982)) .... [1986] 354
Chap.11 (11 U.S.C., ss. 362, 1101–1174 (1982)) .... [1986] 354
Bankruptcy Reform Act (92 Stat. 2549, 2583–85 (1978)) s. 507 .... [1986] 356
Berne CIM and CIV Conventions 1952 .... [1987] 297
Bill C–75, 1st Sess., 33–34 Eliz. II, 1984–85 (Canada) .... [1989] 106
Bills of Exchange Act 1882 ....[1986] 27; [1987] 342; [1988] 382; [1989] 49
s. 3 .... [1986] 196
(1) .... [1986] 191
8(4) .... [1986] 197
10(1)(*a*) .... [1986] 196
(*b*) .... [1986] 197
14(1) .... [1988] 257
31(3) .... [1986] 191
45 .... [1990] 73, 246, 247, 249
(1) .... [1990] 246
(2)(*b*) .... [1990] 70
46(2)(*e*) .... [1990] 249
60(1) .... [1990] 252
80 .... [1988] 371
83(1) .... [1986] 158; [1990] 231
Bill of Exchange Act 1908 (New Zealand) .... [1990] 246
Bills of Exchange Act 1909 (Australia) .... [1990] 246, 252
Bills of Lading Act 1855 .... [1986] 7, 471, [1987] 344; [1988] 259; [1989] 51 *et seq.*, 425, 427, 428, 429

Bills of Lading Act 1855—*cont.*
s. 1 .... [1986] 100, 158, 296, 297, 298, 304, 479; [1987] 257; [1989] 52, 53, 54, 57, 162 *et seq.*, 420, 421, 423, 427, 429; [1990] 1, 2
2 .... [1986] 102; [1989] 173
3 .... [1989] 173
Bills of Lading Act, R.S.C. 1985, c. B–5 (Canada) .... [1986] 344
Bills of Lading Convention 1924 .... [1988] 273
Bills of Sale Act 1878, s. 4 .... [1990] 275
Bills of Sale and Chattel Mortgages Act, R.S.O. 1970, c. 45 .... [1986] 161
British Columbia Chattel Mortgage Act, R.S.B.C. 1979, c. 48 ....[1987] 91
British Columbia Insurance (Marine) Act, R.S.B.C, 1979, c. 203 ....[1989] 96
s. 80(2) ....[1989] 96
British Nationality Act 1948 .... [1989] 105
British Nationality Act 1981 .... [1989] 105
Brussels Civil Liability Convention 1969 .... [1987] 299
Brussels Collision Convention 1952 .... [1987] 297; [1988] 268
Brussels Convention 1924 .... [1990] 316
Brussels Convention and Protocol on Nuclear Ships 1962 .... [1987] 297
Brussels Convention on Arrest of Ships 1952 ....[1987] 283, 296
arts. 1, 3 .... [1987] 297
Brussels Convention on Jurisdiction and the Enforcement of Judgements in Civil and Commercial Matters 1968 .... [1987] 281; [1989] 390, 470; [1990] 146, 193, 277, 296
art. 1 .... [1989] 470
2 .... [1990] 278
arts. 2–6 .... [1988] 100
2–6A .... [1988] 101
art. 4 ....[1988] 97
5(1) .... [1989] 472
(3) ....[1988] 97
6A ....[1988] 99, 100
16(1) .... [1989] 471, 472
(5) .... [1989] 471, 475
17 .... [1988] 101, 255
19 .... [1989] 471, 472, 474
arts. 21, 22, 23 ....[1988] 91
21–23 .... [1990] 277
art. 21 ..... [1988] 93, 94, 95, 96, 97, 98, 99, 102
22 ....[1988] 93, 94, 95, 96, 97, 98, 99, 100, 102
24 ....[1988] 95; [1989] 472–475
arts. 25–31 ....[1988] 97
26–31 ....[1988] 98
art. 27 ....[1988] 98
43(3) .... [1988] 101
57 ....[1988] 93
1971 Protocol ....[1988] 91, 93, 119
arts. 2, 14 .... [1987] 282
Title VII .... [1988] 102
Brussels Convention on Limitation of Liability 1957 ....[1987] 296; [1990] 47
Brussels Convention on Salavage 1910 ....[1990] 32 *et seq.*, 352, 354
art. 15 .... [1990] 437
Brussels Convention Relating to State Owned Ships 1926, arts. 38, 57 .... [1989] 386
Brussels Prevention Convention 1969 ...[1990] 40
Builders Licensing Act 1971 (N.S.W.), Australia, s. 45 .... [1990] 509, 511
Builders Registration and Homeowners Protection Act 1979 (Qld.), Australia, s. 54(5) .... [1990] 512
California Insurance Code—
s. 33 .... [1986] 496
103 .... [1986] 488
252 .... [1986] 489
280 .... [1986] 491
281 .... [1986] 491
283 .... [1986] 491
ss. 330–339 .... [1986] 497
s. 331 .... [1986] 497
332 .... [1986] 497
333 .... [1986] 497
334 .... [1986] 498
335 .... [1986] 498
339 .... [1986] 498
1733 .... [1986] 496
ss. 1880 *et seq.* .... [1986] 491
1880–2010 .... [1986] 497
s. 1900 .... [1986] 498
(*b*) .... [1986] 502
1903 .... [1986] 498
1904 .... [1986] 502
1905 .... [1986] 502
Californian Civil Code, s. 1791(1)(*a*), (3) .... [1988] 511
Canada Act 1982, c. 11 ....[1989] 95
Canada Fisheries Act, R.S.C. 1970, c F–14, s. 58(1)(*b*) ....[1988] 89
Canada Labour Code, R.S.C. 1970, c. L–1 ....[1988] 88
Canada Shipping Act, R.S.C. 1970, c. S–9 .... [1989] 104
s. 1 .... [1989] 105
2 ....[1989] 92
ss. 6, 7 .... [1989] 105
s. 22 .... [1989] 105
ss. 38–40 ....[1988] 86
s. 108 ....[1987] 91
109(1)(3) ....[1989] 95
211 ....[1987] 88
436 ....[1989] 95
466 ....[1989] 95
ss. 647–649 ....[1990] 99, 100
s. 647 ....[1989] 97
(2) ....[1987] 82
ss. 647(2), 649(1) ....[1989] 95

Canada Shipping Act, R.S.C. 1970—*cont.*
Part XV (replaced by Coasting Trade and Commercial Marine Activities Act) .... [1989] 107
Canada Shipping Act, R.S.C. 1970, c. S–9 (Amendments 1987—Bill C–39) .. [1989] 106
Canada Shipping Act, R.S.C. 1985, c. S–9—
ss. 450–472 .... [1987] 346
562 *et seq* .... [1987] 344
574–575, 574–577 ....[1990] 99, 100
574–584 .... [1987] 345
586, 596 .... [1987] 343
Part XV, s. 654 *et seq*. (amended by S.C. 1987, c. 7) .... [1987] 348
Canadian Bank Act, s. 88. See now Stat. Can. 1980, c. 40, ss. 178–180 ...... [1986] 161
Canadian Business Corporation Act 1975, s. 234(2) ....[1988] 69
Canadian Carriage of Goods by Water Act, R.S.C. 1970, c. C–15 ....[1988] 83
Canadian Charter of Rights and Freedoms—
s. 7 ....[1989] 95
ss. 7, 11(*d*) ....[1988] 89
s. 15 ....[1989] 95, 102
(1) ....[1988] 90
para. 6(2)(*b*) ....[1988] 90
Canadian Federal Court Act .... [1988] 534
Canadian State Immunity Act, S.C. 1980–81–82, c. 95 ....[1987] 96
Carriage by Air Act 1961 ....[1989] 91, 133, 428, 429
s. 2 .... [1988] 156
10 .... [1988] 257
Sched. 1, art. 1(1) ....[1989] 37
10 .... [1989] 267
Carriage by Air Acts (Application of Provisions) Order 1967, S.I. 1967 No. 480 .... [1988] 445; [1989] 267
Sched. 1 .... [1988] 257
2 .... [1988] 446, 447
Carriage by Air (Parties to Convention) Order 1988, S.I. 1988 No. 243 ..... [1988] 156
Carriage of Goods by Road Act 1965 (CMR) .... [1988] 177; [1989] 429
Carriage of Goods by Sea Act 1924 .... [1986] 481; [1990] 172, 354
s. 1 .... [1986] 142
Carriage of Goods by Sea Act 1936 (U.S.)—
s. 3(8) .... [1986] 436
4 .... [1986] 436
(2)(*m*) .... [1986] 436
ss. 4(5), 1304(5) .... [1988] 274
Carriage of Goods by Sea Act 1936, c. 229, 49 Stat. 1207 (U.S.) .... [1987] 343, 503
Carriage of Goods by Sea Act 1971 ....[1986] 469, 511; [1987] 305, 343; [1988] 178, 259, 539; [1989] 91, 403 *et seq*.
s. 1(2) .... [1986] 142, 477; [1987] 146
Carriage of Goods by Sea Act 1971—*cont.*
s. 1(3) .... [1987] 306
(4) ....[1986] 476, 477; [1989] 403, 405
(6)(*a*) .... [1989] 405
(*b*) .... [1989] 404–407
2 .... [1987] 306
3 .... [1989] 383
Sched. .... [1986] 481
Sched., art. 1(*b*) .... [1989] 403
arts. III, 4 .... [1986] 158
Sched. IV, arts. 3, 6 .... [1989] 346
Carriage of Goods by Sea Act 1972, s. 3 .... [1987] 235
Carriage of Goods by Sea Act (46 U.S.C., ss. 1300–1315 (1982)) ....[1986] 365, 367
Carriage of Goods by Sea Act No. 1 of 1986 (South Africa) .... [1986] 557
s. 1(1) .... [1987] 305, 306
(*a*) .... [1987] 306
(*b*)(*c*) .... [1987] 307
(*d*) .... [1987] 308, 309
(2) .... [1987] 316
3(1) ....[1987] 312, 313, 314
(2) .... [1987] 314
(6) .... [1987] 316
4 .... [1987] 316
5 .... [1987] 305
(3) .... [1987] 316
6 .... [1987] 305
Carriage of Goods by Sea Act (Singapore) .... [1990] 172
Carriage of Goods by Water Act 1936, R.S.C. 1985, c. C–27 (Canada) ... [1987] 343
Carriage of Goods by Water Act, R.S.C. 1970, c. C–15](Canada)—
art. 3(6) ....[1989] 93
Carriage of Passengers and their Luggage by Sea (Interim Provisions) Order 1980 (S.I. No. 1092) .... [1990] 363
Ceylon Courts of Admiralty Ordinance, s. 23 .... [1987] 170
33 C.F.R.—
s. 153.203 .... [1987] 499
157.03(1) .... [1986] 376
29 .... [1986] 376
37(*a*)(1) .... [1986] 376
43(a) .... [1986] 376
40 C.F.R.—
s. 110.4(*a*) .... [1987] 497
(*b*) .... [1987] 498
110.6 .... [1987] 498
116.4 .... [1987] 497
117.3 and table 117.3 .... [1987] 499
122.62 .... [1986] 377
302.5 .... [1987] 506
306.21(*a*)(1) .... [1987] 507
49 C.F.R.—
s. 1056.1(*b*)(1) .... [1986] 496
11 .... [1986] 496
Charging Orders Act 1979 [1989] 470
s. 1(5) .... [1989] 468

Charging Orders Act 1979—*cont.*
s. 2(1)(*a*)(ii) .... [1989] 467
Cheques Act 1957 .... [1990] 252
s. 4 .... [1986] 181, 191; [1988] 371
5 .... [1986] 191
Cheques Act 1960 (New Zealand) ...... [1990] 252
Cheques and Payment Orders Act 1986 (Australia)—
s. 60(1) .... [1990] 253
ss. 62(1)(*b*), 62(2), 65 .... [1990] 252
62(3), (4), (12), 68(3) .... [1990] 253
s. 68(1), (2) .... [1990] 253
Cheques and Payment Orders Act 1986 (Australia) .... [1989] 239
Chicago Convention 1944 .... [1989] 125, 515
Chinese Constitution 1954—
art. 31 .... [1989] 483
CIM (International Convention concerning Carriage of Goods by Rail) 1961, art. 47 .... [1989] 177
CIV (International Convention concerning Carriage of Passengers and their Luggage by Rail) 1961, art. 43 .... [1988] 177
Civil Aviation (Carriers' Liability) Act 1959 (Cth) .... [1989] 145
Civil Code 1804 (France) .... [1987] 342
Civil Code (BGB) (Germany), s. 304 .... [1990] 383
Civil Code (Holland) para. 1946 .... [1987] 252, 253, 254
Civil Evidence Act 1968—
ss. 14, 18(2) .... [1989] 448
Civil Jurisdiction and Judgments Act 1982 .... [1987] 539, 540; [1988] 537; [1989] 390, 468, 521; [1990] 146, 277, 556
s. 1(1) .... [1987] 281
3 .... [1990] 355
(3) .... [1988] 93
9(1) .... [1988] 102
24 .... [1987] 294
25 .... [1987] 294; [1988] 99; [1989] 472; [1990] 90
(1) .... [1987] 286; [1989] 475
(3)(*a*) .... [1989] 475
26 .... [1986] 67, 281; [1987] 281, 290, 294, 296, 299, [1988] 95
(1) .... [1987] 298
32 .... [1987] 397
(1) .... [1989] 386
(4)(*a*) .... [1989] 386
ss. 41, 42 .... [1987] 284
41–46 .... [1987] 138
s. 42(3) .... [1986] 94
49 .... [1987] 98
Sched. 1 .... [1986] 441; [1990] 278
Sched. 1, Title II, art. 2 .... [1988] 216
5(3) .... [1988] 215
Scheds. 1, 2, 3 .... [1987] 282
Sched. 3 .... [1989] 473
art. 34 .... [1987] 281
Civil Jurisdiction and Judgments Act 1982—*cont.*
Sched. 4 .... [1989] 474
arts. 16(5), 19 .... [1989] 471
13 .... [1987] 281
Civil Jurisdiction and Judgments Act 1982 (Commencement No. 1) Order 1984 (S.I. 1984 No. 1553) .... [1986] 67
Civil Jurisdiction and Judgments Act 1982 (S.I. 1986 No. 2044) .... [1988] 383
Scheds. 1–3 .... [1988] 383
Civil Liability (Contribution) Act 1978 .... [1989] 3, 33
Civil Liability Convention 1969 ..... [1990] 40, 354
Civil Procedure Code 1983 (Iran), art. 440 .... [1987] 274
Civil Procedure Law 1982 (People's Republic of China)—
art. 192 .... [1990] 115
195 .... [1990] 116
Clayton Act (U.S.) .... [1989] 387
Clean Air Act 1956, ss. 1(3)(9), 20(1), 22(3), 34(2) .... [1987] 522
Clean Water Act (U.S.), 33 U.S.C., s. 1321(*f*)(4)–(5) .... [1990] 40
CMR (Convention on the Contracts for the International Carriage of Goods by Road) 1956 .... [1987] 297
art. 27 .... [1988] 177
Coastal Fisheries Protection Act, R.S.C. 1970, c. C–21 (Canada)—
s. 3(1)(2) .... [1989] 100
(2)(*a*) .... [1990] 105
ss. 3(2)(*a*), 8(1)(*b*) .... [1989] 99
s. 8(1), para. 3 .... [1989] 100
Coastal Fisheries Protection Act 1985 (Canada), s. 4(*a*) .... [1990] 105
Coasting Trade and Commercial Marine Activities Act (Coasting Act—Bill C–52, 2nd Sess. 33rd Parliament 1986–87 (Canada)) .... [1989] 104
ss. 2(1), 3 .... [1989] 107
3(3), 4, 5 .... [1989] 108
Code of Civil Procedure (ancien) (France), art. 48 .... [1987] 347
Code of Maritime Procedure of the Republic of Panama, Law No. 8 of 30 March 1982, amended by Law No. 11 of 23 May 1986 .... [1990] 446
Laws Nos. 11 and 83 of 1973 .... [1990] 448
Law No. 43 of 8 November 1984 (Modification of Articles of the Commercial Code) .... [1990] 448
Code of Navigation (Italy), art. 423 ... [1988] 273
Code of Virginia, s. 10–262 (1985) .... [1986] 19
Cohen Committee (1945) (Cmd. 6659) .... [1990] 403
Colonial Courts of Admiralty Act 1890, s. 2(1) .... [1987] 318
Colonial Courts of Admiralty Act 1890 (South Africa) ....[1989] 175, 176, 177, 382

Combines Investigation Act, R.S.C. 1970. c. 23 (Canada) .... [1989] 113
Commerce (Trade Descriptions) Act 1905 (Australia) .... [1987] 217
Commercial Arbitration Act 1984 (Victoria) (Australia)—
s. 48 .... [1986] 285
Commercial Arbitration Act, S.C. 1986. c. 22 (Canada)—
s. 34(2)(*b*)(ii) .... [1989] 93
Commercial Code 1807 (France) .... [1987] 342
Commercial Code (HGB) (Germany), ss. 567 IV, 594 .... [1990] 393
Commonwealth Marine Insurance Act 1909 (Australia) .... [1989] 446
Commonwealth Navigation Act 1912 (Australia) .... [1986] 285
Companies Act 1862 .... [1990] 406, 414
Companies Act 1900—
s. 4 .... [1990] 67
14 .... [1990] 520
Companies Act 1907 .... [1990] 539
s. 10 .... [1990] 521
Companies Act 1927 .... [1990] 539
Companies Act 1928—
s. 43(1) .... [1990] 521
75 .... [1990] 206
Companies Act 1929—
s. 143 (now Companies Act 1985, s. 285) .... [1990] 408
275 .... [1990] 206
Companies Act 1948 .... [1990] 255
s. 72 .... [1988] 60
94(1) .... [1986] 532, 533, 534
95 (now ss. 395–396 of the Companies Act 1985) .... [1986] 1, 2, 424, 525; [1988] 141, 142, 143, 144, 150; [1989] 207
(1) .... [1986] 1, 2
(*e*) .... [1989] 209
(2) .... [1986] 1
(*e*) .... [1989] 206
106 .... [1986] 2
184 (now Companies Act 1985, s. 303) .... [1990] 409
210 .... [1988] 60, 61, 65, 66, 69
(now Companies Act 1985, s. 459) .... [1990] 410
245(1) .... [1986] 384
332 .... [1990] 221
(3) (now Companies Act 1985, s. 458) .... [1990] 413
369(1) .... [1986] 525
399(1) .... [1987] 231
Companies Acts 1948–85 .... [1988] 255
Companies Act 1980—
s. 74 .... [1990] 410
75 .... [1988] 60, 61, 80
(now Companies Act 1985, s. 459) .... [1990] 411
Companies Act 1981 .... [1990] 261, 402
ss. 36–38 (now Companies Act 1985, ss. 131–133 .... [1990] 410
s. 96 .... [1990] 405
Companies Act 1981 (Australia), s. 200(1)(*g*) .... [1990] 526
Companies Act 1985 .... [1987] 188; [1988] 60 *et seq.*; [1990] 29, 275, 401, 520 *et seq.*
s. 9 .... [1988] 75
10 .... [1990] 403
14 .... [1990] 409
ss. 24, 100, 433 .... [1990] 402
s. 35 .... [1990] 412
A (inserted by Companies Act 1989, s. 108) .... [1990] 337
36C, (4) .... [1990] 411
56 .... [1986] 320
ss. 80(1), 89, 91, 95 .... [1988] 71
s. 127 .... [1988] 60
ss. 131–133 .... [1990] 410
134, 179, 251, 256 .... [1990] 414
s. 162 .... [1988] 61
196 (formerly s. 94 of the Companies Act 1948, as substituted by the Insolvency Act 1986, s. 439(1), Sched. 13 Part 1.9 .... [1986] 528
199, 310 (amended), 711A(2) (amended) .... [1990] 30
151–153 .... [1990] 405
221, 241 .... [1990] 212
221, 227 .... [1990] 207
226, 235 (inserted by Companies Act 1989, s. 2 .... [1990] 255
226(4), (5) (inserted by Companies Act 1989), 256(1) (inserted by Companies Act 1989), s. 19 .... [1990] 261
s. 227 (substituted by Companies Act 1989, s. 5) .... [1990] 212, 402
ss. 239, 241(3) .... [1990] 480
s. 285 .... [1990] 408
ss. 296, 297 .... [1987] 189
s. 300 .... [1987] 191
303 .... [1988] 70, 73; [1990] 409
317 .... [1990] 331
322A (inserted by Companies Act 1989, s. 109) .... [1990] 337
(2), (3) .... [1990] 337–338
371 .... [1990] 406
389 .... [1990] 422
ss. 395–396 (formerly s. 95 of the Companies Act 1948) .... [1986] 525
s. 395 .... [1986] 1, 2, 3, 424; [1988] 141, 150; [1989] 196, 211
(inserted by Companies Act 1989, s. 93) .... [1990] 543
(1) (as amended by Sched. 6 to the Insolvency Act 1985 .... [1986] 177; [1989] 199, 200
(2) .... [1990] 525

Companies Act 1985—*cont.*
s. 396 .... [1986] 1; [1988] 143; [1990] 522, 523, 524, 525
(1) .... [1989] 200
(*e*) .... [1989] 200, 206, 207, 208, 214
(*f*) .... [1989] 196, 214
(2)(*e*) .... [1989] 196
(4) .... [1990] 544
397 (inserted by Companies Act 1989, s. 94) .... [1990] 534, 535, 545
(1) .... [1990] 544
(5) .... [1990] 530
398 (inserted by Companies Act 1989, s. 95) .... [1990] 528, 537
399 .... [1990] 529, 530
ss. 399(1)(*b*), 404, 415(2)(*a*), 416 (amended) .... [1990] 29
s. 400(2) (inserted by Companies Act 1989, s. 95) .... [1990] 533
401 (inserted by Companies Act 1989, s. 96) .... [1990] 535, 544
(2)(*b*) .... [1990] 534
402 (inserted by Companies Act 1989, s. 97) .... [1990] 535, 536
403 (inserted by Companies Act 1989, s. 98) .... [1990] 536
ss. 404–406 (inserted by Companies Act 1989, s. 99) .... [1990] 529 *et seq.*
406, 407 .... [1990] 543
s. 407(1) .... [1990] 529, 544
409 .... [1986] 2; [1990] 541, 542
410 (inserted by Companies Act 1989, s. 100) .... [1990] 539, 540, 544
ss. 411, 412 (substituted by Companies Act 1989, s. 101) .... [1990] 543
s. 413 (inserted by Companies Act 1989, s. 102) .... [1990] 534, 544
416 (inserted by Companies Act 1989, s. 103) .... [1990] 545
417 (inserted by Companies Act 1989, s. 103) .... [1990] 536
419(5) (inserted by Companies Act 1989, s. 104) .... [1990] 533
425 .... [1989] 411, 412, 509
ss. 437, 447, 448 .... [1987] 195
s. 458 .... [1987] 190; [1990] 413
459 .... [1988] 60 *et seq.*; [1989] 412, 415, 508; [1990] 406, 411, 415
460 .... [1988] 60
461 .... [1988] 68
(3) .... [1988] 76
614(2)(*b*) .... [1987] 148
651 .... [1989] 504
666 .... [1987] 231
691 .... [1990] 541
ss. 703D(1), (5), 703F(2) (as introduced by Companies Act 1989, s. 105, Sched. 15) .... [1990] 542
703D(3), (5), 703F(3) .... [1990] 543
s. 727 .... [1990] 214, 220, 420

Companies Act 1985—*cont.*
s. 741 .... [1990] 404
744 .... [1987] 191
Sched 4, Part II, s. A. paras. 9–14 ... [1990] 261
ss. B, C .... [1990] 261
Part III, para. 36 .... [1990] 261
36A (inserted by Companies Act 1989, Sched. 1, para. 8) .... [1990] 261
IV .... [1988] 71
XI, Chap. V .... [1990] 29
XII .... [1990] 520 *et seq.*
XIII, Chap. III (inserted by Companies Act 1989) .... [1990] 542
XVII (ss. 459–461) .... [1988] 60
Companies Act 1989 .... [1990] 28 *et seq.*, 261, 275, 520 *et seq.*
s. 46 .... [1990] 414
93 .... [1990] 410
95 .... [1990] 528
97 .... [1990] 533
99 .... [1990] 529
101 .... [1990] 543
108 .... [1990] 402, 412
ss. 113–117 .... [1990] 404
s. 131 .... [1990] 410
142 .... [1990] 545
207 .... [1990] 414
215 .... [1990] 520
396 .... [1990] 523
405 .... [1990] 541
Part IV .... [1990] 520 *et seq.*
VII, ss. 173, 178 .... [1990] 545
Sched. 19, para. 11 .... [1990] 411
Companies Bill 1988—
cl. 79 .... [1989] 196
Companies Consolidation (Consequential Provisions) Act 1985, s. 12 .... [1990] 410
Companies (Floating Charges) (Scotland) Act 1961 .... [1990] 402
Company Directors Disqualification Act 1986 .... [1986] 557
s. 1 .... [1990] 219
(1) .... [1987] 197
(3) .... [1987] 198
2(2) .... [1987] 188
(3)(*a*) .... [1987] 198
ss. 2–5, 6, 8, 10 .... [1987] 197
s. 3(2)(3)(4) .... [1987] 189
(5) .... [1987] 198
ss. 3, 6, 8 .... [1987] 195
s. 4(2) .... [1987] 190, 191
5 .... [1987] 189
(5) .... [1987] 198
ss. 6, 8 .... [1987] 196
s. 6(2)(3) .... [1987] 192
(4) .... [1987] 198
7(1)(3) .... [1987] 192
9(4)(5) .... [1987] 194
10 .... [1990] 215, 219
ss. 10, 11 .... [1987] 196

Company Directors Disqualification Act 1986—*cont.*
s. 13 .... [1987] 198
15 .... [1987] 188
(2), (3)(*b*), (4)(5) .... [1987] 199
16(2) .... [1987] 197
17 .... [1987] 188
18(1)(2) .... [1987] 199
22(5)(6) .... [1987] 191
Sch. 1 .... [1987] 193
Parts I and II .... [1987] 194, 195
Company Directors Liability Act 1890 .... [1990] 410
Company Securities (Insider Dealing) Act 1985 .... [1987] 429; [1989] 245
s. 1(3) .... [1990] 413
Competition Act (Canada)—
s. 34(1)(*c*) .... [1989] 113
Comprehensive Environmental Response, Compensation and Liability Act 1980 (CERCLA) (Superfund Act), P.L. 96–510, 94 Stat. 2767, 42 U.S.C., s. 9601 *et seq.* (U.S.) .... [1987] 348, 496, 505
s. 9607(*f*) .... [1990] 40
Conditional Sales Act, R.S.O. 1970, c. 76 .... [1986] 161
Conservation—National & International Monuments & Memorials, 16 U.S.C. ss. 431–433 .... [1986] 18
Constitution Act 1867 s. 91(10(12) .... [1987] 89
Constitution Act 1867 (Canada) .... [1990] 102
s. 91(10) .... [1989] 91, 95
ss. 91(12), 92(13) .... [1989] 89
Part 1, Sched. B .... [1989] 95
Constitution of India, art. 51(*d*) .... [1988] 15
Consumer Credit Act 1974 .... [1987] 127; [1990] 269 *et seq.*, 280, 555
s. 56 .... [1987] 126
189(1) .... [1989] 512
Consumer Credit (Exempt Agreements) (No. 2) Order 1985 .... [1990] 555–556
Consumer Protection Act 1987 .... [1988] 260; [1989] 371; [1990] 279
s. 1(2) .... [1988] 211
2 .... [1988] 211, 212
(2)(*c*) .... [1988] 211, 516
3 .... [1988] 516
(2)(*b*) .... [1988] 214
4(1)(*d*) .... [1988] 212
(*e*)(*f*) .... [1988] 214
5 .... [1988] 503
(1) .... [1988] 212
(2)(3) .... [1988] 213
7 .... [1988] 214
45 .... [1988] 211
46(2) .... [1989] 378
Parts 2, 3 .... [1990] 280
Part 3 .... [1990] 281
Consumer Safety Act 1978 .... [1987] 137
Consumer Safety (Amendment) Act 1986 .... [1986] 557; [1987] 137
Consumer Transactions (Restriction on Statements) Order 1976 (S.I. 1976 No. 1813) as amended by Consumer Transactions (Restrictions on Statements) (Amendment) Order 1978 (S.I. 1978 No. 127) .... [1988] 507
Continental Shelf Act 1964 .... [1988] 264
Continental Shelf Convention 1958 .... [1990] 289
Contracts Review Act 1980 (Australia)—
s. 7 .... [1990] 168
9 .... [1990] 169
Contracts Review Act 1980 (N.S.W.) .... [1987] 169
Contractual Mistakes Act 1977 (New Zealand)—
ss. 4(1)(2), 5(1) .... [1987] 326
s. 6 .... [1987] 325
(1)(*a*) .... [1987] 328, 330, 332
(i) .... [1987] 326, 327, 331, 335, 337
(ii) .... [1987] 326, 327, 328, 335, 337
(iii) .... [1987] 326, 330, 331, 332, 334, 335, 336, 337
(*b*) .... [1987] 328, 331, 332, 334, 336
(*c*) .... [1987] 329
(2)(*a*) .... [1987] 332, 333, 336
7 .... [1987] 326, 333
(2) .... [1987] 331, 334
Contractual Remedies Act 1979 (New Zealand) .... [1987] 335; [1990] 150
Control of Pollution Act 1974 .... [1988] 413; [1990] 562
Convention for the Conservation of Antarctic Seals 1972 .... [1990] 144
Convention for the Conservation of Marine Living Resources 1980, art. IV .... [1990] 144
Convention for the Reciprocal Recognition and Enforcement of Judgments in Civil and Commercial Matters (U.K. and Canada 24 April 1984, brought into force 1 January 1987) (Cmnd. 9337 (1984) and S.I. 1986 No. 2027) .... [1988] 383
Convention for the Unification of Certain Rules of Law Respecting Assistance and Salvage at Sea, Brussels, 23 September 1910 (Salvage Convention 1910) .... [1990] 32 *et seq.*, 352, 354
art. 15 .... [1990] 437
Convention for the Unification of Certain Rules relating to Carriage by Air 1929 (the Warsaw Convention) .... [1988] 151
Convention for the Unification of Certain Rules relating to Maritime Liens and Mortgages 1926—
art. 3 .... [1988] 166
13 .... [1988] 167
Convention for the Unification of Certain Rules relating to Maritime Liens and Mortgages 1967—
art. 4 .... [1988] 166, 167

Convention for the Unification of Certain Rules relating to Maritime Liens and Mortgages 1967—*cont.*
art. 6(1) .... [1988] 166, 175
7(1) .... [1988] 167
11(3) .... [1988] 171
Convention of 19 June 1980 on the Law Applicable to Contractual Obligations .... [1988] 119
art. 10 .... [1988] 385
Convention on International Bills of Exchange and International Promissory Notes (UN, 1988) .... [1990] 559
Convention on Limitation of Liability for Maritime Claims 1976 .... [1989] 451
Convention Relating to the Arrest of Seagoing Ships 1952 (the Arrest Convention) .... [1990] 354
art. 1(1)(*e*)(*k*)(*l*) .... [1988] 425
(*h*) .... [1988] 427, 428
(*k*) .... [1988] 425, 426
arts. 2, 7 .... [1988] 93
art. 53 .... [1988] 94
Convention Relating to the Limitation of Liability for Maritime Claims 1976 ....[1988] 178; [1990] 354, 363, 437
art. 2(1)(*c*) .... [1990] 361
3 .... [1990] 360
Conventions on Mortgages 1926 and 1967 .... [1987] 301
Copyright Act 1956—
s. 6(4) .... [1989] 159
17(1)(2) .... [1987] 428
(2) .... [1987] 429
48(1) .... [1989] 160
Copyright, Designs and Patents Act 1988—
s. 45 .... [1989] 159
178(1) .... [1989] 160
Cork Report (Cmnd. 8558, para. 1573) .... [1986] 529
Cork Report (Insolvency Law, 1982, Cmnd. 8558 ... [1990] 206, 220, 403, 405, 414
COTIF (Convention concerning International Carriage by Rail) 1980 ....[1988] 177, 268
Credit Contracts Act 1981 (New Zealand) .... [1987] 336
Criminal Code, R.S.C. 1970, c. C–34 (Canada)—
s. 614(1) .... [1989] 100
Crown Liability Act 1970 (Canada)—
s. 3(1) .... [1986] 431
Crown Liability Act, R.S.C. 1970, c. C–28 (Canada)—
ss. 9(3), 23 .... [1989] 90
Crown Liability Act, R.S.C. 1970, c. C–38 (Canada)—
s. 3(1)(*a*) .... [1987] 94
(*b*) .... [1987] 94, 95
Crown Proceedings Act 1947, s. 8 ...... [1990] 362
Customs Act 1901 (Australia) .... [1987] 216
Customs Act, R.S.C. 1970, c. C–40 (Canada) ....[1987] 92; [1989] 102
Customs and Excise Act 1952, s. 44 ... [1987] 214
Customs and Excise Offshore Application Act, S.C. 1984, c. 17 (Canada) .... [1989] 108
Customs Tariff and Excise Tax Act (Canada) .... [1989] 108
Data Protection Act 1984—
s. 1(2) .... [1986] 216
(3) .... [1986] 217
(5) .... [1986] 216
(6) .... [1986] 216
s. 5(2) .... [1986] 216
15 .... [1986] 217
42(1) .... [1986] 216
43(5)–(6) .... [1986] 217
Davey Committee (1895) (C. 7779) .... [1990] 403
Decree No. 66–1078 (France), art. 11 .... [1990] 393
Decree of 12 March 1913 (France) ..... [1987] 345
Decree of 29 November 1935 .... [1987] 347
Decree of 25 March 1937 .... [1987] 343
Decree No. 1299 of 28 September 1955 .... [1987] 346
Decree No. 58–14 of 4 January 1958 ... [1987] 347
Decree No. 58–922 of 7 October 1958 .... [1987] 348
Decree No. 60–456 of 4 May 1960 ...... [1987] 345
Decree No. 66–1078 of 31 December 1966 .... [1987] 343
arts. 33, 49 .... [1987] 344
Decree No. 67–967 of 27 October 1967 .... [1987] 347
arts. 59–70 .... [1987] 346
art. 68 (France) .... [1988] 178
Decree No. 67–967 of 27 October 1967 (as amended by Decree No. 71–161 of 24 February 1971) .... [1987] 347
Decree No. 68–65 of 19 January 1968 .... [1987] 346
Decree No. 49029 of 25 May 1969, art. 4(1)(*a*) (Portugal) .... [1988] 178
Decree No. 74–494 of 17 May 1974 .... [1987] 349
Decree No. 75–553 of 26 June 1975 .... [1987] 349
Decree No. 78–24 of 4 January 1978 ... [1987] 348
Decree No. 78–1000 of 29 September 1978 .... [1987] 349
Decree No. 78–1186 of 18 December 1978 .... [1987] 349
Decree No. 82–426 of 19 May 1982 .... [1987] 349
Decree No. 82–842 of 29 September 1982 .... [1987] 349
Decree No. 86–25 of 3 January 1986 ... [1987] 349
Decree No. 86–1076 of 24 September 1986 .... [1987] 349
Decree No. 86–1371 of 23 December 1986 .... [1987] 346
Deepwater Port Act 1974 .... [1986] 375
Deepwater Port Act 1974, 33 U.S.C. s. 1501 *et seq.* (U.S.) .... [1987] 496

Deepwater Port Act 1974—*cont.*
s. 1517(*d*) .... [1990] 40
Deepwater Port Act 1975, P.L. 93–627, 88 Stat. 2126, amended by Act of 25 September 1984, P.L. 84–419, 98 Stat. 1607 (U.S.) .... [1987] 348
Diamond Report for the D.T.I. on Charge Registration, 1989 .... [1990] 403
Directive on the Interpretation of the Laws (China) 1955 .... [1989] 483
Directive on Strengthening the Interpretation of the Law (China) 1981 ..... [1989] 483
Drug Trafficking Offences Act 1986, s. 2 .... [1987] 214
Dumping at Sea Act 1974 .... [1987] 348
EC Commission Directive on Waste (75/442/EEC), amended by COM (88) 391 Final .... [1990] 16
EC Commission Draft Directive on Civil Liability for Waste (COM (89)) 282 Final .... [1990] 16
EC Council Directives—
73/239 .... [1990] 178, 179, 189
77/187 .... [1990] 412
79/267 .... [1990] 178, 183
83/349 .... [1990] 28
84/253 .... [1990] 28, 29
88/357 .... [1990] 179, 189
88/361 .... [1990] 177
Economic Contract Law (Domestic) (People's Republic of China)—
arts. 11, 13, 17 .... [1989] 485
EEC Convention on Jurisdiction and the Enforcement of Judgments in Civil and Commercial Matters (27 September 1968) ..... [1990] 90, 171, 172, 355
art. 1(2)(*i*) .... [1988] 393,394
5(1) .... [1988] 384, 385, 386, 387
(5) .... [1988] 387, 388
17 .... [1988] 388, 390, 391; [1990] 556
arts. 21, 22 .... [1988] 393
21–23 .... [1988] 391, 392
22(1)(2) .... [1988] 392
24 .... [1990] 90
27(1) .... [1988] 394
(3) .... [1988] 392, 393, 394
(4) .... [1988] 394
36 .... [1988] 393, 394
Titles II, III .... [1988] 393
EEC Convention on Jurisdiction and the Enforcement of Judgments in Civil and Commercial Matters, as amended by Convention of 9 October 1978 .... [1988] 383
EEC Council Directive 77/780 ([1977] O.J. L322/30; [1978] Commercial Laws of Europe 163)—
art. 12(1) .... [1987] 252, 253, 254
(3) .... [1987] 253
EEC Council Regulation No. 4056/86 of 22 December 1986 .... [1988] 182 *et seq.*
EEC Directive 78/659 .... [1988] 413
EEC Directive 79/923 .... [1988] 413
EEC First Directive on Company Law Harmonization .... [1990] 411
EEC Regulation 67/67 .... [1989] 127–128
EEC Regulation 2176/84 .... [1988] 414, 415
EEC Treaty (Treaty of Rome 1957) .... [1988] 536; [1990] 176, 293
art. 7 .... [1990] 181
arts. 9, 38, 39–46, 110 .... [1990] 294
59 *et seq.*, 61(2), 67 .... [1990] 177
art. 85 .... [1989] 127–128
arts. 85, 86 .... [1990] 297, 309
art. 106 .... [1990] 177
177 .... [1987] 253; [1990] 412
215(1) .... [1988] 536
(2) .... [1988] 537
220(4) .... [1990] 146
Electronic Fund Transfer Act 1978 ..... [1986] 196
Electronic Fund Transfer Act 1978 (U.S.) .... [1990] 64
Employers' Liability (Defective Equipment) Act 1969 .... [1988] 211
s. 1(1)(3) .... [1988] 123
(3) .... [1988] 124
Employment Act 1980, s. 17 .... [1990] 348
European Communities Act 1972—
s. 9 .... [1990] 402
(2) (now Companies Act 1985, s. 36(4)) .... [1990] 411
European Community Convention on Jurisdiction and the Recognition and Enforcement of Judgments .... [1988] 535
European Convention on Human Rights (4 November 1950), 1st Additional Protocol, art. 1 .... [1989] 29
European Convention on the Law Applicable to Contractual Obligations—
arts. 1, 3(4), 8(1), 17 .... [1990] 193
art. 3(2) .... [1990] 196
8(2) .... [1990] 199
European Judgments Convention 1968—
art. 1 .... [1987] 282, 283, 290
2 .... [1987] 283, 286, 288, 296, 297, 298
arts. 2–24 .... [1987] 295
art. 4 .... [1987] 288, 301
5 .... [1987] 283, 287, 288, 296, 298
(1) .... [1987] 285, 286, 297, 298
(3) .... [1987] 286, 298, 302
(5) .... [1987] 287, 301, 302
(7) .... [1987] 287, 297
6 .... [1987] 283, 288
(1) .... [1987] 297
6A .... [1987] 283, 296
7 .... [1987] 301
arts. 7, 8, 9 .... [1987] 302
7–12A .... [1987] 283, 301, 303
art. 8 .... [1987] 301, 302
(1)–(3) .... [1987] 302
arts. 9, 10 .... [1987] 302

European Judgments Convention 1968—*cont.*
arts. 12, 12A .... [1987] 301, 303
art. 12(5) .... [1987] 303
12A(1)(*a*)(*b*), (2)(*a*)(*b*) .... [1987] 304
16 .... [1987] 283, 291, 293
(1)(3) .... [1987] 301
(5) .... [1987] 291
17 .... [1987] 283, 289, 293
18 .... [1987] 283
arts. 19–23 .... [1987] 290
19, 20 .... [1987] 285, 291
21, 22 .... [1987] 291, 292
art. 23 .... [1987] 293
24 .... [1987] 287, 292, 294
arts. 25–49 .... [1987] 295
25, 26, 27, 28, 29 .... [1987] 294
31, 33, 34 .... [1987] 295
52, 53 .... [1987] 284
art. 57 .... [1987] 283, 293, 296, 297, 299, 300, 301
68 .... [1987] 282
Title II, ss. 3, 4, 5 .... [1987] 294
Title III .... [1987] 294
Exchange Control Act 1947 .... [1986] 190
Exchange Control (Authorised Dealers and Depositaries) (Amendment) (No. 4) Order 1979 (S.I. No. 1338) .... [1986] 190
Exchange Control (General Exemption) Order 1979 (S.I. No. 1660) .... [1986] 190
Exchange Control (Revocation) Directions 1979 (S.I. No. 1339) .... [1986] 190
Executive Decree No. 42 of 19 September 1986 (Panama) .... [1990] 448
Extension of Admiralty Jurisdiction Act (46 U.S.C., s. 740 (1982)) .... [1986] 364
Factors Acts 1823, 1825, 1877 .... [1988] 298
Factors Act 1889 .... [1987] 248
ss. 2, 8, 9 .... [1988] 298, 299
s. 2 .... [1986] 167
9 .... [1988] 297, 298
Fair Trading Act 1973, s. 6 .... [1990] 30, 281, 440
Family Law Act 1986 .... [1990] 283
Fatal Accidents Act 1976 .... [1988] 215
Federal Arbitration Act (9 U.S.C., ss. 1–14 (1982)) .... [1986] 359
s. 3 .... [1986] 359
4 .... [1986] 360
9 .... [1986] 358
10(*d*) .... [1986] 358
11 .... [1986] 358
Federal Arbitration Act (9 U.S.C., ss. 201–208 (1982)) Chap. 2 .... [1986] 360
Federal Bills of Lading Act 1916
s. 22 (49 U.S.C.A., s. 102) .... [1986] 109
31 (49 U.S.C.A., s. 111) .... [1986] 103
Federal Bills of Lading Act (49 U.S.C.)
ss. 8, 25, 31(*b*) .... [1989] 164, 429
Federal Bills of Lading Act (U.S.) 49 U.S.C.A., ss. 107–112 .... [1990] 4
Federal Court Act, R.S.C. 1970, 2 Supp. C. 10 (Canada)—
s. 17(1)(2) .... [1987] 90
ss. 22(1), 22(2)(*f*), 23 .... [1989] 91
s. 22(1)(2)(*o*) .... [1987] 91
(2)(*i*) .... [1987] 85
Federal Court Act, R.S.C. 1985, c.F–7 (Canada)—
ss. 22, 43(2)(3) .... [1987] 347
s. 43(3) .... [1990] 104
(7)(*c*) .... [1987] 346
Federal Reserve Act 1913 (U.S.) .... [1988] 381
Financial Services Act 1986 .... [1988] 549
s. 62 .... [1988] 379, 380
132 .... [1988] 254, 255
Federal Rules of Civil Procedure—
r. 1 .... [1986] 21
rr. 24(*b*) and 60(*a*) .... [1986] 20
Federal Trade Commission Act 1914 (U.S.) .... [1989] 387; [1990] 281
Federal Water Pollution Control Act (33 U.S.C., ss. 1251–1265, 1281, 1282–1297, 1311–1328, 1341–1345, 1361–1376 (1982) .... [1986] 374
s. 1321(*c*)(1) .... [1986] 374, 375
(*f*) .... [1986] 374, 375
(*g*) .... [1986] 374, 375
(*h*) .... [1986] 374, 375
(2) .... [1986] 375
(*i*) .... [1986] 375
(1) .... [1986] 375
(2) .... [1986] 375
Federal Water Pollution Control Act (FWPCA) (extensively amended and reorganized by Act of 18 October 1972, P.L. 92–500, 86 Stat. 816 and Act of 27 December 1977, P.L. 95–217, 91 Stat. 1566 (also known as Clean Water Act); amended by Act of 21 November 1978, P.L. 95–576, 92 Stat. 2467, amended by Act of 21 October 1980, P.L. 96–483, 94 Stat. 2363) (U.S.) .... [1987] 348, 496, 498, 503
Financial Services Act 1986 .... [1989] 235, 245, 520; [1990] 29, 30, 303, 446
s. 62 .... [1990] 30
ss. 94, 105, 177 .... [1987] 195
s. 114 .... [1990] 414
132 .... [1989] 494
132(1)(6) .... [1987] 206, 207
(3) .... [1987] 207
198(2) .... [1987] 195
Fire Statute (46 U.S.C., s. 182 (1982)) [1986] 369
Fisheries Act, R.S.C. 1970, c. F–14 (Canada)—
s. 19 .... [1987] 86
31(1), para. 3 .... [1989] 101
34(2) .... [1989] 89

Fisheries Act, R.S.C. 1985, c.F–14 (as amended by S.C. 1987, c. 7) (Canada) .... [1987] 348
Florida Statutes Ann. Title 17, s. 267, 11–14 .... [1986] 19
Foreign Awards (Recognition and Enforcement) Act (Act XLV of 1961) (India), ss. 2(*b*), 7(1)(*v*) .... [1988] 14
Foreign Corrupt Practices Act (U.S.) .... [1989] 524
Foreign Economic Contract Law (People's Republic of China) ....[1989] 476 *et seq.*
art. 2 .... [1989] 485
3 .... [1989] 491, 492
4 .... [1989] 487, 491, 492
5 .... [1989] 486, 487, 492
(1)(2) .... [1989] 487, 491
7(1) .... [1989] 492
9 .... [1989] 487
20 .... [1989] 493
37(2) .... [1989] 494
42 .... [1989] 482
Foreign Judgments (Reciprocal Enforcement) Act 1933 .... [1989] 466
Foreign Limitation Periods Act 1984 .. [1988] 255
Foreign Sovereign Immunities Act 1976 (U.S.) .... [1987] 346
Foreign Sovereign Immunities Act (U.S.) .... [1988] 10
Foreign States Immunities Act 1985 (Commonwealth) (Australia)—
s. 18(2) .... [1986] 283
32 .... [1986] 283
French Law of 3 January 1967 .... [1988] 534
Fund Convention 1971 .... [1990] 40
Futures Market Act 1979 (N.S.W. Act No. 176, 1979)—
s. 7 .... [1986] 397
Futures Market (Amendment) Act 1982 (N.S.W. Act No. 128, 1982) .... [1986] 397
Gaming Act 1845—
s. 18 .... [1986] 392, 393, 395; [1989] 300
Gaming Act 1968—
s. 16 .... [1989] 303
Gaming and Betting Act 1912 (Act No. 25, 1912, Australia) .... [1986] 397
General Principles of Civil Law (People's Republic of China)—
art. 145 .... [1989] 490
Geneva Convention 1958 .... [1989] 515, 523; [1990] 289, 430
Geneva Convention on International Multimodal Transport of Goods 1980 .... [1990] 302
Geneva Convention Providing a Uniform Law for Bills of Exchange and Promissory Notes (7 June 1930) .... [1989] 239
Geneva Convention Providing a Uniform Law for Cheques (19 March 1931) .... [1989] 239
German Civil Code, para. 823–1 .. [1988] 405, 406
Glass-Steagull Act (U.S.) .... [1988] 380
Goods Act 1958 (Vic.)—
s. 73 .... [1986] 100
Gower Report (Investor Protection, 1984, Cmnd. 9125) .... [1990] 403
Great Lakes Pilotage Regulations, C.R.C. 1266, s. 4(1)(*c*)(ii) .... [1989] 98
Greek Accession Convention ..... [1988] 119, 537
Greene Committee Report on Company Law Amendment (1926)(Cmnd. 2657) .... [1990] 206, 403
Guatemala Protocol 1971 .... [1988] 230, 233
art. 17 .... [1988] 233
Hague Convention 1984 .... [1989] 386
Hague Convention on Celebration and Recognition of the Validity of Marriages (14 March 1948), art. 3(1) . [1989] 386
Hague Convention on the Service Abroad of Judicial and Extrajudicial Documents in Civil or Commercial Matters .... [1988] 537
Hague Protocol 1955 .... [1988] 445
Hague Rules 1924 .... [1989] 403
art. II .... [1989] 394, 395
III, r. 1 .... [1989] 94
2 .... [1989] 94
6 ...... [1989] 277, 278, 394, 395, 396
8 .... [1988] 84, 85, 285; [1989] 281, 404
IV, r. 4(2)(*c*) .... [1989] 93
(*q*) .... [1989] 94
5 .... [1988] 84, 257, 273, 275; [1989] 278, 280, 281, 396
(*a*) .... [1988] 273
(*e*) .... [1989] 394, 404
(*f*)(*h*) .... [1988] 275
(*g*) .... [1988] 276
Hague Rules (The) (51 Stat. 233, U.S.T. 931, 120 U.N.T.S. 155) .... [1986] 364
Hague-Visby Rules (1968 Protocol) ....[1987] 274, 305, 343
art. I .... [1986] 477
(*b*) .... [1986] 475, 476, 477, 478, 481
(*c*) .... [1987] 308
II .... [1986] 477; [1990] 314
III(3) ... [1986] 475, 476, 477, 478, 479, 481
(*b*) .... [1986] 475, 476, 478
(4) .... [1986] 470, 474, 475, 478, 481, 482, 483
(5) .... [1986] 479, 480
(6) .... [1987] 274; [1990] 172, 314, 316
(8) .... [1987] 260, 261
IV(5)(*a*) .... [1987] 316
(*a*)(*e*) .... [1990] 315
(*e*) .... [1990] 317
bis, (1) .... [1990] 316
V .... [1986] 470, 475, 476, 477, 478, 480
VI .... [1986] 477; [1990] 314
VII .... [1990] 323, 324, 326

Hague-Visby Rules (1968 Protocol)—*cont.*
art. X .... [1988] 445
(*a*)(*b*) .... [1987] 306
(*a*)(*c*) .... [1987] 307
(*a*)(*b*)(*c*) .... [1987] 308
Hamburg Rules 1978 ....[1987] 343; [1988] 259, 268; [1990] 354
art. 6(4) .... [1988] 276
Harbor Workers' Compensation Act (33 U.S.C., s. 902/(13))—
s. 1(13) .... [1986] 356
Harbours, Docks and Piers Clauses Act 1847, s. 56 .... [1990] 358
Harter Act 1893, c. 105, 27 Stat. 445 (U.S.) .... [1987] 342, 344
Harter Act (46 U.S.C., ss. 190–196 (1982) .... [1986] 365
Hazardous Substances Response Trust Fund, 42 U.S.C., s. 9631 (U.S.) .. [1987] 505
Health and Safety at Work Act 1974
s. 6 .... [1990] 279
High Seas Convention 1958, art. 23 ......[1990] 96
Hire Purchase Act (South Australia) (Repealed) ....[1990] 25
Hire Purchase Agreements Act 1931 (South Australia) ....[1990] 21
Hire Purchase Agreements Act 1931 (Western Australia) ....[1990] 21
Hire Purchase Agreements Act 1933 (Queensland, Australia) ....[1990] 21
Hire Purchase Agreements Act 1936 (Victoria, Australia) ....[1990] 21
s. 3 ....[1990] 22
Historic Shipwrecks Act 1976 (Australia) .... [1987] 319
Hong Kong Arbitration Ordinance—
s. 6B ....[1986] 67
29A ....[1986] 68
Hovercraft Act 1968 .... [1989] 133
s. 1(*b*) ....[1989] 91
Hovercraft (Civil Liability) Order 1986 (S.I. No. 1305) .... [1989] 133
H.R. 98–1027, 98th Cong., 2d Sess. (1984) .... [1986] 372
H.R. 5207, 98th Cong., 2d Sess. (1984) .... [1986] 363
H.R. 277, 3156 (99th Cong. 1st and 2nd sess. 1–424 (1985–86) (U.S.) .... [1988] 525
H.R. 277, 99th Cong., 1st Sess. (1985) ......[1986] 363, 366
s. 2(*a*) .... [1986] 363
(*c*) .... [1986] 363
(*e*) .... [1986] 363
5 .... [1986] 363
7(*a*)(1) .... [1986] 363
(*b*) .... [1986] 364
(2) .... [1986] 363
8(*a*) .... [1986] 363
H.R. 3135 (100th Cong. 1st sess. (1987) (U.S.) .... [1988] 526
H.R. 3156 .... [1986] 364

IATA Conditions of Carriage 1927—
arts. 7, 17–21, 22 .... [1989] 125
ICC Rules of Arbitration .... [1990] 430
ICC Uniform Rules for Contract Guarantees .... [1990] 229
IMF Articles of Agreement—
arts. VI, VIII .... [1990] 568
art. VIII, s. 2(*b*) .... [1988] 4; [1990] 559
IMO Convention on Limitation of Liability for Maritime Claims 1976 .... [1988] 517
Inland Water Freight Rates Act, R.S.C. 1970, c. I–12 (Canada) .... [1989] 110
Insolvency Act 1976, s. 9 .... [1987] 191, 194
Insolvency Act 1985 .... [1987] 188, 191; [1989] 120; [1990] 211, 415
ss. 12–16, 18 .... [1987] 188
Sch. 6, para. 15(1)(2) .... [1987] 151
Insolvency Act 1986 .... [1986] 557; [1989] 21, 506 *et seq*. [1990] 29
ss. 8–27 .... [1989] 506
8, 86, 127, 129 .... [1990] 211
s. 8(1) .... [1990] 507
(*b*) .... [1990] 413
(2) .... [1989] 507
(3) .... [1989] 507
(4) .... [1989] 507
9(1) .... [1989] 507
(3) .... [1989] 510
10(1) .... [1989] 509, 510
(*b*) .... [1989] 507
(4) .... [1989] 507
11 .... [1989] 507
(3) .... [1990] 405
(*c*) .... [1989] 507, 508
12(1) .... [1989] 508
15(1)(3) .... [1989] 196
(2)(*b*) .... [1989] 508
(5) .... [1989] 508
(9) .... [1989] 508
21 .... [1989] 508
(1)(*b*) .... [1989] 508
27 .... [1988] 60, 66; [1989] 508
(1)(*a*)(*b*) .... [1989] 508
(2) .... [1989] 508
(3)(*a*)(*b*) .... [1989] 509
ss. 29(2), 40, 175 .... [1990] 540
s. 35(1) .... [1986] 525
40 .... [1987] 151
44(1)(*a*) .... [1900] 529
89 .... [1987] 193
98 .... [1987] 151
ss. 98, 214(2) .... [1990] 214
s. 107 .... [1990] 219, 275
110 ....[1988] 61
122(1)(*g*) .... [1988] 65, 70, 80 [1990] 406
123 .... [1989] 507
ss. 148(1), 165, 167 .... [1990] 219
s. 175(2)(*b*) .... [1987] 148, 151
212 .... [1990] 217
(1)–(3) .... [1990] 218

Insolvency Act 1986—*cont.*
ss. 213–214 .... [1990] 402
s. 213 ......[1987] 196, 197; [1990] 220, 221, 222
(2) .... [1987] 196; [1990] 221
214 ....[1987] 188, 196, 197, 200; 205, 209, 214, 215, 219, 220, 222
(1) ..[1987] 196; [1990] 215, 216, 219, 221
(1), (2) .... [1990] 206
(2)(*c*), 214(4)(*a*), 214(5), (7) .. [1990] 212
(3) ....[1990] 210, 214
(4) ....[1990] 211, 212, 217
(4), (6) .... [1990] 207
216 .... [1987] 188
ss. 240, 245(2)(*a*) .... [1989] 196
s. 247(2) .... [1987] 507
251 [1989] 510, 511; [1990] 213, 403, 404, 540
ss. 251, 323(3) .... [1987] 151
s. 323 .... [1988] 255
344 .... [1990] 525
382 .... [1987] 152
426 .... [1990] 278
436 .... [1989] 512
Part II .... [1990] 211
Sched. 4, Parts I, III .... [1990] 219
Insolvency Rules 1986 (S.I. No. 1925)—
r. 4. 181 .... [1990] 275
r. 7. 51 .... [1989] 509
13. 12 .... [1990] 207
Insurance (Agents and Brokers) Act 1984 (Australia) ......[1989] 234; [1990] 443 *et seq.*
ss. 9, 14, 32, 35 .... [1989] 235
s. 14 .... [1986] 284
Insurance Brokers (Registration) Act 1977 .... [1989] 235
Insurance Companies Act 1947 ....[1987] 37
Insurance Companies Act 1982 .... [1989] 520, 521; [1990] 29
s. 1(1) .... [1987] 201
2 ....[1987] 206, 207
(1) ....[1987] 201, 202
5 .... [1987] 206
Sch. 1, No. 1 .... [1987] 201
Insurance Contracts Act 1984 (Australia) ......[1989] 234; [1990] 443 *et seq.*
s. 9 .... [1986] 284
13 .... [1989] 235
Part III .... [1989] 236
ss. 17, 21, 24, 27, 28, 29, 38, 66, 67 .. [1989] 236
s. 48 .... [1987] 259; [1989] 142
54 .... [1990] 444
Insurance Law Reform Act 1985 (New Zealand) .... [1990] 444
Insurance (Marine) Act, R.S.B.C. 1979, c. 203 (British Columbia)—
s. 80(2) ....[1989] 96
Interest Reduction Act 1931 (New South Wales, Australia), Part III ....[1990] 21
Internal Revenue Code 1986 as amended (U.S.)—
s. 863(*c*)(2) .... [1988] 235
Internal Revenue Code 1986 as amended (U.S.)—*cont.*
s. 864(*b*) .... [1988] 236
871 .... [1988] 245
872(*b*)(5) .... [1988] 239
(6) .... [1988] 240
881 .... [1988] 245
883 .... [1988] 237, 238, 239, 240, 241, 243
(*a*)(4) ....[1988] 239, 240
(*c*) .... [1988] 238, 240, 241, 242, 243
887 .... [1988] 236
911(*d*)(3) .... [1988] 238
International Convention on Civil Liability for Oil Pollution Damage 1969 (The Liability Convention) .... [1987] 275; [1989] 138
International Convention on the Establishment of a Fund for Compensation for Oil Pollution Damage 1971 .... [1989] 138
International Conventions on Liens and Mortgages 1926 and 1967 ..... [1988] 533–534
International Oil Pollution Compensation Fund (The IOPC Fund) FUND/EXC. 16/4 of 22.9.86 .... [1987] 275
International Tin Council (Immunity and Privilege) Order 1972 (S.I. No. 120) .... [1990] 307
International Transport Conventions Act 1983 ....[1988] 177, 268
International Transport Conventions Act 1983 (CIM, COTIF) .... [1989] 429
Interpretation Act 1978—
s. 5, Sched. 1 .... [1990] 405
6(*c*) .... [1990] 405
16(1) .... [1990] 406
Intervention on the High Seas Act, 33 U.S.C., s. 1471 *et seq.* (U.S.) ...... [1987] 518
Iranian Constitution 1979, Principle 4 .... [1987] 274
Irish Companies Acts 1963–1983—
s. 231(1)(*a*) .... [1986] 384
Italian Constitution, arts. 3, 42 .... [1988] 273
Jenkins Committee (1962) (Cmnd. 1749) .... [1990] 403
Joint Stock Companies Act 1844 .... [1990] 402
s. 43 .... [1990] 480
Jones Act 1920, c. 250, 41 Stat. 1007 (U.S.), s. 33 .... [1987] 345
Jones Act (46 U.S.C., s. 688 (1982)) .. [1986] 365
Judicature Act 1873 ....[1989] 162; [1990] 27
Judicature Act No. 2 of 1978 (Sri Lanka)—
s. 13(1) ....[1987] 169, 170, 171
62 .... [1987] 171
Judicature Acts 1873–1875 .... [1990] 322
Judicial Code, 28 U.S.C.A. 1330 *et seq.* ....[1986] 18
Judiciary Act 1789, 18 U.S.C.A. 9 ....[1986] 14, 18, 485
Judiciary Act 1789 (1 Stat. 76–77 (1789)) ....[1986] 364, 485
Justice Law (Sri Lanka), s. 3(2) .... [1987] 170

La. Rev. Stat. Ann.—
s. 22: 655 (West 1978) .... [1986] 381
Labour Code (Panama) .... [1990] 448
Latent Damage Act 1986 .. [1986] 557; [1988] 260
Law 3170 of 1956 (Greece) .... [1986] 434
4502 of 1966 .... [1986] 434
Law of 2 August 1912 (France) .... [1987] 345
Law of 29 April 1916 .... [1987] 346
Law of 21 February 1935 .... [1987] 347
Law of 9 April 1936 .... [1987] 343
Law No. 64–1331 of 26 December 1964, amended by Law No. 73–477 of 16 May 1973 and Law No. 79–5 of 2 January 1979 .... [1987] 348–349
Law No. 66–420 of 18 June 1966 .... [1987] 343
arts. 15, 27, 52 .... [1987] 344
Law No. 67–3 of 3 January 1967—
arts. 58–69 .... [1987] 346
Law No. 67–545 of 7 July 1967 .... [1987] 345, 346
Law No. 67–5 of 3 January 1969 .... [1987] 347
Law No. 69–8 of 3 January 1969—
arts. 31–41 .... [1987] 344
Laws Nos. 11 and 83 of 1973 concerning registration of ships under charter (Panama) .... [1990] 448
Law No. 73–1198 of 27 December 1973 .... [1987] 349
Law No. 76–599 of 7 July 1976 .... [1987] 349
Law No. 76–600 of 7 July 1976 .... [1987] 349
Law No. 76–1180 of 22 December 1976 .... [1987] 349
Law No. 77–530 of 26 May 1977 .... [1987] 349
Law No. 77–1407 of 23 December 1977 .... [1987] 349
Law No. 77–1424 of 27 December 1977 .... [1987] 349
Law No. 79–1103 of 21 December 1979 .... [1987] 343
Law No. 79–1146 of 29 December 1979 .... [1987] 346
Law No. 79–1148 of 29 December 1979 .... [1987] 349
Law No. 81–742 of 5 August 1981 ...... [1987] 349
Law No. 43 of 1984 concerning modification of Articles of the Commercial Code (Panama) .... [1990] 448
Law No. 84–1151 of 21 December 1984 .... [1987] 346
Law No. 84–1173 of 22 December 1984 .... [1986] 346; [1987] 346
Law No. 85–1172 of 12 November 1985 .... [1987] 349
Law No. 86–798 of 3 July 1986 .... [1987] 343
Law No. 86–1292 of 23 December 1986 .... [1987] 343
Law of Property Act 1925 s. 136 (replacing s. 25(6) of Supreme Court of Judicature Act 1873) .... [1986] 197; [1989] 9, 199, 212, 213, 214, 423
s. 136(1) .... [1988] 141, 142; [1989] 162, 291
199 .... [1989] 324
Law of the Organization of the People's Courts of the People's Republic of China of 1 July 1979, art. 33 .... [1989] 483
Law of the Sea Convention 1982 (UNCLOS) .... [1988] 261; [1990] 441, 442
art. 121(3) .... [1990] 289
234 .... [1990] 145
Law on Inland Navigation Matters (Binnenschiffsgesetz) (Germany), s. 48 .... [1990] 385
Law Providing for the Organization of the People's Central Government (People's Republic of China) art. 7 .... [1989] 483
Law Reform Act 1985 (New Zealand) .... [1990] 444
Law Reform Commission Act 1973 (Cth.), s. 6(*d*) .... [1987] 317
Law Reform (Contributory Negligence) Act 1945 ....[1987] 7, 10; [1989] 30, 285, 288; [1990] 52, 422
ss. 1(1), 4 .... [1987] 12; [1988] 8; [1990] 417
s. 1(1) .... [1990] 419
1, 2, 3 ....[1989] 32
4 .... [1990] 418
Law Reform (Married Women and Tortfeasors) Act 1935 ....[1989] 33
Law Reform (Miscellanous Provisions) Act 1934 .... [1988] 180
s. 1 .... [1988] 178
3 .... [1986] 139
(repealed) .... [1987] 417
(1) .... [1987] 417, 418
LDIP (Switzerland) .... [1989] 490
art. 16(1) .... [1989] 491
117(3)(*a*)–(*c*)(*e*) .... [1989] 491
Lien Act 1920 (U.S.) .... [1988] 164
Liens and Mortgages Convention 1926 .. [1989] 14
Life Assurance Act 1774 (Australia) ... [1989] 235
Life Assurance Act 1945 (Australia) ... [1990] 443
Limitation Act 1851, c. 43, 9 Stat. 635 (U.S.), s. 3 .... [1987] 345
Limitation Act 1939—
s. 19(1)(*a*) .... [1989] 314
s. 26 .... [1989] 315
Limitation Act 1980 .... [1986] 557
s. 5 .... [1986] 333
ss. 5, 9 .... [1990] 360
Limitation Act 1984, P.L. 98–498, title II, sub-title A, s. 213(*a*), 98 Stat. 2306 (U.S.) .... [1987] 345
Limitation Convention 1976 .... [1990] 354, 363, 437
art. 2(1)(*c*) .... [1990] 361
3 .... [1990] 360
Limitation of Liability Act, 46 U.S.C., ss. 181–195 (U.S.) .... [1987] 502, 504

Limitation of Liability Act 1935 (46 U.S.C., ss. 181–189 (1982)) .... [1986] 363
s. 183(*a*) .... [1986] 380
Limitation of Liability Act 1984, (Japan), art. 19 [1988] 178
Limitation of Shipowners Liabilty Act 1851 (U.S.), 46 U.S.C.—
ss. 181 *et seq*. .... [1988] 179
181–189 .... [1990] 41
Limited Liability Act 1851 (U.S.) ...... [1988] 179
Limited Liability Act 1855 .... [1990] 402
Liner Conferences Code of Conduct, arts. 12, 23–45 .... [1988] 275
London Convention 1976 .... [1987] 296
art. 6 .... [1988] 526
London Limitation Convention 1976 .... [1990] 41
arts. 1, 6(3) .... [1990] 45
art. 3(*a*) .... [1990] 50
Longshoremen's and Harbor Workers' Compensation Act (33 U.S.C., ss. 901–950 (1982)) .... [1986] 371
s. 2(3) (33 U.S.C., s. 902(3)) .... [1986] 372
(21) (33 U.S.C., s. 902(21)) ...... [1986] 373
3(*a*) (33 U.S.C., s. 903(*a*)) .... [1986] 372
4(*a*) (33 U.S.C., s. 904(*a*)) .... [1986] 372
5(*a*) (33 U.S.C., s. 905(*a*)) .... [1986] 372
(*b*) (33 U.S.C., s. 905(*b*)) ... [1986] 372, 373
Longshore and Harbor Workers' Compensation Act Amendments 1984 (98 Stat. 1639 (1984) amending 33 U.S.C., ss. 901–950) .... [1986] 371
s. 2(*a*) (amending 33 U.S.C., s 902(3)) .... [1986] 371
4 (amending 33 U.S.C., ss. 904(*a*), 905(*a*)) .... [1986] 371
5(*a*)(1) (amending 33 U.S.C., s. 905(*b*)) .... [1986] 373
(*b*) (amending 33 U.S.C., s. 905 by adding sub.-s. 905(*c*)) .... [1986] 371
7, 8, 19 (amending 33 U.S.C., ss. 907, 908, 931) .... [1986] 371
8, 9 (amending 33 U.S.C., ss. 908, 909) .... [1986] 371
11 (amending 33 U.S.C., s. 912(*a*), (*c*), (*d*)) .... [1986] 371
12 (amending 33 U.S.C., s. 913(*b*)) .... [1986] 371
21(*a*) (amending 33 U.S.C., s. 933(*b*)) .... [1986] 371
24(*a*)) (amending 33 U.S.C., s. 944(*c*)) .... [1986] 371
Loreburn Committee (1906) (Cd. 3052) .... [1990] 403
Louisiana Statutes Ann. Title 41, Ch. 13, ss. 1601–1613 .... [1986] 19
Luxembourg Accords 1966 .... [1990] 293
Magistrates Courts Rules .... [1988] 537
Manitoba Personal Property Security Act 1973 (Stat. Man. 1973, c. 5 as am.) .... [1986] 163
Marine Insurance Act 1906 .... [1986] 27; [1987] 342; [1989] 96, 127, 252; [1990] 303
ss. 1–3 .... [1986] 487
s. 4(1) .... [1986] 489
(2)(*a*)(*b*) .... [1986] 489
ss. 4–15 .... [1986] 491
s. 5(2) .... [1986] 491
6(1) .... [1986] 491
17 .... [1986] 29, 31, 320; [1987] 7; [1989] 254, 259, 262
17–18 .... [1986] 485, 500
17–19 .... [1986] 497
18 .... [1986] 29, 31, 320, 500, 501; [1989] 254, 258, 259
(1) .... [1986] 29, 32
(2) ... [1986] 29, 31, 32, 498, 502; [1988] 30
(3) .... [1986] 29
(*b*) .... [1986] 31
(4) .... [1986] 29, 33
19 .... [1986] 502
20(2) .... [1986] 33, 502
(4) .... [1986] 33
21 .... [1986] 497
22 .... [1986] 505
23 .... [1986] 441
26 .... [1986] 441
27 .... [1986] 441
29(3) .... [1986] 449
33(1) .... [1986] 36
(3) .... [1986] 33, 36, 507; [1988] 345; [1989] 261, 262
34(1) .... [1986] 36
(2) .... [1986] 36
(3) .... [1986] 36
35(1) .... [1989] 259
37 .... [1986] 503
39(1) .... [1986] 37; [1988] 352
(1)–(4) .... [1986] 447
(4) .... [1986] 37
(5) .... [1986] 41, 501; [1988] 343, 345, 347, 352, 353
40 .... [1986] 447
41 .... [1988] 127
ss. 45, 46 .... [1989] 262
s. 52(*c*) .... [1986] 445
ss. 55–63 .... [1986] 485
s. 55 .... [1986] 290
(2)(*a*) .... [1986] 44, 444; [1988] 324, 328, 355, 356
(*c*) .... [1986] 444
(4)(*b*) .... [1986] 445
60 .... [1986] 450
62(6) .... [1989] 446
65(*a*) .... [1986] 333
66(6) .... [1986] 444
78(4) .... [1986] 451; [1988] 355, 356, 357; [1989] 410
Schedule .... [1986] 450
Sched. 2, para. 7 .... [1986] 40

Marine Insurance Act 1909 (Commonwealth) (Australia)—
s. 7 .... [1986] 284
8 .... [1986] 284
9 .... [1986] 284
59 .... [1986] 284
61 .... [1986] 290
Marine Insurance (Gambling Policies) Act 1909 .... [1986] 489
Maritime Code 1965 (Iran)—
art. 52 *et seq.* .... [1987] 273
54(6) .... [1987] 274
Maritime Code Act (Canada) .... [1989] 106
Maritime Conventions Act 1911 .... [1987] 344, 346; [1989] 30; [1990] 32, 172, 354
s. 1 .... [1989] 32, 33; [1990] 52
ss. 2, 3 .... [1989] 32
6, 7, 8 .... [1990] 32
s. 6 .... [1986] 331
8 .... [1986] 333; [1990] 360
Maritime Conventions Act 1914, 4 & 5 Geo. 5, c. 13 (Canada) .... [1987] 344, 346
Maritime Lien Act (46 U.S.C., ss. 971–975 (1982) .... [1986] 355
Maryland Securities Act—
s. 11–703(*a*2) .... [1986] 20
Massachusetts G.L. Ch. 6, s. 180 .... [1986] 19
Md. Nat. Res. Code Ann.—
s. 2–201 *et seq.* .... [1986] 19
2–305 .... [1986] 16
9–202 .... [1986] 16
Mercantile Law Act 1908 (N.Z.), s. 13 .... [1986] 100
Mercantile Law Amendment 1856—
s. 5 .... [1989] 10
Merchant Marine Act 1920 (Jones Act, 46 U.S.C. 883 (U.S.)) .... [1989] 108
Merchant Shipping Act 1854, s. 2 .... [1987] 268, 270
s. 458 .... [1988] 450
Merchant Shipping Act 1894 .... [1989] 133, 134, 137 [1990] 355, 357
s. 158 (as amended by s. 1(1) of the Merchant Shipping (International Labour Convention) Act 1925 .. [1987] 268
ss. 331, 332 .... [1987] 268
s. 466 .... [1986] 417
475 .... [1986] 417
483 .... [1986] 417
ss. 492–501 .... [1987] 3
s. 503(1) .... [1990] 47
510 .... [1987] 267, 268, 269, 270, 271, 272
ss. 518, 523 .... [1987] 271, 272
s. 530 .... [1990] 358
544 .... [1986] 325
et seq. .... [1987] 346
(2)(3) .... [1989] 410
546 .... [1988] 450, 451
686(1) .... [1990] 162, 164
Merchant Shipping Act 1894—*cont.*
s. 742 .... [1988] 451; [1990] 15
Parts I, IV .... [1989] 135
Part IX .... [1987] 267, 271, 272
Merchant Shipping Act 1906—
s. 66 .... [1986] 418
s. 72 .... [1987] 271, 272
Merchant Shipping Act 1970—
s. 27 .... [1989] 137
42(2)(repealed) .... [1989] 138
ss. 55–58 .... [1986] 418
Merchant Shipping Act 1974 .... [1988] 264, [1990] 40
s. 5(1) .... [1987] 137
Part I and Sch. 1 .... [1987] 136
Merchant Shipping Act 1976, Sch. 3, Part II, para. 5 .... [1987] 137
Merchant Shipping Act 1977—
s. 44 .... [1989] 137
Merchant Shipping Act 1979 .... [1986] 556, 557; [1988] 214, 264
ss. 14, 17, 20 .... [1988] 178
s. 16 .... [1990] 363
ss. 20, 38 .... [1987] 348
s. 44 .... [1989] 137
Scheds. 3, 4 .... [1990] 354
Sch. 4 ... [1987] 296; [1988] 214, 517; [1990] 360
ss. 17–19 .... [1990] 41
Part I .... [1987] 345
Merchant Shipping Act 1981—
s. 1 .... [1987] 345
2 .... [1987] 343
Merchant Shipping Act 1983 .... [1989] 134
Merchant Shipping Act 1988 .... [1989] 133 *et seq.*; [1990] 302, 358
s. 48 .... [1988] 451
Sched. 4 .... [1989] 138
5 .... [1989] 137
para 3 .... [1988] 451; [1990] 355
Merchant Shipping Act (Commencement No. 10) Order 1986 (S.I. 1986 No. 1052) .... [1986] 556
Merchant Shipping Act No. 57 of 1951 (South Africa)—
s. 2 .... [1987] 307, 308
ss. 307–311 (repealed and replaced) .... [1987] 305, 315, 316
s. 307(3) .... [1987] 311
(5) .... [1987] 307
s. 310(6) .... [1987] 309, 310, 311, 312
Chap. VIII .... [1987] 307, 311
Merchant Shipping (Formal Investigation) Rules 1985 .... [1986] 418
Merchant Shipping (Liability of Shipowners and Others) Act 1958, s. 5 .... [1987] 260, 542
Merchant Shipping (Liability of Shipowners and Others) (Calculation of Tonnage) Order 1986 (S.I. 1986 No. 1040) .... [1986] 557

Merchant Shipping (Liner Conferences) Act 1982 .... [1988] 275
Merchant Shipping (Oil Pollution) Act 1971 .... [1987] 299, 302, 348; [1988] 264; [1989] 3
Merchant Shipping (Oil Pollution) Act 1971 (as amended by the Merchant Shipping Act 1988) .... [1990] 40, 354
ss. 1, 15, 21(2) .... [1990] 15
1, 15 .... [1990] 16
Merchant Shipping (Oil Pollution) Act 1981 (Republic of Singapore)—
ss. 2(1), 6(1)(*b*) .... [1990] 15
s. 18(1) .... [1990] 15, 16
(*b*) .... [1990] 16
Merchant Shipping (Safety Conventions) Act 1949—
ss. 21, 22 .... [1987] 346
s. 22 .... [1986] 331
Merchant Shipping (Tonnage) Regulations 1982—
Regs. 4 to 6 .... [1986] 557
Minnesota House File 1776 (1986) (U.S.), s. 33 .... [1988] 523
Minnesota Statutes (U.S.), s. 549. 22 .... [1988] 523
Misleading Advertisements Regulations 1988 .... [1990] 280, 281
Misrepresentation Act 1967 .... [1987] 248; [1989] 254
s. 2 .... [1987] 7; [1990] 359
(1)(2) .... [1988] 463
(1) .... [1986] 314, 317, 319, 320; [1987] 208; [1990] 148, 149, 150, 459
(2) .... [1986] 314, 319, 320
Misuse of Drugs Act 1971, s. 27 .... [1987] 214
Moneylenders Act 1990 .... [1990] 280
Moneylenders and Infants Loans Act 1941 (N.S.W.), Australia .... [1990] 512
Montreal Agreement 1966 .... [1988] 232
Montreaux Convention 1936—
art. 2 .... [1988] 401, 402
arts. 10, 11, 14 .... [1988] 400
art. 15 .... [1988] 401
18(1)(*d*) .... [1988] 400, 402
23 .... [1988] 402
Annex I .... [1988] 402
II(B)(1)(2) .... [1988] 400
(3)(5) .... [1988] 400, 401
Mortgaging of Aircraft Order 1972 (S.I. 1972 No. 1268) .... [1990] 521
National Bank Act 1864 (U.S.) .... [1988] 381
National Telecommunications Powers and Procedures Act (Canada) .... [1989] 110
National Transportation Act, R.S.C. 1970, c. M–17 (Canada) (amended by National Transportation Act, S.C. 1987, c. 34) .... [1989] 110
s. 22(2) (repealed by National Transportation Act, S.C. 1987, c.34; 24(3)) .... [1989] 110
s. 27 .... [1989] 111
National Transportation Act, S.C. 1987, c. 34 (Canada), repealing Transport Act, R.S.C. 1970, c. T–14—
ss. 35, 58(*c*), 59, 60 .... [1989] 110
46(1)(*a*), 47, 252 .... [1989] 111
Part I .... [1989] 110
V .... [1989] 111
Navigation Act 1912 (Australia) .... [1987] 319
Negligence Act 1979 (B.C.) .... [1987] 51
New Jersey Stat. Ann. 12: 3–8 .... [1986] 427
New South Wales Supreme Court Rules, Part 10, r. 1(*e*) .... [1989] 217
New York Convention on the Recognition and Enforcement of Foreign Arbitral Awards 1958 .... [1987] 311, 313; [1988] 535; [1990] 430
art. II .... [1989] 386
New York Insurance Law—
s. 148 (now s. 3401) .... [1986] 491, 492
1113 .... [1986] 487
(20)(A) .... [1986] 488
(B) .... [1986] 488
(D) .... [1986] 488
(21) .... [1986] 488
2120 .... [1986] 496
2125 .... [1986] 491
3105(*a*) .... [1986] 503
(*b*) .... [1986] 502
(*c*) .... [1986] 502
New Zealand Companies Act 1955, s. 209 .... [1988] 66, 69, 74
New Zealand Insurance Law Reform Act 1977 .... [1987] 125
New Zealand Sea Carriage of Goods Act 1940, Part III, s. 11 .... [1987] 315
Northwest Territories Fishery Regulations (C.R.C. 1978, c. 847) (Canada), s. 22 .... [1987] 89
Norwegian Plan—
s. 75 .... [1989] 454, 459, 462, 463
Ocean Dumping Control Act, R.S.C. 1985, c. 0–2 (Canada) .... [1987] 348
s. 4(1) .... [1990] 102
Oil and Gas Production and Conservation Act (Canada) .... [1989] 106
Oil and Gas Production and Conservation Act, R.S.C. 1985, c. 0–7 (Canada) .... [1987] 348
Oil in Navigable Waters Acts 1955–1971 .... [1987] 348
Ontario Bills of Sale and Chattel Mortgages Act 1849. See 12 Vict. (1849), c. 74 .... [1986] 161

Ontario Business Corporations Act
ss. 169, 184, 247 .... [1989] 411, 412
Ontario Consumer Protection Act (R.S.O. 1980, c. 87 as am.) .... [1986] 165
s. 22 .... [1986] 166
Ontario Corporation Securities Registration Act, R.S.O. 1970, c. 88 (See now R.S.O. 1980, c. 94) .... [1986] 161, 174
s. 2 .... [1986] 174
3(1)(*c*) .... [1986] 166
(*e*) .... [1986] 166
Ontario Draft Revised Personal Property Security Act 1984 .... [1986] 163
s. 1(*a*) .... [1986] 175
2(1)(*a*) .... [1986] 173
(*b*) .... [1986] 173
4 .... [1986] 176
18 .... [1986] 175
23 .... [1986] 175
25(2)-(5) .... [1986] 168
ss. 28–29 .... [1986] 175
s. 45 .... [1986] 176
(2) .... [1986] 167
(3) .... [1986] 167
51 .... [1986] 175
ss. 51–52 .... [1986] 176
s. 58 .... [1986] 174
60(1)(*b*) .... [1986] 169
64(3) .... [1986] 169
65(5) .... [1986] 169
Ontario Occupational Health and Safety Act, s. 1(28) ....[1987] 96
Ontario Personal Property Security Act (originally Stat. Ont. 1967, c. 73) .... [1986] 160
s. 1(*h*) .... [1986] 169
(*w*) .... [1986] 167
(*y*) .... [1986] 165
2 .... [1986] 164
(*a*) .... [1986] 173
(i) .... [1986] 175
(ii) .... [1986] 173
(*b*) .... [1986] 172
3 .... [1986] 165
(1)(*c*) .... [1986] 174
9 .... [1986] 165, 166
12 .... [1986] 175
(1) .... [1986] 166, 175
13(1) .... [1986] 166
14 .... [1986] 166
15 .... [1986] 166
21 .... [1986] 166
22(1)(*a*) .... [1986] 167
(*b*) .... [1986] 167
ss. 24–25 .... [1986] 166
s. 27 .... [1986] 168
(1) .... [1986] 166
(*b*) .... [1986] 168
(*r*) .... [1986] 166
(2) .... [1986] 168
30(1) .... [1986] 167
Ontario Personal Property Security Act (originally Stat. Ont. 1967)—*cont.*
s. 30(2) .... [1986] 167
(3) .... [1986] 167
34(2) .... [1986] 170
35(1)(*a*) .... [1986] 167
38 .... [1986] 169
47(2) .... [1986] 176
(3) .... [1986] 167, 176
(5) .... [1986] 176
53 .... [1986] 176
(1)(*c*) .... [1986] 176
56(2) .... [1986] 169
57(1)(*a*) .... [1986] 169
(*b*) .... [1986] 169
58(*c*) .... [1986] 169
59 .... [1986] 169
60 .... [1986] 169
61(1) .... [1986] 169
(2) .... [1986] 169
62 .... [1986] 169
64 .... [1986] 167
69 .... [1986] 166
72 .... [1986] 162
Outer Continental Shelf Lands Act 1953 (OCSLA), c. 345, 67 Stat. 462, 43 U.S.C., s. 1331 *et seq.* and 1978 amendments enacted by Act of 18 September 1978, P.L. 95–372, title III, 92 Stat. 670, 43 U.S.C., s. 1811 *et seq.* (U.S.) .... [1987] 348, 496, 513
s. 4(*c*) (43 U.S.C., s. 1333(*c*) .... [1986] 373, 374, 375
1813(*b*)(3) ....[1990] 40
Outer Space Act 1986 .... [1986] 557
Panamanian Judicial Code .... [1990] 447
Panamanian Labour Code .... [1990] 447
Partnership Act 1890 .... [1990] 407
s. 46 .... [1990] 401
Patients Act 1977—
s. 6(1) .... [1987] 428
62(1) .... [1987] 429
Petroleum (Consolidation) Act 1928 .. [1988] 264
Pilotage Act 1983 .... [1987] 137
Pilotage Act 1987 .... [1990] 302
Pilotage Act, S.C. 1970–71, c. 52 (Canada)—
ss. 12, 14, 34 ....[1989] 98
Pilotage Law of 30 August 1988, amending Law of 3 November 1967 (Belgium)—
paras. 1, 2 ....[1989] 27
Pipelines Act 1962 .... [1988] 264
P.L. 92–500, 86 Stat. 816 .... [1987] 503
P.L. 95–372, 92 Stat. 674 .... [1987] 513
P.L. 95–576. 92 Stat. 2468 .... [1987] 498
P.L. 96–478, 94 Stat. 2297 .... [1987] 497
P.L. 99–499, 100 Stat. 1613 .... [1987] 505
Police and Criminal Evidence Act 1984 .... [1988] 412
Policyholders Protection Act 1975 ..... [1989] 521
Pomerene Act 1916 (U.S.) ....[1989] 50

Pomerene Act 1916, 49 U.S.C., ss. 81–124 (U.S.) .... [1987] 344
Ports and Tanker Safety Act 1978 (46 U.S.C., s. 391(*a*)(1982)) .... [1986] 376
Ports and Waterways Safety Act 1972, Title II .... [1986] 376
Post Office (Banking Services) Act 1976 .... [1986] 178
Powers of the Criminal Courts Act 1973 .... [1990] 281
s. 43 .... [1987] 214
Prentice Report for the D.T.I. on *ultra vires*, 1986 .... [1990] 403
Prevention of Oil Pollution Act 1971 .... [1986] 557; [1987] 348; [1990] 40
Prevention of Pollution of the Sea Act 1971 (Republic of Singapore), s. 14 .....[1990] 15, 16
P.R. Laws Ann. Title 26 (1976)—
s. 2003(1) ....[1986] 380, 381
Prevention of Oil Pollution Act 1986 .. [1986] 557
Private International Law Act (Yugoslavia)—
arts. 20, 117 .... [1989] 490
Protection of Business Act No. 99 of 1978 (South Africa), s. 3 .... [1987] 313
Protection of Military Remains Act 1986 .... [1986] 557; [1990] 357
Protection of Trading Interests Act 1980 .... [1990] 296
Protection of Wrecks Act 1973 .... [1990] 357
Protocol of 3 June 1971 on the Interpretation of the 1968 EEC Convention on Jurisdiction and the Enforcement of Judgments in Civil and Commercial Matters .... [1988] 384
art. 1(2) .... [1988] 389
Public Buildings, Property & Works—Abandoned Property, 40 U.S.C. 310 ....[1986] 18
Public Law 99–662, 100 Stat. 4199, 33 U.S.C.—
ss. 409, 414, 415 ....[1989] 16
Public Vessels Act (46 U.S.C., 781–790 (1982)) .... [1986] 366
Quebec Civil Code, art. 1715 ....[1987] 82
Quebec Code of Civil Procedure, R.S.Q., c. C–25 (Canada)—
art. 947.2 ....[1989] 93
Railway Act, R.S.C. 1970, c. R–2 (Canada)—
s. 262 ....[1989] 91
Recognition and Enforcement of Foreign Arbitral Awards Act No. 40 of 1972 (South Africa), s. 2 .... [1987] 313
Recognition of Trusts Act 1987 ... [1989] 386, 468
Registration Act 1981 (Australia) ...... [1987] 319
Report and Sale and Supply of Goods (Law Com. No. 160, Scot. Law Com. No. 104) (1987) Cm. 137 ...... [1988] 462, 514
paras. 4.21, 4.24 .... [1988] 462
Responses of the People's Supreme Court to Questions arising out of the Application of the Foreign Economic Contract Law of 19 October 1987 (People's Republic of China) ....[1989] 476 *et seq.*
art. 1(1) .... [1989] 476, 485
(2) .... [1989] 476, 490
(3) .... [1989] 477
2(1) ....[1989] 477, 486, 487, 492
(2) ....[1989] 477, 486, 490
(4) .... [1989] 477, 486
(5) .... [1989] 477
(6)(iv-ix) ....[1989] 478, 486, 490
(vi), (viii-ix), (xi) .... [1989] 478, 486
(7) .... [1989] 479, 486
(10) ....[1989] 479, 487, 492
(11) .... [1989] 479, 491
3(7)(ii-iii) .... [1989] 480, 493
5(1) .... [1989] 486
(2) .... [1989] 480, 494
6(2) .... [1989] 481, 493
Restatement (Second) of Conflicts of Law—
s. 6 .... [1986] 353
188 .... [1986] 353
Restrictive Trade Practices Act 1956 .. [1986] 181
Restrictive Trade Practice Act 1976 .... [1988] 264
Rhine Convention 1868 .... [1987] 297
Rivers and Harbors Act (33 U.S.C. s. 403) (1982) .... [1986] 379
Rivers and Harbours Act 1899 (Refuse Act) (33 U.S.C.)—
ss. 401–418 .... [1989] 15 *et seq.*
s. 407 .... [1987] 496, 517
Road Traffic Act 1972—
s. 143 *et seq.* .... [1987] 210
149 .... [1987] 230
Rome Convention 1933 .... [1989] 515
R.S.C. (Rules of the Supreme Court) 1883, Ords. 31, 54, r. 12 .... [1990] 321
R.S.C. (Rules of the Supreme Court)—
Ord. 11 ....[1989] 216, 221, 385, 391, 392; [1990] 193, 202, 277
r. 1 .... [1987] 1, 391
(1)(*f*) .... [1986] 514; [1988] 215
(i)(*d*)(iii) .... [1986] 514
(*f*)(iii) .... [1987] 1
(2) .... [1987] 138, 295
(3) .... [1987] 295
12, r. 8 .... [1986] 276, 277
14 .... [1986] 386, 420; [1989] 295; [1990] 472, 474, 476
r. 2 .... [1989] 390
15, r. 2 .... [1990] 328
(4) .... [1989] 294
6 ....[1987] 232; [1990] 89
12(1) .... [1989] 391, 392
(5) .... [1989] 391, 392

R.S.C. (Rules of the Supreme Court)—*cont.*
Ord. 15, r. 16 .... [1990] 211
18, r. 17 .... [1990] 476
r. 19 .... [1986] 276
20 .... [1990] 170
22 rr. 1–3 .... [1990] 27
24 .... [1989] 469; [1990] 322
27, r. 3 .... [1990] 330
29 .... [1990] 320, 321, 322
r. 2(5) .... [1990] 321
r. 10 .... [1987] 173
rr. 11, 12 .... [1987] 175; [1990] 307
32, r. 11 .... [1990] 320
48 .... [1989] 465–470, 472, 473, 475
r. 1(1) .... [1989] 465, 466, 471
49 .... [1988] 430
r. 1(1) .... [1989] 467, 468, 470
Ords. 55, 57 .... [1986] 418
Ord. 62, rr. 12(2), 29(1) .... [1990] 97
71, rr. 25–39 .... [1987] 295
74, r. 2 .... [1986] 418
75 .... [1990] 320
r. 16 .... [1987] 324
114 .... [1987] 282
R.S.C. (Rules of the Supreme Court) (Singapore)—
Ord. 20 .... [1990] 169
rr. 5(1), (2), (3) .... [1990] 170, 171
Rarotonga Treaty and Protocols .... [1990] 564
Restrictive Trade Practices Act 1976—
s. 6 .... [1990] 309
35(3) .... [1990] 440
Safety at Sea Act 1986 .... [1986] 557
Sale of Goods Act 1983 .... [1986] 27, 165; [1987] 342; [1989] 259, 260, 379; [1990] 280, 364
s. 14(1) .... [1987] 401; [1988] 508, 509
(2) .... [1989] 380
Sale of Goods Act 1979 .... [1987] 342; [1989] 428; [1990] 284
s. 2(1) .... [1989] 23, 24
13 .... [1990] 457, 458, 459
ss. 13, 14 .... [1988] 506; [1989] 371
13–15 .... [1988] 507
s. 14(2) .... [1987] 400, 401, 403; [1989] 148, 380; [1990] 459
(2) (3) .... [1988] 508, 511, 514
(3) .... [1987] 401, 403, 405; [1990] 458, 459, 460
(6) .... [1987] 400, 401, 402, 403, 404
16 .... [1986] 6, 7, 108; [1987] 257; [1989] 53, 163, 420, 421, 424, 425, 430
17 .... [1989] 424, 506
18 .... [1988] 502
(5) .... [1986] 300; [1989] 424
19 .... [1989] 506
(2) .... [1990] 2
ss. 21–25 .... [1986] 226, 229
25, 26 .... [1986] 167
25, 47 .... [1990] 273

Sale of Goods Act 1979—*cont.*
s. 33 .... [1987] 181
ss. 34, 35 .... [1988] 457
s. 35 .... [1988] 507
39(2) .... [1986] 300
43(1)(*a*) .... [1986] 300
44 .... [1989] 194
ss. 49, 50 .... [1990] 307
s. 50(3) .... [1990] 305, 309, 310, 311, 314
53(1) .... [1988] 457
59 .... [1990] 376
ss. 61, 62 .... [1988] 508
s. 61(1) .... [1989] 261, 372
131(3) .... [1990] 456
Sale of Goods Act (Canada), s. 25 .... [1990] 273
Sale of Goods Act (R.S.A. 1970, c. 327) (Canada), s. 17(2) .... [1988] 510
Sale of Goods Act (R.S.P.E.I. 1951, c. 144) (Canada), s. 16(1) .... [1988] 510
Sale of Goods and Supply of Services Act 1980 (Republic of Ireland)—
ss. 2, 3 .... [1989] 373
Salmon and Freshwater Fisheries Act 1975 .... [1988] 412
Salvage Act 1912 (U.S.), 46 U.S.C.—
ss. 727–730 .... [1990] 32
Salvage Act 1912, c. 268, 37 Stat. 242 (U.S.) .... [1987] 346
Salvage Convention 1910 .... [1987] 276; [1990] 32 *et seq.*, 352, 354
art. 15 .... [1990] 437
Salvage Convention 1989 .... [1990] 32 *et seq.*, 352 *et seq.*
art. 13(1)(*a*)-(*j*) .... [1989] 416, 418
(*h*)-(*j*) .... [1989] 417
14 .... [1989] 416, 417, 418
(4) .... [1989] 418
Saskatchewan Consumer Products Warranties Act 1977 (Canada)—
s. 10 .... [1988] 511
Saskatchewan Personal Property Security Act (Stat. Sask. 1979–80, c.P. 6.1) .... [1986] 163, 171
s. 3(*b*) .... [1986] 173
Sea—Carriage of Goods Act 1904 (Cth.) .... [1987] 342
Sea Fisheries Act 1968, s. 17 .... [1987] 271
Second Treaty of Erzeroum 1847 .... [1990] 300
Sherman Act (U.S.) .... [1989] 387
Ship Mortgage Act 1920 (U.S.) .... [1988] 166
Ship Mortgage Act (46 U.S.C. ss. 911–984 (1982)) .... [1986] 356
s. 30(M) (46 U.S.C., s. 953) .... [1986] 356
Shipping Act 1916 (U.S.) .... [1988] 182
Shipping Act 1984 (U.S.) .. [1988] 182; [1989] 112
ss. 6(*g*), 10(*b*) .... [1988] 183
Shipping Conferences Exemption Act 1978–79, c. 15 (Canada) .... [1989] 112
Shipping Conferences Exemption Act, S.C. 1987, c. 22 (Canada)—
s. 4(1)(*b*)(*c*), (3) .... [1989] 112

Shipping Conferences Exemption Act, S.C. 1987, c. 22 (Canada)—*cont.*
ss. 4(1), 5 .... [1989] 113
S.I. 1983 No. 236 .... [1986] 139
Single European Act 1987 .... [1989] 522
Sirovich Amendment of 1936 (Act of 5 June 1936, c. 521, 49 Stat. 1480 (U.S.) .... [1987] 345
S.R. & O 1923 No. 752 .... [1986] 417
State Immunity Act 1978, s. 10 .... [1987] 346
State Immunity Act, R.S.C. 1985, c. S–18 (Canada), s. 7 .... [1987] 346
State Immunity Act, S.C. 1980–81–82–83, c. 95 (Canada), s. 7(2) .... [1988] 87
Statute of Frauds 1677 .... [1990] 510
s. 4 .... [1988] 292
Submerged Lands Act, 43 U.S.C.—
s. 13101 *et seq.* .... [1986] 18, 19
ss. 1301–1315 (1976) (U.S.) .... [1987] 27
Suits in Admiralty Act (46 U.S.C.—
ss. 741–752 (1982)) .... [1986] 366
Sunday Observance Act 1677—
s. 6 .... [1989] 66
Superfund Amendments and Reauthorization Act 1986, P.L. 99–499, 100 Stat. 1613 (U.S.) .... [1987] 505
Supplemental Rules for certain Admiralty and Maritime Claims, 28 U.S.C.A. Rules (1970)—
r. C(1*a*) .... [1986] 18
(2) .... [1986] 20
E(3*a*) .... [1986] 20
F .... [1986] 22
Supplemental Rules B & C, Supplemental Rules for Certain Admiralty and Maritime Claims, Federal Rules of Civil Procedure, 28 U.S.C., as amended 1985 (U.S.) .... [1987] 347
Supply of Goods and Services Act 1982 .... [1987] 249; [1989] 23, 24
ss. 4, 9 .... [1989] 371
s. 13 .... [1988] 35; [1990] 417
Part II .... [1986] 557
Supply of Goods (Implied Terms) Act 1973 .... [1988] 508
s. 7(2) .... [1987] 400
10 .... [1989] 371
Supreme Court Act 1981—
ss. 20, 21 .... [1987] 347, 542
21, 21(4) .... [1990] 361
20–24 .... [1987] 323; [1988] 423
s. 20(1) .... [1986] 276
(*j*) .... [1987] 262; [1988] 450
(*m*)(*n*) .... [1988] 425
(2) .... [1986] 276
(*h*)(*m*)(*n*) .... [1988] 424, 425
(*h*) .... [1986] 333; [1987] 85; [1988] 425
(*j*) .... [1986] 278, 333
(*m*) .... [1988] 423, 426, 427, 428
21 .... [1986] 276; [1988] 424
(4) .... [1986] 281; [1988] 96, 428
Supreme Court Act 1981—*cont.*
ss. 21(2)-5, 37(3) .... [1987] 347
s. 24(1) .... [1986] 277; [1989] 91
35A .... [1986] 139, 140, 141; [1987] 417
(1) .... [1986] 140, 141
(3) .... [1986] 140, 141
37 .... [1990] 241
(1) .... [1989] 472, 474; [1990] 321
(3) .... [1987] 320
50 .... [1987] 70
Part II
ss. 21, 22, 23, 24 .... [1986] 382
Supreme Court Act No. 59 of 1959 (South Africa), s. 19 *bis* .... [1987] 314
Supreme Court of Judicature Act 1873 .... [1989] 293
s. 25(6) (replaced by s. 136 of Law of Property Act 1925) .... [1989] 9, 199, 212, 213, 215
Supreme Court of Judicature Act 1875 .... [1989] 293
Supreme Court of Judicature (Consolidation) Act 1925 .... [1988] 426
Sched. 1 .... [1990] 27
Tax Reform Act 1986 (U.S.) .... [1988] 235 *et seq.*
Technical Corrections Act 1988 (H.R. 4333, S.2238, 31 March 1988) (U.S.) .... [1988] 238
Territorial Waters Jurisdiction Act 1878 .... [1990] 163
Texas Civil Practice and Remedies Code (Wrongful Death Statute), s. 71.031 (U.S.) .... [1987] 392
Theft Act 1968 .... [1989] 381
Theft Act 1968, s. 5(1)(3) .... [1988] 130
Third Parties (Rights Against Insurers) Act 1930 .... [1987] 302, 406; [1989] 393, 495 *et seq.*, 521; [1990] 446
s. 1 .... [1987] 211, 230
(1)(3) .... [1987] 229, 407; [1989] 389, 496, 498
(3) .... [1987] 230, 234
(4)(5) .... [1987] 239
2(1) .... [1987] 230
(2) .... [1987] 229
3 .... [1987] 229
Torts (Interference with Goods) Act 1977—
s. 2(2) .... [1988] 41
ss. 2(2), 11(1) .... [1987] 51
s. 8 .... [1986] 229; [1988] 37, 42
(1) .... [1986] 229
11(1) .... [1986] 231
Trade Descriptions Act 1968 .... [1989] 371, 372, 376, 381; [1990] 281
Trade Practices Act 1974 (Commonwealth) (Australia)—
s. 4B .... [1990] 373
52 .... [1990] 167, 168
74 .... [1986] 283; [1990] 166
(3) .... [1990] 167

Trade Practices Act 1974 (Commonwealth) (Australia)—*cont.*
s. 87 .... [1990] 168
(2)(*a*) .... [1990] 167
Part V .... [1987] 169
Trans-Alaska Pipeline Authorization Act 1973, P.L. 93–153, title II, s. 204, 87 Stat. 586, 43 U.S.C., s. 1651 *et seq.* (U.S.) .... [1987] 348, 496, 515
s. 1653(*a*)(1), (*c*)(1) .... [1990] 40
Transfer of Undertakings (Protection of Employment) Regulations 1981 (EC Council Directive 77/187), art. 5 .. [1990] 412
Transport Act, R.S.C. 1970, c. T–14 (Canada) (repealed by National Transportation Act, S.C. 1987, c. 34) .... [1989] 110
Treaty of Rome—
arts. 38–43 .... [1989] 522
art. 84(2) .... [1988] 183, 184
85 .... [1988] 136, 182, 183, 184, 185, 191, 193, 194, 195; [1989] 388
(1) .... [1988] 184, 185, 186, 188, 189; [1989] 387
(*d*) .... [1988] 187
(1)(2) .... [1988] 188
(2) .... [1988] 187
(3) .... [1988] 184, 185, 189, 191, 192, 193, 194
86 .... [1988] 136, 138, 182, 183, 184, 185, 189, 191, 193, 194, 195; [1989] 387
(3) .... [1989] 387
UCC—
1–102(4) .... [1987] 187
1–201(37) .... [1986] 162
1–201(46) .... [1986] 196
2–105(4) .... [1989] 424, 425, 430
2–313 to 315 incl .... [1987] 121
2–314 .... [1988] 511
2–319 to 2–325 incl .... [1986] 492
2–320 .... [1987] 187
2–321 .... [1987] 180, 187
2–501(1) .... [1986] 493
2–508 .... [1990] 364, 369, 370, 372, 373
(1) .... [1990] 372
(2) .... [1990] 370, 372, 376
2–509 .... [1986] 493
2–510 .... [1986] 493
(2) .... [1986] 494
(3) .... [1986] 494
2–601 .... [1990] 369
2–706(2), (3) .... [1990] 314
2–711(3) .... [1988] 458
2A–101, 9 .... [1988] 281
4–104(*g*) .... [1986] 196
7–307, 7–403(2), 7–502(1)(*d*) ... [1989] 164, 429
7–501, 502 .... [1990] 4
9 .... [1986] 160ff; [1989] 205
9–101 .... [1986] 171

UCC—*cont.*
9–102 .... [1986] 162, 172
9–103(3) .... [1990] 543
9–302(1)(*e*) .... [1986] 173
9–307 .... [1986] 167
9–312 .... [1986] 177
9–315 .... [1986] 169
UNCID Uniform Rules of Conduct for Interchange of Trade Data by Teletransmission 1988 .... [1990] 302
UNCTAD Code of Conduct for Liner Conferences 1983 .... [1990] 565
UNCTAD Convention on Conditions of Registration of Merchant Ships ... [1990] 564
Unfair Contract Terms Act 1977 .... [1986] 201; [1987] 80, 169, 248, 404; [1989] 122, 371 *et seq.*, 493; [1990] 280, 284, 285, 555
s. 2 .... [1988] 505, 507
(1) .... [1988] 475
(2) .... [1988] 474, 475
ss. 3, 11 .... [1990] 309
s. 3 .... [1988] 475, 507
(2) .... [1988] 474, 475
5 .... [1988] 504
(2)(*a*) .... [1988] 504; [1989] 380
(*b*) .... [1988] 505
6 .... [1988] 507, 513
(2), (3) .... [1988] 507
8 .... [1986] 201
10 .... [1988] 476, 505, 507
11(4) .... [1988] 475
12 .... [1988] 504; [1989] 371, 376
(1) .... [1990] 373
13 .... [1988] 366, 367, 505, 507, 513
(1) .... [1987] 536; [1988] 475
14 .... [1988] 507
ss. 26, 27 .... [1990] 549
s. 28 .... [1987] 137
Sched. 1, para. 2 .... [1986] 313
Unidroit Convention on International Factoring 1988 .... [1990] 559
Uniform Customs and Practice for Documentary Credits (ICC, 1983) ...... [1990] 559
Uniform Law on the International Sale of Goods (ULIS) 1972—
arts. 33(1), 43, 44(1) .... [1990] 371
art. 44(1) .... [1990] 378
Uniform Personal Property Security Act 1982 .... [1986] 164
s. 1(*c*) .... [1986] 172
(*k*. 1) .... [1986] 173
(*w*) .... [1986] 172
2 .... [1986] 173
(*b*) .... [1986] 172, 173
32(1) .... [1986] 170
54(1) .... [1986] 169
59(3) .... [1986] 169
61 .... [1986] 169
(1)(*b*) .... [1986] 169
61(2) .... [1986] 169

Uniform Personal Property Security Act 1982—*cont.*
s. 61(2)(*b*) ..... [1986] 169
(5) ..... [1986] 169
66 ..... [1986] 176
Uniform Rules for Collections (ICC, 1978) ..... [1990] 559
Uniform Rules on Liquidated Damages and Penalty Clauses (UNIDROIT)—
art. 8 ..... [1990] 19
Uniform Sale of Goods Act (Canada) ..... [1990] 272, 367, 380
Uniform Sales Act 1906 ..... [1986] 7
s. 1321 ..... [1986] 374
(*b*)(3)(*i*) ..... [1986] 377
(6)(A) ..... [1986] 377
(*c*)(1) ..... [1986] 375
(*f*) ..... [1986] 374, 375
(1) ..... [1986] 375
(*g*) ..... [1986] 374
(*h*)(2) ..... [1986] 374, 375
(*i*) ..... [1986] 375
(1) ..... [1986] 375
(2) ..... [1986] 375
ss. 1341–1345 ..... [1986] 374
s. 1342(*a*)(1) ..... [1986] 377
(*b*) ..... [1986] 377
ss. 1361–1376 ..... [1986] 374
s. 1370 ..... [1986] 377
United Nations Commission on International Trade Law Draft Convention on International Bills of Exchange and International Promissory Notes 1986—
art. 4(10) ..... [1990] 250
United Nations Convention on the Law of the Sea 1982 (UNCLOS) ..... [1989] 517 *et seq.*, 523; [1990] 561
9 U.S.C.—
ss. 1–14 ..... [1986] 358, 359
s. 3 ..... [1986] 359
4 ..... [1986] 360
8 ..... [1986] 67
ss. 201–208 ..... [1986] 360
11 U.S.C.—
s. 362 ..... [1986] 354
363(*e*) ..... [1986] 354
ss. 701–766 ..... [1986] 354
1101–1174 ..... [1986] 354
12 U.S.C.—
ss. 24, 378(*a*)(1), 1841–1850 ..... [1988] 381
18 U.S.C.—
ss. 1961–1968 ..... [1986] 82
28 U.S.C.— ..... [1987] 347
s. 1291 ..... [1986] 358
1292(*a*)(3) ..... [1986] 22
(*b*) ..... [1986] 22
ss. 1330, 1332(*a*), 1391(*f*), 1441(*d*), 1602–1611 ..... [1987] 346
s. 1333 ..... [1986] 364
2415(*a*)(*b*) ..... [1987] 504
28 U.S.C.—*cont.*
s. 2415(*a*) ..... [1986] 376
(*b*) ..... [1986] 376
2416(*c*) ..... [1986] 376
33 U.S.C.—
ss. 401–418 ..... [1989] 15
s. 403 ..... [1986] 379
407 ..... [1987] 517
408 ..... [1989] 18
409 ..... [1986] 379
ss. 409–415 ..... [1989] 15 *et seq.*
s. 411 ..... [1986] 379
412 ..... [1986] 379
414 ..... [1986] 379
415 ..... [1986] 379
ss. 901–950 ..... [1986] 371
s. 902(3) ..... [1986] 371, 372
(13) ..... [1986] 356
(21) ..... [1986] 373
903(*a*) ..... [1986] 372
904(*a*) ..... [1986] 371, 372
905 ..... [1986] 371
(*a*) ..... [1986] 371, 372
(*b*) ..... [1986] 372, 373
(*c*) ..... [1986] 371
907 ..... [1986] 371
908 ..... [1986] 371
909 ..... [1986] 371
912(*a*) ..... [1986] 371
(*c*) ..... [1986] 371
(*d*) ..... [1986] 371
913(*b*) ..... [1986] 371
931 ..... [1986] 371
933(*b*) ..... [1986] 371
944(*c*) ..... [1986] 371
1251 *et seq.* ..... [1987] 348
ss. 1251–1265 ..... [1986] 374
s. 1251(*h*) ..... [1986] 377
1281 ..... [1986] 374
1282–1297 ..... [1986] 374
1311–1328 ..... [1986] 374
1311(*b*)(1) ..... [1986] 377
1321(*a*)(2) ..... [1987] 497
(*b*)(3) ..... [1987] 497, 498
(i) ..... [1987] 497
(B) ..... [1987] 497
(5) ..... [1987] 499
(6)(A)(B) ..... [1987] 499
(*c*)(1) ..... [1987] 500
(*d*) ..... [1987] 518
(*f*)(1) ..... [1987] 503, 504
(4)(5) ..... [1987] 501
(*g*) ..... [1987] 503
(i)(1) ..... [1987] 500
(3)(A) ..... [1987] 497
1371(*a*) ..... [1987] 518
1471 *et seq.* ..... [1987] 518
ss. 1472, 1479(*c*) ..... [1987] 518
s. 1501 ..... [1987] 518
et seq. ..... [1987] 348
1502(10) ..... [1987] 518

33 U.S.C.—*cont.*
1517(*a*)(1)(2), (*b*)(*d*) .... [1987] 518
1901 *et seq.* .... [1987] 521
42 U.S.C.—
s. 9601 *et seq.* .... [1987] 348
(14) .... [1987] 506
(16) .... [1987] 507
9603(*b*)(3) .... [1987] 506
9607 .... [1987] 505
(1) .... [1987] 506
(*a*) (as amended 1986) .... [1987] 507
(*a*)(1)(4) .... [1987] 508
(4)(C) .... [1987] 507
(*b*)(3) .... [1987] 509
(*h*) .... [1987] 512
(*j*) .... [1987] 506
(*l*)(*m*) .... [1987] 511
9613(*c*) .... [1987] 511
(*f*)(1) .... [1987] 510
(*g*)(1)(A) .... [1987] 510
9631 .... [1987] 505
9651(*c*)(1) .... [1987] 511
(2) .... [1987] 507
43 U.S.C.—
s. 1333 .... [1986] 374
(*c*) .... [1986] 373
1651 *et seq.* .... [1987] 515
1653 .... [1987] 348
(*c*)(1)(2)(3)(5)(7) .... [1987] 516
(8)-(11) .... [1987] 517
1811 *et seq.* .... [1987] 348, 513
(8) .... [1987] 514
1813(*a*)(1)(2)(A) .... [1987] 513
(2)(B)(C) .... [1987] 513
(D)(E)(F) .... [1987] 514
(*b*)(2)(3)(4)(5)(6) .... [1987] 514
1814(*b*) .... [1987] 515
(1)(2) .... [1987] 514
(*e*)(1)(2) .... [1987] 514
(i) .... [1987] 513
1815 .... [1987] 514
1817(*a*)(*c*) .... [1987] 515
(i)(6) .... [1987] 515
1820(*a*)(*c*) .... [1987] 513
46 U.S.C.—
s. 181 *et seq.* .... [1988] 179
ss. 181–189 .... [1986] 363; [1989] 18
s. 182 .... [1986] 369
ss. 183, 185, 186, 189 .... [1987] 345
s. 183 .... [1988] 519
(*b*) .... [1986] 363
ss. 190–196 .... [1986] 365; [1987] 342, 344
s. 391(*a*) .... [1986] 376
603 .... [1986] 351
604 .... [1986] 351
688 .... [1986] 365; [1987] 345
ss. 727–731 .... [1987] 346
s. 740 .... [1986] 364
ss. 741–752 .... [1986] 366
761–767 .... [1986] 365
781–790 .... [1986] 366
46 U.S.C.—*cont.*
s. 785 .... [1986] 366
ss. 801 *et seq.*, 1701 *et seq.* .... [1988] 182
s. 883 .... [1989] 108
ss. 911–984 .... [1986] 356
951, 952(*b*), 953(*a*) .... [1988] 166
951–954, 971–975 .... [1987] 347
s. 953 .... [1986] 356
ss. 971–975 .... [1986] 355
1300–1315 .... [1986] 365, 367; [1987] 343
s. 1304(2)(*b*) .... [1986] 369
(5) .... [1986] 367
ss. 1701–1720 .... [1989] 112
2101–13110 .... [1986] 364
49 U.S.C.—
ss. 8, 25 .... [1989] 164
s. 31(*b*) .... [1989] 164, 429
ss. 81–124 .... [1987] 344
15 U.S.C.A.—
s. 1012 (McCarron-Ferguson Act) .. [1986] 486
1693(*a*) .... [1986] 196
28 U.S.C.A.—
s. 41 .... [1986] 487
1333 .... [1986] 485
1873 .... [1986] 487
46 U.S.C.A.—
s. 181–189 ....[1986] 22
183(*a*) ....[1986] 22, 23
(*b*) ....[1986] 23
764 ....[1986] 23
885 .... [1986] 486
1281 *et seq.* .... [1986] 486
49 U.S.C.A.—
s. 102 .... [1986] 109
111 .... [1986] 103
10101 *et seq.* .... [1986] 496
U.S. Carriage of Goods by Sea Act 1936 (COGSA) (46 U.S.C. 1303 *et seq.*)—
s. 1304(3) .... [1989] 346, 351
(6) ....[1989], 346, 350, 352, 353
U.S. Code Cong, and Admin. News, 100 Stat. 4199 (1986) ....[1989] 17
U.S. Code Cong, and Admin. News, 6639, 6738 (1986) ....[1989] 16, 17
U.S. Const., Art. 1, s. 9, cl. 3 .... [1986] 377
IV, ss. 1, 2 .... [1986] 485
U.S. Federal Regulations, Title 46 (subchapters N and O, Parts 146–154) .... [1989] 343
Title 49, Parts 171–177 .... [1989] 343
U.S. Public Law 99–514 (H.R. 3838) 22 October 1986 .... [1988] 235
U.S. Shipping Act 1984 .... [1988] 404
Usury Acts 1854 (repealed) ....[1989] 41
Usury Laws Repeal Act 1854 .... [1990] 280, 489
Variation of Trusts Act 1958 .... [1989] 435
Vice-Admiralty Courts Act 1863 ...... [1987] 170
s. 14 .... [1987] 171
Victorian Hire Purchase Act 1959 (Australia), s. 3 ....[1990] 25

Victorian Instruments Act 1958 (Australia), s. 30(5) .... [1990] 27
Vienna Convention on Contracts for the International Sale of Goods 1980 (UNICITRAL Convention)—
arts. 34, 37, 39, 48 .... [1990] 372
34, 37, 48(1) .... [1990] 378
46, 49 .... [1990] 371
art. 46(2), (3) .... [1990] 372
(3) .... [1990] 379
48(1) .... [1990] 376
Vienna Convention on the Law of Treaties 1969—
art. 31(3)(*c*) .... [1988] 401; [1989] 519
40(1)(5) .... [1988] 153
Warsaw Convention 1929 .... [1987] 297
art. 22 .... [1988] 446
Warsaw Convention as amended at The Hague 1955 .... [1988] 445; [1989] 37
art. 1(2) .... [1988] 217
arts. 10(2), 12, 13, 14, 15(3), 17, 18, 19, 24(1), (2), 30(3) .... [1989] 38
art. 17 .... [1988] 218, 220, 223, 224, 228, 229, 230, 231, 232, 234
18, 19 .... [1988] 154
20 .... [1988] 155
(1) .... [1988] 218, 219, 224, 232
21 .... [1988] 154
arts. 22, 25 .... [1989] 145 *et seq.*
art. 22 .... [1988] 179, 180
(1) .... [1988] 230, 231
(2) .... [1988] 155
23 .... [1988] 155
(2) .... [1988] 154
Warsaw Convention as amended at The Hague 1955—*cont.*
art. 24 .... [1988] 155
(2) .... [1988] 231
(3) .... [1988] 154
25 .... [1988] 231, 232, 233, 234
28(2) .... [1989] 147
34 .... [1988] 218
36 .... [1988] 181
Water Act 1973 .... [1990] 562
Water Act 1989 .... [1990] 562
Water Carriage of Goods Act 1910 (Canada) .... [1987] 342
Water Resources Development Act 1986 (U.S.)—
s. 939 .... [1989] 17
Weights and Measures Act 1985 .... [1990] 280
Wet Toezicht Kredietwezen (the Banking Act (Holland)), para. 46(1) .... [1987] 252
Wreck Act (U.S.) (33 U.S.C.)—
ss. 409–415 .... [1989] 15 *et seq.*
409, 411, 412, 414, 415, (1982) [1986] 379
Wreck and Salvage Act 1846 .... [1987] 268
Wreck Removal Act, 33 U.S.C. ss. 409, 414 .... [1986] 18
Wrongful Death Act (46 U.S.C., ss. 761–767 (1982)) .... [1986] 365
York-Antwerp Rules .... [1989] 127
York-Antwerp Rules 1974 .... [1988] 268
rr. A, X(*b*), XI(*b*) .... [1988] 89
r. A .... [1990] 173
VI .... [1990] 45, 358
Yukon Territory Ordinance (Ord. Yukon Terr 1980 (2nd) c.20) .... [1986] 163

Index 1974–1990

"A DIRECTORY OF 154 PERIODICALS USEFUL TO TRANSPORT RESEARCHERS: INFORMATION DATABASES IN THE FIELD OF TRANSPORTATION", [1990] 152
"A GUIDE TO MARITIME BOUNDARY DELIMITATION", [1988] 121
"A GUIDE TO THE CIVIL JURISDICTION AND JUDGMENTS CONVENTION", [1988] 118
"A GUIDE TO THE HAGUE–VISBY RULES", [1986] 414
"A MODERN INTRODUCTION TO INTERNATIONAL LAW" (6th Edn.), [1988] 540
"A PRACTICAL GUIDE TO CONTRACTS OF AFFREIGHTMENT AND HYBRID CONTRACTS", [1987] 130
"A TEXTBOOK ON CONTRACT", [1988] 408
ACCEPTANCE
communications of (*Jacobs*), [1983] 663
ACCIDENTAL ERRORS
power of arbitrators to cure (*Thomas*), [1985] 263
ACCOUNTING
some problems with foreign exchange, losses in translation (*Owles*), [1980] 411
ACT
Bills of Lading Act 1855 (The) (Case and comment), [1990] 1
Companies Act 1989 (The) (Case and comment), [1990] 28
Merchant Shipping Act 1988 (Case and comment), [1989] 133
Sale of Goods Act 1979: seller cure in the sale of goods (*Ahdar*), [1990] 364
Wreck Removal Act (U.S.): recent amendments (Case and comment), [1989] 15
ACT, OF 1984, US, [1985] 515
ACTION *IN REM*
gaps in (*Hazelwood*), [1982] 210
plugged? (*Hazelwood*), [1982] 422
time-charterer, one-ship company and sister-ship action (*Tettenborn*), [1981] 507
ACTION *IN REM*, THE SISTER SHIP
(*Thomas*), [1979] 158
ADMINISTRATION OF JUSTICE ACT 1956
"damage done by any ship" (*Clarke*), [1976] 412
ADMINISTRATIVE CAUTION
(*de Lacy*), [1989] 506
ADMIRALTY AND SHIPPING LAW
recent developments in US (*Healy*), [1984] 607
ADMIRALTY CLAIMS
non-maritime (Case and comment), [1986] 276
ADMIRALTY COURT
Canadian decisions 1983–1984 (*Tetley*), [1985] 326
of Sri Lanka (*Ratnasabapathy*), [1985] 260
ADMIRALTY COURT ACT 1861
"damage done by any ship" (*Clarke*), [1976] 412
ADMIRALTY JURISDICTION
changes in South Africa (*Rycroft*), [1984] 417
in US (*Foremost Insurance Co.* v. *Richardson*) (*Sargent*), [1984] 112
over agency contracts (*Peralta Shipping Corp.* v. *Smith & Johnson Corp.*) (Case and comment), [1986] 12
proposed reforms of in Australia (*Davenport*), [1987] 317

ADMIRALTY JURISDICTION—*continued*
Supreme Court Act 1981 (*Jackson*), [1982] 236
tort claims (*The Antonis P. Lemos*) (*Case and comment*), [1984] 374
"ADMIRALTY JURISDICTION AND PRACTICE IN SOUTH AFRICA", [1989] 382
ADMIRALTY JURISDICTION REGULATION ACT
South Africa, implementation of (*Staniland*), [1985] 462
ADMIRALTY LAW
Singapore, recent developments (*Selvam*), [1985] 209
some issues in Canadian offshore oil and gas development (*Spicer*), [1982] 5
US, continuing problems after supposed demise of *Ryan* indemnity (*Bagwell*), [1982] 556
ADMIRALTY RULES
upheld in Sri Lanka (*The Ayesha*) (Case and comment), [1987] 169
ADMISSIBILITY
and enforcement of foreign court decisions and arbitration awards in Greece (*Timagenis*), [1984] 488
ADMIXTURE OF GOODS
in English law (*Indian Oil Corp. Ltd.* v. *Greenstone Shipping S.A.* (*Panama*)) (Case and comment), [1988] 286
AFFREIGHTMENT
contract of (*Crump*), [1985] 19
AGENCY
admiralty jurisdiction over contracts (*Peralta Shipping Corp.* v. *Smith & Johnson Corp.*) (Case and comment), [1986] 12
"Bowstead on Agency", [1977] 202; [1978] 633
AGENT
Japanese agent's liability for delivery without presentation of bill of lading (*Daiwa Bank* v. *Mankai Shipping and Fast Marine* (*The Taichun*)) (Case and comment), [1989] 35
port, his rights, liabilities and problems (*Morris*), [1982] 218
"The gratuitous agent's liability" (*Chaudhry* v. *Prabhakar*) (Case and comment), [1989] 148
AGENTS
commercial, Benelux law not incorporated in Dutch Commercial Code (*Calkoen*), [1978] 395
AGREEMENTS
arbitration
as signpost of the proper law (*Thomas*), [1984] 141
proper law of (*Thomas*), [1984] 304
salvage, master's authority (*Goddard*), [1984] 255
AIR
limitation of liability in the air and at sea (*McGilchrist*), [1975] 256
AIR CARGO
recovery for loss of valuable cargo under Warsaw Convention (*Soloman and Goldman*), [1982] 453
AIR TRAFFIC CONTROL
the operator's liability (*McGilchrist*), [1977] 204
AIR TRANSPORT
air and maritime transport and the EEC competition rules (*Ministère Publique* v. *Asjes*, *Nouvelles Frontières et al*) (Case and comment), [1987] 14
European Community instruments on (Case and comment), [1988] 135
"AIRCRAFT FINANCE: REGISTRATION, SECURITY AND ENFORCEMENT", [1989] 515
AIRCRAFT HIJACKING
liability for injuries sustained by passengers in the event of hijacking of aircraft and other violations of aviation security (*Gam*), [1988] 217
AIRLINE
as plaintiff in US (*McGilchrist*), [1980] 328
"ALL JANGLE AND RIOT", [1987] 249
"ALONGSIDE VESSELS OR LIGHTERS REACHABLE ON HER ARRIVAL" (*Ventris*), [1980] 174
AMERICAN ACADEMY OF FOREIGN LAW
(Information), [1987] 561
AMERICAN EXPRESS
unsuitable (*Heather*), [1982] 157
"AMERICAN TORT PROCESS (THE)", [1990] 132

AMOCO CADIZ, THE
some legal aspects of (*Dubais*), [1979] 292
"AN INTRODUCTION TO COMPARATIVE LAW" (2nd Edn.), [1990] 271
"AN INTRODUCTION TO THE HONG KONG LEGAL SYSTEM", [1989] 130
"AN INTRODUCTION TO THE LAW OF OBLIGATIONS", [1986] 413
"AN INTRODUCTION TO THE LAW OF RESTITUTION", [1986] 540
"AN INTRODUCTION TO THE SCOTS LAW OF CONTRACT", [1990] 138
"AN INTRODUCTORY GUIDE TO EEC COMPETITION LAW AND PRACTICE", [1987] 129
"ANNOTATED ADMIRALTY LEGISLATION", [1989] 382
"ANNUAL REVIEW OF OCEAN AFFAIRS: LAW AND POLICY, MAIN DOCUMENTS 1985–1987. Vols. I and II", [1990] 563
"ANTARCTIC LEGAL REGIME (THE)", [1990] 144
"ANTI-DUMPING AND ANTI-SUBSIDY LAW: THE EUROPEAN COMMUNITIES", [1988] 414
"ANTITRUST LAWS OF THE USA", THE, [1981] 512
"ANUARIO DE DERECHO MARITIMO", [1985] 516
APPORTIONMENT OF LOSS
collisions and contributions (*Fitzgerald* v. *Lane*) (Case and comment), [1989] 30
ARAB WORLD
property law in, [1985] 279
ARBITRATION
a New Yorker looks at London maritime arbitration (*Cohen*), [1986] 57
abandonment of by silence or inactivity (*Food Corporation of India* v. *Antclizo Shipping Corporation (The Antclizo)*) (Case and comment), [1987] 263
abandonment of by silence or inactivity (*The Antclizo*; *The Multitank Holsatia*) (Case and comment), [1988] 302
agreements
as signpost of the proper law (*Thomas*), [1984] 141
proper law of (*Thomas*), [1984] 304
an appraisal of the 1979 Act (*Thomas*), [1981] 199
and arrest (*The Andria*; *The Tuyuti*) (*Case and comment*), [1984] 370
and forum, and choice of law clauses, Hague-Visby Rules (*Jackson*), [1980] 159
and general average adjustment in People's Republic of China (*Hudson*), [1976] 135
and grain contracts, [1984] 679
appeals and charterparty construction (*The Antaios*)(*Case and comment*), [1984] 547
"Arbitration in Sweden", [1978] 634
awards in New York involving shipowner withdrawals from charter upon late payment (*Murray*), [1976] 164
basis and validity of a restricted reasons agreement (*Thomas*), [1986] 235
charterparties, "*stare decisis et non quieta movere*" (*Arnold*), [1977] 24
commercial
Admiralty security and the arbitral process (*Thomas*), [1983] 495
discretion and issues of technical misconduct (*Thomas*), [1982] 288
in commodity trades (*Mackie*), [1976] 278
injunctive jurisdiction of Commercial Court (*Thomas*), [1981] 389
international agreements, enforcement of foreign arbitral awards (*Thomas*), [1981] 17
judge-arbitrators (*Thomas*), [1983] 120
law and practice of, [1984] 137
legal remedies for dilatoriness (*Thomas*), [1983] 315
power of court to extend time for commencing proceedings (*Thomas*), [1981] 529
removal of arbitrators by the court (*Thomas*), [1982] 186
restraining concurrent foreign legal proceedings (*Thomas*), [1983] 692
security for costs in (*Thomas*), [1982] 463
the vexed issue of interest awards (*Thomas*), [1982] 667
consequential damages and duty to mitigate in New York maritime arbitrations (*Bulow*), [1984] 622
costs and Lloyd's Form salvage arbitrations (*The Ios I*) (Case and comment), [1987] 172
curial law of proceedings (*Thomas*), [1984] 491
difference between legal and arbitration approach in petroleum shortage disputes (*Textor*), [1983] 392
disclosure requirements imposed on arbitrators in maritime arbitrations under US law (*Meade*), [1975] 399

ARBITRATION—*continued*
foreign awards, admissibility and enforcement in Greece (*Timagenis*), [1984] 488
fundamental changes in Italian law (*Costabel*), [1983] 440
hazards of invoking Indian law (*Oil & Natural Gas Commission* v. *Western Company of North America*) (Case and comment), [1988] 12
in Piraeus, "a growing trend" (*Timagenis*), [1977] 319
international (*Naviera Amazonica Peruana S.A.* v. *Compania Internacional de Seguros del Peru*) (Case and comment), [1988] 23
laytime problems and comparison of law (*Trappe*), [1986] 251
leave to appeal under 1979 Act (*Lewis*), [1982] 271
"manifest disregard of the law" doctrine (*Bauer*), [1979] 142
maritime arbitration in the People's Republic of China (*Shum*), [1990] 114
New York arbitration as seen by a Londoner (*Wodehouse*), [1986] 43
New York charter arbitrations and pre-hearing discovery (*Kuffler*), [1978] 557
power of English arbitrators to make awards in foreign currencies, [1976] 255
problems with and solutions for New York maritime arbitration (*Jarvis*), [1986] 535
procedures, need for reform, a High Court comment, [1978] 267
rivals for centres of (*The Lord Hacking*), [1979] 435
Second International Congress of Maritime Arbitrators, [1974] 61
some rules of practice and procedure and methods of appeal under Scots law (*Inglis*), [1976] 289
stale arbitrations (*The Leonidas D*) (*Case and comment*), [1985] 293
table of comparative maritime arbitration procedures (*Cohen*), [1976] 422
the Centrocon clause, an appreciation of *The Astraea* and *The Evje* cases (*Hudson*), [1974] 301
"The dog that slept" (Case and comment), [1988] 307
"the sleeping and the dead" (*Matthews*), [1982] 401
the unauthorized publication of arbitration awards (Case and comment), [1989] 158
the USSR maritime arbitration commission (*Timmermans*), Part 1, [1987] 350; Part 2, [1987] 468
Third International Congress of Maritime Arbitrators, [1976] 377
US
obtaining security in aid of arbitration (*Healy*), [1976] 267
time not of the essence in nominating arbitrator (*Ashworth*), [1976] 266
US Arbitration Act and "manifest disregard of law" (*Berg*), [1975] 129
when proceedings become stale (*Lewis*), [1983] 289
"ARBITRATION: A PRACTICAL GUIDE", [1986] 134
ARBITRATION ACT 1950
the end of s. 27? (Case and comment), [1986] 142
ARBITRATION ACT 1979
an appraisal (*Thomas*), [1981] 199
leave to appeal under (*Lewis*), [1982] 271
"ARBITRATION AND CONCILIATION UNDER THE UNCITRAL RULES: A TEXTUAL ANALYSIS", [1990] 268
ARBITRATION AWARDS
publication of (Case and comment), [1987] 139
"ARBITRATION IN SWEDEN", [1978] 634
"ARBITRATION INTERNATIONAL", [1986] 405
ARBITRATIONS
maritime, in London, recent developments in the law (*McIntosh*), [1983] 235
ARBITRATORS
commercial, removal of by court (*Thomas*), [1982] 186
disclosure requirements imposed in maritime arbitrations under US law (*Meade*), [1975] 399
power of to cure accidental errors (*Thomas*), [1985] 263
Second International Congress of Maritime Arbitrators, [1974] 61
Third International Congress of Maritime Arbitrators, [1976] 377
table of comparative maritime arbitration procedures, (*Cohen*), [1976] 422
"ARNOULD'S LAW OF MARINE INSURANCE", [1983] 679
ARREST
after judgment (*Case and comment*), [1985] 186
and arbitration (*The Andria; The Tuyuti*) (*Case and comment*), [1984] 370
ARREST OF SHIP
arrest of associated ship not retrospective in operation (Case and comment), [1986] 279

ARREST OF SHIPS
"arresting the misconception" (*Robinson*), [1982] 261
(*Goffey*), [1975] 34
in Greece (*Timagenis*), [1984] 90
in Japan (*Hosoi*), [1980] 322; (*Hosoi and Tsurusaki*), [1981] 359
in Panama, "anatomy of" (*Pardini*), [1983] 456
on insurance claims (*Case and comment*), [1985] 173
owned by charterers (*Tabbush*), [1982] 585
releasing from (*Matthews*), [1983] 99
ARREST OF VESSELS
in the States of the Arab Gulf Cooperation Council (*Price and Haberbeck*), [1985] 392
"ARRESTS, LIENS AND MORTGAGES: MODERN NEEDS AND MODERN DEVELOPMENTS", [1988] 548
"ARRIVED SHIP"
some considerations of *The Johanna Oldendorff* and *The Loucas N* cases (*Davies*), [1974] 1
"ASBATANKVOY CHARTER (THE)", [1986] 414
"ASIAN PACIFIC REGIONAL TRADE LAW SEMINAR", [1986] 412
ASSUMPSIT DUTIES
(*The Zephyr*) (*Case and comment*), [1984] 376; [1985] 414
ASTRAEA, THE
([1971] 2 Lloyd's Rep. 494), the Centrocon arbitration clause (*Hudson*), [1974] 301
ATTACHMENT
Mareva injunction and *saisie conservatoire* (*Tetley*), [1985] 58
ATTACHMENT *IN PERSONAM*
Mareva injunction (*Rose*), [1981] 1, 177
ATTORNEY'S FEES
expenses in *custodia legis*, court costs (*Tetley*), [1984] 1
AUDITORS
auditor's duties: a narrow approach (*Caparo Industries Plc* v. *Dickman*) (Case and comment), [1990] 477
contributory neligence: a viable defence for auditors? (*Marshall and Beltrami*), [1990] 416
extent of liability (*Alexander* v. *Cambridge Credit Corp. Ltd.*) (Case and comment), [1988] 19
true and fair revisited (*Evans*), [1990] 255
AUSTRALIA
articles 22 and 25 of the Warsaw Convention—an Australian contribution (*S.S. Pharmaceutical Co. Ltd.* v. *Qantas Airways Ltd.*) (Case and comment), [1989] 145
aviation policy rewritten to avoid effects of *Maclean* v. *Maclean* (*Pyne*), [1981] 525
contracts for the supply of services in (*Case and comment*), [1984] 557
miscellaneous developments in law (Case and comment), [1986] 283
privity of contract in Australia: the beginning of the end? (*Trident General Insurance Co. Ltd.* v. *McNiece Bros. Pty. Ltd.*) (Case and comment), [1989] 139
product liability in (*Goldring*), [1977] 351
proposed reforms of admiralty jurisdiction in (*Davenport*), [1987] 317
the Hague Rules in Australia (*P.S. Chellaram & Co. Ltd.* v. *China Ocean Shipping Co.*) (Case and comment), [1989] 277
"wider still and wider: the bounds of Australian exorbitant jurisdiction" (*Briggs*), [1989] 216
"AUSTRALIAN INSURANCE LAW", [1990] 443
"AUSTRALIAN LAW OF CHEQUES AND PAYMENT ORDERS", [1989] 239
AUSTRIA
General Freight Forwarding Conditions and Freight Forwarding Insurance Scheme (*Blasche*), [1976] 374
AVERAGE DISBURSEMENTS
insurance of (*Hudson*), [1987] 443
AVIATION
insurance, a recent decision (*Margo*), [1980] 335
liability insurance claims in general aviation (*McGilchrist*), [1980] 196
litigation, punitive damages in (*McGilchrist*), [1979] 48
mental anguish, before and after the crash (*McGilchrist*), [1984] 311
"AVIATION INSURANCE", [1980] 451; (2nd Edn.), [1990] 135
AVIATION LITIGATION
in US (*McGilchrist*), [1980] 59

AVIATION (POLICY)
rewritten in Australia to avoid effects of *Maclean* v. *Maclean* (*Pyne*), [1981] 525
AVIATION SECURITY
liability for injuries sustained by passengers in the event of hijacking of aircraft and other violations of aviation security (*Gam*), [1988] 217
AWARDS
and commercial judgments, recognition of in the Commonwealth, [1986] 129
arbitration, in Greece, admissibility and enforcement of foreign (*Timagenis*), [1984] 488
enhanced salvage (*Brice*), [1985] 33
international commercial arbitration agreements, enforcement of foreign arbitral awards (*Thomas*), [1981] 17
the unauthorized publication of arbitration awards (Case and comment), [1989] 158
BAILMENT
"from bailment to bailment" (*Rose*), [1982] 200
BALTIME CLAUSE 13
(*The TFL Prosperity*) (*Case and comment*), [1984] 196
BANK ACCOUNTS
restitution and theft (*Case and comment*), [1985] 180
BANKER AND CUSTOMER
implied terms in the relationship (*The Maira (No. 3)*) (Case and comment), [1989] 40
BANKERS
and performance bonds (*Penn*), [1985] 132
"BANKERS DOCUMENTARY CREDITS", [1985] 273
BANKING
bank manuals and instructions to staff, some legal aspects (*Weerasooria*), [1974] 295
banks and extra-territorial orders (*Ellinger*), [1989] 363
giro system and electronic transfers of funds (*Ellinger*), [1986] 178
implied terms in the banker and customer relationship (*The Maira (No. 3)*) (Case and comment), [1989] 40
legal position of banks in Performance Bond cases (*Arora*), [1981] 264
money transfer, future developments in (*Arora*), [1981] 56
money transfer methods, recent developments (*Arora*), [1980] 416
the banker's right to compound interest (*The Maira (No. 3)*) (Case and comment), [1990] 488
the legal implications of cheque truncation (*Vroegop*), [1990] 244
the role of correspondent banks in direct funds transfers (*Vroegop*), [1990] 547
the time of payment in paper-based and electronic funds transfer systems (*Vroegop*), [1990] 64
when payment is made (*Ryder*), [1974] 286; [1977] 174
worldwide *Mareva* injunctions: the position of international banks (*Malek and Lewis*), [1990] 88
"BANKING ACT (THE)", [1987] 249
"BANKING AND FINANCE LAW REVIEW", [1988] 262
BANKING LAW
understanding banking law (*Cranston*), [1988] 360
"BANKING LAW. VOL. 1: THE LAW RELATING TO DOMESTIC BANKING. VOL. 2: THE LAW AND PRACTICE OF INTERNATIONAL BANKING", [1989] 240
"BANKING SUPERVISION (REGULATION OF THE U.K. BANKING SECTOR UNDER THE BANKING ACT 1987), [1990] 434
BANKRUPTCY
effect upon mortgages of future property (*Matthews*), [1981] 40
BANKS
CHAPS transfer of funds (*Geva*), [1988] 477
duties to principal debtor and guarantor (*Barclays Bank Plc* v. *Quincecare Ltd.*) (Case and comment), [1988] 441
EEC secrecy provisions (*Hillegom Municipality* v. *Hillenius*) (Case and comment), [1987] 251
freezing a joint account (*Matthews*), [1984] 651
freezing foreign bank accounts (*Libyan Arab Foreign Bank* v. *Bankers Trust Co.*) (Case and comment), [1988] 1
in Socialist Eastern Europe (*Kovats*), [1975] 173
issuing bank, dilemma of (*Arora*), [1984] 81
legal position of in Performance Bond cases (*Arora*), [1981] 264
"Liggett" defence, banker's last resort (*Ellinger and Lee*), [1984] 459

BANKS—*continued*
money transfer, future developments in (*Arora*), [1981] 56
reforming the banking laws, Stage One (*Morgan*), [1979] 30
BARRATRY
scuttler's easy route to the "golden prize" (*Hazelwood*), [1982] 383
BELGIUM
liability for pilot's negligence under Belgian law (Case and comment), [1989] 27
"BENJAMIN'S SALE OF GOODS", [1981] 510; (3rd Edn.), [1990] 302
"BERNAERTS' GUIDE TO THE UNITED NATIONS CONVENTION ON THE LAW OF THE SEA", [1990] 441
BILL OF LADING
in the oil tanker trade (*Ventris*), [1981] 479
the, as a receipt, missing oil in unknown quantities (*Debattista*), [1986] 468
BILLS OF EXCHANGE
"Byles on Bills of Exchange", [1984] 682
"BILLS OF EXCHANGE AND BANKERS' DOCUMENTARY CREDITS", [1987] 380
BILLS OF LADING
and implied contracts (*Treitel*), [1989] 162
and third parties (*Treitel*), [1986] 294
authority of charterers to sign under standard time charter terms (*Pritchett*), [1980] 21
"delivery orders" in lieu of (*Teare*), [1976] 29
Japanese agent's liability for delivery without presentation of bill of lading (*Daiwa Bank* v. *Mankai Shipping and Fast Marine* (*The Taichun*)) (Case and comment), [1989] 35
references to charterparties in (*Mankabady*), [1974] 53
simplification of documentation and document replacement (*Gronfors*), [1976] 250
the bill of lading: do we really need it? (*Sir Anthony Lloyd*), [1989] 47
BILLS OF LADING ACT 1855 (THE)
passing of property under c.i.f. contracts and the Bills of Lading Act 1855 (*The Delfini*) (Case and comment), [1990] 1
"BIOGRAPHICAL DICTIONARY OF THE COMMON LAW", [1984] 512
BIRD-STRIKES
airport operator's liability for (*McGilchrist*), [1979] 494
"BLACKSTONE'S STATUTES ON COMMERCIAL LAW", [1990] 438
BONDS
performance
are bankers free from the underlying contract? (*Penn*), [1985] 132
use and usefulness (*Williams*), [1983] 423
BOOK DEBTS
fixed charge over (*Case and comment*), [1985] 409
"BOWSTEAD ON AGENCY", [1987] 125
"BOWSTEAD ON AGENCY", [1977] 202; [1978] 633
"BRAEKHUS & REIN'S HANDBOOK ON P. & I. INSURANCE" (3rd Edn.), [1990] 292
BREACH
anticipatory breach of condition (*The Afovos*) (*Case and comment*), [1984] 189
contracts, impracticability of performance, is it grounds for breach? (*Arnold*), [1977] 346
BREACH OF DUTY
fundamental, contracts (*Rose*), [1980] 396
BRITISH FLAG
"a privilege or an encumbrance—or just an anachronism?" (*Jones*), [1981] 241
BROKERS
insurance, rights and duties of (*Bamford*), [1976] 59
reinsurance, brokers and the conflict of laws (*Forsikringsaktieselskapet Vesta* v. *Butcher*) (Case and comment), [1988] 5
BROKERS (INSURANCE)
duty of care (*Glass*), [1978] 619
intermediaries, recent and projected developments, Insurance Brokers (Registration) Act 1977 (*Morgan*), [1978] 39
BULK CARGOES
ownership of (*The Gosforth*) (Case and comment), [1986] 4
BULK OIL CARGOES
claims for short delivery, some recent trends (*Weale*), [1978] 405

BUNKERS
sampling in oil tankers (*The Othoni*: *The Erikoussa*) (*Case and comment*), [1985] 10
BUSINESS
acting in the course of a business (*Pearce*), [1989] 371
and State taxes in the US (*Owles*), [1982] 253
commercial, and trade laws, [1982] 162
essential business law, [1979] 510
insurance, [1979] 512
essential law, leases of business premises, [1980] 210
in Saudi Arabia, legal aspects of, [1985] 279
insolvency, [1980] 212
US and income tax (*Owles*), [1982] 650
"BUSINESS LAW", [1988] 418
BUSINESSMAN, THE
the law and the EEC (*Ryder*), [1978] 291
BUSINESSMEN
receiver/contractor relationships (*Tugendhat*), [1974] 39
"BUSINESSMEN'S GUIDE TO EEC LEGAL DEVELOPMENTS (THE)", [1986] 415
"BUTTERWORTHS BANKING AND FINANCIAL LAW REVIEW 1987", [1989] 243
"BUTTERWORTHS COMMERCIAL LAW HANDBOOK", [1990] 438
"BUTTERWORTHS INSURANCE LAW HANDBOOK", [1986] 553
"BUTTERWORTHS INSURANCE LAW HANDBOOK" (2nd Edn.), [1988] 270
"BYLES ON BILLS OF EXCHANGE", [1984] 682
C.I.F. CONTRACTS
passing of property under c.i.f. contracts and the Bills of Lading Act 1855 (*The Delfini*) (Case and comment), [1990] 1
CANADA
Admiralty decisions 1983–1984 (*Tetley*), [1985] 326
Admiralty law, some issues in offshore oil and gas development (*Spicer*), [1982] 5
Canadian maritime law decisions: 1987–88 (*Tetley*), [1989] 89; 1988–1989 (*Tetley, Q.C.*), [1990] 99
country's approach to marine pollution (*Lowry*), [1975] 10
group life assurance in (*Merkin*), [1981] 485
law, new personal property security legislation (*Ziegel*), [1986] 160
law, per package limitation, diverging approach in Canadian courts (*McEwen*), [1976] 269
marine insurance law in (*McEwen*), [1984] 671
maritime law decisions 1985–86 (*Tetley*), [1987] 82
maritime law judgments in 1980 (*Tetley*), [1981] 489
maritime law judgments in 1981 (*Tetley*), [1982] 542
maritime law judgments in 1982 (*Tetley*), [1983] 603
oppression and preferred shares—a heady Canadian brew (*Palmer* v. *Carling O'Keefe Breweries of Canada Ltd.*) (Case and comment), [1989] 411
Supreme Court liberalizes the rules re measuring damages for breach of a chattel lease (*Langille* v. *Keneric Tractor Sales Ltd.*) (Case and comment), [1988] 276
the lack of uniformity and the very unfortunate state of maritime law in (*Tetley*), [1987] 340
transport deregulation in the Canadian maritime industry (*Cathcart*), [1989] 104
"CAREER PREPARATION AND OPPORTUNITIES IN INTERNATIONAL LAW", [1987] 248
CARGO
damage by fire (*Bauer*), [1982] 1
damaged, actions in tort (*Case and comment*), [1985] 1
division of liability as between ship and cargo (*Diamond*), [1977] 39
liability after discharge (*The Bunga Teratai*) (Case and comment), [1990] 323
marine cargo claims, identity of the carrier, the Hague Rules, Visby Rules UNCITRAL (*Tetley*), [1977] 519
"Marine Cargo Claims", [1978] 627
recovery actions in US (*Carey*), [1980] 184
remedies, defences and insurers' liabilities (*Hudson*), [1981] 471
special charges on, obligations of ship and cargo owners (*Hudson*), [1981] 315
the new Institute Cargo Clauses (*George*), [1986] 438
CARGO (AIR)
recovery for loss of valuable cargo under Warsaw Convention (*Solomon and Goldman*), [1982] 453

"CARGO LIABILITY STUDY—FINAL REPORT", [1976] 191
CARGOES
bulk oil, claims for short delivery, some recent trends (*Weale*), [1978] 405
CARRIAGE BY AIR
forum non conveniens, the continuing debate (*McGilchrist*), [1980] 439
air disaster and associated problems (*Binney*), [1981] 101
air traffic control—the operator's liability (*McGilchrist*), [1977] 204
airline passenger tickets, duty to give notice (*McGilchrist*), [1979] 353
airport operator's liability for bird-strikes (*McGilchrist*), [1979] 494
Art. 25, an English approach to recklessness (*McGilchrist*), [1983] 488
aviation litigation in the US (*McGilchrist*), [1980] 59
BAA v. *BAB*. A licence upon terms, requirement of reasonableness (*McGilchrist*), [1981] 381
can the US courts denounce the Warsaw Convention? (*McGilchrist*), [1983] 111
carriage outside the international Conventions (*Holmes* v. *Bangladesh Biman Corp.*) (Case and comment), [1989] 267
claims against the product supplier (*McGilchrist*), [1978] 487
delivery of a passenger ticket (*McGilchrist*), [1981] 296
delivery of a passenger ticket (reprise) (*McGilchrist*), [1981] 378
denial of boarding
a perspective from the Philippines (*McGilchrist*), [1981] 518
to airline passengers (*McGilchrist*), [1981] 93
does the Warsaw Convention govern non-contractual liability? (*McGilchrist*), [1983] 685
Dutch Civil Code, a method of drafting a "code of transport" (*Schadee*), [1977] 37
four new Protocols to Warsaw Convention (*McGilchrist*), [1976] 186
hijacking (*McGilchrist*), [1978] 298
in the U.S. Court of Appeals (*Re Korean Air Lines Disaster of September 1, 1983*) (Case and comment), [1988] 150
is Warsaw Convention liability contractual in nature? (*McGilchrist*), [1979] 181
legislative history as an aid to interpretation (*McGilchrist*), [1978] 68
liability insurance claims in general aviation (*McGilchrist*), [1980] 196
limitation of liability under Warsaw Convention, further developments in US (*McGilchrist*), [1983] 308
notices in the passenger ticket (*McGilchrist*), [1982] 444
obtaining jurisdiction in US (*McGilchrist*), [1978] 609
punitive damages in aviation litigation (*McGilchrist*), [1979] 48
special contracts and the Malta Agreement (*McGilchrist*), [1977] 366
the airline as plaintiff, recent developments in US (*McGilchrist*), [1980] 328
the gold franc in the US—after *Franklin Mint* (*McGilchrist*), [1982] 281
The People ex rel. Air France v. *Louis J. Giliberto* (*McGilchrist*), [1979] 351
what is a Poincaré gold franc worth? (*McGilchrist*), [1982] 164
"when does loss mean damage?" (*McGilchrist*), [1977] 370
when may domestic carriage be characterised as international? (*McGilchrist*), [1982] 660
wilful misconduct and the Warsaw Convention (*McGilchrist*), [1977] 539
CARRIAGE BY RAIL
international, of passengers and luggage (*Hodgin*), [1976] 1
CARRIAGE BY ROAD
international, of passengers and luggage (*Hodgin*), [1976] 1
CARRIAGE BY SEA
common law liability of public carrier (*Kirkham*), [1976] 282
contract to carry passenger by (*The Mikhail Lermontov*) (Case and comment), [1990] 164
"dangerous" cargoes: the responsibilities and liabilities of the various parties (*Bulow*), [1989] 342
general average, new forms for general average security (*Hudson*), [1977] 501
identity of the carrier, the Hague Rules, Visby Rules, UNCITRAL (*Tetley*), [1977] 519
"Law of Shipping and Carriage in South Africa", The, [1974] 314
legal problems arising from transport of liquefied natural gas, [1975] 387
the significance of tort in claims in respect of (*Reynolds*), [1986] 97
"CARRIAGE OF DANGEROUS GOODS BY SEA (THE)", [1990] 151
CARRIAGE OF GOODS
freight forwarder's status from a comparative viewpoint (*Hill*), [1975] 27
future of deviation in the law (*Mills*), [1983] 587

CARRIAGE OF GOODS—*continued*
gold values in Conventions (*Costabel*), [1979] 326
international carriage of perishable goods and ATP, combined transport (*Hill*), [1977] 546
simplification of documentation and document replacement (*Gronfors*), [1976] 250
CARRIAGE OF GOODS BY LAND
carriage of dangerous goods (*Hill*), [1978] 74
CARRIAGE OF GOODS BY RAIL
law of, in South Africa, [1974] 314
CARRIAGE OF GOODS BY ROAD
CMR, contracts for the international carriage, [1986] 131
deductions from freight (*R. H. & D. International Ltd.* v. *I.A.S. Animal Air Services Ltd.*) (*Case and comment*), [1984] 199
hi-jacking in road transport law (*Quick Smith*), [1974] 11
integration of CMR Rules in Swedish domestic regulations (*Petersson and Wetter*), [1978] 567
law of, in South Africa, [1974] 314
CARRIAGE OF GOODS BY ROAD (CMR)
an outline and its history (*Donald*), [1975] 420
aspects of the limitation of actions under (*Hardingham*), [1979] 362
case update (*Glass*), [1982] 173
CMR and hired trailers (*Glass*), [1981] 384
Continental case law, loss by theft (*Wijffels*), [1977] 30
contractual relationship between shipper, forwarder and carrier by road (*Hill*), [1975] 137
damages under CMR, the decision of the House of Lords (*Hardingham*), [1978] 51
delay provisions in combined transport (*Hardingham*), [1979] 193
interpretation in the English courts (*Hill*), [1977] 212
safeguarding the parties' interests (*Hardingham*), [1981] 306
the time bar regulations in the Convention (*Wetter*), 504
CARRIAGE OF GOODS BY SEA
insurance of household goods shipments (*Rossmere*), [1976] 173
Payne & Ivamy's, [1986] 136
"Payne & Ivamy's Carriage of Goods by Sea", [1980] 73
the Italian Constitutional Court and the limits on the liability of the carrier of goods by sea (Case and comment), [1988] 273
the new Act in South Africa (*Staniland*), [1987] 305
"CARRIAGE OF GOODS BY SEA", [1988] 258
CARRIAGE OF GOODS BY SEA ACT
customary reduction of COGSA liability (*Sun Oil Co.* v. *Carlisle*) (Case and comment), [1986] 436
CARRIAGE OF GOODS BY SEA ACT 1971
and sea waybills (*The European Enterprise*) (Case and comment), [1989] 403
CARRIER
common law liability of public carrier by sea (*Kirkham*), [1976] 282
contractual relationship between shipper, forwarder and carrier by road (*Hill*), [1975] 137
forwarding and sub-contracting complications (*Hill*), [1976] 63
the Italian Constitutional Court and the limits on the liability of the carrier of goods by sea (Case and comment), [1988] 273
CASE LAW
Continental, loss by theft, CMR (*Wijffels*), [1977] 30
"CASEBOOK ON AGENCY" (3rd Edn.), [1988] 271
"CASEBOOK ON CARRIAGE BY SEA", [1986] 415
"CASEBOOK ON PARTNERSHIP", A, [1983] 486
"CASEBOOK ON SALE OF GOODS" (5th Edn.), [1988] 271
"CASEBOOK ON SHIPPING LAW" (4th Edn.), [1988] 271
CASES, COLLISION—JUDGMENTS AND DIAGRAMS, [1985] 141
"CASES AND MATERIALS ON ADMIRALTY" (2nd Edn.), [1990] 151
"CASES AND MATERIALS ON THE LAW OF INTERNATIONAL TRADE", [1982] 160
CENTROCON, ARBITRATION CLAUSE
an appreciation of *The Astraea* and *The Evje* cases (*Hudson*), [1974] 301
"CHALMERS' SALE OF GOODS", [1982] 278
"CHANGES IN THE WORLD SHIPPING ENVIRONMENTS AND COUNTER-STRATEGIES TOWARD THE YEAR 2000", [1990] 564

CHAPS [1988]
transfer of funds (*Geva*), [1988] 477
CHARGE CARDS [1989]
supply of goods and charge cards (*Re Charge Card Services Ltd.*) (Case and comment), [1989] 22
CHARGES
fixed and floating (*Re Brightlife Ltd.*) (Case and comment), [1987] 147
"CHARLESWORTH AND CAIN COMPANY LAW", [1978] 296
CHARTERER (TIME)
third party liability in Japan (*Hosoi*), [1985] 254
CHARTERERS
arrest of ships owned by (*Tabbush*), [1982] 585
authority to sign bills of lading under standard time charter terms (*Pritchett*), [1980] 21
warranty of safe port/berth, master's negligence (*Herman and Goldman*), [1983] 615
"CHARTERERS' LIABILITY INSURANCE", [1987] 373
"CHARTERERS' LIABILITY INSURANCE", [1988] 548
CHARTERING
demurrage, "*quot homines tot sententiae*" (*Ventris*), [1977] 533
fundamental breach of charterparty (*Clarke*), [1978] 472
seaworthiness in time charters (*Clarke*), [1977] 493
some NYPE time charter problems (*Mabbs*), [1978] 456
"time lost in waiting for berth to count as . . . laytime" (*Costabel*), [1975] 150
CHARTERPARTIES
"alongside vessels or lighters reachable on her arrival" (*Ventris*), [1980] 174
comparative study of South African, English and American law, [1984] 135
demurrage, "*quot homines tot sententiae*" (*Ventris*), [1977] 533
disputes, withdrawals, repudiation, frustration (*Barclay*), [1975] 412
fixed "subject to details" (*Ball*), [1984] 250
insurance covenants in leases and insurance provisions in (Case and comment), [1986] 149
late payment of hire, when payment is made (*Ryder*), [1977] 174
New York arbitration awards, withdrawals from charter upon late payment (*Murray*), [1976] 164
orders under (*The Kanchenjunga*) (Case and comment), [1989] 415
orders under (*The Kanchenjunga*; *The Epaphus*) (Case and comment), [1987] 408
references to charterparties in bills of lading (*Mankabady*), [1974] 53
Scrutton on, [1985] 513
sub details (*The Junior K*) (case and comment [1988] 439
tanker voyage charterparties, need for modernisation (*Ventris*), [1974] 44
the off-hire clause in the New York Produce Exchange time charterparty (*Davies*), [1990] 107
time charter, doctrine of overlap-underlap in US courts (*Besman*), [1974] 49
time charters, speed and consumption warranties (*Barclay*), [1974] 13
"time lost in waiting for berth to count as . . . laytime" (*Costabel*), [1975] 150
"time lost waiting for berth", some considerations of *The Johanna Oldendorff* and *The Loucas N* cases (*Davies*), [1974] 1
"CHARTERPARTIES, A COMPARATIVE STUDY OF SOUTH AFRICAN, ENGLISH AND AMERICAN LAW", [1984] 135
CHARTERPARTIES (TIME)
default in payment of hire (Case and comment), [1986] 1
CHARTERPARTY
construction, arbitration appeals (*The Antaios*) (*Case and comment*), [1984] 547
fixtures "subject details" (*Debattista*), [1985] 241
fundamental breach of (*Clarke*), [1978] 472
incorporation of terms (*The Varenna*) (*Case and comment*), [1984] 194
CHARTERPARTY (TIME)
Intertanktime (*Michelet*), [1978] 287
CHARTERS
New York arbitrations and pre-hearing discovery (*Kuffler*), [1978] 557
tanker voyage charterparties, need for modernisation (*Ventris*), [1974] 44
time, doctrine of overlap-underlap in US courts (*Besman*), [1974] 49
"time lost in waiting for berth to count as . . . laytime" (*Costabel*), [1975] 150
CHARTERS (TIME)
speed and consumption warranties (*Barclay*), [1974] 13

CHATTEL LEASE
measuring damages for breach of: Supreme Court of Canada liberalizes the rules (*Langille* v. *Keneric Tractor Sales Ltd.*) (Case and comment), [1988] 276
CHEQUES
wrongful dishonour of: general or special damages (*Rae* v. *Yorkshire Bank Plc*) (Case and comment), [1988] 138
"CHERNOBYL: LAW AND COMMUNICATION", [1990] 568
"CHESHIRE, FIFOOT & FURMSTON'S LAW OF CONTRACT" (11th Edn.), [1987] 387
"CHESHIRE & NORTH'S PRIVATE INTERNATIONAL LAW" (11th Edn.), [1989] 385
CHINA
Chinese Supreme Court: the responses to questions arising out of the application of the Foreign Economic Contract Law of 19 October 1987 (*Guojian and Samuel*), [1989] 476
CHINA (PEOPLE'S REPUBLIC OF)
general average adjustment and arbitration in (*Hudson*), [1976] 135
maritime arbitration in (*Shum*), [1990] 114
resolution of collision claims in (*Griggs*), [1979] 138
the Peking Adjustment Rules, [1976] 141
"CHITTY ON CONTRACTS" (26th Edn.), [1990] 555
CHOICE OF LAW CLAUSES
and forum, arbitration, and Hague-Visby Rules (*Jackson*), [1980] 159
"CHORLEY & GILES' SHIPPING LAW", [1988] 543
C.I.F.
damages for breach of a c.i.f. contract (*Treitel*), [1988] 457
"C.I.F. AND F.O.B. CONTRACTS", [1985] 398
C.I.F. CONTRACTS
out-turn clauses in, in the oil trade (*Lightburn and Nienaber*), [1987] 177
C.I.F. SALES
rights of rejection under (*Treitel*), [1984] 565
"CITY DIRECTORY 1988 (THE)", [1988] 549
"CIVIL JURISDICTION AND ENFORCEMENT OF FOREIGN JUDGMENTS", [1988] 535
CIVIL JURISDICTION AND JUDGMENTS
recent decisions of the European Court (*Stone*), [1988] 383
"CIVIL JURISDICTION AND JUDGMENTS", [1984] 511
CIVIL JURISDICTION AND JUDGMENTS ACT 1982
lis alibi pendens and *forum non conveniens* in collision actions (*Blackburn*), [1988] 91
CIVIL JURISDICTION AND JUDGMENTS ACT 1982, THE
(Information), [1987] 138
"CIVIL JURISDICTION AND JUDGMENTS ACT 1982", THE, [1984] 320
"CIVIL JURISDICTION IN SCOTLAND", [1990] 146
CIVIL LAW
development of and common law, the contrasts (*Jolowicz*), [1982] 87
CIVIL LIABILITY
Royal Commission on, and compensation for personal injury (The Pearson Report), [1978] 399
CIVIL LIABILITY PROCEEDINGS
relevance of "formal investigation" findings (*The European Gateway*) (Case and comment), [1986] 417
"CIVIL LIABILITY STATUTES", [1987] 249
CLAIMS
carriage by air, against the product supplier (*McGilchrist*), [1978] 487
carriage by sea, the significance of tort in respect of (*Reynolds*), [1986] 97
Convention on limitation of liability for maritime, [1977] 73
demurrage, "non-maritime" (*Ventris*), [1984] 657
foreign currency, and the English courts (*Isaacs*), [1977] 356
hull, UNCTAD report (*Goodacre*), [1979] 315
insurance, and consequential loss, [1978] 67
marine cargo claims, identity of the carrier (*Tetley*), [1977] 519
"Marine Cargo Claims", [1978] 627
marine collision, set-off in (*Knott*), [1981] 269
"Marine Insurance Claims", [1975] 308
mistaken settlements of disputable claims (*Andrews*), [1989] 431
resolution of collision claims in China (*Griggs*), [1979] 138

CLAIMS—*continued*
settlement between Iran and US (*Amin*), [1983] 248
CLAIMS (INSURANCE)
arrest of ships on (*Case and comment*), [1985] 173
CLAUSES
demise clause in US courts (*Pritchett*), [1980] 387
demurrage (Oilvoy) (*Textor*), [1985] 343
exclusion, negligence (*Palmer*), [1983] 557
exclusion and limitation (*Darlington Futures Ltd.* v. *Delco Australia Pty. Ltd*) (Case and comment), [1987] 165
floating choice of law clauses (*Beck*), [1987] 523
jurisdiction clauses, the validity of "floating" choice of law (*Briggs*), [1986] 508
penalties and forfeiture: contractual remedies specified by the parties (*Jobson* v. *Johnson*) (Case and comment), [1990] 158
Romalpa, further developments (*Davies*), [1984] 280
the construction of *force majeure* clauses and self-induced frustration (*The Super Servant Two*) (Case and comment), [1990] 153
the Himalaya Clause (*Powles*), [1979] 331
the new Institute Cargo Clauses (*George*), [1986] 438
the off-hire clause in the New York Produce Exchange time charterparty (*Davies*), [1990] 107
CLAUSES, TITLE
reservation of (*Davies*), [1984] 49
CLAUSES (EXCLUSION)
after the Unfair Contract Terms Act, [1978] 297
CLUBS, P & I
(*Coghlin*), [1984] 403
CMI CONFERENCE 1977
report of proceedings, [1978] 14
CMR
an outline and its history (*Donald*), [1975] 420
and hired trailers (*Glass*), [1981] 384
aspects of the limitation of actions under (*Hardingham*), [1979] 362
case update (*Glass*), [1982] 173
combined transport, actions against successive carriers under (*Hardingham*), [1978] 499
Continental case law, loss by theft (*Wijffels*), [1977] 30
contracts for the international carriage of goods by road, [1986] 131
contractual relationship between shipper, forwarder and carrier by road (*Hill*), [1975] 137
damages under, the decision of the House of Lords (*Hardingham*), [1978] 51
delay provisions in combined transport (*Hardingham*), [1979] 193
integration of Rules in Swedish domestic road transportation regulations (*Petersson and Wetter*), [1978] 567
"International Carriage of Goods by Road", [1983] 681
interpretation of in the English courts (*Hill*), [1977] 212
putting practice into theory (*Glass*), [1984] 30
safeguarding the parties' interests (*Hardingham*), [1981] 306
the time bar regulations in the Convention (*Wetter*), [1979] 504
"CMR: CONTRACTS FOR THE INTERNATIONAL CARRIAGE OF GOODS BY ROAD", [1986] 131
COASTAL LIMITS
of England (*Gibson*), [1978] 616
COGSA
customary reduction of liability (*Sun Oil Co.* v. *Carlisle*) (Case and comment), [1986] 436
"COLLECTION OF INTERNATIONAL CONCESSIONS AND RELATED INSTRUMENTS, A", [1983] 105
COLLISION AT SEA
coming into force of International Regulations for Preventing Collisions at Sea 1972 (*Mankabady*), [1977] 330
"COLLISION AT SEA—A GUIDE TO THE LEGAL CONSEQUENCES", [1978] 630
COLLISION CASES 1974
(*Harley*), [1975] 156
"COLLISION CASES—JUDGMENTS AND DIAGRAMS", [1985] 141

COLLISION CLAIMS
resolution of in China (*Griggs*), [1979] 138
COLLISION (MARINE)
set-off in collision claims (*Knott*), [1981] 269
"COLLISION REGULATIONS", [1985] 141
COLLISION REGULATIONS (THE) 1972
(*Harley*), [1977] 178
in question (*Kemp*), [1979] 347
COMBINED TRANSPORT
actions against successive carriers under CMR (*Hardingham*), [1978] 499
aspects of the limitation of actions under CMR (*Hardingham*), [1979] 362
delay provisions of CMR (*Hardingham*), [1979] 193
freight liner conditions (*Hill*), [1977] 88
ICC Uniform Rules (*Wheble*), [1976] 145, 148
in perspective, ICC Rules for a combined transport document (*McGilchrist*), [1974] 25
international carriage of perishable goods and ATP (*Hill*), [1977] 546
interpretation of CMR in the English courts (*Hill*), [1977] 212
text of ICC Uniform Rules, [1974] 29
the carriage of dangerous goods by land (*Hill*), [1978] 74
the time bar regulations in the CMR Convention (*Wetter*), [1979] 504
to and from the US (*Ullman*), [1976] 157
to Europe (*Hill*), [1975] 303
warehousing and the sub-contractor (*Hill*), [1977] 373
COMFORT LETTERS
"a very comfortable comfort letter" (*Kleinwort Benson Ltd.* v. *Malaysia Mining Corp. Bhd.*) (Case and comment), [1988] 290
"COMMENCEMENT OF LAYTIME", [1989] 122
"COMMENTARIES ON TANKER VOYAGE CHARTERPARTIES", [1990] 565
"COMMERCIAL AGREEMENTS AND COMPETITION LAW: PRACTICE AND PROCEDURE IN THE UK AND EEC", [1987] 378
COMMERCIAL ARBITRATION
Admiralty security and the arbitral process (*Thomas*), [1983] 495
costs, discretion and issues of technical misconduct (*Thomas*), [1982] 288
injunctive jurisdiction of Commercial Court (*Thomas*), [1981] 389
international agreements, enforcement of foreign arbitral awards (*Thomas*), [1981] 17
judge-arbitrators (*Thomas*), [1983] 120
legal remedies for dilatoriness (*Thomas*), [1983] 315
power of court to extend time for commencing proceedings (*Thomas*), [1981] 529
removal of arbitrators by the court (*Thomas*), [1982] 186
restraining concurrent foreign legal proceedings (*Thomas*), [1983] 692
security for costs in (*Thomas*), [1982] 463
the vexed issue of interest awards (*Thomas*), [1982] 667
COMMERCIAL ARBITRATION BILL 1984
New South Wales (*Scotford*), [1985] 136
"COMMERCIAL ARBITRATION IN THE ARAB MIDDLE EAST", [1988] 246
"COMMERCIAL BUSINESS AND TRADE LAWS (UK)", [1982] 162
COMMERCIAL CONTRACTS
and the Commercial Court (*Goff*), [1984] 382
COMMERCIAL COURT, THE
commercial contracts and (*Goff*), [1984] 382
(Information), [1987] 136
practice and procedure of, [1984] 322
COMMERCIAL CRIME
international, Commonwealth perspective (*Rider*), [1985] 217
"COMMERCIAL DISPUTES SETTLEMENT IN CHINA", [1988] 546
COMMERCIAL JUDGMENTS
and awards, recognition of in the Commonwealth, [1986] 129
COMMERCIAL LAW
in Israel (*Naschitz*), [1977] 84
"COMMERCIAL LAW IN A CHANGING ECONOMIC CLIMATE", [1982] 279

"COMMERCIAL LAW IN THE ARAB MIDDLE EAST: THE GULF STATES", [1990] 119
"COMMERCIAL LAW IN THE GULF STATES", [1985] 279
"COMMERCIAL LAW OF SINGAPORE", [1987] 134
"COMMERCIAL LITIGATION: PRE-EMPTIVE REMEDIES", [1988] 403
COMMERCIAL NEGLIGENCE
(*Dawson*), [1983] 209
COMMERCIAL TRANSACTIONS
payment obligations in, [1984] 327
COMMODITIES
commercial arbitration in commodity trades (*Mackie*), [1976] 278
security over, equitable pledges and conversion (*Palmer*), [1986] 218
COMMON CARRIERS
control over agreements and practices in US, Federal Maritime Commission, antitrust exemption in Shipping Act 1916 (*Meade*), [1976] 401
COMMON LAW
and oil pollution (*Gibson*), [1979] 498
and sovereign immunity (*Lewis*), [1979] 460
Biographical Dictionary of, [1984] 512
development of and civil law, the contrasts (*Jolowicz*), [1982] 87
liability of public carrier by sea (*Kirkham*), [1976] 282
"no fault" in America (*Owles*), [1976] 396
"COMMON LAW OF OBLIGATIONS (THE)", [1990] 432
"COMMON LAW OF RESTRAINT OF TRADE (THE): A LEGAL AND ECONOMIC ANALYSIS", [1989] 126
"COMMON MARITIME ADVENTURE" (York-Antwerp Rules 1974)
not such a common adventure (*The Alppi* v. *The Bjorn Eskil*) (Case and comment), [1990] 173
COMMONWEALTH
perspective on combating international commercial crime (*Rider*), [1985] 217
COMPANIES
essential law, finance, takeovers and mergers, [1980] 212
insolvency, [1980] 212
receiver/contractor relationships (*Tugendhat*), [1974] 39
COMPANIES ACT 1948
s. 95 (Case and comment), [1986] 1
COMPANIES ACT 1985
registration of retention of title clauses under s. 395 (*E. Pfeiffer Weinkellerei-Weineinkauf G.m.b.H. & Co.* v. *Arbuthnot Factors Ltd.*) (Case and comment), [1988] 140
section 459—a code of conduct for the quasi-partnership? (*Hannigan*), [1988] 60
s. 395 (Case and comment), [1986] 1
COMPANIES ACT 1989 (THE)
(Case and comment), [1990] 28
COMPANIES ACTS
another in the series (*Owles*), [1980] 315
the courts and the Companies Acts: the judicial contribution to company law (*Milman*), [1990] 401
COMPANY DIRECTOR
liability of, as seen by American courts (*Owles*), [1978] 422
COMPANY DIRECTORS
disqualifying of (*Hannigan*), [1987] 188
COMPANY LAW
"Charlesworth and Cain Company Law", [1978] 296
in Great Britain, [1983] 301
registration of company charges: the new law (*McCormack*), [1990] 520
the courts and the Companies Acts: the judicial contribution to company law (*Milman*), [1990] 401
true and fair revisited (*Evans*), [1990] 255
wrongful trading (*Oditah*), [1990] 205
"COMPANY LAW AND CAPITALISM", [1978] 65
"COMPANY LAW IN GREAT BRITAIN", [1983] 301
COMPARATIVE LAW
legal relations of stevedores in (*Cigoj*), [1975] 296
"COMPARATIVE LAW OF MONOPOLIES", [1990] 439

COMPENSATION
for pollution damage by ships, report on international conference (*Popp*), [1985] 118
COMPETITION LAW
an introduction to UK's, [1978] 505
"COMPETITION LAW : ANTITRUST POLICY IN UK AND EEC", [1985] 276
"COMPETITION LAW", [1986] 548
COMPULSORY PILOTAGE
"a jurisdictional collision" (*Gibson*), [1979] 356
COMPUTERS
the lawyer and the computer (*Stephens*), [1975] 166
"CONCEPT AND PRACTICE", [1990] 152
CONDITIONS
of towage, and fundamental breach (*Lux*), [1979] 148
CONDITIONS OF CARRIAGE
combined transport (*Hill*), [1977] 88
CONFERENCE (CMI)
report of proceedings, [1978] 14
CONFERENCE LINES
new lines for (*Rose*), [1982] 636
CONFERENCE ON THE LAW OF THE SEA (UN)
third session, report on (*Lake*), [1975] 383
CONFERENCES
liner, anti-trust implications of (*McIntosh*), [1980] 139
shipping, [1984] 325
CONFLICT OF LAWS
maritime securities and, some problems (*Tettenborn*), [1980] 404
multi-party insurances and the conflict of laws (*The Irish Rowan*) (Case and comment), [1989] 389
reinsurance, brokers and the conflict of laws (*Forsikringsaktieselskapet Vesta* v. *Butcher*) (Case and comment), [1988] 5
time limitation (*Stone*), [1985] 497
"CONFLICT OF LAWS", [1990] 282
"CONFLICT OF LAWS IN THE EUROPEAN COMMUNITY", [1988] 535
"CONFLICTS OF INTEREST IN THE CHANGING FINANCIAL WORLD", [1989] 128
CONFUSION
anticipating confusion (*Sanko Steamship Co. Ltd.* v. *Eacom Timber Sales Ltd.* (*The Sanko Iris and Sanko Venus*)) (Case and comment), [1988] 21
"CONSEQUENTIAL LOSS AND INSURANCE CLAIMS", [1978] 67
CONSERVATION
marine, and right of navigation (*Gibson*), [1980] 203
CONSIGNMENT NOTE
simplification of documentation and document replacement (*Gronfors*), [1976] 250
CONSORTIUM
and related operations in the UK (*Wooldridge*), [1978] 427
CONSTRUCTION
problems at Lloyd's (*Christian*), [1982] 152
CONSTRUCTIVE TOTAL LOSS
rights and liabilities of underwriters on payment of (*Hudson*), [1978] 1
CONSUMER CREDIT ACT 1974, THE
(*Goode*), [1974] 264
"CONSUMER CREDIT LAW", [1990] 269
"CONSUMER LAW STATUTES", [1987] 248
CONSUMER PROTECTION
current legislation in Finland (*Sevon*), [1978] 592
CONSUMER PROTECTION ACT 1987
maritime consumers? (*Tettenborn*), [1988] 211
CONSUMERS
maritime consumers?—the Consumer Protection Act and shipping law (*Tettenborn*), [1988] 211
"CONSUMERS AND THE LAW", [1986] 553
"CONTAINERISATION IN THE EIGHTIES", [1990] 152

CONTAINERS
supplied to a ship for her operation? (*The River Rina*) (Case and comment), [1988] 423
the transport of goods in refrigerated: an Australian perspective (*Springall*), [1987] 216
"CONTAINERS: CONDITIONS, LAW AND PRACTICE OF CARRIAGE AND USE", [1990] 291
CONTAMINATION
liability for mixed and refined cargoes shipped in distribution tankers (*Cameron*), [1975] 281
"CONTEMPORARY PROBLEMS IN INTERNATIONAL ARBITRATION", [1990] 142
CONTRACT
breach of, damages on rescission for (*Lombard North Central Plc* v. *Butterworth*) (Case and comment), [1987] 143
damages for breach of a c.i.f. contract (*Treitel*), [1988] 457
illegality of, insurance of goods (*Euro-Diam Ltd.* v. *Bathurst*) (Case and comment), [1988] 124
mental distress damages in, decade of change (*Burrows*), [1984] 119
mistake in (*Associated Japanese Bank (International) Ltd.* v. *Credit du Nord S.A.*) (Case and comment), [1988] 300
more points on the *Brandt* v. *Liverpool* contract (*The Aramis*) (Case and comment), [1987] 255
of affreightment (*Crump*), [1985] 19
privity of contract in Australia: the beginning of the end? (*Trident General Insurance Co. Ltd.* v. *McNiece Bros. Pty. Ltd.*) (Case and comment), [1989] 139
proper law of a *Brandt* v. *Liverpool* contract (*The Elli 2*) (*Case and comment*), [1985] 188
restitutionary damages for breach of (*Birks*), [1987] 421
Unfair Contract Terms Act 1977, The (*Reynolds*), [1978] 201, 211
"CONTRACT CASES AND MATERIALS", [1987] 239
CONTRACT LAW
the higher altitudes (*Carter*), [1989] 81
"CONTRACT LAW IN AUSTRALIA", [1988] 113
"CONTRACT LAW IN PERSPECTIVE", [1987] 239
"CONTRACT LAW TODAY (ANGLO-FRENCH COMPARISONS)", [1990] 556
CONTRACT STATUTES, THE
New Zealand (*Dawson*), [1985] 42
CONTRACT TERMS
standard, new law on in Germany (*von Marschall*), [1979] 278
CONTRACTOR
relationship with receiver (*Tugendhat*), [1974] 39
CONTRACTS
admiralty jurisdiction over agency contracts (*Peralta Shipping Corp.* v. *Smith & Johnson Corp.*) (Case and comment), [1986] 12
bills of lading and implied contracts (*Treitel*), [1989] 162
certainty in, House of Lords, *Hongkong Fir* revisited (*Applebey and Meisel*), [1982] 592
C.I.F. and F.O.B., [1985] 398
commercial, and the Commercial Court (*Goff*), [1984] 382
commodity futures contracts and the Gaming Act (*Chaikin and Moher*), [1986] 390
contract to carry passenger by sea (*The Mikhail Lermontov*) (Case and comment), [1990] 164
exchange, and the international sale of goods (*Corbett*), [1977] 310
f.o.b. contracts: substitution of vessels (*Cargill U.K. Ltd.* v. *Continental U.K. Ltd.*) (Case and comment), [1990]] 465
for supply of services under 1982 Act (*Murdoch*), [1983] 652
for the international carriage of goods by road, [1986] 131
for the supply of services in Australia (*Case and comment*), [1984] 557
formation and repudiation by international telex (*Lewis*), [1980] 433
fundamental breach of duty (*Rose*), [1980] 396
grain, and arbitration, [1984] 679
impracticability of performance, is it grounds for breach? (*Arnold*), [1977] 346
insurance
materiality in (*Brooke*), [1985] 437
problems in defining (*Hodgin*), [1980] 14
law of commercial contracts in Iran (*Amin*), [1982] 416
limitation on relief for affirmed (*The Alaskan Trader (No. 2)*) (*Case and comment*), [1984] 378
Lloyd's Open Form and contractual remedies (*Gaskell*), [1986] 306
marine insurance, UNCTAD report (*Goodacre*), [1979] 315
of hire and the Supply of Goods and Services Act 1982 (*Palmer*), [1983] 377

CONTRACTS—*continued*
penalties and forfeiture: contractual remedies specified by the parties (*Jobson* v. *Johnson*) (Case and comment), [1990] 158
penalties and the financial contract (*Esanda Finance Corp.* v. *Plessnig*) (Case and comment), [1990] 16
sale of goods, "of soya beans, circles and strings" (*Powles*), [1978] 306
services rendered under ineffective contracts (*Carter*), [1990] 495
shipbuilding, legal problems associated with (*Mankabady*), [1978] 477
shipbuilding (*Clarke*), [1981] 234
the formation of international contracts (*Briggs*), [1990] 192
third party rights on insurance contracts (*Trident General Insurance Co. Ltd.* v. *McNiece Bros. Pty. Ltd.*) (Case and comment), [1987] 258
towage, and fundamental breach (*Lux*), [1979] 148
with consignees and indorsees (*Todd*), [1984] 476
CONTRACTUAL OBLIGATIONS
EEC Convention on law applicable (*Williams*), [1981] 250
CONTRIBUTION
and double insurance (*Hodgin*), [1977] 515
CONTRIBUTORY NEGLIGENCE
a viable defence for auditors? (*Marshall and Beltrami*), [1990] 416
contributory negligence in contract—again (*Forsikringsaktieselskapet Vesta* v. *Butcher*) (Case and comment), [1987] 10
"CONTROL OF EXCLUSION CLAUSES IN ENGLAND AND INDIA", [1990] 284
"CONTROL OF MARINE POLLUTION IN INTERNATIONAL LAW", [1987] 375
"CONVENIOS INTERNACIONALES MARITIMOS", [1987] 381
CONVENTION
International
for the prevention of pollution from ships 1973, [1974] 232
for the reciprocal recognition and enforcement of judgments in civil and commercial matters, [1974] 109
International Convention on the Limitation Period in the International Sale of Goods, [1975] 105
the European Judgments Convention, maritime claims (*Brice*), [1987] 281
United Nations Convention on Conditions for Registration of Ships (*Sturmey*), [1987] 97
CONVENTION ON LIMITATION OF LIABILITY FOR MARITIME CLAIMS 1976, [1977] 73
CONVENTIONS
carriage by air outside the international Conventions (*Holmes* v. *Bangladesh Biman Corp.*) (Case and comment), [1989] 267
gold values in carriage of goods (*Costabel*), [1979] 326
the enactment of the 1989 Salvage Convention in English law: policy issues (Case and comment), [1990] 352
the new Salvage Convention: green seas and grey areas (*Brice, Q.C.*), [1990] 32
The Salvage Convention 1989—who pays? (Case and comment), [1989] 416
COPYRIGHT
(*Haines*), [1974] 289
COUNTERCLAIM
and set-off—the necessary connection (*Dole Dried Fruit and Nut Co.* v. *Trustin Kerwood Ltd.*) (Case and comment), [1990] 471
"COUNTRY RISK ANALYSIS", [1986] 553
COURT, THE COMMERCIAL
and commercial contracts (*Goff*), [1984] 382
COURT COSTS
expenses in *custodia legis* and attorney's fees (*Tetley*), [1984] 1
COURTS
the courts and the Companies Acts: the judicial contribution to company law (*Milman*), [1990] 401
CRAWFORD & FALCONBRIDGE: BANKING AND BILLS OF EXCHANGE" (8th Edn.), [1988] 108
CREDITS, BANKERS' DOCUMENTARY, [1985] 273
CRIME
international commercial, Commonwealth perspective (*Rider*), [1985] 217
on board foreign ships on high seas, jurisdiction of English courts (*Bentil*), [1983] 60
piracy, "the current crime"(*Wiener*), [1979] 469

CRIME—*continued*
profits of and their recovery, [1985] 401
CRIMINAL LIABILITY
of ships' masters (*Taylor*), [1981] 499
CROWN, THE
liability of, negligence by customs officials, imported goods (*Zien* v. *The Queen*) (Case and comment), [1986] 430
C.T.I. v. *OCEANUS*
chipping away at—(*Barclay Holdings (Australia) Pty. Ltd.* v. *British National Ins. Co. Ltd.*) (Case and comment), [1988] 30
CURRENCY
foreign, judgments (*Powles*), [1979] 485
CUSTODIA LEGIS
expenses in, court costs and attorney's fees (*Tetley*), [1984] 1
CUSTOMS
negligence by officials, imported goods, liability of the Crown (*Zien* v. *The Queen*) (Case and comment), [1986] 430
CUSTOMS AND EXCISE
appointment of Customs ports (*Gibson*), [1981] 303
DAMAGE
cargo, by fire (*Bauer*), [1982] 1
"damage done by any ship", Admiralty Court Act 1861, Administration of Justice Act 1956 (*Clarke*), [1976] 412
oil pollution, maritime claims, London Convention (1976) (*Selvig*), [1979] 21
P pays X for the physical damage due to D's negligence (*The Esso Bernicia*) (Case and comment), [1989] 1
pollution
by ships, liability and compensation report on international conference (*Popp*), [1985] 118
new definition of (*Brodecki*), [1985] 382
to cargo, actions in tort (*Case and comment*), [1985] 1
to goods in transit, how to recover for loss, [1980] 344
"when does loss mean damage?", carriage by air (*McGilchrist*), [1977] 370
DAMAGES
against insurers in US, policy disputes (*Barrett*), [1980] 131
and the late payer (*The Lips*) (Case and comment), [1987] 414
assessable against marine insurers (*Allen*), [1976] 258
for breach of a c.i.f contract (*Treitel*), [1988] 457
"how remote can you get?"(*Gibson*), [1978] 497
mental distress, decade of change (*Burrows*), [1984] 119
restitutionary damages for breach of contract (*Birks*), [1987] 421
"too remote" (*Trappe*), [1982] 427
under CMR, decision of the House of Lords (*Hardingham*), [1978] 51
"DAMAGES RECOVERABLE IN MARITIME MATTERS", [1985] 141
"DANGEROUS" CARGOES
the responsibilities and liabilities of the various parties (*Bulow*), [1989] 342
DANGEROUS GOODS
the carriage of by land, combined transport (*Hill*), [1978] 74
DATA PROTECTION ACT 1984, THE
(*Austin*), [1984] 663
DEATH
wrongful, maritime (*Bodden* v. *American Offshore Inc.*) (*Fries*), [1984] 295
DEBENTURE HOLDERS
and judgment creditors, problems of priority (*Hare and Milman*), [1982] 57
DEBT
late payment of (*La Pintada*) (*Case and comment*), [1984] 365
DEBTORS
examination of judgment debtors as to their assets abroad: courts' powers and jurisdiction (*Kaye*), [1989] 465
"DEBTORS AND CREDITORS (A SOCIO-LEGAL PERSPECTIVE)", [1988] 103
DEBTS
trade, factoring of, its framework of law (*Salinger*), [1977] 184

DECK STOWAGE
extension of time, and the time bar (*Kenya Railways* v. *Antares Pte. Ltd.* (*The Antares*)) (Case and comment), [1987] 146
DEFECTIVE SHIP
liability for (*Coltman* v. *Bibby Tankers Ltd.* (*The Derbyshire*)) (Case and comment), [1988] 123
DELAY
uncollected goods: the penalties of delay (*Palmer*), [1987] 43
DELIMITATION
maritime boundary, [1985] 144
of sea fisheries districts (*Gibson*), [1978] 495
DELIVERY ORDERS
ship's (*Teare*), [1976] 29
DEMISE CLAUSE
in American courts (*Pritchett*), [1980] 387
the, and the Hague Rules (*Kaleej International Pty. Ltd.* v. *Gulf Shipping Lines Ltd.*; *Carling O'Keefe Breweries of Canada Ltd.* v. *C.N. Marine Inc.* (*The Newfoundland Coast*) (Case and comment), [1987] 259
the demise clause again (*Carling O'Keefe Breweries of Canada* v. *C.N. Marine Inc.* (*The Newfoundland Coast*) (Case and comment), [1990] 493
The Jalamohan (Case and comment), [1988] 285
DEMURRAGE
"*quot homines tot sententiae*" (*Ventris*), [1977] 533
charterparties, "*stare decisis et non quieta movere*" (*Arnold*), [1977] 24
claims, "non-maritime" (*Ventris*), [1984] 657
Oilvoy clauses (*Textor*), [1985] 343
"DEVELOPMENT OF CONSUMER LAW AND POLICY", THE, [1984] 685
DICTIONARY
Biographical of the Common Law, [1984] 512
"DICTIONARY OF INSURANCE LAW", [1982] 277
"DICTIONARY OF SHIPPING LAW", [1986] 414
"DICTIONARY OF SHIPPING TERMS", [1986] 555
"DICTIONARY OF SHIPPING TERMS: ITALIAN-ENGLISH AND ENGLISH-ITALIAN", [1988] 549
"DICTIONARY OF SHIPPING TERMS: SPANISH-ENGLISH AND ENGLISH-SPANISH", [1988] 549
DIRECT FUNDS TRANSFERS
the role of correspondent banks in direct funds transfers (*Vroegop*), [1990] 547
DIRECTORS
disqualifying company directors (*Hannigan*), [1987] 188
DISCLOSURE
of criminal information to insurers (*Clarke*), [1984] 100
requirements imposed under US law on arbitrators in maritime arbitrations (*Meade*), [1975] 399
the duty of (*La Banque Financière* v. *Westgate* (*The Good Luck*)) (Case and comment), [1989] 251
the insurer's duties of good faith and disclosure (*The Good Luck*) (Case and comment), [1988] 27
DOCK WORK
(*Gordon*), [1975] 142
DOCUMENTARY CREDITS
ICC Code of Practice (*Wheble*), [1976] 8
rules for, [1976] 15
UCP, effect of incorporation; question of leave to defend action to enforce documentary credit (*Forestal Mimosa Ltd.* v. *Oriental Credit Ltd.*; *Esal* (*Commodities*) *Ltd.* v. *Oriental Credit Ltd.*) (Case and comment), [1986] 420
DOCUMENTARY CREDITS, BANKERS', [1985] 273
DOCUMENTS
rejection of (*Gill & Duffus S.A.* v. *Berger & Co. Inc.*) (*Case and comment*), [1984] 191
service of in shipping under Greek law (*Timagenis*), [1984] 275
short form and waybills, a lawyer's view (*Williams*), [1979] 297
"DOCUMENTS ON THE INTERNATIONAL COURT OF JUSTICE", [1980] 72
"DOUBLE TAXATION RELIEF FOR SHIPPING", [1989] 226
"DROIT DES TRANSPORTS", [1978] 632

"DROIT MARITIME PRECIS", [1980] 208
DUE DILIGENCE
general average, defences and disputes (*Hudson*), [1976] 416
DURESS
the travails of duress (*Crescendo Management* v. *Westpac Banking*; *Williams* v. *Roffey Bros.*; *The Evia Luck (No. 2)*) (Case and comment), [1990] 342
DUTCH CIVIL CODE
a method of drafting a "code of transport" (*Schadee*), [1977] 37
DUTIES OF CONFIDENCE AND LOYALTY
International Corona Services v. *Lac Minerals* (Case and comment), [1990] 4
DUTY
the duty of disclosure (*La Banque Financière* v. *Westgate* (*The Good Luck*)) (Case and comment), [1989] 251
DUTY OF CARE
insurance brokers (*Glass*), [1978] 619
ECONOMIC DURESS
clarity or confusion? (*Atlas Express Ltd.* v. *Kafco* (*Importers and Distributors*) *Ltd.* (*The Alev*)) (Case and comment), [1989] 270
ECONOMIC LOSS
in collision cases (*Case and comment*), [1985] 407
in maritime context (*Gaskell*), [1985] 81
ECONOMIC TAX RECOVERY ACT 1981, THE (*Owles*), [1982] 81
EEC
air and maritime transport and the EEC competition rules (*Ministère Publique* v. *Asjes, Nouvelles Frontières et al*) (Case and comment), [1987] 14
and insurance (*Hodgin*), [1978] 621; (*Mankabady*), [1975] 1
and international agreements (*Hendry*), [1980] 117
and the businessman and the law (*Ryder*), [1978] 291
aspects of industrial property rights in (*Haines*), [1977] 64
bank secrecy provisions (*Hillegom Municipality* v. *Hillenius*) (Case and comment), [1987] 251
competition rules and maritime transport (*Rabe and Schutte*), [1988] 182
Convention on law applicable to contractual obligations (*Williams*), [1981] 250
exclusive dealing agreements in, [1984] 688
insurance companies freedom of establishment within, implementation in Italy (*Costabel*), [1978] 606
insurance market and 1992: significance of fiscal and tariff issues (*Dassesse*), [1990] 176
legislation controlling dangerous substances (*Guruswamy*), [1983] 464
Regulations 67/67 replaces, [1984] 688
the Fourth Council Directive on Accounts (Treaty of Rome, Art. 54(3)(g)) (*Wooldridge*), [1980] 27
"EEC BANKING LAW", [1988] 420
"EEC COMPETITION LAW", [1989] 237
"EEC FISHERIES LAW", [1989] 521
"EFFECTIVE RETENTION OF TITLE CLAUSES", [1989] 118
"ELECTRONIC BANKING: THE LEGAL IMPLICATIONS", [1987] 126
ELECTRONIC FUNDS TRANSFER SYSTEMS (Banking)
the time of payment in paper-based and electronic funds transfer systems (*Vroegop*), [1990] 64
"ELEMENTS OF INSURANCE", [1979] 199
EMPLOYMENT AND INDEMNITY CLAUSES
the safe port/berth obligation and employment and indemnity clauses (*Baker*), [1988] 43
"EMPLOYMENT OF MERCHANT SEAMEN", THE, [1980] 448
"ENCYCLOPEDIA OF ARBITRATION LAW", [1986] 402
"ENCYCLOPEDIA OF CARRIAGE LAW SOURCES", [1988] 267
"ENCYCLOPEDIA OF COMPETITION LAW", [1989] 127
"ENCYCLOPEDIA OF INTERNATIONAL COMMERCIAL ARBITRATION", [1986] 402
"ENCYCLOPEDIA OF OIL AND NATURAL GAS LAW", [1988] 263
"ENCYCLOPEDIA OF SHIPPING LAW SOURCES (U.K.)", [1986] 402
"ENCYCLOPEDIA OF SHIPPING LAW SOURCES (U.K.) SERVICE ISSUE NO.4", [1986] 554

ENFORCEMENT
and admissibility of foreign court decisions and arbitration awards in Greece (*Timagenis*), [1984] 488
"ENFORCEMENT OF MARITIME CLAIMS", [1987] 537
ENGLAND
coastal limits of (*Gibson*), [1978] 616
foreign maritime liens in English courts, principle and policy (*Jackson*), [1981] 335
foreign personal and proprietary judgments, recognition and enforcement (*Stone*), [1983] 1
law, comparative study of charterparties, [1984] 135
law, deductions from freight and hire under (*Rose*), [1982] 33
staying of actions on grounds of *forum non conveniens* (*Briggs*), [1984] 227
ENGLISH COURTS
and US letters rogatory (*Isaacs*), [1978] 464
ENGLISH LAW
Admixture of goods in (*Indian Oil Corp. Ltd.* v. *Greenstone Shipping S.A.* (*Panama*)) (Case and comment), [1988] 286
ENVIRONMENTAL LAW
EEC legislation controlling dangerous substances (*Guruswamy*), [1983] 464
protection and the UN Convention on the Law of the SEA (*Guruswamy*), [1983] 705
EQUIPMENT LEASING
a decade of growth (*DAVIES*), [1983] 631
EQUITY
personal restitution in (*Islamic Republic of Iran Shipping Lines* v. *Denby*) (Case and comment), [1988] 128
"EQUITY AND COMMERCIAL RELATIONSHIPS", [1990] 128
ERRORS
accidental, power of arbitrators to cure (*Thomas*), [1985] 263
"ESSENTIAL BUSINESS LAW— AND THE LEGAL SYSTEM", [1979] 510
"ESSENTIAL BUSINESS LAW—INSURANCE", [1979] 512
"ESSENTIAL BUSINESS LAW—LEASES OF BUSINESS PREMISES", [1980] 210
ESSO MALAYSIA, THE ([1974] 2 Lloyd's Rep. 143; [1974] 2 ALL ER 705)
the practical effects of (*Gault*), [1975] 5
"EURO-ARAB ARBITRATION", [1989] 231
EUROPE
combined transport to (*Hill*), [1975] 303
EUROPEAN COMMUNITIES
note on the activities of (*Lake*), [1975] 418
EUROPEAN COMMUNITY
instruments on air transport (Case and comment), [1988] 135
EUROPEAN COURT
recent decisions re civil jurisdiction and judgments (*Stone*), [1988] 383
EUROPEAN JUDGMENTS CONVENTION
jurisdiction clauses, in bills of lading (*Case and comment*), [1985] 177
EUROPEAN JUDGMENTS CONVENTION, THE
maritime claims (*Brice*), [1987] 281
EVJE, THE
([1974] 3 WLR 269; [1974] 2 Lloyd's Rep. 57), the Centrocon arbitration clause (*Hudson*), [1974] 301
EXCHANGE CONTROL REGULATIONS
exchange contracts and the international sale of goods (*Corbett*), [1977] 310
"EXCHANGE RATES IN INTERNATIONAL LAW AND ORGANIZATION", [1990] 567
EXCLUSION AND LIMITATION CLAUSES
(*Darlington Futures Ltd.* v. *Delco Australia Pty. Ltd.*) (Case and comment), [1987] 165
EXCLUSION CLAUSES
negligence (*Palmer*), [1983] 557
"EXCLUSION CLAUSES AFTER THE UNFAIR CONTRACT TERMS ACT", [1978] 297
"EXCLUSIVE DEALING AGREEMENTS IN THE EEC: REGULATIONS 67/67 REPLACED", [1984] 688
EXCLUSIVE ECONOMIC ZONE
Nigeria's (*Okere*), [1982] 124
"EXCLUSIVE ECONOMIC ZONE CLAIMS", [1987] 128

"EXPORT PRACTICE AND DOCUMENTATION" (3rd Edn.), [1988] 256
EXTENSION OF TIME
deck stowage and the time bar (*Kenya Railways* v. *Antares Pte. Ltd.* (*The Antares*)) (Case and comment), [1987] 146
"EXTRATERRITORIAL JURISDICTION: AN ANNOTATED COLLECTION OF LEGAL MATERIALS", [1984] 507
FACTORING OF DEBTS
modern, its framework of law (*Salinger*), [1977] 184
FACTORS ACT
and *nemo dat* (*National Employers' Mutual Gen. Ins. Assn. Ltd.* v. *Jones*) (Case and comment), [1988] 297
"FALCONER'S MARINE DICTIONARY", [1979] 61
"FAMILY STORY", THE, [1981] 374
"FARWELL'S RULES OF THE NAUTICAL ROAD", [1983] 484
FATAL ACCIDENTS ACTS 1846 to 1959
The Esso Malaysia, practical effects of (*Gault*), [1975] 5
FAULT
and marine losses (*Mustill*), [1988] 310
FEDERAL MARITIME COMMISSION (FMC)
control over agreements and practices of common carriers in US, Shipping Act 1916 (*Meade*), [1976] 401
FIDUCIARY RELATIONSHIP
duties of confidence and loyalty (*International Corona Services* v. *Lac Minerals*) (Case and comment), [1990] 4
FINANCE
company, takeovers and mergers, essential law, [1980] 212
insolvency, [1980] 212
new problems of financing oil shipments (*Ventris*), [1975] 38
"Raising Finance: The Guardian Guide for the Small Business", [1983] 682
"FINANCE OF INTERNATIONAL TRADE", [1982] 655
FINANCIAL SERVICES ACT, THE
(Information), [1987] 137
"FINANCIAL TIMES LAW REPORTS", [1986] 551
FINANCIAL TRANSACTIONS
payment obligations in, [1984] 327
"FINANCING CONSUMER SALES AND PRODUCT DEFENCES (IN CANADA AND THE UNITED STATES)", [1986] 401
"FINANCING OF COUNTERTRADE (THE)", [1987] 554
FINLAND
current consumer protection legislation in (*Sevon*), [1978] 592
FISHERIES
coastal limits of England (*Gibson*), [1978] 616
in the Gulf (*Amin*), [1983] 671
local sea, legislation (*Gibson*), [1980] 340
"FISHERIES REGIME OF THE EXCLUSIVE ECONOMIC ZONE (THE)", [1989] 521
FIXED CHARGES
fixed and floating charges (*Re Brightlife Ltd.*) (Case and comment), [1987] 147
FIXTURES
charterparties, "subject to details" (*Ball*), [1984] 250
charterparty, "subject details" (*Debattista*), [1985] 241
FLAG
maritime, and international law, [1979] 58
FLOATING CHARGES
fixed and floating charges (*Re Brightlife Ltd.*) (Case and comment), [1987] 147
the crystallization of, subordination agreements and priority conflicts (*Chiaw*), [1986] 519
F.O.B. AND C.I.F. CONTRACTS, [1985] 398
FORCE MAJEURE CLAUSES
self-induced frustration and *force majeure* clauses (*The Dan King*) (Case and comment), [1989] 3
the construction of *force majeure* clauses and self-induced frustration (*The Super Servant Two*) (Case and comment), [1990] 153

FORDHAM CORPORATE LAW INSTITUTE
"International Regulations of Maritime Transportation", [1979] 514
"FOREIGN AFFAIRS IN ENGLISH COURTS", [1987] 383
FOREIGN COURT
decisions, enforcement and admissibility in Greece (*Timagenis*), [1984] 488
FOREIGN CURRENCIES
judgments in (*Hene*), [1975] 19
FOREIGN CURRENCY
judgments (*Powles*), [1979] 485
FOREIGN CURRENCY CLAIMS
and the English courts (*Isaacs*), [1977] 356
FOREIGN ECONOMIC CONTRACT LAW
the responses of the Chinese Supreme Court to questions arising out of the application of the Foreign Economic Contract Law of 19 October 1987 (*Guojian and Samuel*), [1989] 476
FOREIGN EXCHANGE
losses, "the passing of risk?" (*Hudson*), [1979] 288
some problems, losses in translation, accounting (*Owles*), [1980] 179
taxation (*Owles*), [1980] 411
FOREIGN PROCEEDINGS
restraining (*British Airways Board* v. *Laker Airways Ltd.*) (*Case and comment*), [1984] 563
"FOREIGN TRADE, INVESTMENT AND THE LAW IN THE PEOPLE'S REPUBLIC OF CHINA", [1989] 129
FORFEITURE
penalties and forfeiture: contractual remedies specified by the parties (*Jobson* v. *Johnson*) (Case and comment), [1990] 158
FORMAL INVESTIGATION FINDINGS
relevance of to civil liability proceedings (*The European Gateway*) (Case and comment), [1986] 417
FORUM
Hague-Visby Rules, and arbitration, and choice of law clauses (*Jackson*), [1980] 159
FORUM NON CONVENIENS
an update (*Briggs*), [1985] 360
carriage by air, the continuing debate (*McGilchrist*), [1980] 439
forum non conveniens—the last word? (*Spiliada Maritime Corporation* v. *Cansulex Ltd.*) (Case and comment), [1987] 1
staying of actions in England (*Briggs*), [1984] 227
FORWARD TRADING
in Brent crude (*The Aragon*) (Case and comment), [1989] 143, 418
"FOUNDATIONS OF EUROPEAN COMMUNITY LAW (THE)" (2nd Edn.), [1990] 141
"FOUNDATIONS OF THE LAW OF TORT", [1985] 403
FRANCE
the lack of uniformity and the very unfortunate state of maritime law in (*Tetley*), [1987] 340
FRAUD
definition and classification of maritime (*Kapoor*), [1983] 29
maritime, international, [1982] 442
return to the Macmillan doctrine (*Tai Hing Cotton Mill Ltd.* v. *Liu Chong Hing Bank Ltd.*) (Case and comment), [1986] 8
transnational (*Teik*), [1985] 418
FREIGHT
deductions from
and hire under English law (*Rose*), [1982] 33
for carriage of goods by road (*R. H. & D. International Ltd.* v. *I.A.S. Animal Air Services Ltd.) (Case and comment)*, [1984] 199
earned freight: how sacrosanct? (*The Dominique*) (Case and comment), [1989] 289
FREIGHT FORWARDER
combined transport Europe (*Hill*), [1975] 303
contractual relationship between shipper, forwarder and carrier by road (*Hill*), [1975] 137
his status from a comparative viewpoint (*Hill*), [1975] 27
FREIGHT FORWARDING
Austrian General Freight Forwarding Conditions and Freight Forwarding Insurance Scheme (*Blasche*), [1976] 374

FREIGHT FORWARDING—*continued*
forwarding and sub-contracting complications (*Hill*), [1976] 63
FREIGHT LINER CONDITIONS
combined transport (*Hill*), [1977] 88
FREIGHT RATE
effect of quotation of (*Case and comment*), [1985] 412
"FRESHWATER FISHERY LAW", [1988] 412
FRUSTRATION
in charterparty disputes, withdrawals, repudiation (*Barclay*), [1975] 412
self-induced frustration and *force majeure* clauses (*The Dan King*) (Case and comment), [1989] 3
FUNDAMENTAL BREACH
of charterparty (*Clarke*), [1978] 472
of towage conditions (*Lux*), [1979] 148
"FUNDAMENTAL DUTIES", [1981] 294
FUNDS
misdirected funds: restitution from the recipient (*Birks*), [1989] 296
"FUTURES AND OPTIONS FOR SHIPPING", [1990] 287
GAMING ACT (THE)
the Act and commodity futures contracts (*Chaikin and Moher*), [1986] 390
GARNISHMENT
of English debt: foreign complications (*Deutsche Schachtbau* v. *S.I.T. Co.*) (Case and comment), [1988] 429
GAS
Canadian offshore development, some Admiralty law issues (*Spicer*), [1982] 5
GENERAL AVERAGE
adjustment and arbitration in People's Republic of China (*Hudson*), [1976] 135
and marine insurance in the US, [1981] 516
and salvage, insurance of average disbursements (*Hudson*), [1980] 168
(*Crump*), [1985] 19
defences and "due diligence" disputes (*Hudson*), [1976] 416
ground for refusal to contribute (*Buglass*), [1975] 390
law of shipping and carriage in South Africa, [1974] 314
new forms for general average security (*Hudson*), [1977] 501
the future of non-separation agreements (*Ellermand Lines Ltd.* v. *Gibbs, Nathaniel (Canada) Ltd. et al*) (Case and comment), [1987] 160
"GENERAL PRINCIPLES OF INSURANCE LAW" (5th Edn.), [1989] 520
GERMAN DEMOCRATIC REPUBLIC
new maritime code (*Richter-Hannes and Richter*), [1977] 197
"GERMAN LAW OF TORT (THE): A COMPARATIVE INTRODUCTION TO", [1988] 405
GERMANY
new law on standard contract terms (*von Marschall*), [1979] 278
GIRO SYSTEM
and electronic transfers of funds (*Ellinger*), [1986] 178
GOLD FRANC
replacement of unit of account (*Bristow*), [1978] 31
GOLD VALUES
in carriage of goods Conventions (*Costabel*), [1979] 326
GOOD FAITH
the insurer's duties of good faith and disclosure (*The Good Luck*) (Case and comment), [1988] 27
"GOODBYE TO THE MEMORANDUM", [1989] 246
GOODS
liability for labelling of goods and instructions for use (*Brown*), [1988] 502
preservation after release, shipowners' liens (*Tettenborn*), [1985] 376
rejection of goods, restitution for services and incontrovertible benefit (*The Manila*) (Case and comment), [1989] 397
transport of, general conditions for, in the Netherlands (*Klinkhamer*), [1979] 26
transport of goods in refrigerated containers: an Australian perspective (*Springall*), [1987] 216
uncollected: the penalties of delay (*Palmer*), [1987] 43
GOODS IN TRANSIT
how to recover for loss of, [1980] 344
non-apparent damage to (*Clarke*), [1982] 533

"GRAIN CONTRACTS AND ARBITRATION", [1984] 679
GREAT BRITAIN (TERRITORIAL WATERS)
Territorial Waters (Amendment) Order in Council 1979 (*Gibson*), [1980] 67
GREECE
admissibility and enforcement of foreign court decisions and arbitration awards in (*Timagenis*), [1984] 488
arbitration in Piraeus (*Timagenis*), [1977] 319
arrest of ships in (*Timagenis*), [1984] 90
NAT tax illegal in Sri Lanka (Case and comment), [1986] 434
service of documents in shipping cases (*Timagenis*), [1984] 275
shipping case law in (*Timagenis*), [1976] 46
GUARANTEE AND INDEMNITY CLAUSE
Norwegian Saleform (*The Barenbels) (Case and comment*), [1984] 553
GUARANTEES
a guarantee signed by mistake (*Lloyds Bank Plc* v. *Waterhouse*) (Case and comment), [1990] 338
performance guarantees (*Coleman*), [1990] 223
undertaken without the request of the debtor (*The Zuhal K and Selin*) (Case and comment), [1989] 7
"GUIDE TO DOCUMENTARY OPERATIONS", [1979] 371
"GUIDE TO THE INSURANCE OF PROFESSIONAL NEGLIGENCE RISKS, A", [1983] 481
GULF STATES, THE
control of marine pollution (*Amin*), [1982] 104
legal systems in (*Amin*), [1983] 71
"HAGUE CONVENTION: SERVICE OF PROCESS ABROAD", [1984] 685
HAGUE RULES
in Australia (*P.S. Chellaram & Co. Ltd.* v. *China Ocean Shipping Co.*) (Case and comment), [1989] 277
HAGUE RULES, THE
and the demise clause (*Kaleej International Pty. Ltd.* v. *Gulf Shipping Lines Ltd.*; *Carling O'Keefe Breweries of Canada Ltd.* v. *C.N. Marine Inc.* (*The Newfoundland Coast*)) (Case and comment), [1987] 259
and Visby Rules and UNCITRAL, identity of the carrier (*Tetley*), [1977] 519
application of in post-revolutionary Iran (Case and comment), [1987] 273
"from radical revolution to questionable reformation" (*Righetti*), [1977] 192
interpretation of (*Mankabady*), [1974] 125
recommendations relating to the revision of, [1974] 134
the new Rules (*McGilchrist*), [1974] 255
HAGUE-VISBY PROTOCOL, THE
(Information), [1987] 559
HAGUE-VISBY RULES, THE
and transhipment (*Mayhew Foods Ltd.* v. *Overseas Containers Ltd.) (Case and comment*), [1984] 202
(*Diamond*), [1978] 225
forum, arbitration, and choice of law clauses (*Jackson*), [1980] 159
(Information), [1987] 559
now operative in UK, [1977] 512
"HAGUE-ZAGREB ESSAYS 3", THE, [1981] 112
"HALCYON ISLE"
The Halcyon Isle revisited: a South African perspective (*Staniland*), [1989] 174
HALCYON ISLE, The
in defense of (Case and comment), [1987] 152
HAMBURG RULES, THE
(Information), [1987] 559
HAMBURG RULES, THE, [1978] 439
a commentary (*Tetley*), [1979] 1
"HANDBOOK OF ARBITRATION PRACTICE", [1988] 107
"HANDBOOK ON MARINE POLLUTION", [1988] 109
"HARBOUR LAW", [1984] 509
HIGH COURT
a High Court comment on need for reform of arbitration procedures, [1978] 267

HIJACKING
aerial, carriage by air (*McGilchrist*), [1978] 298
in road transport law (*Quick Smith*), [1974] 11
HIMALAYA CLAUSE, THE
(*Powles*), [1979] 331
HIRE
late payment of, when payment is made (*Ryder*), [1977] 174
HOLLAND
Benelux law on commercial agents now incorporated in Dutch Commercial Code (*Calkoen*), [1978] 395
Dutch Civil Code, a method of drafting a "code of transport" (*Schadee*), [1977] 37
HONG KONG
developments in maritime law in 1983 (*Quennell*), [1984] 434
"Macmillan" doctrine reviewed in (*Tai Hing Cotton Mill Ltd.* v. *Liu Chong Hing Bank Ltd.) (Case and comment*), [1984] 559
recent developments in maritime law (*Quennell*), [1986] 382
HOUSE OF LORDS
certainty in contracts, *Hongkong Fir* revisited (*Applebey and Meisel*), [1982] 592
decision of, damages under CMR (*Hardingham*), [1978] 51
"HOW TO RECOVER FOR LOSS OR DAMAGE TO GOODS IN TRANSIT", [1980] 344
"HOW TO SECURE A MARITIME LIEN", [1983] 109
HULL CLAIMS
UNCTAD report (*Goodacre*), [1979] 315
ICC
Documentary Credits, Code of Practice (*Wheble*), [1976] 8
in perspective, Rules for a combined transport document (*McGilchrist*), [1974] 25
rules for Documentary Credits, [1976] 15
text of ICC Uniform Rules, [1974] 29
Uniform Customs and Practice, their nature and the 1983 revision (*Ellinger*), [1984] 578
Uniform Rules for a Combined Transport Document (*Wheble*), [1976] 145, 148
ILLEGAL INSURANCE
(*Clarke*), [1987] 201
IMO, [1985] 146
and liability for oil pollution from ships (*Abecassis*), [1983] 45
"IMPACT OF MARINE POLLUTION", THE, [1980] 451
IMPLIED TERMS
in the banker and customer relationship (*The Maira (No. 3)*) (Case and comment), [1989] 40
IMPLIED WARRANTY
of seaworthiness in time policies, the American view (*Pritchett*), [1983] 195
IN PERSONAM
attachment, *Mareva* injunction (*Rose*), [1981] 1, 77
IN REM
action, time-charterer, one-ship company and sister-ship action *in rem* (*Tettenborn*), [1981] 507
gaps in action of (*Hazelwood*), [1982] 210
plugged? (*Hazelwood*), [1982] 422
sister ship action (*Thomas*), [1979] 158
INCOME TAX
U.S. federal, consequences to foreign corporations engaged in international shipping (*Donna Marie Zerbo*), [1988] 235
INDUSTRIAL PROPERTY
aspects of rights in EEC (*HAINES*), [1977] 64
INFORMATION
the remedies for abuse of confidential information (*Lac Minerals* v. *International Corona Services Ltd.*; *Aquaculture Corp.* v. *N.Z. Mussel Co. Ltd.* (Case and comment), [1990] 460
INFORMATION , CRIMINAL
disclosure of to insurers (*Clarke*), [1984] 100
INJUNCTION
Mareva
attachment *in personam* (*Rose)*, [1984] 1, 177
recent developments (*Meisel*), [1980] 38

INJUNCTION—*continued*
(*Tetley*), [1985] 58
INJUNCTIONS
worldwide *Mareva* injunctions: the position of international banks (*Malek and Lewis*), [1990] 88
INJURY
accidental, insurance (*Case and comment*), [1985] 12
INLAND WATERWAYS ASSOCIATION
report on Continental waterways, [1977] 203
IN REM
amendment of writ *in rem* (*The Kusu Island*) (Case and comment), [1990] 169
INSTITUTE CARGO CLAUSES
the new (*George*), [1986] 438
INSTITUTE CLAUSES
The new (*O'May*), [1985] 191
"INSTITUTE CLAUSES HANDBOOK (THE)", [1987] 385
"INSTITUTE FOR THE LAW OF THE SEA (THE) (NILOS): INTERNATIONAL ORGANIZATIONS AND THE LAW OF THE SEA (VOL. 2, 1986)", [1989] 525
INSTITUTE OF MARITIME LAW (THE)
the law of marine insurance, has it a future? (*Diamond*), [1986] 25
"INSTITUTE TIME CLAUSES HULLS", [1989] 246
INSURANCE
accidental injury (*Case and comment*), [1985] 12
and the EEC (*Hodgin*), [1978] 621; (*Mankabady*), [1975] 1
Austria, Freight Forwarding Insurance Scheme (*Blasche*), [1976] 374
Avoidance of policy or repudation of claim? (*Gordon* v. *A.A. Mutual Ins. Assn. Ltd.*) (Case and comment), [1988] 452
brokers, duty of care (*Glass*), [1978] 619
claims and consequential loss, [1978] 67
companies freedom of establishment within EEC, implementation in Italy (*Costabel*), [1978] 606
covenants in leases and insurance provisions in charterparties (Case and comment), [1986] 149
directors' liability, some legal aspects of in US (*Owles*), [1977] 163
disclosure of criminal information (*Clarke*), [1984] 100
disputes in the US, a period of uncertainty for the insurer (*Liederman*), [1986] 79
double, and contribution (*Hodgin*), [1977] 515
EEC insurance market and 1992: significance of fiscal and tariff issues (*Dassesse*), [1990] 176
elements of, [1979] 199
"illegal" (*Bedford Insurance Co.* v. *I.R.B.: B. A. Stewart* v. *Oriental Fire & Marine Insurance Co.) (Case and comment*), [1984] 368
illegal (*Clarke*), [1987] 201
in Poland, comparative review (*Marek*), [1984] 643
in US, policy disputes, damages against insurers (*Barrett*), [1980] 131
insurer's liability extended (*Banque Keyser Ullmann S.A.* v. *Skandia (U.K.) Insurance Ltd.*) (Case and comment), [1987] 5
intermediaries, recent and projected developments, Insurance Brokers (Registration) Act 1977 (*Morgan*), [1978] 39
law
a fundamental principle of (*Lewis*), [1979] 275
dictionary of, [1982] 277
recent causes (*Clarke*), [1983] 576
law reform (*Hodgin*), [1981] 284
materiality in contracts (*Brooke*), [1985] 437
mortgagee's interest insurance (*The Alexion Hope*) (Case and comment), [1988] 282
multi-party insurances and the conflict of laws (*The Irish Rowan*) (Case and comment), [1989] 389
new Israeli insurance contract law 1981 (*Naschitz*), [1982] 249
of average disbursements (*Hudson*), [1987] 443
of goods, illegality of contract (*Euro-Diam Ltd.* v. *Bathurst*) (Case and comment), [1988] 124
of pleasure craft and the doctrine of proximate cause (*J.J. Lloyd Instruments Ltd.* v. *Northern Star Insurance Co. Ltd.* (*The Miss Jay Jay*)) (Case and comment), [1987] 22
Ombudsman Bureau, first annual report (*Merkin*), [1982] 266
"personal accident, life and other insurances", [1981] 111
problems in defining contracts (*Hodgin*), [1980] 14

INSURANCE—*continued*
rights and duties of brokers (*Bamford*), [1976] 59
the Anglo-American scene (*Margo*), [1981] 83
the Law Commission and insurance law (*Merkin*), [1981] 347
third party rights against insurers (*Michel and Congdon*), [1989] 495
third party rights on insurance contracts (*Trident General Insurance Co. Ltd.* v. *McNiece Bros. Pty. Ltd.*) (Case and comment), [1987] 258
under Saudi Arabian law (*Haberbeck*), [1986] 246
INSURANCE (AVIATION)
a recent decision (*Margo*), [1980] 335
liability claims in general aviation (*McGilchrist*), [1980] 196
regulation in US (*White*), [1985] 453
INSURANCE BROKERS (REGISTRATION) ACT 1977
(*Morgan*), [1978] 39
"INSURANCE CONTRACT LAW", [1989] 246
INSURANCE CONTRACTS
variation and affirmation in (*Hadenfayre* v. *British National Insurance Society Ltd.) (Case and comment*), [1985] 3
"INSURANCE INTERMEDIARIES AND THE LAW", [1990] 302
INSURANCE LAW
in Australia (*Scotford*), [1985] 201
"INSURANCE LAW JOURNAL", [1990] 133
"INSURANCE LEGISLATION MANUAL", [1989] 234
INSURANCE (LIFE)
and personal accident and other insurances, [1981] 111
INSURANCE (MARINE)
and General Average
in the US, [1981] 516
insurance of average disbursements (*Hudson*), [1980] 168
"Arnould's Law of Marine Insurance", [1983] 679
damages assessable against insurers for wrongful failure to pay property losses (*Allen*), [1976] 258
in South Africa (*Bamford*), [1975] 171
law, in Canada (*McEwen*), [1984] 671
law of shipping and carriage in South Africa, [1974] 314
"Marine Insurance Claims", [1975] 308; [1983] 103
marine insurance law: can the lawyers be trusted? (*O'May*), [1987] 29
of household goods shipments (*Rossmere*), [1976] 173
Piracy (*The Andreas Lemos) (Hazelwood*), [1983] 283
proper law of marine policy (*Stone*), [1984] 438
Templeman on, [1981] 373
the law of, has it a future? (*Diamond*), [1986] 25
the making of the marine insurance contract, a comparison of English and US law (*Condon*), [1986] 484
the practice of scuttling (*O'May*), [1974] 6
UNCTAD report, as related to hull claims (*Goodacre*), [1979] 315
wilful misconduct of the assured (*Case and comment*), [1984] 415
"INSURANCE OF COMMERCIAL RISKS: LAW AND PRACTICE (THE)", [1987] 244
"INSURANCE OF PROFESSIONAL NEGLIGENCE RISKS (THE): LAW AND PRACTICE", [1990] 559
INSURANCE OMBUDSMAN BUREAU
first annual report (*Merkin*), [1982] 266
INSURANCE (PERSONAL ACCIDENT)
and life and other insurances, [1981] 111
INSURANCE (WAR RISKS)
(*O'May*), [1976] 180
INSURANCE (WET MARINE)
regulation in US (*White*), [1985] 453
INSURER
the insurer's duties of good faith and disclosure (*The Good Luck*) (Case and comment), [1988] 27
INSURERS
in US, policy disputes, damages against (*Barrett*), [1980] 131

INTEREST
on debts paid late (Case and comment), [1986] 139
on maximum sums (*Mann and Kurth*), [1988] 177
INTEREST AWARDS
the vexed issue in commercial arbitration (*Thomas*), [1982] 667
INTERLOCUTORY ORDERS
for inspection of property (*The Mare del Nord*) (Case and comment), [1990] 319
INTERMEDIARIES
insurance, recent and projected developments, Insurance Brokers (Registration) Act 1977 (*Morgan*), [1978] 39
INTERNATIONAL
and national organisations concerned with shipping (*Mankabady*), [1974] 274
carriage of goods by road, contracts for, [1986] 131
carriage of passengers and luggage by rail and road (*Hodgin*), [1976] 1
carriage of perishable goods and ATP, combined transport (*Hill*), [1977] 546
regulations of maritime transportation, [1979] 514
"INTERNATIONAL AGENCY, DISTRIBUTION AND LICENSING AGREEMENTS", [1988] 264
INTERNATIONAL AGREEMENTS
and the EEC (*Hendry*), [1980] 117
"INTERNATIONAL AND LEGAL PROBLEMS OF THE GULF", [1982] 441
INTERNATIONAL ARBITRATION
Naviera Amazonica Peruana S.A. v. *Compania Internacional de Seguros del Peru* (Case and comment), [1988] 23
"INTERNATIONAL ARBITRATION: THREE SALIENT PROBLEMS", [1988] 416
"INTERNATIONAL BUSINESS AND NATIONAL JURISDICTION", [1989] 229
"INTERNATIONAL CARRIAGE OF GOODS BY ROAD (CMR)", [1989] 236
"INTERNATIONAL CARRIAGE OF GOODS BY ROAD: CMR", [1983] 681
"INTERNATIONAL CARRIAGE OF GOODS: SOME LEGAL PROBLEMS AND POSSIBLE SOLUTIONS", [1990] 302
INTERNATIONAL CHAMBER OF COMMERCE
Documentary Credits, Code of Practice (*Wheble*), [1976] 8
rules for Documentary Credits, [1976] 15
Uniform Customs and Practice, their nature and the 1983 revision (*Ellinger*), [1984] 578
Uniform Rules for a Combined Transport Document (*Wheble*), [1976] 145, 148
"INTERNATIONAL CHAMBER OF COMMERCE ARBITRATION", [1988] 246
INTERNATIONAL CHAMBER OF COMMERCE (ICC)
in perspective, Rules for a combined transport document (*McGilchrist*), [1974] 25
text of ICC Uniform RULES, [1974] 29
"INTERNATIONAL CIVIL LITIGATION IN UNITED STATES COURTS", [1990] 296
"INTERNATIONAL COMMERCIAL AGREEMENTS", [1990] 298
"INTERNATIONAL COMMERCIAL AND MARITIME ARBITRATION", [1990] 130
"INTERNATIONAL COMMERCIAL ARBITRATION IN BELGIUM", [1990] 429
INTERNATIONAL CONGRESS
second, of maritime arbitrators, [1974] 61
INTERNATIONAL CONGRESS OF MARITIME ARBITRATORS (THIRD), [1976] 377
table of comparative maritime arbitration procedures (*Cohen*), [1976] 422
INTERNATIONAL CONTRACTS
the formation of (*Briggs*), [1990] 192
INTERNATIONAL CONVENTION FOR THE PREVENTION OF POLLUTION FROM SHIPS 1973, [1974] 232
INTERNATIONAL CONVENTION FOR THE RECIPROCAL RECOGNITION AND ENFORCEMENT OF JUDGMENTS IN CIVIL AND COMMERCIAL MATTERS, [1974] 109
INTERNATIONAL CONVENTION ON CIVIL LIABILITY FOR OIL POLLUTION DAMAGE
application to *The Urquiola* case (*Arroyo*), [1977] 337
INTERNATIONAL CONVENTION ON THE LIMITATION PERIOD IN THE INTERNATIONAL SALE OF GOODS, [1975] 105
INTERNATIONAL CONVENTIONS
carriage by air outside the international Conventions (*Holmes* v. *Bangladesh Corp.*) (Case and comment), [1989] 267

INTERNATIONAL COURT OF JUSTICE
documents on, [1980] 72
INTERNATIONAL CRIME
commercial, Commonwealth perspective (*Rider*), [1985] 217
"INTERNATIONAL DISPUTE SETTLEMENT", [1989] 246
"INTERNATIONAL HANDBOOK AND LEGAL GUIDE FOR THE INSURER AND REINSURER (1982)", [1982] 659
INTERNATIONAL LAW
and maritime flag, [1979] 58
new horizons in, [1980] 71
torts in violation of international law (*Amerada Hess Shipping Corp* v. *Argentine Repubic* (*The Hercules*)) (Case and comment), [1988] 10
"INTERNATIONAL LAW", [1987] 247
"INTERNATIONAL LAW OF THE SEA", THE, [1984] 684
"INTERNATIONAL LAW" (2nd Edn.), [1988] 261
"INTERNATIONAL MARITIME FRAUD", [1982] 442
"INTERNATIONAL MARITIME LAW CONVENTIONS", [1984] 329
"INTERNATIONAL MARITIME ORGANIZATION", THE, [1985] 146
"INTERNATIONAL MARITIME ORGANIZATION (THE)" (2nd Edn. Vol. 1), [1987] 387
"INTERNATIONAL REGULATION OF SALVAGE AT SEA", [1990] 436
INTERNATIONAL REGULATIONS FOR PREVENTING COLLISIONS AT SEA 1972
coming into force of (*Mankabady*), [1977] 330
"INTERNATIONAL REGULATIONS OF MARITIME TRANSPORTATION", [1979] 514
INTERNATIONAL SALE OF GOODS
and exchange contracts (*Corbett*), [1977] 310
Convention on Limitation Period, [1975] 105
(*Eckersley*), [1975] 265
"INTERNATIONAL SALE OF GOODS", [1987] 534
"INTERNATIONAL SHIP ARREST", [1990] 570
INTERNATIONAL SHIPPING
U.S. federal income tax consequences to foreign corporations engaged in (*Donna Marie Zerbo*), [1988] 235
"INTERNATIONAL STRAITS OF THE WORLD" (VOLS. I and II), [1979] 372
INTERNATIONAL TELEX
formation and repudiation of contracts by (*Lewis*), [1980] 433
INTERNATIONAL TIN COUNCIL (THE)
the saga of (Case and comment), [1990] 305
INTERNATIONAL TRADE
accommodations of the law of (*Cigoj*), [1974] 309
and payments, [1979] 201
cases and materials on the law of, [1982] 160
"Finance of International Trade", [1982] 655
theory of changed circumstances in (*Amin*), [1982] 577
US reports, [1982] 162
"INTERNATIONAL TRADE AND PAYMENTS", [1979] 201
"INTERNATIONAL TRADE REGULATION (GATT, THE UNITED STATES AND THE EUROPEAN COMMUNITY)" (2nd Edn.), [1988] 248
"INTERPRETATION OF CONTRACTS (THE)", [1990] 428
INTERTANKTIME
(*Michelet*), [1978] 287
"INTRODUCTION TO THE CONFLICT OF LAWS", [1990] 282
"IOANNIS DASKALELIS"
in defence of *The Ioannis Daskalelis* (Case and comment), [1989] 11
IRAN
application of the Hague Rules (Case and comment), [1987] 273
claims settlement with US (*Amin*), [1983] 248
law of commercial contracts in (*Amin*), [1982] 416
ISRAEL
commercial and maritime law in (*Naschitz*), [1977] 84
new insurance contracts law 1981 (*Naschitz*), [1982] 249

ISRAEL—*continued*
warehouseman not entitled to benefit from Warsaw Convention (*Naschitz*), [1985] 479
ITALIAN CONSTITUTIONAL COURT
and the limits on the liability of the carrier of goods by sea (Case and comment), [1988] 273
ITALY
fundamental changes in arbitration law (*Costabel*), [1983] 440
implementation in of insurance companies freedom of establishment within EEC (*Costabel*), [1978] 606
JAPAN
arrest of ships in (*Hosoi and Tsurusaki*), [1981] 359
arrest of vessels in (*Hosoi*), [1980] 322
Japanese agent's liability for delivery without presentation of bill of lading (*Daiwa Bank* v. *Mankai Shipping and Fast Marine* (*The Taichun*)) (Case and comment), [1989] 35
time charterer's third party liability in (*Hosoi*), [1985] 254
JOHANNA OLDENDORFF, THE ([1973] 2 Lloyd's Rep. 333)
some considerations of the case (*Davies*), [1974] 1
"JOURNAL OF CONTRACT LAW", [1989] 228
"JOURNAL OF INTERNATIONAL ARBITRATION", [1986] 405
"JOURNAL OF INTERNATIONAL BANKING LAW", [1986] 405
JUDGE-ARBITRATORS
commercial arbitration (*Thomas*), [1983] 120
JUDGMENT CREDITORS
and debenture holders, problems of priority (*Hare and Milman*), [1982] 57
JUDGMENT DEBTORS
examination of judgment debtors as to their assets abroad: courts' powers and jurisdiction (*Kaye*), [1989] 465
JUDGMENTS
in foreign currencies (*Hene*), [1975] 19
JUDGMENTS AND DIAGRAMS—COLLISION CASES, [1985] 141
JURISDICTION
Admiralty, Supreme Court Act 1981 (*Jackson*), [1982] 236
carriage by air, obtaining jurisdiction in US (*McGilchrist*), [1978] 609
civil, and judgments, [1984] 511
examination of judgment debtors as to their assets abroad: courts' powers and jurisdiction (*Kaye*), [1989] 465
extraterritorial
an annotated collection of legal materials, [1984] 507
of US antitrust laws (*Sornarajah*), [1981] 365
of English courts, crimes committed in foreign ships on high seas (*Bentil*), [1983] 60
offences on board ships (*R.* v. *Cumberworth*) (Case and comment), [1990] 162
over claims for damage done by any ship (*Clarke*), [1976] 412
"wider still and wider: the bounds of Australian exorbitant jurisdiction" (*Briggs*), [1989] 216
writ, a new approach for service (*Case and comment*), [1985] 6
JURISDICTION CLAUSES
in bills of lading and the European Judgments Convention (*Case and comment*), [1985] 177
the validity of "floating" choice and law and (*Briggs*), [1986] 508
"KENNEDY'S LAW OF SALVAGE", [1986] 539
"KITCHIN'S ROAD TRANSPORT LAW", [1979] 515
"LA GIURISPRUDENZIA ITALIANA IN TEMA DI TRASPORTI", [1988] 411
LATE PAYER
damages and the (*The Lips*) (Case and comment), [1987] 414
LATE PAYMENT
maritime arbitration awards in New York involving shipowner withdrawals from charter (*Murray*), [1976] 164
of debt (*La Pintada) (Case and comment*), [1984] 365
LAW
Admiralty
and shipping law in US, recent developments (*Healy*), [1984] 607
recent developments in Singapore (*Selvam*), [1985] 209
some issues in Canadian offshore oil and gas development (*Spicer*), [1982] 5
US, continuing problems after supposed demise of *Ryan* indemnity (*Bagwell*), [1982] 556

LAW—*continued*
Admixture of goods in English law (*Indian Oil Corp. Ltd.* v. *Greenstone Shipping S.A.* (*Panama*)) (Case and comment), [1988] 286
air, Dutch Civil Code, a method of drafting "a code transport" (*Schadee*), [1977] 37
air, the operator's liability in air traffic control (*McGilchrist*), [1977] 204
airport operator's liability for bird-strikes (*McGilchrist*), [1979] 494
and the businessman and the EEC (*Ryder*), [1978] 291
banking, bank manuals and instructions to staff, some legal aspects (*Weerasooria*), [1974] 295
Benelux law on commercial agents now incorporated in Dutch Commercial Code (*Calkoen*), [1978] 395
Canada
country's approach to marine pollution (*Lowry*), [1975] 10
marine insurance in (*McEwen*), [1984] 671
per package limitation, diverging approach in Canadian courts (*McEwen*), [1976] 269
Canada, new personal property security legislation (*Ziegel*), [1986] 160
Canada: Supreme Court liberalizes the rules re measuring damages for breach of a chattel lease (*Langille* v. *Keneric Tractor Sales Ltd.*) (Case and comment), [1988] 276
Canadian maritime law decisions 1985–86 (*Tetley*), [1987] 82
Canadian maritime law decisions 1986–87 (*Tetley*), [1988] 82
Canadian maritime law decisions: 1987–88 (*Tetley*), [1989] 89
Canadian maritime law decisions: 1988–89 (*Tetley, Q.C.*), [1990] 99
Chinese Supreme Court: the responses to questions arising out of the application of the Foreign Economic Contract Law of 19 October 1987 (*Guojian and Samuel*), [1989] 000
choice of law clauses (*Jackson*), [1980] 159
CMR, interpretation of, in English courts (*Hill*), [1977] 212
collision cases in English courts in 1974 (*Harley*), [1975] 156
commercial
in a changing economic climate, [1982] 270
in the Gulf States, [1985] 279
commercial arbitration, [1984] 137
common law, liability of public carrier by sea (*Kirkham*), [1976] 282
company
and capitalism, [1978] 65
"Charlesworth and Cain Company Law", [1978] 296
in Great Britain, [1983] 301
insolvency, [1980] 212
company law: wrongful trading (*Oditah*), [1990] 205
comparative, legal relations of stevedores in (*Cigoj*), [1975] 296
Competition, antitrust policy in UK and EEC, [1985] 276
consumer law and policy, development of, [1984] 685
controlling mercury pollution, issues and implications for UK (*Guruswamy*), [1982] 611
curial, of arbitration proceedings (*Thomas*), [1984] 491
decision of the House of Lords, damages under CMR (*Hardingham*), [1978] 51
deductions from freight and hire under English law (*Rose*), [1982] 33
determining ownership of shipwreck in the U.S. (*Klein* v. *Unidentified Wrecked and Abandoned Vessel*) (Case and comment), [1987] 24
developments in Australia, miscellaneous (Case and comment), [1986] 283
difference between legal and arbitration approach in petroleum shortage disputes (*Textor*), [1983] 392
Dr Lushington's contribution to the law of maritime salvage (1838–67) (*Waddams*), [1989] 59
Dutch Civil Code, a method of drafting a "code of transport" (*Schadee*), [1977] 37
enactment of the Salvage Convention 1989 in English law: policy issues (Case and comment), [1990] 352
England, recognition and enforcement of foreign personal and proprietary judgments (*Stone*), [1983] 1
environmental
EEC legislation controlling dangerous substances (*Guruswamy*), [1983] 464
protection and the UN Convention on the Law of the Sea (*Guruswamy*), [1983] 705
essential business law, [1979] 510
company finance, takeovers and mergers, [1980] 212
insurance, [1979] 512

LAW—*continued*
examination of judgment debtors as to their assets abroad: courts' powers and jurisdiction (*Kaye*), [1989] 465
factoring of debts (*Salinger*), [1977] 184
floating choice of law clauses (*Beck*), [1987] 523
for small business, [1983] 682
foreign currency
claims and the English courts (*Isaacs*), [1977] 356
judgments (*Powles*), [1979] 485
foundations, of law of tort, [1985] 403
future deviation in law of carriage of goods (*Mills*), [1983] 587
Germany, new law on standard contract terms (*von Marschall*), [1979] 278
Greece, NAT tax illegal in Sri Lanka (Case and comment), [1986] 434
Greece, shipping case law (*Timagenis*), [1976] 46
ground for refusal to contribute in general average (*Buglass*), [1975] 390
harbour, [1984] 509
hi-jacking in road transport law (*Quick Smith*), [1974] 11
in Australia, product liability (*Goldring*), [1977] 351
in Iran, of commercial contracts (*Amin*), [1982] 416
in Israel, commercial and maritime (*Naschitz*) [1977] 84
in Middle East, of personal injuries (*Amin*), [1983] 446
in US, the airline as plaintiff (*McGilchrist*), [1980] 328
India, arbitration, hazards of invoking Indian law (*Oil & Natural Gas Commission* v. *Western Company of North Amercia*) (Case and comment), [1988] 12
insurance
a fundamental principle of (*Lewis*), [1979] 275
and the Law Commission (*Merkin*), [1981] 347
dictionary of, [1982] 277
in Australia (*Scotford*), [1985] 201
recent causes (*Clarke*), [1983] 576
reform (*Hodgin*), [1981] 284
international
and maritime flag, [1979] 58
new horizons in, [1980] 71
note on the activities of the European Communities (*Lake*), [1975] 418
international, torts in violation of (*Amerada Hess Shipping Corp.* v. *Argentine Republic* (*The Hercules*)) (Case and comment), [1988] 10
International Convention for the reciprocal recognition and enforcement of judgments in civil and commercial matters, [1974] 109
international maritime conventions, [1984] 329
international trade
accommodations of the law of (*Cigoj*), [1974] 309
cases and materials on law of, [1982] 160
Israel, new insurance contract law 1981 (*Naschitz*), [1982] 249
Italy, fundamental changes in arbitration law (*Costabel*), [1983] 440
judgments in foreign currencies (*Hene*), [1975] 19
jurisdiction, carriage by air, obtaining jurisdiction in US (*McGilchrist*), [1978] 609
leases of business premises, [1980] 210
legal aspects of safety of offshore installations (*Cadwallader*), [1977] 53
legal position of banks in Performance Bond cases (*Arora*), [1981] 264
legal problems
arising from the transport of liquefied natural gas, [1975] 387
associated with shipbuilding contracts (*Mankabady*), [1978] 477
liability for pilot's negligence under Belgian law (Case and comment), [1989] 27
"manifest disregard of" and US Arbitration Act (*Berg*), [1975] 129
"manifest disregard of the law" doctrine (*Bauer*), [1979] 142
marine insurance, can the lawyers be trusted? (*O'May*), [1987] 29
marine insurance, the making of the contract, a comparison of English and US law (*Condon*), [1986] 484
maritime
Canadian judgments in 1982 (*Tetley*), [1983] 603

LAW—*continued*
decision-making (*Mustill*), [1985] 314
judgments in Canada in 1980 (*Tetley*), [1981] 489
maritime, recent developments in Hong Kong (*Quennell*), [1986] 382
maritime terrorism and the law (Case and comment), [1987] 18
of competition—an introduction to UK's law, [1978] 505
of marine insurance, has it a future? (*Diamond*), [1986] 25
of maritime arbitrations in London, recent developments (*McIntosh*), [1983] 235
of the sea, report on third session of UN Conference (*Lake*), [1975] 383
of tug, tow and pilotage, [1983] 107
our law of theirs? (*Holmes* v. *Bangladesh Biman Corp.*; *McElderry* v. *Cathay Pacific Airways* (Case and comment), [1988] 445
parol evidence rule (Law Commission Report No. 154) (Case and comment), [1986] 157
pilotage, [1984] 514
power of English arbitrators to make awards in foreign currencies, [1976] 255
proper, of a *Brandt* v. *Liverpool* contract (*The Elli 2) (Case and comment*), [1985] 188
property, in the Arab world, [1985] 279
proposed reforms of admiralty jurisdiction in Australia (*Davenport*), [1987] 317
registration of company charges: the new law (*McCormack*), [1990] 520
role of, in conflict between fishing and sand gravel industries in Scottish coastal waters (*Forte*), [1984] 263
Royal Commission on civil liability and compensation for personal injury (The Pearson report), [1978] 399
Saudi Arabia, insurance (*Haberbeck*), [1986] 246
Scots law, some rules of practice and procedure in arbitrations, methods of appeal (*Inglis*), [1976] 289
service of documents in shipping cases in Greece (*Timagenis*), [1984] 275
shipping, the Consumer Protection Act and (*Tettenborn*), [1988] 211
South Africa
comparative study of charterparties, [1984] 135
marine insurance in (*Bamford*), [1975] 171
of shipping and carriage, [1974] 314
South Africa, the new Carriage of Goods by Sea Act (*Staniland*), [1987] 305
Sri Lanka, Admiralty Rules upheld (*The Ayesha*) (Case and comment), [1987] 169
State immunity, the case of the Cuban sugar (*Lewis*), [1982] 96
staying of actions on grounds of *forum non conveniens* in England (*Briggs*), [1984] 277
"table tennis for marine lawyers" (Case and comment), [1986] 286
the higher altitudes of contract law (*Carter*), [1989] 81
the lack of uniformity and the very unfortunate state of maritime law in Canada, the United States, the United Kingdom and France (*Tetley*), [1987] 340
the lawyer and computer (*Stephens*), [1975] 166
the legal implications of cheque truncation (*Vroegop*), [1990] 244
the New Zealand Contractual Mistakes Act: a lesson in legislation (*Beck*), [1987] 325
transference of risk under comparative and internationally unified law (*Cigoj*), [1978] 56
UK, Hague-Visby Rules now operative in, [1977] 512
understanding banking law (*Cranston*), [1988] 360
uniform, for international sales, [1982] 657
United States, liability under for spills of oil or chemicals from vessels (*Bagwell*), [1987] 496
US
antitrust laws, extraterritorial jurisdiction (*Sornarajah*), [1981] 365
disclosure requirements imposed on arbitrators in maritime arbitrations (*Meade*), [1975] 399
liability of company director as seen by American courts (*Owles*), [1978] 422
"no fault" in (*Owles*), [1976] 396
product liability, a trial lawyer's view of (*Tozer*), [1977] 488
product liability, "like fleas to a dog" (*Owles*), [1977] 498
product liability (*Kuffler*), [1976] 33
time charter, doctrine of overlap-underlap in American courts (*Besman*), [1974] 49
U.S. admiralty and shipping law, recent developments (*Healy and Scowcroft*), [1986] 350
"what next in the law?", [1982] 438
worldwide *Mareva* injunctions: the position of international banks (*Malek and Lewis*), [1990] 88
"LAW AND PRACTICE OF MARINE INSURANCE AND AVERAGE (THE)", [1990] 278

"LAW, ECONOMY AND SOCIETY, 1750–1914", [1986] 270
"LAW, FORCE AND DIPLOMACY AT SEA", [1987] 245
"LAW AND JUSTICE IN CONTEMPORARY YEMEN", [1988] 270
"LAW AND PRACTICE OF BANKING (THE) " (VOL. 1 BANKER AND CUSTOMER (4th Edn.); VOL. 2 SECURITIES FOR BANKERS' ADVANCES (7th Edn.)), [1988] 266
"LAW AND PRACTICE OF COMMERCIAL ARBITRATION", THE, [1984] 137
"LAW AND PRACTICE OF INTERNATIONAL COMMERCIAL ARBITRATION (THE)", [1988] 398
"LAW AND PRACTICE OF REINSURANCE (THE)", [1988] 116
"LAW AND THE CULTURAL HERITAGE (VOL. 1: DISCOVERY AND EXCAVATION)", [1986] 546
LAW BOOKS
 lawyers', a practical index to legal literature, [1978] 66
LAW COMMISSION (THE)
 and insurance law (*Merkin*), [1981] 347
"LAW DICTIONARY (ENGLISH–GERMAN)", [1987] 558
"LAW FOR THE SMALL BUSINESS: THE DAILY TELEGRAPH GUIDE", [1983] 682
"LAW IN SINGAPORE ON CARRIAGE OF GOODS BY SEA (THE)", [1987] 235
"LAW OF CONTRACT (THE)", [1987] 242
"LAW OF CONTRACT IN SCOTLAND (THE)", [1990] 138
"LAW OF CONTRACTS AND RELATED OBLIGATIONS IN SCOTLAND (THE)", [1987] 131
"LAW OF DAMAGES (THE)" (15th Edn.), [1990] 137
"LAW OF GUARANTEE (THE) (A TREATISE ON GUARANTEE, INDEMNITY AND THE STANDBY LETTER OF CREDIT"), [1989] 225
"LAW OF INSURANCE (THE)", [1986] 260
"LAW OF INTERNATIONAL TRADE", THE, [1982] 160; [1986] 268
"LAW OF INTERNATIONAL TRADE FINANCE (THE)", [1990] 558
"LAW OF LIEN (THE)", [1988] 545
"LAW OF PILOTAGE", THE, [1982] 514
"LAW OF RESTITUTION (THE)" (3rd Edn.), [1989] 115
"LAW OF SHIPPING AND CARRIAGE IN SOUTH AFRICA, THE", [1974] 314
"LAW OF THE NATIONAL RIVERS AUTHORITY (THE)", [1990] 562
LAW OF THE SEA
 UN Conference on, report on third session (*Lake*), [1975] 383
"LAW OF THE SEA (THE)" (2nd Edn.), [1990] 561
"LAW OF THE SEA AND INTERNATIONAL SHIPPING (THE): ANGLO-SOVIET POST-UNCLOS PERSPECTIVES", [1988] 407
"LAW OF THE SEA AND MARITIME BOUNDARY DELIMITATION IN SOUTH-EAST ASIA (THE)", [1990] 289
"LAW OF TORT (THE)", [1987] 236
"LAW OF TUG, TOW AND PILOTAGE", THE, [1983] 107
"LAW OF TUGS, TOW AND PILOTAGE (THE)", [1986] 275
"LAW OF WAR (THE)", [1989] 238
"LAW REPORTS OF THE COMMONWEALTH", [1987] 544
"LAW REPORTS OF THE COMMONWEALTH 1985: COMMERCIAL LAW REPORTS", [1986] 551
LAWS
 reforming the banking laws, Stage One (*Morgan*), [1979] 30
"LAWSUIT", [1981] 110
LAWYERS
 marine insurance law: can the lawyers be trusted? (*O'May*), [1987] 29
 maritime, and the market-place (*Summerskill*), [1984] 205
 the lawyer and the computer (*Stephens*), [1975] 166
"LAWYERS' LAW BOOKS: A PRACTICAL INDEX TO LEGAL LITERATURE", [1978] 66
LAYTIME
 an inconsistency of approach? (*The Kyzikos*) (Case and comment), [1989] 263
 laytime problems and comparison of law (*Trappe*), [1986] 251
 recent developments in laytime cases (*Trappe*), [1990] 383
"LAYTIME", [1983] 306
"LAYTIME AND DEMURRAGE", [1988] 249

LEASES
of business premises, essential law, [1980] 210
LEASING, EQUIPMENT
a decade of growth (*Davies*), [1983] 631
LEGAL
decisions and developments, [1979] 60
system, essential business law and the, [1979] 510
"LEGAL ASPECTS OF AGRICULTURE IN THE EUROPEAN COMMUNITY", [1990] 293
"LEGAL ASPECTS OF BUSINESS IN SAUDI ARABIA", [1985] 279
"LEGAL ASPECTS OF BUSINESS TRANSACTIONS AND INVESTMENT IN THE FAR EAST", [1990] 566
"LEGAL ASPECTS OF DOING BUSINESS IN AFRICA", [1990] 152
"LEGAL ASPECTS OF DOING BUSINESS IN EASTERN EUROPE AND THE SOVIET UNION", [1988] 541
"LEGAL ASPECTS OF SYNDICATED LOANS", [1987] 549
"LEGAL DECISIONS", [1986] 554
"LEGAL DECISIONS AND DEVELOPMENTS", [1979] 60
"LEGAL DECISIONS 1987", [1988] 548
"LEGAL IMPLICATIONS OF DISCLOSURE IN THE PUBLIC INTEREST (THE)", [1988] 105
"LEGAL INSTITUTIONS—THE DEVELOPMENT OF DISPUTE SETTLEMENT", [1986] 265
LEGAL LITERATURE
a practical index to, [1978] 66
"LEGAL PROBLEMS OF CREDIT AND SECURITY" (2nd Edn.), [1990] 431
"LEGAL PROBLEMS OF INTERNATIONAL BANKING", [1988] 421
"LEGAL STATUS OF BERLIN (THE)", [1988] 112
LEGAL SYSTEMS
in the Gulf States (*Amin*), [1983] 71
"LEGALITY OF NON-FORCIBLE COUNTERMEASURES IN INTERNATIONAL LAW (THE)", [1990] 290
LEGISLATION
Benelux law on commercial agents now incorporated in Dutch Commercial Code (*Calkoen*), [1978] 395
current consumer protection legislation in Finland (*Sevon*), [1978] 592
local sea fisheries (*Gibson*), [1980] 340
of EEC, controlling dangerous substances (*Guruswamy*), [1983] 464
State Immunity Act 1978 (*Hodgin*), [1979] 55
LETTER OF CREDIT
dilemma of issuing bank (*Arora*), [1984] 81
LETTERS ROGATORY
US and the English courts (*Isaacs*), [1978] 464
LEX MERCATORIA
(*Deutsche Schachtbau-und Tiefbohrgessellschaft mbH* v. *The R'As Al Khaimah National Oil Co. and Shell International Petroleum Co. Ltd.*) (Case and comment), [1987] 277
LIABILITY
airport operator's, for bird-strikes (*McGilchrist*), [1979] 494
Conventions, Special Drawing Right in (*Tobolewski*), [1979] 169
criminal, of master in ship routeing schemes (*Warbrick*), [1984] 23
division of as between ship and cargo (*Diamond*), [1977] 39
extent of auditors' liability (*Alexander* v. *Cambridge Credit Corp. Ltd.*) (Case and comment), [1988] 19
for contamination of mixed and refined cargoes shipped and distribution tankers (*Cameron*), [1975] 281
for defective ship (*Coltman* v. *Bibby Tankers Ltd.* (*The Derbyshire*)) (Case and comment), [1988] 123
for injuries sustained by passengers in the event of hijacking of aircraft and other violations of aviation security (*Gam*), [1988] 217
for labelling of goods and instructions for use (*Brown*), [1988] 502
for pilot's negligence under Belgian law (Case and comment), [1989] 27
for pollution damage by ships, report on international conference (*Popp*), [1985] 118
insurance claims in general aviation (*McGilchrist*), [1980] 196

LIABILITY—*continued*
insurer's liability extended (*Banque Keyser Ullmann S.A.* v. *Skandia (U.K.) Insurance Ltd.*) (Case and comment), [1987] 5
Japanese agent's liability for delivery without presentation of bill of lading (*Daiwa Bank* v. *Mankai Shipping and Fast Marine* (*The Taichun*)) (Case and comment), [1989] 35
liability after discharge (*The Bunga Teratai*) (Case and Comment), [1990] 323
limitation of, at sea and in the air (*McGilchrist*), [1975] 256
limits of, in present economic situation (*Tobolewski*), [1980] 47
of company director, as seen by American courts (*Owles*), [1978] 422
of masters, provisions and changes (*Taylor*), [1984] 446
of shipowner or operator for physical injuries to persons in the sea (*Luksic*), [1979] 44
rights and liabilities of underwriters on payment of a constructive total loss (*Hudson*), [1978] 1
shipowner's, limitation of (*The Marion) (Case and comment*), [1984] 363
some legal aspects of directors' liability insurance in US (*Owles*), [1977] 163
the gratuitous agent's liability (*Chaudhry* v. *Prabhakar*) (Case and comment), [1989] 148
the operators's in air traffic control (*McGilchrist*), [1977] 204
third party in Japan (*Hosoi*), [1985] 254
under U.S. law for spills of oil or chemicals from vessels (*Bagwell*), [1987] 496
Warsaw Convention, is liability contractual in nature? (*McGilchrist*), [1979] 181
who has got his cross-liabilities crossed? (*Wilmot*), [1989] 450
"LIABILITY FOR DAMAGE TO LUGGAGE IN INTERNATIONAL AIR TRANSPORT", [1989] 124
LIABILITY (PRODUCT)
US statutes of limitations as applicable to (*Owles*), [1978] 9
"LIBER AMICORUM FOR LORD WILBERFORCE", [1988] 396
LIEN
maritime, how to secure, [1983] 109
on sub-freights need not be perfected under US UCC (*In re Pacific Caribbean Shipping* (*U.S.A.*) *Inc.* (*The Alicia*) (Case and comment), [1986] 424
on sub-freights registrable as a charge (*In re Welsh Irish Ferries Ltd.* (*The Ugland Trailer*)) (Case and comment), [1986] 1
the sub-contractor's (*Glass*), [1979] 189
LIEN HOLDERS AND MORTGAGEES
who should prevail? (*Berlingieri*), [1988] 157
LIENS
foreign maritime liens in English courts (*Jackson*), [1981] 335
maritime, protecting against for supplies and services on chartered ships calling at US ports (*Love and Kimball*), [1984] 290
maritime (Case and comment), [1986] 159
on sub-freights and priorities (*G. & N. Angelakis Shipping Co. S.A.* v. *Compagnie National Algerienne de Navigation* (*The Attika Hope*)) (Case and comment), [1988] 148
shipowners', preservation after release of goods (*Tettenborn*), [1985] 376
the juridical nature of a lien on sub-freights (*Oditah*), [1989] 191
US maritime and new arrest and attachment rules (*Owen*), [1985] 424
LIENS (MARITIME)
an American view (*Burke*), [1978] 269
"arresting the misconception" (*Robinson*), [1982] 261
in Polish law (*Adamczak*), [1982] 433
LIFE ASSURANCE (GROUP)
in Canada (*Merkin*), [1981] 485
"LIGGETT" DEFENCE
banker's last resort (*Ellinger and Lee*), [1984] 459
LIMITATION
per package limitation, diverging approach in Canadian courts (*McEwen*), [1976] 269
LIMITATION OF ACTIONS
aspects of under CMR (*Hardingham*), [1979] 362
LIMITATION OF LIABILITY
at sea and in the air (*McGilchrist*), [1975] 256
Convention on, maritime claims, [1977] 73
(Information), [1987] 559
shipowners' right to a limitation of liability adrift on a sea of tort changes (*Hughes*), [1988] 517

LIMITATION OF LIABILITY—*continued*
the application of foreign overall limitation statutes (*The M/V Swibon*) (Case and comment), [1986] 22
tug and tow, the flotilla issue (*Kovats*), [1977] 19
under Warsaw Convention, further developments in US (*McGilchrist*), [1983] 308
"LIMITATION OF LIABILITY", [1986] 274
"LIMITATION OF LIABILITY FOR MARITIME CLAIMS", [1988] 117
"LIMITATION OF SHIPOWNERS' LIABILITY: THE NEW LAW", [1988] 117
LIMITATION STATUTES
the application of foreign overall limitation statutes (*The M/V Swibon*) (Case and comment), [1986] 22
LIMITATION (TIME)
in English conflict of laws (*Stone*), [1985] 497
LIMITATIONS
statutes of, US, as applicable to product liability claims (*Owles*), [1978] 9
"LIMITED LIABILITY IN COLLISION CASES", [1986] 274
LIMITS OF LIABILITY
in present economic situation (*Tobolewski*), [1980] 47
LINER CONFERENCES
anti-trust implications of (*McIntosh*), [1980] 139
LIQUEFIED NATURAL GAS (LNG)
legal problems arising from transport of, [1975] 387
LIS ALIBI PENDENS
staying or discontinuing English proceedings (*Australian Commercial* v. *ANZ Bank*; *Attorney-General* v. *Arthur Anderson*) (Case and comment), [1990] 326
LIS ALIBI PENDENS AND *FORUM NON CONVENIENS*
in collision actions after the Civil Jurisdiction and Judgments Act 1982 (*Blackburn*), [1988] 91
LISBON RULES, THE
(Information), [1987] 561
LITIGATION
aviation, in US (*McGilchrist*), [1980] 59
aviation, punitive damages (*McGilchrist*), [1979] 48
LLOYD'S
construction problems at (*Christian*), [1982] 152
"LLOYD'S ARBITRATION REPORTS", [1989] 231
LLOYD'S FORM
Costs and Lloyd's Form salvage arbitrations (*The Ios I*) (Case and comment), [1987] 172
LLOYD'S OPEN FORM
and 1910 Salvage Convention under pressure, [1984] 139
role of (*Bessemer Clark*), [1980] 297
LLOYD'S OPEN FORM (THE)
and contractual remedies (*Gaskell*), [1986] 306
LLOYD'S STANDARD FORM OF SALVAGE AGREEMENT, [1980] 304
a descriptive and analytical scrutiny (*Thomas*), [1978] 276
an examination of (*Griggs*), [1974] 138
text of, [1974] 145
LMAA TERMS (1987), THE
(Information), [1987] 136
LNG
risk sharing in LNG shipping (*Abecassis*), [1982] 138
LOCAL AUTHORITIES
and offshore petroleum development (*Gibson*), [1978] 305
LOF
salvage arbitrations: publication of awards, and appeals (Case and comment), [1988] 454
LONDON
practice in of maritime arbitrations, recent developments (*McIntosh*), [1983] 235
LONDON CONVENTION ON LIMITATION OF LIABILITY FOR MARITIME CLAIMS 1976
and oil pollution damage (*Selvig*), [1979] 21
"LORD ATKIN", [1984] 506
"LORD DENNING: THE JUDGE AND THE LAW", [1988] 269

LOSS
by theft, Continental case law, CMR (*Wijffels*), [1977] 30
economic
in collision cases (*Case and comment*), [1985] 407
in the maritime context (*Gaskell*), [1985] 81
"when does loss mean damage?", carriage by air (*McGilchrist*), [1977] 370
LOSSES
foreign exchange, "the passing of risk?" (*Hudson*), [1979] 288
LOUCAS N, THE
([1970] 2 Lloyd's Rep. 482; [1971] 1 Lloyd's Rep. 215) some considerations of the case (*Davies*), [1974] 1
"MACGILLIVRAY & PARKINGTON ON INSURANCE LAW", [1989] 246
"MACMILLAN" DOCTRINE
reviewed in Hong Kong (*Tai Hing Cotton Mill Ltd.* v. *Liu Chong Hing Bank Ltd.*) (*Case and comment*), [1984] 559
"MALACCA, SINGAPORE AND INDONESIA", [1979] 372
MALTA AGREEMENT, THE
carriage by air, special contracts (*McGilchrist*), [1977] 366
"MANIFEST DISREGARD OF LAW"
and US Arbitration Act (*Berg*), [1975] 129
"MANIFEST DISREGARD OF THE LAW" DOCTRINE (*Bauer*), [1979] 142
MAREVA INJUNCTION
attachment and *saisie conservatoire* (*Tetley*), [1985] 58
attachment *in personam* (*Rose*), [1981] 1, 177
recent developments (*Meisel*), [1980] 38
"MAREVA INJUNCTION AND ASSOCIATED ORDERS (THE)", [1986] 410
"MAREVA INJUNCTION AND RELATED ORDERS (THE)", [1986] 410
"MAREVA INJUNCTION (THE) AND ANTON PILLER ORDER (PRACTICE AND PRECEDENTS)", [1988] 120
MAREVA INJUNCTIONS
worldwide *Mareva* injunctions: the position of international banks (*Malek and Lewis*), [1990] 88
"MAREVA INJUNCTIONS", [1990] 286
"MAREVA INJUNCTIONS: LAW AND PRACTICE", [1988] 120
"MARINE CARGO CLAIMS", [1978] 627
"MARINE CARGO CLAIMS" (3rd Edn)., [1990] 126
MARINE DICTIONARY
Falconer's, [1979] 61
"MARINE ENCYCLOPAEDIC DICTIONARY (THE)" (2nd Edn.), [1988] 549
MARINE INSURANCE
wilful misconduct of the assured (*Case and comment*), [1985] 415
"MARINE INSURANCE", [1980] 447
"MARINE INSURANCE AND GENERAL AVERAGE IN THE US", [1981] 516
"MARINE INSURANCE CLAIMS", [1975] 308; [1983] 103
"MARINE INSURANCE. VOL. 1: PRINCIPLES AND BASIC PRACTICE", [1989] 246
"MARINE INSURANCE" (4th Edn.), [1989] 246
"MARINE INSURANCE LAW OF CANADA", [1990] 303
MARINE LOSSES
and fault (*Mustill*), [1988] 310
MARINE POLICY AND INSTITUTE CLAUSES
The new (*O'May*), [1985] 191
"MARINE POLICY FOR AMERICA" (2nd Edn.), [1990] 440
MARINE POLLUTION
Canada's approach (*Lowry*), [1975] 10
impact of, [1980] 451
"MARITIME AFFAIRS—A WORLD HANDBOOK," [1988] 548
MARITIME ARBITRATION COMMISSION (THE) (USSR)
(*Timmermans*), Part 1, [1987] 350; Part 2, [1987] 468
"MARITIME BOUNDARY DELIMITATION", [1985] 144
MARITIME CLAIMS
Convention on limitation of liability for, [1977] 73
for oil pollution damage, London Convention (1976) (*Selvig*), [1979] 21

MARITIME CLAIMS—*continued*
the European Judgments Convention (*Brice*), [1987] 281
MARITIME CODE
new, of German Democratic Republic (*Richter-Hannes and Richter*), [1977] 197
"MARITIME CODES—1: PANAMA", [1990] 446
MARITIME DEATH
wrongful (*Bodden* v. *American Offshore Inc.*) (*Fries*), [1984] 295
"MARITIME FLAG AND INTERNATIONAL LAW", [1979] 58
MARITIME FRAUD
definition and classification of (*Kapoor*), [1983] 29
international, [1982] 442
"MARITIME FRAUD: AN OVERVIEW", [1986] 415
MARITIME LAW
Canadian decisions 1985–86 (*Tetley*), [1987] 82
Canadian decisions 1986–87 (*Tetley*), [1988] 82
Canadian decisions: 1987–88 (*Tetley*), [1989] 89
Canadian decisions: 1988–89 (*Tetley, Q.C.*), [1990] 99
Canadian judgments in 1981 (*Tetley*), [1982] 542
decision-making in (*Mustill*), [1985] 314
developments in Hong Kong in 1983 (*Quennell*), [1984] 434
in Israel (*Naschitz*), [1977] 84
international conventions, [1984] 329
judgments in Canada in 1980 (*Tetley*), [1981] 489
judgments in Canada in 1982 (*Tetley*), [1983] 603
maritime arbitration in the People's Republic of China (*Shum*), [1990] 114
offences on board ships: jurisdiction (*R.* v. *Cumberworth*) (Case and comment), [1990] 162
of salvage, [1984] 139
products liability in U.S. (*DiBiagio*), [1987] 118
recent developments in Hong Kong (*Quennell*), [1986] 382
"table tennis for marine lawyers" (Case and comment), [1986] 286
the lack of uniformity and the very unfortuante state of maritime law in Canada, the United States, the United Kingdom and France (*Tetley*), [1987] 340
maritime law, products liability in (*DiBiagio*), [1987] 118
"MARITIME LAW", [1986] 400
"MARITIME LAW" (3rd Edn.), [1990] 302
MARITIME LAW ASSOCIATION OF AUSTRALIA AND NEW ZEALAND, [1982] 32
"MARITIME LAW HANDBOOK", [1988] 267
"MARITIME LAW OF SALVAGE", [1984] 139
"MARITIME LAWS OF THE ARABIAN GULF CO-OPERATION COUNCIL STATES (THE)", [1987] 386
MARITIME LAWYERS
and the market-place (*Summerskill*), [1984] 205
MARITIME LIEN
how to secure, [1983] 109
MARITIME LIENS
an American view (*Burke*), [1978] 269
"arresting the misconception" (*Robinson*), [1982] 261
(Case and comment), [1986] 159
foreign maritime liens not to be recognized in South Africa (*The Andrico Unity*) (Case and comment), [1990] 491
in Polish law (*Adamczak*), [1982] 433
protecting against, for supplies and services on chartered ships calling at US ports (*Love and Kimball*), [1984] 290
shipowners', preservation after release of goods (*Tettenborn*), [1985] 376
US liens and new arrest and attachment rules (*Owen*), [1985] 424
"MARITIME LIENS", [1981] 514
foreign liens in English courts, principle and policy (*Jackson*), [1981] 335
"MARITIME LIENS AND CLAIMS", [1988] 533; [1989] 249
MARITIME SALVAGE
Dr Lushington's contribution to the law of maritime salvage (1838–67) (*Waddams*), [1989] 59

MARITIME SECURITIES
and the conflict of laws (*Tettenborn*), [1980] 404
MARITIME TERRORISM
and the law (Case and comment), [1987] 18
"Violence at Sea", [1987] 546
MARITIME TRANSPORT
air and maritime transport and the EEC competition rules (*Ministère Publique* v. *Asjes, Nouvelles Frontières et al*) (Case and comment), [1987] 14
EEC competition rules and maritime transport (*Rabe and Schutte*), [1988] 182
"MARITIME TRANSPORT", [1983] 304
MASTER
authority in salvage agreements (*Goddard*), [1984] 255
criminal liability, ship routeing schemes (*Warbrick*), [1984] 23
criminal liability of, provisions and changes (*Taylor*), [1984] 446
MASTERS
criminal liabilities of (*Taylor*), [1981] 499
MEDICAL MALPRACTICE
in US (*Gusmano*), [1976] 50
MENTAL ANGUISH
before and after the crash (*McGilchrist*), [1984] 311
MERCHANT SEAMEN
employment of, [1980] 448
MERCHANT SHIPPING
Merchant Shipping Act 1988 (The) (Case and comment), [1989] 133
"MERCHANT SHIPPING ACT 1970", [1988] 270
"MERCHANT SHIPPING ACT 1979", [1988] 549
"MERCHANT SHIPPING (LINER CONFERENCES) ACT 1982", [1987] 557
"MERCHANT SHIPPING (STERLING EQUIVALENTS) (VARIOUS ENACTMENTS) ORDER 1986
(Information), [1987] 136
MERCHANTABLE QUALITY
meaning of in sales of goods (Case and comment), [1987] 400
MERCURY POLLUTION
laws controlling, issues and implications of UK (*Guruswamy*), [1982] 611
"MERGER CONTROL IN THE EEC", [1990] 297
MIDDLE EAST
international and legal problems of the Gulf, [1982] 441
law, of personal injuries (*Amin*), [1983] 446
The Gulf, fisheries in (*Amin*), [1983] 671
"MIDDLE EAST LEGAL SYSTEMS; COMMERCIAL LAW OF IRAN; ISLAMIC LAW IN THE CONTEMPORARY WORLD", [1990] 119
MISDELIVERY
and time bars (*The Captain Gregos*) (Case and comment), [1989] 394; [1990] 314
MISDIRECTED FUNDS
restitution from the recipient (*Birks*), [1989] 296
"MISREPRESENTATION", [1990] 147
"MODERN BILLS OF LADING", [1988] 538
"MODERN INSURANCE LAW", (2nd Edn.), [1990] 445
"MODERN LAW OF PILOTAGE", THE, [1984] 514
"MODERN LINER CONTRACTS", [1986] 414
MONEY
judgments in foreign currencies (*Hene*), [1975] 19
MONEY TRANSFER
future developments in (*Arora*), [1981] 56
methods, recent developments (*Arora*), [1980] 416
MORTGAGEE
mortgagee's interest insurance (*The Alexion Hope*) (Case and comment), [1988] 282
MORTGAGES
effect of bankruptcy on mortgages of future property (*Matthews*), [1981] 40
"MORTGAGES OF SHIPS: MARINE SECURITY IN CANADA", [1987] 379
"MOTOR CARRIER CARGO CLAIMS", [1989] 236

"MOZLEY & WHITELEY'S LAW DICTIONARY" (10th Edn.), [1989] 528
MULTI-MODAL TRANSPORT
(Information), [1987] 559
"NAFTIKO DIKEO (MARITIME LAW)", [1987] 132
NATIONAL
and international organisations concerned with shipping (*Mankabady*), [1974] 274
NAVIGATION
"errors of" in NYPE form, reflections on *The Emmanuel C* (*Koh*), [1983] 597
right of, marine conservation (*Gibson*), [1980] 203
"NAZIONALITA DELLA NAVE: TRA CODIFICAZIONE E DECODIFICAZIONE", [1986] 408
NEGLIGENCE
by customs officials, imported goods, liability of the Crown (*Zien* v. *The Queen*) (Case and comment), [1986] 430
contributory, in contract (*Forsikringsaktieselskapet Vesta* v. *Butcher*) (Case and comment), [1987] 10
contributory negligence: a viable defence for auditors? (*Marshall and Beltrami*), [1990] 416
exclusion clauses (*Palmer*), [1983] 557
in the commercial sphere (*Dawson*), [1983] 209
liability for pilot's negligence under Belgian law (Case and comment), [1989] 27
master's, charterers' warranty of safe port/berth (*Herman and Goldman*), [1983] 615
"no fault" in America (*Owles*), [1976] 396
P pays X for the physical damage due to D's negligence (*The Esso Bernicia*) (Case and comment), [1989] 1
receiver's liability for (*Arora*), [1983] 294
salvorial negligence and its consequences (*Thomas*), [1977] 167
who is to pay for the stevedore's negligence? (*Kovats*), [1974] 121
NEMO DAT AND THE FACTORS ACT
National Employers' Mutual Gen. Ins. Assn. Ltd. v. *Jones* (Case and comment), [1988] 297
NETHERLANDS, THE
general conditions for the transport of goods (*Klinkhamer*), [1979] 26
"NEW DIRECTIONS IN MARITIME LAW", [1988] 538
"NEW FOUNDATIONS FOR INSURANCE LAW", [1988] 251
"NEW HORIZONS IN INTERNATIONAL LAW", [1980] 71
NEW SOUTH WALES
commercial arbitration bill (*Scotford*), [1985] 136
NEW YORK ARBITRATIONS
and pre-hearing discovery (*Kuffler*), [1975] 557
NEW ZEALAND
contract damages for exchange losses (*Rickett*), [1982] 566
contract statutes, the (*Dawson*), [1985] 42
NEW ZEALAND CONTRACTUAL MISTAKES ACT (THE)
a lesson in legislation (*Beck*), [1987] 325
NIGERIA
exclusive economic zone (*Okere*), [1982] 124
"NIGERIAN SHIPPING CASES. VOL. 2: 1980–1986", [1989] 242
"NORTH AMERICAN COMMERCIAL LAW", [1988] 269
NORTH SEA
blow-out in, Norwegian viewpoints on liability (*Brask*), [1975] 271
"NORTHEAST ARCTIC PASSAGE", [1979] 372
NORWEGIAN SALEFORM
guarantee and indemnity clause (*The Barenbels*) (*Case and comment*), [1984] 553
(*The Barenbels*) (*Case and comment*), [1985] 306
NOTICE OF READINESS
the persistence of uncertainty (*The Aktion*) (Case and comment), [1989] 152
NOTICE OF UNREADINESS
(*Aktion Maritime Corporation of Liberia* v. *S. Kasmas & Bros. Ltd.* (*The Aktion*)) (Case and comment), [1987] 410
NOTICES
in air passenger's ticket (*McGilchrist*), [1982] 444

NYPE
"errors of navigation" in form, reflections on *The Emmanuel C* (*Koh*), [1983] 597
some NYPE time charter problems (*Mabbs*), [1978] 456
the off-hire clause in the New York Produce Exchange time charterparty (*Davies*), [1990] 107
OFF-HIRE
the off-hire clause in the New York Produce Exchange time charterparty (*Davies*), [1990] 107
OFFSHORE
petroleum development and local authorities (*Gibson*), [1978] 305
OFFSHORE INSTALLATIONS
legal aspects of safety (*Cadwallader*), [1977] 53
OIL
bulk oil cargoes, claims for short delivery, some recent trends (*Weale*), [1978] 405
Canadian offshore development, some Admiralty law issues (*Spicer*), [1982] 5
forward trading in Brent crude (*The Aragon*) (Case and comment), [1989] 143, 418
new problems of financing oil shipments (*Ventris*), [1975] 38
the bill of lading as a receipt, missing oil in unknown quantities (*Debattista*), [1986] 468
OIL CARGOES
liability for contamination of mixed and refined cargoes shipped in distribution tankers (*Cameron*), [1975] 281
OIL POLLUTION
"a circular argument" (*Gibson*), [1979] 186
and the common law (*Gibson*), [1979] 498
blow-out in the North Sea, Norwegian viewpoints on liability (*Brask*), [1975] 271
compensation for, the future of Tovalop (*Bessemer Clark*), [1978] 572
control of marine pollution in the Gulf States (*Amin*), [1982] 104
(Information), [1987] 560
International Convention for the prevention of, from ships, [1974] 232
liability under U.S. law for spills of oil or chemicals from vessels (*Bagwell*), [1987] 496
making the polluter pay, a note on *The Zoe Colocotroni* case (*Brown*), [1981] 323
marine claims for, London Convention (1976) (*Selvig*), [1979] 21
of the sea, and the Swedish *Tsesis* decision (*Tiberg*), [1984] 218
"ships" and "liability" (*The Stolt Avance*) (Case and comment), [1990] 14
(*The Patmos*) (Case and comment), [1987] 275
"OIL POLLUTION FROM SHIPS: INTERNATIONAL, UNITED KINGDOM AND UNITED STATES LAW AND PRACTICE", [1987] 374
OIL TANKERS
bill of lading in oil tanker trade (*Ventris*), [1981] 479
sampling of bunkers in (*The Othoni: The Erikoussa*) (*Case and comment*), [1985] 10
"some topical considerations in the event of a casualty" (*Abecassis*), [1979] 449
OIL TRADE
out-turn clauses in c.i.f. contracts in the oil trade (*Lightburn and Nienaber*), [1987] 177
OILVOY
demurrage clauses (*Textor*), [1985] 343
ORDERS
under charterparties (*The Kanchenjunga*) (Case and comment), [1989] 415
"OUTER SPACE (NEW CHALLENGES TO LAW AND POLICY)", [1986] 404
OUT-TURN CLAUSES
in c.i.f. contracts in the oil trade (*Lightburn and Nienaber*), [1987] 177
OVERLAP-UNDERLAP
time charter, doctrine of, in US courts (*Besman*), [1974] 49
OWNERSHIP
of bulk cargoes (*The Gosforth*) (Case and comment), [1986] 4
P. & I. ASSOCIATIONS
direct recovery from (*The Fanti and The Padre Island*) (Case and comment), [1987] 406
P. & I. CLUBS
(*Coghlin*), [1984] 403
P. & I. LIABILITY
for compulsory wreck removal (*East Coast Tender Services Inc.* v. *Robert T. Winzinger Inc.*) (Case and comment), [1986] 427
PANAMA
"anatomy of arrest" in (*Pardini*), [1983] 456

"PANORAMICA ESPANOLA DEL ARBITRAJE COMERCIAL INTERNACIONAL", [1977] 538
"PARALLEL IMPORTS", [1989] 123
PAROL EVIDENCE RULE
Law Commission Report No. 154 (Case and comment), [1986] 157
PARTNERSHIP
casebook on (*Ivamy*), [1983] 486
PASSENGER TICKETS
air, and the duty to give notice (*McGilchrist*), [1979] 353
notices in air passenger's ticket (*McGilchrist*), [1982] 444
PASSENGERS
(Information), [1987] 560
liability for injuries sustained by passengers in the event of hijacking of aircraft and other violations of aviation security (*Gam*), [1988] 217
PASSING OFF
and unfair competition (*Lewis*), [1981] 341
"PATENT LICENSING AND EEC COMPETITION RULES: REGULATION 2349/84", [1986] 547
PAYMENT (Banking)
the time of payment in paper-based and electronic funds transfer systems (*Vroegop*), [1990] 64
"PAYMENT OBLIGATIONS IN COMMERCIAL AND FINANCIAL TRANSACTIONS", [1984] 327
PAYMENT OF HIRE
default, time charterers (Case and comment), [1986] 1
PAYMENTS
and international trade, [1979] 201
"PAYNE & IVAMY'S CARRIAGE OF GOODS BY SEA", [1980] 73
"PAYNE & IVAMY'S CARRIAGE OF GOODS BY SEA", [1986] 136
PEARSON REPORT, THE
Royal Commission on civil liability and compensation for personal injury, [1978] 399
PEKING ADJUSTMENT RULES, [1976] 141
PENALTIES
and the financial contract (*Esanda Finance Corp.* v. *Plessnig*) (Case and comment), [1990] 16
penalties and forfeiture: contractual remedies specified by the parties (*Jobson* v. *Johnson*) (Case and comment), [1990] 158
PERFORMANCE
impracticability of, contracts, is it grounds for breach? (*Arnold*), [1974] 346
PERFORMANCE BONDS
are bankers free from the underlying contract? (*Penn*), [1985] 132
legal position of banks (*Arora*), [1981] 264
use and usefulness (*Williams*), [1983] 423
PERFORMANCE GUARANTEES
(*Coleman*), [1990] 223
"PERSIAN GULF (THE) AND THE STRAIT OF HORMUZ", [1979] 513
"PERSONAL ACCIDENT, LIFE AND OTHER INSURANCES", [1981] 111
PERSONAL INJURIES
law in the Middle East (*Amin*), [1983] 446
PERSONAL INJURY
compensation for, Royal Commission on (The Pearson Report), [1978] 399
PERSONAL PROPERTY SECURITY
new Canadian legislation (*Ziegel*), [1986] 160
PETROLEUM
shortage of, disputes, difference between legal and arbitration approach (*Textor*), [1983] 392
PHYSICAL INJURIES
to persons in the sea, tort liability of shipowner or operator (*Luksic*), [1979] 44
PILOT
liability for pilot's negligence under Belgian law (Case and comment), [1989] 27
PILOTAGE
compulsory, "a jurisdictional collision" (*Gibson*), [1979] 356
law of, [1983] 107; [1984] 514
"PILOTAGE ACT 1987 (THE)", [1990] 151

PIRACY
marine insurance, *The Andreas Lemos* (*Hazelwood*), [1983] 283
"the current crime" (*Wiener*), [1979] 469
PLAINTIFF
the airline as, recent developments in US (*McGilchrist*), [1980] 328
POINCARE GOLD FRANC
what is its worth? (*McGilchrist*), [1982] 164
POLAND
insurance system, comparative review (*Marek*), [1984] 643
law, maritime liens (*Adamczak*), [1982] 433
POLLUTION
International Convention for the prevention of pollution from ships 1973, [1974] 232
laws controlling mercury pollution, issues and implications for UK (*Guruswamy*), [1982] 611
liability and compensation for damage by ships, report on international conference (*Popp*), [1985] 118
marine, impact of, [1980] 451
new definition of (*Brodecki*), [1985] 382
oil
IMO and liability for pollution from ships (*Abecassis*), [1983] 45
of the sea and the Swedish *Tsesis* decision (*Tiberg*), [1984] 218
US response to water pollution by ships (Water Pollution Control Act 1972) (*Kuffler*), [1977] 1
POLLUTION (MARINE)
Canada's approach (*Lowry*), [1975] 10
control of in Gulf States (*Amin*), [1982] 104
POLLUTION (OIL)
"a circular argument" (*Gibson*), [1979] 186
and the common law (*Gibson*), [1979] 498
application of International Convention on Civil Liability for Oil Pollution Damage to *The Urquiola* case (*Arroyo*), [1977] 337
blow-out in the North Sea, Norwegian viewpoints on liability (*Brask*), [1975] 271
compensation for, the future of Tovalop (*Bassemer Clark*), [1978] 572
PORT AGENT
his rights, liabilities and problems (*Morris*), [1982] 218
PORTS
appointment of Customs ports (*Gibson*), [1981] 303
the concept of safe ports (*Reynolds*), [1974] 179
the politically unsafe port (*Baker and David*), [1986] 112
PRACTICE
and procedure of the Commercial Court, [1984] 322
of commercial arbitration and law of, [1984] 137
of maritime arbitrations in London, recent developments in the law (*McIntosh*), [1983] 235
"PRACTICE AND PROCEDURE OF THE ADMIRALTY COURTS (THE) (FORMS AND PRECEDENTS)", [1988] 547
"PRACTICE AND PROCEDURE OF THE COMMERCIAL COURT", THE, [1984] 322
PRACTICE AND PROCEDURE OF THE COMMERCIAL COURT (THE)", [1986] 554
PREFERRED SHARES
oppression and preferred shares—a heady Canadian brew (*Palmer* v. *Carling O'Keefe Breweries of Canada Ltd.*) (Case and comment), [1989] 411
PRINCIPAL AND AGENT
duties, obligations and liabilities of ship's agent to his principal (*Trappe*), [1978] 595
PRIORITY CONFLICTS
the crystallization of floating charges and subordination agreements (*Chiaw*), [1986] 519
"PRIVATE INTERNATIONAL LITIGATION", [1990] 277
PRIZE COMPETITIONS
the lottery of legality (*Merkin*), [1981] 66
PROCEDURE
and practice of the Commercial Court, [1984] 322
PRODUCT LIABILITY
a trial lawyer's view of in US (*Tozer*), [1977] 488
in Australia (*Goldring*), [1977] 351

PRODUCT LIABILITY—*continued*
in US
(*Kuffler*), [1976] 33
"like fleas to a dog" (*Owles*), [1977] 498
US statutes of limitations as applicable to claims (*Owles*), [1978] 9
"PRODUCT LIABILITY ACTIONS BY FOREIGN PLAINTIFFS IN THE UNITED STATES", [1989] 131
PRODUCT SUPPLIER
claims against, carriage by air (*McGilchrist*), [1978] 487
PRODUCTS LIABILITY
in U.S. maritime law (*DiBiagio*), [1987] 118
PROFESSIONAL LIABILITY
medical malpractice in US (*Gusmano*), [1976] 50
"PROFESSIONAL LIABILITY TODAY", [1986] 415
"PROFITS OF CRIME AND THEIR RECOVERY", [1985] 401
PROOF OF SCUTTLING
The Captain Panagos D.P. (Case and comment), [1989] 25
PROPER LAW
arbitration agreements as signpost of (*Thomas*), [1984] 141
of a *Brandt* v. *Liverpool* contract (*The Elli 2*) (*Case and comment*), [1985] 188
of a marine insurance policy (*Stone*), [1984] 438
of arbitration agreements (*Thomas*), [1984] 304
PROPERTY
interlocutory orders for inspection of property (*The Mare del Nord*) (Case and comment), [1990] 319
passing of property under c.i.f. contracts and the Bills of Lading Act 1855 (*The Delfini*) (Case and comment), [1990] 1
"PROPERTY LAW IN THE ARAB WORLD", [1985] 279
PROPERTY RIGHTS
industrial, aspects of in EEC (*Haines*), [1977] 64
PROPOSED LEGISLATION
(Information), [1987] 137
"PROPRIETARY RIGHTS AND INSOLVENCY IN SALES TRANSACTIONS", [1989] 116
PROTECTION
of trading interest Bill (*Owles*), [1980] 55
PROTECTION AND INDEMNITY CLUBS
(*Coghlin*), [1984] 403
PROTECTION OF TRADING INTERESTS BILL
(*Owles*), [1980] 55
"PROTECTIONISM AND THE FUTURE OF INTERNATIONAL SHIPPING", [1986] 542
"PROVISIONAL DAMAGES", [1987] 133
PROXIMATE CAUSE
insurance of pleasure craft and the doctrine of (*J.J. Lloyd Instruments Ltd.* v. *Northern Star Insurance Co. Ltd.* (*The Miss Jay Jay*)) (Case and comment), [1987] 22
PUNITIVE DAMAGES
in aviation litigation (*McGilchrist*), [1979] 48
QUASI-BAILMENT
Metaalhandel J.A. Magnus B.V. v. *Ardfields Transport Ltd.*; *Transcontainer Express Ltd.* v. *Custodian Security Ltd.* (Case and comment), [1988] 34
QUASI-PARTNERSHIP
section 459 of the Companies Act 1985—a code of conduct for the quasi-partnership? (*Hannigan*), [1988] 60
"QUIS CUSTODES CUSTODIET"
(*Ventris*), [1983] 442
"R & D AND THE EEC COMPETITION RULES REGULATION 418/85", [1987] 238
"RAISING FINANCE: THE GUARDIAN GUIDE FOR THE SMALL BUSINESS", [1983] 682
RECEIVER
liability for negligence (*Arora*) [1983] 294
relationship with contractor (*Tugendhat*), [1974] 39
"RECOGNITION AND THE UNITED NATIONS", [1988] 265
"RECOGNITION OF COMMERCIAL JUDGMENTS AND AWARDS IN THE COMMONWEALTH", [1986] 129

RECOVERY ACTIONS
cargo, in US (*Carey*), [1980] 184
"RED HAND" RULE
Interfoto Picture Library Ltd. v. *Stiletto* (*Visual Programmes Ltd.*) (Case and comment), [1988] 294
"REFERENCE BOOK OF MARINE INSURANCE CLAUSES" (58th Edn.), [1989] 246
"REGULATING THE AIRLINES (ADMINISTRATIVE JUSTICE AND AGENCY DISCRETION)", [1986] 409
REGULATION
of wet marine and aviation insurance in US (*White*), [1985] 453
"REGULATION AND SUPERVISION OF FINANCIAL INSTITUTIONS (THE)", [1990] 434
"REGULATION OF FOREIGN LAWYERS (THE)", [1987] 248
REGULATIONS
Collision (The), in question (*Kemp*), [1979] 347
REGULATIONS, COLLISION, [1985] 141
REINSURANCE
follow settlements and claims co-operation clauses (Case and comment), [1986] 145
Forsikringsaktieselskapet Vesta v. *Butcher* (Case and comment), [1989] 285
reinsurance, brokers and the conflict of laws (*Forsikringsaktieselskapet Vesta* v. *Butcher*) (Case and comment), [1988] 5
"REINSURANCE LAW", [1988] 254
"REMEDIES (COMMENTARY AND MATERIALS)", [1990] 276
"REMEDIES FOR TORTS AND BREACH OF CONTRACT", [1989] 121
"REMEDIES IN CONTRACT AND TORT", [1990] 276
REPORT, THE PEARSON, [1978] 399
"REPORT ON CONTINENTAL WATERWAYS", [1977] 203
REPUDIATION
in charterparties, withdrawals, frustration (*Barclay*), [1975] 412
RESERVATION OF TITLE
by unpaid seller (*Lewis*), [1980] 309
the controversy continues (*McCormack*), [1989] 198
"RESERVATION OF TITLE CLAUSES", [1989] 118
RESTITUTION
the travails of duress (*Crescendo Management* v. *Westpac Banking*; *Williams* v. *Roffey Bros.*; *The Evia Luck* (*No. 2*)) (Case and comment), [1990] 342
without counter-restitution (*Guinness Plc* v. *Saunders*) (Case and comment), [1990] 330
RESTRAINT
of foreign proceedings (*SNIAS* v. *Lee*) (Case and comment), [1987] 391
RESTRICTIVE TRADE PRACTICES ACT 1976
registration defences (*Merkin*), [1983] 224
"RETENTION OF TITLE—A PRACTICAL GUIDE TO 19 NATIONAL LEGISLATIONS", [1990] 451
"REVIEW OF INTERNATIONAL BUSINESS LAW", [1989] 524
"RICHARDS BUTLER ON LATENT DAMAGE", [1988] 260
RIGHTS AND LIABILITIES
of underwriters on payment of a constructive total loss (*Hudson*), [1978] 1
RISK
transference of under comparative and internationally unified law (*Cigoj*), [1978] 56
RISK SHARING
in LNG shipping (*Abecassis*), [1982] 138
ROAD TRANSPORT
hi-jacking in road transport law (*Quick Smith*), [1974] 11
ROMALPA CLAUSE
unpaid seller's reservation of title, not effective un US (*Murray*), [1981] 278
ROMALPA CLAUSES
Clough Mill Ltd. v. *Martin* (*Case and comment*), [1985] 15
further developments (*Davies*), [1984] 280
"ROMAN-DUTCH INSURANCE LAW", [1990] 285
ROYAL COMMISSION
on civil liability and compensation for personal injury (The Pearson Report), [1978] 399

R.S.C., ORD. 29
interim payment: having your cake and eating it? (*Shearson Lehman Brothers Inc.* v. *J.H. Rayner (Mincing Lane) Ltd.*) (Case and comment), [1987] 173
RULES, THE HAMBURG
a commentary (*Tetley*), [1979] 1
SAFE PORT/BERTH
master's negligence, charterers' warranty of (*Herman and Goldman*), [1983] 615
the safe port/berth obligation and employment and indemnity clauses (*Baker*), [1988] 43
SAFE PORTS
the concept of (*Reynolds*), [1974] 179
SAFETY
offshore installations, legal aspects of safety (*Cadwallader*), [1977] 53
SAISIE CONSERVATOIRE
Mareva injunction, attachment (*Tetley*), [1985] 58
SALE OF GOODS
"Benjamin's Sale of Goods", [1981] 510
"Chalmers' Sale of Goods", [1982] 278
contracts, of "of soya beans, circles and strings" (*Powles*), [1978] 306
description, reliance and the sale of goods (*Harlingdon and Leinster Enterprises Ltd.* v. *Christopher Hull Fine Art Ltd.*) (Case and comment), [1990] 455
international (*Eckersley*), [1975] 265
and exchange contracts (*Corbett*), [1977] 310
Convention on Limitation Period, [1975] 105
seller cure in the sale of goods (*Ahdar*), [1990] 364
transference of risk under comparative and internationally unified law (*Cigoj*), [1978] 56
"SALE OF GOODS", [1990] 272
SALE OF GOODS ACT 1979 (THE)
seller cure in the sale of goods (*Adhar*), [1990] 364
SALES FROM BULK
(*Hudson*), [1989] 420
SALES OF GOODS
meaning of merchantable quality (Case and comment), [1987] 400
"SALES PROMOTION LAW", [1988] 417
SALVAGE
agreements, master's authority (*Goddard*), [1984] 255
an examination of Lloyd's Standard Form of Salvage Agreement (*Griggs*), [1974] 138
and General Average, insurance of average disbusements (*Hudson*), [1980] 168
costs and Lloyd's Form salvage arbitrations (*The Ios I*) (Case and comment), [1987] 172
Dr Lushington's contribution to the law of maritime salvage (1838–67) (*Waddams*), [1989] 59
enhanced awards (*Brice*), [1985] 33
enhancement of awards (Case and comment), [1986] 152
in non-tidal waters (*The Goring*) (Case and comment), [1987] 262
Lloyd's Standard Form of Salvage Agreement, [1980] 304
a descriptive and analytical scrutiny (*Thomas*), [1978] 276
maritime law of, [1984] 139
non-tidal (*The Goring*) (Case and comment), [1988] 449
of ancient treasure ships (*Subaqueous Exploration & Archaeology Ltd., and Atlantic Ship Historical Society Inc.* v. *The Unidentified, Wrecked and Abandoned Vessel, etc. et al*) (Case and comment), [1986] 16
present and future (*Brice*), [1984] 394
role of Lloyd's Open Form (*Bessemer Clark*), [1980] 297
salvorial negligence and its consequences (*Thomas*), [1977] 167
text of Lloyd's Form, [1974] 145
the new Salvage Convention: green seas and grey areas (*Brice, Q.C.*), [1990] 32
towage or salvage? (*The Manchester*) (Case and comment), [1988] 16
SALVAGE CONVENTION (THE) 1989
enactment in English law: policy issues (Case and comment), [1990] 352
who pays? (Case and comment), [1989] 416
"SALVAGE CONVENTION (1910) AND LLOYD'S OPEN FORM UNDER PRESSURE", [1984] 139

SAUDI ARABIA
insurance under Saudi Arabian law (*Haberbeck*), [1986] 246
legal aspects of business in, [1985] 279
"SAUDI BUSINESS AND LABOUR LAW (ITS INTERPRETATION AND APPLICATION)", [1986] 406
"SCHMITTHOFF'S EXPORT TRADE (THE LAW AND PRACTICE OF INTERNATIONAL TRADE)" (8th Edn.), [1988] 256
SCOTLAND
conflict between fishing and sand gravel industries in coastal waters, the role of law (*Forte*), [1984] 263
"SCOTTISH CASES AND MATERIALS IN COMMERCIAL LAW", [1990] 139
SCOTTISH RULES OF PRACTICE AND PROCEDURE IN ARBITRATIONS
and methods of appeal (*Inglis*), [1976] 289
"SCRUTTON ON CHARTERPARTIES", [1985] 513
SCUTTLING
"Barratry—the scuttler's easy route to the golden prize" (*Hazelwood*), [1982] 383
proof of (*The Captain Panagos D.P.*) (Case and comment), [1989] 25
the practice of (*O'May*), [1974] 6
SEA
limitation of liability at sea and in the air (*McGilchrist*), [1975] 256
SEA FISHERIES
delimitation of districts (*Gibson*), [1978] 495
"SEA LAWYER: A GUIDE FOR YACHTSMEN" (2nd Edn.), [1988] 270
SEA WAYBILLS
and the Carriage of Goods by Sea Act 1971 (*The European Enterprise*) (Case and comment), [1989] 000
"SEA-BED ENERGY AND MINERAL RESOURCES AND THE LAW OF THE SEA", [1986] 272
SEABED EXPLORATION AND MINING
foreshadowed global legal regime of (*Bentil*), [1983] 260
SEAMEN
employment of, [1980] 448
SEAWORTHINESS
implied warranty in time policies, the American view (*Pritchett*), [1983] 195
in time charters (*Clarke*), [1977] 493
SECURITY ARRESTS
in South Africa (*The Dimitris*) (Case and comment), [1990] 9
"SECURITY ON MOVEABLE PROPERTY AND RECEIVABLES IN EUROPE", [1990] 273
SET-OFF
and counterclaim—the necessary connection (*Dole Dried Fruit and Nut Co.* v. *Trustin Kerwood Ltd.*) (Case and comment), [1990] 471
in marine collision claims (*Knott*), [1981] 269
SETTLEMENT OF CLAIMS
mistaken settlements of disputable claims (*Andrews*), [1989] 431
"SHATT-AL-ARAB BOUNDARY QUESTION (THE)", [1990] 300
SHIP
division of liability as between ship and cargo (*Diamond*), [1977] 39
SHIP CLASSIFICATION
determining the indeterminate class (*The Morning Watch*) (Case and comment), [1990] 481
SHIP OPERATOR
tort liability of (*Luksic*), [1979] 44
"SHIP REGISTRIES—1: PANAMA", [1990] 448
SHIP ROUTEING SCHEMES
criminal liability of master (*Warbrick*), [1984] 23
SHIPBUILDING CONTRACTS
(*Clarke*), [1981] 234
legal problems associated with (*Mankabady*), [1978] 477
"SHIPHANDLING WITH TUGS", [1989] 525
SHIPMENTS (OIL)
new problems of financing (*Ventris*), [1975] 38

SHIPOWNER
tort liability of (*Luksic*), [1979] 44
SHIPOWNER'S LIABILITY
limitation of (*The Marion*) (*Case and comment*), [1984] 363
SHIPOWNERS' LIENS
preservation after release of goods (*Tettenborn*), [1985] 376
SHIPPER
contractual relationship between shipper, forwarder and carrier by road (*Hill*), [1975] 137
SHIPPING
British flag (*Jones*), [1981] 241
case law in Greece (*Timagenis*), [1976] 46
international and national organisations concerned with (*Mankabady*), [1974] 274
"Law of Shipping and Carriage in South Africa", The, [1974] 314
offences on board ships: jurisdiction (*R.* v. *Cumberworth)* (Case and comment), [1990] 162
risk sharing in LNG shipping (*Abecassis*), [1982] 138
ship's delivery orders (*Teare*), [1976] 29
US response to water pollution by ships (*Kuffler*), [1977] 1
use of reasonable endeavours to save a vessel from sinking (*The Talisman*) (Case and comment), [1989] 408
SHIPPING ACT OF 1984, US, [1985] 515
"SHIPPING CONFERENCES", [1984] 325
"SHIPPING IN INTERNATIONAL TRADE RELATIONS", [1990] 448
"SHIPPING LAW", [1979] 378
"SHIPPING STATISTICS YEARBOOK 1988", [1990] 288
SHIPS
arrest of
(*Goffey*), [1975] 34
in Greece (*Timagenis*), [1984] 90
criminal liability of masters (*Taylor*), [1981] 499
foreign, jurisdiction of English courts in crimes committed on high seas (*Bentil*), [1983] 60
in consideration of building ships (*Clarke*), [1981] 234
oil pollution and IMO (*Abecassis*), [1983] 45
pollution from, International Convention 1973, [1974] 232
registration of, UN Convention (*Sturmey*), [1987] 97
releasing from arrest (*Matthews*), [1983] 99
speed and consumption warranties under time charters (*Barclay*), [1974] 13
technical aspects of unseaworthiness (*Barclay*), [1975] 288
SHIP'S AGENT
duties, obligations and liabilities of to his principal (*Trappe*), [1978] 595
SHIPS' NAMES
substitution of, on writ (*The Kusu Island*) (*Case and comment*), [1985] 309
"SHIP'S VALUE" (2nd Edn.), [1990] 299
SHIPWRECK
law determining ownership of in the U.S. (*Klein* v. *Unidentified Wrecked and Abandoned Vessel*) (Case and comment), [1987] 24
SHORT DELIVERY
claims for, bulk oil cargoes, some recent trends (*Weale*), [1978] 405
SHORT FORM DOCUMENTS
and waybills, a lawyer's view (*Williams*), [1979] 297
SILENCE
may not be golden (*Excomm Ltd.* v. *Guan Guan Shipping (Pte.) Ltd.* (*The Golden Bear*)) (Case and comment), [1987] 155
SINGAPORE
recent developments in Admiralty law (*Selvam*), [1985] 209
"SIR WILLIAM SCOTT, LORD STOWELL", [1988] 528
SISTER SHIP ACTION *IN REM*, THE
(*Thomas*), [1979] 158
SMALL BUSINESS
"Law for the Small Business: The Daily Telegraph Guide", [1983] 682
"Raising Finance: The Guardian Guide for the Small Business", [1983] 682

"SMALL COMFORT" LETTERS
Kleinwort Benson Ltd. v. *Malaysia Mining Corp. Bhd.* (Case and comment), [1989] 281
SOUTH AFRICA
changes in Admiralty jurisdiction (*Rycroft*), [1984] 417
foreign maritime liens not to be recognized in South Africa (*The Andrico Unity*) (Case and comment), [1990] 491
implementation of Admiralty Jurisdiction Regulation Act (*Staniland*), [1985] 462
law, comparative study of charterparties, [1984] 135
marine insurance law in (*Bamford*), [1975] 171
security arrests in (*The Dimitris*) (Case and comment), [1990] 9
shipping and carriage in, law of, [1974] 314
The Halcyon Isle revisited: a South African perspective (*Staniland*), [1989] 174
the new Carriage of Goods by Sea Act (*Staniland*), [1987] 305
SOVEREIGN IMMUNITY
and the common law (*Lewis*), [1979] 460
the case of the Cuban sugar (*Lewis*), [1982] 96
"SOVIET LAW" (2nd Edn.), [1990] 294
SPECIAL DRAWING RIGHT
in liability Conventions (*Tobolewski*), [1979] 169
"SPECIFIC PERFORMANCE", [1987] 551
SRI LANKA
Admiralty Court (*Ratnasabapathy*), [1985] 260
Admiralty Rules upheld (*The Ayesha*) (Case and comment), [1987] 169
Greek NAT tax illegal in (Case and comment), [1986] 434
"STANDARD BUSINESS CONTRACTS", [1987] 535
STANDARD CONTRACT TERMS
new law on, in Germany (*von Marschall*), [1979] 278
STANDARD TERMS (OF TIME CHARTERS)
authority of charterers to sing bills of lading under (*Pritchett*), [1980] 21
STATE IMMUNITY
the Act of 1978 (*Lewis*), [1980] 1
the case of the Cuban sugar (*Lewis*), [1982] 96
STATE IMMUNITY ACT 1978
(*Hodgin*), [1979] 55
(*Lewis*), [1980] 1
"STATE IMMUNITY: SOME RECENT DEVELOPMENTS", [1990] 450
STATES OF THE ARAB GULF COOPERATION COUNCIL
arrest of vessels (*Price and Haberbeck*), [1985] 392
"STATUTES AND REGULATIONS OF THE PEOPLE'S REPUBLIC OF CHINA", [1988] 253
"STATUTORY INTERPRETATION", [1986] 262
STAY OF ACTION
foreign tonnage limitation not a ground for refusing (*The Benarty*) (*Case and comment*), [1984] 545
STAYING OR DISCONTINUING PROCEEDINGS
lis alibi pendens: staying or discontinuing English proceedings (*Australian Commercial* v. *ANZ Bank*; *Attorney-General* v. *Arthur Anderson*) (Case and comment), [1990] 326
STERLING EQUIVALENTS ORDER
(Information), [1987] 560
STEVEDORES
legal relations of in comparative law (*Cigoj*), [1975] 296
who is to pay for the stevedore's negligence? (*Kovats*), [1974] 121
"STRAIT OF DOVER (THE)", [1988] 400
STRAIT OF HORMUZ
and the Persian Gulf, [1979] 513
SUB-BAILMENT
sub-bailment on terms (*Palmer*), [1988] 466
SUB-CONTRACTOR
freight forwarding and sub-contracting complications (*Hill*), [1976] 63
the sub-contractor's lien (*Glass*), [1979] 189
warehousing and the sub-contractor, combined transport (*Hill*), [1977] 373
SUB-FREIGHTS
the juridical nature of a lien on sub-freights (*Oditah*), [1989] 191

SUBORDINATION AGREEMENTS
the crystallization of, floating charges and priority conflicts (*Chiaw*), [1986] 519
SUPPLY OF GOODS
supply of goods and charge cards (*Re Charge Card Services Ltd.*) (Case and comment), [1989] 22
SUPPLY OF GOODS AND SERVICES ACT 1982
contracts for supply of services under (*Murdoch*), [1983] 652
contracts of hire (*Palmer*), [1983] 377
SUPREME COURT ACT 1981
"arresting the misconception" (*Robinson*), [1982] 261
SUPREME COURT (US)
opinion of (*Franklin Mint Corpn.* v. *Trans World Airlines Inc.*) (*McGilchrist*), [1984] 499
SWEDEN
"Arbitration in Sweden", [1978] 634
integration of CMR Rules in domestic road transportation regulations (*Petersson and Wetter*), [1978] 567
Tsesis decision, and oil pollution of the sea (*Tiberg*), [1984] 218
"TALES FROM A PALM COURT", [1988] 270
TANKER VOYAGE CHARTERPARTIES
need for modernisation (*Ventris*), [1974] 44
"TANKER VOYAGE CHARTERPARTIES", [1987] 553
TANKERS
liability for contamination of mixed and refined cargoes (*Cameron*), [1975] 281
TAXATION
income tax and American business (*Owles*), [1982] 650
some problems with foreign exchange, losses in translation (*Owles*), [1980] 411
State taxes and business in the US (*Owles*), [1982] 253
the US collector and the foreigner (*Owles*), [1983] 93
US, and the Economic Tax Recovery Act 1981 (*Owles*), [1982] 81
"TAXATION OF LLOYD'S UNDERWRITERS", [1987] 134
"TEMPLEMAN ON MARINE INSURANCE", [1981] 373
"TEMPLEMAN ON MARINE INSURANCE: ITS PRINCIPLES AND PRACTICE" (6th Edn.), [1989] 126
TERRITORIAL WATERS (BRITISH)
Territorial Waters (Amendment) Order in Council 1979 (*Gibson*), [1980] 67
TERRORISM
maritime, and the law (Case and comment), [1987] 18
"Violence at Sea", [1987] 546
THE *AMOCO CADIZ*
some legal aspects of (*Dubais*), [1979] 292
the lack of uniformity and the very unfortunate state of maritime law in (*Tetley*), [1987] 340
THEFT
loss by, Continental case law, CMR (*Wijffels*), [1977] 30
THIRD INTERNATIONAL CONGRESS OF MARITIME ARBITRATORS, [1976] 377
table of comparative maritime arbitration procedures (*Cohen*), [1976] 422
THIRD PARTIES
and bills of lading (*Treitel*), [1986] 294
THIRD PARTIES (RIGHTS AGAINST INSURERS) ACT 1930
in a modern context (*Michel*), [1987] 228
THIRD PARTY RIGHTS
against insurers (*Michel and Congdon*), [1989] 495
on insurance contracts (*Trident General Insurance Co. Ltd.* v. *McNiece Bros. Pty. Ltd.*) (Case and comment), [1987] 258
TIME BAR
extension of time, deck stowage and the time bar (*Kenya Railways* v. *Antares Pte. Ltd.* (*The Antares*)) (Case and comment), [1987] 146
regulations in the CMR Convention (*Wetter*), [1979] 504
TIME BARS
misdelivery and time bars (*The Captain Gregos*) (Case and comment), [1989] 394; [1990] 314
TIME CHARTER
authority of charterers to sign bills of lading under standard terms (*Pritchett*), [1980] 21

"TIME CHARTER WITHDRAWALS", [1986] 554
TIME CHARTERER
third party liability in Japan (*Hosoi*), [1985] 254
TIME CHARTERPARTY
Intertanktime (*Michelet*), [1978] 287
TIME CHARTERPARTIES
the off-hire clause in the New York Produce Exchange time charterparty (*Davies*), [1990] 107
TIME CHARTERS
default in payment of hire (Case and comment), [1986] 1
doctrine of overlap-underlap in US courts (*Besman*), [1974] 49
lien on sub-freights (Case and comment), [1986] 1
seaworthiness in (*Clarke*), [1977] 493
some NYPE time charter problems (*Mabbs*) [1978] 456
"TIME LOST IN WAITING FOR BERTH TO COUNT AS . . . LAYTIME"
(*Costabel*), [1975] 150
"TIME LOST WAITING FOR BERTH"
some considerations of *The Johanna Oldendorff* and *The Loucas N* cases (*Davies*), [1974] 1
"TIME-BARRED ACTIONS", [1986] 274
TITLE CLAUSES
reservation of (*Davies*), [1984] 49
TITLE TO SUE
in the Warsaw Convention system: opening the gate wide? (*Gatewhite Ltd.* v. *Iberia Lineas Aereas de Espana Sociedad*) (Case and comment), [1989] 37
"TOO REMOTE"
(*Trappe*), [1982] 427
TORT
actions for damaged cargo (*Case and comment*), [1985] 1
claims, Admiralty jurisdiction (*The Antonis P. Lemos*) (*Case and comment*), [1984] 374
foundations of law of, [1985] 403
liability of the shipowner or operator (*Luksic*), [1979] 44
the shipowner's right to a liquidation of liability adrift on a sea of tort changes (*Hughes*), [1988] 517
the significance of in claims in respect of carriage by sea (*Reynolds*), [1986] 97
TORTS (INTERFERENCE WITH GOODS) ACT 1977
(*Hodgin*), [1978] 80
TOVALOP
the future of (*Bessemer Clark*), [1978] 572
TOW
law of, [1983] 107
TOWAGE
conditions and fundamental breach (*Lux*), [1979] 148
towage or salvage? (*The Manchester*) (Case and comment), [1988] 16
"TOWARDS A GENERAL DUTY TO TRADE FAIRLY?", [1990] 279
TRADE
"Finance of International Trade", [1982] 655
international
accommodations of the law of (*Cigoj*), [1974] 309
and payments, [1979] 201
cases and materials on the law of, [1982] 160
laws and commercial business, [1982] 162
oil tanker trade, bill of lading in (*Ventris*), [1981] 479
Protection of Trading Interests Bill (*Owles*), [1980] 55
theory of changed circumstances in international (*Amin*), [1982] 577
US international reports, [1982] 162
TRADE DEBTS
factoring of, its framework of law (*Salinger*), [1977] 184
TRADE DESCRIPTIONS ACT 1968
restructuring the control of price indications (*Oughton*), [1982] 117
"TRADE WINDS—AN INTRODUCTION TO THE UK'S LAW OF COMPETITION", [1978] 505
TRADING
wrongful trading (*Oditah*), [1990] 205

"TRAMP SHIP AGENCY PRACTICE", [1988] 410
TRANSHIPMENT
and the Hague-Visby Rules (*Mayhew Foods Ltd.* v. *Overseas Containers Ltd.*) (*Case and comment*), [1984] 202
TRANSPORT
deregulation in the Canadian maritime industry (*Cathcart*), [1989] 104
hi-jacking in road transport law (*Quick Smith*), [1974] 11
in perspective, ICC Rules for a combined transport document (*McGilchrist*), [1974] 25
legal problems arising from transport of liquefied natural gas, [1975] 387
maritime, [1983] 304
of goods in refrigerated containers: an Australian perspective (*Springall*), [1987] 216
text of ICC Uniform Rules, [1974] 29
TRANSPORT BY ROAD
Dutch Civil Code, a method of drafting a "code of transport" (*Schadee*), [1977] 37
TRANSPORT (COMBINED)
actions against successive carriers under CMR (*Hardingham*), [1978] 499
aspects of the limitation of actions under CMR (*Hardingham*), [1979] 362
delay provisions of CMR (*Hardingham*), [1979] 193
freight liner conditions (*Hill*), [1977] 88
ICC Uniform Rules (*Wheble*), [1976] 145, 148
international carriage of perishable goods and ATP (*Hill*), [1977] 546
interpretation of CMR in the English courts (*Hill*), [1977] 212
the carriage of dangerous goods by land (*Hill*), [1978] 74
the time bar regulations in the CMR Convention (*Wetter*), [1979] 504
to and from the US (*Ullman*), [1976] 157
to Europe (*Hill*), [1975] 303
warehousing and the sub-contractor (*Hill*), [1977] 373
"TRANSPORT: INTERNATIONAL TRANSPORT TREATIES", [1988] 267
TRANSPORT (MARINE)
"International Regulations of Maritime Transportation", [1979] 514
TRANSPORT OF GOODS
general conditions for in the Netherlands (*Klinkhamer*), [1979] 26
TRANSPORT (ROAD)
"Kitchin's Road Transport Law", [1979] 515
TREATY OF ROME (ART. 54(3)(*g*))
the Fourth Council Directive on Accounts (*Wooldridge*), [1980] 27
TUG
law of, [1983] 107
TUG AND TOW
limitation of liability, the flotilla issue (*Kovats*), [1977] 19
"TURKISH STRAITS (THE)", [1988] 400
UCP
effect of incorporation; question of leave to defend action to enforce documentary credit (*Forestal Mimosa Ltd.* v. *Oriental Credit Ltd.*; *Esal* (*Commodities*) *Ltd.* v. *Oriental Credit Ltd.*) (Case and comment), [1986] 420
U.K.
consortium and related operations in (*Wooldridge*), [1978] 427
Hague-Visby Rules now operative in, [1977] 512
issues and implications for UK in control of mercury pollution (*Guruswamy*), [1982] 611
the lack of uniformity and the very unfortunate state of maritime law in (*Tetley*), [1987] 340
"U.K. MARINE POLLUTION LAW", [1988] 548
"U.K. OIL POLLUTION LEGISLATION", [1988] 270
UN CONFERENCE ON THE LAW OF THE SEA
third session, report on (*Lake*), [1975] 383
UNCITRAL
and the Hague Rules and the Visby Rules, identity of the carrier (*Tetley*), [1977] 519
UNCLOS (UN CONFERENCE ON LAW OF THE SEA)
"the sea law changeth" (*Harley*), [1983] 86

UNCOLLECTED GOODS
the penalties of delay (*Palmer*), [1987] 43
UNCTAD
report, as related to hull claims (*Goodacre*), [1979] 315
"UNDERSTANDING CONTRACT LAW", [1988] 529
UNDERWRITERS
rights and liabilities of on payment of a constructive total loss (*Hudson*), [1978] 1
"UNDERWRITERS' BEDSIDE BOOK (THE)", [1990]151
UNFAIR COMPETITION
and passing off (*Lewis*), [1981] 341
UNFAIR CONTRACT TERMS
evaluating an EEC perspective (*Forte*), [1985] 482
UNFAIR CONTRACT TERMS ACT 1977
exclusion clauses after, [1978] 297
(*Reynolds*), [1978] 201, 211
UNIFORM COMMERCIAL CODE (US)
lien on sub-freights need not be perfected under (*In re Pacific Caribbean Shipping* (*U.S.A.*) *Inc.* (*The Alicia*)) (Case and comment), [1986] 424
UNIFORM CUSTOMS AND PRACTICE (ICC)
their nature and the 1983 revision (*Ellinger*), [1984] 578
"UNIFORM LAW FOR INTERNATIONAL SALES", [1982] 657
UNIFORM RULES (ICC)
text of Uniform Rules for a combined transport document, [1974] 29
"UNIFORM SALES LAW", [1987] 534
UNIT OF ACCOUNT
gold franc, replacement of (*Bristow*), [1978] 31
UNITED NATIONS
conference on law of the sea (UNCLOS), "the sea law changeth" (*Harley*), [1983] 86
Convention on Conditions for Registration of Ships (*Sturmey*), [1987] 97
"UNITED NATIONS CONVENTION ON THE LAW OF THE SEA 1982: A COMMENTARY", [1989] 517
UNPAID SELLER
reservation of title (*Lewis*), [1980] 309
UNSAFE PORT
the politically unsafe port (*Baker and David*), [1986] 112
UNSEAWORTHINESS
technical aspects of (*Barclay*), [1975] 288
UPDATE
on *forum non conveniens* (*Briggs*), [1985] 360
U.S.
a New Yorker looks at London maritime arbitration (*Cohen*), [1986] 57
Admiralty and shipping law, recent developments (*Healy*), [1984] 607
admiralty and shipping law, recent developments (*Healy and Scowcroft*), [1986] 350
Admiralty jurisdiction (*Foremost Insurance Co.* v. *Richardson*) (*Sargent*), [1984] 112
Admiralty law, continuing problems after supposed demise of *Ryan* indemnity (*Bagwell*), [1982] 556
American business and income tax (*Owles*), [1982] 650
antitrust laws, extraterritorial jurisdiction (*Sornarajah*), [1981] 365
arbitration
obtaining security in aid of arbitration (*Healy*), [1976] 267
time not of the essence in nominating arbitrator (*Ashworth*), [1976] 266
arbitration awards in New York involving shipowner withdrawals from charter upon late payment (*Murray*), [1976] 164
aviation litigation in (*McGilchrist*), [1980] 59
cargo recovery actions in (*Carey*), [1980] 184
carriage by air in the U.S. Court of Appeals (*Re Korean Air Lines Disaster of September 1, 1983*) (Case and comment), [1988] 150
claims settlement with Iran (*Amin*), [1983] 248
combined transport to and from (*Ullman*), [1976] 157
common law, "no fault" in America (*Owles*), [1976] 396
directors' liability insurance in, some legal aspects of (*Owles*), [1977] 163

U.S.—*continued*
federal income tax consequences to foreign corporations engaged in international shipping (*Donna Marie Zerbo*), [1988] 235
Fire statute, what has become of? (*Bauer*), [1982] 1
insurance coverage disputes in, a period of uncertainty for the insurer (*Liederman*), [1986] 79
insurance in, policy disputes, damages against insurers (*Barrett*), [1980] 131
law, comparative study of charterparties, [1984] 135
law, determining ownership of shipwreck in (*Klein* v. *Unidentified Wrecked and Abandoned Vessel*) (Case and comment), [1987] 24
law, marine insurance, a comparison of English and US law (*Condon*), [1986] 484
letters rogatory and the English courts (*Isaacs*), [1978] 464
liability of a company director as seen by American courts (*Owles*), [1978] 422
lien on sub-freights need not be perfected under UCC (*In re Pacific Caribbean Shipping* (*U.S.A.*) *Inc.* (*The Alicia*)) (Case and comment), [1986] 424
limitation of liability under Warsaw Convention, further developments (*McGilchrist*), [1983] 308
"manifest disregard of law" and US Arbitration Act (*Berg*), [1975] 129
marine insurance, household goods shipments (*Rossmere*), [1976] 173
marine insurance and general average in, [1981] 516
maritime arbitrations, disclosure requirements imposed on arbitrators under US law (*Meade*), [1975] 399
maritime liens, new arrest and attachment rules (*Owen*), [1985] 424
medical malpractice in (*Gusmano*), [1976] 50
New York arbitration as seen by a Londoner (*Wodehouse*), [1986] 43
product liability, a trial lawyer's view of (Tozer), [1977] 488
product liability in
(*Kuffler*), [1976] 33
"like fleas to a dog" (*Owles*), [1977] 498
recent amendments to the U.S. Wreck Removal Act (Case and comment), [1989] 15
Shipping Act of 1984, [1985] 515
Shipping Act 1916, antitrust exemption, "should it be eliminated or modified?" (*Meade*), [1976] 401
State taxes and business (*Owles*), [1982] 253
statutes of limitations as applicable to product liability claims (*Owles*), [1978] 9
tax collector, the, and the foreigner (*Owles*), [1983] 93
taxation and the Economic Tax Recovery Act 1981 (*Owles*), [1982] 81
the airline as plaintiff, recent developments (*McGilchrist*), [1980] 328
"the antitrust laws of the USA", [1981] 512
the demise clause in US courts (*Pritchett*), [1980] 387
the gold franc in, after *Franklin Mint (McGilchrist)*, [1982] 281
time charter, doctrine of overlap-underlap in US courts (*Besman*), [1974] 49
unpaid seller's reservation of title under *Romalpa* clause, not effective un US (*Murray*), [1981] 278
Water Pollution Control Act 1972 (*Kuffler*), [1977] 1
U.S. COURTS
can they denounce the Warsaw Convention? (*McGilchrist*), [1983] 111
"U.S. SHIPPING ACT OF 1984: A SCRUTINY OF CONTROVERSIAL PROPOSALS", [1988] 404
USSR
the maritime arbitration commission (*Timmermans*), Part 1, [1987] 350; Part 2, [1987] 468
"VESSEL TRAFFIC SYSTEMS", [1987] 556
"VIOLENCE AT SEA", [1987] 546
VISBY RULES, THE
and the Hague Rules and UNCITRAL, identity of the carrier (*Tetley*), [1977] 519
VOYAGE CHARTERPARTIES
tankers, need for modernisation (*Ventris*), [1974] 44
WAIVER
the notions of waiver (*The Kanchenjunga*) (Case and comment), [1990] 453
WAR RISKS
insurance (*O'May*), [1976] 180
WAREHOUSEMAN
and the Warsaw Convention, another point of view (Case and comment), [1986] 292
not entitled to benefit from Warsaw Convention in Israel (*Naschitz*), [1985] 479

WAREHOUSING
and the sub-contractor, combined transport (*Hill*), [1977] 373
WARRANTIES
speed and consumption under time charters (*Barclay*), [1974] 13
WARSAW CONVENTION
Art. 25, an English approach to recklessness (*McGilchrist*), [1983] 488
articles 22 and 25—an Australian contribution (*S.S. Pharmaceutical Co. Ltd.* v. *Qantas Airways Ltd.*) (Case and comment), [1989] 145
can the US courts denounce? (*McGilchrist*), [1983] 111
does the Convention govern non-contractual liability? (*McGilchrist*), [1983] 685
four new Protocols (*McGilchrist*), [1976] 186
is Convention liability contractual in nature? (*McGilchrist*), [1979] 181
limitation of liability under, further developments in US (*McGilchrist*), [1983] 308
recovery under for loss of valuable air cargo (*Solomon and Goldman*), [1982] 453
title to sue in the Warsaw Convention system: opening the gate wide? (*Gatewhite Ltd.* v. *Iberia Lineas Aereas de Espana Sociedad*) (Case and comment), [1989] 37
warehouseman and the Convention, another point of view (Case and comment), [1986] 292
warehouseman not entitled to benefit in Israel (*Naschitz*), [1985] 479
WARSAW CONVENTION, THE
and wilful misconduct (*McGilchrist*), [1977] 539
WATER POLLUTION CONTROL ACT 1972 (US)
(*Kuffler*), [1977] 1
"WATER POLLUTION LAW", [1990] 562
WATERWAYS
Continental, report on, [1977] 203
WAYBILLS
and short form documents, a lawyer's view (*Williams*), [1979] 297
simplification of documentation and document replacement (*Gronfors*), [1976] 250
"WHAT LAW NOW FOR THE SEAS?", [1987] 248
"WHAT NEXT IN THE LAW?",[1982] 438
WILFUL MISCONDUCT
and the Warsaw Convention (*McGilchrist*), [1977] 539
WINDING UP
winding up a foreign company (*International Westminster Bank Plc* v. *Okeanos Maritime Corp.*) (Case and comment), [1989] 20
"WORLD ARBITRATION REPORTER: VOL. 1: INTERNATIONAL LEGAL FRAMEWORK", [1987] 376
"WORLD COURT (THE) AND THE CONTEMPORARY INTERNATIONAL LAW-MAKING PROCESS", [1979] 376
WRECK
is there a right to? (*Goddard*), [1983] 625
or *wreccum maris*? (*The Lusitania*) (Case and comment), [1987] 267
WRECK REMOVAL
compulsory, P. & I. liability for (*East Coast Tender Services Inc.* v. *Robert T. Winzinger Inc.*) (Case and comment), [1986] 427
WRECK REMOVAL ACT (U.S.)
recent amendments (Case and comment), [1989] 15
WRIT
amendment of writ *in rem* (*The Kusu Island*) (Case and comment), [1990] 169
service out of jurisdiction, a new approach (*Case and comment*), [1985] 6
substitution of ships' names on (*The Kusu Island*) (*Case and comment*), [1985] 309
WRONGFUL DEATH
maritime (*Bodden* v. *American Offshore Inc.*) (*Fries*), [1984] 295
"YEARBOOK, COMMERCIAL ARBITRATION" (Vol. X, 1985), [1986] 267
"YEARBOOK COMMERCIAL ARBITRATION", [1989] 513
"YEARBOOK MARITIME LAW" (Vol. 1: 1984), [1988] 110
"YEARBOOK OF EUROPEAN LAW 7: 1987" [1989] 387
YORK-ANTWERP RULES, THE
revision of, [1974] 151
text of, [1974] 153

YORK-ANTWERP RULES, THE—*continued*
the new Rules examined (*Hudson*), [1974] 162
YORK-ANTWERP RULES 1974
not such a common adventure (*The Alppi* v. *The Bjorn Eskil*) (Case and comment), [1990] 173
"ZAHLUNG UND ZAHLUNGSSICHERUNG IM AUSSENHANDEL" (6th Edn.), [1989] 234